Foundations of Personal Fitness

Any
Body
Can...Be Fit!

Don Rainey
Edward Marcus High School
Flower Mound, Texas

Tinker D. Murray
Southwest Texas State University
San Marcos, Texas

West Publishing Company
Minneapolis/St. Paul   New York   Los Angeles   San Francisco

Composition: Parkwood Composition Services, Inc.
Cover Image: David Hanover, Hanover Photography

WEST'S COMMITMENT TO THE ENVIRONMENT
In 1906, West Publishing Company began recycling materials left over from the production of books. This began a tradition of efficient and responsible use of resources. Today, 100% of our legal bound volumes are printed on acid-free, recycled paper consisting of 50% new paper and 50% paper that has undergone a de-inking process. We also use vegetable-based inks to print all of our books. West also recycles nearly 27,700,000 pounds of scrap paper annually—the equivalent of 229,300 trees. West has devised ways to capture and recycle waste inks, solvents, oils, and vapors created in the printing process. We also recycle plastics of all kinds, wood, glass, corrugated cardboard, and batteries, and have eliminated the use of Styrofoam book packaging. We at West are proud of the longevity and the scope of our commitment to the environment. West pocket parts and advance sheets are printed on recyclable paper and can be collected and recycled with newspapers. Staples do no have to be removed. Bound volumes can be recycled by removing the cover. Production, Prepress, Printing and Binding by West Publishing Company.

British Library Cataloguing-in-Publication Data.
A catalogue record for this book is available from the British Library.

Copyright © 1997   By WEST PUBLISHING COMPANY
                          610 Opperman Drive
                          P.O. Box 64526
                          St. Paul, MN 55164-0526

04 03 02 01 00 99   8 7 6 5 4 3 2

Library of Congress Cataloging-in-Publication Data

Foundations Of Personal Fitness (student edition) ISBN 0-314-08465-7
Foundations Of Personal Fitness (Texas Teachers Wraparound edition) ISBN 0-314-08466-5
Foundations Of Personal Fitness (National Teachers Wraparound edition) ISBN 0-314-0622-1

The *FOUNDATIONS OF PERSONAL FITNESS: Any Body Can Be Fit* textbook program consists of the following components:

- *Foundations of Personal Fitness* Student Text
- *Foundations of Personal Fitness* Teacher Wraparound Edition
- *Foundations of Personal Fitness* Teacher Resource Package
- *Foundations of Personal Fitness* Video Library
- *Foundations of Personal Fitness* Nutrition CD-ROM
- *Foundations of Personal Fitness* Professional Reference Library
- *Foundations of Personal Fitness* WESTEST
- *Foundations of Personal Fitness* Nutrition Videodisc
- *Foundations of Personal Fitness* Diet Analysis software
- *Foundations of Personal Fitness* Student Activity Workbook
- CNN Annual Health and Fitness Video Update

Each component listed above is described in the following pages. Making yourself familiar with the components and their relationships to each other will help you obtain maximum benefit from the individual components and from the program as a whole.

Student Textbook

FOUNDATIONS OF PERSONAL FITNESS: Any Body Can Be Fit is a new textbook written for high school personal fitness courses. The text is divided into eleven chapters that collectively provide students with a range of knowledge and skills that will enable them to understand the importance of an active lifestyle and to design effective and appropriate personal fitness programs throughout their lives.

The text is comprehensive, covering all the basic information and skills related to personal fitness. Included are extensive discussions of the scientific principles overload, specificity, and progression, as well as the components of fitness: cardiovascular fitness, flexibility, muscular strength, muscular endurance, and body composition. The text also makes students aware of the differences between health-related and skill-related fitness, alerts them to the importance of safety precautions, explains the health risks that they can minimize by maintaining an active lifestyle, and delineates the steps involved in performing proper warm-ups, exercise routines, and cool-downs.

The major theme of the textbook is perhaps best expressed in the subtitle *Any Body Can Be Fit.* Throughout the text the authors emphasize to students that while not everyone has the genetic makeup and the drive to be a successful and competitive athlete, everyone does have the ability to make themselves physically fit. Developing and maintaining personal fitness begins with knowledge, characterized in the textbook as the ABCs—the initial letters of *Any Body Can.* Students need to learn the components of fitness, the advantages of fitness, and the proper way to go about developing an appropriate fitness program for the students' personal goals. At the outset of the course, in the introduction to Chapter 1, and throughout the text, the authors remind students that Any Body Can Be Fit. You will also notice as you read through the text that many passages end with the expression "Any Body Can ..." as a way of emphasizing to students that they can achieve and maintain good to high levels of personal fitness.

Features

This idea that all people can achieve fitness is also emphasized in one of the textbook's special features, the "Any Body Can" feature. At least one time per chapter, students read about a real person who has made outstanding accomplishments in the area of fitness. In many cases these individuals have overcome adversity or suffered through an adversity to achieve their high levels of fitness. Students will enjoy reading about and will be motivated by the amazing accomplishments of people such as Jack LaLanne and "Babe" Didrikson Zaharias. Each of these features concludes with the reminder to students that while not everyone is capable of superior athletic performance, everyone is capable of achieving and maintaining personal fitness.

Another special feature in the text is the *Active Mind/Active Body* feature, which highlights for students the theme that personal fitness is both a mental and a physical activity. All people in today's society need the knowledge contained in *Foundations of Personal Fitness* to enable them to develop and adjust their own personal exercise and physical activity program now and in the future. In addition to having this knowledge of exercise science principles and the components of both health- and skill-related fitness, students must be active—it goes without saying, that they cannot become physically fit without engaging in exercise and sport. The *Active Mind/Active Body* activity is perhaps the best example of how the textbook encourages the students to be active and to learn the information they need.

You will notice as you flip through the book that in some cases the logo for this activity highlights the phrase *Active Mind;* in others, it highlights the phrase *Active Body.* The highlighted phrase indicates whether or not the activity is primarily a cognitive activity or a physical activity. More importantly, seeing the two terms together repeatedly throughout the text will help students realize that achieving and maintaining personal fitness is both a mental and a physical activity.

Regarding the organization of the text, you should be aware that *Foundations of Personal Fitness* does not have separate chapters on stress and consumerism, as do many fitness texts. One reason for this is that many students study consumer issues and learn about stress in sufficient depth during their required health courses—thus, they do not need or want extensive lessons on these topics again in their fitness courses. The authors also feel strongly that students understand and retain more information about stress and consumer issues if the information is provided to them in short sections related to other fitness topics. Therefore, as the information becomes relevant within a given section of the text, consumer topics and stress topics are discussed throughout the text. For example, you will find a lengthy discussion of how to assess and compare fitness centers in Chapter 11, "Shaping Your Current and Future Personal Fitness Program;" and you will find a discussion of different criteria for purchasing athletic shoes in Chapter 2, "Making Physical Activity and Exercise Safe for You." These consumer issues are discussed as they relate to the main body of the text. While there are discussions of consumer topics and concepts about stress within the text itself, there are also special features—"Stress Break" and "Consumer Corner" appearing in specially designed boxes throughout the text. Teaching consumer and stress issues in this manner, rather than devoting full chapters to these topics, has worked well in the authors' classrooms for many years.

Other special features that you will find throughout the text are:

- *Fitness Check*—The Fitness Checks provide you with opportunities to formally assess students' knowledge and physical progress in a particular area of fitness.
- *Remember This*—These short, margin features highlight key messages from the text to increase the likelihood that students will read and remember the most important points in the text.
- *Quotes*—Scattered throughout the text are quotes that emphasize the importance of fitness in an

attempt to motivate students to develop an active lifestyle.
- *Believe It Or Not*—The colorful *Believe It Or Not* boxes contain short statements of fact and fiction regarding fitness to check, in a nonthreatening way, whether or not students are aware of some of the myths surrounding fitness topics. Answers to the *Believe It Or Nots* are found within the student text so that students can check for themselves whether or not they were aware of the myth.

Study Aids

Included in the Student Text are several pedagogical features that will help your students master the content in the textbook. You will be able to make a variety of homework assignments depending upon the ability levels of your students. It is not expected that you would use all of the study material in a given chapter, but rather that you would pick and choose the items that are most beneficial to your students.

At the beginning of each chapter, in addition to the opening photos, you will find *Contents, Outcomes,* and *Key Terms.* Having your students preview these items before they begin reading the chapter will improve their comprehension of the chapter. You might even want to question the students as they look through the Contents and Outcomes, asking them what they would expect to find under these headings. You could also quiz them on their knowledge of the Key Terms before they read the chapter.

Within the chapters themselves, you will find definitions in the margin, which call out the Key Terms in the chapter so that students will be able to find the definitions easily. The Section Reviews provide two or three questions to check that students have read and understood the key points in any particular section.

At the end of each chapter you will find a variety of study materials, including a summary, true/false section, multiple choice questions, discussion questions, a vocabulary exercise, critical thinking activities, and, in most chapters, a case study. The true/false and multiple choice questions are objective questions, which students should be able to answer easily after reading the chapter. The discussion questions and critical thinking questions will require more thought. You may want to have the students work on these in groups, or deal with these items in a class discussion. The vocabulary experience exercise deals with just a select few of the terms in the chapter. For further vocabulary work, you will

Overview of the Textbook Program

want to use the handouts in the Teacher's Resource Package. Students should enjoy doing the case studies, which provide realistic situations that require students to pull together the main concepts and skills from the chapter to develop an exercise plan or rationale.

As a group, these different study aids should provide you with a range and type of exercises that will satisfy the needs of your particular class, regardless of your students' ability levels or learning styles.

Illustrations

You will see at a glance that *Foundations of Personal Fitness* is a heavily illustrated text. Because the authors have worked extensively with high school students for many years, they were aware of the importance of visual appeal. Therefore, a greater than usual number of graphs, charts, drawings, and photographs have been included to supplement the textual material. Cartoons and "Hearty" (the cartoon heart character who becomes increasingly more physically fit as you move through the book) add humor. Overall, the illustrations in the text should help create a positive attitude toward fitness for your students. They should provide you with tools for starting discussions and for motivating your students to become physically fit.

Teacher's Wraparound Edition

The *Foundations of Personal Fitness* Teacher's Wraparound Edition was designed to make the most effective use possible of the Student Text. This Wraparound Edition is probably similar to many others that you've seen. In the Wraparound Edition, the pages of the Student Text have been reduced to approximately 85% of their actual size, which allows more space for the teacher notes that appear along both sides of the text and across the bottom.

In this Teacher's Wraparound Edition, you will have a wide variety of activity suggestions to help you reinforce and supplement the content of the Student Text. The activity suggestions come from not only the authors of the Student Text, but from eight additional physical education teachers from both the college and high school levels. In these activity suggestions and background information notes, you have the benefit of many years of classroom experience teaching personal fitness courses, which will be of great help to you,

especially if you are teaching a personal fitness course for the first time.

Following is a brief look at the organization and content of your Teacher's Wraparound Edition.

Chapter Opener Pages

Each chapter in the Student Textbook opens with a two-page spread. The information contained in your Teacher's Wraparound Edition around these two chapter-opener pages is different from the information in the rest of the Wraparound since these pages contain information that will help you preview the chapter and organize your teaching of the chapter. Included on these two pages are the following:

- **Chapter Overview**—One or two paragraphs that summarize the key concepts and skills taught in this chapter.
- **Teacher Resource Material**—A listing of various handouts, transparencies, etc. contained in the Teacher Resource Package that will help you teach this chapter.
- **Discuss the Photo**—Questions you can use to prompt classroom discussion of the photos on the opening two-page spread. Using these questions to discuss the photos can be an effective way to lead students into the chapter.
- **Pacing Chart**—Perhaps the most useful piece of information on the opening two-page spread, this Pacing Chart offers suggestions from the authors on ways that you might want to teach the chapter given a limited amount of time for that particular chapter. Within the Pacing Chart, the authors have identified the activities and passages from the chapter that they believe to be most important in the chapter. This information should help you make the most effective use of the textbook within your particular situation as determined by your time frame and student makeup.

Side Columns Throughout the Text

In the side columns of your Teacher's Wraparound Edition, you will find background information, teaching suggestions, discussion questions, references, and a variety of other information that will help you teach the chapter. This information in the side columns is organized into a four-part teaching sequence for each section of the chapter. The four parts of the teaching sequence are: *Focus, Teach & Apply, Assess,* and *Close.*

Overview of the Textbook Program

Focus

You will find several items under the Focus heading that will help you prepare the students for a particular section. First are the *Outcomes*, which show you exactly what the students should have learned after completing the section.

Following the Outcomes are *Focus Activities*. Included under this head are activity suggestions for motivating students and drawing their attention to the primary concepts of the section.

Teach and Apply

Under the Teach & Apply heading you will find a variety of teaching suggestions, including both guided and independent practice for teaching the section. In most cases you will find many more activities than you will be able to use. You should pick and choose those that you think will work best for you and your students. In addition to activities, you will find the following under the Teach & Apply heading.

- **Discussion**—The Discussion questions will help you initiate classroom discussion. In most cases these questions are specific to content on a particular page. For example, you may find questions to help you quiz students as to their understanding of a particular figure or one of the Key Terms. Other questions are more open-ended, calling for students to speculate about the ways in which a particular concept discussed on the page might impact their own lives.
- **Teacher Support Notes**—The Teacher Support Notes provide bits of information for you, which you may or may not decide to pass on to the students. In many cases, these include statistics about health and fitness in the United States.
- **Teaching Strategies**—Under the Teaching Strategies heading you will find suggestions from the authors with regard to points that you should emphasize in the text. You will also find suggestions for methods that you can use to deliver content in the Student Text in the most effective way.
- **Teacher Notes**—In some cases you will want discussion questions and activity suggestions to help you teach the special features in the text such as the *Stress Break, Consumer Corner, Fitness Check,* and the *Active Mind/Active Body* activities. You will find the teacher suggestions for these special features under headings of the same name.
- ***Healthy People 2000***—Periodically, throughout the text, the *Healthy People 2000* Objectives are provided for your general information. You may or may not want to read these to the students or write them on the board.
- ***Teacher Readings***—Also scattered throughout the Teacher's Wraparound Edition are boxes listing books and other references that the authors felt might be helpful to you if you have time for more background information.

Assess

Under the Assess heading you will find suggestions for assessing students' comprehension of the text material and for evaluating their skills levels. Also located under this heading are the answers to the Section Review questions.

Close

Under the Close heading you will find a suggestion for an activity or discussion that will help the students remember the key concepts and skills of that particular section prior to going on to the next section.

Special Features

Within all four headings of the teaching sequence you will find special logos for videos, software, CNN Update, and handouts. These logos serve as reminders that for each lesson in the text you will find a variety of print and multimedia support in the *Foundations of Personal Fitness* Teacher Resource Package. You will read more about each of these components later in this section.

Bottom Panels

Across the bottom of the Teacher's Wraparound Edition, you will find activity suggestions and background information of a slightly more general nature than what you will find in the side columns. The side columns will provide you with more specific information about teaching material on the student pages. The topics included are **Ability Levels, Across the Disciplines, Special Needs, Critical Thinking, Science and Technology, Equipment Options, Wellness Connection, Cooperative Learning,** and **Cultural Diversity.**

Teacher Resource Package

Accompanying the *Foundations of Personal Fitness* Student Text and Teacher's Wraparound Edition is a

Overview of the Textbook Program

comprehensive, already prepared package of classroom material for you and your students. Here is a brief listing of what you will find in the supplementary material:

- **Detailed Daily Lesson Plans**—Included in your Teacher Resource Package are several different sets of complete lesson planning information to help you use the *Foundations of Personal Fitness* and its accompanying material in your course. Included are lesson plans for block scheduling and traditional semester course. The lesson plans have been developed by the authors of the text over a period of many years, thus providing you with workable, field-tested, daily lesson plans from which you can design your own course.
- **Vocabulary Worksheets**—A variety of games and puzzles to help you teach the key terms in each chapter are provided in the Teacher Resource Package.
- **Reteaching Worksheets**—The reteaching sheets shown at the bottom of your Teacher's Wraparound Edition are included in the Teacher Resource Package.
- **Transparency Masters**—Approximately 100 transparency masters, primarily of figures from the text, are provided in the supplement package.
- **Color Acetates**—50 color transparencies of key figures are also provided in the supplement package.
- **Chapter Tests**—For each chapter of the Student Text, you will find a complete chapter test.
- **Handouts**—You will find a variety of handouts in your Teacher Resource Package. For example, all of the evaluation sheets and questionnaires from the *Active Mind/Active Body* activities in the textbook are reproduced in the supplement package. A variety of additional handouts are also included to enrich the content.

Videos

The *Foundations of Personal Fitness* Video Library is available with the text. Included in the library are videos on all of the different topics covered in the book, such as cardiovascular fitness, muscular strength and endurance, flexibility, weight training, aerobics, and much more.

CNN Video Updates

Accompanying the *Foundations of Personal Fitness* text are health and fitness annual updates from CNN.

These updates provide 15 to 20 short segments covering the most important news stories in the areas of health and fitness as covered by one of the world's leading news agencies, CNN. For each video clip there is corresponding teaching material, which includes questions and teaching suggestions to help you prepare for and follow up on each video segment. You will receive the video updates each year of the textbook adoption.

Nutrition Laser Disks and CD-ROM

Depending upon your hardware capabilities and personal preferences, additional nutrition information is available on videodisc and CD-ROM formats. Live-action video footage, animations, and interactive activities are included. You will find these multimedia packages extremely motivational and of high interest to students.

Diet Analysis Software

The Diet Analysis Software is available for IBM PCs and Macintosh computers. Students are able to use the software to analyze their diets. After filling out a food recall form, students go through the step-by-step program to analyze their intakes of major nutrients, results are printed out, and the students can analyze the nutritional content of up to three-days intake of as many as 30 foods for each day. Percentages of RDA, calories, fats, proteins, carbohydrates, vitamins, and minerals for the individual foods are provided. There is also an exercise option that allows students to enter type and duration of exercise so that the program can alter the personal RDA recommendations accordingly.

WESTEST

This computerized testing software is available for the IBM PCs, compatibles, and Macintosh. It includes all of the questions contained on the printed chapter tests in the supplementary material. The program allows you to create, edit, store, and print your own individual tests.

Philosophy of the Course

Foundations of Personal Fitness: Any Body Can Be Fit—it's as simple as A, B, C. The ABC concept has been used by the authors to show students and teachers that developing and maintaining an active lifestyle is a reasonable and attainable goal that all adolescents can achieve. This ABC theme is promoted throughout each chapter of the text. The ABCs, that promote personal fitness for adolescents in the text, are consistent with the belief that education should prepare one for life. The philosophy and content of the course are based on the extensive combined personal and professional experience of the authors (see biographical sketches) who have successfully developed and implemented this course at the high school physical education level for the past 12 years.

Strong, extensive, and consistent research evidence shows that low levels of physical activity in adults are associated with increased risks for chronic diseases and premature death. The amounts, or the dose-relationship, of physical activity and exercise necessary for good health and higher levels of physical fitness are also becoming better defined for adults. The promotion of physical activity in children, adolescents, and adults is supported by national initiatives like those contained in the *Healthy People 2000* Objectives and the 1995 Centers for Disease Control and Prevention (CDC) and the American College of Sports Medicine (ACSM) Public Health Statement. The CDC/ACSM Statement encourages all Americans to accumulate 30 minutes of daily, moderate, physical activity. Additionally, in the Spring of 1996 the National Institutes of Health and the U.S. Surgeon General's Office released official statements encouraging all Americans to adopt active lifestyles as a primary health care prevention strategy.

There are no research data as of yet that provide an optimal dose of physical activity or exercise during childhood or adolescence. However, experts have recently produced physical activity recommendations for adolescents based on the idea that active adolescents will most likely become active adults. The guidelines follow and are included for students in the *Any Body Can Be Fit* text.

Guideline 1 – All adolescents should be physically active daily, or nearly every day, as part of play, games, sports, work, transportation, recreation, physical education, or planned exercise, in the context of family, school, or community activities.

Guideline 2 – Adolescents should engage in three or more sessions per week of activities that last 20 minutes or more at a time and that require moderate to vigorous levels of exertion.

For too long, physical education has not been given the same resources or attention in the high school curricula as math, science, or English. However, with the current attention and emphasis focused on health care in the U.S., it is hard to believe that there is content more important to be taught to all adolescents than personal health/fitness concepts.

The current national awareness of the importance of personal fitness has focused the spotlight on school physical education programs as an essential way to promote active lifestyles in adolescents. However, the effectiveness of current school physical education programs at promoting physical activity and the quality of those programs is of concern. For example, data from the 1990 Youth Risk Behavior Survey suggest that adolescents are less active now than they were a decade ago. Only 37 percent of teenagers in grades 9 through 12 reported performing at least 20 minutes of vigorous exercise three or more times per week. About 50 percent of students reported they did not participate in physical education classes, 25 percent said they do not do any physical activity.

It is our belief that personal fitness courses in high school physical education should prepare students to develop, experience, and adopt the behaviors they will need for a lifetime of healthy, active living. We also believe that the high school personal fitness course should be the foundation of the physical education curriculum. It should be structured such that students have the opportunity to be physically active at least 20 to 30 minutes daily. Other courses in the curriculum should support the concepts presented in the personal fitness course and allow students to experience a wide variety of lifetime activity options.

The *Any Body Can Be Fit* approach to teaching personal fitness to adolescents goes beyond just the explanation of why an active lifestyle is important. The *Any Body Can Be Fit* philosophy and methods are uniquely different from most typical physical education curricula, which emphasize skill acquisition, team sports, and competition. The *Any Body Can Be Fit* materials have been designed to significantly improve upon the traditional adolescent high school physical education experience. Specifically, we achieve this by providing opportunities for students to learn about personal fitness, successfully experience personal fitness, assess their own changes in personal fitness, and at the same time enjoy the process.

Role of the Teacher

Physical education programs across the country are presently being critiqued as to their importance in public schools. While it may be difficult to support the benefits of some traditional physical education courses, virtually everyone supports the teaching of personal fitness courses. This is most likely due to the fact that personal fitness courses can provide students with a foundation for living active and healthy lives. Personal fitness courses in physical education are being developed and implemented at the high school level nationwide. State and national leaders are recognizing the fact that personal fitness is something all students should learn and experience.

Now, not just *Any Body Can*, or should, teach personal fitness. One of the most critical factors that will determine whether a personal fitness course in physical education is successfully implemented, is the commitment and dedication of the teacher for the course. Teachers of this course should value the concepts and behaviors typically promoted in personal fitness. This does not mean that the teachers' personal appearance has to necessarily represent the ultimate picture of health and fitness. However, the teachers should be physically active themselves and promote healthy fitness behaviors. As a teacher, you have the responsibility to portray a lifestyle that shows that you value personal fitness, and this lifestyle should be readily identifiable by your students. We believe that you will have a longer-lasting impact on students in this course if students observe that you are actively practicing what you preach. Teachers who are good role models for personal fitness should take pride in their accomplishments, knowing that they have provided students with the knowledge and experiences that they can use for a lifetime of health and fitness.

Any Body Can Be Fit has been designed to provide you with the latest updated information about personal fitness. However, new information is constantly being added to the field of personal fitness. In order to stay informed, teachers of personal fitness should make every effort to be active in their state, regional, and national professional organizations. And, administrators and school districts should support these professional development efforts.

Teachers implementing a personal fitness course for the first time need to realize that they will face some unique challenges compared to those encountered in other traditional physical education courses. Teaching personal fitness requires a combination of lectures, written assignments, laboratories, and physical activities. This may require you to spend more time, initially, preparing for your daily lessons. It may take you some time to really feel comfortable teaching personal fitness. However, the *Any Body Can Be Fit* Teacher's Edition and Teacher Resource Package have been developed to assist you in making your teaching experiences both enjoyable and worthwhile. The text has been developed *by* practitioners, *for* practitioners.

There is no single best way to teach personal fitness. Teachers will have to consider the facilities and equipment they have available, their student population, and their class sizes. Teachers will also have to evaluate their own personalities and content strengths and weaknesses to fully develop and successfully implement this course.

It does appear that the teaching of personal fitness is here to stay, particularly with the national emphasis on controlling health-care costs and the move toward preventive medicine. Your contribution of teaching personal fitness to adolescents will have a tremendous impact on the future lives of students and on their personal attitudes about taking self-responsibility for their future health and fitness. We are proud that we can help you teach personal fitness. Good luck to you!

Physical Fitness Testing

Physical fitness testing of children and adolescents is often expected in school physical education programs. It is usually thought that physical fitness testing will promote good health in children and youth. It is even required by law in some states. However, fitness testing may not be warranted if it is not effective at encouraging youth to adopt active lifestyles.

Many experts have recommended that physical fitness testing be eliminated in schools. This may be appropriate if teachers only rely on older, traditional testing methods that have not been effective at stimulating youth to become active. For example, some teachers just administer a physical fitness test and assign a grade based on the results. They don't necessarily prepare students to be assessed or allow students to experience the benefits of participating in physical activities or exercise. When this technique is used by teachers, they tend to disregard factors such as age, physical maturation, gender, and trainability (genetics), which can significantly influence student performances.

For those teachers who like to use pre- and post-testing on physical fitness measures, we suggest you proceed with caution if you try to use this technique in the personal fitness course. Typically the personal fitness course will last only nine to eighteen weeks, and this will probably not be enough time for your students with low levels of fitness to realize significant improvement in physical fitness measures. Also, pre- and post-testing of physical fitness may encourage students to not do as well on their first assessment, especially if they know they will be retested later for a grade. The goal of physical fitness testing should not necessarily be to see gains in fitness. The ultimate goal is to get adolescents to have positive experiences with physical activity and exercise so they will want to continue these behaviors.

The authors support the belief that physical fitness testing, or more importantly, self-assessment of fitness, should never be done if it creates an atmosphere that promotes negative experiences for youth. Physical fitness testing can really only be effective if students are allowed to prepare for fitness assessments, are evaluated with reasonable performance standards based on each student's self-assessment, and are given opportunities to improve upon low levels of fitness. If you use physical fitness testing, you should use criterion-referenced tests (there are many of these, such as the Prudential *Fitnessgram* in the text), which are based on behavioral objectives for the course. Students can recognize success in their personal fitness if they are allowed to participate in physical activities long enough to experience and value the concept that *Any Body Can Be Fit*.

We do not profess to have all the answers for promoting adolescents to adopt physically active lifestyles, but we do advocate the use of the *Any Body Can Be Fit* personal fitness model that has worked successfully in Don Rainey's class. The model is based on the following educational concepts:

1. Teach students the whys of personal fitness.
2. Allow students to experience success with physical activity and exercise by having them engage in moderate conditioning.
3. Teach and conduct student self-assessments of their personal fitness levels.
4. Reinforce students' progress and encourage students to continue the development or maintenance of their personal fitness levels by having them continue conditioning or enter a maintenance program.
5. Allow students to explore physical activity and exercise options.
6. Allow students to design a personal fitness program that meets their individual needs.
7. Reassess students if necessary.
8. Encourage and reinforce continued student success.

The model includes integrating physical activities and moderate levels of conditioning into the personal fitness course. This is achieved by focusing the delivery of the course in three stages or components. In stage one, a cardiovascular conditioning unit is introduced to students during which they learn about aerobic conditioning and are exposed to developing (by walking or jogging) and assessing their own levels of aerobic fitness. In stage two, students learn about and participate in a strength and muscular development unit, which combines flexibility, sound nutrition, and body composition concerns. In stage three, students are exposed to a variety of activities, consumer issues, and stress management issues. During this stage students design their own personal fitness plan for now and the future.

The *Any Body Can Be Fit* text has been developed to help you teach the personal fitness course in a variety of ways (see Philosophy of the Course). We believe that physical fitness testing or student self-assessment can be an important part of the personal fitness course in high school. Physical fitness testing or student self-assessment can effectively be used by teachers to encourage adolescents to be physically active for a lifetime. However, as Dr. James Morrow (Chair of the Department of Kinesiology, Health Promotion, and Recreation at the University of North Texas) has said, "High school physical fitness testing is useless, unless teachers and administrators focus less on testing and evaluation, and more on the knowledge, experiences, and attitudes which lead directly to desired behaviors."

Student Evaluation

There are numerous ways to evaluate whether students have met the objectives of the personal fitness course. We recommend that you consider the following guidelines when developing your criteria for evaluating course objectives.

Students who are taking the personal fitness course should:

1. Learn and understand why physical activity and exercise are important to disease prevention and the maintenance of functional health.
2. Understand and apply safety practices associated with physical fitness. This includes correct application of biomechanical and physiological principles related to physical activity and exercise training.
3. Learn and understand the components of physical fitness.
4. Learn and understand the relationship between physical fitness activities or exercise to stress, nutrition, and consumer issues.
5. Experience the development and maintenance of an acceptable health-related level of physical fitness.
6. Select and experience a variety of dynamic activities that can improve or maintain physical fitness levels.
7. Assess individual personal fitness levels.
8. Design a personal fitness program that meets the individual's needs and interests. This should be based on the results of their personal fitness assessments.
9. Demonstrate successful participation in a variety of physical activities and exercises based on the requirements of the course.

A variety of evaluation strategies can be used to determine whether students have met the personal fitness course objectives. We recommend that you consider using the following evaluation strategies:

1. *Chapter tests, quizzes, and mid-term or final exam.*
   These can be used to assess cognitive understanding of the *Any Body Can Be Fit* text. (Many assessment materials are provided in the Teacher Resource Package.) These assessments should require students to use their thinking, reasoning, analyzing, predicting, estimating, and problem-solving skills. The *Any Body Can Be Fit* philosophy and materials support the goal of having students understand and apply personal fitness concepts, instead of merely exposing them to the information.
2. *Laboratory and cooperative learning experiences.*
   These activities stimulate students to explore, expe-

rience, and apply the cognitive concepts of personal fitness. These also allow students to share learning experiences and provide opportunities for peer teaching.
3. *Written projects and/or homework.*
   Written projects can further allow students to use their critical thinking skills (for example solving case studies, researching consumer issues, and extra credit assignments). The reteaching and enrichment activities provided in the Teacher Resource Package can be used effectively as homework for students.
4. *Physical activity projects.*
   Physical activity projects can be individual or group projects that require preparation and demonstration of a variety of physical activities or exercises. Examples might include having students design an aerobic dance routine, aqua aerobic routine, isometric resistance routine, or circuit weight training routine.
5. *Physical fitness evaluations.*
   These include a battery of both skill- and health-related fitness evaluations. Examples of skill-related evaluations include speed, balance, power, agility, coordination, and reaction time. Examples of health-related evaluations include cardiovascular, flexibility, muscular strength and endurance, and body composition.
6. *Physical fitness program design.*
   Students should be able to write personal fitness plans specifically for cardiovascular fitness, flexibility fitness, muscular strength and endurance, sound nutrition, body composition concerns, stress control, and consumer issues. These plans should be written based on an analysis of individual needs and interests.
7. *Participation.*
   Participation should include a variety of activities and experiences. Daily class participation time should include 20 to 30 minutes of regular physical activity or exercise. Students should participate by engaging in a combination of activities in class, such as aerobic conditioning, strength and endurance conditioning, flexibility routines, exercise program design, and laboratory experiences. Students should participate long enough in physical activities to successfully experience and value the concept that *Any Body Can Be Fit.*

Grading in the personal fitness course should be based on your evaluation strategies. Grading will also have to be designed based on your school or school district's criteria for determining student grades. The

Student Evaluation

following are options that are currently being used by practitioners to grade students in high school personal fitness courses. You may find an option, or combination of options, that will work well for your course.

Option 1

10-25%	1.	Chapter tests, quizzes.
10-25%	2.	Mid-term or final exam.
10-20%	3.	Laboratory and cooperative learning experiences.
5-10%	4.	Written projects and/or homework.
10-25%	5.	Physical activity projects.
5-15%	6.	Physical fitness evaluations.
10-20%	7.	Physical fitness program design.
20-30%	8.	Participation.

Option 2

25-30%	1.	Chapter tests, quizzes, and mid-term or final exam.
20-30%	2.	Laboratory and cooperative learning experiences.
10-15%	3.	Written projects and/or homework, physical activity projects, and physical fitness evaluations.
10-15%	4.	Physical fitness program design.
20-30%	5.	Participation.

Option 3

30%	1.	Chapter tests, quizzes, mid-term or final exam, and written projects and/or homework.
15%	2.	Laboratory and cooperative learning experiences, and physical activity projects.
15%	3.	Physical fitness evaluations and physical fitness program design.
40%	4.	Participation.

There are certain aspects of grading that remain controversial. For example, should you assign a grade based on the outcomes of personal fitness assessments (fitness testing)? Or should you assign the grade based on the student's ability to accurately administer and explain the fitness assessment (fitness testing)? Or both? Some schools or school districts require teachers to administer fitness assessments and assign grades accordingly. In our opinion, this should be done only when students have had sufficient time to condition and prepare themselves for the assessments. Teachers also need to realize that factors such as age, physical maturation, gender, and trainability (genetics) will influence student performances. Above all, you should not use fitness assessments in a way that will discourage students from wanting to engage in regular physical activity or exercise.

Inclusion is the practice of educating all students, both disabled and nondisabled, in regular classes. In physical education, inclusion means that students with disabilities are placed in classes with their age-appropriate peers with instruction that meets their individual needs. It is a chance for children with and without disabilities to have the opportunity to interact and work together toward common goals.

Students can be safely included and achieve success in regular physical education classes without the need to completely change the program or cause undue burden on the physical educator. Some modifications may need to be made to accommodate the student with disabilities in class, but these changes can be positive for the entire class. Each activity needs to be carefully considered for the types of modifications necessary for success for all students.

There are other methods of including the special student in regular physical education. Often times a peer tutor is all the student with disabilities needs to be able to experience success in physical education class. The type of disability will determine the style and extent of tutoring a student may need.

Some disabled students may need a professional assistant to accompany them to physical education class. This determination needs to be made with input from the school's multidisciplinary team that works with the special education students.

The Adapted Physical Education specialist assigned to the school can offer a wealth of information to teachers working with students with disabilities in the regular physical education setting. This specialist can offer modifications, specialized equipment, or suggestions for accommodating the special student in physical education.

Cerebral Palsy

Cerebral palsy is a non-progressive, permanent, neurological condition that is the result of damage to a specific motor area of the brain thereby affecting the development of the central nervous system. The extent of the damage and the age at which it happens has a direct effect on what neurological impairment occurs. Cerebral palsy can occur before, during, or anytime after birth. Approximately 30% of all cases are the result of prenatal difficulties, 60% occur during birth, and 10% occur later in life as a result of an accident or illness.

General characteristics of cerebral palsy include muscular weakness, poor coordination, paralysis, and other disturbances to voluntary motor control. Often, mental retardation, seizure disorders, perceptual disorders, and speech deficits are also present.

Individuals with cerebral palsy are classified according to the amount of dysfunction and the associated motor involvement. The basic classifications of cerebral palsy include:

1. monoplegia—dysfunction in one extremity (rare)
2. paraplegia—dysfunction in the lower extremities
3. hemiplegia—dysfunction in both the upper and lower extremities on the same side of the body
4. triplegia—dysfunction in three extremities (usually both legs and one arm)
5. quadriplegia—dysfunction in all four extremities

Implications for Physical Education

A multidisciplinary approach is advised when planning physical activity for the cerebral palsy student since the psychomotor characteristics vary vastly according to the type of cerebral palsy, the severity of the condition, and associated disorders. Consideration must also be given to the presence of primitive reflexes and perceptual-motor deficits that may exist. Programs should focus on what the student can do and should be designed to enhance the student's functional abilities.

Instructional Strategies/ Adaptations

1. Become familiar with the student's complete medical condition. Obtain program recommendations for the student from physicians, occupational therapists, physical therapists, and any other member of the multidisciplinary team involved with the student.
2. Allow time at the beginning and end of each class for the student to do relaxed stretching of various muscle groups.
3. Utilize gross motor activities as opposed to fine motor activities.
4. Limit activities to those that do not require highly coordinated movements and/or good balance.
5. Include activities and movements that do not elicit any primitive reflexes that may be present.
6. Allow plenty of time for the student to repeat a skill or parts of a skill as many times as necessary.
7. Adjust the skill/activity requirements to each student's muscular strength and joint flexibility.
8. Provide leisure/recreation activities that have carry-

over value into the community as opposed to "sport type" activities.

9. Mobility during activities can be greatly enhanced through the use of walkers, scooters, and other assistive devices.

10. Make use of adaptive equipment such as Velcro, special grips, etc. that enhance the student's ability to manipulate objects.

Spinal Cord Injuries

A spinal cord injury is a permanent condition that results when damage occurs to the spinal cord and/or spinal nerves. The degree of impairment that results is dependent upon:

- the site of the injury. The higher the injury, the more damage and the greater the loss of function.
- whether the injury is partial or complete. If the injury is partial, there is a possibility of regaining lost function. The nerves do not regenerate themselves, but as pressure from trauma and swelling is relieved some function may be restored. If the injury is complete, it is permanent and no function will be regained since the nerves are unable to regenerate themselves.

Spinal cord injuries are classified into two basic categories:

Paraplegia results from severance at, or below, the second thoracic (T-2) vertebrae. Paralysis and impaired function occur in the lower limbs.

Quadriplegia results from severance of the spinal cord above the second thoracic (T-2) vertebrae. Paralysis and impaired function occurs in all four limbs.

Implications for Physical Education

The most important consideration to make when planning an activity program for students with a spinal cord injury is to correctly assess their medical condition. The program must be planned and developed around the severity and level of injury. Realistic goals need to be established based on the student's capabilities and/or skills that must be relearned.

Instructional Strategies/Adaptations

1. All activity programs need to be developed in collaboration with the medical personnel involved in the rehabilitation of students with a spinal cord injury.

2. Assess the movement capabilities of the students and adapt to those capabilities activities that will allow maximum participation and success.

3. Encourage the students to help plan their own physical education program.

4. The students should be encouraged to perform all parts of an activity or skill that they can.

5. Focus on developing strength and endurance in the unaffected muscle groups.

6. Be sure to include activities and exercises that can assist students in achieving and maintaining physical fitness.

7. Developing upper body strength, flexibility, and endurance are particularly important for the paraplegic. It will not only assist them in propelling the wheelchair but it will also make transferring to and from the chair easier.

8. Exercises and activities that increase circulation to the lower limbs are important in alleviating some of the secondary complications that can occur.

9. If the student is able to transfer to and from the chair, encourage them to do so. This will not only enhance upper body development but will help to improve lower limb circulation.

10. It may be necessary to make modifications such as distance requirements, accuracy, and/or form so that the students experience success.

11. All activities should allow for maximum participation with the students' peers.

12. Be aware that students with spinal cord injuries are unable to regulate heat dissipation from the injury site down.

13. Watch for the development of ulcers and/or pressure sores that may result from a particular exercise or activity.

14. Seek the assistance of physical and occupational therapists in developing aids and assistive devices for students' wheelchairs to facilitate their participation in activities.

Muscular Dystrophy

Muscular dystrophy is a term that is used to describe a group of related degenerative muscle diseases. It is a chronic, progressive deterioration of the voluntary musculature. Although the exact cause of muscular dystrophy is unknown, it is known that muscle protein is lost, causing weakness and atrophy of the skeletal muscles. The protein is gradually replaced by fat and connective tissue.

Implications for Physical Education

Programs of physical activity for the student with muscular dystrophy are critical to the maintenance of the best possible physical health. The more activities utilized to maintain existing function, the more likely it is that the debilitative effects of the disease can be delayed. The actual adaptations and activities for individual students will depend upon the type of muscular dystrophy that they have and how far the disease has actually progressed.

Instructional Strategies/Adaptations

1. Recommendations from a student's physician are critical when planning a program to ensure that the activities and modifications are not contraindicated.
2. Activities should focus on maintaining existing function.
3. Moderate exercise for the unaffected muscle groups is critical.
4. When activities involve the affected muscle groups, no resistance other than gravity should be utilized.
5. Any exercise or activity that causes undue strain or fatigue should be avoided.
6. Activity periods should be frequent, but short in duration. The students should be encouraged to participate to their fullest capacity.
7. Frequent rest periods should be provided for students who fatigue easily.
8. Students should be encouraged to participate in as many different activities as possible.
9. Activities requiring locomotion should be utilized as long as possible to increase and/or prolong independent movement.
10. As the disease begins to progress, use adaptations and modifications that will allow the student to successfully complete assigned tasks.
11. It is important to be particularly sensitive to the emotional needs of the student with muscular dystrophy.
12. Utilize the "buddy" system to help compensate for students' weaknesses while still allowing them some independence in movement.

Cardiovascular Conditions

Cardiovascular conditions include any and all diseases involving the heart and/or blood vessels. Disorders that are prevalent in children include congenital heart conditions and rheumatic heart disease.

The most common occurrence of cardiovascular disease in children results from rheumatic fever complications. The exact cause of rheumatic fever is not known although it occurs following a streptococcus infection. The heart is not always affected, but when it is, it causes the mitral and aortic valves of the heart to become inflamed, resulting in such severe scarring that the valves are unable to function properly.

Implications for Physical Education

Most students affected with either rheumatic or congenital cardiovascular disorders can benefit from a well planned physical education program that allows the students to work within their capabilities. It is critical when planning a program for students with cardiac conditions that the intensity and tolerance level for exercise of the individual students be established. Restrictions for students will vary based on the severity of their condition. Activities that are within tolerance levels for a student can be determined using the American Heart Association's functional classification system. The classification system is as follows:

Class I (A)	No significant limitations of physical activity.
Class II (B)	Slight restrictions on physical activity.
Class III (C)	Moderately limited physical activity. Strenuous activity is contraindicated.
Class IV (D)	Severe limitations of physical activity. Unable to participate in activity without fatigue, dyspanea, and pain. These and other symptoms of cardiac insufficiency may be present even at rest.

Instructional Strategies/Adaptations

1. Activities that are too strenuous and/or involve body contact need to be modified.
2. Frequently monitor the student's pulse rate so that the level of activity can be adjusted accordingly. It is important to know what the student's resting heart rate is and to obtain a baseline measurement under a variety of situations.
3. Students with cardiac problems must be continually monitored during activity for any signs of distress (change in skin color, shortness of breath, etc.)
4. Try to design a total fitness program that does not

place great demands on the cardiovascular system.

5. Exercise and activity programs should be progressive in nature. Begin with short periods of activity with frequent rest periods and progress to longer periods of duration (as the student develops tolerance).

6. *Never* push students who indicate they are experiencing difficulties. Some students may need to be encouraged to stop activities when they seem fatigued.

7. Competitive activities should be avoided. Often, just the emotions involved in these situations will push the stress of the activity above the tolerance level of the student.

8. Take into consideration the personality of students when they are involved in physical activity. Some students become too competitive even in noncompetitive activities.

9. Keep the emotional stress of participating in an activity to a minimum.

10. Modify activities with respect to pace, distances traveled, and/or duration of activity to reduce stress on the cardiovascular system.

11. In team sports, have the student rotate positions frequently so that the intensity of the level of activities are modified.

12. Special considerations must be given to weather conditions. During hot or humid weather, limit activity since it causes an increase in expenditure of energy.

Mildly Retarded/Educable Mentally Retarded (EMR)

Mildly retarded students (IQ 68-52) possess social and motoric skills that are similar to their nondisabled peers. Academic performance is the most apparent difference. Much of a student's academic difficulties originate from the inability to deal with higher cognitive functioning and abstract thinking.

Implications for Physical Education

Many students who are classified as mildly retarded can, and do, participate in regular physical education activities without difficulty. They are much more like their "normal" peers in physical abilities and capabilities than in any other respect. Physical education classes and sports are often a primary opportunity for them to experience success and develop self-esteem.

It is important that mildly retarded students receive a well-rounded physical education program that provides them with numerous opportunities to experience and practice a variety of skills in varied situations. It is critical that activities also provide ample opportunities for positive social interactions with nondisabled peers. This will ensure that the younger mildly retarded student has the chance to develop play skills that may not develop naturally. It also affords the older student the opportunity to learn leisure skills that will enable them to successfully participate in community recreational activities.

Instructional Strategies/Adaptations

1. Most activities will require little or no modification. Students should be allowed to participate in all activities.

2. Activities and tasks should be age-appropriate and consistent with the students' levels of maturity.

3. All instruction should be progressive and success oriented.

4. Instructions need to be concise, concrete, and brief. Directions should be simple and sequential.

5. Provide a variety of activities that utilize the same skills so that transfer can occur.

6. To enhance mastery of a skill, utilize repetition but vary methods to maintain student interest.

7. Allow ample opportunities for practice. Practice periods should be short with frequent changes in activities to provide for success and to maintain motivation.

8. Provide the students with individual practice sessions so that they can repeat skill performance over and over.

9. Assist the students in developing a "movement vocabulary" by reinforcing key concepts and words involving the movement or skills being taught.

10. If necessary, provide mildly retarded students with "buddies" to assist them during activities.

Moderately Retarded/Trainable Mentally Retarded (TMR)

The student who is classified as moderately retarded (IQ 51-36) generally experiences more pronounced deficits in social, emotional, mental, and motoric development than the mildly retarded student. As the student becomes older, these deviations from the norm become more apparent.

The moderately retarded student generally exhibits significant problems with attention span, memory, and recognition/generalizations of learned skills. Socially, rudimentary behaviors are more significant than in the mildly retarded necessitating frequent reminders of socially appropriate responses.

Implications for Physical Education

Motorically, the moderately retarded student demonstrates more pronounced deficits in psychomotor skills and performance. It is possible that some of the deficits may be a result of failure to understand the movement skill rather than the actual inability to perform the skill.

Increased deficits in the moderately retarded seem to exist in balance, fundamental locomotor skills, general body coordination, and fitness levels. The presence of these deficits necessitates a more individualized program of motor skill development in order for the student to receive maximum benefit from the program.

Instructional Strategies/Adaptations

1. Provide ample time for learning to occur. Remember that the learning ability (rate) is diminished in the moderately retarded.
2. When teaching skills, utilize the parts vs. the whole approach. Breakdown each skill into distinct parts and work on each part before attempting to teach the whole skill.
3. Utilize concrete examples and demonstrations of tasks to be learned to enhance skill development. It may be necessary to physically manipulate the student through the desired pattern or task.
4. Provide plenty of independent practice time that is short and spaced out so that maximum success occurs.
5. All activities should be geared to providing the student with opportunities to experience success.
6. Often, progress is slow in the moderately retarded, so be certain to reinforce all attempts at completing tasks, as well as accomplishments that occur.
7. Use strong visual, tactile, kinesthetic, and auditory stimuli to enhance student learning.
8. Provide a variety of activities that assist the student in transferring skills from one activity to another.
9. Simplify all instructions and repeat them frequently to reinforce key concepts.

10. Keep game and movement activity terminology to a minimum. Frequently reinforce any terms that are used.

Severely and Profoundly Retarded (SMR)

The severely retarded (IQ 35-20) and the profoundly retarded (IQ less than 19) exhibit extreme developmental delays in all areas of growth and development. In addition to mental retardation, secondary disabling conditions such as cerebral palsy, visual deficits, hearing and speech problems, and delayed maturation often exist. These students rarely interact with others and require complete and total care.

Inappropriate social behaviors are often more pronounced in the severely and profoundly retarded. They have a tendency to become worse if intervention does not occur. The most common behaviors that are seen are self-stimulating behaviors such as rocking and self-mutilation.

Implications for Physical Education

With the severe and profound population, even the most fundamental skills must be taught. The emphasis of physical education programming for the severe and profound population should be on motor skill development. Tasks such as reaching and grasping, which normally develop with maturation, must be taught to the severe and profound student. Physical education activities as well as the development of fundamental movement patterns and skills must also be taught.

Instructional Strategies/Adaptations

1. One-on-one instruction is essential if any meaningful learning is to occur.
2. Provide activities that elicit any possible purposeful movement.
3. Activities should focus on assisting the students in understanding cause and effect, especially the effects that their own actions elicit.
4. Many times it is necessary to manually guide a student's body parts through the desired movement pattern.
5. The environment must be carefully structured so that maximum learning can occur.
6. Equipment should be modified to enable the stu-

dents to move more proficiently and effectively in their environment.

Learning Disabilities

Students with learning disabilities comprise the largest and perhaps the least understood group of students who experience learning difficulties. Many students with learning disabilities exhibit average or above average intellectual capabilities but their actual achievement is delayed due to a breakdown in one or more of the information processing steps. Normally, information processing is a continuous cycle that includes the following steps:

Receiving sensor input. Stimuli is received through visual, auditory, kinesthetic, vestibular, and/or tactile systems.

Processing and/or decision making. The stimuli is sorted, organized, and synthesized.

Motor output. The actual movement or action occurs.

Feedback. The stimuli that results from the motor output is received through the sensory systems and the process begins again.

Implications for Physical Education

Just as there is no one set of characteristics that describe a student with learning disabilities, there is also no clear profile of the motor performances of these students. Some students with learning disabilities will exhibit average or above average motor abilities and skills while others will exhibit significant perceptual-motor deficits. Often, students with learning disabilities will experience the following motoric difficulties: inaccurate perceptions of sensory cues, general awkwardness and/or clumsiness, poor static and dynamic balance, delayed and/or immature motor patterns and skills, difficulty in sequencing and motor planning, and difficulty with fine motor tasks.

It is imperative when planning a physical education program for students with learning disabilities that the unique learning characteristics of each student are taken into consideration. Physical education activities that are carefully and individually designed for success can provide excellent opportunities for the student with learning disabilities to develop a positive self-concept.

Instructional Strategies/Adaptations

1. Be aware of and understand the specific nature of each student's learning difficulties.
2. To eliminate frustration and failure, provide activities that are challenging but within the capabilities of a student.
3. Make sure that each student experiences success during each activity and/or lesson by task analyzing the activities and using progressions to teach skills.
4. Activities should proceed from simple to more complex in small increments.
5. Class routines should be highly structured and consistent from day to day.
6. Activities should concentrate on developing perceptual-motor abilities.
7. Instruction should be multi-sensory. Verbal directions need to be clear, concise, accompanied by visual demonstrations and, when appropriate, tactile assistance.
8. Highly competitive and elimination games should be avoided.
9. Allow the student with learning disabilities ample time to think through a task. Asking the student to verbalize instructions may also prove to be beneficial.
10. Reinforce academic concepts through movement activities as frequently as possible.
11. When planning a sequence of activities, make sure each part of the activity is distinctly different from the others.
12. Carefully sequence movement activities so that each student experiences success and a sense of direction.
13. Eliminate as much extraneous stimuli from the learning environment as possible.
14. Utilize various group formations to enhance each student's role as being a contributing member of a group.

Lesson Plans

The *Any Body Can Be Fit* book of personal fitness consists of eleven chapters. Each chapter has specific information pertaining to an important component of personal fitness. In the opinion of the authors, the eleven chapters should not be taught separately and independently of the other chapters. We do not suggest that you try to teach the course starting at chapter one and continuing from chapter to chapter until reaching chapter eleven. It is recommended that these eleven chapters be taught by selectively integrating specific sections from specific chapters. Optimal personal fitness requires the coordination of many fitness components. Therefore, the integrating of these chapters will provide the best opportunity for understanding and successfully experiencing the **A**ny **B**ody **C**an approach.

AM/AB=Active Mind/Active Body
TRP=Teacher Resource Package
FC=Fitness Check
TM=Teacher-made

It is also important to note the three major stages of activity throughout the course. Stage one includes a cardiovascular and flexibility unit. Stage two focuses on developing muscular strength and endurance while combining sound nutrition and body composition concerns. In stage three, students are exposed to a variety of activities including an aerobic dance unit, consumer issues, and stress management issues. Students are also encouraged to design their own personal fitness plan in stage three.

Lesson Plans

Accelerated Block*

Nine-week Lesson Plans

WEEK 1

Monday   **Discuss:** Ch. 1, Introduction, Sec. 1. **Activity:** AM/AB p. 6 and AM/AB p. 10.

Tuesday   **Discuss:** Ch. 1, Sec. 2; Ch. 5, Sec. 4. **Activity:** AM/AB p. 15, AM/AB p. 22, and Cardiovascular Conditioning (TRP); AM/AB p. 91; Flexibility Conditioning (TRP).

Wednesday **Discuss:** Ch. 1, Sec. 3, 4. **Review:** Ch. 1. **Activity:** Cardiovascular/ Flexibility Conditioning (TRP); Video.

Thursday   **Test:** Ch. 1. **Discuss:** Ch. 2, Sec. 1, 2. **Activity:** Physical Activity Readiness Questionnaire, p. 40 (TRP).

Friday   **Discuss:** Ch. 2, Sec. 3, 4. **Activity:** AM/AB p. 55; Cardiovascular/Flexibility Conditioning (TRP).

WEEK 2

Monday   **Discuss:** Ch. 2, Sec. 5. **Activity:** AM/AB p. 59; Cardiovascular/Flexibility Conditioning (TRP).

Tuesday   **Discuss:** Ch. 2, Sec. 6, 7. **Review:** Ch. 2. **Activity:** Cardiovascular/ Flexibility Conditioning (TRP); **Homework:** Case Study p. 67.

Wednesday **Test:** Ch. 2. **Discuss:** Ch. 3, Sec. 1; Ch. 5, Sec. 1. **Activity:** FIT Worksheet for Ch. 3 (TRP).

Thursday   **Discuss:** Ch. 3, Sec. 2. **Activity:** AM/AB p. 75; AM/AB p. 76; AM/AB p.161.

Friday   **Discuss:** Ch. 3, Sec. 3, 4; Ch. 6, Sec. 3. **Activity:** AM/AB p. 95; Cardiovascular/Flexibility Conditioning (TRP).

WEEK 3

Monday   **Discuss:** Ch. 3, Sec. 5, 6; Ch. 5, Sec. 5. **Review:** Ch. 3. **Activity:** AM/AB p. 99; Cardiovascular/Flexibility Conditioning (TRP). **Homework:** Case Study p. 103.

Tuesday   **Test:** Ch. 3. **Discuss:** Ch. 4, Sec. 1. **Activity:** AM/AB pp. 112–113; Skill-Related Fitness Worksheet (TRP); Cardiovascular/Flexibility Conditioning (TRP).

Wednesday **Discuss:** Ch. 4, pp. 114–115; Ch. 5, Sec. 2, 3; Ch. 6, Sec. 2, 4. **Activity:** AM/AB pp. 122–123; Health-Related Fitness Worksheet (TRP); FC p.198; and AM/AB p. 205.

Thursday   **Discuss:** Ch. 4, pp. 116–120; Ch. 9, Sec. 1. **Review:** Ch. 4. **Activity:** AM/AB pp. 122–123; Cardiovascular/Flexibility Conditioning (TRP).

Friday   **Quiz:** (TM) Ch. 4. **Activity:** FC pp. 126–134; Cardiovascular/Flexibility Conditioning (TRP).

Lesson Plans

WEEK 4

Monday **Activity:** FC pp. 135–137 (cont.), 140–142. Cardiovascular Conditioning (TRP).

Tuesday **Discuss:** Ch. 7, Sec. 1. **Activity:** FC pp. 142–145; Cardiovascular Conditioning (TRP).

Wednesday **Discuss:** Ch. 9, Sec. 3. **Activity:** FC, pp. 145–147; FC pp. 316–319.

Thursday **Discuss:** Ch. 6, Sec. 1. **Review:** Chs. 4–6. **Activity:** FC pp. 138–140; FC pp. 177–180; AM/AB pp. 149–151. **Homework:** Case Study, p. 187.

Friday **Test:** Chs. 4–6. **Discuss:** Ch. 7, Sec. 2; Ch. 8, Sec. 1, 2.

WEEK 5

Monday **Discuss:** Ch. 7, Sec. 5; Ch. 8, Sec. 3, pp. 251–253. **Activity:** AM/AB p. 239; AM/AB p. 277: Bench press p. 277.

Tuesday **Activity:** AM/AB p. 277: Front military press, p. 280; Bent-over row, p. 285; Squat, p. 287; Arm curl, p.291; French press, p. 292; Abdominal crunch, p. 293.

Wednesday **Discuss:** Ch. 8, Sec. 4 pp. 261–266. **Activity:** FC p. 263 (pretest).

Thursday **Review:** Chs. 7, 8. **Discuss:** Ch. 8, Sec. 4, pp. 267–268. **Activity:** FC p. 263 (cont.).

Friday **Test:** Chs. 7, 8. **Discuss:** Ch. 8, Sec. 3, pp. 253–261, **Activity:** AM/AB p. 254; AM/AB p. 277: Incline press, p. 278; Back shoulder press, p. 280; Back and Front lat pull, p. 286; Lunge, p. 289; Upright row, p. 283; Heel raises, p. 291.

WEEK 6

Monday **Review:** Ch. 8, Sec 3 (Muscles and exercises). **Activity:** Ch. 8, Sec. 3, Weight training circuit (see TRP).

Tuesday **Discuss:** Ch. 7, Sec. 3, pp. 223–226; **Activity:** Ch. 7, Sec. 3, Isometric exercise (see TRP); AM/AB p. 277; Bench press dumbbell, p. 277; Flat bench fly, p. 279; Shrug, p. 282; Good morning, p. 287; Leg extension, p. 290; Leg curl, p. 289; Shoulder raises, p. 284.

Wednesday **Review:** Ch. 8, Sec. 3 (Muscles and exercises). **Activity:** Ch. 8, Sec. 3, Weight training circuit (see TRP).

Thursday **Quiz:** (TM) Chs. 7, 8. **Discuss:** Ch. 7, Sec. 3, pp. 227–231. **Activity:** AM/AB p. 277: Incline press dumbbell, p. 278; Incline fly, p. 279; Shoulder press dumbbell, p. 280; Leg press, p. 287; Kickback, p. 293; Arm curl dumbbell, p. 291.

Friday **Discuss:** Ch. 7, Sec. 4. **Activity:** Ch. 8, Sec. 3, Weight training circuit (see TRP).

* These lesson plans can also be used with the AB Block.

Lesson Plans

Accelerated Block

Nine-week Lesson Plans (continued)

WEEK 7

Monday **Discuss:** Ch. 10, Sec. 1. **Review:** Chs. 7, 8. **Activity:** Ch. 8, Sec. 3, Weight training circuit (see TRP).

Tuesday **Test:** Chs. 7, 8. **Discuss:** Ch. 10, Sec. 2. **Activity:** AM/AB p. 351; AM/AB p. 352.

Wednesday **Discuss:** Ch. 9, Sec. 2. **Activity:** AM/AB p. 312; Ch. 8, Sec. 3, Weight training circuit (see TRP).

Thursday **Discuss:** Ch. 9, Sec. 4, 5; Ch. 10, Sec. 3; Ch. 11, Sec. 1. **Review:** Chs. 9, 10. **Activity:** AM/AB p. 377.

Friday **Test:** Chs. 9, 10. **Discuss:** Ch. 8, Sec. 5. **Activity:** Ch. 8, Sec. 3, Weight training circuit (see TRP); AM/AB p. 377 (cont.).

WEEK 8

Monday **Discuss:** Ch. 8, Sec. 6, AM/AB p. 295. **Activity:** Ch. 8, Sec. 3, Weight training circuit (see TRP); AM/AB, p. 377 (cont.).

Tuesday **Discuss:** Ch. 11, Sec. 2. **Activity:** AM/AB p. 377 (cont.).

Wednesday **Activity:** Ch. 8, Sec. 3, Weight training circuit (see TRP); AM/AB p. 377 (cont.).

Thursday **Discuss:** Ch. 11, Sec. 3. **Activity:** AM/AB, p. 387; AM/AB p. 377 (cont.).

Friday **Activity:** Ch. 8, Sec. 3, Weight training circuit (see TRP); AM/AB p. 377 (cont.).

WEEK 9

Monday **Activity:** FC p. 263 (post-test) (may use 1 RM); AM/AB p. 377 (cont.).

Tuesday **Activity:** FC p. 263 (post-test) (may use 1 RM); AM/AB p. 377 (cont.).

Wednesday **Activity:** AM/AB p. 377 presentations.

Thursday **Test:** Ch. 11. **Review:** All chapters. **Activity:** AM/AB p. 377 presentations; AM/AB pp. 7–9.

Friday **Test:** Final

Lesson Plans

Eighteen-week Lesson Plans

AM/AB=Active Mind/Active Body
TRP=Teacher Resource Package
FC=Fitness Check
TM=Teacher-made

WEEK 1

Monday	**Discuss:** Ch. 1, Introduction. **Activity:** AM/AB pp. 6–9; AM/AB pp. 10–11.
Tuesday	**Discuss:** Ch. 1, Secs. 1, 2. **Activity:** AM/AB pp. 15–16; AM/AB p. 22.
Wednesday	**Discuss:** Ch. 1, Sec. 3. **Activity:** Cardiovascular conditioning (see TRP).
Thursday	**Discuss:** Ch. 1, Sec. 4. **Review:** Ch. 1. **Activity:** Cardiovascular conditioning (see TRP). **Video.**
Friday	**Test:** Ch. 1. **Activity:** Cardiovascular conditioning (see TRP).

WEEK 2

Monday	**Discuss:** Ch. 2, Sec. 1. **Activity:** Physical Activity Readiness Questionnaire, p. 40; Cardiovascular conditioning (see TRP).
Tuesday	**Discuss:** Ch. 2, Sec. 2. **Activity:** AM/AB p. 95; Flexibility conditioning (see TRP).
Wednesday	**Discuss:** Ch. 2, Sec. 3. **Activity:** Cardiovascular/Flexibility conditioning (see TRP).
Thursday	**Discuss:** Ch. 2, Sec. 4. **Review:** Ch. 2. **Activity:** AM/AB p. 55.
Friday	**Quiz:** Ch. 2, Sec. 1–4. **Discuss:** Ch. 2, Sec. 5. **Activity:** AM/AB p. 59; Cardiovascular/Flexibility conditioning (see TRP).

WEEK 3

Monday	**Discuss:** Ch. 2, Sec. 6. **Activity:** Cardiovascular/Flexibility conditioning (see TRP).
Tuesday	**Discuss:** Ch. 2, Sec. 7. **Review:** Ch. 2. **Activity:** Case Study p. 67.
Wednesday	**Test:** Ch. 2. **Activity:** Cardiovascular/Flexibility conditioning (see TRP).
Thursday	**Discuss:** Ch. 3, Sec. 1. **Activity:** AM/AB p. 75; AM/AB p. 76.
Friday	**Discuss:** Ch. 3, Sec. 2. **Activity:** Cardiovascular/Flexibility conditioning (see TRP); FIT worksheet (see TRP).

WEEK 4

Monday	**Discuss:** Ch. 3, Sec. 3. **Activity:** Cardiovascular/Flexibility conditioning (see TRP).
Tuesday	**Discuss:** Ch. 3, Sec. 4; Ch. 6, Sec. 3, 4. **Activity:** AM/AB p. 95; AM/AB p. 205.
Wednesday	**Discuss:** Ch. 3, Sec. 5. **Activity:** Cardiovascular/Flexibility conditioning (see TRP).

Lesson Plans

Eighteen-week Lesson Plans (continued)

AM/AB=Active Mind/Active Body
TRP=Teacher Resource Package
FC=Fitness Check
TM=Teacher-made

Thursday	**Discuss:** Ch. 3, Sec. 6. **Review:** Ch. 3. **Activity:** AM/AB p. 99; Case Study p. 103.
Friday	**Test:** Ch. 3. **Activity:** Cardiovascular/Flexibility conditioning (see TRP).

WEEK 5

Monday	**Discuss:** Ch. 4, Sec. 1. **Activity:** AM/AB p. 112; Cardiovascular/Flexibility conditioning (TRP).
Tuesday	**Discuss:** Ch. 4, Sec. 1. **Review:** Ch. 4. **Activity:** AM/AB p. 112; Skill-related and Health-related worksheets (TRP).
Wednesday	**Quiz:** Ch. 4, Secs. 1 & 2. **Discuss:** Ch. 4, Sec. 3. **Activity:** FC, pp. 126–129, Cardiovascular/Flexibility conditioning (TRP).
Thursday	**Discuss:** Ch. 4, Sec. 3. **Activity:** FC pp. 130–137.
Friday	**Discuss:** Ch. 4, Sec. 4; Ch. 6, Sec. 2. **Activity:** FC pp. 140–142; FC p. 198.

WEEK 6

Monday	**Discuss:** Ch. 4, Sec. 4. **Activity:** FC pp. 142–145, Cardiovascular/Flexibility conditioning (TRP).
Tuesday	**Discuss:** Ch. 4, Sec. 4; Ch. 9, Sec. 3. **Activity:** FC pp. 145–147; FC pp. 316–319.
Wednesday	**Discuss:** Ch. 4, Sec. 4. **Activity:** FC pp. 138–140.
Thursday	**Discuss:** Ch. 5, Sec. 4. **Review:** Ch. 4. **Activity:** FC 177–180.
Friday	**Test**: Ch. 4. **Activity:** AM/AB pp. 149–151.

WEEK 7

Monday	**Discuss:** Ch. 5, Sec. 1. **Activity:** AM/AB p. 161; AM/AB p. 166.
Tuesday	**Discuss:** Ch. 5, Sec. 2, 3 and 5. **Review:** Ch. 5. **Activity:** Case Study p. 187.
Wednesday	**Test:** Ch. 5. **Discuss:** Ch. 7, Sec. 1, 2.
Thursday	**Discuss:** Ch. 8, Secs. 1, 2. **Activity:** AM/AB p. 277: Bench press, pp. 277–278.
Friday	**Discuss:** Ch. 7, Sec. 5, pp. 236–237; Ch. 8, Sec. 3, pp. 251–253. **Activity:** AM/AB p. 277: Squat pp. 287–288.

Lesson Plans

WEEK 8

Monday	**Discuss:** Ch. 8, Sec. 4, pp. 261–266. **Activity:** FC p. 263: Bench press (only).
Tuesday	**Discuss:** Ch. 8, Sec. 4, pp. 269–270. **Activity:** FC p. 263: Squat (only).
Wednesday	**Discuss:** Ch. 8, Sec. 6. **Activity:** AM/AB p. 277: Front Military press, p. 280; Bent-over row, pp. 285–286; Arm curl, p. 291; French press, p. 292; Abdominal crunch, pp. 293–294.
Thursday	**Activity:** FC p. 263 (pre-test).
Friday	**Review:** Ch. 7, 8. **Activity:** FC p. 263 (pretest cont.).

WEEK 9

Monday	**Test:** Chs. 7, 8. **Discuss:** Ch. 8, Sec. 3, pp. 253–261. **Activity:** AM/AB p. 254.
Tuesday	**Discuss:** Ch. 8, Sec. 6. **Activity:** AM/AB p. 277: Incline press, pp. 278–279; Back shoulder press, p. 280; Back and Front lat pull, p. 286; Lunge, p. 289; Upright row, p. 283; Heel raises, p. 291.
Wednesday	**Activity:** Ch. 8, Sec. 3. Weight training circuit (see TRP).
Thursday	**Discuss:** Ch. 7, Sec. 5, pp. 238–240. **Activity:** AM/AB p. 233; AM/AB p. 277: Bench press dumbbell, p. 277; Flat bench fly, pp. 279–280.
Friday	**Activity:** Ch. 8, Sec. 3. Weight training circuit (see TRP).

WEEK 10

Monday	**Activity:** Ch. 8, Sec. 3. Weight training circuit (see TRP).
Tuesday	**Discuss:** Ch. 7, Sec. 3, pp. 223–226. **Activity:** Ch. 7, Sec. 3, Isometric exercise (see TRP).
Wednesday	**Activity:** Ch. 8, Sec. 3, Weight training circuit (see TRP).
Thursday	**Discuss:** Ch. 7, Sec. 3, pp. 227–231. **Review:** Chs. 7, 8. **Activity:** AM/AB p. 277: Incline press dumbbell, pp. 278–279; Incline fly, pp. 279–280; Shoulder press dumbbell, pp. 280–281.
Friday	**Test:** Chs. 7 & 8. **Activity:** Ch. 8, Sec. 3, Weight training circuit (see TRP).

WEEK 11

Monday	**Activity:** Ch. 8, Sec. 3, Weight training circuit (see TRP).
Tuesday	**Discuss:** Ch. 7, Sec. 4. **Activity:** AM/AB p. 277: Shoulder raises, pp. 284–285; Leg press, p. 287; Kickback, p. 293; Arm curl dumbbell, pp. 291–292.
Wednesday	**Activity:** Ch. 8, Sec. 3, Weight training circuit (see TRP).
Thursday	**Discuss:** Ch. 8, Sec. 5. **Review:** Chs. 7, 8. **Activity:** AM/AB p. 277: Shrug, p. 282; Good Morning, p. 287; Leg extension, p. 290; Leg curl, pp. 289–290.
Friday	**Quiz:** Chs. 7, 8, **Activity:** Ch. 8, Sec. 3, Weight training circuit (see TRP).

Lesson Plans

Eighteen-week Lesson Plans (continued)

WEEK 12

Monday	**Activity:** Ch. 8, Sec. 3, Weight training circuit (see TRP).
Tuesday	**Discuss:** Ch. 9, Sec. 1, 2. **Activity:** AM/AB p. 312.
Wednesday	**Activity:** Ch. 8, Sec. 3, Weight training circuit (see TRP).
Thursday	**Discuss:** Ch. 9, Secs. 4, 5. **Activity:** Case Study, Ch. 9.
Friday	**Activity:** Ch. 8, Sec. 3, Weight training circuit (see TRP).

WEEK 13

Monday	**Activity:** Ch. 8, Sec. 3, Weight training circuit (see TRP).
Tuesday	**Activity:** AM/AB p. 295.
Wednesday	**Activity:** FC p. 263 (post-test), (may use 1 RM).
Thursday	**Review:** Chs. 7, 8. **Activity:** FC p. 263 (post-test), (may use 1 RM).
Friday	**Test:** Chs. 7, 8.

WEEK 14

Monday	**Discuss:** Ch. 10, Sec. 1. **Activity:** Nutrient worksheet (see TRP).
Tuesday	**Discuss:** Ch. 10, Sec. 1. **Activity:** Nutrient worksheet (see TRP).
Wednesday	**Discuss:** Ch. 10, Sec. 2. **Activity:** AM/AB p. 351; AM/AB p. 352.
Thursday	**Discuss:** Ch. 11, Sec. 1, AM/AB p. 377 (aerobic dance exercise), **Activity:** AM/AB p. 377 (Begin aerobic dance exercise routine).
Friday	**Discuss:** Ch. 10, Secs. 3, 4. **Review:** Ch. 10. **Activity:** AM/AB p. 377.

WEEK 15

Monday	**Test:** Ch. 10. **Activity:** AM/AB p. 377.
Tuesday	**Discuss:** Ch. 11, Sec. 2. **Activity:** AM/AB p. 377.
Wednesday	**Discuss:** Ch. 11, Sec. 3. **Activity:** AM/AB p. 387; AM/AB, p. 377.

Lesson Plans

| Thursday | **Activity:** AM/AB p. 377. (Design and practice the warm-up section.) |
| Friday | **Activity:** AM/AB p. 377. (Design and practice the arm section.) |

WEEK 16

Monday	**Activity:** AM/AB p. 377. (Design and practice the aerobic section.)
Tuesday	**Activity:** AM/AB p. 377. (Design and practice the leg and abdominal section.
Wednesday	**Activity:** AM/AB p. 377. (Design and practice the cool-down section.)
Thursday	**Activity:** AM/AB p. 377. (Practice entire routine.)
Friday	**Activity:** AM/AB p. 377. (Presentations.)

WEEK 17

Monday	**Activity:** AM/AB p. 377. (Presentations.)
Tuesday	**Review:** Ch. 11. **Activity:** AM/AB p. 377. (Presentations.)
Wednesday	**Test:** Ch. 11. **Activity:** AM/AB p. 377 (Designing your complete personal fitness program.)
Thursday	**Activity:** AM/AB p. 381 (Designing your complete personal fitness program), Ch. 11, Sec. 1, Class participation in lifetime activities (basketball, volleyball tennis, walking, jogging, etc.).
Friday	**Activity:** AM/AB p. 381 (Designing your complete personal fitness program), Ch. 11, Sec. 1, Class participation in lifetime activities (basketball, volleyball tennis, walking, jogging, etc.).

WEEK 18

Monday	**Activity:** AM/AB p. 381. (Designing your complete personal fitness program); Ch. 11, Sec. 1, Class participation in lifetime activities (basketball, volleyball tennis, walking, jogging, etc.).
Tuesday	**Discuss:** AM/AB p. 381. (Designing your complete personal fitness program. Turn it in.)
Wednesday	**Review for Test.**
Thursday	**Review for Test.**
Friday	**Final Test.**

Resources

American College of Sports Medicine
P.O. Box 1440
Indianapolis, IN 46206-1440
Ph: 317-637-9200
Fax: 317-634-7817
E-mail: PIP.ACSM@ACSM.ORG

**American Master Teacher Program
for Children's Physical Education**
Human Kinetics Publishers
P.O. Box 5076
Champaign, IL 61825-5076
Ph: 217-351-5076, Ext. 2258
Fax: 217-351-2674

American School Health Association
P.O. Box 708
Kent, OH 44240
Ph: 216-678-1601
Fax: 216-678-4526

Division of Adolescent and School Health
National Center for Chronic Disease Prevention and
Health Promotion
Centers for Disease Control and Prevention
MSK32
4770 Buford Highway N.E.
Atlanta, GA 30341-3724
Ph: 770-488-5356
Fax: 770-488-5972

International Association of Fitness Professionals
6190 Cornerstone Ct. East
Suite 204
Sand Diego, CA 92121-3773
Ph: 619-535-8979, ext. 7/800-999-4332, ext. 7
Fax: 619-535-8234

**National Association for Physical
Education in Higher Education**
Dr. Gail Evans, Executive Secy.-Treasurer
Dept. of Human Performance
San Jose State University
San Jose, CA 95192-0054
Ph: 408-924-3029
Fax: 408-924-3053
E-mail: grant@sjsuvm1.sjsu.edu

**National Assoc. of Governor's
Councils on Physical Fitness and Sports**
201 S. Capitol Avenue, Suite 560
Indianapolis, IN 46225
Ph: 317-237-5630
Fax: 317-237-5632

National School Health Education Coalition
1400 Eye Street, NW, Suite 520
Washington, DC 20005
Ph: 202-408-0222
Fax: 202-408-8922

National Wellness Institute, Inc.
1045 Clark Street, Suite 210
P.O. Box 827
Stevens Point, WI 54481-0827
Ph: 715-342-2969
Fax: 715-342-2979
E-mail: nwelli@wis.com

**President's Council on
Physical Fitness and Sports**
701 Pennsylvania Ave. NW, Suite 250
Washington, DC 20004
Ph: 202-272-3421
Fax: 202-504-2064

**Society of State Directors of Health,
Physical Education, and Recreation**
9805 Hillridge Drive
Kensington, MD 20895
Ph: 301-949-0709
Fax: 301-949-0799

United States Physical Education Foundation
P.O. Box 5076
Champaign, IL 61825-5076
Ph: 217-351-5076, Ext. 2258

Youth Fitness Coalition, Inc. / Project ACES
P.O. Box 6452
Jersey City, NJ 07306-0452
Ph: 201-433-8993
Fax: Same, but call first

Manufacturers and Suppliers

Weightlifting Belts

Champion Glove Mfg. Co
2200 E. Ovid
Des Moines, IA 50313
Ph: 515-265-2551 / 800-247-4537
Fax: 515-265-7210

Ironclad Sports, Inc.
18 Eldorado Drive
East Northport, NY 11731
Ph: 800-685-2535
Fax: 516-462-5295

Pioneer Products
Div. General Leathercraft Mfg.
1330 Northwestern Dr.
El Paso, TX 79912
Ph: 915-833-9892 / 800-445-5262
Fax: 915-585-1412

Exercise Benches

Atlantic Fitness Products
Div. Fitness Corp. of America, Inc.
6701 Moravia Park Dr.
Baltimore, MD 21237
Ph: 410-488-2020 / 800-445-1855
Fax: 410-488-3059

Cemco Physical Fitness Products
2453 Chico Avenue
South El Monte, CA 91733
Ph: 818-442-2295 / 800-782-6377
Fax: 818-444-5157

National Barbell Supply
23550 Commerce Park Road
Beachwood, OH 44122
Ph: 216-595-1700 / 800-835-1091
Fax: 216-595-1708

Blood Pressure Meters

American Medical Screening
2923 N. 33rd Avenue
Phoenix, AZ 85017
Ph: 602-269-0655
Fax: 602-269-2128

Blood Pressuring Monitoring, Inc.
11350 Gladwin Street
Los Angeles, CA 90049
Ph: 310-476-8033
Fax: 310-476-8033

Her-Mar, Inc.
P.O. Box 402916
Miami Beach, FL 33140
Ph: 305-532-5413 / 800-327-8209
Fax: 305-532-6803

Bodybuilding, Training Aids

All Pro Exercise Products, Inc.
135 Hazelwood Drive
Jericho, NY 11753-1799
Ph: 516-938-9287 / 800-735-9287
Fax: 516-932-9849

Health for Life
8033 Sunset Blvd., Suite 483
Los Angeles, CA 90046
Ph: 310-306-0777 / 800-874-5339
Fax: 310-305-7672

JBBA Publishing
Div. JBBA, Inc.
P.O. Box 842
Appleton, WI 54912-0842
Ph: 414-731-5222 / 800-535-2366
Fax: 414-731-5749

Video Cassettes

Body Wise Int'l, Inc.
6350 Palomar Oaks Ct.
Carlsbad, CA 92009
Ph: 619-438-8977
Fax: 619-438-9033

Destination Fitness
Div. CVT Productions, Inc.
440 Charnelton Street, Suite 220
Eugene, OR 97401
Ph: 541-345-9635 / 800-624-4952
Fax: 541-345-2977

Video Learning Library
15838 N. 62nd Street
Scottsdale, AZ 85254-1988
Ph: 602-596-9970 / 800-383-8811
Fax: 602-596-9973

Dynamix
733 W. 40th St., #10
Baltimore, MD 21211-2142
Ph: 410-243-9755 / 800-843-6499
Fax: 410-243-9759

Stretching Inc.
P.O. Box 767
Palmer Lake, CO 80133
Ph: 800-333-1307
Fax: 719-481-9058

Karen Westfall Productions
P.O. Box 2504
St. George, UT 84770
Ph: 800-566-2182
Fax: 801-628-3160

InLytes Productions
610 B. Distillery Commons
Louisville, KY 40206
Ph: 502-584-5197 / 800-243-7867
Fax: 502-584-5289

Fitness Arts Distributors
1455 19th Street
Santa Monica, CA 90404
Ph: 800-735-3315
Fax: 310-264-1628

Bergh International Holdings
5428 Lyndale Avenue South
Minneapolis, MN 55419
Ph: 612-827-0254 / 800-423-9685
Fax: 612-827-1103

Computer Software, Activity Tracking

Alternate Computer Services/ Club-Pac
609 W. Lunt Avenue
Schaumburg, IL 60193
Ph: 708-893-1992
Fax: 708-893-1974

Body Logic
P.O. Box 162101
Austin, TX 78716
Ph: 512-327-0050 / 800-285-8212
Fax: 512-327-6770

Custom Design Systems, Inc.
200 Daniels Way, Suite 210
Freehold, NJ 07728
Ph: 908-294-0003 / 800-CDS-SALE
Fax: 908-294-9397

Computer Software, Exercise Prescription

BioAnalogics Systems, Inc.
9000 S.W. Gemini
Beaverton, OR 97005-7151
Ph: 503-626-8000 / 800-327-7953
Fax: 503-641-4031

Computerized Bodyweight Management Systems (CBMS)
P.O. Box 62597
Colorado Springs, CO 80962
Ph: 800-743-9750
Fax: 510-937-2618

Integrated Fitness Corp.
26 Sixth St., Suite 305
Stamford, CT 06905
Ph: 203-961-9192
Fax: 203-961-9663

Computer Software, Fitness Assessment

Bioelectrical Sciences, Inc.
5580 La Jolla Blvd., Suite 714
La Jolla, CA 92037
Ph: 619-270-8536
Fax: 619-270-8536

Computer Outfitters
639 N. Swan Road
Tucson, AZ 85711
Ph: 602-795-4722 / 800-827-2567
Fax: 602-795-5465

Peak Performance Technologies, Inc.
7388 S. Revere Pkwy., #601
Englewood, CO 80112
Ph: 303-799-8686 / 800-PIK-PEAK
Fax: 303-799-8690

Computer Software,
Nutrition/Diet

CSI Software
15425 North Fwy., #180
Houston, TX 77090
Ph: 713-872-0984 / 800-247-3431
Fax: 713-873-7240

Pro Body Comp, Inc.
430 Dickinson Street
Springfield, MA 01108
Ph: 413-733-8700 / 800-732-2004
Fax: 413-734-2790

Fat Calipers

Accu-Measure, Inc.
P.O. Box 4040
Parker, CO 80134
Ph: 303-690-4211 / 800-866-2727
Fax: 303-690-4219

Country Technology, Inc.
P.O. Box 87
Gays Mills, WI 54631
Ph: 608-735-4718
Fax: 608-735-4859

Isorobic Exercise Equip.
5521 Scotts Valley Drive
Scotts Valley, CA 95066
Ph: 408-439-9898 / 800-538-7790
Fax: 408-439-9504

Free Weights

Badger Fitness Equip.
1010 Davis Avenue
South Milwaukee, WI 53172
Ph: 414-764-4068
Fax: 414-768-7047

**Dynamic Fitness Products, Inc./
  Bodymasters**
139 Route 9W North, P.O. Box 367
Garnerville, NY 10923
Ph: 914-429-0062 / 800-669-2660
Fax: 914-429-0104

Hoist Fitness Systems
9990 Empire Street, #130
San Diego, CA 92126
Ph: 619-578-7676 / 800-541-5438 (CA)
800-548-5438
Fax: 619-578-9558

Heart Rate Meters

CardioAnalysis Systems, Inc.
255 N. Washington Street, #202
Rockville, MD 20850-1703
Ph: 301-279-7300 / 800-543-2850
Fax: 301-279-7303

Her-Mar, Inc.
P.O. Box 402916
Miami Beach, FL 33140
Ph: 305-532-5413 / 800-327-8209
Fax: 305-532-6803

Trinity Fitness and Sports Co.
2410 J Street
Sacramento, CA 95816-4806
Ph: 916-442-8500
Fax: 916-441-6301

Progressive Resistance
Machines, Multistation

**David Fitness Systems/
  Kinetic Resources Inc.**
3725 Cockrell Avenue
Fort Worth, TX 76110
Ph: 817-921-9981 / 800-933-2600
Fax: 817-921-1407

Fitness Equip. Source, Inc.
870 East, 9400 South, Suite 203
P.O. Box 68
Sandy, UT 84094
Ph: 801-576-0063 / 800-748-5125
Fax: 801-576-5631

Panatta Sport USA
Div. Dynakaz, Inc.
P.O. Box 1974
Auburn, AL 36830
Ph: 205-749-4994 / 800-892-2425
Fax: 205-821-3174

Stretching Equipment

Body Fit, Inc.
3925 Triumvera, Suite 17-E
Glenview, IL 60025
Ph: 708-296-7500 / 800-393-7227
Fax: 708-657-8690

Innovative Fitness Products
15 Kinross Drive
San Rafael, CA 94901
Ph: 415-454-2976 / 800-677-0871
Fax: 415-454-6401

Physical Research Corp.
451 Worcester Road
Charlton, MA 01507
Ph: 508-248-5244
Fax: 508-248-3627

Timers, Circuit Interval Timing Equipment

Precise Int'l
15 Corporate Drive
Orangeburg, NY 10962
Ph: 914-365-3500 / 800-431-2996
Fax: 914-425-4700

Chronomix Corp.
650-F Vaqueros Avenue
Sunnyvale, CA 94086
Ph: 408-737-1920 / 800-538-1548
Fax: 408-737-0160

Sprint/Rothhammer
P.O. Box 5579
Santa Maria, CA 93456-5579
Ph: 805-481-2744 / 800-235-2156
Fax: 805-489-0360

Weight Training - Accessories

American Body Building Products
4701 N. Federal Highway, Suite 360
Lighthouse Point, FL 33064
Ph: 305-786-9009 / 800-456-9105
Fax: 305-786-8835

Body Masters Sports Indus., Inc.
700 E. Texas Avenue, P.O. Box 259
Rayne, LA 70578
Ph: 318-334-9611 / 800-325-8964
Fax: 318-334-4827

Weight Training - Systems

Anterion Conditioning Equip.
4809 Miami Street
St. Louis, MO 63116
Ph: 314-351-9778

Bob Block Sports Fitness Equipment
8128 Castleway Court West
Indianapolis, IN 46250
Ph: 800-852-4168
Fax: 317-845-7704

Computer Sports Medicine, Inc.
135 Beaver Street
Waltham, MA 02154
Ph: 617-894-7751
Fax: 617-894-7754

Foundations of Personal Fitness

Any
Body
Can...Be Fit!

Foundations of Personal Fitness

Any
Body
Can...Be Fit!

Don L. Rainey
Edward Marcus High School
Flower Mound, Texas

Tinker D. Murray
Southwest Texas State University
San Marcos, Texas

West Publishing Company
Minneapolis/St. Paul   New York   Los Angeles   San Francisco

Copyedit: Mary Berry, Naples Editing Service
Composition: Parkwood Composition Services, Inc.
Index: Terry Casey
Illustrations: Precision Graphics, Gary Carroll
Exercise & weightlifting images: David Hanover, Hanover
Photography (complete photo credits follow the index)
Cover image: David Hanover, Hanover Photography

WEST'S COMMITMENT TO THE ENVIRONMENT

In 1906, West Publishing Company began recycling materials left over from the production of books. This began a tradition of efficient and responsible use of resources. Today, 100% of our legal bound volumes are printed on acid-free, recycled paper consisting of 50% new paper pulp and 50% paper that has undergone a de-inking process. We also use vegetable-based inks to print all of our books. West recycles nearly 27,700,000 pounds of scrap paper annually—the equivalent of 229,300 trees. Since the 1960s, West has devised ways to capture and recycle waste inks, solvents, oils, and vapors created in the printing process. We also recycle plastics of all kinds, wood, glass, corrugated cardboard, and batteries, and have eliminated the use of polystyrene book packaging. We at West are proud of the longevity and the scope of our commitment to the environment.

West pocket parts and advance sheets are printed on recyclable paper and can be collected and recycled with newspapers. Staples do not have to be removed. Bound volumes can be recycled after removing the cover.

Production, Prepress, Printing and Binding by West Publishing Company.

British Library Cataloguing-in-Publication Data. A catalogue record for this book is available from the British Library.

04 03 02 01 00 99   8 7 6 5 4 3 2

Library of Congress Cataloging–in–Publication Data

Murray, Tinker Dan, 1951–
   Foundations of Personal Fitness: Any Body Can Be Fit (student edition) ISBN #- 0-314-08465-7
   Foundations of Personal Fitness: Any Body Can Be Fit (Texas Teachers Wraparound edition)
      ISBN #- 0-314-08466-5
   Foundations of Personal Fitness: Any Body Can Be Fit (National Teachers Wraparound edition)
      ISBN #- 0-314-0622-1
   Includes index.
   Summary: Discusses the foundations of physical fitness, the benefits of regular exercise, and the advantages of weight training and proper nutrition.
   ISBN 0-314-08466-7 (Hard : alk paper)
1. Physical fitness—Health aspects—Juvenile literature.   2. Exercise—Physiological effect—
Juvenile literature.   (1. Physical fitness.   2. Exercises.   3. Health.] I. Rainey, Don.   II. Title.
RA781.M778 1997
613.7—dc20   96-4956
                                                                     CIP

About The Authors

Don L. Rainey

Don L. Rainey, M.S., is a physical educator and coordinator of health and physical education at Marcus High School in Flower Mound, Texas. He earned a bachelor of science degree in Health and Physical Education at Lamar University in 1971. He also earned a master of science degree in Health and Physical Education at Lamar in 1972, and has completed postgraduate studies at East Texas State University in Commerce, Texas. Don has taught the Foundations of Personal Fitness Course at Marcus High School for the past 12 years. He served as a national fitness consultant to the Boy's Clubs of America from 1983 to 1984. From 1985 to 1988 Don was a sub-committee member for the Governor's Commission on Physical Fitness that developed the Fit Youth Today Program. He served as Chair for the Texas Association for Health, Physical Education, Recreation, and Dance (TAHPERD) from 1985 to 1986. He was a founding member of the TAHPERD Foundations of Personal Fitness Course Committee in 1991, and continues to serve on that committee. He was named Teacher of the Year in Secondary Physical Education by TAHPERD in 1989 and was part of the Texas Teacher of the Year "Tour of Texas" in 1992. He was given the Honor Award from TAHPERD in 1994. He also was awarded a Physical Education Public Information (PEPI) Award in 1994. Don has conducted over forty workshops about the Foundations of Personal Fitness Course for physical educators. He has also presented and published numerous papers related to physical education and exercise science issues.

Tinker D. Murray

Tinker D. Murray, Ph.D., FACSM, is a professor and director of the human performance laboratory in the Health, Physical Education, and Recreation Department at Southwest Texas State University in San Marcos, Texas. He earned a bachelor of science degree in Physical Education and Biology from the University of Texas in 1973. He earned his master of education degree in Physical Education from Southwest Texas State University in 1976, and completed his Ph.D. in Physical Education from Texas A&M University in 1984. Tinker served as Director of Cardiac Rehabilitation at Brooke Army Medical Center from 1982 to 1984. Tinker has been a lecturer and examiner for the U.S.A. Track and Field Level II Coaching Certification Program since 1988. He served as the Vice Chair of the Governor's Commission for Physical Fitness in Texas from 1993-1994. Tinker was awarded a Physical Education Public Information (PEPI) Award in 1993 by the Texas Association for Health, Physical Education, Recreation, and Dance (TAHPERD) and was named TAHPERD Scholar for 1995. He also was given the Honor Award from TAHPERD in 1995. Tinker is a Fellow of the American College of Sports Medicine (ACSM) and certified as an ACSM Program Director. He served as the Chair of the TAHPERD Foundations of Personal Fitness Course Committee from 1991–1995 and is currently a member of the committee. He has conducted over twenty-five workshops about the Foundations of Personal Fitness Course for physical educators. Tinker has presented and published numerous papers related to physical education and exercise science issues.

Contents in Brief

Table of Contents

Chapter 7   # Developing Muscular Strength and Endurance through the Science of Weight Training   **216**

Chapter 8   # Start Lifting — Safely and Correctly   **244**

Chapter 9   # Your Body Composition   **300**

CONSUMER CORNER

Foreword

Health-related fitness programs are now clearly established to be important in the prevention of lifestyle generated diseases, including heart disease, diabetes, obesity, and even certain cancers.

The principles and concepts in *FOUNDATIONS OF PERSONAL FITNESS: Any Body Can Be Fit* are ones that will help with the understanding and development of health-related fitness programs for our students. These programs should be supported by all parents, teachers, physicians, and health care personnel. I strongly support them.

Steven P. Van Camp, M.D.
President,
American College of Sports Medicine,
1995–1996

Acknowledgements

To both of our wives, we appreciate you for helping make this book a reality and encouraging us to live up to what we said we ought to be able to do. A special thanks to all of our contributors who provided timely professional input and inspired us throughout this project. To Steven Van Camp, M.D. thanks for your medical advice and the foreword for this text. To Bill Squires, Ph.D. a special thanks for serving as our exercise science advisor for the text. We would also like to thank our editors, Bob Cassel, Mario Rodriguez, and Glenda Samples. We would like to thank all of our professional colleagues and friends from the Texas Association for Health, Physical Education, Recreation, and Dance (TAHPERD), the American Alliance of Health, Physical Education, Recreation, and Dance (AAHPERD), the American College of Sports Medicine (ACSM) and the Texas Regional Chapter of the American College of Sports Medicine (TACSM) for their support and guidance throughout our professional careers.

Reviewers

We would also like to acknowledge the following manuscript reviewers who made many valuable comments and suggestions during the early development stages of the project.

Jennifer Arant
Green County Technical Schools
Paragould, AR

Cinda Baer
Nimitz High School
Irving, TX

Dr. Robert Case
Sam Houston State University
Huntsville, TX

Dr. Paula Dohoney
Oklahoma State University
Stillwater, OK

Deanna Harris
Lake Highlands Junior High School
Dallas, TX

Dr. Mary McCabe
Hurst-Euless-Bedford ISD
Bedford, TX

Manuel Pacheco
J.M. Hanks High School
El Paso, TX

Sue Rehm
Byrd Middle School
Tulsa, OK

Marie Rossman
Trinity High School
Euless, TX

Thomas Schlarbaum
Hillsborough County Schools
Tampa, FL

Dr. Fred Wheeler
Pope High School
Marietta, GA

James Whitman
Charles Henderson Middle School
Troy, AL

Elly Zanin
Broward County Schools
Ft. Lauderdale, FL

Dedication

To my lovely wife, Julie — Thanks for all your love, patience, motivation, and professional expertise.
To my parents Louise and Bob — Thanks for your love and for encouraging me in my educational pursuits.
And, to my grandmother Rose — Thanks for your love and the great example of active living you provide at age 90.

Tinker

To my best and closest friend, my wife Reneé. Your support, encouragement, and assistance will be forever appreciated. To all of my family and friends, thank you for being a part of the successful completion of this book.

Don

Introduction

Many research studies show the positive influence of physical fitness on physical and mental health, self-esteem, and learning. Physical fitness promotes self-confidence, enhances learning, and is society's wise investment in the future.

Emphasis on academic achievement produces knowledgeable individuals. However, an educated mind cannot repay society's investment when that mind resides in a body poorly prepared for a long, productive, and healthy life. All too often an individual's contribution to society is cut short by disability, sickness, or premature death. Society's investment in education yields maximum returns only when there is a sound mind in a healthy body.

This book has been designed to allow you to experience and become educated about the **ABCs** of a healthy, active, and fit lifestyle. It is our hope that in this course, you will develop positive health and fitness attitudes, skills, and behaviors that you will adopt and enjoy for the rest of your long and healthy life.

Don Rainey
Tinker D. Murray

Chapter Overview

Chapter 1 is 34 pages long and divided into four sections listed to the right. Major learning outcomes of the chapter are also listed to the right. Briefly, this chapter introduces students to the concept of personal fitness and the positive outcomes associated with it. It emphasizes the importance of the individual's daily choices in determining that person's level of fitness. It also gives students some key concepts and skills about modifying their health risk factors.

Teacher Resource Material

In the Teacher Resource Package accompanying the textbook, you will find the following materials to help you teach this chapter.

Activity Sheets

One Reteaching Worksheet is provided in the Teacher Resource Package for each section of this chapter. Handouts are also provided for the following Active Mind/Active Body activities:

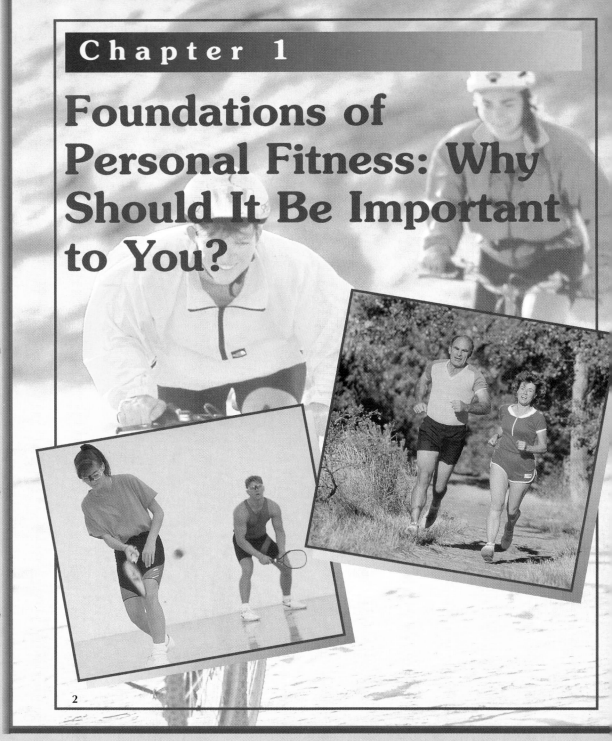

Chapter 1

Foundations of Personal Fitness: Why Should It Be Important to You?

2

PACING CHART

You could easily spend 4 to 5 days teaching this chapter if students read the entire chapter, do all of the Active Mind/Active Body activities, and complete several of the handouts from the Teacher Resource Package. However, you can cover the material in this chapter in 2 to 3 days. It is recommended that physical activity be a regular part of each class period (20–30 minutes minimum). Following are some examples of how to cover the main topics if you are pressed for time.

Contents

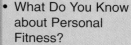

Outcomes

After reading and studying this chapter, you will be able to:

1. Define and explain the terms related to personal fitness.
2. Explain how negative or positive attitudes and beliefs about personal fitness can influence your health and physical fitness.
3. Explain and identify modifiable and less modifiable risk factors and how they influence life expectancy.
4. Explain and identify the positive outcomes that physical activity, exercise, or both can have on your health and physical fitness level.
5. Explain and discuss the national goals and recommendations for physical activity, exercise, or both, for adolescents.
6. Define and explain the stages of your personal fitness continuum.

Key Terms

After reading and studying this chapter, you will be able to understand and provide practical definitions for the following terms:

personal fitness	hypertension	low-density lipoprotein (LDL)
health	osteoporosis	very low density lipoprotein
wellness	obesity	(VLDL)
functional health	cholesterol	stress
physically active lifestyle	triglyceride	stressor
sedentary lifestyle	heart attack	distress
exercise	stroke	eustress
physical fitness	atherosclerosis	predisposition
risk factor	high-density lipoprotein	life expectancy
hypokinetic	(HDL)	longevity
cardiovascular disease		

3

- What Do You Know about Personal Fitness?
- What Are Your Current Attitudes and Beliefs about Physical Activity, Exercise, and Physical Fitness?
- How Physically Active Are You Now?
- What Are Your Health Risk Factors?

A Chapter Test for this chapter is available in the Teacher Resource Package.

Transparencies/Masters

A transparency or master is provided in the Teacher Resource Package for each of the following figures: 1.1, 1.2, 1.3, 1.4, 1.5, and 1.6.

Discuss the Photo

Ask students how often they go biking or running. Then discuss the benefits of being fit and healthy throughout their lives. Discuss with students their past experiences with achieving or failing to reach reasonable levels of physical fitness.

Time	Suggestions
Day 1	Assign students to read Sections 1 and 2 prior to class. In class do the Active Mind/Active Body activities on pp. 6–9 and pp. 10–11. Also include a variety of discussions about photos and figures.
Day 2	Assign students to read Sections 3 and 4 prior to class. In class do the Active Mind/Active Body activities on pp. 15–16 and p. 22.
Day 3	Discuss the benefits of personal fitness. Use Figures 1.2, 1.3, 1.4, 1.5, and 1.6 to enhance discussion. Discuss Guidelines 1 and 2 and the Personal Fitness Continuum.

Focus

Outcomes

In **Section 1** students will learn:

1. To define and explain the terms related to personal fitness.

2. To explain how negative and positive attitudes and beliefs about physical fitness can influence their health and physical fitness.

Focus Activities

1. Write the following on the board for students to work on while you are taking attendance: *Describe the activities that you performed in your past physical education class experiences.*

INTRODUCTION

Welcome to your course on the foundations of personal fitness! This course is different from any of the physical education courses that you may have taken in elementary, junior high, or middle school. In those courses you primarily played games or participated in sports activities. In this course you will learn that **A**ny **B**ody **C**an develop a plan for a physically active lifestyle that you can use now and throughout your adult life. You are about to start a journey during which you will learn about and experience personal fitness in a positive and successful way. Personal fitness is both obtainable and enjoyable. It is as easy as **A**, **B**, **C**: **A**ny **B**ody **C**an be fit!

This book and course have been designed to challenge you to do these things:

- Become educated about your personal levels of physical activity and physical fitness.
- Successfully experience the benefits of physical activity and physical fitness conditioning.
- Assess your own level of physical fitness and progress in the course.
- Design a physical activity and physical fitness program that can meet your individual needs now and in the future.

Throughout this book, you will be asked to explain, demonstrate, and experience the concepts presented to you by completing the "Active Mind/Active Body" activities. These activities will help you become responsible for planning, developing, and maintaining your own healthy lifestyle. In the first "Active Mind/Active Body" activity, on page 6, you will examine your current knowledge about what a physically active lifestyle is and what it involves. Completing this activity will increase your knowledge and help you identify the areas of fitness requiring further study.

SECTION 1 Personal Fitness: What's It All About?

personal fitness

the result of a way of life that includes living an active lifestyle, maintaining good or better levels of physical fitness, consuming a healthy diet, and practicing good health behaviors throughout life.

health

a state of well-being that includes physical, mental, emotional, spiritual, and social aspects.

Personal fitness has many definitions because the term means many different things to different people. In this section you will learn about some of the key concepts that are common to any definition of personal fitness. After concluding this section, you might want to create your own definition of fitness.

Personal Fitness and Its Benefits

Personal fitness is the result of a way of life that includes living an active lifestyle, maintaining good or better levels of physical fitness, consuming a healthy diet, and practicing good health behaviors throughout life. **Health** is a state of well-being that includes physical, mental, emotional, spiritual, and social aspects. Good health is

ABILITY LEVELS

Reteaching

Some students may need help mastering the concepts contained in this section. In your Teacher Resource Package, you will find the reproducible worksheet shown here. This worksheet should help students who have been absent and those needing additional help to improve their comprehension and retention of the content in this section.

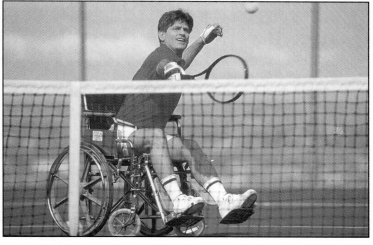

• *You can participate in personal fitness activities in a number of different ways. With such a wide range of sports and exercises to choose from, you will be sure to find activities that match your interests and abilities.*

2. Use Active Mind/Active Body on p. 6 to have students assess their current knowledge about what a physically active lifestyle is and what it involves.

Teach & Apply

Discussion

• Have students brainstorm ways they can add more physical activity to their daily lives. Then have them discuss barriers that may keep them from being physically active.

• Stress to students how important functional health is in later life. Then, discuss why being a "couch potato" can be dangerous to one's health. Refer to the cartoon on page 10 and remind students that "couch potatoes" start off as "tater tots."

• Have students discuss how their fitness and exercise habits can be affected by any of the negative attitudes.

---

wellness

the attainment and maintenance of a moderate to high level of physical, mental, emotional, spiritual, and social health.

functional health

a person's physical ability to function independently in life, without assistance.

physically active lifestyle

a way of living that regularly includes physical activity such as walking, climbing stairs, or participating in recreational movements.

sedentary lifestyle

an inactive lifestyle.

important to teens and adults, regardless of their age. Good health is necessary for performing normal daily tasks.

Wellness is the attainment and maintenance of a moderate to high level of physical, mental, emotional, spiritual, and social health. Wellness is a goal that requires a lifetime of commitment, from young adulthood through the Golden Years. In striving for wellness, you are trying to reach your full potential in all the areas of your life.

Functional health is a term that describes a person's physical ability to function independently in life, without assistance. If your functional health status drops below minimal levels, you can lose your physical independence in daily living. Examples of the loss of physical independence include losing the ability to walk, to drive a car, or to feed yourself. A person may have functional health but may possess a low level of wellness. For example, a person may still be able to drive his or her car but have the signs and symptoms of cardiovascular disease.

A **physically active lifestyle** is a way of living that regularly includes physical activity such as walking from class to class, climbing stairs, or participating in recreational activities. Researchers have recently shown that people who live a physically active lifestyle are able to maintain their functional health status longer than people who lead an inactive lifestyle, or **sedentary lifestyle**. Inactive people are often referred to as "couch potatoes."

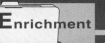

This activity will allow you to provide a more challenging learning experience for some of your students.

Have students complete the following activity: Pretend that you have lost your physical independence. With the cooperation of at least two friends, pretend that you cannot walk, drive a car, feed yourself, or perform any task that requires physical activity. Your friends must carry you (or push you in a wheelchair), drive you, and feed you, as well as perform any other task for you that would require physical independence. Make a list of the things that are the most difficult to adapt to in this condition. Trade roles with your friends, and compare your lists. How does this experience affect your feelings about being elderly and losing your physical independence?

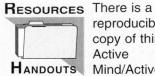

RESOURCES

HANDOUTS

There is a reproducible copy of this Active Mind/Active Body activity in your Teacher Resource Package.

Active Mind!
Active Body!

Use this questionnaire at the beginning of the course. Have the students give their honest opinions, with no grade attached. Save these surveys and return them to the students at the end of the course. Allow them to see if their knowledge of personal fitness has changed.

Answers

1. False. Cardiovascular fitness is related to your heart and lungs, not well-toned muscles.

2. True.

3. True.

4. True. A single bout of exercise can stress the cardiovascular system. However, multiple bouts of exercise for several weeks are required to have lasting effects and benefits on the cardiovascular system.

5. False. Muscle does not turn to fat. They are different types of tissue. However, you can lose muscle and increase fat in a specific area.

6. True.

7. True.

Active Mind! *Active* Body!
What Do You Know Now about Personal Fitness?

The following is a series of 50 statements about personal fitness. They are designed to evaluate your current knowledge about health and physical fitness. Some of the statements are true, and some are false. Try to be as honest as you possibly can with each of your answers. (Write your answers on a separate sheet of paper. **Do Not** write in this book.) If you are unsure about your answer, mark "unsure" for your response. There will be no grade assigned to this activity, so feel free to express your opinions. At the completion of the course, do this activity again to determine if your knowledge about physical fitness has increased.

	A I Am Certain It Is True	B I Think It Is True	C I Am Unsure	D I Think It Is False	E I Am Certain It Is False
1. People who have well-toned, fit muscles are automatically also cardiovascularly fit.	—	—	—	—	—
2. Regular exercise can reduce the heart rate at rest.	—	—	—	—	
3. Many of the cardiovascular benefits that result from regular exercise are gradually lost if exercise is not continued.	—	—	—	—	—
4. A single exercise session will have little lasting effect on the cardiovascular system.	—	—	—	—	—
5. Unexercised muscles can turn to fat.	—	—	—	—	—
6. Regular exercise can help reduce a person's resting blood pressure.	—	—	—	—	—
7. Regular exercise can increase the strength of your bones.	—	—	—	—	—
8. Ballistic stretching is an unsafe method for improving flexibility.	—	—	—	—	—
9. Isometric exercises involve static muscle contractions with little or no movement.	—	—	—	—	—
10. Regular exercise has little effect on the body's ability to use fat.	—	—	—	—	—
11. Swimming is an excellent way to increase one's cardiorespiratory endurance capacity.	—	—	—	—	—

Across the Disciplines

Math/Language Arts

Software programs have been developed that assist people in defining their level of personal fitness. Seldom, however is the user encouraged to reflect on and synthesize the results of the program. The results can aid in personal goal setting.

Using an integrated applications software program, have students develop an electronic spreadsheet that includes information from the "Active Mind/Active Body" on pp. 15–16. Students will have to design a spreadsheet format that will allow them to document and automati-

	A I Am Certain It Is True	B I Think It Is True	C I Am Unsure	D I Think It Is False	E I Am Certain It Is False
12. Muscular strength is the ability to move a heavy weight one time.	——	——	——	——	——
13. Playing soccer regularly can improve one's cardiorespiratory endurance capacity.	——	——	——	——	——
14. Weight training is a good way to improve one's cardiorespiratory endurance capacity.	——	——	——	——	——
15. Disorders such as obesity, high blood pressure, and back pain can be a result of no exercise.	——	——	——	——	——
16. A person with a high level of muscular strength has little danger of heart attack.	——	——	——	——	——
17. Skill-related components of fitness measure such things as balance, agility, coordination, and speed.	——	——	——	——	——
18. The overload principle involves three factors: intensity, duration, and frequency.	——	——	——	——	——
19. Jogging, swimming, cross-country skiing, and cycling are all examples of aerobic activity.	——	——	——	——	——
20. Cardiorespiratory endurance activities must be repeated at least five times per week in order to get any benefit.	——	——	——	——	——
21. Cardiorespiratory endurance refers to the body's ability to perform exercises for an extended period of time.	——	——	——	——	——
22. The target heart rate level for a healthy person building cardiorespiratory endurance is 60 to 80 percent of one's maximum heart rate.	——	——	——	——	——
23. Cool-down activities help prevent blood pooling.	——	——	——	——	——
24. Warm-up and stretching exercises will reduce the muscle soreness often felt when first starting an exercise program.	——	——	——	——	——
25. Cool-down periods are just as important as warm-up periods.	——	——	——	——	——
26. A weight training program is best used for building muscular endurance.	——	——	——	——	——

(Continued on next page)

8. True. Ballistic stretching is a quick, jerking process that can cause muscle tear to unconditioned muscle or muscles that have not been properly warmed-up.

9. True.

10. False. Regular exercise will burn calories and speed up your metabolism, both of which can help burn fat.

11. True. If swimming is done for a sustained time (20–30 minutes) on a regular basis (3–4 days/week), it will produce good cardiorespiratory capacity.

12. True.

13. True.

14. False. The use of light weights with high numbers of reps (15–25) can produce minimal cardiovascular endurance gains. Aerobic activities are the best way to produce cardiovascular gains.

15. True.

16. False. See #1.

17. True.

18. True.

19. True.

20. False. As few as 2 days a week can provide some benefits, however 3–4 days a week are recommended.

21. True.

22. True.

23. True.

24. True.

25. True.

26. True.

cally calculate numeric points for daily behaviors and weekly results for the duration of this fitness course. Using the word processing application, students will begin an electronic journal that allows them to integrate the information from the spreadsheet, set personal goals, evaluate their progress, and write about their reaction to their fitness experience.

If students are successful in this activity, they will have created a personal document that encourages them to develop, evaluate, and modify personal goals, enables them to chart their fitness experiences, and becomes a record of their personal reactions to the process.

What Do You Know Now about Personal Fitness? (continued)

27. True.
28. False. The length of time for these activities will depend on the type of activity and the intensity of the activity and the condition of the person. Mild walking may need less time while vigorous activities such as soccer, basketball, tennis, or running may need more time. Five is typically recommended.
29. False. Most healthy, young adults will only need a medical screening and not a complete medical examination.
30. True.
31. False. Regular exercise can enhance your sleep.
32. True.
33. False. Fit, healthy students are more alert, have more energy, and have higher attendance. Therefore, they do better in school.
34. True.
35. True.
36. True.
37. True. The type is important because it may have a direct effect on the intensity. If the intensity is too high, you will not be able to sustain the activity and therefore, you will burn fewer calories.
38. False. They use considerably more calories.
39. True.
40. True.
41. False. A person may have poor health-related fitness and still have a healthy looking body. They may have poor cardiovascular fitness, poor flexibility, or weak muscles.
42. True.

	A I Am Certain It Is True	B I Think It Is True	C I Am Unsure	D I Think It Is False	E I Am Certain It Is False
27. The benefits gained from exercise depend in part on the number of days and the length of time that a person exercises.					
28. The warm-up and stretching period of an exercise session need not be more than one or two minutes.					
29. All individuals should have a complete physical exam before starting an exercise program.					
30. Participating in an activity program where everyone exercises at the same intensity and frequency can be dangerous.					
31. Participation in a regular exercise program can reduce one's ability to sleep soundly.					
32. Exercise can provide an opportunity to reduce stress.					
33. Experts believe there is very little relationship between physical fitness and academic performance.					
34. Regular exercise can slow down the natural aging process.					
35. Physically active individuals are less likely than inactive individuals to develop cardiovascular disease.					
36. Regular exercise combined with dieting is a more effective way to reduce fat than just exercising.					
37. The number of calories burned during exercise depends on the type and the intensity of the exercise.					
38. An obese person uses the same number of calories as a light person during comparable exercise periods.					
39. An individual's body fat can be determined by skinfold measurements.					
40. Regular exercise increases the amount of oxygen the body can use while exercising.					
41. A person's health-related fitness refers to how that person's body looks.					
42. Exercising abdominal muscles may help prevent lower back muscle pain.					
43. Hypokinetic diseases are a result of too much activity.					

Special Needs

Disabled people need physical, motor, and health-related fitness as much as nondisabled individuals. Personal fitness, functional health, and a physically active lifestyle can be limited, however, by a physical disability. If you have students who are restricted in their ability to be physically active because of a disability, encourage them to strive for personal fitness, functional health, and an active lifestyle, within their limitations. All forms of fitness will aid in developing self-reliance and confidence among disabled groups.

	A I Am Certain It Is True	B I Think It Is True	C I Am Unsure	D I Think It Is False	E I Am Certain It Is False
44. Static stretching is the recommended method for conducting flexibility exercises.	___	___	___	___	___
45. A well-balanced diet can provide you with all the vitamins and minerals you need.	___	___	___	___	___
46. High repetitions during an exercise will produce more strength benefits.	___	___	___	___	___
47. You can never have too much flexibility.	___	___	___	___	___
48. The principle of progression deals with exercise improvement.	___	___	___	___	___
49. Exercise workouts should be at least 30 minutes long to provide any benefit.	___	___	___	___	___
50. The benefits of regular exercise are reduced as you become older.	___	___	___	___	___

exercise

physical activity that is planned, structured, repetitive, and results in the improvement or maintenance of personal fitness.

physical fitness

a level of individual physical ability that allows a person to perform daily physical tasks effectively with enough energy reserves for recreational activities or unexpected physical challenges.

By engaging in regular physical activity or **exercise**, you can improve or maintain an acceptable level of physical fitness. Physically active people are more likely to live life to its fullest. They add more than just years to their life. They add life to their years, by feeling and looking better.

Physical fitness is defined as a level of individual physical ability that allows a person to perform normal daily physical tasks effectively with enough energy reserves for recreational activities or unexpected physical challenges. Physical fitness is an outcome of a physically active lifestyle or exercise program that is practiced over time. A more detailed explanation of the different types of physical fitness will be presented in Chapter 4.

Moderate to high levels of physical fitness are associated with good health and wellness. Physical fitness is also related to how efficiently the heart, lungs, circulation, bones, and muscles function. Young adults who maintain a physically active lifestyle now and remain physically fit throughout life can expect a higher quality of life. They also reduce their risks for developing chronic diseases (high blood pressure, heart disease, stroke, and so on). Sedentary living habits and low physical fitness levels have a negative impact on both health and daily living.

It is important for you to understand that you *do not* have to be an athlete to reach moderate to high levels of physical fitness. Remember, **A**ny **B**ody **C**an be fit! Will you?

43. False. Hypokinetic refers to a low level of activity.
44. True.
45. True.
46. False. High repetitions are associated with muscular endurance.
47. False. Research suggests that hypermobility may be associated with joint problems.
48. True.
49. False. Thirty minutes would be nice, but any activity time on a daily basis can be beneficial.
50. This is true to some extent. Exercise is still important throughout your life to maintain functional health and fitness.

Activities

• Place students into groups and have them develop their own definitions of physical fitness. Then have one member of each group read his or her group's definition to the class. Once each group has reported, encourage the class to agree on a single definition. Afterwards, discuss why they may have had trouble reaching a consensus (confounding factors like age, gender, weight, general health, and genetics).

Assess

Use the Section 1 Review questions to assess students' comprehension of the concepts presented in Section 1.

These students should be required to see their physicians before starting any program. A topic for discussion might include how the meaning of fitness varies with the nature and severity of the disability. The physical educator might find any information the doctor can share about the student's disability to be helpful in assisting the student in designing a personal fitness program.

Possible teacher resources: *Fitness for Special Populations,* Roy J. Shephard, Human Kinetics Books, Champaign, IL, 1990. *Fitness for the Handicapped: An Instructional Approach,* James V. Sullivan, Charles C Thomas, Publisher, Springfield, IL, 1984.

CHAPTER 1
SECTION 1
10

Attitudes and Beliefs about Personal Fitness

Both young and old people often fail to realize the importance of being physically active or engaging in exercise to maintain good health. They have negative attitudes or beliefs about physical activity, exercise, and physical fitness programs for a variety of reasons. Some of these reasons follow:

- They lack time.
- They are in poor physical condition.
- They have a high percentage of body fat.
- They have unrealistic physical fitness goals or expectations.
- They lack accurate knowledge about physical fitness.
- They feel that they are not athletic.
- They are afraid of physically overstraining themselves.
- They have had negative experiences with physical activity, exercise, or both.
- They have concerns about negative peer pressure.

If you have many of these negative attitudes, the odds are that you will live a sedentary lifestyle as you get older. By learning more about your own personal fitness you can develop positive experiences leading to an active and more productive lifestyle.

At this point, we challenge you to explore your attitudes and beliefs about physical activity, exercise, and physical fitness programs. From the questionnaire in the "Active Mind/Active Body" activity on the next two pages, identify your current attitudes and beliefs. If you do not already have positive attitudes about physical activity, exercise, and physical fitness, we hope you will develop them through your experiences in this course. If you are inactive or do not exercise regularly, we challenge you to change your behaviors and improve your physical fitness. You can do it. In fact, **A**ny **B**ody **C**an!

- *Physical activity and exercise can promote positive mental attitudes.*

SECTION 1 REVIEW

Answer the following questions on a separate sheet of paper:

1. What is the difference between functional health and the absence of disease?
2. Why is it important for you to pursue wellness throughout your life?
3. List five negative attitudes and beliefs that are associated with becoming a "couch potato."

Ask students to explain the most important concepts discussed in Section 1.

CRITICAL THINKING

Have students interview people of different ages who are currently involved in an exercise program. They should ask questions similar to the following:
- What kind of exercise do you do?
- For how long do you do the exercise?
- When did you start your exercise program?
- What physiological and psychological benefits have you noticed?
- How does the program fit with your lifestyle and schedule?
- What motivates you to stick with the exercise program?

Active Mind! Active Body!

What Are Your Current Attitudes and Beliefs about Personal Fitness?

The following is a series of 25 statements of attitudes and beliefs about physical activity, exercise, and physical fitness. They are designed to evaluate your current attitudes and beliefs about physical activity, exercise, and physical fitness. Use the scale to rate how you feel about the statements presented. Try to be as honest as you possibly can with each of your answers. If you are unsure about your answer, mark "unsure" for your response. (Write your answers on a separate sheet of paper. **Do Not** write in this book.) There will be no grade assigned to this activity, so feel free to express your opinions. At the completion of the course do this activity again and determine if your attitudes and beliefs about physical activity, exercise, and physical fitness have changed.

	A I Agree Strongly	B I Agree	C I Am Unsure	D I Disagree	E I Disagree Strongly
1. I don't have time to exercise.	___	___	___	___	___
2. Regular physical activity and exercise make me feel better.	___	___	___	___	___
3. I am not very athletic.	___	___	___	___	___
4. I have always enjoyed participation in physical activities and exercise.	___	___	___	___	___
5. I enjoy physical education classes.	___	___	___	___	___
6. I have a moderate to high level of health and physical fitness.	___	___	___	___	___
7. I am happy with my physical appearance.	___	___	___	___	___
8. I like to walk and jog.	___	___	___	___	___
9. I like team games and sports.	___	___	___	___	___
10. I like to lift weights.	___	___	___	___	___
11. I like to engage in physical activities with friends.	___	___	___	___	___
12. Exercising twice a week is all I need to do to stay in shape.	___	___	___	___	___
13. Athletes, cheerleaders, and band members should be excused from taking physical education.	___	___	___	___	___

(Continued on next page)

RESOURCES HANDOUTS

There is a reproducible copy of this Active Mind/ Active Body activity in your Teacher Resource Package.

Active Mind! Active Body!

This Active Mind/Active Body activity will help students become more aware of their own attitudes about personal fitness. Be sure that they understand there will be no grade. As with the first AM/AB activity, save the surveys and return them to the students at the end of the course to see if their attitudes have changed.

Teacher Readings

Blair, S. N., Kohl, H. W., Paffenbarger, R. S., Jr., Clark, D. G., Cooper, K. H., and Gibbons, L. W., Physical fitness and all-cause mortality: a prospective study of healthy men and women. *Journal of the American Medical Association,* 262:2395–2401, 1989.

Then have students interview people of different ages who are not exercising on a regular basis. They should ask questions similar to the following:
• Why aren't you involved in an exercise program?
• Do you feel you have adequate knowledge about exercise and diet? Why or why not?
• Describe your past attempts at developing an exercise program.
• Describe your current lifestyle (work, leisure-time activities, risk factors).

After the interviews are completed, have students analyze the information they collected and draw conclusions. Encourage them to find similarities in the people of both groups.

Healthy People 2000

The Role of the Schools—The challenge set out through *Healthy People 2000* is one directed to people throughout the Nation. Each of us, whether acting as an individual, an employee or employer, a member of a family, community group, professional organization, or government agency, has both an opportunity and an obligation to contribute to the effort to improve the Nation's health profile. To arrive at the established goals and objectives, we must chart a common course that depends upon commitment and action from every level of our society. Then the challenge can be met.

The individual is both the starting point and the ultimate target of the campaign towards *Healthy People 2000.*

Our worksites can provide a smoking cessation program and a fitness center, for example, but we have to enroll. Fast-food chains can offer salads, but we have to choose them. Legislators can mandate food labeling, but we must care enough to read the labels. Our health care providers can provide the necessary screening tests and immunization, but we must take the initiative to obtain them.

What Are Your Current Attitudes and Beliefs about Personal Fitness? *(continued)*

	A I Agree Strongly	B I Agree	C I Am Unsure	D I Disagree	E I Disagree Strongly
14. Learning about personal fitness will be valuable to me later in life.	___	___	___	___	___
15. Physical education classes have always been boring to me.	___	___	___	___	___
16. Physical education should be a required class.	___	___	___	___	___
17 Engaging in physical activity or exercise helps me forget my problems and reduces my stress levels.	___	___	___	___	___
18. Grades should not be given in physical education.	___	___	___	___	___
19. I would take physical education as an elective class even if it were not a required course.	___	___	___	___	___
20. I know how to design my own personal fitness program.	___	___	___	___	___
21. Personal fitness teaches self-discipline.	___	___	___	___	___
22. Doing physical activity and exercise can improve your health.	___	___	___	___	___
23. After a day at school, I am too tired to exercise.	___	___	___	___	___
24. I would rather watch sports on television than actually participate in sports.	___	___	___	___	___
25. I feel guilty when I don't exercise everyday.	___	___	___	___	___

SECTION 2 Risk Factors and Your Personal Fitness

In the United States today people can expect to live about seventy-five years. By the time you are seventy-five, however, the number of years a person can expect to live may be higher.

It may be difficult for you to think of yourself becoming older. Eventually you will age, though, just as your parents and grandparents have. Therefore, it is important for you to understand and develop healthy personal fitness habits now.

Science and Technology

Many physical education teachers are reluctant to accept and use new technology, usually due to their inability to see its relevance to physical education. In most cases, however, the usefulness of new technology is limited only by the teacher's perceptions of technology and its applications.

Computers, for example, can be extremely helpful to the physical education teacher. Many physical education departments may find that computers are less accessible to them than they are to other departments, due to cost

Risk Factors for Heart and Artery Disease

- Heredity (history of CVD prior to age 55 in family members).
- Gender (being male).
- Smoking.
- Hypertension.
- High blood cholesterol, high LDL, and/or low HDL.
- Glucose intolerance (diabetes).
- Lack of exercise.
- Obesity (30 percent or more overweight).
- Stress.

risk factor

a condition or trait that increases the likelihood that people will develop chronic diseases.

BELIEVE IT? ... OR NOT?

Every year, 500,000 Americans die of heart disease, and over 1 million suffer nonfatal heart attacks.

See page 25 for answer.

Unfortunately, many adults die or become disabled prematurely (at age fifty or sixty, for example) because of chronic diseases for which they are at high risk. Chronic diseases are illnesses that usually develop over several years. They can cause disability and even death. Examples of chronic diseases include heart disease, cancer, hypertension, and osteoporosis. The good news is that you can reduce your chance for developing many chronic diseases.

Health **risk factors** are variables or conditions that increase the likelihood that people will develop chronic diseases. You can modify or influence many risk factors, at least in part, if you practice positive health behaviors. In fact, research has shown that the health behaviors that you establish as a young adult will most likely continue into your later adult life. The health behaviors you adopt now may either benefit or injure your health. Thus, it is important that you be able to recognize the risk factors that you currently have. You can then develop and practice a plan to reduce or eliminate your risk factors, if possible.

• *Are you a couch potato? It is okay to relax in front of the television from time to time, if you don't overdo it and you get plenty of exercise.*

Focus

Outcomes

In **Section 2**, students will learn:

1. To explain and identify health risk factors that can be modified.
2. To explain and identify health risk factors that are less modifiable.

Focus Activities

1. Have students design and present posters that compare and contrast the characteristics of a person who is "physically fit" with a person who lives a sedentary lifestyle.
2. After each person or group has presented the posters, have everyone determine the amount of time they are sedentary or active by using the Active Mind/Active Body activity on pp. 15–16.

and budget restraints. This is true if the school or department is trying to buy "cutting edge" systems. Cutting edge computers are not necessary, however, for most applications in physical education. Low-end computers (the machines that are considered obsolete by most people) work just as well for most physical education needs as their cutting-edge brothers, and cost one-third less.

Take the challenge: Determine how accessible computers are to your department, and what the possibilities are for obtaining new computer systems.
Remember: Most computer companies have marketing strategies to help the education community obtain the necessary funds to purchase computers.

Teach & Apply

Discussion

- Have students discuss the word hypokinetic. Define "hypo" (under or low) and "kinetic" (movement activity).
- Identify the diseases commonly associated with a hypokinetic lifestyle (cardiovascular disease, hypertension, osteoporosis, obesity, high blood cholesterol).
- Discuss Figure 1.1 and how simply moving from a low fitness level to a moderate fitness level can be very beneficial to your health.
- Have students discuss reasons why teens start smoking (insecurity in social settings, peer pressure, attractive ads, lack of knowledge about the dangers of smoking).

hypokinetic

physically inactive, or sedentary.

cardiovascular disease

heart and blood vessel disease.

hypertension

high blood pressure.

osteoporosis

a condition in which the bones are porous and brittle.

obesity

excessive body fat; excessive weight (20% or more above appropriate weight).

cholesterol

a blood fat.

triglyceride

a blood fat.

Risk Factors You Can Modify

You can control many health risk factors. Others you can do little about, but your lifestyle can help you control their effects on your life.

A person who is **hypokinetic** throughout life is at an increased risk for problems such as **cardiovascular disease**, **hypertension**, low back pain, **osteoporosis**, **obesity**, negative emotional stress, colon cancer, and high blood **cholesterol** and **triglyceride** levels.

Research has shown that adults who are sedentary die from chronic diseases at a much higher rate than do more active individuals. Figure 1.1 shows that when adults move from low fitness levels (sedentary) to moderately active fitness levels, they significantly reduce their risk of dying from chronic disease. (An example of a moderate level is walking two miles in about thirty minutes, four days per week.) If adults obtain a higher fitness level (for example, jog two

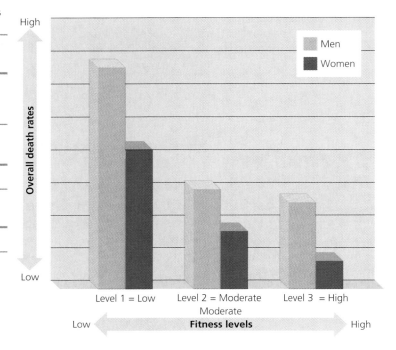

- **Figure 1.1**   *The Relationship Between Levels of Physical Fitness and All Causes of Death.*
Source: Adapted with permission from Blair, S.N. "Exercise and Health," *Sports Science Exchange* (Gatorade Sports Science Institute, 1990), Vol. 3, no. 29: 1–6.

Reteaching

ABILITY LEVELS

Reteaching

Some students may need help mastering the concepts contained in this section. In your Teacher Resource Package, you will find the reproducible worksheet shown here. This worksheet should help students who have been absent and those needing additional help to improve their comprehension and retention of the contents in this section.

Active Mind! *Active* Body!

How Physically Active Are You Now?

On a separate sheet of paper, answer the questions below "yes" or "no." For each question answered yes, give yourself the number of points indicated. Add the points to determine your level of physical activity.

Occupation and Daily Activities

1. I usually walk to and from school and work (at least ½ mile each way). (1 point)
2. I usually take the stairs rather than use elevators or escalators. (1 point)
3. My typical daily physical activity is best described by the following statement:
   a. Most of my day is spent walking to class, sitting in class or at home, or in light activity. (0 points)
   b. Most of the day is spent in moderate activity such as fast walking. (4 points)
   c. My typical day includes several hours of heavy physical activity (football, volleyball, basketball, gym workout, or the like). (9 points)

Leisure Activities

4. I spend a few hours in light leisure activity each week (such as slow canoeing or slow cycling). (1 point)
5. I hike or bike (at a moderate pace) once a week or more on the average. (1 point)
6. At least once a week, I participate for an hour or more in vigorous dancing, such as aerobic or folk dancing. (1 point)
7. I play racquetball or tennis at least once a week. (2 points)
8. I often walk for exercise or recreation. (1 point)
9. When I feel bothered by pressures at school, work, or home, I use exercise as a way to relax. (1 point)
10. Two or more times a week, I perform calisthenic exercises (sit-ups, push-ups, etc.) for at least 10 minutes per session. (3 points)
11. I regularly participate in yoga or perform stretching exercises. (2 points)
12. Twice a week or more, I engage in weight training for at least 30 minutes. (4 points)
13. I participate in active recreational sports such as volleyball, baseball, or softball.

(Continued on next page)

Active Mind! *Active* Body!

This is another assessment Active Mind/Active Body activity that will not be graded. Students should realize that the purpose of the activity is to help them determine where they are located in the range between inactive and very active. You will probably want to discuss the results in class but only in a general way. Make sure they realize that anything less than 12 points means that they need to become more active. Have students keep their worksheets and do the activity again at the end of the semester to see if they have became more active.

Teacher Readings

Morrow, J. R. and Gill, Diane, Editors. The Academy Papers, No. 28—The role of physical activity in fitness health, *Quest,* 47(3), 261–410, 1995.

Enrichment *This activity will allow you to provide a more challenging learning experience for some of your students.*

Have students complete the following activity: Read a recent article in a news magazine about cigarette smoking. Does the article mention that cigarette smoking is linked as a likely cause to certain cancers?

—cigarette smoking is an addiction to nicotine, and is treated and cured as such?

—cigarette smoking is increasing among youth and teenagers?

—there is increasing legislation that limits cigarette smoking, and places stricter controls on the tobacco industry?

Make an oral report to your class about the article you read, and be sure to include any information about the above questions.

Teacher Readings

Blair, S. N., Exercise and health. *Gatorade Sports Science Exchange,* 3(29), 3, 1990.

How Physically Active Are You Now? (continued)

    a. about once a week. (2 points)

    b. about twice a week. (4 points)

    c. three times a week or more. (7 points)

14. At least once a week, I participate in vigorous fitness activities like jogging or swimming (at least 20 continuous minutes per session).

    a. about once a week. (3 points)

    b. about twice a week. (5 points)

    c. three times a week or more. (10 points)

Total Points Earned _____

Scoring:

0–5 points—inactive.   This amount of physical activity leads to a steady decline in fitness.

6–11 points—moderately active.   This amount of physical activity slows fitness loss but will not maintain fitness.

12–20 points—active.   This amount of physical activity will build or maintain an acceptable level of physical fitness.

21 points or over—very active.   This amount of physical activity will maintain a high level of fitness.

Source: Reprinted with permission from F. S. Sizer, E. N. Whitney, L. K. DeBruyne, *Making Life Choices: Health Skills and Concepts* (St. Paul: West, 1994), 240. Activity adapted from Russell Pate (University of South Carolina, Department of Exercise Science).

miles in about twenty minutes, four days per week), they reduce their risk even further. The most important point, however, is that people should increase their physical activity enough to get out of the low fitness category.

    To figure out how your current level of physical fitness would rate health-wise, please do the "Active Mind/Active Body" activity that begins on the preceding page.

    Smoking.   Chronic smokers (people who have smoked consistently for ten, twenty, or even thirty years) have an increased risk for heart and lung disease compared with nonsmokers. For example, smokers are two times as likely as nonsmokers to have a **heart attack**. Smokers tend to be less active than nonsmokers, which increases their risk of premature chronic disease.

heart attack

the blockage of vessels feeding the heart, causing the death of heart tissue.

Equipment Options

    In the past, physical education teachers found innovative ways to develop their own equipment. They made weights from coffee cans filled with concrete and attached to iron rods, springs with handles were attached to the wall, and "tennis shoes" were bought at the local five and dime.

    Today, fitness equipment is a booming, multibillion-dollar industry with hundreds of manufacturers for all kinds of weight-lifting equipment, treadmills, stairsteppers, and shoes. For example, in addition to tennis shoes, we now have

• *Smoking increases your risk for chronic heart and lung diseases.*

BELIEVE IT? ... OR NOT?

Only 22 percent of Americans aged eighteen and older engage in light to moderate physical activity for at least thirty minutes, five or more times per week. In addition, 24 percent do not engage in any leisure-time physical activity.

See page 25 for answer.

stroke

blockage of blood flow to the brain.

Smokers who stop smoking and choose an active lifestyle can reduce their heart attack risk level to that of nonsmokers in two to three years. Although it is very difficult to stop smoking, it is never too late to quit smoking and begin a more active lifestyle. (Obviously, it is best never to start.)

Hypertension.   A person with high blood pressure (hypertension) is at increased risk for **stroke** and heart attack. There are few symptoms of hypertension, which is one reason why it can be so dangerous. Hypertension is associated with genetic makeup, aging, a high salt or sodium intake, obesity, and also by excessive alcohol consumption.

Blood pressure is easy to measure. Do you know what yours is? Everyone should know what it is (see Chapter 5).

When physicians diagnose people as having hypertension, they usually recommend weight loss (if appropriate). People are also told to modify their diets (for example, consume less sodium) and to become more physically active.

Discussion

Discuss problems associated with smoking (heart disease, lung cancer, throat cancer, birth defects, increased blood pressure, increased cases of bronchitis, lower life expectancy, premature wrinkling of skin).

Teacher Support Notes

You may want to tell students the following:

• Seventy-five percent of lung cancer deaths in women and 83 percent in men are caused from smoking.
• Risk of sudden death from a heart attack is twice as great in smokers, as compared to nonsmokers.
• The number of adult Americans who smoke dropped 11 percent between 1965 and 1990.
• It takes a former smoker about fifteen years to completely recover from the effects of smoking.

Activity

Have the school nurse attend class to demonstrate how blood pressure is taken. The nurse can also

running shoes, basketball shoes, weight-lifting shoes, crosstrainers, and aerobics shoes, making it very difficult to explain to students what type of shoe they need to buy. For weight-lifting equipment you can purchase hydraulic machines, free standing weights, counterbalanced machines, and stepped-resistance machines. **Take the challenge:** Make a list of the equipment that you feel is necessary for your students to achieve physical fitness, then browse through local sporting goods stores to determine the number of options available for each type of equipment you need. **Remember:** *Flash, Glitter* and *Price* are not always the best way to choose a piece of equipment.

describe how blood cholesterol is measured and what levels are considered safe or unsafe.

Teaching Strategies

Emphasize that fat is the major concern when dealing with body composition. Chapter 9 is devoted entirely to body composition. Before this course is completed, each student should have the opportunity to have his or her body composition measured. Each student should also have an opportunity to determine his or her percentage of body fat.

Discussion

Discuss the two types of stressors. Have students identify five examples of distress and five examples of eustress that are common to teens.

Activity

Have students collect articles, cartoons, or comic strips about any of the risk factors. Choose some of the examples to use as discussion starters.

BELIEVE IT? ... OR NOT?

A healthy, active lifestyle practiced over time can add 2.5 years to your life. This is important for maintaining physical independence later in life.

See page 25 for answer.

• *Many foods that we eat are high in fat and cholesterol.*

atherosclerosis

a disease process that causes substances to build up inside arteries, blocking blood flow.

high-density lipoprotein (HDL)

"good cholesterol"; the type of cholesterol that is associated with a lower atherosclerosis risk.

low-density lipoprotein (LDL)

"bad cholesterol"; a type of cholesterol that is associated with higher atherosclerosis risk.

very low density lipoprotein (VLDL)

"bad cholesterol"; a type of cholesterol that is associated with higher atherosclerosis risk.

High Levels of Cholesterol and Triglycerides.   A person with an elevated level of cholesterol is at an increased risk for the development of **atherosclerosis**. The total amount of cholesterol in the blood is determined by the combination of the fats we eat, as well as the fats produced by our bodies.

Cholesterol is usually classified as either "good cholesterol" or "bad cholesterol." **High-density lipoprotein (HDL)** is "good cholesterol" and is associated with a lower atherosclerosis risk. **Low-density lipoprotein (LDL)** and **very low density lipoprotein (VLDL)** are types of "bad cholesterol" and are associated with higher atherosclerosis risk.

Triglycerides are another type of blood fat. Triglycerides are also usually associated with a higher atherosclerosis risk. Therefore, it is important to control and limit fat intake in the diet. In that way we can help lower our cholesterol and triglyceride levels or maintain acceptable levels. Maintaining appropriate levels of personal fitness can also help control normal cholesterol and triglyceride levels.

Body Composition.   The amount of water, bone, muscle, and fat in your body determines your body composition. A person who carries too much body fat is at an increased risk for problems such as hypertension, heart disease, and diabetes mellitus (high blood sugar disease). Obesity (excessive body fat) often begins in childhood

Wellness Connection

A Stress-Free Life: Is It for You?

Ask students if they would really want to live a life that was absolutely and completely free of stress. Tell them that they might think that that sounds like a good idea, but in reality they would hate it. While it is true that continuously high levels of stress are undesirable and can be harmful, an absolutely stress-free life would not be desirable either. Such a life would most likely be dull and boring, with no challenges or excitement.

Most of us function best with stress lev-

REMEMBER This!

Smoking, reducing stress, eating right, and being physically active are all behaviors that you decide to include or exclude in your lifestyle. A wise and healthy person recognizes the importance of this point. Make *your* lifestyle choices wisely.

stress

the physical and psychological responses of your body as you try to adapt to stressors.

stressor

anything that requires you to adapt and cope with either positive or negative situations.

distress

excess negative stress, such as fear, anger, or confusion.

eustress

positive stress; an enjoyable type of stress.

and usually persists into adulthood, unless an obese person alters his or her diet and adopts an active lifestyle.

A person with too little body fat (excessive leanness), in contrast, is at risk for problems such as osteoporosis and certain forms of cancer. Excessive leanness is usually associated with abnormal eating and psychological or addictive behaviors that require professional attention.

Stress. **Stress** is defined as the physical and psychological responses of your body as you try to adapt to stressors. A **stressor** is anything that requires you to adapt and cope with either positive or negative situations.

Distress is excess negative stress, such as fear, anger, confusion, or other similar mood states in your life. Distress can increase your risk for chronic disease (such as heart attack) or can make a disease process worse. Distress can produce negative physical responses (increased heart rate, increased hormone levels, headaches, and so on). It can also have negative emotional effects (anxiety, sleeplessness, depression, and so on).

Eustress is positive stress. It is an enjoyable type of stress, such as what you might feel in being elected class president, scoring well on an exam, or obtaining your driver's license.

A few ways to cope positively with stress include changing your diet (eating breakfast regularly and reducing caffeine intake), meditation (reflecting about a pleasant event in your life), or physical activity (brisk walking or weight lifting). Dealing with stress in a positive way is something that will challenge you daily for the rest of your life. Therefore, future chapters in this text will present discussions and activities that focus on teaching you to cope with stress in positive ways. Look for the "Stress Break" strategies in the margins throughout the remainder of the book.

Less Modifiable Risk Factors

Three health risk factors related to death or disability due to chronic disease are age, gender (sex), and heredity (genetics). You cannot change or even completely modify these risks. You can, however, live an active lifestyle that minimizes the consequences of these factors on your good health.

Age. An older person tends to be at increased risk for diseases such as high blood pressure, heart disease, and cancer as compared with younger individuals. This makes sense when you realize that most people who die in old age (at ages seventy, eighty, ninety, and beyond) die as the result of chronic disease processes. You cannot change your age. However, you can optimize your functional health as you age and live a higher-quality lifestyle by being physically active and by eating a healthy diet throughout your life.

Teacher Support Notes

You may want to tell students the following:

• Regular exercise can help prevent osteoporosis in the elderly.
• Regular exercise is associated with better memories, reaction time, and reasoning powers.

Have students take the Active Mind/Active Body on p. 22 to determine what risk factors they do or do not have. They should then discuss ways to modify or change their behaviors.

els that fluctuate around the mid ranges, between high and low. The fluctuations result from events such as a big test. As the test gets closer and closer, your stress level goes up; when the test is over, your stress level goes down. Maybe you have a fight and break up with your boyfriend or girlfriend, but then you find someone you like even better,

and your stress level goes back down.

Keep in mind that long-term exposure to high levels of stress can be harmful to your health and should be avoided or properly handled. A moderate amount of stress in your life, however, is normal and to be expected. Use that stress as a motivating or driving force to enrich and improve the quality of your life.

Stress Break

Explain that the "Stress Break" is a feature dealing with all aspects of stress and will be highlighted in each chapter. Students should understand the positive relationship between stress, regular physical activity, and good nutrition.

Assess

Use the Section 2 Review questions to assess the students' comprehension of the concepts presented in Section 2.

ANSWERS TO SECTION 2 REVIEW

1. *a.* Sedentary lifestyle: Get active, start an exercise program, find ways to include activity throughout your day. Move from a low fitness level to a moderate fitness level.
b. Smoking: Stop smoking, it is never too late to stop.
c. Hypertension: Start an exercise program, lower your salt intake, and lose weight.
d. High cholesterol and triglycerides: Maintain appropriate levels of personal fitness and limit your fat intake.
e. Body composition: Adopt an active lifestyle and eat sensible, nutritious meals.

REMEMBER This!

You cannot change your age, your gender, or your heredity. However, you can choose to be physically active and to eat wisely. These behaviors will help you maximize your functional health for years to come and reduce your health risks as much as possible.

predisposition

susceptibility to increased health risk due to genetic makeup.

Gender (Sex). Some health risk factors are influenced by gender. For example, men between the ages of forty and fifty have a higher risk for heart disease than do women of the same age range. The risk for heart disease for women increases dramatically after age fifty and then matches that of men. Women have a higher risk than men for osteoporosis beginning at ages forty-five to fifty. The risk for osteoporosis for men increases dramatically after age seventy and then matches that of women.

It is important that you recognize the health risk factors associated with your gender. Even if you have an increased health risk due to your gender, there are behaviors that can help you modify and minimize that risk. For example, a woman is at an increased risk for osteoporosis. However, she can take calcium and hormone supplements and exercise regularly to modify and reduce that risk (see Chapters 7 and 10).

Heredity (Genetics). A person may be born with a **predisposition** to increased health risk for various disease processes. For example, some individuals are born with extremely high blood cholesterol levels. They develop atherosclerosis at an early age (in their

• *Heredity can influence your health risks.*

COOPERATIVE LEARNING

You have probably been using group activities in your class for as long as you have been teaching. Your reasons might include the need for sharing limited equipment or your desire to help with the students' socialization. Now, more than ever before, the need for structured group work, or *cooperative learning* as it is frequently called, is becoming more evident.

In the workplace, it is becoming apparent that many young people have not learned the skills necessary for them to be successful. Among the unlearned

Stress Break

Have you ever noticed what happens to your heart rate and rate of breathing when you get angry or frightened? Both your heart rate and your breathing speed up very quickly, which is a normal response of your body to stress. This response is caused by a chemical that is released into your bloodstream. The chemical, called *adrenaline,* can be very helpful in times of emergency. Other reactions to adrenaline include muscle tension, pupil dilation, increased blood nutrients, and raised blood pressure.

Frequent and prolonged sessions of stress or high levels of adrenaline can be dangerous. Problems such as high blood pressure, ulcers, and diabetes can result. However, a good fitness program can help use up or metabolize excess adrenaline. Be active!

twenties or thirties), which can cause them to have heart attacks and die prematurely.

Fortunately, even if your family has a history of a disease, you can often modify your behaviors or lifestyle to minimize your own risks. For example, if your father or grandfather had a heart attack before age sixty, you have most likely inherited some heart disease risk. However, by controlling such health risk factors as cholesterol intake, obesity, physical inactivity, and so on, you can significantly reduce your overall risk for a heart attack.

Now you know about the modifiable and less modifiable risk factors associated with chronic diseases or disease processes. Next, it is important for you to identify the risk factors you already have. Take a moment and check off the risks that you have in the "Active Mind/Active Body" activity on the next page. It is not unusual for young adults to have at least one or more risk factors. However, it is important that you develop a personal risk factor modification plan to minimize the risks that you do have.

SECTION 2 REVIEW

Answer the following questions on a separate sheet of paper:

1. How can you eliminate each of the six modifiable health risk factors?
2. What is the significance of moving from a low level of fitness to a moderate level of fitness? (See Figure 1.1.)
3. Identify two positive and two negative behaviors you might use to deal with the stress in your life. Give examples and explain them.

f. Stress: Consume regular and nutritious meals, reduce caffeine intake, practice relaxation activities, and start a physical activity program. It may also be helpful to avoid stressful situations when possible.
2. By moving from the low fitness category into the moderate fitness category, people significantly reduce their risk of dying from chronic diseases.
3. Answers will vary, but could include: Positive—changing your diet, meditation, or physical activity. Negative—anxiety, sleeplessness, depression, ulcers, fatigue, anger, headaches, fear, and other chronic diseases.

SECTION 3 — Personal Fitness and Positive Outcomes

Numerous health benefits of physical activity and exercise have been documented for adults. National organizations have recommended physical activity and exercise programs as ways to provide health benefits to young adults as well. People who are physically active and have a personal fitness program can expect many benefits. Section 3 will discuss the benefits of personal fitness.

Close

Ask students to design a "Health Risk Pyramid." This can be done by placing the health risk factors they feel are the most important on the bottom of a pyramid. The second most important will be the next level, and so on, until all risk factors have been placed into the construction of the pyramid. Students should be prepared to discuss why they have determined their specific order.

skills are problem-solving skills, creative-thinking skills, and skills to enhance teamwork. Cooperative learning is designed not only to encourage teamwork but also to teach the skills necessary for *effective* teamwork. In addition, it is an effective way to give students practice with problem-solving and creative-thinking activities.

The main difference between unstructured group work and cooperative learning is *interdependence.* Interdependence, as you may have guessed, means depending on one another. When group members are interdependent, the success of the group as a whole depends on the contribution of each individual member of that group.

CHAPTER 1
SECTION 3
22

Focus

Outcomes

In **Section 3**, students will learn:

1. To identify the positive outcomes that physical activity and exercise can have on health and fitness level.
2. To discuss how many of the positive outcomes of physical activity are interrelated to one another.

Focus Activities

1. Have students discuss factors associated with a healthy self-esteem.
2. Have students discuss the factors associated with your physical self-concept.
3. Study Figures 1.3 and 1.4. Discuss how an active lifestyle can influence your functional health.

Improvements in Physical Appearance

Almost everyone is concerned, to some degree, about physical appearance. Young adults are particularly preoccupied with their appearance. Often people base much of their feelings of self-esteem and self-worth on how they look. Physical size and shape, to some degree, can determine if a person is to be an athlete or a nonathlete, or if a person is accepted in certain social settings.

During your young adult years, you may experience periods of growth that are governed by your genetic makeup. By engaging in regular physical activity or exercise, combined with a sound nutrition plan, you can help bring about some of your desired physical growth changes. These include increased strength, muscle tone, and body size, along with weight control and reduced levels of body fat. Your personal fitness behaviors will have an influence on your physical appearance both now and in the future.

> " Health and intellect are the two blessings of life.
>
> **Menander**
> c. 342–292 BC "

Active Mind! Active Body!

What Are Your Health Risk Factors?

Identify the health risk factors that you have from the list below. Then determine which ones you can modify. Mark your answers on a separate sheet of paper.

	Yes	No	Don't Know	Can Modify	Cannot Modify
1. Sedentary lifestyle					
2. Smoking					
3. Hypertension					
4. High level of blood fats					
5. Obesity					
6. Excessive stress					
7. Age					
8. Gender					
9. Heredity					

ABILITY LEVELS

Reteaching

Some students may need help mastering the concepts contained in this section. In your Teacher Resource Package, you will find the reproducible worksheet shown here. This worksheet should help students who have been absent and those needing additional help to improve their comprehension and retention of the content in this section.

Enhancement of Self-Esteem

Most people agree that self-esteem is a powerful force within each individual. It enables people to cope better with the basic challenges of life. A healthy, fit person is more likely to experience the feelings of happiness, self-worth, and a sense of enjoying their accomplishments. Simply put, people who are fit, healthy, and feel good about their health and physical appearance are more likely to live an enjoyable, productive life. Look at Figure 1.2 to see some of the more important factors affecting your self-esteem, and especially your *physical* self-concept.

BELIEVE IT? ... OR NOT?

Along with stopping smoking, maintaining a physically active lifestyle is one of the least expensive and most productive health behaviors available to the public.

See page 25 for answer.

BELIEVE IT? ... OR NOT?

Physical activity or exercise can not help you live longer.

See page 25 for answer.

Intelligent thinking

Emotional centeredness

Spiritual centeredness

SELF-ESTEEM

Honors

Finances

Accomplishments

Family status

Friends

Social acceptance

Personality

Physical self-concept

Appearance (body image)

Physical fitness and condition

Aquired competence

Inborn talent

• **Figure 1.2** *Factors Influencing Self-Esteem.*

Teach & Apply

Discussion

• Have students discuss what they value about good physical appearance.
• How does physical appearance affect their day-to-day routines?
• Have students identify people who are examples of good physical appearance.
• Have students discuss barriers that may keep them from having the physical appearance they would like to have.

Activity

Ask students to write a short story in which the lives of two people are affected differently because they have different physical appearances. Ask them to show how their lifestyle decisions can affect the rest of their lives. You may choose to select some of the stories to read in class.

 **E**nrichment

This activity will allow you to provide a more challenging learning experience for some of your students.

Have students complete the following activity: Make two lists of the things about your own physical appearance which you (a) like and want to maintain, and (b) dislike and would like to change. Include such items as muscle tone, body size, weight, and body fat. How many items on your "like" list can be maintained by physical activity or exercise? How many items on your "dislike" list can be enhanced by physical activity or exercise?

Discussion

• Have students examine and discuss Figure 1.2. Check to see that they understand how their self-esteem can be positively or negatively affected by any of the self-esteem factors.
• Dispel the myth that exercise only has physical benefits. Clarify that exercise can have both physical and psychological benefits. The psychological benefits may include the following: enhanced self-esteem, social benefits, reduction of stress, better ability to cope with depression.

Teacher Support Notes

RESOURCES **TRANSPARENCIES** Draw Maslow's Hierarchy of Needs on the chalkboard or use the overhead transparency/master provided in the Teacher Resource Package. The hierarchy is similar to a pyramid in that the needs of the bottom level must be met before the needs of the next level can be obtained.

The first level is physiological needs (food, water, sleep, etc.).

• *Physical activity and exercise can have a positive influence on your academic and physical performance.*

life expectancy

the number of years a person can expect to live.

longevity

the actual length of a person's life.

Stress Reduction

As mentioned earlier, there are two kinds of stress: positive and negative. As a young adult, you can't escape being bombarded every day with stressors that lead to both types of stress. How you deal with stressors, however, can and will have a large impact on your life. Will you respond in positive, productive ways, or will you respond in negative, possibly unhealthy ways? You will need to consider and develop coping strategies that work for you. Regular physical activity or exercise combined with a sound nutrition plan can be a good step in the right direction.

Improvements in Academic and Physical Performance

Regular participation in physical activity, exercise, or both has been shown to enhance student academic performance, as well as to speed up the rate at which we learn physical skills. These observations are based on the fact that active students often have greater attention spans, have higher energy levels, and miss fewer days of school. Similarly, workers in business and industry settings who participate in wellness programs have higher physical working capacities and are absent fewer days than workers who do not participate. Furthermore, active employees have enhanced social interactions, reduced boredom, and improved mental attitudes. Therefore, adopting a physically active lifestyle can improve your academic success, as well as your job and physical performance.

Increased Life Expectancy and Improved Functional Health

Physical activity and exercise increase muscular strength and endurance and cause people to burn or expend energy. Researchers have shown that an active lifestyle improves blood cholesterol and triglyceride levels. Physical activity, exercise, or both help people feel better and help them cope with emotional stress. Physically active people are also less likely to smoke or begin smoking. For these reasons, physical activity and exercise not only have positive influences on cardiovascular disease risks, hypertension, preventable cancers, obesity, osteoporosis, and low back pain but also can increase **life expectancy** and **longevity**.

Figure 1.3 shows two different ways in which fifteen-year-old students might age and influence their functional health. It is important to note that in theory, the physically inactive person (life expectancy = seventy-five) would not live as long as the physically active person (life expectancy = eighty-six). The graph also illustrates that the inactive person would most likely lose functional health at age sixty-

CULTURAL DIVERSITY

The Philippines

The most popular sport in the Philippines is basketball. Many people find this surprising, since the Filipinos don't have the height or the build to play this game in which height is an advantage.

Filipinos find it easy to construct basketball courts just about anywhere. A harvested field or a dirt road might become a court. (Playing on a field or a road would make dribbling a real challenge.) They can turn old wooden planks and the rim of an old tin can into a back-

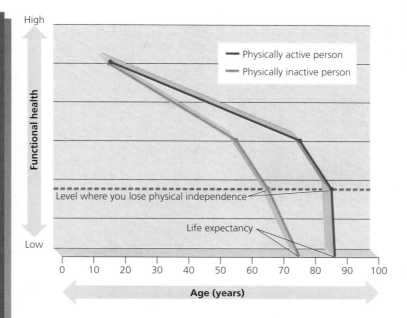

• **Figure 1.3** *The Influence of a Physically Active Lifestyle on Functional Health.*

Source: Theory adapted from S. N. Blair (Cooper Institute for Aerobics Research, 1996).

The second level involves safety and security.

The third level involves love, affection, and healthy relationships.

The fourth level involves self-esteem, the need to feel respected and needed, and self-worth. Self-esteem is about experiencing success and learning to become independent.

The fifth and top level is the need for self-actualization. This includes realizing your talents and capabilities, and utilizing them to their fullest potential.

Discussion

• Have students discuss why it would be beneficial for corporate presidents to have wellness and fitness centers available for their employees. Discussion might include: long- and short-term benefits such as productivity, employee satisfaction, reduced sick days, less turnover, and less "burnout."

• Students should study and discuss Figure 1.3. Clarify how and why the active person is more likely to be independent longer.

two—earlier than the active person, who probably would lose it at age eighty-five. The physically active person not only would live longer but would probably have a higher quality of life. Furthermore, the active person would minimize the time that he or she was physically dependent on others.

As you have probably heard, government leaders are very concerned about controlling the costs of health care in the United States. One of the least expensive and most productive methods for reducing health-care costs is to encourage people to develop and maintain healthy, physically active lifestyles. It is estimated that 60 percent of all current U.S. health-care costs can be attributed to unhealthy lifestyles. As an adult, wouldn't you rather spend your hard-earned money on new cars and vacations than on doctor and hospital bills? An active lifestyle can make the difference.

As you can see in Figure 1.4 on the next page, functional health changes with age in different ways, depending on the changes in a person's physical activity patterns and percentage of body fat. For

board and basket. The ease with which they can put together a court probably adds to the popularity of the game.

Young athletes play a game called *sipa,* which is played by kicking a small ball made of woven cane. *Jai alai* is a game enjoyed by skilled athletes. This game is played on a court with two walls by players with long, hand-shaped bas-

kets strapped to their wrists. The players use the baskets to propel the ball against the walls in this extremely fast-moving game.

Filipinos also participate in their own martial arts, *arnis.* During an *arnis* match, the contestants use twisting movements and a wooden stick to defeat their opponents.

26   Foundations of Personal Fitness

Activity

Have students complete interviews with members of their extended families (parents, grandparents, aunts, and uncles) to gain information about illnesses and health and fitness behaviors. From their findings, have them construct a family tree that contains information about the family's health history. Then have students match their family members' health and fitness behaviors with their illnesses. Compare the family tree results with Figure 1.4.

Assess

Use the Section 3 Review questions on p. 28 to assess students' comprehension of the concepts presented in Section 3.

Teacher Readings

Jackson, A. S., Beard, E. F., Weir, L. T., Ross, R. M., Stuteville, J. E., and Blair, S. N. Changes in aerobic power of men, ages 25–70 yr, *Medicine and Science in Sports and Exercise*, 27(1), 113–120, 1995.

B ELIEVE IT? ... OR NOT?

It is much cheaper and more effective to maintain good health than it is to regain it once it is lost.

See page 25 for answer.

• *You have a choice—Be Active!*

example, let's imagine a thirty-year-old male who is moderately active (4, for example, on a Personal Activity Rating (PAR) scale of 0 to 7, with 0 = inactive and 7 = highly active).

Let's further imagine that this moderately active male has 20 percent body fat. Now let's look at how our imaginary 30-year-old might age in several different ways. Suppose that the person moves to a high physical activity level (PAR = 7) and, as he ages, reduces his body fat by five percent. He will maintain a high level of functional health. If, however, the person increases his physical activity level slightly (PAR = 5) and maintains his present percentage of body fat, he will still have a moderate level of functional health at age seventy. But, more importantly, if the person becomes sedentary (like many adults) and increases his body fat to 30 percent, he will most likely lose his functional health by age seventy (which is premature).

Remember, health-care costs are lower for people who maintain higher levels of functional health. In other words, the greatest amount of health-care dollars are spent on people who have lost their functional health.

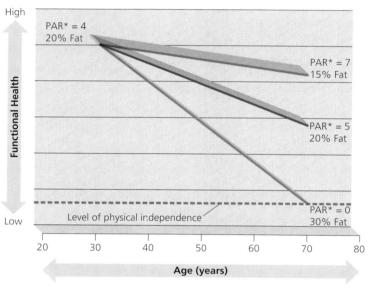

* PAR = Personal Activity Rating

• *Figure 1.4* *Projected Changes in Functional Health with Regard to Age, Changes in Physical Activity Patterns, and Percentage of Body Fat.*

Source: Adapted with permission from A. S. Jackson, et al. "Changes in Aerobic Power of Men, Ages 25–70 Years," *Medicine and Science in Sports and Exercise,* Vol. 27, no. 1 (1995): 113–120.

Across the Disciplines

Social Studies/Economics

Personal fitness is big business in the United States. Have groups of students research the impact of the fitness industry on the national economy over the past 20 years. They could research the increase in fitness-related businesses, growth of employment in various components of the industry, or the proliferation of new products. Ask students to brainstorm about fitness products they have used, heard of, or seen advertised. They should be able to identify some of the

Any Body Can!

Jack LaLanne

Jack LaLanne, the godfather of physical fitness, opened the nation's first health club in 1936. He was one of the first people to promote active lifestyles, and at eighty-one, he still vigorously works out for two hours a day.

In the late 1950s he began the first televised aerobic exercise program. The Jack LaLanne Show, promoting nutrition and fitness, lasted 34 years. During the early shows, LaLanne encouraged women to exercise, to take charge of their appearance and their health. At the time, the idea that women should work out was an unusual philosophy, and LaLanne was one of the first to proclaim that exercising is both healthy and sensible.

Jack was among the first individuals to recommend that athletes use weights to develop strength. In the 1940s and 1950s he invented and built some of the first exercise machines for his gym, including a cable-pulley machine, a leg-extension machine, and a safety system for doing squats (a weightlifting technique explained in Chapter 8).

Jack was not always as physically fit as he is today. As a teenager, Jack was skinny and shy. When he was a young man, his mother took him to hear a nutritionist lecture. He was so motivated by the talk that he began to exercise and learn all he could about nutrition.

Jack is known for his Herculean feats of muscular strength and endurance. For example, he has done 100 handstand push-ups in 6 minutes and over 1,000 push-ups in 23 minutes. He swam across the San Francisco Bay while handcuffed. He also towed a 2000 pound boat the length of the Golden Gate Bridge (about 2 miles) while swimming underwater with air tanks but no swim fins. At the age of 70, he towed 70 friends in 70 different boats across Long Beach Harbor, near Los Angeles, California.

At an age when most people are quietly reflecting back on their lives, Jack is as busy as ever. He lectures regularly about the benefits of an active lifestyle and about false advertising in health and fitness issues. Currently he is in training for a 20 mile swim underwater from Catalina Island to Los Angeles.

Not everyone can be a fitness expert like Jack LaLanne, but Any Body Can lead an active lifestyle, exercise regularly, and make physical fitness an important part of their everyday life. That's right, you can do it!

CNN Health and Fitness Updates

You can update your coverage of health and fitness topics, as well as spark lively classroom discussion and deeper understanding, by using the **CNN Health and Fitness Updates.** These video updates are produced by Turner Educational Services, using the resources of CNN, the world's first 24-hour, all-news network.

With the introduction of the **CNN Health and Fitness Updates,** West Educational Publishing is proud to be the exclusive partner of CNN for textbook/video integration in high school fitness. By making use of the **CNN Health and Fitness Updates** you can bring the power of CNN, the network known for providing in-depth, live coverage and analysis of breaking news events, to your fitness class.

For assistance in using and incorporating the **CNN Health and Fitness Updates** into your classroom presentations, see the *Classroom Guide to the CNN Health and Fitness Updates.* The **CNN Health and Fitness Updates** are available with West Educational Publishing's *Foundations of Personal Fitness* by Don Rainey and Tinker Murray.

following products: apparel (i.e., Reebok, Nike); equipment (i.e., Nautilus, Nordic Track); media (i.e., magazines—*Shape*, *Prevention*); health-related diet food (i.e., Healthy Choice, Lean Cuisine); training (i.e., Gold's Gym, local health clubs); health information literature (i.e., books such as *How to Lower Your Fat Thermostat* by Dennis Remington

(M.D.), et. al., or *Jane Brody's Nutrition Book);* video/audio tapes, television programs, or software (i.e., *Fitness by Jake, Basic Training,* and so on). From their research, students should be able to explain what factors have contributed to fluctuations in the economic growth during this period of time.

ANSWERS TO SECTION 3 REVIEW

1. *a.* Answers should include some of the following: increased muscular strength, muscle tone, body size, better weight control, and reduced levels of fat.

b. By improving your physical fitness level, you can enhance your physical self-concept, which can have a positive impact on your social acceptance, your personality, and others. All of these combine to determine your self-esteem.

c. Regular fitness activities are a positive method of coping with stress.

d. Improved fitness levels enhance academic performance, increase attention span, and increase energy levels.

e. Physically active people have a higher life expectancy.

f. Health-care cost is lower for those individuals who are moderately active and maintain physical fitness levels throughout their lives.

REMEMBER This!

Personal fitness is not something that you can develop and automatically keep for the rest of your life. You must continually practice personal fitness to maintain it. Make personal fitness as much a part of your lifestyle as brushing your teeth is. Participate in it daily.

Throughout future chapters in this text, discussions and activities will teach you about various consumer issues (such as health-care costs) related to your personal fitness. Look for the "Consumer Corner" boxes throughout the book.

SECTION 3 REVIEW

Answer the following question on a separate sheet of paper:

1. Explain how obtaining or maintaining physical fitness can benefit each of the following:
   a. Physical appearance.
   b. Self-esteem.
   c. Stress.
   d. Academic performance.
   e. Life expectancy.
   f. Health-care costs.

CONSUMER CORNER

Stay Active and Save Money

Health-care costs in the United States have been rising dramatically over the past several years. You've probably heard your parents and other adults talk about how much they have had to pay for a trip to the doctor's office, a tiny bottle of medicine, or a short stay in the hospital. People who suffer from chronic diseases and ailments that require surgery or constant medication often find themselves overloaded with medical bills they can never seem to overcome.

The federal government and many state governments are searching for ways to hold the line on escalating health-care costs and to provide quality health care to everyone at affordable prices. Until a solution is found, however, we all must be prepared to deal with these high costs. Even if you are fortunate enough to be healthy for most of your life, health insurance costs will take a significant part of your income.

Although the situation doesn't look promising, you should realize that you can do something about health-care costs. You can get started now on a plan for lifetime fitness and good health by developing and sticking with a personal physical fitness plan, which will greatly increase your chances of avoiding illnesses and injuries that result in doctor and hospital bills. Of course there are no guarantees. As you know from reading this chapter, many health risks are beyond your control. There is no doubt, however, that you can prevent or reduce many health risks by staying active.

Special Needs

It should be noted that those students who have difficulty with the written word (i.e. students with learning disabilities or mildly mentally retarded students) should be given special consideration when instruction revolves around the textbook content. Some students are auditory learners; they learn by hearing. Some are visual learners; they learn by seeing. Some students are kinesthetic learners; they learn by doing. Many students who display learning difficulties fall into this last category of learners. Kinesthetic learners need active lessons that are

SECTION 4　Personal Fitness: How Much Is Enough?

Healthy People 2000 Goals

Listed below are the goals of *Healthy People 2000*, a government publication that also contains a long list of objectives that will help people reach these goals.

- Increase the span of healthy life for Americans
- Reduce health disparities (differences) among Americans
- Achieve access to preventative services for all Americans

Regular physical activity and exercise have been recommended by the U.S. Public Health Service for children, adolescents, and adults as part of the *Healthy People 2000* health promotion and disease prevention objectives for the nation. The *Healthy People 2000* objectives are designed to encourage all Americans to develop and maintain healthy, active lifestyles. Experts have found that by becoming more active, Americans can improve both their health and their physical fitness levels.

Your Health versus Your Physical Fitness Level

Figure 1.5 on the next page shows that improvements in health versus physical fitness come about at different levels of physical activity or exercise. Health benefits can be obtained from minimal levels of physical activity or exercise. In contrast, higher levels of activity or exercise are required to stimulate moderate to high physical fitness benefits. This means that sedentary people can improve their health immediately just by raising their level of physical activity or exercise from low to moderate. However, to achieve higher personal fitness goals (for example, preparing for sports participation, running a 5K road race, or increasing your bench press maximum by 25 pounds), you will need to engage in higher levels of physical activity, exercise, or both. (See Chapter 3 for more details.)

Recently, researchers developed general physical activity and exercise guidelines for adolescents (ages eleven to twenty-one years). These guidelines were designed to help you develop and maintain your health and physical fitness. No one knows for sure the amount of physical activity or exercise needed for optimal health and physical fitness for young adults. However, the following guidelines were designed to provide you with target goals now, as well as to encourage you to continue to be active throughout your life:

- *Guideline 1.* All adolescents should be physically active daily or nearly every day, as part of play, games, sports, work, transportation, recreation, physical education, or planned exercise, in the context of family, school, or community activities.

- *Guideline 2.* Adolescents should engage in three or more sessions per week of activities that last twenty minutes or more at a time and that require moderate to vigorous levels of exertion.

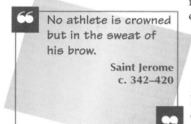

> No athlete is crowned but in the sweat of his brow.
>
> **Saint Jerome**
> c. 342–420

Close

Ask students to respond to the question, Is there anything in life more valuable than your good health?

broken down into steps to assure that learning takes place. It's also important that these learners successfully complete a particular step in the lesson before progressing to the next step.

• *You can make personal fitness a pleasurable social experience with others.*

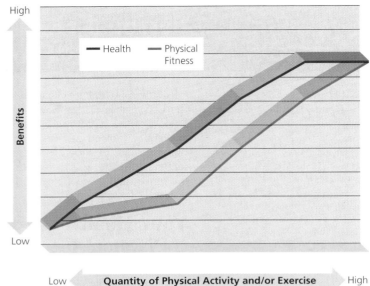

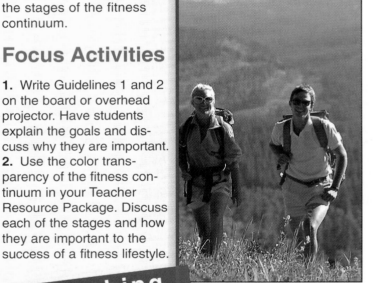

• *Being physically active can positively influence your health and physical fitness.*

CHAPTER 1 SECTION 4
30

Focus

Outcomes

In **Section 4**, students will learn:

1. To explain and discuss the national goals and recommendations for physical activity, exercise, or both, for adolescents.
2. To define and explain the stages of the fitness continuum.

Focus Activities

1. Write Guidelines 1 and 2 on the board or overhead projector. Have students explain the goals and discuss why they are important.
2. Use the color transparency of the fitness continuum in your Teacher Resource Package. Discuss each of the stages and how they are important to the success of a fitness lifestyle.

• **Figure 1.5**   *Comparing Health Benefits and Physical Fitness Benefits of Physical Activity, Exercise, or Both.*

As you learn to design your personal fitness program during the rest of this course, keep these guidelines in mind, and use them as you develop your program.

The personal fitness continuum in Figure 1.6 is designed to help you visualize how you can achieve and maintain personal fitness (level 5 in Figure 1.6). Initially, (1), when someone has low fitness, he needs to learn about the concepts of how to achieve physical fitness by participating safely in physical activity, exercise, or both. Once the person begins to (2) experience physical activity and exercise successfully, he will begin to have improved fitness levels. At that point, the individual should explore his activity options (3) and become actively and safely involved in a variety of physical activities. Then he can decide which activities are the most enjoyable and beneficial personally. By evaluating (4) the level of physical fitness, the individual can then modify his personal fitness program to meet individual needs for ongoing success (5).

Now that you understand the process of moving from low fitness levels to moderate or high fitness levels, it is important for you to motivate yourself to begin experiencing physical activity, exercise, or both. Remember, **A**ny **B**ody **C**an be fit! Will you?

ABILITY LEVELS

Reteaching

Some students may need help mastering the concepts contained in this section. In your Teacher Resource Package, you will find the reproducible worksheet shown here. This worksheet should help students who have been absent and those needing additional help to improve their comprehension and retention of the content in this section.

BELIEVE IT? ...
OR NOT?

Former high school athletes are at less risk for heart disease during their adult years than are members of the general population.

See page 25 for answer.

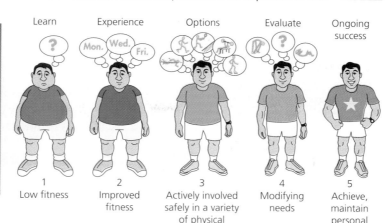

Learn	Experience	Options	Evaluate	Ongoing success

1 Low fitness — 2 Improved fitness — 3 Actively involved safely in a variety of physical activities — 4 Modifying needs — 5 Achieve, maintain personal fitness

• **Figure 1.6** *Your Personal Fitness Continuum.*

REMEMBER **This!**

The knowledge and activity experiences from this course will prepare you to solve your fitness problems for the future. What is important to your personal fitness is not just what you do today. It's what you do today, tomorrow, and in the extended future that is important.

Let's Get Started!

In this course you will participate in a conditioning program that will allow you to experience the benefits of physical activity and regular exercise in a positive way. The conditioning program can be designed by you and your instructor and should consist of a cardiovascular component (such as walking, jogging, or aerobic dance), a flexibility component (for example, stretching or range-of-motion activities), and a muscular strength and endurance component (weight lifting, calisthenics, and so on). You'll learn more about each of these components of fitness as you read this text.

It is important for you to get started *now* on your personal conditioning program so that later (starting in Chapter 4) you will be able to assess your fitness levels accurately and safely. It is also important that you follow the personal conditioning program for *several weeks* prior to your physical evaluations. Doing so will help you improve your levels of physical fitness.

Begin your conditioning program at a low to moderate level. Gradually increase this level over a period of *several weeks* to reduce injury risk. When you first start your program, it will be difficult to include all the fitness components at one time. It is best to start with the cardiovascular and flexibility components and add the muscular strength and endurance components later.

Teach & Apply

Activities

• Have students list the activities they do each day that meet the goals of Guideline 1.
• Have students list the activities they do weekly that meet the goals of Guideline 2.

Discussion

Have students discuss their lists for Guidelines 1 and 2, along with how and when additional opportunities for increased activity might be utilized.

Assess

Use the Section 4 Review questions on p. 32 to assess students' comprehension of the concepts presented in Section 4.

**E**nrichment *This activity will allow you to provide a more challenging learning experience for some of your students.*

Have students complete the following activity: Use Figure 1.5 on page 30 to answer the following questions.

Suppose that a person increased his or her quantity of physical activity and/or exercise from low to medium. What effect would this increase have on his or her (a) health, and (b) physical fitness? Do lower levels of physical activity and/or exercise have a greater benefit for health or physical fitness? (Answers: Both health and physical fitness would benefit from increased physical activity. Lower levels of physical activity have a greater benefit for health.)

**CHAPTER 1
SECTION 4
32**

ANSWERS TO SECTION 4 REVIEW

1. Guideline 1 is concerned with incorporating a variety of physical activities into your daily lives. Guideline 2 is concerned with activities that are more vigorous and are sustained for 20 or more minutes and should be done three or more times per week.

2. *Step 1*—Learn about correct, safe fitness concepts.
Step 2—Experience successful physical activity.
Step 3—Participate in a variety of physical activities.
Step 4—Continually evaluate your level of fitness in order to make any needed modifications to your activities.
Step 5—Continued participation and success with an on-going fitness program.

BELIEVE IT? ... OR NOT?

If you have enough money, you do not have to worry about your personal fitness level.

See page 25 for answer.

SECTION 4 REVIEW

Answer the following questions on a separate sheet of paper:

1. How do the first two physical activity guidelines for adolescents differ from one another?

2. Describe the process and stages in moving from low fitness levels to moderate or high fitness levels.

SUMMARY

Numerous scientific studies have documented the beneficial effects of physical activity, exercise, or both, in groups of men and women across the entire adult age range. Research has also shown that physical activity patterns and fitness levels established during childhood and adolescence are likely to carry over into adult life. Sound physical activity and nutrition habits developed in these early years provide the foundation for a lifetime of physical fitness.

Many scientific studies over the past twenty years support the value of regular exercise as part of a healthy lifestyle. Studies have documented a sedentary lifestyle as a risk factor for major chronic diseases. In many cases of fatigue, the cause is a lack of regular physical exercise. National health studies indicate that a high percentage of visits to physicians are for vague complaints such as chronic fatigue.

Regular, vigorous physical activity throughout life significantly reduces the risk of disability and premature death from stroke and heart disease. It can also effectively alter many of the important risk factors for cardiovascular disease by lowering body weight and blood cholesterol levels, raising HDL ("good cholesterol"), and promoting the maintenance of normal blood pressure. Regular exercise also has several potential benefits for people with diabetes. In addition, preliminary evidence indicates that active individuals may have a lower risk of dying of cancer.

The benefits of regular exercise on psychological health have also been clearly documented. People with anxiety and depression do better if exercise training is combined with other treatments. In fact, the vast majority of individuals who take up regular physical activity, exercise, or both, report an improved sense of general well-being and an enhanced self-image.

The health benefits of lifelong exercise habits and a high level of physical fitness are clear. This course and text are designed to help you develop the skills and behaviors you need to establish healthy, active lifestyle habits now and in the future.

Close

Have students begin a 4–5 week cardiovascular training protocol. Then, have the students use a variety of evaluations. Chapter 5 includes a sample of a safe conditioning program.

CRITICAL THINKING

Have each student select three people of different ages that they know fairly well. Students are to analyze the lifestyles of these people, noting the ways in which technology makes life easier for each person. Things students might look for include: use of automobiles, remote controls, microwave ovens, computers, fax machines, etc.

After they have collected the information, have students write an essay on each person identifying ways in which technology affects the physical, social, and mental aspects of the person's life.

Chapter 1 Review

True/False

On a separate piece of paper, mark each question below either T for True or F for False.

1. Moderate to high levels of physical fitness are associated with good health and wellness.
2. The best way to develop fitness is to become an athlete.
3. A lack of accurate physical fitness knowledge can contribute to a negative attitude about physical activity, exercise, or both.
4. The fitness behaviors that you develop as a young adult will have little effect on you and your health as an adult.
5. A sedentary lifestyle is one of the major risk factors for early death.
6. To significantly reduce your chances of early death from chronic disease, you will need to maintain a *high level* of fitness.
7. Eustress is the positive stress we all must deal with in our lives.
8. Men between the ages of fifty and sixty are more likely to die of heart disease than women of the same age.
9. Physical fitness is associated with enhanced self-esteem.
10. The *Healthy People 2000* objectives are designed to encourage all Americans to develop and maintain healthy, active lifestyles.

Multiple Choice

1. Health is a state of well-being that includes which of the following?
   a. physical aspects
   b. social aspects
   c. mental-emotional aspects
   d. spiritual aspects
   e. all of the above
2. The ability to maintain physical independence throughout your life is called
   a. sedentary health.
   b. functional health.
   c. physical fitness.
   d. less modifiable risk.
3. People who lead sedentary lifestyles are often referred to as
   a. couch potatoes.
   b. athletes.
   c. physically fit.
   d. low-health-risk people.
4. Smokers who stop smoking and adopt an active lifestyle can reduce their heart attack risk level to that of nonsmokers in ____ year(s).
   a. one-half
   b. one
   c. one to two
   d. two to three

Answers

True/False

1. T
2. F
3. T
4. F
5. T
6. F
7. T
8. T
9. T
10. T

Multiple Choice

1. e
2. b
3. a
4. d

(For example, students might note that using a remote control to change the television channels can create "couch potatoes," which affects the physical aspect of a person's life.) Then ask students to recommend changes each person could make to improve the physical, social, and mental aspects of their lives that have been affected by technology.

(For example, students could recommend that a person go to a gym to work out instead of sitting in front of the television with the remote control.)
   Students should gain an understanding that advances in technology have both positive and negative effects on our lifestyles.

Chapter 1 Review

Multiple Choice (continued)

5. a
6. d
7. d
8. b
9. c
10. a

Discussion

1. It is possible for one of the individuals to have heart disease and the other not. The individual with heart disease has less wellness but could still have his or her functional health. That means that he or she was still able to take care of himself or herself.

2. Even though there is a history of heart disease in your family, it is possible for you to reduce your chances of heart disease. This can be done by exercising regularly, eating properly, not smoking, and reducing stress.

3. Answers may vary and include any of the following:
  a. improved appearance
  b. improved muscular endurance
  c. improved muscular strength
  d. feelings of personal self-control
  e. enjoyment of life
  f. improved health
  g. increased energy
  h. improved physical performance
  i. improved school work
  j. better stress-coping abilities
  k. better sleep
  l. increased life expectancy

5. The average life expectancy for adults in the United States today is about ___ years.
  a. seventy-five
  b. seventy
  c. sixty-five
  d. sixty

6. Which of the following is the most easily modified risk factor?
  a. age
  b. gender
  c. genetics
  d. stress

7. People who are physically active throughout their lives may add about ___ year(s) to their life expectancy.
  a. 1
  b. 1.5
  c. 2
  d. 2.5

8. Cholesterol is usually classified as "good" or "bad." Which of the following refers to the "good" cholesterol?

  a. LDL
  b. HDL
  c. VLDL
  d. Triglycerides

9. Which of the following is *not* a positive outcome of personal fitness?
  a. improved physical appearance
  b. enhanced self-esteem
  c. hypertension
  d. stress reduction

10. Which of the following is the correct order for designing your personal fitness continuum?
  a. learn, experience, options, evaluate, and ongoing success
  b. experience, learn, evaluate, options, and ongoing success
  c. evaluate, experience, learn, ongoing success, and options
  d. options, ongoing success, evaluate, learn, and experience

Discussion

1. Explain how two seventy-five-year-old adults could both have their functional health but at the same time differ in relation to their wellness levels. Give examples.

2. Explain how you can adjust your lifestyle and behaviors to reduce your risk for premature death due to inherited genes.

3. In your opinion, which positive outcome of physical fitness is the most important, and why?

Vocabulary Experience

Match the correct term in Column A to the definition in Column B by writing the appropriate number in each blank.

Column A
____ wellness

____ physical fitness

Column B
1. Variables or conditions that increase the likelihood that you will develop chronic diseases.

2. The attainment and maintenance of a moderate to high level of physical, mental, emotional, spiritual, and social health.

Wellness Connection

Overweight vs. Overheavy

What does it really mean to say a person is overweight? Would you say that Arnold Schwarzenegger or Sylvester Stallone are overweight? Well, the answer would actually be, "Yes, they are."

The term overweight, as used by most people, refers to a person's body weight in relation to a height-weight chart, which indicates that if you are a certain height then you should weigh within a certain range of pounds. The charts allow for gender (male or female) or even bone

_____ risk factors

_____ predisposition

_____ sedentary lifestyle

_____ hypokinetic

3. Physically inactive.

4. Susceptibility to increased health risk due to genetic makeup.

5. Individual physical abilities that allow you to perform normal daily physical tasks effectively.

6. Inactive lifestyle.

Critical Thinking

1. Evaluate your self-esteem. Do you think that living a physically active lifestyle can have a positive influence on your self-esteem? Why or why not?

2. What advantages does a physically fit person have over a person with a low level of physical fitness on a day-to-day basis? Explain your answer.

3. How can living a physically active lifestyle improve your academic performance? Explain your answer.

Case Study — Raul Cuts Class

Raul is a seventeen-year-old junior who has become an expert at avoiding physical education classes. Since his first days in middle school, he has managed to develop a bag of tricks that allow him to sit out more days than he participates, and in some cases, avoid the physical education course entirely.

His problems with physical education classes began years ago. It seemed that he was always being required to take physical fitness tests that he was not prepared for. Later he would be sore and uncomfortable. He also hates sweating and messing up his hair. He spends the better part of his morning before school getting his hair just right, and then, after just five minutes of P.E., his hair is a mess and all that careful styling has been wasted.

What Raul doesn't mention is that he is also overweight and out of shape. He doesn't like to admit it, but he is embarrassed by his physical appearance when he has to wear anything other than his loose-fitting clothes, and it only takes about half a lap around the football field before he is totally winded.

There is a history of heart trouble in his family, and Raul thinks he heard somewhere that there is a connection between heart attacks and working out, but he is not sure. He thinks that there is probably nothing to this—it's just another trick to get you to come to class.

Here is your assignment:

Assume that you are Raul's friend. Write a letter to Raul trying to convince him not only to enroll in a P.E. class this semester, but to work hard during this class to get himself into shape. Use the information that you have read in this chapter to support your case.

KEYS TO HELP YOU
• Consider Raul's self-esteem
• Be sure you mention health risks

structure (ectomorph, endomorph, mesomorph), at which point most of us suddenly decide that we have a large frame. The height-weight charts do not, however, distinguish between weights due to muscle development or fat deposits. Because of this, many individuals who have large muscle mass development are "overweight" according to the charts.

Point out to students that their total body weight as determined by a scale and compared to height-weight charts has less to do with their wellness than does their body composition. To determine an accurate representation of their body composition, students should find their percentage of body fat. They will learn more about this in Chapter 9.

Chapter 2 is 32 pages long and divided into seven sections listed to the right. Major learning outcomes of the chapter are also listed to the right. Briefly, this chapter introduces students to the concept of how to safely engage in physical activity and exercise. It emphasizes the importance of medical evaluations and screenings, environmental issues, clothing options, basic biomechanics, injury prevention and care, and adherence to personal fitness. It also gives students some key concepts about walking and jogging techniques.

Teacher Resource Material

In the Teacher Resource Package accompanying the textbook you will find the following material to help you teach this chapter.

Activity Sheets

One Reteaching Worksheet is provided in the Teacher Resource Package for each section of this chapter. Handouts are also provided for the following

Chapter 2

Making Physical Activity and Exercise Safe for You

36

PACING CHART

You could easily spend five to six days teaching this chapter if students read the entire chapter, do the Active Mind/Active Body activities, and complete several of the handouts from the Teacher Resource Package. However, you can cover the material in this chapter in three to four days. It is recommended that physical activity be a regular part of each class period (20 to 30 minutes minimum). Following are some examples to help you cover the main topics in the chapter if you are pressed for time.

Contents

1. Medical Evaluations
2. Weather Conditions
3. The Outdoor Environment: It Can Be Hazardous
4. Dressing for Safety and Enjoyment
5. How to Put Your Best Foot Forward
6. Injury Prevention and Care
7. Adherence to a Personal Fitness Program

Outcomes

After reading and studying this chapter, you will be able to:

1. Define and explain the terms related to physical activity participation and safe exercise.
2. Explain the importance of having a medical evaluation prior to beginning a personal fitness program.
3. Tell how you can determine whether or not you need to undergo medical screening.
4. Discuss how weather conditions can influence the safety of your personal fitness program.
5. Explain how the outdoor environment can be hazardous. Identify specific situations that would cause you to modify your physical activity or exercise plans.
6. Explain the importance of choosing appropriate clothing and safety equipment for your personal fitness program. Identify specific items you will need.
7. Describe the proper way to walk and jog, based on the principles of biomechanics.
8. Identify and describe the injuries commonly experienced in personal fitness programs and how you might prevent and treat them.
9. Explain the importance of adherence to your personal fitness program, and how you can improve your adherence.

Key Terms

After reading and studying this chapter, you will be able to understand and provide practical definitions for the following terms:

medical screening	rehydration	strain
medical examination	diuretic	tendon
hyperthermia	heat stress index	stitch
dehydration	hypothermia	ligament
heat cramps	frostbite	cartilage
heat exhaustion	supination	stress fracture
heat stroke	pronation	adherence
acclimatization	biomechanics	

37

Active Mind/Active Body activity:

- Biomechanically Correct Walking and Jogging Checklist

A handout is also provided for the following:

- Physical Activity Readiness Questionnaire

Transparencies/ Masters

A transparency or master is provided in the Teacher Resource Package for each of the following figures: 2.1, 2.2, 2.3, 2.4, 2.5, 2.6, 2.7, and 2.8

Discuss the Photo

Ask students if they have been skiing. Ask what precautions they took while they were skiing. Then discuss why it is important to consider safety issues in planning and participating in personal fitness programs. Discuss with students their past experiences with injuries or threats to their personal safety while they were engaged in physical activities or exercise. Then discuss ways in which they could have avoided injury or a dangerous situation.

CHAPTER 2

Time	Suggestions
Day 1	Assign students to read Sections 1 and 2 prior to class. In class, do the Physical Activity Readiness Questionnaire on page 40. Include discussions about photos and figures.
Day 2	Assign students to read Sections 3 and 4. In class, discuss outdoor hazards. Discuss safe and effective fitness clothing and equipment. Do the Active Mind/Active Body activity on page 55.
Day 3	Assign students to read Sections 5 and 6 prior to class. Discuss biomechanics. In class, do the Active Mind/Active Body activity on page 59. Discuss injury prevention and care.
Day 4	Assign students to read Section 7 prior to class. Complete discussion of Section 6. Introduce the concept of adherence to personal fitness programs and discuss factors that influence it.

Focus

Outcomes

In **Section 1** students will learn:

1. To define and explain the terms related to physical activity participation and safe exercises.

2. To explain the importance of having a medical evaluation prior to beginning a personal fitness program, and whether students need to undergo medical screening.

Focus Activities

1. Discuss reasons for having medical examinations.

2. Use the Personal Activity Readiness Questionnaire on page 40 to have students evaluate whether they need to have a medical evaluation or medical screening.

INTRODUCTION

*T*he previous chapter clearly established the benefits of participating in regular physical activity and exercise throughout your life. This new knowledge, it is hoped, has motivated you to start or upgrade your personal fitness program. Should you jump right in and get going with the program that you have been putting off for so long? No, you should consider many things before you start or revise a personal fitness program.

The first step is to learn how to plan a safe and reasonable program that will not only be productive for you but also will increase the likelihood of your adherence to your personal fitness program. Many people start personal fitness programs with the best intentions. However, a 40 to 50 percent dropout rate is typical due to poor planning, unrealistic goals, and unsafe practices.

A journey of 1,000 miles starts with the first step. The material in Chapter 2 can help make this first step not only a safe one but also one that can be continued throughout your journey so that you can obtain your goals. Personal fitness is a journey that should have no end. A major goal of your long personal fitness journey is to make it enjoyable.

SECTION 1   Medical Evaluations

We generally think of physical activity and exercise as being good for us. However, safety risks can be involved. If you consider important medical guidelines, you can minimize these risks. Some questions you should consider are whether or not you should have a medical evaluation, how often you should be evaluated, and what should be included in the evaluation.

Who Needs an Evaluation?

Many people should have medical evaluations before beginning physical activity or exercise programs. Some people increase their risks for injury and other health problems if they start a program without medical clearance. If you have any known chronic disease, it is strongly recommended that you get medical clearance before beginning any formal exercise program, regardless of your age. Examples of chronic diseases could include any of the following:

- Heart disease or cardiovascular disorders.
- Severe obesity.

Reteaching

ABILITY LEVELS

Reteaching

Some students may need help mastering the concepts contained in this section. In your Teacher Resource Package, you will find the reproducible worksheet shown here. This worksheet should help students who have been absent and those needing additional help to improve their comprehension and retention of the content in this section.

* *Everyone needs regular medical evaluations. As you age, you will need to be evaluated more frequently.*

- High blood pressure.
- Kidney disease.
- Diabetes.

Men forty years old and above and women fifty and above who have not exercised vigorously for a number of years, and who have not had a medical examination in the past two to three years, are also encouraged to see a physician. A young adult with no medical history of heart problems in the family and no more than one risk factor (see Chapter 1) may begin an exercise program without a medical evaluation.

How Often Is the Evaluation Recommended?

There are no absolute guidelines for how often a person needs a medical evaluation. Some general guidelines for healthy people would include the following:

- Between the ages of six and fifteen: once every three years.
- Between the ages of fifteen and thirty-four: once every two years.
- Between the ages of thirty-five and fifty-nine: once a year.
- Sixty years old and older: twice a year.

What Should the Evaluation Include?

Most healthy young adults will be evaluated with a **medical screening**. During a medical screening any or all of the following will be assessed: eyes, ears, nose, throat, blood pressure, hernia, height, weight, and a check of how the heart and lungs sound. If a more serious **medical examination** is needed, the physician may examine the heart with an exercise stress test. In this test, the heart is monitored very closely as the patient walks or runs on a treadmill. Other parts of a medical examination may include a blood test, a urinary analysis, and a study of the family health-risk history.

The Physical Activity Readiness Questionnaire on the next page is an example of a simple health screening questionnaire. This type of questionnaire is often used by adults to determine whether or not they may safely begin an exercise program without a medical evaluation. Complete the questionnaire carefully. Then determine whether it may or may not be safe for you to begin a physical activity and exercise program.

medical screening

a basic evaluation of the eyes, ears, nose, throat, blood pressure, height, weight, and a check for possible hernia.

medical examination

a more extensive evaluation than is done in a medical screening, assessing any or all of the following: exercise stress test, blood test, urinary analysis, or family health-risk history.

Teach & Apply

Discussion

- Have students respond to the statement, "Personal fitness is a journey that should have no end."
- Ask students why they have or don't have a personal fitness program. Then ask them if they have ever worried about their safety while doing physical activity or while exercising.
- Have students list reasons why they would need to go see a physician. Ask students when they made their last visit to a physician. Ask them what types of tests they had done at the physician's office. What kinds of information did the tests give to their physicians and themselves?
- Ask students when they had their last medical screening. Discuss with the class how a medical examination is more rigorous than a medical screening.

Enrichment

This activity will allow you to provide a more challenging learning experience for some of your students.

Have students complete the following activity: Call your family doctor or any other physician, and ask about a preparticipation medical examination for an exercise program. Ask some of the following questions:
a. How are heart disease and other cardiovascular diseases diagnosed?
b. What are the procedures for a "medical screening"?
c. What health problems are related to obesity?
d. How is high blood pressure treated?
e. How is diabetes diagnosed and treated?
Write a one-page report on the answers to the questions, and explain why it may be important for many people to have a medical evaluation before beginning a personal fitness program.

Teacher Support Notes

You may want to tell students the following: Typically, if a medical examination is needed prior to beginning an exercise program (to rule out evidence of heart disease, for example), the physician will do an exercise treadmill or bicycle test with an electrocardiogram (ECG or EKG). This is often called a graded exercise test (GXT). The ECG is used to rule out evidence of ischemia (or lack of blood flow) to the heart.

Activity

Have students use the Personal Activity Readiness Questionnaire on this page to determine if they can safely begin an exercise program. This form can be used by you to effectively screen your class for health risks of which you are unaware.

Teaching Strategy

Questionnaires are often used to assess one's health risks prior to beginning exercise programs, particularly if someone who is very sedentary is planning on working out at a vigorous intensity level. Extensive medical screening and medical examinations are not needed for the vast majority of youth with whom you will work. However, they are helpful at screening out the few youths

---

PAR - Q & YOU
(Physical Activity Readiness–Questionnaire)
(A Questionnaire for People Aged 15 to 69)

Regular physical activity is fun and healthy, and increasingly more people are starting to become more active every day. Being more active is very safe for most people. However, some people should check with their doctor before they start becoming much more physically active.

If you are planning to become much more physically active than you are now, start by answering the seven questions in the box below. If you are between the ages of 15 and 69, the PAR-Q will tell you if you should check with your doctor before you start. Common sense is your best guide when you answer these questions. Please read the questions carefully and answer each one honestly: check YES or NO.

YES	NO	
☐	☐	1. Has your doctor ever said that you have a heart condition *and* that you should only do physical activity recommended by a doctor?
☐	☐	2. Do you feel pain in your chest when you do physical activity?
☐	☐	3. In the past month, have you had chest pain when you were not doing physical activity?
☐	☐	4. Do you lose your balance because of dizziness or do you ever lose consciousness?
☐	☐	5. Do you have a bone or joint problem that could be made worse by a change in your physical activity?
☐	☐	6. Is your doctor currently prescribing drugs (for example, water pills) for your blood pressure or heart condition?
☐	☐	7. Do you know of *any other reason* why you should not do physical activity?

NOTE: If the PAR-Q is being given to a person before he or she participates in a physical activity program or a fitness appraisal, this section may be used for legal or administrative purposes.

I have read, understood and completed this questionnaire. Any questions I had were answered to my full satisfaction.

NAME _____ DATE _____
SIGNATURE _____ WITNESS _____
SIGNATURE OF PARENT _____
or GUARDIAN (for minors)

If you answered

YES to one or more questions

Talk with your doctor by phone or in person BEFORE you start becoming much more physically active or BEFORE you have a fitness appraisal. Tell your doctor about the PAR-Q and which questions you answered YES to.

- You may be able to do any activity you want—as long as your start slowly and build up gradually. Or, you may need to restrict your activities to those which are safe for you. Talk with your doctor about the kinds of activities you wish to participate in and follow his/her advice.
- Find out which community programs are safe and helpful for you.

DELAY BECOMING MUCH MORE ACTIVE:
- if you are not feeling well because of a temporary illness such as a cold or a fever—wait until you feel better; or
- if you are or may be pregnant—talk to your doctor before you start becoming more active.

NO to all questions

If you answered NO honestly to all PAR-Q questions, you can be reasonably sure that you can:
- start becoming much more physically active—begin slowly and build up gradually. This is the safest and easiest way to go.
- take part in a fitness appraisal—this is an excellent way to determine your basic fitness so that you can plan the best way for you to live actively.

Please note: If your health changes so that you then answer YES to any of the above questions, tell your fitness or health professional. Ask whether you should change your physical activity plan.

- *The Physical Activity Readiness Questionnaire will help you determine whether or not you can safely participate in physical activity.*

Source: Reprinted with permission from S. Thomas, J. Reading, R. J. Shephard: Revision of the Physical Activity Readiness Questionnaire (PAR-Q), *Canadian Journal of Sports Science* 17 (1992): 338–345 (based on the British Columbia Department of Health, PAR-Q Validation Report, 1975).

Across the Disciplines

Psychology

The ability to establish and maintain a successful personal fitness plan is a life-enhancing skill that must be learned. Setting realistic, attainable goals is a significant factor in a person's realizing a successful personal fitness plan. Goal-setting alone does not assure success. Self-motivation is also a critical factor. The term "Yo-Yo Syndrome" has been used to describe the upward and downward path of people who unsuccessfully begin diet and/or exercise plans only to

SECTION 1 REVIEW

Answer the following questions on a separate sheet of paper:

1. Describe the differences between a medical screening and a medical examination.
2. Would the responses of one or both of your parents to the "Physical Activity Readiness Questionnaire" differ from yours? If so, how?

SECTION 2   Weather Conditions

hyperthermia

overheating; body temperature above 98.6 degrees Fahrenheit.

dehydration

excess fluid loss from the body; symptoms include weakness and fatigue.

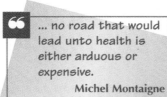

> " ... no road that would lead unto health is either arduous or expensive.
>
> **Michel Montaigne**

Another important safety consideration for your exercise program is weather conditions. If the environment is too hot, or too humid, or too cold, you will significantly increase your risk for injuries.

The Dangers of Physical Activity in Heat and Humidity

During physical activity or exercise, your body produces heat and raises your body temperature above what is normal at rest (98.6 degrees Fahrenheit). To control overheating (**hyperthermia**), your body sweats. The sweat evaporates on your skin to cool your body. When the weather is hot and humid, you sweat excessively and lose excess fluids (**dehydration**), which can produce weakness and fatigue. In hot, humid weather it can be difficult for you to maintain a normal body temperature during physical activity. This can put you at a higher risk for developing heat injuries, including heat cramps, heat exhaustion, and heat stroke.

Heat Cramps.   **Heat cramps** are painful contractions of the muscles used during physical activity or exercise due, at least in part, to dehydration. Heat cramps are the mildest form of heat injury and can be minimized by drinking plenty of fluids and maintaining a normal body fluid balance. Normal body fluid balance refers to your ability to balance the amount of water you consume with the amount that you lose or excrete daily (see Chapter 10 for more details).

nationwide that are at risk for sudden death during exercise. Screenings are also important to use so that students recognize that they should have a screening later in life if they have been sedentary and want to return to a personal fitness program.

Assess

Use the Section 1 Review Questions to assess students' comprehension of the concepts presented in Section 1.

ANSWERS TO SECTION 1 REVIEW

1. Medical screenings are simple checkups. The medical examination is more rigorous and often requires several different diagnostic tests.
2. Answers will vary.

Close

Ask students why their responses on the questionnaire were or were not different from their parents. (See Section 1 Review question #2.) Ask them if they might ever have to answer yes to one of the questions and why.

quit when they reach their goals or grow tired of the prescribed routine. The medical field has emphasized the negative physical and psychological effects this up-and-down process has on the individual. Discuss this syndrome with your class. Have students brainstorm a list of reasons why people begin fitness programs and a list of reasons why those plans tend to fail. Explain how learning to set realistic, attainable fitness goals is an invaluable lifelong skill and how self-motivation is another vital skill that facilitates the realization of one's goals. The personal fitness class can be a perfect setting in which students can experience successful goal-setting and understand the importance of self-motivation.

Focus

Outcome

In **Section 2** students will learn:

1. To determine how weather conditions can influence the safety of their personal fitness program.

Focus Activities

1. Discuss the types of injuries associated with exercising in very hot or very cold environmental conditions.

RESOURCES

TRANSPARENCIES

2. Use the transparencies/masters of Figures 2.1, 2.2, and 2.3 to illustrate to students the concepts of fluid loss, the heat stress index, and wind chill.

REMEMBER This!

It is important to continue the rehydration process after an exercise session has been completed. It may take up to twelve hours to achieve complete fluid replacement after strenuous exercise in the heat. An easy way to monitor whether fluids are being adequately replaced, from day to day, is by weighing yourself. If you have weight loss on a daily basis that exceeds 3 percent of your total body weight, the rehydration process is probably not complete. For example, if you weigh 120 pounds, a 3 percent weight loss would be 3.6 pounds. If this happens to you, you should not participate in heavy physical activity until your body weight is back to normal.

Heat Exhaustion.   **Heat exhaustion** is an overheating condition that includes feelings of weakness; headache; rapid pulse; stomach discomfort; dizziness; heavy sweating; muscle cramps; and cool, clammy skin. If you have the symptoms of heat exhaustion, you should stop physical activity or exercise immediately. You should then get to a cool, dry environment and drink plenty of fluids. You should not return to your normal personal fitness program again until you have had a chance (usually a day or two) to replace your normal fluid balance.

Heat Stroke.   **Heat stroke** can be life threatening. Its symptoms include fainting or nearly fainting; a lack of sweating; hot, dry skin; and a very high body temperature. Heat stroke requires immediate medical treatment.

• *Learn to recognize the symptoms of heat stress during physical activity and exercise.*

Reteaching

ABILITY LEVELS

Reteaching

Some students may need help mastering the concepts contained in this section. In your Teacher Resource Package, you will find the reproducible worksheet shown here. This worksheet should help students who have been absent and those needing additional help to improve their comprehension and retention of the contents of this section.

Any Body Can!

The Tarahumara Indians

The Tarahumara Indians from Mexico's Copper Canyon are known as the "Raramuri," or foot runners. They live at high altitudes and are famous for their 50- to 200-mile foot races. Known for their Spartan-like lifestyle, they consume a diet that is very low in fat and total calories.

For decades, the Tarahumara have had competitions between villages where runners wearing sandals kick wooden balls along trails. Contests can last for several days, and runners often cover more than 100 miles before they give up due to fatigue. Legends about their long distance running capabilities include stories of their running up to 70 miles a day, 170 miles without stopping, and 500 miles a week carrying 40 pounds of mail.

The unusual endurance capabilities of the Tarahumara have been recognized by outsiders ever since the 1920s, and they have been encouraged to compete nationally and internationally in long distance running events. However, with the exception of the 1928 and 1968 Olympic Games, few Indians have left their native land to compete. This has been due in part to the differences in cultural habits of the Indians and the outside world.

In 1992, a group of five Tarahumara were coaxed out of Copper Canyon to compete in the Leadville, Colorado, 100-mile Race (run over mountainous trails) by a wilderness guide who had befriended them and had become their sponsor and coach. The Indians were expected to do very well in the race because it was at high altitudes (9,000 to over 12,000 feet), similar to their native environment. However, after leading the race for 40 miles, the five Tarahumara dropped out because they were unfamiliar with the course and with racing strategies needed for success.

In the 1993 Leadville 100-miler, three better prepared Tarahumara Indians placed first, second, and fifth. And, in the 1994 race, two of the Tarahumara placed first and third. The Tarahumara Indians are gaining international fame as endurance running champions.

Not everyone can conquer fierce environmental challenges during exercise like the Tarahumara Indians, but Any Body Can live a healthy lifestyle and make physical fitness an important part of their everyday life. That's right, you can do it!

Teach & Apply

Discussion

Ask students if they sweat during physical activity or exercise in very cold conditions. For example, have them compare running outside for 20 minutes in International Falls, Minnesota (the icebox of the U.S.), during January versus Dallas, Texas, in July.

Teacher Support Notes

You may want to tell students the following: We sweat during exercise whether it is cold or hot. However, students will not perceive that they sweat when it is cold because it is usually less humid when it is cold and sweat evaporates more effectively in these conditions. It is usually more humid when it is hot and sweat does not evaporate as readily. Therefore, students notice that

Enrichment

This activity will allow you to provide a more challenging learning experience for some of your students.

Have students complete the following activity: In your local grocery store, look at the nutrition labels for the various sports drinks sold. Compare the carbohydrate (sugar) content of each drink. How many of these drinks have a sugar content greater than 8 percent? Next, go to the soft-drink section, and look at the nutrition labels for the various canned and bottled soft drinks. Record the sugar content for these drinks. Next, go to the fruit juice section, and record the sugar content of the various canned or bottled fruit juices that are sold. Write a report on your findings. If a drink with greater than 8 percent sugar content will be absorbed into your system much slower than water, which drinks would you recommend for quick fluid replacement in hot weather?

their clothing gets soaked when they exercise in hot conditions. It is possible to get dehydrated in either hot or cold conditions.

Discussion

• Ask students if they or anyone they know has had a heat injury. Ask them if they observed any symptoms of heat problems mentioned in the text.

• Discuss why professional athletes who are from a cold climate might have trouble competing if they compete in a warm environment.

Teacher Support Notes

You may want to tell students the following: Some professional football teams conduct summer preseason drills in northern states where it is cool while other teams workout in southern states where it is much warmer. It is not unusual to see a team acclimatized to the heat in early season games perform much better than a team that is not acclimatized.

Activity

Divide the class into groups of three and have each group fill up three 1-liter bottles with water. Then have each member of the group hold up the filled water bottles to experience the potential amount of weight lost as sweat (water) in one hour during vigorous exercise.

acclimatization

the process of allowing the body to adapt slowly to new conditions.

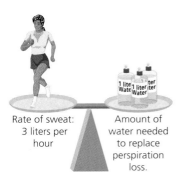

Rate of sweat: 3 liters per hour

Amount of water needed to replace perspiration loss.

• **Figure 2.1** *Maintaining Water Balance. Think about how much soda there is in a 3-liter soda bottle. That's how much water your body can sweat in an hour-long workout.*

rehydration

the process of replacing fluids that have been lost or excreted from the body.

diuretic

a substance that promotes water loss through urination.

How to Avoid Heat Injury. You may have noticed that activities that are easily accomplished in cool weather become much more difficult to accomplish, and are more physically demanding, in hot, humid weather. If exercising in the heat is unavoidable, try to allow your body to adapt slowly to the heat—a process called **acclimatization**. It has been shown that you can become acclimatized to working out in the heat after five to ten days. The first few physical activity or exercise sessions in the heat should be light and last for only about twenty minutes. After you get acclimatized to the heat, you can increase your exercise gradually in both duration and intensity.

It is important to drink plenty of fluids prior to and during physical activity in the heat. Your body needs fluids to maintain sweating for body cooling. Inadequate fluid intake can lead to dehydration. Dehydration leads to a reduction in sweating and, ultimately, a significant rise in body temperature. A balance of water loss and water intake must be maintained.

Water loss through sweating during vigorous physical activity or exercise can reach as much as 3 liters per hour (see Figure 2.1). To maintain water balance, you should consume between 1.5 and 2.5 cups (1 cup = 8 ounces) of cold water ten to twenty minutes *before* exercising in the heat. During physical activity in the heat, attempt to match fluid loss with fluid intake. A rule of thumb would be approximately 1 cup of water *every* ten to fifteen minutes.

The body's thirst mechanism may lag behind the body's actual need for fluid. Therefore, to prevent heat injuries, you must continue to replace fluids despite the fact that you may not feel thirsty. Water is an excellent fluid to consume when you exercise in the heat. For most situations, water works as well as anything for preventing dehydration. However, numerous sports drinks are also on the market, and you may want to try some of them.

The following are some guidelines for consuming fluids when exercising in hot weather:

• Look for fluids that have an appealing taste during heavy exercise.

• A sports drink that provides an optimal fluid replacement has a 5 to 8 percent carbohydrate (sugar) content. You can find the contents of these drinks by reading the container labels or nutrition facts (more about this in Chapter 10).

• Replacement fluids containing carbonation, fruit juices, and fruit drinks are not the best choices because they may upset your stomach. They also are absorbed at a much slower rate than plain water or specially made sports drinks.

• Drinks containing caffeine may slow **rehydration** attempts, because caffeine acts as a **diuretic**.

Clothing is also important for safe exercise in the heat. Choose clothing that is loose and light in color to promote optimal heat loss

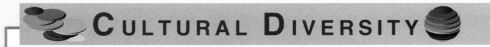

CULTURAL DIVERSITY

Canada

Love of the outdoors and sports seems to be in the blood of Canadians. Whether they're participating on organized sports teams or cross-country skiing, Canadians enjoy staying active.

Many of the sports that are popular in the United States are also popular in Canada. Baseball, volleyball, and football are all played by Canadians. Few people realize how many of today's popular sports owe their beginnings to Canadians. For example, basketball was

Relative Humidity	Air Temperature (°F)										
	70°	75°	80°	85°	90°	95°	100°	105°	110°	115°	120°
0%	64	69	73	78	83	87	91	95	99	103	107
10%	65	70	75	80	85	90	95	100	105	111	116
20%	66	72	77	82	87	93	99	105	112	120	130
30%	67	73	78	84	90	96	104	113	123	135	148
40%	68	74	79	86	93	101	110	123	137	151	
50%	69	75	81	88	96	107	120	135	150		
60%	70	76	82	90	100	114	132	149			
70%	70	77	85	93	106	124	144				
80%	71	78	86	97	113	136					
90%	72	80	91	108							

Low Risk 90 or Less	Medium Risk 90 – 105	Higher Risk 105 to 130	Probable Injury 130 or More

RISK OF HEAT INJURY

• **Figure 2.2** *Heat Stress Index. Use this chart to calculate the heat stress index when you exercise if you know the temperature and humidity. For example, if it were 90 degrees Fahrenheit and the humidity was 70 percent, the heat stress index would be 106, which places you at higher risk for heat injury.*

heat stress index

a number that reflects a combination of high temperatures and high humidity.

hypothermia

a condition in which the body temperature drops below normal (98.6 degrees Fahrenheit).

frostbite

damage to the body tissues due to freezing.

as you sweat. Tight clothes do not allow air to circulate between the skin and the clothing. Dark clothing absorbs heat, whereas light clothing reflects heat rays. Cotton fabrics are best, as they absorb moisture rapidly and promote evaporation and cooling. Never wear sweatshirts or rubber suits, which limit your ability to have excessive sweat evaporate and cool your body.

You can reduce your risk for heat injury by limiting your activity when the **heat stress index** reaches or exceeds 105 (see Figure 2.2). You can also reduce your risk for heat injuries by exercising during the cooler parts of the day, either in the early morning or the evening.

The Dangers of Physical Activity in Cold Weather

When you are physically active or exercise in cold weather, your body temperature can drop below normal (a condition called **hypothermia**). In extremely cold conditions you significantly increase your risk for tissue damage from freezing (**frostbite**). It is important to consider the combined influences of wind and temper-

invented by James Naismith, who was born in Canada. Lacrosse, which is popular in Australia, England, New Zealand, and the United States, was invented by Canadian Plains Indians.

Hockey, too, was invented in Canada. It probably evolved from a type of field hockey that was played by soldiers. Many of hockey's outstanding players

have come from Canada.

Because of Canada's climate, people have ample opportunity to enjoy snow skiing, sledding, and tobogganing, which are all very popular activities. During the summer months, baseball, softball, soccer, and bicycling are some of the many ways Canadians stay active.

Assess

Use the Section 2 review questions to assess students' comprehension of the concepts presented in Section 2.

ANSWERS TO SECTION 2 REVIEW

1. Heat cramps are less severe than heat exhaustion and are the mildest form of heat injuries. Heat exhaustion includes weakness, headache and rapid pulse.
2. The wind chill would be −5°.

Close

Discuss the topics covered in Section 2 that were the most beneficial to students in developing and following a personal fitness plan.

Consumer Corner

Ask students if they have ever noticed that an article of clothing they wore during exercise caused them to sweat more than another outfit. Have them explain why.

Wind Speed (mph)	Air Temperature (°F)														
Calm	40	35	30	25	20	15	10	5	0	−5	−10	−15	−20	−25	−30
5	37	33	27	21	16	12	6	1	−5	−11	−15	−20	−26	−31	−35
10	28	21	16	9	4	−2	−9	−15	−21	−27	−33	−38	−46	−52	−58
15	22	16	11	1	−5	−11	−18	−25	−36	−40	−45	−51	−58	−65	−70
20	18	12	3	−4	−10	−17	−25	−32	−39	−46	−53	−60	−67	−76	−81
25	16	7	0	−7	−15	−22	−29	−37	−44	−52	−59	−67	−74	−83	−89
30	13	5	−2	−11	−18	−26	−33	−41	−48	−56	−63	−70	−79	−87	−94
35	11	3	−4	−13	−20	−27	−35	−43	−49	−60	−67	−72	−82	−90	−96
40	10	1	−6	−15	−21	−29	−37	−45	−53	−62	−69	−76	−85	−94	−101

Low Risk Warmer than −21	Increasing Risk −22 to −67	High Risk Colder than −67

RISK OF FROSTBITE

• **Figure 2.3** *Wind Chill Index. Use the chart to calculate the wind chill if you know air temperature and wind speed. If it were 15 degrees Fahrenheit and the wind was blowing at 30 mph, the wind chill would be −26, which places you at a higher risk for injury.*

ature, or the wind chill factor, before you decide to be active on a cold and windy day (see Figure 2.3).

When you exercise in cold weather, wear warm, loose-fitting clothing in layers. Pay attention to media weather forecasts. Finally, be sure to protect your extremities (hands, feet, head, ears, and so on) from extreme cold.

BELIEVE IT? ... OR NOT?

Death during vigorous exercise is rare. It is estimated that there is one death per year in a population of 15,000 to 20,000 adult exercisers.

See page 57 for answer.

SECTION 2 REVIEW

Answer the following questions on a separate piece of paper:

1. Describe the differences between heat cramps and heat exhaustion.
2. When the outside temperature is 20 degrees Fahrenheit and the wind is blowing at 15 miles per hour, what is the wind chill factor?

Special Needs

It is important to note that those students with physical disabilities or medical limitations need a thorough medical evaluation prior to the beginning of any exercise program. The physical education teacher should encourage the student to ask his or her attending physician to include the following information in the evaluation: the student's health history, the student's disabling condition, any medication(s) the student is currently taking, any contraindications related to an exercise program, and information from the student's physical therapist.

Danger under -22 degrees

• *When you exercise in cold weather, dress appropriately for the challenge.*

 Health and Fitness Updates

You can update your coverage of health and fitness topics, as well as spark lively classroom discussion and deeper understanding, by using the **CNN Health and Fitness Updates.** These video updates are produced by Turner Educational Services, using the resources of CNN, the world's first 24-hour, all-news network.

With the introduction of the **CNN Health and Fitness Updates,** West Educational Publishing is proud to be the exclusive partner of CNN for textbook/video integration in high school fitness. By making use of the **CNN Health and Fitness Updates** you can bring the power of CNN, the network known for providing in-depth, live coverage and analysis of breaking news events, to your fitness class.

For assistance in using and incorporating the **CNN Health and Fitness Updates** into your classroom presentations, see the *Classroom Guide to the CNN Health and Fitness Updates.* The **CNN Health and Fitness Updates** are available with West Educational Publishing's *Foundations of Personal Fitness* by Don Rainey and Tinker Murray.

CONSUMER CORNER

Beware of the "Quick Fix"

Many people still believe they can speed up the loss of fat by wearing a plastic or rubber suit during exercise sessions. This is a false belief, as well as a dangerous one. Most of the weight you lose is fluid, not fat, and will quickly be replaced when you drink fluids following your activity. Using this type of suit places you at risk for dehydration.

You should always be aware of the fact that there are many false advertisements about health and fitness "quick fixes." Be sure you thoroughly investigate any quick-weight-loss or fitness gimmicks before you buy or use them.

Some of the claims that should alert you to gimmicks and unreliable products are:

• ads that rely solely upon identification of a product with a famous person, such as a movie star or sports hero

• weight-loss promises that say you will lose large amounts of weight in a short period of time

• solutions to weight loss that involve products other than regular foods. Try not to get yourself into a position in which you are dependent upon special products. These products are often expensive, and they usually do not contain the variety of nutrients that you consume with natural foods.

Remember, nothing worthwhile comes easy. If you want to lose weight, you will need to work at it. You will learn more about the sensible way to lose weight in Chapters 9 and 10.

The physical education teacher should be aware of the professional resources available when working with the disabled or medically limited population. The student's parents, school nurse, physical therapist, occupational therapist, and special education teacher(s) are all excellent sources of information.

Individuals with physical and medical disabilities, particularly those with central nervous system damage, are more apt to be prone to problems with body temperature maintenance because the body is unable to properly regulate heat loss or gain. Certain medications may have an affect on their bodies' ability to stay properly hydrated.

Focus

Outcome

In **Section 3** students will learn:

1. To explain how the outdoor environment can be hazardous and how to identify ways to modify their physical activity or exercise plans to be safe.

Focus Activities

1. Discuss the hazards associated with physical activity or exercise in regard to air pollution, altitude, bad dogs, and crime.
2. Use the "Stress Break" information to highlight the fact that environmental elements can be stressful in everyday life.

SECTION 3   The Outdoor Environment: It Can Be Hazardous

Your medical evaluation came up with no problems. Now you are ready to head outdoors to begin your exercise program. It sounds safe enough, but first you should be aware of some serious environmental concerns. Your community may have any or all of these safety hazards. Take some time to determine if any of these hazards are present in your physical activity and exercise environment.

Air Pollution: Industrial and Automobile Emissions

Industrial pollutants and carbon monoxide (a gas created by combustion engines, including those in cars and trucks) have created potentially dangerous exercise environments in many cities. Many of the industrial pollutants can restrict our breathing passages making it difficult to breathe, especially when large amounts of air are needed during exercise. You might compare the difficulty caused by these pollutants to the difficulty you'd experience if you had to do all your breathing through a long, narrow straw.

In addition, harmful materials can collect in our lungs. Carbon monoxide is dangerous because it is more readily absorbed by the

BELIEVE IT? ... OR NOT?

Of the five hundred young people who die each year riding bikes, only 20 percent are victims of head trauma.

See page 57 for answer.

• *Air pollution can make physical activity and exercise hazardous.*

Reteaching

ABILITY LEVELS

Reteaching

Some students may need help mastering the concepts contained in this section. In your Teacher Resource Package, you will find the reproducible worksheet shown here. This worksheet should help students who have been absent and those needing additional help to improve their comprehension and retention of the contents of this section.

Stress Break

•••••••••••••••••••

One of the reasons why millions of people participate in regular physical activity is to reduce the stress in their lives. A regular walk through the park, a bike ride around the neighborhood, or even a vigorous game of tennis can help you relax. It may be the only time of the day that you get to do something just for yourself. Find a place and a time of day that insures the experience will be a positive one. If you are concerned about traffic, dogs, potential violence, or time constraints, you may find that your workouts are more stress producing than stress reducing. Plan your workout to make it positive and enjoyable. You need opportunities to deal with stress in positive ways.

bloodstream than is the needed oxygen. If you exercise regularly in an environment with polluted air, you will increase your risk for respiratory problems.

You can take several steps to minimize your risks from air pollution. First, pay attention to media reports of high pollution levels. Next, identify the areas and the times of day that have less traffic. During peak traffic or high-pollution periods, limit or eliminate completely your exercise, especially if you have respiratory problems. Finally, find suitable indoor physical activity and exercise opportunities if you cannot avoid peak traffic or high-pollution periods.

Altitude

High altitude (starting at about 5,000 feet above sea level) can reduce your ability to exercise or perform work, especially if you have been living at lower altitudes. Moving from lower to higher altitudes will reduce the ability of your heart and lungs to deliver and utilize oxygen. This causes you to get tired more quickly than you would at sea level. It can also cause high altitude sickness (upset stomach, headache, dehydration, and so on). A person who moves from a low to a high altitude and then lives and trains in the high altitude over a period of time can increase the work capacity of the heart and lungs. However, this person's capacity will never be as high as it would be at sea level.

When you move from a low altitude to a high altitude, gradually increase the amount you exercise over a period of days. If possible, change altitude slowly over several hours. This can help prevent altitude sickness. Drink plenty of fluids. This can also help prevent altitude sickness. Individuals with heart or lung problems, of course, should consult a doctor before attempting vigorous exercise at any altitude.

Bad Dogs

Even if the air quality is good and the weather is great, you may encounter other outdoor hazards. For example, the exercise environment may have loose dogs. Nothing is worse than having a pleasant jog, walk, or bike ride interrupted by an unfriendly canine.

As you exercise outdoors, be alert for dogs. If you encounter a dog, do not unnecessarily frighten or threaten it. If confronted by a dog, it may be best to face it and yell, "***Bad dog! Stop!***" Then walk slowly away—never run.

Crime

It is a sad fact, but a necessary consideration, that crime is commonplace in our society. Women should be especially concerned

Teach & Apply

Discussion

• Ask students to discuss the photo on p. 48. Have them identify which elements (air quality, sunlight/ozone, automobiles, etc.) of the environment would make exercising hazardous to their health.
• Ask students if they ever got stuck behind a city bus and had to breathe the polluted air. Then ask them why it might be even worse if they were exercising.

Discussion

Ask students if they have traveled to a high altitude and tried to exercise (for example, a ski trip). Have them list any problems they encountered.

Enrichment

This activity will allow you to provide a more challenging learning experience for some of your students.

Have students complete the following activity: Call your local weather station and ask the following questions:
a. What level of pollution might be dangerous for a person exercising outdoors?
b. What times of the day are best and worst for air pollution?
c. What are the most likely causes of the air pollu- **tion in your area?**
d. What recommendations can be made for a person with respiratory problems exercising outdoors on high-pollution days?

Write a one-page paper on the answers to these questions, and report to the class on the effect that air pollution might have on outdoor physical activity in your community.

Assess

Use the Section 3 Review questions to assess students' comprehension of the concepts presented in Section 3.

ANSWERS TO SECTION 3 REVIEW

1. Answers will vary, but should include respiratory problems and high carbon dioxide levels.
2. Plan ahead of time, exercise in well-lit areas, exercise with friends, avoid verbal confrontations, and let someone know where you are going and when you expect to return.

Close

Have students discuss the "Stress Break" information on p. 49 and how it relates to outdoor exercise hazards they face. Have students provide ways to optimize their chances of having positive physical activity and exercise experiences.

Teacher Readings

Runner's World Magazine, Rodale Press, Volume 31, Number 2, 1996.

BELIEVE IT? ...
OR NOT?

More than 60 million Americans walk for exercise.

See page 57 for answer.

• *Being aware of potential hazards in your exercise environment will enable you to minimize injuries.*

about when and where they exercise. Take some time to examine and plan your outdoor exercise routes and routines to avoid crime.

The following guidelines can help you avoid crime or threatening situations:

• Exercise in well-lighted areas.
• Exercise with friends.
• Avoid high-crime neighborhoods.
• Avoid verbal confrontations, if possible.
• Let someone know where you are going and when you expect to return.

SECTION 3 REVIEW

Answer the following questions on a separate sheet of paper:

1. Explain the hazards associated with physical activity or exercise in environments with polluted air.
2. List precautions you can take to avoid bad dogs and crime in your exercise environment.

Equipment Options

Manufacturers today make a major effort to provide safe equipment. Although most fitness equipment is safe, physical education teachers still need to review their equipment needs and investigate the safety of a piece of equipment prior to purchase. A major emphasis in

today's market is protective head gear for cyclists and in-line skaters. Helmets for cyclists can range in price from $9.99 to $150.00 or more and are made from a range of materials. Look for a DOT inspection emblem on the helmet. This emblem assures that the helmet and its

SECTION 4 Dressing for Safety and Enjoyment

If you dress properly for physical activity and exercise, you will be more comfortable. You will also reduce your risk for injury. An understanding of clothing and safety needs for specific physical activities can enhance your adherence to, and enjoyment of, your personal fitness program.

Clothing

On mild to warm days, wear loose, comfortable clothes (shorts, T-shirts, tank tops, socks, and the like). Avoid clothes that restrict your movements or that cause you to overheat (see Section 2, earlier in the chapter). When it is cold, wear sweatshirts and pants, tights, windbreakers, and gloves or mittens. Wear different layers of clothing when it is cold. That way, you can remove a layer or two if you get too warm.

Clothing does not need to be expensive to be effective for physical activity and exercise. However, you should be a wise consumer when selecting clothing. For example, consider the temperature of your exercise environment, safety factors (reflective clothing might be useful), price, quality of material, and type of cleaning required before you decide to buy anything.

Some considerations in selecting your physical activity and exercise clothing are specific to your gender. For example, to provide additional exercise safety and comfort, women may want to purchase a sports bra. For the same reasons, men may want to purchase sport briefs or an athletic supporter.

Safety Equipment

If you participate in an activity such as bicycling, skateboarding, or in-line skating, you should always wear protective equipment. For example, you should always wear a helmet. Statistics show that the likelihood of head injury is reduced 85 percent by using a bike helmet. When skateboarding or in-line skating, wear elbow pads, knee pads, and wrist guards.

A protective helmet should have a foam liner inside to absorb blows to the head in case of a fall. Choose a helmet that meets the standards set by either the American National Standards Institute (ANSI) or the Shell Memorial Foundation. Make sure the helmet has a snug but comfortable fit. Finally, check the helmet for a chin strap and buckle, so it will stay securely fastened.

REMEMBER This!

Your safety and successful participation in your personal fitness program may depend upon your choice, purchase, and proper care of exercise clothing and equipment. Therefore, when you decide to buy personal fitness gear, make informed consumer choices as you shop.

manufacturers meet or exceed the quality necessary to protect a person from injury designated by the Department of Transportation.

Physical education teachers may want to suggest protective clothing for runners during the cold months. Advancements in materials for running apparel have produced lightweight clothes that act as an insulation against cold, are waterproof, and remain flexible. This clothing is half the weight of the traditional cotton sweatsuits. **Take the challenge:** Go to your nearest sporting goods store and inspect their equipment. **Remember:** Look at the manufacturers' labels and compare materials to price.

Focus

Outcomes

In **Section 4** students will learn:

1. To explain the importance of choosing appropriate clothing and safety equipment for their personal fitness program.
2. To identify specific items of clothing and safety equipment they will need.

Focus Activities

1. Discuss the factors that should be considered when selecting physical activity and exercise equipment.
2. Use the *Healthy People 2000* Objective 9.13 (page 53) to emphasize the importance of using safety equipment (bicycle helmets).
3. Use the transparency/master of Figure 2.4 to explain the characteristics of proper personal fitness footwear.
4. Use Figure 2.5 and the Active Mind/Active Body activity on page 55 to help students determine their foot type and kinds of shoes they should purchase.

Teacher Readings

ACSM Guidelines for Exercise Testing and Prescription, American College of Sports Medicine, 4th Edition, Lea & Febiger, Philadelphia, PA: 1995.

Footwear

Shoes are essential for your personal fitness program. You should select the right shoe based on your activities and type of exercise. Numerous types of shoes are specifically designed for particular activities and sports. You can significantly reduce your risk for skeletal and muscular injuries by making wise footwear choices.

Teach & Apply

Discussion

Ask students to describe the type of clothing they currently wear when they engage in physical activity or exercise. Ask them if clothing that looks good, is trendy, or fashionable is always effective for their exercise environment.

Teacher Support Notes

You may want to tell students the following: Appropriate clothing doesn't always look the best and/or cost the most. For example, running tights fit well and look good on many people, but they can cause individuals to overheat on moderate

High-cut vs low-cut exersice shoes

High-cut exercise shoe
Provides ankle support and excellent cushioning

Low-cut exercise shoe
Provides better flexibility for all-around movement.

Parts of a good exercise shoe

Upper
Flexibility and comfort are necessary for workouts

Toe Box
The part of the shoe that surrounds the toes

Sockliner
Provides cushioning and reduces heat build-up inside shoe

Heel cushion
Cushions and protects the foot from impact shock

Forefoot cushion
Cushions the metatarsal heads from impact shock

Midsole
Cups and supports the foot during lateral movement and provides arch support

Outsole
Made of abrasion-resistant rubber, with toe wrap

Figure 2.4   *Features of an Exercise Shoe.*

ABILITY LEVELS

Reteaching

Some students may need help mastering the concepts contained in this section. In your Teacher Resource Package, you will find the reproducible worksheet shown here. This worksheet should help students who have been absent and those needing additional help to improve their comprehension and retention of the content in this section.

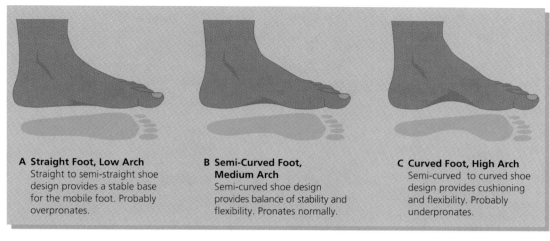

A Straight Foot, Low Arch
Straight to semi-straight shoe design provides a stable base for the mobile foot. Probably overpronates.

B Semi-Curved Foot, Medium Arch
Semi-curved shoe design provides balance of stability and flexibility. Pronates normally.

C Curved Foot, High Arch
Semi-curved to curved shoe design provides cushioning and flexibility. Probably underpronates.

• **Figure 2.5**   *Matching Feet and Shoes.*

to warm days and can put an individual at increased risk for a heat injury. Looking good, trendy, or fashionable may not always be functional.

Discussion

Ask students if they wore a helmet the last time they rode a bicycle. If not, ask them why.

Healthy People 2000

Objective 9.13—**Increase use of helmets to at least 80 percent of motorcyclists and at least 50 percent of bicyclists.** Place Objective 9.13 on the board or overhead projector to stimulate a discussion about exercising with the proper safety equipment. One of the first things people often hit when falling off a bicycle is their heads. Ask students to think about falling off a bicycle (3 to 6 feet to the ground) and landing on their heads and whether they think it might cause a serious injury.

Select a style of shoe that will meet your specific needs. For example, if you are going to engage primarily in a walking program, you need to buy a "walking shoe." If you are going to play basketball, you need to buy a shoe specifically designed for basketball. Of course, if you are going to do a variety of activities, you may want to buy an all-purpose (cross-training) pair of shoes. Figure 2.4 shows the features you should look for in a physical activity or exercise shoe.

It is a good idea to visit a local sporting goods store to seek out advice before you buy shoes for physical activity or exercise. If you cannot find a knowledgeable salesperson to help you when you shop for shoes, ask your physical education instructor for advice.

The shape of your shoe should match the shape of your foot (see Figure 2.5). If you have a normal foot shape (Type B), your foot will strike the ground on the outside of the heel when you walk, a movement called **supination**. Your foot will then roll inward (a movement referred to as **pronation** as you walk or jog. Pronation and supination are normal foot movements. However, too much pronation causes excessive wear on the inside of the heels of shoes. Too much supination causes excessive wear on the outside of the heels of shoes. In addition, too much pronation or supination can increase the risk for leg and knee injuries.

If you have a normal foot shape, with normal amounts of pronation and supination (Type B in Figure 2.5), a shoe without special motion control features should work for you. If you have a foot that has too much pronation (Type A), you have a more mobile foot when you walk or jog. You may need a shoe that provides stability and reduces the overpronation. If your foot has too little pronation when you walk or jog (Type C), you have a less mobile foot. You

supination

a movement of the foot when walking or jogging in which the foot strikes the ground on the outside of the heel.

pronation

an inward rolling of the foot in walking or jogging.

Enrichment   *This activity will allow you to provide a more challenging learning experience for some of your students.*

Have students complete the following: For this activity you will need several cycling helmets and cantaloupes.
a. Place newspapers or other appropriate covering over a spot on the floor about 10 feet in diameter. From a step ladder, drop a cantaloupe from about 8 to 10 feet above the floor. Observe how much of the cantaloupe splatters on impact.

b. Strap a cantaloupe into one of the cycling helmets. Drop the cantaloupe from the same height, with the helmet protecting the underside of the cantaloupe. Observe the splatter from this impact.
c. Repeat Step B with each of the different helmets.
d. Write a report of the results of this experiment. What does this exercise demonstrate about the importance of wearing a helmet while cycling?

Activity

RESOURCES

TRANSPARENCIES

Use the transparency/master of Figure 2.4 to stimulate a discussion about what features students should look for in a good personal fitness shoe. Ask students why one type of shoe, such as for basketball, would probably have different features than a shoe for golf.

Activity

RESOURCES

TRANSPARENCIES

Use the transparency/master of Figure 2.5 and the Active Mind/Active Body activity on page 55 to have students determine their foot shape. Make sure students do this on a safe nonslippery surface and have towels to clean up afterwards.

Consumer Corner

Ask students if they ever had a pair of shoes that were too big or too small for them. Ask them why they bought shoes that did not fit. What mistakes did they make? (Didn't try them on? Didn't walk around in them in the store? Tried them on with socks that were too thick?) Remind students that if they do have more than one pair of shoes, they will get better wear out of them by alternating which ones they wear daily.

REMEMBER This!

Try on shoes before you buy them. Walk around in the store to make sure the shoes are comfortable. Be sure to try on shoes when you're wearing the same type of socks that you intend to wear during physical activity or exercise.

• *Before you buy a new pair of athletic shoes, find a store that has knowledgeable salespeople.*

CONSUMER CORNER

Smart Shoe Shopping

You can spend anywhere from $25 to $200 for a pair of athletic shoes. If you plan to be physically active—and hopefully you do—you need to purchase a pair of quality shoes. Unless you feel you must have the latest, "hottest" shoe from companies such as Nike and Reebok, you will be able to find a fine shoe for around $50. The features to look for are comfort, cushioning, flexibility, stability, and ventilation.

Buy your shoes at a store that has knowledgeable clerks who can help you find the shoes that are right for your feet and your needs.

The kind of shoes you wear are important, but it is just as important to know when to replace your shoes. Once a fitness shoe starts to lose its support and cushion, it should no longer be used for fitness activities. This shoe could do more harm than good to your feet and joints. If it is financially possible, you should have two pairs of fitness shoes and alternate their use. This will give the shoes time to dry out and regain their cushioning effect. This strategy will provide you with the support you need and can extend the life of your shoes significantly.

Wellness Connection

You may want to tell students the following: You may wonder why it would be important to evaluate the health of your eyes, ears, nose, and throat before beginning an exercise program. The eyes are important to be able to see dangers and hazards that you may encounter during your exercise program. If you have difficulty seeing uneven ground or some object in your path while jogging, you may become injured. The ears allow you to be aware of unseen dangers such as traffic, dogs, running water, or machinery. The ears also need

probably need a shoe that has greater cushioning and flexibility features. Once you determine your foot type, a knowledgeable salesperson or your physical education teacher can advise you about the type of shoe that will be best for your foot type and personal fitness needs. To analyze your foot shape, see the "Active Mind/Active Body" activity on this page.

Determine your foot size as well. The size of your physical activity and exercise shoes will probably differ from the size of your dress shoes. Physical activity and exercise shoes should have a snug heel and a space of about a half-inch between your longest toe and the end of the shoe. A roomy toe box (the part of the shoe that surrounds the toes) will allow your foot to swell during activity. (Refer back to Figure 2.4 on page 52.)

SECTION 4 REVIEW

Answer the following questions on a separate sheet of paper:

1. Explain why exercising in hot, humid environments requires special clothing.
2. It is especially important to select and wear proper footwear for physical activity and exercise. Give some reasons to support this statement.

Active Mind! Active Body!   Wet Foot Test

Lay a piece of paper (colored paper, if possible) on a hard floor. Get your foot wet. Then stand on the paper. Straight feet (Type A) leave an imprint that is oval shaped. Semi-curved feet (Type B) show the forefoot and the heel connected by a band about 2 inches wide or more. Curved feet (Type C) have a narrow band connecting the forefoot and heel. (See Figure 2.5.)

to function well for communication during team sports and for verbal warnings in activities such as racquetball or snow skiing.

The nose may alert you to a potential hazard such as fire or a chemical leak. It is also important for the nose to function well for air exchange during endurance-type exercise. The throat needs to function well in order to transport sufficient air to your lungs.

SECTION 5 — How to Put Your Best Foot Forward

Now that you know how to choose the right size, shape, and kind of footwear, you need to learn about the proper techniques for walking and jogging. The movements used in walking and jogging are often used in other activities that you might participate in, such as in-line skating, tennis, and other recreational sports. As you learn new skills and participate in new activities, you should be aware that biomechanical factors can influence how well you perform in terms of both efficiency and safety.

Biomechanics is the study of the principles of physics applied to human motion. For example, when you jog slowly, your foot strikes the ground with a force that is three to five times your body weight. This activity places tremendous force and stress on the feet, lower legs, knees, upper legs, hips, and back. By understanding the biomechanics of walking and jogging, you can minimize these forces and stresses. You then can avoid injuries and reduce excessive wear and tear on your footwear.

The following suggestions will help you walk and jog safely and efficiently from a biomechanical standpoint:

- Start slowly. Follow the recommendations for efficient, gentle walking and jogging in Figure 2.6.
- Breathe deeply through your nose and mouth, rather than through your nose only.
- Relax your fingers, hands, arms, shoulders, neck, and jaw.
- Bend your arms at the elbows at about 90 degrees. Swing your arms straight forward and back instead of across your body.
- Stand nearly erect. Hold your head up, and minimize your head motion.
- Develop a smooth, even stride that feels natural and comfortable to you.
- When your foot strikes the ground, it should land on the heel. Try to point your toes straight ahead as your heel strikes the ground. You should push off on the ball of your foot.
- Do not pound noisily as you walk or jog. Avoid slapping your feet and excessive bouncing.
- Try to walk or jog on a soft surface, such as a dirt road, track, or grassy area, as opposed to a concrete or asphalt surface. Avoid hilly surfaces, because they can place unusual stress on your muscles and joints.

biomechanics

the study of the principles of physics applied to human motion.

> " A sound mind in a sound body, is a short but full description of a happy state in this world.
>
> **John Locke**
> 1632–1704, from *Some Thoughts Concerning Education*, 1693. "

Reteaching

Name _____ Date _____ Period _____

Chapter 2 Section 5 — How To Put Your Best Foot Forward

Directions: Answer the questions in the blanks provided.
1. What is the study of the principles of physics applied to human motion?
Biomechanics
2. How great is the force of a person's foot striking the ground when they jog slowly?
Three to five times the person's body weight
3. List six (6) parts of the body on which jogging places tremendous forces and stresses.
Feet   **Upper legs**
Lower legs **Back**
Knees   **Hips**
4. List six (6) parts of the body that should be relaxed while walking or jogging.
Fingers   **Shoulders**
Hands   **Neck**
Arms   **Jaw**
5. How many degrees should your arms be bent at the elbows while walking or jogging?
90 degrees
6. In front of each of the following movements, put YES if the movement is suggested for biomechanical efficiency in walking and jogging, and NO if it is not.
No a. breathe through your nose only
No b. swing your arms across your body
Yes c. stand nearly erect
Yes d. breathe deeply through your nose and mouth
No e. bounce excessively

Reteaching Worksheets   20   © 1997 West Publishing Co.

Use the "Active Mind/Active Body" activity on page 59 to evaluate your walking and jogging form. This information will help you prevent injuries and may improve your form.

Answers to
BELIEVE IT? ... OR NOT?

Pg. 46 True.
Pg. 48 False. Eighty percent of the young people who die each year riding bikes are victims of head trauma.
Pg. 50 True.
Pg. 55 True.
Pg. 59 False. The midsole and heel (cushioning parts) of sport shoes usually become compressed in six months to one year and lose a significant amount of their original cushioning. This can increase your risk for injuries, so purchase new shoes regularly.
Pg. 60 True.
Pg. 62 True.
Pg. 64 False. Wearing a rubber suit is not a good way to lose weight. Wearing a rubber suit can cause you to become dehydrated rapidly and increase your risk for heat injury. The quick weight loss you experience is only temporary. The weight returns once you rehydrate afterward.

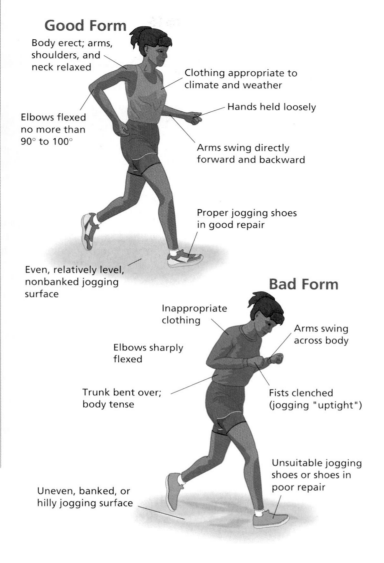

Good Form

Body erect; arms, shoulders, and neck relaxed

Clothing appropriate to climate and weather

Hands held loosely

Elbows flexed no more than 90° to 100°

Arms swing directly forward and backward

Proper jogging shoes in good repair

Even, relatively level, nonbanked jogging surface

Bad Form

Inappropriate clothing

Arms swing across body

Elbows sharply flexed

Trunk bent over; body tense

Fists clenched (jogging "uptight")

Unsuitable jogging shoes or shoes in poor repair

Uneven, banked, or hilly jogging surface

• **Figure 2.6**   Good and Bad Jogging Form. Start Slow and Follow the Illustrated Mechanics for Efficient Gentle Jogging.

Teach & Apply

Discussion

Ask students if they have ever seen someone walking or jogging whose actions looked very inefficient or who had a lot of wasted motion. Ask them what factors they saw that could be corrected.

Classroom Management

Have each student get a partner and use the Active Mind/Active Body activity worksheet, Biomechanically Correct Walking and Jogging Checklist, to analyze his or her partner's walking and jogging technique. If a student needs improvement, have him or her repeat the activity until he or she is doing it correctly.

Enrichment

This activity will allow you to provide a more challenging learning experience for some of your students.

Videotape students as they are walking/jogging. Have them watch their own videos and make notes on the following:
a. Relaxation in the head, neck, jaw.
b. Relaxation in the shoulders, arms, and hands.
c. The bend in the arms at the elbow.
d. The swing in the arms—is it straight?
e. Erect posture.
f. Head motion.
g. Stride evenness.
h. Foot strike—heel, midfoot, or toe.
i. Toe direction at foot strike.
j. Foot push-off.
k. Body movement, bouncing, etc.
    Students should write a report on both the correct and incorrect biomechanical patterns observed.

CHAPTER 2
SECTION 6
58

Assess

Use the Active Mind/ Active Body activity on page 59 to assess student progress. Then use the Section 5 Review questions to assess students' comprehension of the concepts presented in Section 5.

ANSWERS TO SECTION 5 REVIEW

1. Biomechanics is the study of the principles of physics applied to human motion.
2. Correct biomechanical walking and jogging techniques include: start slowly; breathe deeply through your nose and mouth; relax fingers, hands, arms, shoulders, neck, and jaw, etc. (See preceding bullet points in text.)

Close

Collect a group of older-style athletic shoes and show the class how the shoe styles and features have changed over the years. Ask the class to look for differences between worn-out shoes and newer shoes. Then ask the students how worn-out shoes can have a negative effect on their walking and jogging biomechanics.

SECTION 5 REVIEW

Answer the following questions on a separate sheet of paper:

1. What is biomechanics?
2. List and compare correct and incorrect biomechanical walking and jogging techniques.

SECTION 6 Injury Prevention and Care

Injuries often occur in personal fitness programs. The best way to prevent injuries is by recognizing the common types of injuries. You also need to care for injuries properly and, when necessary, have them evaluated by medical professionals.

The most common types of fitness injuries are to the skin, muscles, connective tissue, and bones. Most of the injuries you encounter will probably be minor. However, you should always pay close attention to any injury, and seek out medical attention if the injury continues to interfere with your personal fitness program for more than a week or two. Discuss injuries that might happen to you with your physical education instructor, the school nurse, your parents, and your personal doctor.

Injuries to the Skin

Common skin injuries include cuts, scrapes, bruises, and blisters. Minor cuts and scrapes usually heal in a few days if you keep them clean, apply antiseptic medicine to the injured area, and cover the injury site with a bandage. Most minor bruises will not need treatment and will disappear in a week or so.

Blisters are usually caused by excessive friction between the skin and another surface. Foot blisters are common when you first start conditioning. They can be prevented by gradually breaking your shoes in and wearing socks that fit well. If you get a blister, treat it like a cut or scrape, and do not let it dry out.

Muscle Injuries

Muscle injuries usually involve **strains** or muscle cramps. A strain can be a pull, tear, or rip in a muscle or tendon. (**Tendons** are bands

REMEMBER This!

A little thought and planning can help you avoid many injuries. However, if you do get injured, take care of even the most minor cases. You can then prevent injuries from getting worse. For example, you can avoid letting a cut get infected.

strain

a pull, tear, or rip in a muscle or tendon.

tendon

a band of tissue that connects muscle to bone.

 **Science and Technology**

Safety is a major issue during physical activity because many factors can contribute to damage and injury. Damage is also a possibility when operating a computer. A few simple rules can prevent damage to the computer (and you).
1. *Always* make copies of your files onto floppy disks. Then, it doesn't matter what disappears on the computer.
2. *Frequently* save the files with which you are working. If you remember these two rules, you have a 98% chance of not losing any files.
3. *Never* keep open containers of liquid

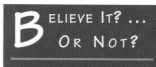

Active Mind! *Active* Body!

Biomechanically Correct Walking and Jogging Checklist

Use the questions below to analyze your walking and jogging form. Be sure to mark your answers on a separate sheet of paper, not in your book.

	I'm Doing Fine!	Improvement Needed!
1. Is my breathing relaxed and rhythmical?	_____	_____
2. Are my hands, arms, shoulders, neck, and jaw relaxed?	_____	_____
3. Are my arms at about 90 degrees and swinging straight forward, not across my body?	_____	_____
4. Is my upper body erect, with minimal head motion?	_____	_____
5. Is my stride length not too long, not too short?	_____	_____
6. Is my foot stride heel to toe, with toes pointed straight ahead?	_____	_____
7. Is there excessive bouncing or slapping of my feet?	_____	_____

BELIEVE IT? ... OR NOT?

Sport shoes can easily last for two to three years and still have plenty of cushioning for walking or jogging.

See page 57 for answer.

of tissue that connect muscles to bones.) Strains may result from insufficient warm-up, lack of flexibility, overtraining, or other situations. Strains often cause the injured area to swell. You should seek medical attention for any swelling. Proper first aid for a strain that has swelling includes rest (*R*), ice (*I*), compression (*C*), and elevation (*E*), or *RICE*. For example, if you get a strain, stop activity. Apply ice to the area. (Do not apply ice directly to the skin. Use an ice pack or ice in a towel.) Wrap the area in an elastic bandage. Finally, raise the body part. Never immediately apply heat to a strain because this can cause additional swelling and slow the recovery process.

Muscle cramps are painful spasms that can occur during physical activity or exercise. Muscle cramps are usually associated with dehydration or an imbalance in minerals in the body. You can avoid most muscle cramps by making sure you are not dehydrated. One com-

Focus

Outcome

In **Section 6** students will learn:

1. To identify and describe the injuries commonly experienced in personal fitness programs and how they can prevent and treat the injuries.

Focus Activities

1. Discuss the common personal fitness injuries that occur and how students can prevent them or care for them.
2. Use the transparency/master of Figure 2.7 to explain the differences between muscles, tendons, ligaments, and cartilage.

Teacher Readings

Powers, S. K. and Howley, E. T.: *Exercise Physiology: Theory and Application to Fitness and Performance.* 2nd Edition. Madison, WI: Brown & Benchmark, 1994.

around your computer.
4. Purchase a copy of some type of disk tool software (Norton Utilities, Disk Utilities, etc.), which are developed to help correct problems that occur with the computer.
5. *Never* put a pirated copy of a program on your hard drive. Many pirated software titles contain code or "viruses," that are

designed to wipe out computer systems.
Take the challenge: Go to a software seller and ask about the different software utilities made for both IBM-PC and Macintosh computers. **Remember:** When beginning to use a computer, you may find that you have to re-boot the system when you have done something wrong. That is OK, it happens to everyone.

Teach & Apply

Activity

Demonstrate the proper technique for applying RICE to a lateral ankle sprain. Place an ice pack on a student volunteer's ankle. Use an elastic bandage to hold the ice pack in place and to apply compression. Then have the student elevate the leg.

Discussion

Ask students if they have experienced shinsplints. Some students may have developed shinsplints since they started walking and jogging. Tell them that shinsplints usually go away after 6 to 8 weeks of conditioning.

stitch

a sharp pain on the side or sides of the abdomen; a common form of muscle cramp most commonly caused by improperly conditioned breathing muscles.

ligament

a band of tissue that connects bone to bone and limits the movement of a joint.

cartilage

a soft, cushioned material that surrounds the ends of bones at a joint to prevent the bones from rubbing against each other.

stress fracture

a bone injury caused by overuse; also called *fatigue fracture.*

Believe It? ... Or Not?

If your best time in the mile at sea level is ten minutes, you will be able to run the mile in about eleven minutes at an altitude of 7,000 feet.

See page 57 for answer.

mon form of a muscle cramp is a **stitch**, a sharp pain on the side or sides of your upper abdomen. The most common cause for stitches is a lack of proper conditioning for the breathing muscles. Stitches often occur when you are not used to breathing deeply for several minutes at a time. Side stitches usually disappear as you become conditioned and improve your personal fitness level.

Connective Tissue Injuries

Connective tissue can be injured by overuse. The kinds of connective tissue (soft tissue material that helps hold bones and joints in place) usually involved are tendons, ligaments, and cartilage. **Ligaments** are bands of tissue that connect bone to bone and limit the movement of joints. **Cartilage** surrounds the ends of bones at a joint to prevent the bones from rubbing against each other (see Figure 2.7).

Two of the most common connective tissue injuries you may see are shinsplints and sprains. A *shinsplint* is an inflammation of a tendon or muscle, which causes several types of pain in the front or side of the lower leg. Shinsplints can have a variety of causes. They can usually be treated by wearing proper footwear and using RICE. Sometimes shinsplints can get severe and require care by a doctor. Sprains usually involve a partial tear of a ligament. (A familiar cause is twisting your ankle.) Sprains can be minor or severe and are often treated with RICE. Always have a doctor evaluate a sprain immediately for proper care.

Injuries to Bones

Injuries to bones are serious and require medical care. Some bone injuries, such as **stress fractures**, are caused by overuse. Your doctor may not be able to diagnose such an injury until several weeks after it occurs. Stress fractures start as a small crack in a bone. There is usually pain above and below the crack in the bone, and it is very tender to touch. Over time (four to six weeks), the stress fracture will get worse. At that time it can often be noticed by your doctor upon X-ray examination.

Preventing Injuries

You may be asking yourself, "Why should I be active if I am going to get injured?" In terms of your health, it is far more hazardous to be inactive than to face the risks of injury by being active. To prevent or safely treat common injuries, follow these guidelines:

- Pay attention to your body. If you feel unusually sore or fatigued, postpone activity or exercise until you feel better.

ABILITY LEVELS

Reteaching

Some students may need help mastering the concepts contained in this section. In your Teacher Resource Package, you will find the reproducible worksheet shown here. This worksheet should help students who have been absent and those needing additional help to improve their comprehension and retention of the content in this section.

Muscle

Tendon

Ligament — — Cartilage

Figure 2.7   *A Joint and Its Connective Tissue.*

- Include a proper warm-up and cool-down in your personal fitness program. You'll learn about warm-ups and cool-downs in the next chapter.
- Monitor the frequency, intensity, and time/duration of your exercise closely, and make your progression slow and steady (more about this in Chapter 3).
- If you run or walk in traffic, always face the oncoming traffic.
- Wear reflective clothing during night physical activities or exercise (walking, jogging, and so on).
- Use proper safety equipment for activities with a higher injury risk (skateboarding, in-line skating, cycling, and the like).
- Always seek out proper medical advice when you have an injury.

Teacher Support Notes

You may want to tell students the following: The exact cause of side stitches is unknown. They may be due to lack of blood flow to the working muscles of breathing (diaphragm, intercostals, and abdominals). They also can occur if a student has just eaten or consumed fluids immediately prior to exercise. Once students have experienced 6 to 8 weeks of conditioning, the incidence of stitches is rare.

Discussion

Stress this point with students: It is far more hazardous to their long-term health to be inactive than to face the risk of injury they might incur by being active.

Assess

Use the Section 6 Review questions on the next page to assess students' comprehension of the concepts presented in Section 6.

Enrichment

This activity will allow you to provide a more challenging learning experience for some of your students.

Have students complete the following activity: Call your family doctor or local orthopedic clinic and ask the following questions about injury prevention and care:
a. What are the most common muscle injuries for both athletes and nonathletes?
b. What type of treatment is recommended for shinsplints?

c. What type of shoes or footwear is recommended to avoid shinsplints?
d. What procedure is used to detect stress fractures?
e. How severe must a connective tissue or bone injury be before surgery is used in the treatment?
   Write a report on the answers to these questions, and comment on the importance of injury prevention in a personal fitness program.

SECTION 6 REVIEW

Answer the following questions on a separate sheet of paper:

1. What is RICE?

2. For treatment of a strain, why should heat not be applied to the injured area?

**ANSWERS TO
SECTION 6 REVIEW**

1. RICE is the first aid technique for strains and sprains. RICE = *Rest, Ice, Compression,* and *Elevation.*

2. You will only make it swell more and prolong the healing time.

Close

Have your school's athletic trainer or an orthopedic specialist come to your class as a guest and discuss common injuries he or she sees and treats.

Focus

Outcome

In **Section 7** students will learn:

1. To explain the importance of adherence to your personal fitness program, and how you can improve your adherence.

Focus Activities

1. Discuss adherence to a personal fitness program.
2. Use the transparency/master of Figure 2.8 to explain ways students can improve their adherence.

SECTION 7 — Adherence to a Personal Fitness Program

adherence

the ability to continue something, such as your chosen personal fitness program, over a period of time.

Adherence refers to your ability to continue, or stick to, your personal fitness program. If you adhere to it, your program is a success. Unfortunately, many people stop participating in their personal fitness programs. Many of the factors with a negative impact on adherence were listed in Chapter 1's discussion of attitudes and beliefs about personal fitness. These factors are repeated here:

* Lack of time.
* Poor physical condition.
* High percentage of body fat.
* Unrealistic personal fitness goals or expectations.
* Lack of accurate knowledge about physical fitness.
* Feelings of being unathletic.

BELIEVE **I**T? ... **O**R **N**OT?

Ten to fifteen high school athletes die every year from heat injuries that are preventable.

See page 57 for answer.

• *Working out with a friend can help you improve your adherence.*

CRITICAL THINKING

For this activity you will need one index card for each student in your class. On half of the cards, write an injury or exercise-related problem such as a strained ankle. (Write a different one on each card.) On the rest of the cards, write a first aid treatment or action such as RICE (rest, ice, compression, elevation). (Again, write a different one on each card.) Distribute one card to each student.

Students with injury or exercise-related problems on their cards should role-play situations in which the injuries could

Stress Break

Don't let your workouts become a source of stress in your life. Instead, let your workouts fit into your life. If you have a tight schedule, and other priorities sometimes interfere with your workout time, don't get too worried. Deal with your priorities and, as soon as possible, get back on your routine. This way you won't resent your working out. In fact, often you will notice that the lay-off was good for your mental attitude. You may find that after a break you are more relaxed and enjoying your workout time even more.

- Fear of physical overstrain.
- Past negative experiences with physical activity, exercise, or both.
- Concerns about negative peer pressure.

By understanding some of the factors that might interfere with your adherence, you can increase your odds for achieving a successful personal fitness program. Remember, it is your right and your duty to yourself to develop personal fitness. Figure 2.8 highlights several factors that can help you improve your adherence.

What can you do to improve your adherence to your program? First, make a contract with yourself to participate regularly in personal fitness.

Second, set reasonable, achievable, and specific goals. Develop realistic expectations. For example, you may want to be able to swim one mile continuously, in thirty minutes. You will need to start with a program that helps you work up to that level—for example, swimming steadily for five minutes, then ten minutes, and so on up to thirty minutes. It may be several weeks before you can achieve your goal. This is normal.

Third, be patient. The positive changes and benefits of your personal fitness program will occur gradually. Control your initial enthusiasm. Listen to your body for any signs that you are working too hard, too soon (see the previous discussion on preventing injuries).

Fourth, develop a schedule for your regular participation in physical activity and exercise. If a conflict interferes with your schedule, get back to your personal fitness program as soon as you can. Remember, do not dwell on feelings of guilt if you occasionally have to skip your physical activity or exercise. Focus on the positive aspects of your personal fitness program, and recognize that it is what you do over the long haul that is important.

Fifth, participate with friends or family members when you can. Make physical activity or exercise a social experience as well as a physical one.

- Choose activities of moderate intensity
- Choose low-impact weight-bearing activities
- Start slowly
- Progress gradually
- Emphasize activities you prefer
- Avoid injuries
- Participate in cross-training
- Make your program convenient
- Expand your total time up to thirty to sixty minutes

- **Figure 2.8** *How to Improve Your Adherence.*

occur. Students with first aid treatments on their cards should offer the solutions/treatments given on their cards if they fit the situations.

Encourage discussion as students analyze possible solutions/treatments. Then have students draw conclusions about possible outcomes if no action or improper action is taken in each of the injury situations.

This activity works well as either a small-group or whole-class activity.

Discussion

Ask students if they have ever started a personal fitness program and then discontinued it for one reason or another. Have those who have had this experience share with the class the main reason they did not adhere to the program.

Activity

Divide the class into groups of three or four. Have each group develop an example of a personal adherence contract. Allow them 10 minutes to generate ideas, then let one member of each group share his or her group's ideas with the rest of the class.

Stress Break

Have students read the "Stress Break" and have them react to whether they have felt stressed out by the fact that exercising is trendy.

Assess

Use the Section 7 Review questions on the next page to assess students' comprehension of the concepts presented in Section 7.

BELIEVE **I**T? ...
OR **N**OT?

Wearing a rubber suit that makes you sweat heavily during physical activity or exercise is a good way to lose weight.

See page 57 for answer.

Sixth, develop a progress chart to plot your improvements. Occasionally assess your physical fitness level to determine if you are maintaining reasonable levels of personal fitness. (Chapters 4, 5, 6, 8, and 9 will discuss this further.)

Finally, engage in physical activities and exercises that you like to do. Vary your routine with a variety of activities. Adherence levels are usually higher if you choose activities of low impact (low stress on the joints) and do them at a moderately intense level.

SECTION 7 REVIEW

Answer the following questions on a separate sheet of paper:

1. Give three reasons why people drop out of personal fitness programs.
2. What are some things you could do to improve your adherence to your personal fitness program?

ANSWERS TO SECTION 7 REVIEW

1. Answers will vary but could include lack of time, poor physical condition, etc.
2. To improve adherence: a) make a contract with yourself, b) set reasonable goals, c) be patient, d) develop a schedule, e) participate with friends or family, and f) develop a chart to plot improvements.

Close

Ask students for examples of activities that they have discontinued because they tried to do too much too soon. Why do they think this happened?

SUMMARY

Participation in physical activity and exercise programs can benefit your health and well-being. However, to maximize the benefits of participation, you need to make sure that your physical activity and exercise are safe for you.

You should recognize the factors (heart disease, severe obesity, high blood pressure, kidney disease, and diabetes) that determine whether you need to have a medical evaluation prior to beginning your personal fitness program. You should be able to identify the dangers (heat injuries or frostbite) of participating in physical activity or exercise when it is very hot or very cold, as well as be able to minimize your injury risks. Various outdoor environmental problems (including air pollution, dogs, and crime) can also be hazardous to you. Investigate your environment before you begin your program.

Choosing the right clothing and footwear for physical activity and exercise will help you be more comfortable and safe. Proper safety equipment (helmets, elbow pads, knee pads, and so on) will significantly reduce your risks for muscle and skeletal injuries. If you apply an understanding of biomechanics to activities such as walking and jogging, you will avoid injuries and minimize excessive wear and tear on your footwear.

You can significantly reduce the risk of injuries in your personal fitness program by safely and slowly changing the frequency, intensity, and time/duration of your exercise. Finally, you can improve your personal fitness adherence by paying attention to conflicts that will interfere with your success and by developing a realistic plan to enhance your opportunities to be physically active.

Reteaching

ABILITY LEVELS

Reteaching

Some students may need help mastering the concepts contained in this section. In your Teacher Resource Package, you will find the reproducible worksheet shown here. This worksheet should help students who have been absent and those needing additional help to improve their comprehension and retention of the content in this section.

Chapter 2 Review

True/False

On a separate sheet of paper, mark each question below either T for True or F for False.

1. Healthy young adults with no history of heart problems are unlikely to need a medical examination before starting an exercise program.

2. Healthy young adults should be encouraged to have a medical evaluation every two to three years.

3. In cold weather, exercise clothing should be made of a heavy material and be tight fitting. This will help prevent heat loss.

4. Carbon monoxide, a dangerous gas, is associated with streets and highways that have high volumes of traffic.

5. Exercising at low or high altitudes has little effect on your performance.

6. A good pair of basketball shoes, a T-shirt, and a pair of shorts are all the things you need to get started with a jogging program.

7. It is always a good idea to try on exercise shoes with socks before you purchase them.

8. Statistics show that wearing a helmet when skateboarding is really not necessary.

9. It is a good idea to match the shape of your foot with the shape of the shoe you buy.

10. *RICE* stands for rest, ice, compression, and elevation.

Multiple Choice

1. A medical examination would include tests to study which of the following?
   a. blood pressure, hernia, and lung sounds
   b. exercise stress test, urine, and blood
   c. medical history, eyes, and ears
   d. nose, throat, and heart sounds

2. Which of the following is not an example of a chronic disease?
   a. heart disease
   b. kidney disease
   c. diabetes
   d. two or three colds per year

3. Which of the following should be considered when purchasing a new pair of shoes?
   a. the shape of the shoe
   b. pronation support
   c. supination support
   d. flexible sole
   e. all of the above

4. When the weather is hot and humid, you will sweat excessively and lose large amounts of fluids. What is this condition called?
   a. hyperthermia
   b. dehydration
   c. heat cramps
   d. heat stroke

5. Anyone exercising in warm and humid environments should pay attention to which of the following?
   a. drinking plenty of fluids
   b. proper clothing
   c. heat injury symptoms
   d. all of the above

6. If you decide to drink a commercially made sports drink when you exercise in the heat, what percentage of carbohydrates should you look for in the drink?
   a. 1 percent
   b. 2 to 3 percent
   c. 5 to 8 percent
   d. 9 to 10 percent
   e. greater than 15 percent

Answers

True/False

1. T
2. T
3. F
4. T
5. F
6 F
7. T
8. F
9. T
10. T

Multiple Choice

1. b.
2. d.
3. e.
4. b.
5. d.
6. c.
7. c.
8. c.
9. c.
10. c.

Discussion

1. It is important to prevent heat injuries. Heat and humidity can cause dehydration, heat cramps, heat exhaustion, and heat stroke. It can also limit how much work you can do.

Enrichment

This activity will allow you to provide a more challenging learning experience for some of your students.

Interview the manager of a local fitness club. Ask him or her about the reasons for adherence and nonadherence in the customers of his or her facility. Ask him or her some of the following questions:

a. What are some of the reasons that customers fail to renew their memberships in the facility?

b. If a customer does not renew his or her membership, is it most likely that they have adopted another form of exercise or activity, or that they have stopped exercising?

c. What percentage of his/her customers fail to renew their memberships after one month? two months? six months? one year?

d. What percent of his/her customers have lifetime memberships, if offered?

2. Heat exhaustion includes feelings of weakness, headache, rapid pulse, etc. Heat stroke causes one to faint or nearly faint; have hot, dry, skin; and have very high body temperatures. To treat heat exhaustion, get to a cool, dry environment and drink plenty of fluids. He or she should not resume his or her fitness program until he or she has replaced his or her fluids. Heat stroke requires immediate medical attention.

3. Select a style and size of shoe that suits your needs. Determine your shoe type. Try on the shoes with socks and walk around in the store to make sure they fit. When in doubt, ask for advice in selecting a shoe.

Vocabulary Experience

<u>2</u> medical screening
<u>5</u> hypothermia
<u>6</u> heat exhaustion
<u>1</u> pronation
<u>3</u> adherence
<u>4</u> biomechanics

Critical Thinking

1. Answers will vary but might include roller hockey, skateboarding, in-line skating, mountain biking, etc. Safety equipment might include helmets, knee and elbow pads, mouthpieces, wrist guards, etc. Solid scientific evidence clearly shows that safety equipment can reduce the risks for injuries and even death in higher-risk physical activities and exercises.

Chapter 2 Review

7. When exercising in extreme cold conditions, it is possible for your body temperature to drop below normal (98.6 degrees Fahrenheit). What is this condition called?
   a. frostbite
   b. hyperthermia
   c. hypothermia
   d. none of the above

8. Which of the following is *not* a guideline for exercising in high altitudes?
   a. Drink plenty of fluids.
   b. Gradually change altitude.
   c. Eat meals more often to prevent altitude sickness.
   d. Gradually increase exercise over a period of time.

9. If you were going to exercise in a potentially dangerous area, which of the following guidelines would you *not* use?
   a. avoid verbal confrontation
   b. exercise in well-lit areas
   c. exercise alone, when possible
   d. let someone know where you have gone

10. Which of the following will not improve your adherence to your personal fitness program?
   a. working at moderate intensities
   b. starting slowly
   c. engaging in high-impact, weight-bearing activities
   d. making your program convenient
   e. participating in cross-training

Discussion

1. Explain why it is important to know the air temperature and the amount of humidity in the air. How can this affect exercise?

2. Identify and explain the main differences between symptoms of heat exhaustion and heat stroke. What are the treatments for each condition?

3. Tell what you should consider and do before you ever buy a pair of physical activity or exercise shoes.

Vocabulary Experience

Match the correct term in Column A to the definition in Column B by writing the appropriate number in each blank.

Column A	Column B
_____ medical screening	1. An inward roll of the foot during jogging.
_____ hypothermia	2. An evaluation of the *eyes, ears, nose, throat, blood pressure,* and so on.
_____ heat exhaustion	3. Continued success with a personal fitness program.
_____ pronation	4. The study of the principles of physics applied to human motion.
_____ adherence	5. A drop in body temperature to below normal.
_____ biomechanics	6. A condition with symptoms that include weakness; headache; stomach discomfort; and cool, clammy skin.

COOPERATIVE LEARNING

You can help the students in your class develop a sense of interdependence with their classmates. You can help them become "teammates." Here are a few suggestions:
• When grouping students, it is best to make sure there is a mixture of ability levels in each group. This can usually be accomplished by grouping students randomly. You can number students according to how many groups you will have. All of the ones will be in a group, all of the twos will be in a group, and so on. You can also group students alphabetically.

Critical Thinking

1. What kinds of physical activities that you like to do require protective safety equipment? List the safety equipment you feel you would need to perform these activities. Explain how the equipment would help you prevent injuries.

2. What is your level of adherence to physical activity and exercise? Why?

3. Explain the importance of using replacement fluids following vigorous exercise in the heat. Which fluids do you use? Why?

Case Study — David's Fitness Program

David is an unfit, overweight fifteen-year-old who has lived all his life in Anchorage, Alaska. His father recently made a career change that required the family to move to central Texas. David has never been very athletic or physically active, and he has not paid much attention to his health or personal fitness.

Now that he has moved to a much warmer climate and the different weather conditions of Texas, he would like to make some improvements in his fitness habits (behaviors). He feels he should take advantage of his new environment by starting a physical activity and exercise program. His goals are to lose 20 pounds and to improve his cardiovascular fitness level.

David has no experience with personal fitness programs and knows little about them. He does realize that he needs the help of someone knowledgeable about designing and implementing fitness programs—someone like you!

Here is your assignment: David—Part I

Assume you are David's neighbor, and he has asked you to help him plan his new physically active lifestyle. Organize a list of things David should consider and do before beginning a moderate to vigorous personal fitness program.

KEYS TO HELP YOU

- Consider David's current medical status.
- List the concerns David must deal with as he changes from his previous environment to his new environment.
- Consider David's needs and desires.

2. Answers will vary and be based on factors like poor physical condition, high percentage of body fat, etc.
3. Replacement fluids help the body rehydrate after exercise. This allows your body to recover and respond more quickly for another bout of exercise. Students will use a variety of replacement fluids, usually based on taste.

KEYS TO CASE STUDY

David needs to start slowly and set reasonable goals. He should evaluate his health status before beginning a program by completing the health screening questionnaire in this chapter. He will have to acclimatize to the warm Texas climate. David would be wise to improve his adherence by making a contract with himself, being patient, developing a regular schedule, participating with friends or family, and developing a progress chart to plot his improvements.

The first four people on your attendance sheet will be in a group, etc.
• When your students work in groups, make sure each member of the group has a specific job to complete. Divide the task into parts so that each team member has a responsibility. The individual tasks can be fairly complex, depending on the skill level of your students, or they can be as simple as watching the clock so that the group doesn't run out of time.
• Allow time at the end of your group work for class discussion about what happened in the groups. Let students tell you what was right and what was wrong in the groups. Help them come up with suggestions for correcting the "wrongs."

RESOURCES **HANDOUTS** A chapter test is provided for Chapter 2 in your Teacher Resource Package.

Chapter Overview

Chapter 3 is 36 pages long and divided into six sections listed to the right. Major learning outcomes of the chapter are also listed to the right. Briefly, this chapter introduces students to the concept of how to design physical activity and exercise programs. It emphasizes the scientific principles of exercise science that students should learn to use in the development and maintenance of their personal fitness. It also provides students with examples of warm-up and cool-down activities.

Teacher Resource Material

In the Teacher Resource Package accompanying the textbook, you will find the following material to help you teach this chapter.

Activity Sheets

One Reteaching Worksheet is provided in the Teacher Resource Package for each section of this chapter. Handouts are also provided for the following Active Mind/Active Body activities:

Chapter 3

Designing Physical Activity and Exercise Programs

68

PACING CHART

You could easily spend seven to nine days teaching this chapter if students read the entire chapter, do the Active Mind/Active Body activities, and complete several of the handouts from the Teacher Resource Package. However, you can cover the material in this chapter in four to five days. It is recommended that physical activity be a regular part of each class period (20 to 30 minutes minimum). The following are some examples of how to help you cover the main topics in the chapter if you are pressed for time.

Contents

1. The Scientific Principle of Overload (Do More!)
2. The Scientific Principle of Specificity (Be Specific!)
3. The Scientific Principle of Progression (Improve!)
4. Warm It Up, First!
5. Work It Out!
6. Cool It Down, Afterward!

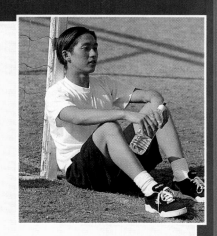

Outcomes

After reading and studying this chapter, you will be able to:

1. Define and explain the terms related to designing physical activity and exercise programs.
2. Explain the importance of understanding exercise science principles and how they apply to the workout component of your personal fitness program.
3. Explain the purpose of proper warm-up, and describe the different types of warm-up.
4. Describe how you would design your personal fitness prescription for working out.
5. Explain the purpose of proper cool-down, and describe the different types of cool-down.

Key Terms

After reading and studying this chapter, you will be able to understand and provide practical definitions for the following terms:

dose	conditioning	warm-up
overload principle	mode	active warm-up
FIT	progression principle	muscle/skeletal warm-up
personal fitness prescription	overuse injury	static body stretches
frequency	trainability	cardiovascular warm-up
intensity	plateau effect	specific active warm-up
heart rate	detraining	general active warm-up
maximum heart rate	cross-train	passive warm-up
perceived exertion	overtraining	blood pooling
talk test	physical activity zealot; exercise zealot	cardiovascular cool-down
time/duration	acute	stretching cool-down
specificity principle	chronic	

69

- The Effect of Intensity on Heart Rate
- Learning to Stretch Correctly

Transparencies/ Masters

A transparency or master is provided in the Teacher Resource Package for each of the following figures: 3.1, 3.2, 3.3, 3.4, 3.5, 3.6, 3.7, 3.8, 3.9, 3.10, 3.11, 3.12, 3.13 and 5.21.

Discuss the Photo

Ask students what they think the student in the photo is doing with the notebook and what the letters F.I.T. mean. Ask students how they have determined how often, how hard, and how long they exercised. Ask them how hard they would work out if you told them to exercise moderately. This should help them to understand that the term "moderate" is often too general in nature because it is interpreted differently by students. What is moderate for one person is hard for another.

CHAPTER 3

Time	Suggestions
Day 1	Assign students to read Section 1. Do the Active Mind/Active Body activities on page(s) 75 and 76.
Day 2	Assign students to read Section 2. Discuss the specificity principle, situations related to FIT, and how to do record keeping. Have students develop an exercise log.
Day 3	Assign students to read Sections 3 and 4. Discuss progression, trainability, detraining, overtraining, and warm-up. Do the Active Mind/Active Body activities on page(s) 91 and 95.
Day 4	Assign students to read Sections 5 and 6 prior to class. Discuss how to design a workout and proper cool-down. In class, do the Active Mind/Active Body activity on page 99.

Focus

Outcomes

In **Section 1** students will learn:

1. To define and explain the terms related to the scientific principle of overload.
2. To explain the application of overload in designing personal fitness programs.

Focus Activities

1. Discuss the concepts of frequency, intensity, and time/duration as they relate to physical activity and exercise.
2. Use the Active Mind/Active Body activities on pages 75 and 76 to have students determine their resting and exercise heart rates.

INTRODUCTION

*P*hysical activity and exercise can be prescribed much like medication because the benefits of physical activity or exercise are dose related. In other words, amount and frequency of physical activity and exercise in your life will determine the benefits that you can gain by participating in your personal fitness program. For example, the dose of physical activity or exercise necessary for health benefits (reduced risk of chronic disease) is often less than the dose needed for physical fitness benefits (such as higher personal fitness goals). After taking this course, you will not have to go to the doctor to get a prescription for physical activity or exercise. You will be highly qualified to write your own personal fitness prescription.

A personal fitness prescription includes several factors: how often you work, how hard you work, length of time you work, the type of activity or exercise you do, and other factors that will be discussed later. It is important for you to learn how to design a personal fitness prescription to safely and effectively achieve Guidelines 1 and 2 below. You first encountered these guidelines in Chapter 1:

- *Guideline 1. All adolescents should be physically active daily, or nearly every day, as part of play, games, sports, work, transportation, recreation, physical education, or planned exercise, in the context of family, school, or community activities.*

- *Guideline 2. Adolescents should engage in three or more sessions per week of activities that last twenty minutes or more at a time and that require moderate to vigorous levels of exertion.*

To meet the objective of Guideline 1, it is important for you to adopt an active lifestyle that encourages you to spend time in physical activity or exercise every day. A simple personal fitness plan is all that is necessary to achieve Guideline 1. Include physical activity as part of your daily lifestyle. Make it a simple and common occurrence, like brushing your teeth.

To meet the objective of Guideline 2, you will find it helpful to develop a more detailed personal fitness prescription that will meet your individual goals and interests. To carry out Guideline 2, you will need to set reasonable goals, engage in moderate to vigorous physical activity or exercise, and keep records of your progress.

Before you can design your personal fitness prescription, you must understand the scientific principles of physical activity and exercise. You must also learn about the art of applying these scientific principles to insure that your program is safe and effective. The material in the first two sections of this chapter is based on recommendations from the leading exercise science organization in the world, the American College of Sports Medicine (ACSM). Let's begin by exploring some of the primary scientific principles you'll need.

REMEMBER This!

Get off the couch and move! Find ways to be active. Take the stairs, not the elevator. Walk to school when possible, instead of riding in a car. Engage in recreational activities regularly.

* Reprinted with permission from "A Consensus on Physical Activity Guidelines for Adolescents" by J. F. Sallis and Kevin Patrick, *Pediatric Exercise Science*, Vol. 6, no. 4 (1994): 302–314.

Reteaching

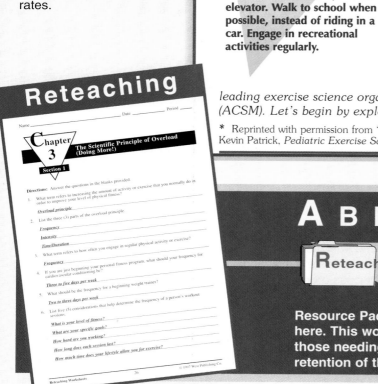

Name _____ Date _____ Period _____

Chapter 3
Section 1
The Scientific Principle of Overload (Doing More!)

Directions: Answer the questions in the blanks provided.

1. What term refers to increasing the amount of activity or exercise that you normally do in order to improve your level of physical fitness?

Overload principle

2. List the three (3) parts of the overload principle.

Frequency

Intensity

Time/Duration

3. What term refers to how often you engage in regular physical activity or exercise?

Frequency

4. If you are just beginning your personal fitness program, what should your frequency for cardiovascular conditioning be?

Three to five days per week

5. What should be the frequency for a beginning weight trainer?

Two to three days per week

6. List five (5) considerations that determine the frequency of a person's workout sessions.

What is your level of fitness?

What are your specific goals?

How hard are you working?

How long does each session last?

How much time does your lifestyle allow you for exercise?

26   © 1997 West Publishing Co.

Reteaching Worksheets

ABILITY LEVELS

Reteaching

Some students may need help mastering the concepts contained in this section. In your Teacher Resource Package, you will find the reproducible worksheet shown here. This worksheet should help students who have been absent and those needing additional help to improve their comprehension and retention of the content in this section.

SECTION 1

The Scientific Principle of Overload (Do More!)

dose

the amount and frequency of an activity or substance.

overload principle

the principle that says to improve your level of physical fitness, you must increase the amount of activity or exercise that you normally do.

FIT

the three components of the overload principle: Frequency, Intensity, and Time/Duration; a level of physical conditioning that is desirable and obtainable by everyone.

personal fitness prescription

an exercise or physical activity plan that includes frequency, intensity, time/duration, mode, and other factors.

frequency

in a personal fitness prescription, how often you work.

To improve your level of physical fitness, you must increase the **dose** (amount) of activity or exercise that you normally do. This is called the **overload principle**. The amount of overload can be increased in three different ways, as shown in Figure 3.1. The three parts of the overload principle—frequency, intensity, and time/duration—can be remembered by using the first letter of each word to form the word **FIT**. The word *FIT* describes a level or dose of physical conditioning that is desirable and obtainable by everyone.

Any **B**ody **C**an be FIT! The beginning exerciser, as well as the high-performance athlete, should incorporate the use of FIT into daily and weekly **personal fitness prescriptions** and records.

Frequency

Frequency refers to how often you engage in regular physical activity or exercise. Exercise that is too infrequent results in limited progress. Too frequent exercise can increase the possibility of injury. If you are just beginning your personal fitness program, your frequency for cardiovascular conditioning should be three to five days per week. Cardiovascular conditioning consists of specific activities that improve the efficiency of your heart, lungs, blood, and blood vessels. The frequency for a beginning weight trainer should be two to three days per week (Figure 3.2 on the next page).

Individuals of average to high fitness levels will need to consider their specific goals before they determine how frequently they will

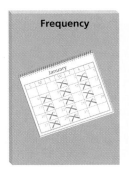
Frequency

Intensity

Time/Duration

• *Figure 3.1*   *The FIT Formula Includes Three Ways to Increase Overload.*

Activity	Frequency for Beginners	Frequency for Those of Average to High Fitness Levels
Cardiovascular conditioning	3–5 days per week	4–6 days per week
Weight training	2–3 days per week	3–5 days per week

Figure 3.2 *Activity Frequency for Exercisers of Varying Fitness Levels.*

cise science to maintain and enhance physical performance, fitness, health, and quality of life. For more information about the ACSM, call (317) 637-9200.

Activity

Have students prepare large posters that define and provide examples of FIT.

Teaching Strategies

As an alternative to the activity above, you might want to make posters with misspelled words and then have students study the posters to find the misspellings.

Discussion

• Discuss the meaning of frequency ("how often" students should work out). Ask students to tell the minimum frequency for physical activity and exercise for good health. Use Figure 3.2 to emphasize these points.
• Discuss how the walking and jogging protocol that you have had students doing thus far relates to FIT. Ask them how their conditioning program relates to the overload principle.

BELIEVE IT? ... OR NOT?

You can never get enough physical activity or exercise.

See page 96 for answer.

intensity

in a personal fitness prescription, how hard you work.

heart rate

the number of times your heart beats per minute.

maximum heart rate

the maximum number of times your heart can beat in a minute.

need to be active (Figure 3.2). For example, a competitive cyclist interested in competition will need to work four to six days per week. The cyclist may even occasionally want to work out multiple times per day.

The frequency of your workout sessions should be determined by the following considerations:

• What is your level of fitness?
• What are your specific goals (health or performance)?
• How hard are you working (intensity)?
• How long does each session last (time/duration)?
• How much time does your lifestyle allow you for exercise (determined by how much time you devote to jobs, schoolwork, and other commitments)?

Intensity

Intensity refers to the difficulty of your physical activity or exercise. If the intensity is too low, progress is limited. If you work too hard, you fatigue quickly and increase your risk for injury.

Suggested Heart Rate and Weight Lifting Intensities. **Heart rate** is the number of times your heart beats per minute. It is recommended that the beginning exerciser work at an intensity that is 60 to 70 percent of his or her maximum heart rate for cardiovascular conditioning. **Maximum heart rate** is the maximum number of times your heart can beat per minute. Maximum heart rate is determined, to a great extent, by age. It will be discussed in greater detail in Chapter 5. Figure 3.3 shows the range of predicted maximum heart rates for students fourteen to eighteen years of age.

A beginning heart rate level for cardiovascular fitness would be about 120 to 145 beats per minute. If you are of an average to high fitness level, you can and should work at moderate to higher intensities, or heart rates of about 145 to 185 beats per minute.

The beginning weight trainer should determine intensity of exercise differently. He or she should use as a guide 60 to 70 percent of the maximum amount of weight he or she can lift one time for any exercise. For example, say your maximum lift for the bench press is

Across the Disciplines

Music

Various companies have produced exercise audio tapes that many people use for assistance in their exercise programs. These tapes are similar in that they usually contain music and verbal

instructions that guide a person through a prescribed fitness activity. Some people have found that music alone can direct their exercise programs, from the warm-up to the cool-down.

Discuss how students can determine the number of beats to a measure in

• *These water polo players are working at high intensity.*

Age	Predicted Maximum Heart Rate
14	206
15	205
16	204
17	203
18	202

• **Figure 3.3** *Your Predicted Maximum Heart Rate.*

100 pounds. You would then bench press 60 or 70 pounds eight to twelve times. The weight trainer of average to high fitness levels can work at moderate to higher intensities, or 70 to 85 percent of the maximum amount of weight he or she can lift one time for any exercise. These recommendations are summarized in Figure 3.4.

The intensity of your workout sessions should be determined by the following considerations:

• What is your level of fitness?

• What are your specific goals (health or performance)?

Activity	Intensity for Beginners	Intensity for Those of Average to High Fitness Levels
Cardiovascular conditioning	120–145 beats/min.	145–185 beats/min.
Weight training	60–70% of max. lift	70–85% of max. lift

• **Figure 3.4** *Activity Intensity for Exercises of Varying Fitness Levels.*

their music and what kinds of music facilitate appropriate fitness activities. Have students design their own exercise tapes using music that assists them with their prescribed fitness programs. The tape should include selections that enable them to slowly bring their heart rates up and warm up their bodies, followed by music that keeps them at their appropriate target heart rates for the desired amount of time. The tape should also contain music that brings their heart rates down slowly following the intense exercise segment and ends with a relaxing cool-down. Have students share their music and exercise programs with their classmates, and encourage them to use their programs during their free time.

• Discuss the meaning of intensity ("how hard" students should work out). Ask students to tell the minimum intensity for physical activity and exercise for good health.

• Ask students why heart rate can be used to determine the intensity of physical activity and exercise. It is hoped that many of them already know that as intensity increases, heart rate also increases. Use Figure 3.3 to help students calculate their maximum heart rates.

• Discuss the initial recommendations for weight training intensity in Figure 3.4.

Teacher Support Notes

Maximum heart rate (MHR) is often predicted by subtracting one's age from 220. While this provides a quick estimate of MHR, you should recognize that there is a wide variation in maximum heart rate among individuals. MHR on average varies by plus or minus 10 beats per minute. In some students it will vary by as much as plus or minus 20 beats per minute. In other words, if a 15-year-old student's predicted MHR is $220 - 15 = 205$ beats per minute, then it probably will actually be between 195–215 beats per minute. It could be as low as 185 and higher than 215 and still be normal for that student.

Teaching Strategies

Have students make large posters of Figure 5.21 from Chapter 5, which shows heart rate zones for people of various ages. Discuss how the target zone changes with age.

Discussion

• Ask students to explain the talk test.
• Use Figure 3.5 to explain the concept of perceived exertion. Ask students to rate (with a number) how hard they have been working while doing their previous walking and jogging conditioning in the course.
• Discuss the concept of time/duration for personal fitness prescription. Ask students how long they usually exercise for cardiovascular conditioning, muscular strength or endurance, and flexibility.

---

perceived exertion

how hard a person feels he or she is working during physical activity or exercise.

talk test

a test that uses a person's ease or difficulty in carrying on a conversation while engaged in physical activity or exercise to measure exercise intensity.

time/duration

in a personal fitness prescription, the length of time you work.

6	No exertion at all
7	Extremely light
8	
9	Very light
10	
11	Light
12	
13	Somewhat hard (moderate)
14	
15	Hard/heavy
16	Vigorous
17	Very hard
18	
19	Extremely hard
20	Maximal exertion

• ***Figure 3.5*** *Perceived Exertion Scale. How hard a person feels he/she has worked during physical activity or exercise.*

Source: Adapted with permission from G. Borg, "Psychophysical Bases of Perceived Exertion," *Medicine and Science in Sports and Exercise,* Vol. 14, no. 5 (1982), 377.

• How often do you engage in physical activities or exercise (frequency)?
• How long does each session last (time/duration)?

You have learned that an important way to determine your target physical activity or exercise intensity is by measuring your heart rate. The "Active Mind/Active Body" activities on pages 75 and 76 will give you experience in measuring your resting and exercising heart rates.

Perceived Exertion.   Another simple method of determining intensity is based on Figure 3.5. Use the figure to rate how hard overall you feel you are working during physical activity or exercise (**perceived exertion**). The perceived exertion scale in Figure 3.5 ranges in value from 6 to 20. If you were sitting at rest, your rating of perceived exertion would probably be 6 and would represent "no exertion at all." If you were cycling, you would monitor your feelings of how hard you were breathing, your heart rate, your body temperature, and any muscle or skeletal discomfort to get your overall perceived exertion. You then might rate the intensity of your cycling as 13 if you were working moderately hard, or 16 if you were working vigorously. The perceived exertion method of determining intensity is easy to use once you have gained experience with physical activity and exercise in your personal fitness program.

Talk Test.   Another way to use perceived exertion to monitor your intensity is with the **talk test**. The talk test determines how easily you are able to carry on a conversation while you are engaged in physical activity or exercise. For example, if you rate your intensity between 11 and 16 (light to vigorous), you should be able to carry on a conversation with an exercising partner. This is an appropriate intensity level for your fitness program. However, if you and your partner are struggling to talk to each other, you are probably working harder than the *vigorous* level, which is harder than you need to work for basic personal fitness goals.

Time/Duration

Time/duration refers to how long in minutes, hours, or days you engage in physical activities or exercise sessions. A time/duration that is too short may result in limited progress. A time/duration that is too long will increase your risk for overuse injuries.

Beginning exercisers should accumulate twenty to thirty minutes of cardiovascular activity or exercise three to five days a week. You may accumulate your twenty to thirty minutes in one continuous workout session, or you may choose to collect your thirty minutes in three separate, ten-minute activity or exercise sessions. For example, you might take a brisk walk for ten minutes in the morning, another at noon, and another in the evening.

Teacher Readings

Kenney, W. L., Senior Editor. *ACSM Guidelines for Exercise Testing and Prescription,* American College of Sports Medicine, 4th Edition, Lea & Febiger, Philadelphia, PA: 1995.

Special Needs

When active muscle mass is limited by paralysis, amputation, or muscular dystrophies, persons normally have lower MHR (maximum heart rates). Any student with central nervous system damage, i.e. cerebral palsy or minimal brain damage, will also have lower MHRs, as will persons on certain medications. These students should be encouraged to "under work," thus beginning a program with a low number of repetitions and lighter weight and gradually increasing at a slower rate than the regular physical education student. For the disabled stu-

Active Mind! Active Body!

Taking Your Resting Pulse

The photographs below show you how to locate and take your pulse at two sites (the carotid artery, located at your throat, and the radial artery, located on the thumb side of your wrist). Use your index and middle fingers together on your dominant hand (preferred writing hand) to locate your pulse at either your neck or wrist. To measure your carotid pulse, put your fingers on the side of your throat by your Adam's apple, and press lightly. (Do not use both hands, as you may cut off the circulation of blood to your head.) Use a clock or watch to count for six seconds. Record the number of beats you get in six seconds. Then multiply that number by 10 to get your heart rate for one minute.

What did you get? Try it again on yourself. Then get a partner, and measure each other. To get your true resting pulse, you will need to take your pulse immediately when you wake up in the morning. Measure your resting pulse the next two mornings. What did you get?

Now that you know how to get your resting pulse, let's explore how different levels of work (intensities) influence your physical activity or exercise heart rate. Do the "Active Mind/Active Body" activity on the next page.

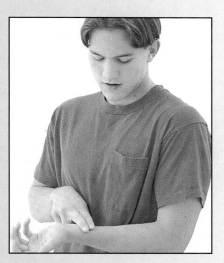

dent, long-duration, low-intensity activities are as effective as short-duration, high-intensity activities.

The medically impaired and physically impaired students would benefit by having their physicians or physical therapists review their exercise plans, looking at mode as well as the FIT. Generally, with the disabled population, goals should be geared toward maintaining function and range of motion.

Progression will vary with the disabled population. The loss of function or type of loss varies greatly, so there are no set guidelines. Progression will be slower. Many disabled students will not only reach a plateau but that plateau may be "permanent" due to their limitations.

Active Mind! Active Body!

Have students do the Active Mind/Active Body activity on this page. You should pair students up for this activity. Use Figure 3.6 to summarize the effects that different kinds of exercises have on heart rate. Discuss why heart rate will vary from one activity to another. Discuss the answers to the questions at the bottom of Figure 3.6.

Classroom Management

Have pencils ready for the students before beginning the Active Mind/Active Body activity on this page. Have soft, soothing music playing when students walk in the classroom and have mats for them to lie down on to get relaxed for measuring their resting pulse. Instruct them when they enter class not to talk and to be still to get best results. When students start moving about after getting resting values, make sure they are not running with their pencils in their hands. Demonstrate the hopping motion exercise. You should lead the jumping jacks so that all the students do them at the same pace. Make sure you space students out and allow plenty of room for the sprint exercise.

Active Mind! Active Body!
The Effect of Intensity on Heart Rate

Carefully record your pulse rate on a separate sheet of paper after each of the following activities:

1. Lie down for five minutes. Be as still and quiet as possible. Record your pulse rate. (This is not a true resting rate, because you have been up and active for some time. To measure your true resting heart rate, you would need to take it just when you woke up in the morning, before you got out of bed.)

2. Stand up, and record your pulse rate.

3. Walk around the gym for one minute, and record your pulse rate.

4. Jog slowly around the gym for one minute, and record your pulse rate.

5. Bound, jump, or hop around the gym for forty seconds, and record your pulse rate.

6. Do thirty jumping jacks, and record your pulse rate.

7. Do an all-out sprint for forty seconds, and record your pulse rate. Be sure to keep good spacing between you and your classmates. Take your pulse at the completion of your run, but remember to continue to walk for an additional three minutes after you take your pulse.

8. After you do a three-minute walk, sit down and do static stretching for an additional two minutes, then record your pulse. Keep stretching for another two minutes, and record your pulse rate again. These pulse readings will be used as recovery pulse rates.

Look at the sample graph on the next page. In this graph the nine pulse rates you just recorded have been plotted for an imaginary person. After studying this sample, plot your pulse rates to create your own personal graph. Then answer the questions below the graph.

REMEMBER This!

A quick and easy way to estimate your exercise heart rate is to count your pulse rate for six seconds immediately after activity. Then add a 0 to the number of beats you counted, and you will automatically have your estimated exercise heart rate. The number you get should be in your intensity zone (for example, beginner, or average to high fitness level).

CRITICAL THINKING

Have students develop a questionnaire for analyzing individual exercise programs. Students should use the questionnaire to interview members of health clubs, faculty/staff at your school, and owners of health clubs in your community. Questions could include: What caused you to be interested in an exercise program? Why? What motivation roadblocks have you experienced? What type of exercise do you do? Do you do cross-training? What limitations, if any, do you have? What have been the results of your exercise program? What

Sample Effects of Different Exercises on Your Heart Rate

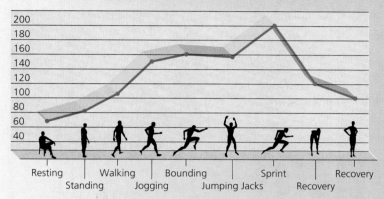

1. Which activity generated the highest pulse rate?
2. Which activity generated the lowest pulse rate?
3. Which activity was the easiest and which was the most difficult?
4. What is the relationship between your pulse rate and the intensity of the physical activity (work load)?
5. If two people start and finish a 1-mile run at the same time, making sure to remain side by side during the entire activity, how could you determine which person worked the hardest?
6. Which of these activities would be the best choice for a daily 20-minute aerobic activity and why?

• **Figure 3.6**   *Use the graph above as a reference to plot all nine of your pulse recordings. On a separate sheet of paper, draw a graph similar to the one shown above. Make a small circle to indicate the beats per minute. Then connect the circles with a thin line. Be sure to discuss the questions below the graph.*

Teaching Strategies

Have students make two to three large posters of Figure 3.6 that you can hang up in the gym (or your activity area). Then let students practice using the chart to rate how hard they are working.

Teacher Support Notes

Dr. Steve Van Camp is a cardiologist from San Diego, California, and was president of the American College of Sports Medicine from 1995–1996. He teaches his patients to use perceived exertion to monitor their exercise intensity.

Teacher Readings

Powers, S. K. and Howley, E. T.: *Exercise Physiology: Theory and Application to Fitness and Performance,* 2nd Edition. Madison, WI: Brown & Benchmark, 1994.

is your occupation?

After sharing questionnaire results with the class, have students write a newspaper story (complete with catchy headline) extolling the benefits of personal exercise programs and including the results of the survey of your local community. Students can be creative but should include important points. They should focus on analyzing the individual exercise programs reported by the people interviewed, how the people have improved their overall wellness, and the keys to their success.

Teacher Support Notes

Exercising at lower intensities for longer durations (for example, 55% of maximum heart rate for 45 minutes at a time) is best for those adolescents interested in weight loss. If students complain that they can't exercise for that long all at one time, you can point out that they could schedule several shorter sessions per day during which they can get active.

Healthy People 2000

Objective 1.3—Increase to at least 30 percent the proportion of people aged 6 and older who engage regularly in light to moderate physical activity for at least 30 minutes per day. (Light to moderate physical activity requires sustained, rhythmic muscular movements, is at least the equivalent to sustained walking, and is performed at less than 60 percent of maximum heart rate for age.) Place Objective 1.3 on the chalkboard and discuss whether students think this is a reasonable goal.

Discussion

Use Figure 3.7 to discuss the concept of time/duration for weight training. Ask students why this concept would be different for weight training than for cardiovascular conditioning.

CONSUMER CORNER

High Tech vs. Low Tech Heart Monitors

Many exercisers are using technology to monitor their heart rates. There are a variety of shapes, styles, and prices in the heart rate monitoring business. One type of heart rate monitor is the pulse bar, which you hold in your hand. Another type can fit on your ear or on your finger to give you a pulse readout. The most accurate type fits around your chest right over the heart and transmits a signal of your pulse to a wristwatch. You may want to experiment with one of these heart rate monitors when you work out.

Heart rate monitors provide a simple, accurate way to measure your heart rate, and thereby, the intensity of your workout.

Do not think, however, that heart rate monitors are necessary for a safe, effective personal fitness program.

You will find directions and photos that will help you learn to take your own pulse with nothing more than a watch on page 75 of this text. You will probably feel uncertain and clumsy the first few times you try to take your pulse. With a little practice, however, you will become very skilled at measuring your heart rate accurately.

Remember, you do not need a lot of expensive equipment to make yourself physically fit. With a pair of exercise shoes and the desire to be fit, you can be successful at obtaining and maintaining personal fitness.

BELIEVE IT? ... OR NOT?

The Centers for Disease Control in Atlanta, Georgia, has found that 13 percent of all male runners and 17 percent of all female runners seek medical attention for running-related injuries during any given year.

See page 96 for answer.

Continue these beginning cardiovascular workout sessions for the first two to three weeks, which will allow you to improve slowly and safely. As you become more fit, increase the length of time for each session anywhere from 35 minutes to 1 hour. The American College of Sports Medicine recommends 20 to 60 minutes of continuous or noncontinuous activity per physical activity or exercise session. Your specific goals will determine the time/duration for your prescription. For example, your goal may be to lose weight. Longer workout sessions of lower intensity, in your case, will result in a greater loss of weight.

If you are already of an average to high fitness level, you may find that the length of your daily workouts needs to be longer based on your personal goals. One way you can adjust your time/duration is by alternating harder days (45 minutes to 1 hour) with easier days (20 to 40 minutes).

If you are doing weight training, the time/duration will be determined by the number of exercises you perform. The beginning weight trainer will spend twenty to thirty minutes, whereas the individual of average to high fitness level will spend forty-five minutes to one hour. These recommendations are summarized in Figure 3.7.

Science and Technology

Designing a physical activity program can be simplified by using a computer. Computer software, which allows any person to set a time management scheme, can be purchased for both IBM-PCs and Macintosh systems. Most time management software bundles

come with daily and monthly planners as well as personal logs. Personal logs allow users to keep track of their daily routines.

For the bolder individual, a personal activity log can be designed using any simple database program. Microsoft

Activity	Time/Duration for Beginners	Time/Duration for Those of Average to High Fitness Levels
Cardiovascular conditioning	20–30 minutes	35 minutes to 1 hour
Weight training	20–30 minutes	45 minutes to 1 hour

• **Figure 3.7**   *Activity, Time/Duration for Exercisers of Varying Fitness Levels.*

REMEMBER This!

Intensity and time/duration for physical activity or exercise are difficult to determine separately. The higher the intensity of your activity, the shorter your activity time/duration will typically be. The lower the intensity of your activity, the longer your activity time/duration can be.

The time/duration of your workout sessions should be determined by the following considerations:

• What is your level of fitness?
• What are your specific goals (health or performance)?
• How hard are you working (intensity)?
• How often are you working (frequency)?
• How much time does your lifestyle allow you for exercise (determined by how much time you devote to jobs, schoolwork, and other commitments)?

SECTION 1 REVIEW

Answer the following questions on a separate sheet of paper:

1. What is the overload principle, and why is it important to your personal fitness program?
2. What are the relationships between FIT and your personal fitness program?
3. What is the talk test, and how and when should you use it?

SECTION 2   The Scientific Principle of Specificity (Be Specific!)

Improvements in your personal fitness will occur in the particular muscles that you overload during physical activity or exercise. This is called the **specificity principle**. You will see personal fitness adaptations your body makes according to your involvement in different

Access, Dbase, FoxPro, Claris FilePro, and HyperCard are among the many software databases that are available. These software titles will also allow the teacher to develop grade tracking forms and activity logs for students. A teacher can customize tracking logs to suit the individual student, and develop grading systems within the software. **Take the challenge:** Inquire about the types of database software available at your school, or go to your nearest software dealer and let them show you database software. **Remember:** Most software dealers now have access to trial copies of software that you can try before you buy.

Focus

Outcomes

In **Section 2** students will learn:

1. To define and explain the terms related to the scientific principle of specificity.
2. To explain the application of specificity in designing personal fitness programs.

Focus Activity

Discuss the concepts of mode, special situations, and record keeping as they apply to the specificity principle.

---

specificity principle

the principle that says improvements in your personal fitness will occur in the particular muscles that you overload during physical activity or exercise.

conditioning

engaging in regular physical activity or exercise that results in an improved state of physical fitness.

mode

in a personal fitness prescription, the type of activity or exercise you do.

BELIEVE IT? ... OR NOT?

"No train, no gain!" is a good way to describe physical activity or exercise; if you do not engage in physical activity or exercise on a regular basis, you will not acquire the positive benefits of a personal fitness program.

See page 96 for answer.

---

activities. For example, if you lift weights, the muscles that you move to lift the weights will get stronger as you overload them. Muscles that are not required to help move the weights will not change in terms of strength.

The specific changes that you see following a period of **conditioning** occur in different ways, depending on the activities or exercise you engage in. For example, if your goal is to become a better in-line skater, you will get the best results by focusing on improving your skills and conditioning while in-line skating. You may see some improvements in your in-line skating if you perform other activities, such as cycling on a regular basis, but the changes will not be as great as they would be if you were more specific in your conditioning. Also, if you condition yourself specifically to improve your strength, you will see minimal changes in your cardiovascular endurance.

To apply the specificity principle effectively, you need to evaluate your personal fitness goals and determine the realistic improvements you want to achieve. You can then choose specific activities or exercises to help yourself achieve your goals.

Mode of Activity

You do have a choice in the type of physical activity in which you participate. **Mode** refers to the type of physical activity or exercise you choose to do. For example, modes of cardiovascular conditioning include walking, jogging, swimming, and cycling. The mode of physical activities and exercises you do should be determined by the following considerations:

- What are your specific goals?
- How much time do you have?
- What do you like to do for fun?
- How much money do you have to spend on equipment?
- How do you plan to achieve Guidelines 1 and 2 (discussed previously) in your personal fitness plan?

Special Situations

In certain situations, such as those in which you are injured, sick, or on medication, you will need to adjust your personal fitness plan. For example, if you suffer a leg injury during a jogging program, you may have to stop jogging and engage in other cross-training activities (cycling, swimming, and so on) until your leg heals. If you get sick for several days, you should modify your personal fitness plan so you can gradually return to your previous conditioning level over a few weeks. Your personal fitness program should be designed to optimize your health and well-being. Thus, you should adjust your program to accommodate situations that might negatively influence your benefits.

Reteaching

Name _____ Date _____ Period _____

Chapter 3 Section 2 — The Scientific Principle of Specificity (Be Specific!)

Directions: Answer the questions in the blanks provided.

1. What term refers to the specific improvement in fitness performance in the muscles that are overloaded in a personal fitness program?

   Specificity principle

2. What term refers to the type of physical activity or exercise a person chooses to do?

   Mode

3. List four (4) modes of cardiovascular conditioning:

   Walking   *Swimming*
   Jogging   *Cycling*

4. List four (4) considerations that determine the mode of physical activities and exercises that you do.

   What are your specific goals?
   How much time do you have?
   What do you like to do for fun?
   How much money do you have to spend on equipment?

5. Give three (3) examples of certain situations in which you may have to adjust your FIT and progression rate.

   When you are injured
   When you are sick
   When you are on medication

6. Give two (2) examples of other cross-training activities a person may engage in if they have had to stop jogging due to a leg injury.

   Cycling
   Swimming

© 1997 West Publishing Co.

Reteaching Worksheets   28

ABILITY LEVELS

Reteaching

Some students may need help mastering the concepts contained in this section. In your Teacher Resource Package, you will find the reproducible worksheet shown here. This worksheet should help students who have been absent and those needing additional help to improve their comprehension and retention of the content in this section.

• *The variety of physical activities that you can choose to include in your personal fitness program is almost limitless. Try to find new activities that you enjoy.*

Record Keeping

Record keeping is just as important to the beginning exerciser as it is to the high-performance athlete. Anyone involved in physical activity or exercise should have specific goals and a plan to reach those goals. A physical activity and exercise record book can help you safely and successfully reach your goals. Your record-keeping book should consider any or all of the following items:

- Your goals (for example, to lose weight, get stronger, reduce stress, or run a marathon).
- How many and which days you exercise (try not to miss more than one day between exercise sessions).
- Time, distance, and intensity (heart rate, amount of weight lifted on hard and easy days).
- Weather conditions (temperature, smog, or humidity).
- Different routes you may have taken; places you exercised.
- Specific activities or exercises you did (weight training, swimming, backpacking, in-line skating, lawn mowing, etc.).
- Injuries.
- Foods and liquids consumed.
- Weight loss or gain.
- Progress.

REMEMBER This!

Performance goals require more specific and detailed personal fitness prescriptions than those for moderate levels of fitness and health. For example, if your goal is to take a 50-mile mountain-bike trip and you spend most of your preparation time lifting weights and doing flexibility exercises, you probably won't realize your goal. You would be better off conditioning yourself specifically, by doing more mountain-bike riding on hilly courses. A mountain-bike trip would require more cardiovascular fitness than strength and flexibility fitness.

Teach & Apply

Discussion

Ask students to explain the scientific principle of specificity. Ask them for examples of exercises that will make them stronger, increase their endurance, improve their flexibility, and have a positive influence on their body composition.

Activities

- Have students make posters listing physical activities and exercises that will provide specific benefits, as mentioned in the discussion above.
- On the board or overhead projector, list 15–20 recreational activities and sports. Ask students to determine what specific kinds of conditioning activities they would recommend a person do to improve at the items on the list.

Enrichment

This activity will allow you to provide a more challenging learning experience for some of your students.

Have students complete the following activity: Answer the following questions to assess the specificity of your own personal fitness program:
a. What are the goals I want to accomplish with my personal fitness program?
b. What specific activities did I participate in?
c. Is my current distribution of activities consistent with the accomplishment of my goals?
d. How often do I want to participate in each type of activity? Considering my goals, and the satisfaction I have with my progress toward those goals, how enjoyable is each activity?
e. How often do I want to participate in each type of activity, considering that my fitness level has improved (or not improved)?

Discussion

• Ask students what modes of physical activity or exercise they would recommend for getting stronger, more flexible, or changing body composition in a positive way.

• Ask students which modes of activities and exercises they enjoy and dislike. Then ask them why they feel that way.

• Ask students to discuss other special situations that would require them to adjust their FIT temporarily or for longer periods of time.

• Discuss with the class whether they think keeping records of their personal fitness conditioning is important. Then ask why they feel the way they do.

Activity

Have students develop an individual exercise log. Have them write down what activities and exercises they have done thus far in the course. Have them use the bulleted points in Section 2 under the head "Record Keeping" to customize their record keeping. Discuss with them why these records will be important to them six months from now, one year from now, five years from now, etc.

Assess

Use the Section 2 Review questions to assess students' comprehension of the concepts presented in Section 2.

Any Body Can!

David B. ("D. B.") Dill

David B. "D. B." Dill (1891–1986) was a pioneer in the area of exercise science and the development of scientific principles that apply to physical activity and exercise programs. He did extensive research on the body's responses to working in different environments, and on the effects of aging.

Orphaned at a young age, Dill moved to California with his uncle in 1905. He attended Santa Ana High School in California, where he was a member of the track team. Following high school, he spent a year working as a ranch foreman in Santa Fe, New Mexico.

In 1913 he earned a Bachelor of Science degree in Chemistry from Occidental College in California. The next year he earned a Master of Science degree in Chemistry from Stanford University. Following college, he taught high school chemistry in Salt Lake City, Utah, where he also coached and served as principal.

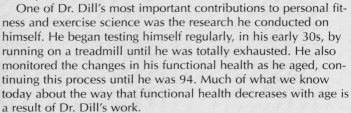

During World War I, D. B. Dill began work on his Doctor of Philosophy degree in Physiology at Harvard University. He was particularly interested in physiology related to physical activity and exercise. In 1927 he became a professor at Harvard and Director of the Harvard Fatigue Laboratory. From 1927 to 1947, Dr. Dill and his colleagues conducted some of the first research projects related to physical activity and exercise.

One of Dr. Dill's most important contributions to personal fitness and exercise science was the research he conducted on himself. He began testing himself regularly, in his early 30s, by running on a treadmill until he was totally exhausted. He also monitored the changes in his functional health as he aged, continuing this process until he was 94. Much of what we know today about the way that functional health decreases with age is a result of Dr. Dill's work.

Dr. Dill continued to conduct research until he died at the age of 95. He wrote three books and more than 325 research papers. He served as president of the American Physiological Society from 1950–1951 and president of the American College of Sports Medicine from 1960–1961. He continued to be physically active throughout his life. Dr. Dill is perhaps best known for putting the results of scientific research into practice.

Not everyone can be an exercise scientist like Dr. Dill, but **A**ny **B**ody **C**an live an active lifestyle and make physical fitness an important part of their everyday life. That's right, you can do it!

Wellness Connection

Exercise—How Much is Too Much?

We all agree that a regular program of physical exercise is good for us. However, extremely excessive exercise may actually have a negative effect. This situation, called exercise addiction or exercise dependency, may be recognized by a compulsion to exercise without regard to illness or injury. In this situation, exercise may take the place of very important things such as family, friends, church, schoolwork, boyfriends, or girlfriends. Injuries, depression, and mood distur-

SECTION 2 REVIEW

Answer the following questions on a separate sheet of paper:

1. What is the specificity principle, and why is it important to your personal fitness?
2. What is the relationship between mode and your personal fitness?
3. How can record keeping contribute positively to your personal fitness program?

SECTION 3 — The Scientific Principle of Progression (Improve!)

progression principle

the rate at which you change the frequency, intensity, and time/duration (FIT) of your personal fitness prescription.

overuse injury

an injury caused by doing too much, too soon, too often in an exercise program.

The **progression principle** refers to the rate at which you change the FIT (frequency, intensity, and time/duration) of your personal fitness prescription. Your FIT should be gradually increased over time. The rate of progression should be based on your listening to your body and analyzing how you feel as you adapt to physical activity and exercise. You should never increase all the factors in your program (frequency, intensity, and time/duration) at the same time or increase any one factor too fast or too soon. This would probably overload your body too much and increase your risk for an **overuse injury** such as straining a muscle.

Stages of Progression

Progression in your personal fitness program should occur in stages, including an initial stage, an improvement stage, and a maintenance stage. Figure 3.8 on the next page shows how a person might move through the progression stages. The initial stage in the figure takes about eight weeks. Note the quick improvements in the fitness level of the person charted. This indicates that the person probably was very inactive at the start. (Remember, each person will adapt differently.)

From nine to thirty weeks the figure shows the improvement stage of conditioning. During this stage more gradual improvements in fitness are usually observed as FIT increases. The line extending from thirty-one weeks to one year illustrates the maintenance stage of conditioning. During this stage your FIT levels off, but don't forget that you must continue your program to keep your FIT at this level.

BELIEVE IT? ... OR NOT?

Physical activity and exercise are panaceas (cure-alls).

See page 96 for answer.

bances may become commonplace.

Remember the information presented in Chapter 1. Health is a state of well-being that includes physical, mental, emotional, spiritual, and social aspects.

To attain true wellness, you must go beyond just the physical aspects of exercise and reach for the balance that will give you a well-rounded and fulfilling life.

ANSWERS TO SECTION 2 REVIEW

1. The specificity principle refers to the improvements in your personal fitness that will occur in the particular muscles that you overload during physical activity or exercise.
2. The mode refers to the type of physical activity or exercise you choose to do and helps determine the specific personal fitness benefits you may achieve.
3. Record keeping can help you set and achieve your personal fitness goals. Records can help you recognize what helped make you successful or what went wrong with your program.

Close

Have students go to a bookstore and look for manuals that are used as exercise logs (an example might be a running log or calendar). Have them discuss the different types of logs available and how they differed from the one they developed in class.

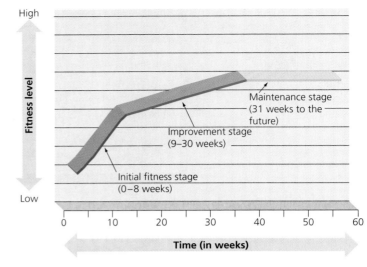

• **Figure 3.8** *Example of the Progression Principle. Improvement usually occurs in stages.*

Focus

Outcomes

In **Section 3** students will learn:

1. To define and explain the terms related to the scientific principle of progression.
2. To explain the application of progression in designing personal fitness programs.

Focus Activities

1. Discuss the stages of progression, trainability, detraining, and overtraining.
2. Use Figures 3.8 and 3.9 to discuss the concepts of progression and trainability.

> 66 **"Those who think they have not time for bodily exercise will sooner or later have to find time for illness"**
> (Edward Stanley, Earl of Derby, in an 1873 speech). 99

trainability

the rate at which a person improves personal fitness following physical activity or exercise conditioning. Trainability is determined, to a large extent, by genetic makeup.

Remember, the body can have a variety of responses to progressive overload from physical activity and exercise. Your own improvement response will depend on the following factors:

• Your initial fitness level (the lower you start, the more quickly you usually improve).

• Your genetic makeup and trainability (to be discussed shortly).

• The rate at which you overload your body or change FIT.

• Your specific goals (health or performance).

You will become better at designing and changing the progression of your personal fitness program as you gain experience with a variety of physical activities and exercise.

Trainability

Trainability refers to the rate at which a person improves personal fitness following physical activity or exercise conditioning. Trainability is determined, to a large extent, by genetic makeup. For example, athletes have unusual physical abilities due, at least in part, to inherited traits. These traits allow athletes to work out at higher levels than the average person and to improve more quickly. The concept of trainability is illustrated in Figure 3.9.

ABILITY LEVELS

Reteaching

Some students may need help mastering the concepts contained in this section. In your Teacher Resource Package, you will find the reproducible worksheet shown here. This worksheet should help students who have been absent and those needing additional help to improve their comprehension and retention of the content in this section.

BELIEVE IT? ...
OR NOT?

Exercise science principles developed by a professional organization called the American College of Sports Medicine are important to use in the design of personal fitness prescriptions.

See page 96 for answer.

R**EMEMBER** This!

Not everyone can reach certain goals, such as running a mile in six minutes or becoming a champion body builder. However, given enough time and proper conditioning *Any Body Can* achieve Guidelines 1 and 2 and have positive influences on their health and well-being.

plateau effect

the leveling off of physical fitness improvement in a personal fitness program.

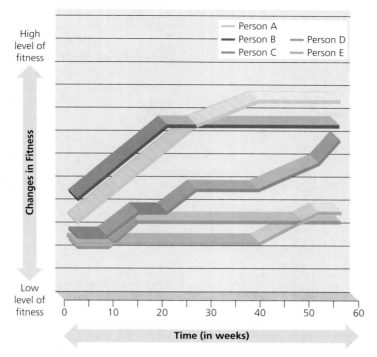

• **Figure 3.9** *Differences in Trainability Among Individuals.*

Figure 3.9 shows that Person A has a moderate initial fitness level and improves steadily during one year of conditioning to a high level of fitness. Individual B has a moderately high initial fitness level, improves rapidly in fitness for about twenty weeks, and then experiences a **plateau effect**. *Plateau effect* refers to the fact that there is a period of time when little, if any, fitness improvement occurs.

Individual C begins with an average initial fitness level and improves significantly during one year of conditioning. Individual D begins with a below-average level of fitness and does not improve to average levels until after a half-year of conditioning. Individual E begins at about the same fitness level as Individual D and experiences early modest improvements in fitness with a later plateau effect in fitness.

Individuals D and E were not able to improve as much as A, B, and C. However, both D and E were able to improve over time with conditioning. These differences could have occurred, even if all five people used exactly the same fitness program, due to inherited differences in trainability.

Teach & Apply

Discussion

Ask students to explain the scientific principle of progression. Ask them to discuss their experiences with progressing too fast or not fast enough in their past fitness experiences.

Teaching Strategies

Make a poster that has a male and female endurance athlete (for example, triathletes) on the left and a male and female body builder on the right. Draw an arrow from left to right and write, "You can look like this after six weeks of weight training." Then have students react to whether they think this is possible. Ask them which males and females are fitter. This poster will help tie the principles of specificity and progression together for the students.

Enrichment

This activity will allow you to provide a more challenging learning experience for some of your students.

Have the students complete the following activity: Keep a training log that records the activities in your personal fitness program. Keep in mind the guidelines for progression in your program. Record your progression for each type of activity. Be sure to record your frequency for each week, the intensity (heart rate or weight lifted) of each workout, and duration (time) for each workout. After each week of participation, average your heart rate or amount of weight lifted for that week. After an eight week period, reassess your program and take any necessary steps to adjust your FIT progression to be consistent with your fitness goals.

Discussion

Ask students to discuss what detraining means to them. Ask them if they ever felt like they were in very good shape and then had to lay off from training for a while. How fast did they feel they lost fitness?

Teacher Support Notes

Dr. Ed Coyle from the University of Texas has studied the effects of detraining (also known as the reversibility principle) on the cardiovascular system. He evaluated the effects of 84 days of detraining on previously high fit endurance individuals. He found that the subjects lost one-half of the pretest values on stroke volume (the amount of blood pumped with each beat of the heart) after 10–12 days of detraining. Dr. Coyle's work illustrates the medication-like effect that exercise has in terms of losing benefits if it is discontinued for extended periods of time. This has been called the half-life effect. For example, you lose one-half of the cardiovascular fitness benefits you might have gained in 10–12 days of no training. The half-life for losing strength with detraining is longer, as pointed out in the text (probably 20–30 days).

detraining

the loss of health and fitness benefits when a personal fitness program is stopped.

cross-train

to vary activities and exercises from day to day to prevent detraining, especially after an injury.

overtraining

being too active or exercising too much. Overtraining leads to overuse injuries and addictive behaviors.

Detraining

Chapter 1 discussed some of the benefits of engaging in physical activity or exercise. **Detraining** is the loss of health or physical fitness benefits when a personal fitness program is stopped. For example, if you become ill and have to remain in bed for several days with no activity, you will notice that you are weak and have less fitness, which will require some time to regain.

Most of the benefits of a physical fitness program (such as improved functional health, enhanced self-esteem, and reduced stress) are lost, at least to some extent, over time if the program is stopped. For example, if you are able to walk or jog 2 miles in twenty minutes and then stop all conditioning for two to three weeks, you will probably find that you are unable to do 2 miles in twenty minutes when you start back on your program. It may take you three to six weeks of new conditioning to get back to the same level of fitness.

It is important to recognize that the benefits of physical activity or exercise are lost at different rates following detraining. For example, if you detrain for four weeks, you may notice that your cardiovascular fitness level has dropped significantly, whereas your levels of strength have not decreased as much. You should also realize that you cannot lose your personal fitness benefits in a day, or two, or even three. In fact, it is always a good idea to take off a day or two if you are unusually tired, you are sick, or you have a significant schedule conflict. However, it is important not to discontinue your program for too long (one to two weeks), or you will detrain.

You may also find that it is to your advantage to **cross-train** to prevent detraining, particularly if you are injured. In that way you can rest your injury while maintaining the most fitness benefits. For example, if you like to lift weights and you hurt your shoulder, you may still be able to ride a stationary cycle and lift leg weights to maintain some fitness.

A knowledge of detraining will help you *maintain* a reasonable level of personal fitness—which is much easier than *obtaining* the level in the first place. You should also realize that just about everyone has to start and stop his or her personal fitness program several times in adult life. To maximize your personal fitness benefits, simply minimize your periods of detraining.

Overtraining

Overtraining is being too active or exercising too much. Overtraining can produce abnormal physical and mental stress and is associated with increased overuse injuries (muscle and skeletal problems caused by overexercising). Overtraining is also characterized by behaviors characteristic of addiction (for example, believing you will lose fitness if you miss just one day of conditioning).

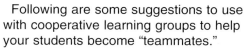

COOPERATIVE LEARNING

Following are some suggestions to use with cooperative learning groups to help your students become "teammates."

Individually, each student must be responsible, not only for completing his or her individual part of a task but also for learning the material necessary for

the completion of the whole task. For example, if students are working in groups to learn the stages of progression, each group member should have an individual responsibility. Not only would each member be responsible for his or her own part of the task, but each

• *Working hard is good, but be careful not to overtrain. An injury resulting from overtraining can bring a quick halt to your fitness program, which could mean starting from the beginning once your injury heals.*

BELIEVE IT? ...
OR NOT?

Less than 50 percent of adults say they feel better after physical activity or exercise.

See page 96 for answer.

physical activity zelot; exercise zealot

a person who is addicted to a physical activity or exercise program.

It is very important that you be able to recognize the symptoms of overtraining. You may have chronic fatigue, for example. You feel tired all the time, especially after starting a personal fitness program or after overloading your body. You may have constant muscle soreness.

Another sign of overtraining is insomnia. You may not be able to sleep at night, particularly after a day or two of vigorous activity or exercise. You may have a rapid weight loss because your physical activity or exercise program leaves you so tired that you do not feel like eating. Your morning resting pulse rate may be elevated since overtraining is often associated with an elevated pulse rate of about 10 beats above normal.

Other signs of overtraining include mental stress or "burnout". You are not only tired physically, but you are also mentally stressed or feel burned out. The physical activities and exercises you usually like to do are just not fun anymore.

If you are becoming a physical activity or exercise zealot, you are overtraining. A **physical activity zealot**, or **exercise zealot**, is a person who believes that if a little bit of activity or exercise is good, then more is better. Zealots can become addicted to their physical activity or exercise programs and do serious harm to themselves by overloading themselves too much.

Teacher Support Notes

Individuals who are at high risk for becoming physical activity or exercise zealots are often low to moderately physically talented but highly motivated. They believe that if a little bit of activity or exercise is good for you, then more is better. They believe in the concept of, "no pain—no gain!" This kind of attitude is not always bad, but when carried to extremes, students who practice this philosophy can expose themselves to unnecessary injury risk. They also may develop negative addictive behaviors such as anorexia and bulimia, which can become quite serious. (See Chapter 9.)

Discussion

Ask students if they have ever known a physical activity or exercise zealot. What behaviors did they exhibit that suggest that they might be addicted to exercise?

Assess

Use the Section 3 Review questions on the next page to assess students' comprehension of the concepts presented in Section 3.

member would also be responsible for knowing the information contained in the entire analysis and how it all fits together. Everyone in the group is responsible for making sure other members understand the material. Asking questions of different group members will let you know who understands the material.

While the students are working in

groups, communication skills are important. You, as the teacher, need to set guidelines for the students' interaction and communication while they are in their groups. You must insist that they speak positively to each other, using encouragement rather than insult. And you must monitor their interaction while they are in groups.

acute

occurring over a short time.

chronic

occurring over an extended time.

REMEMBER This!

Some rest may be just what you need if you are physically and mentally stressed out, are sick, or have other significant schedule conflicts.

Overtraining can be **acute** (occur over a short period of time), or it can be **chronic** (occur over an extended time). An example of acute overtraining is the two-a-day or three-a-day practices that an athlete might do for two or three weeks before the football or volleyball season. In this case, the acute overtraining is planned to be an intense learning and practice time for sports preparation. This type of overtraining can only last two or three weeks. Most athletes would burn out and increase their overuse injury rate if they continued to overload themselves at these high levels. If you ever feel like you are suffering from acute overtraining, you will usually recover rapidly by taking a few days off from your physical activity or exercise program.

Chronic overtraining is more serious than acute overtraining. Chronic overtraining occurs over several weeks or months and often leads to serious mental distress. It is important to avoid chronic overtraining by recognizing the symptoms of overdoing your personal fitness program. Most people will not recover from chronic overtraining by just taking a few days off from their personal fitness program. Several weeks or months can be required to recover from chronic overtraining. Physical activity or exercise zealots may even require special counseling in order to recover.

SECTION 3 REVIEW

Answer the following questions on a separate sheet of paper:

1. What is the progression principle, and why is it important to your personal fitness program?
2. Why do some individuals realize more improvement and improve at faster rates than others?
3. Explain the differences between overtraining and detraining. How can these concepts affect your personal fitness?

SECTION 4 Warm It Up, First!

warm-up

a variety of low-intensity activities that are designed to prepare your body for moderate to vigorous activities.

The **warm-up** portion of a personal fitness program should always be done before any moderate or vigorous physical activities are performed. Unfortunately, many people do their warm-up too quickly, or not at all. A well-designed warm-up will help you participate in a safe, successful, and enjoyable workout.

ANSWERS TO SECTION 3 REVIEW

1. The progression principle refers to the rate at which you change the FIT of your personal fitness program.
2. Improvement varies based on the concept of trainability, which is determined to a large extent by genetics.
3. Overtraining is related to overloading the body too much and not allowing enough time for one to adjust to the frequency, intensity, or time/duration of the personal fitness prescription. Detraining refers to the loss of health and physical fitness benefits when someone stops his or her program for a significant period of time. Both overtraining and detraining can have negative effects on your personal fitness.

Close

Have an athlete who has been injured and who had to detrain speak to the class about how long it took to lose his or her healthy fitness level. Ask him or her to speak about his or her cross-training program (if he or she has one) and rehabilitation efforts.

CULTURAL DIVERSITY

Colombia

Geographical characteristics affect the types of recreational activities enjoyed by Colombians. Along the coasts, water sports are very popular, particularly surfing. Water skiing, scuba diving, and snorkeling are done in the Pacific bays.

Because much of the land is covered with mountains, hiking, climbing, and cycling have gained popularity. Skiing the 19,000-foot Sierra Nevada range is a thrill enjoyed by the wealthy.

City dwellers are more likely to have

* *Be sure to warm up before starting the workout phase of your personal fitness program or before engaging in any sports activities. By warming up you reduce your chance of injury and increase the effectiveness of your workout.*

REMEMBER This!

For most personal fitness programs, stretches should be static. It is not necessary to use quick, jerking movements.

active warm-up

a warm-up that attempts to raise the body temperature by actively involving the muscular, skeletal, and cardiovascular systems.

muscle/skeletal warm-up

a warm-up that usually involves a series of static body stretches.

static body stretches

stretches that are done slowly, smoothly, and in a sustained fashion.

Purpose of the Warm-up

The warm-up should raise your heart rate gradually before physical activity or exercise. This gradual increase causes a slight rise in muscle temperature, which enables your muscles to work safely and more efficiently. In fact, your whole body benefits. Muscles, bones, and nerves seem to perform better when the body temperature is slightly increased. Evidence suggests that warm-up helps minimize physical activity and exercise injuries and may help reduce some of the symptoms of muscle soreness.

Active Warm-up

Warm-up may be active or passive. In **active warm-up**, you attempt to raise your body temperature by actively involving the muscular, skeletal, and cardiovascular (heart and circulation) systems. The **muscle/skeletal warm-up** is usually performed by doing a series of static body stretches. (This will be covered in detail in Chapter 6.) Body stretches can loosen up muscles and better prepare them for working out. **Static body stretches** are stretches that are done slowly, smoothly, and in a sustained fashion.

Focus

Outcome

In **Section 4** students will learn:

1. To explain the importance of proper warm-up and to describe the different types of warm-up.

Focus Activities

1. Discuss the purpose of warm-up and the differences between active and passive warm-up.
2. Use Figure 3.10 on page 92 to help students learn to stretch properly during a warm-up.

Teach & Apply

Discussion

Ask students what the term "warm-up" means to them. What types of activities should be included in a warm-up? How long should a warm-up last?

Teacher Readings

Wilmore, J. H. and Costill, D. L.: *Physiology of Sport and Exercise,* Champaign, IL: Human Kinetics, 1994.

access to recreational facilities and be interested in the health benefits of sports than are rural residents. Regular exercise programs such as aerobics are available in big cities like Bogotá.

Sports clubs and leagues thrive in rural areas. Volleyball and bicycle racing are popular, but soccer is the king of sports. Baseball and basketball are other favorite team sports. Almost every Colombian town has a *tejo* court, too, for playing a traditional game resembling horseshoes. A smooth piece of stone or metal, the *tejo,* is thrown at a pipe that has been sunk in a dirt mound and filled with a small amount of an explosive. The object of the game is to make an explosion!

Assess

Use the Section 4 Review questions to assess students' comprehension of the concepts presented.

ANSWERS TO SECTION 4 REVIEW

1. To increase muscle temperature.
2. It is an active warm-up technique that includes stretching in a slow, smooth, and sustained fashion.
3. In active warm-up you do stretches to involve the muscular, skeletal, and cardiovascular systems and raise body temperature. In a passive warm-up outside sources are used to raise body temperature.

cardiovascular warm-up

a warm-up that gradually increases the heart rate and internal body temperature.

specific active warm-up

a warm-up structured primarily for a specific skill or game activity.

general active warm-up

a warm-up tailored to individual physical activities. It is less structured than a specific active warm-up.

passive warm-up

a warm-up that raises the body temperature using outside heat sources such as blankets, and hot baths.

• Safety reminder—wear proper exercise shoes during all phases of your workout.

In addition to stretching, it is necessary to do a cardiovascular warm-up. The **cardiovascular warm-up** gradually increases your heart rate and your internal body temperature. Both the muscle/skeletal and cardiovascular warm-ups should be done prior to moderate or vigorous physical activity or exercise.

There are two types of active warm-up: general and specific. A **specific active warm-up** is structured primarily for skill or game activities (football, volleyball, basketball). A **general active warm-up** is less structured and is usually used for individual physical activities. For example, a specific warm-up designed to be performed before a game of basketball might include layups, jump shots, and upper and lower leg stretches. A general warm-up designed for swimming or jogging might include running in place, calisthenics, and various stretches.

Passive Warm-up

The **passive warm-up** raises body temperature through the use of outside heat sources such as covering oneself with blankets, taking hot baths or saunas, or applying skin creams. This process is not very effective because it does not involve adequate muscle/skeletal or heart activity.

Warm-up Guidelines

Follow these guidelines for a safe warm-up:
• Do both heart and muscle/skeletal warm-ups.
• Start slowly, and gradually increase intensity.
• Warm-up for five to fifteen minutes (colder weather may require more time).
• Design a specific warm-up intended for your exercises or physical activities.
• Make your warm-up intensity high enough to produce an increase in heart and breathing rates and a light sweat.

The "Active Mind/Active Body" activities on pages 91 and 95 will give you practice in designing your own warm-up program.

SECTION 4 REVIEW

Answer the following questions on a separate sheet of paper:
1. Why is it important to warm up prior to exercise?
2. What is the static stretching technique?
3. What is the difference between active and passive warm-up?

Reteaching

Name _____ Date _____ Period _____

Chapter 3
Section 4
Warm It Up, First!

Directions: Answer the questions in the blanks provided.

1. What term refers to a variety of low intensity activities that are designed to prepare your body for moderate to vigorous activities?

   Warm-up

2. How should a warm-up affect your heart rate before physical activity or exercise?

   It should raise your heart rate gradually.

3. During a warm-up, what happens to your muscle temperature, which enables your muscles to work safely and more efficiently?

   The warm-up causes a slight rise in muscle temperature.

4. How does an increased body temperature affect the way that muscles, bones, and nerves perform?

   They perform better when the body temperature is slightly increased.

5. What effect does a warm-up have on the symptoms of muscle soreness?

   It helps minimize muscle soreness.

6. In what type of warm-up do you attempt to raise your body temperature by actively involving the muscular, skeletal, and cardiovascular systems?

   The active warm-up

7. What type of stretches are done slowly, smoothly, and in a sustained fashion?

   Static body stretches

8. What type of warm-up gradually increases your heart rate and your internal body temperature?

   Cardiovascular warm-up

9. What type of active warm-up is structured for skill or game activities?

   Specific active warm-up

32   © 1997 West Publishing Co.

Reteaching Worksheets

ABILITY LEVELS

Reteaching

Some students may need help mastering the concepts contained in this section. In your Teacher Resource Package, you will find the reproducible worksheet shown here. This worksheet should help students who have been absent and those needing additional help to improve their comprehension and retention of the content in this section.

Active Mind! Active Body!

Learning to Stretch Correctly

As you begin a walking/jogging program, it is important that you use appropriate warm-up stretches. Practice performing each of the warm-up stretches shown in Figure 3.10 correctly and safely. The exercises can be used to stretch the whole body. For best results, you should do these after a light cardiovascular warm-up. Start slowly, and hold static positions.

The numbers in the following list refer to the exercises in Figure 3.10 on the next page.

1. Single knee press—stretches lower back and gluteals:
    *   Lie on your back, and bring your left leg toward your chest by placing both hands under the left knee and slowly pulling.
    *   Exhale while pulling your leg.
    *   Hold this position for eight to twelve seconds; then change legs and repeat.

2. Side stretcher—stretches obliques:
    *   From a standing position with feet a shoulders' width apart, put your right hand on the back of your neck.
    *   Place your left hand near the side of your left knee, and bend sideways (to the left) as far as possible.
    *   Do not lean forward or backward.
    *   Hold the position for eight to twelve seconds, and then repeat on the other side.

3. Thigh stretcher—stretches quadriceps:
    *   From a standing position, bend your right knee backward and up.
    *   With your left hand, grasp your right foot, and gently pull upward toward the gluteals.
    *   Avoid leaning forward.
    *   It may be helpful to hold onto a wall or chair with the other hand.
    *   Hold this position for eight to twelve seconds, and then change legs and repeat.

4. Chest and arm stretch—stretches pectoralis and deltoids:
    *   From a standing or sitting position, raise your arms and hands to a shoulder-high position.
    *   Straighten your arms, and place your hands palm down.
    *   Try to touch your hands behind your back.
    *   Hold this position for eight to twelve seconds.

(Continued on next page)

Active Mind! Active Body!

Prior to having students do the warm-up stretches in the Active Mind/Active Body activity on this page you should spread out the class and demonstrate each stretch. Let students practice each stretch as you move through the group to critique students.

Close

Use the Active Mind/Active Body activity on page 95 as homework for students.

Enrichment   *This activity will allow you to provide a more challenging learning experience for some of your students.*

Have students attend three different sports competitions (football, basketball, volleyball, baseball, etc.) Observe the pregame warm-up, and any postgame cool-down for each team. Answer the following questions concerning these activities:

a. How much time was spent on muscle/skeletal warm-up?

b. How much time was spent on static body stretches?

c. How much time was spent on a cardiovascular warm-up?

d. How much of the warm-up could be considered a specific active warm-up?

e. How much time was spent in cooling-down after the game?

Health and Fitness Updates

You can update your coverage of health and fitness topics, as well as spark lively classroom discussion and deeper understanding, by using the **CNN Health and Fitness Updates.** These video updates are produced by Turner Educational Services, using the resources of CNN, the world's first 24-hour, all-news network.

With the introduction of the **CNN Health and Fitness Updates,** West Educational Publishing is proud to be the exclusive partner of CNN for textbook/video integration in high school fitness. By making use of the **CNN Health and Fitness Updates** you can bring the power of CNN, the network known for providing in-depth, live coverage and analysis of breaking news events, to your fitness class.

For assistance in using and incorporating the **CNN Health and Fitness Updates** into your classroom presentations, see the Classroom Guide to the CNN Health and Fitness Updates. The **CNN Health and Fitness Updates** are available with West Educational Publishing's Foundations of Personal Fitness by Don Rainey and Tinker Murray.

• **Figure 3.10** Recommended Warm-up Stretches. These stretches can help you meet flexibility goals safely.

Across the Disciplines

Mathematics

To assist students with understanding the concept of overload, have them design a spreadsheet that will enable them to record how often they were exercising (frequency), their heart rates as a measure of how hard they are working (intensity), and the duration of their workouts (time). Also included in this spreadsheet should be their personal evaluation of how they feel after they work out. Students should use a scale from 0 to 10 to describe them-

Learning to Stretch Correctly *(continued)*

5. Trunk twist—stretches back and hips:
   - Sit on the floor with both legs straight in front of you.
   - Bend the left knee far enough to place the left foot flat on the floor next to the right knee.
   - Now cross the left leg over the right leg, and place the left foot flat on the floor next to the right knee.
   - Place your right elbow on the left side of your left leg.
   - Place your left arm and hand on the floor behind you.
   - While pressing with your right arm, try to twist your body and head as far to the left as possible.
   - Hold this position for eight to twelve seconds. Then change your leg and arm position and repeat.

6. Single leg toe touch—stretches hamstrings and lower back:
   - Sit on the floor, with both legs straight in front of you.
   - Bend your right knee far enough to place your right foot flat on the floor next to the left knee.
   - Reach for your left ankle with both hands.
   - Gently pull your body forward while trying to touch your head to your knee.
   - Hold this position for eight to twelve seconds. Then change your leg and arm position and repeat.

7. "Yes," "no," "maybe"—stretches head and neck:
   - Slowly tilt your head backward as far as possible. Then bring your head forward and touch your chin to your chest. This is the "yes" stretch.
   - Slowly turn your head as far to the right as possible, then back to the left as far as possible. This is the "no" stretch.
   - Now pull both of your shoulders up toward your ears. This is the "maybe" stretch.
   - Avoid rotating your head and neck in a complete circle.
   - Hold each position for eight to twelve seconds.

8. Side lunge—stretches inner thigh and groin:
   - From a standing position, step to the right with your right foot and leg.
   - Bend your left knee, and balance most of your weight on your left leg.
   - Keep your right leg straight out to the side.
   - Balance yourself with one or both hands touching the floor.
   - Hold this position for eight to twelve seconds. Then change legs and repeat.

(Continued on next page)

Healthy People 2000

Objective 1.5—Reduce to no more than 15 percent the proportion of people aged 6 and older who engage in no leisure-time physical activity.

Although the protective effect of a more active lifestyle is seen for both occupational and leisure-time physical activity, the amount of physical activity at work and in the home has declined steadily. For most people, the greatest opportunity for physical activity is during leisure. Unfortunately, 24 percent of men and women aged 18 and older report no leisure-time physical activity.

It is important for those who are sedentary during their leisure time to take the first step towards developing a pattern of regular physical activity. Public education efforts need to address the specific barriers that inhibit the adoption of physical activity by different population groups.

Teacher Readings

Baumgartner, T. A. and Jackson, A. S. *Measurement for Evaluation in Physical Education and Exercise Science*, 5th Edition, Dubuque, IA: W. C. Brown, 1994.

selves on a range from extremely fatigued to extremely energized. Students should record this information in their journals. Encourage students to develop an electronic spreadsheet and enter their data weekly. By using formulas, the spreadsheet will automatically calculate the information entered. Formulas can also be used to enable stu-dents to play "what if?" to calculate projected increases or decreases in the frequency, intensity, and duration of activity or exercise. Emphasize to students that they are trying to find a personal FIT combination that enables them to achieve their desired levels of physical conditioning without experiencing undue fatigue or injury.

Healthy People 2000

Objective 1.6—**Increase to at least 40 percent the proportion of people aged 6 and older who regularly perform physical activities that enhance and maintain muscular strength, muscular endurance, and flexibility.**

Muscular strength and endurance describe the ability of skeletal muscles to perform hard and/or prolonged work. Strength and endurance greatly affect the ability to perform the tasks of daily living without undue physical stress and fatigue. Regular use of skeletal muscles helps improve and maintain strength and endurance. Engaging in regular physical activity and engaging in a variety of physical activities can help to satisfy this objective. Although weight training (exercising with free weights or weight machines) can increase muscle strength and endurance, weight training is not necessary to meet this objective and may not be appropriate for all age groups and individuals.

Flexibility describes the range of motion in a joint or sequence of joints. Those with greater flexibility may have a lower risk of future back injury.

Learning to Stretch Correctly

9. Forward lunge—stretches hip flexors:
   - From a standing position, step directly to the front with your right leg.
   - Bend your right knee to a 90-degree angle while keeping your left leg back and straight. Your left foot should be on its toes.
   - Be sure not to let your right knee extend past your right foot.
   - Balance yourself with one or both hands on the floor.
   - Hold this position for eight to twelve seconds. Then change legs and repeat.

10. Reverse hurdle—stretches hamstrings and lower back:
   - Sit on the floor, with both legs straight in front of you.
   - Bend your left knee far enough to place the bottom of your left foot against the side of your right knee.
   - Reach for your right ankle with both hands.
   - Gently pull your body forward while trying to touch your head to your knee.
   - Hold this position for eight to twelve seconds. Then change your leg and arm position and repeat.

11. Butterfly—stretches groin:
   - From a sitting position, bend both knees, and place the bottoms of both feet against each other.
   - Lean forward, and place both hands on your feet.
   - Slowly pull the heels of your feet toward your body.
   - You may slightly lean forward.
   - Try to keep your knees out and down.
   - Hold this position for eight to twelve seconds.

12. Calf stretch—stretches gastrocnemius:
   - From a standing position, face a wall. Place your feet 3 feet from the wall.
   - Step forward with your left foot, and support your weight by placing your hands on the wall.
   - Your right foot should remain in its position and should stay flat on the floor as you lean forward.
   - There should be no weight on your left foot.
   - Hold this position for eight to twelve seconds. Then change legs and repeat.

Special Needs

Any warm-up exercises that disabled students use should be based on their actual work-out programs. The warm-up exercises could be the actual exercises but fewer in number and with lower intensity.

Any workout program should be based on information gathered from physicians, physical therapists, etc. and assessments of the beginning level of fitness. Training levels will be much different with disabled students than with regular students. Some students may exhibit extremely low levels of cardiovascular

Active Mind! Active Body! Designing a Sample Warm-up

Design a specific active warm-up program for softball. (*Hint:* What body parts are most often used by a softball player?) Then design a general active warm-up program for cycling.

SECTION 5 Work It Out!

The workout phase of your personal fitness program is the period of time that you should spend daily, or almost daily, in physical activity or exercise. A well-designed workout phase should be based on scientific exercise principles. Your workout phase should also be tailored to your personal fitness goals and experiences with physical activity and exercise.

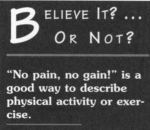

BELIEVE IT? ... OR NOT?

"No pain, no gain!" is a good way to describe physical activity or exercise.

See page 96 for answer.

• *Girls, as well as boys, benefit greatly from a well-designed weight training program.*

fitness but high levels of muscular strength and endurance. Programming should keep functionality for independence in mind.

Cool-down exercises should, like warm-up exercises, be the same basic workout program but of lower intensity. Cool-down periods for the disabled student may need to be of longer duration due to the body's inability to recover quickly.

It is often beneficial for the disabled student to include an additional 10–15 minutes of post-workout exercises while all muscles are still warm and the blood supply is high. The same exercises that were used in the warm-up can be repeated during this time.

Focus

Outcome

In **Section 5** students will learn:

1. To describe how to design their personal fitness prescriptions for working out.

Focus Activity

Discuss the elements involved in designing a workout by using Figures 3.11 and 3.12.

Teach & Apply

Discussion

• Ask students if they have ever designed a workout for themselves according to guidelines that are presented in the example in Figure 3.12.
• Discuss Figure 3.11 and ask students how their walking and jogging program has been going compared to that shown. Students should be provided with opportunities to increase their walking or jogging distances in a progressive manner.

Teacher Support Notes

The conditioning protocol in Figure 3.11 was designed by the authors based on their previous research, which has shown that the vast majority of students (barring significant orthopedic problems) can successfully meet these standards in 5–8 weeks. The walking conditioning program mentioned in Chapter 5 provides you with an alternative for those students who cannot jog. You should note that the walking protocol requires students to walk briskly for longer periods of time to expend similar amounts of energy as those students who jog.

Answers to

BELIEVE IT? ... OR NOT?

Pg. 72 False. Physical activity and exercise are dose (amount) related. For example, if you engage in physical activity or exercise very infrequently, you will not be able to develop or maintain adequate levels of personal fitness. If you do too much physical activity or exercise, you can increase your risk of injuries caused by overuse.

Pg. 78 True.

Pg. 80 True.

Pg. 83 False. Physical activity or exercise will not solve all health problems. However, physical activity or exercise may be a valuable part of the treatment for various physical and mental disorders.

Pg. 85 True.

Pg. 87 False. Ninety percent of adults say they feel better after they participate in physical activity or exercise.

Pg. 95 False. You can achieve an acceptable level of personal fitness by engaging in moderate physical activities or exercise. Physical activity or exercise does not have to be painful to help you achieve many personal fitness goals.

Designing a Workout

Figure 3.12 on the next page gives an example of a personal fitness prescription. You might want to use this prescription in designing your workout. The figure shows you how to combine the modes of your conditioning with FIT.

Figure 3.11 below provides an example of a six-week walking/jogging conditioning program designed to help you walk/jog 1.6 to 2.0 miles (for boys) or 1.4 to 1.8 miles (for girls) in twenty minutes. These standards are consistent with good to better levels of cardio-

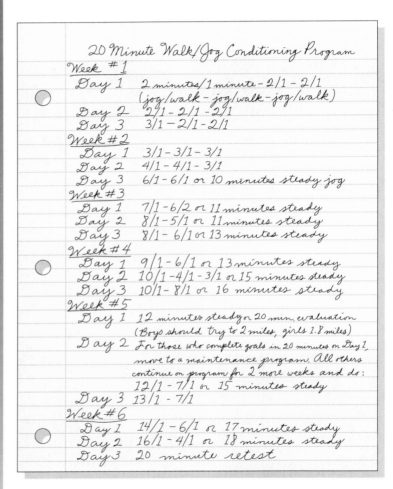

20 Minute Walk/Jog Conditioning Program

Week #1
Day 1   2 minutes/1 minute – 2/1 – 2/1
        (jog/walk – jog/walk – jog/walk)
Day 2   2/1 – 2/1 – 2/1
Day 3   3/1 – 2/1 – 2/1

Week #2
Day 1   3/1 – 3/1 – 3/1
Day 2   4/1 – 4/1 – 3/1
Day 3   6/1 – 6/1 or 10 minutes steady jog

Week #3
Day 1   7/1 – 6/2 or 11 minutes steady
Day 2   8/1 – 5/1 or 11 minutes steady
Day 3   8/1 – 6/1 or 13 minutes steady

Week #4
Day 1   9/1 – 6/1 or 13 minutes steady
Day 2   10/1 – 4/1 – 3/1 or 15 minutes steady
Day 3   10/1 – 8/1 or 16 minutes steady

Week #5
Day 1   12 minutes steady or 20 min. evaluation
        (Boys should try to 2 miles, girls 1.8 miles)
Day 2   For those who complete goals in 20 minutes on Day 1,
        move to a maintenance program. All others
        continue on program for 2 more weeks and do:
        12/1 – 7/1 or 15 minutes steady
Day 3   13/1 – 7/1

Week #6
Day 1   14/1 – 6/1 or 17 minutes steady
Day 2   16/1 – 4/1 or 18 minutes steady
Day 3   20 minute retest

● **Figure 3.11**   20-Minute Walk/Jog Conditioning Program.

ABILITY LEVELS

Reteaching

Some students may need help mastering the concepts contained in this section. In your Teacher Resource Package, you will find the reproducible worksheet shown here. This worksheet should help students who have been absent and those needing additional help to improve their comprehension and retention of the content in this section.

Frequency	3–5 days per week
Intensity	Moderate to vigorous and continuous, if possible
Time/Duration	Accumulate 20–60 minutes each session
Modes	Walk–hike, run–jog, bike, cross-country ski, dance, skip rope, row, stair climb swim, skate, in-line skating, endurance games
Resistance-Weight Training	8–10 exercises, 2–3 times per week
Flexibility	Include warm-up and cool-down stretches

• **Figure 3.12**   *Example of a Personal Fitness Prescription for Fitness in Young Adults.*

REMEMBER This!

Workout sessions with lower intensity (60 percent) and longer duration (fifty to sixty minutes) will usually cause you to expend more energy than workout sessions of higher intensity (80 percent) and shorter duration (twenty minutes).

Stress Break
. . . .

How we feel about ourselves, and what we believe others think about us, can influence the amount of positive and negative stress in our lives. By organizing our daily routines, improving our self-esteem, or improving our fitness levels, we can greatly improve our ability to deal with stress. Stress is always going to be in our lives, so how we deal with and avoid stress is important.

Here are some ways to deal positively with exercise, improve adherence, and consequently reduce stress:

• Plan your days ahead of time. Don't put things off to the last minute. Decide on the most important things that must get done. Planning ahead can save you a lot of confusion, frustration, and stress.

• Remember that fitness does not happen overnight. It takes time and patience. A consistent, well-organized fitness plan will improve your fitness level. With this kind of plan, reasonable gains are made quickly, and you obtain all the benefits that go along with being fit.

• Eat a sensible diet and follow a consistent workout schedule to reduce body fat and stress.

• Don't set your goals too high. Set short-term goals that will keep you motivated. Don't be in a hurry. You have the rest of your life to be fit!

• Start slowly, and have reasonable goals. You will then be less likely to overtrain. In fact, by progressing slowly, you are more likely to find out that you are capable of many things you didn't believe you could do.

• Remember that being fit is a personal choice. Your choice to be fit should not be determined by others. However, working out can be a pleasant experience to share with a partner who values fitness as much as you do. It is also a great way to meet new friends.

Teacher Support Notes

It is very important to teach students that their personal progress will vary based on their genetics, gender, body composition, initial fitness levels, and how much physical activity or exercise they do. Significant conditioning effects also depend on what you are measuring. For example, significant strength gains may appear in students in 4–6 weeks while significant changes in body composition take longer. It is important to also recognize that if you like to grade on a pre- and posttest basis, some students may not have enough time to achieve (due to slower progression) the standards you might use.

Assess

Use the Section 5 Review questions on the next page to assess students' comprehension of the concepts presented in Section 5.

Enrichment

This activity will allow you to provide a more challenging learning experience for some of your students.

Have students complete the following activity: Keep a training log that records the activities in your personal fitness program. Keep in mind your goals for improvements in fitness. For cardiovascular conditioning, activities that require endurance and stamina are best. For increased strength, weight training and heavy lifting exercises are best. For flexibility, stretching exercises are essential. After each week of participation, list the different types of activities you have participated in for your personal fitness program. Have these activities been consistent with your fitness goals? Reassess your program and take any necessary steps to alter the activities you participate in to be consistent with your fitness goals.

vascular fitness. This walking/jogging program is designed to increase your FIT over time and to provide you with the choice of combining walking and jogging or doing continuous jogging. If you prefer a continuous walking program, you can follow the sample walking conditioning program explained later in Chapter 5. It is hoped, as recommended in Chapter 1, that you are already involved in a cardiovascular conditioning program similar to the one shown in Figure 3.11.

SECTION 5 REVIEW

Answer the following questions on a separate sheet of paper:

1. How do you combine your mode of physical activity with FIT?
2. List a variety of physical activities that are modes of cardiovascular conditioning.

SECTION 6   Cool It Down, Afterward!

The cool-down portion of a personal fitness program should always be done after any moderate or vigorous physical activities or exercises are performed. Like the warm-up, the cool-down is often done too quickly or not at all. A well-designed cool-down will help you recover from physical activity or exercise safely and more effectively.

It is important to lower your heart rate gradually following physical activity or exercise. This gradual decrease in heart rate will help you prevent blood pooling in the lower body. **Blood pooling** is a condition, following exercise, in which blood collects in the large veins of the legs and lower body (Figure 3.13). It can cause you to become dizzy and feel like you are going to faint because less blood is pumped to your brain. Blood pooling typically follows moderate or vigorous physical activity or exercise, especially if you stop abruptly and just sit or lie down. You can prevent blood pooling by moving about slowly and continuously (walking, standing in place and moving your feet up and down, and jogging slowly) for about three to five minutes following physical activity or exercise. This is called **cardiovascular cool-down**.

blood pooling

a condition, following exercise, in which blood collects in the large veins of the legs and lower body, especially when the exercise is stopped abruptly.

cardiovascular cool-down

a period after exercise in which you try to prevent blood pooling by moving about slowly and continuously for about three to five minutes.

Equipment Options

It is necessary to have the proper equipment available to determine the baseline cardiovascular fitness of a person. The most extensively used pieces of equipment for a P.E. teacher are the whistle and the stopwatch. These generally become the main components during health-fitness field tests. Other pieces of equipment, which are necessary when designing and preparing for a field test, are balance scales, equipment for measuring height, and pedometers.

Balance scales, which come in many different sizes and shapes, measure the

stretching cool-down

a period after cardiovascular cool-down in which you perform stretching exercises for three to five minutes to minimize stiffness and muscle soreness.

Following your three- to five-minute cardiovascular cool-down recovery period, it is important for you to stretch for another three to five minutes to minimize stiffness and muscle soreness. This is called your **stretching cool-down**. Cool-down stretches should use the same static stretching exercises that were discussed for warming up prior to exercise (see the discussion on warm-up). Try designing your own cool-down program in the "Active Mind/Active Body" activity on this page.

• *Cool-down is just as important as warm-up. Be sure to always include a cool-down in each workout session.*

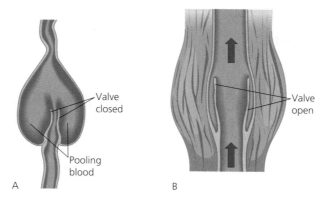

Valve closed

Pooling blood

A

Valve open

B

• **Figure 3.13**   *Blood Pooling. [A] Valves in the large veins (like the legs) close and cause blood to pool while the body is at rest or when there is no muscle contraction. [B] During a proper cool-down the muscles contract against the leg veins and squeeze blood back towards the heart.*

Active Mind! Active Body!

Your Cool-Down Program

Design a cool-down program for a physical activity or exercise that you like to do. Include both a cardiovascular and a stretching component.

weight of an individual. P.E. teachers can perform height measurements by purchasing a balance scale with a height attachment in place, or by purchasing a seamstress tape measure at the local fabric store and affixing it to the wall of the gym. Pedometers measure walking and running distances, and, for schools

without jogging tracks, this piece of equipment is essential. **Take the challenge:** Do an inventory of the equipment that you have available and then price the other equipment listed that you don't have. **Remember:** The cost and effort can be minimal for conducting a fitness field test.

Focus Activities

1. Use Figure 3.13 to discuss the concept of blood pooling.
2. Discuss the difference between the cardiovascular cool-down and a stretching cool-down.
3. Use the Active Mind/Active Body activity on this page.
4. Use Figure 3.14 to summarize the components of a typical conditioning program.

Teach & Apply

Discussion

Use Figure 3.13 to discuss blood pooling. Emphasize what happens to blood flow returning to the heart via the large veins if one stops suddenly after exercise and does not gradually cool-down (blood pools and venous blood flow is reduced).

Assess

Use the Active Mind/Active Body activity on this page to assess students' progress. Then use the Section 6 Review questions to assess students' comprehension of the concepts presented in Section 6.

ANSWERS TO SECTION 6 REVIEW

1. Cool-down properly. Do not suddenly stop and do nothing or sit down after physical activity or exercise. This can cause blood pooling and make you dizzy or feel like you're going to faint.

2. They differ very little because they are very similar in nature. For example, stretching is an important fitness component that is common to both the warm-up and cool-down.

REMEMBER This!

A complete workout includes several components. Figure 3.14 shows an example of the necessary workout considerations you can use to design your personal fitness program.

Component	Activity	Duration (min)
Warm-up	Stretch, low-level calisthenics, walking	10
Muscular Conditioning	Calisthenics, weight training	15-30
Cardiovascular Conditioning	Walk, jog/run, swim, bike, cross-country ski, dance, stair step, in-line skating	20-50
Cool-down	Walk, stretch	5-10

• *Figure 3.14*   *Necessary Workout Considerations.*

SECTION 6 REVIEW

Answer the following questions on a separate sheet of paper:

1. Why and how can you prevent blood pooling?
2. How do warm-up and cool-down activities differ?

Close

Use Figure 3.14 to summarize the typical components that students should identify with a conditioning program.

SUMMARY

An understanding of exercise principles can help you successfully design your personal fitness prescription to achieve Guidelines 1 and 2 in Chapter 1. It is important for you to accumulate time daily or nearly every day in physical activity or exercise to improve and maintain your good health and to achieve Guideline 1.

To achieve Guideline 2, you will need to apply the scientific conditioning principles of overload, specificity, and progression when you plan your workout. To reduce significantly your risk of injuries in your personal fitness program, apply the concepts of FIT:

frequency, intensity, and time/duration. As you gain more experience in the art of applying other scientific principles, such as trainability, detraining, and overtraining, you will be better at modifying your personal fitness program to meet special situations.

When you do a proper warm-up, you will be better prepared to work out safely. Your workout will vary from day to day.

Following your workout, it is very important for you to cool down. A proper cool-down can help you prevent blood pooling and minimize stiffness and muscle soreness.

Reteaching

Name _____ Date _____ Period _____

Chapter 3 Section 6 — Cool It Down, Afterward!

Directions: Answer the questions in the blanks provided.

1. What portion of a personal fitness program should always be done after any moderate or vigorous physical activities or exercises are performed?

   The cool-down

2. How fast should you lower your heart rate following physical activity or exercise?

   The heart rate should be lowered gradually.

3. What is a condition, following exercise, in which blood collects in the large veins of the legs and lower body?

   Blood pooling

4. Explain why blood pooling would cause a person to become dizzy and feel like they are going to faint.

   Less blood is pumped to the brain.

5. What type of cool-down will prevent blood pooling?

   A cardiovascular cool-down

6. What should you do for three to five minutes following your cardiovascular cool-down recovery period to minimize stiffness and muscle soreness?

   A stretching cool-down

7. What type of stretching exercises should be included in cool-down stretches?

   Static body stretches

Reteaching Worksheets   35   © 1997 West Publishing Co.

ABILITY LEVELS

Reteaching

Some students may need help mastering the concepts contained in this section. In your Teacher Resource Package, you will find the reproducible worksheet shown here. This worksheet should help students who have been absent and those needing additional help to improve their comprehension and retention of the content in this section.

Chapter 3 Review

True/False

On a separate sheet of paper, mark each question below either T for True or F for False.

1. The three parts of the overload principle are frequency, intensity, and type.

2. Young adults just beginning an aerobic exercise program should maintain a heart rate of 130 to 150 beats per minute.

3. The workout frequency is the length of time your workout takes each day.

4. Beginning exercisers can prevent injury if their intensity stays between 70 and 90 percent of their maximum heart rate.

5. If the workload on the heart increases, the pulse rate will decrease.

6. A primary purpose of a warm-up is to increase the heart rate gradually prior to exercise.

7. An active warm-up can be either specific or general.

8. Moderate to vigorous exercise sessions should always include a warm-up phase and a cool-down phase.

9. The warm-up phase and cool-down phase can help prevent injury and soreness.

10. Blood pooling can be prevented by sitting down and relaxing after vigorous exercise.

Multiple Choice

1. The overload principle involves which of the following?
   a. an increase in physical activity or exercise above what you normally do
   b. an increase in the improvement you would normally expect
   c. an increase in the changes that occur in your body
   d. an increase in the negative effects that occur in your body

2. Your exercise intensity is affected by which of the following?
   a. level of fitness
   b. fitness goals
   c. length of each workout session
   d. number of workout sessions per week
   e. all of the above

3. Which of the following would be recorded in an exercise record book?
   a. food eaten
   b. FIT
   c. goals
   d. all of the above

4. Potential differences in physical fitness improvement between two people training the same way for the same length of time is due to which of the following?
   a. overload
   b. specificity
   c. progression
   d. trainability

5. Which principle refers to the rate at which you change your personal fitness prescription?
   a. specificity
   b. progression
   c. overload
   d. mode

6. Which of the following is not a symptom of overtraining?
   a. constant muscle soreness
   b. mental burnout
   c. high performance
   d. chronic fatigue

Answers

True/False

1. F
2. F
3. F
4. F
5. F
6. T
7. T
8. T
9. T
10. F

Multiple Choice

1. a.
2. e.
3. d.
4. d.
5. b.
6. c.

Enrichment

This activity will allow you to provide a more challenging learning experience for some of your students.

Have students complete the following activity: Answer the following questions to assess the frequency, intensity, and time of your own personal fitness program:

a. What was my beginning level of fitness when I started my personal fitness program?

b. What goals have I set for myself in planning my personal fitness program?

c. How frequently have I been able to participate in my personal fitness program in the past several weeks?

d. How has my frequency, intensity, and time of participation changed from the beginning of my program to now?

e. What have been the biggest obstacles to participation in my personal fitness program?

Multiple Choice
(continued)

7. d.
8. e.
9. a.
10. b.

Discussion

1. Generally, the harder you work the higher your heart rate will be. You should also rate harder work higher than lighter work on the perceived exertion scale. Therefore, the higher your physical activity heart rate, the higher your perceived exertion number will be.

2. Detraining occurs when you have to discontinue a personal fitness program for extended periods of time. Signs of detraining include weakness or lost fitness levels.

3. Generally, the frequency, intensity, and time/duration must be considered together when planning a personal fitness prescription. For example, you'll find that the higher your intensity, the shorter your time/duration will probably be and you may not recover as fast from day-to-day activity. This might require you to adjust your frequency in order to fully recover.

Vocabulary Experience

_6_ blood pooling
_4_ static body stretch
_2_ overload principle
_1_ FIT
_3_ mode
_5_ frequency

Chapter 3 Review

7. Which of the following is an example of a passive warm-up?

  a. toe touch
  b. walk around the gym
  c. basketball layups
  d. whirlpool bath

8. Which of the following is a static stretching technique?

  a. slowly stretching
  b. smoothly stretching
  c. sustained stretching
  d. none of the above
  e. a, b, and c

9. Which of the following would _not_ be a specific warm-up for basketball?

  a. jumping jacks
  b. layups
  c. passing drills
  d. free throw shooting

10. Which cool-down procedure is best for preventing blood pooling?

  a. leg stretches
  b. slow walk
  c. arm stretches
  d. deep breathing techniques

Discussion

1. Explain how the perceived exertion scale and your heart rate can be used to determine your exercise intensity. How are they similar?

2. Identify and explain the common signs of detraining.

3. Explain how each of the components of the overload principle (FIT) are related to one another.

Vocabulary Experience

Match the correct term in Column A to the definition in Column B by writing the appropriate number in each blank.

Column A	Column B
____ blood pooling	**1.** Frequency, intensity, and time/duration.
____ static body stretch	**2.** The need to increase the amount of activity or exercise above what you normally do to improve your fitness level.
____ overload principle	**3.** The type of activity or exercise you do.
____ FIT	**4.** A slow, smooth, sustained stretch.
____ mode	**5.** How often you engage in physical activity or exercise.
____ frequency	**6.** A condition in which blood collects in the large veins of the legs and lower body.

CRITICAL THINKING

Have students pair with a parent, school staff member, friend, or classmate for a four-week "exercise experience." Students should begin their experience by analyzing their partners' lifestyle, time constraints, schedule, needs, etc. Then students will design a four-week program of diet and exercise for their partners. Students are responsible to keep a daily log in which they record distance traveled, calories spent, weight lost, etc. They are also responsible to motivate and monitor their partners on a daily basis.

Critical Thinking

1. How can you influence your personal fitness progression by changing your FIT? Explain your answer.

2. If a friend tells you that she started an exercise program to improve her physical fitness but quit after two weeks because she didn't see any improvements, what would you tell her? Why wasn't she successful? How can she improve her chances for personal fitness success?

3. What advice can you give someone you know who has the symptoms of being an exercise zealot? He is concerned that if he misses a workout for one or two days, he will get out of shape. Explain your answer.

Case Study — David—Part 2

Do you remember David from Chapter 2? He is an overweight fifteen-year-old who has lived all his life in Anchorage, Alaska. His father recently made a career change that required the family to move to central Texas. David has never been very athletic or physically active, and he has not paid much attention to his health or personal fitness.

Now that he has moved to a much warmer climate and the different weather conditions of Texas, he would like to make some improvements in his fitness habits (behaviors). He feels he should take advantage of his new environment by starting a physical activity and exercise program. His goals are to lose 20 pounds and to improve his cardiovascular fitness levels. David needs your personal fitness expertise again.

Design a beginning physical activity and exercise plan for David. Prepare a detailed two-week warm-up, workout, and cool-down program for David. Try to be as specific as possible when choosing activities and exercises. It is possible to design many programs that would benefit David. Use your knowledge and imagination to create a safe and effective personal fitness program.

KEYS TO HELP YOU

The following tips may help you design David's program:
- Consider his history of personal activity and exercise.
- Consider his current fitness level.
- Consider his needs and goals.
- Determine a reasonable intensity, duration, and frequency for a beginning program.

Four weeks is suggested as being a realistic time frame for this activity. At the conclusion of four weeks, have students discuss with their partners the results/benefits that have been attained.

Walk: The Four Seasons by Rob Sweetgall (Creative Walking, Inc.—Walking and Cross-Training Logbook) is suggested for use with this activity.

Critical Thinking

1. When you change your FIT you can either overload the body for continued improvements in fitness, keep it the same for maintenance purposes, or decrease it to recover from an illness, for example.

2. She didn't stay with the program long enough to see the benefits. She wasn't successful because she probably worked too hard, too soon. She may have unrealistic expectations as well. She can improve her chances for success by learning more about personal fitness from someone like you.

3. Encourage him to lighten up a bit about his physical activity and exercise program. Tell him that he will not lose any significant fitness by missing a day or two of conditioning. In fact, doing too much physical activity or exercise can have negative effects.

KEYS TO CASE STUDY

Programs will vary but should include the material included in Figures 3.11, 3.12, and 3.14 from the text.

RESOURCES

HANDOUTS

A chapter test is provided for Chapter 3 in your Teacher Resource Package.

Chapter Overview

Chapter 4 is 52 pages long and divided into the four sections listed to the right. Major learning outcomes of the chapter are also listed to the right. Briefly, this chapter introduces students to the two specific parts of physical fitness. It emphasizes the differences between skill-related fitness and health-related fitness. It also introduces students to a variety of both skill- and health-related fitness evaluations that will allow students to assess their personal fitness levels.

Teacher Resource Materials

In the Teacher Resource Package accompanying the textbook, you will find the following material to help you teach this chapter.

Activity Sheets

Reteaching Worksheets are provided in the Teacher Resource Package for Sections 1 and 2 of this chapter. Handouts are also provided for the Active Mind/ Active Body activity, Evaluating Fitness Levels.

Chapter 4

Skill-related and Health-related Fitness

PACING CHART

You could easily spend ten days teaching this chapter if students read the entire chapter, do the Active Mind/Active Body activities, and complete several of the handouts from the Teacher Resource Package. However, you can cover the material in this chapter in six days. It is recommended that physical activity be a regular part of each class period (20 to 30 minutes minimum). The following are some examples of how you can cover the main topics in the chapter if you are pressed for time.

Contents

1. Whats and Whys of Skill-related Fitness
2. Whats and Whys of Health-related Fitness
3. Skill-related Fitness Evaluations
4. Health-related Fitness Evaluations

Outcomes

After reading and studying this chapter, you will be able to:

1. Explain how health-related fitness and skill-related fitness are related to physical fitness.
2. Explain the differences between health-related fitness and skill-related fitness.
3. Identify and explain examples of skill-related fitness.
4. Identify and explain examples of health-related fitness.
5. Identify and explain examples of skill-related fitness evaluations.
6. Identify and explain examples of health-related fitness evaluations.
7. Describe your personal fitness profile.

Key Terms

After reading and studying this chapter, you will be able to understand and provide practical definitions for the following terms:

skill-related fitness	power	energy cost
agility	reaction time	muscular endurance
balance	health-related fitness	body composition
center of gravity	cardiovascular fitness	percentage of body fat
coordination	flexibility	kilocalorie
speed	muscular strength	energy expenditure

105

Transparencies/Masters

A transparency or master is provided in the Teacher Resource Package for each of the following figures: 4.1, 4.2, 4.3, 4.10, 4.11, 4.12. A transparency or master is also provided for Active Mind/Active Body activities:
- Skill-related Fitness
- Health-related Fitness
- Evaluating Fitness Levels

and for Fitness Check Activities:
- Evaluating Skill-related Fitness
- Evaluating Health-related Fitness

Discuss the Photo

Ask students to discuss why it is important to consider a variety of physical activities for good fitness. Tell them this chapter will present the eleven components of physical fitness and ways to evaluate an individual's level of physical fitness.

CHAPTER 4

Time	Suggestions
Day 1	Assign students to read Sections 1 and 2 prior to class. In class, do the Active Mind/Active Body activities on pages 112–113 and 122–123. Include discussion about photos and figures.
Days 2,3	Assign students to read Section 3 prior to class. In class, discuss the skill-related evaluations and their purposes. Have students take the skill-related evaluations.
Days 4,5	Assign students to read Section 4 prior to class. In class, discuss the health-related evaluations and their purposes. Have students begin taking the health-related fitness evaluations.
Day 6	Continue the health-related fitness evaluations. Do the Active Mind/Active Body activity on pp. 149–151.

Focus

Outcomes

In **Section 1**, students will learn:

1. To explain how health-related fitness and skill-related fitness are related to physical fitness.
2. To explain the differences between health-related fitness and skill-related fitness.
3. To identify and explain components of skill-related fitness.
4. To demonstrate physical activities associated with components of skill-related fitness.

Focus Activities

1. Identify the eleven parts of physical fitness.
2. Explore each of the skill-related fitness components in detail.

INTRODUCTION

*B*y now you understand the need for regular physical activity or exercise and, it is hoped, value that need. Chapter 4 will guide you through a variety of physical activities and physical evaluations that can help you determine your path to developing and maintaining moderate to high levels of physical fitness.

What is physical fitness? Is it the high cardiovascular capacity of a marathoner, or is it the sculptured body of Arnold Schwarzenegger? Maybe your picture of a physically fit person is an Olympic gymnast or a highly skilled soccer player. The truth is that you do not need to be an athlete to be physically fit.

Many components contribute to the state of being physically fit. These components can be categorized as skill-related fitness or health-related fitness (Figure 4.1). Skill-related fitness, or performance fitness, has six parts, which are primarily associated with the ability to perform successfully during games and sports. Health-related fitness has five parts, which are primarily associated with disease prevention and functional health. You need both skill- and health-related fitness, because both types of fitness can contribute to your ability to do everyday life activities. Activities such as walking, climbing stairs, bending over, lifting things, or any of the recreational activities that many of us do daily require some degree of physical fitness. This means that our bodies will perform and function more efficiently and effectively if we maintain acceptable levels of physical fitness.

This course places a greater emphasis on the health-related aspects of physical fitness than on the skill-related aspects. Knowing how to correctly perform health-related physical activities and evaluations can help you prepare for a long, happy, productive, and fit life. Health-related fitness is an obtainable goal that *A*ny *B*ody *C*an reach.

REMEMBER This!

*P*hysical fitness depends on physical abilities that allow you to perform daily physical tasks effectively, with enough energy reserves to engage in recreational activities or to meet unexpected physical challenges. Physical fitness is an outcome of a physically active lifestyle or exercise program that occurs over time.

SECTION 1   Whats and Whys of Skill-related Fitness

skill-related fitness

the ability to perform successfully during games and sports; also called *performance fitness*. Skill-related fitness has six components: agility, balance, coordination, power, speed, and reaction time.

Skill-related fitness, or performance fitness, includes the six components of physical fitness that are often associated with games and sports. Also, many of the chores and jobs we do daily require the use of one or more of these six physical abilities. The six skill-related components of fitness are agility, balance, coordination, speed, power, and reaction time (Figure 4.2).

The highly skilled athlete will possess a high level of ability in most, if not all, of the six components. The weekend athlete, often referred to as the "weekend warrior," will also possess a certain level of pro-

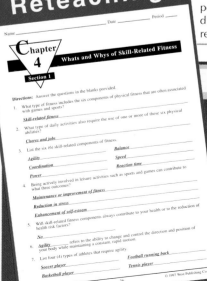

Reteaching

ABILITY LEVELS

Reteaching

Some students may need help mastering the concepts contained in this section. In your Teacher Resource Package, you will find the reproducible worksheet shown here. This worksheet should help students who have been absent and those needing additional help to improve their comprehension and retention of the content in this section.

Skill-related Fitness

Agility
Balance
Coordination
Speed
Power
Reaction Time

Health-related Fitness

Cardiovascular Fitness
Muscular Endurance
Flexibility
Muscular Strength
Body Composition

• **Figure 4.1**
Components of Fitness.

• *Prior to his movie career, Arnold Schwarzenegger was a body-builder. Do you think he is exhibiting health-related or skill-related fitness in this photo?*

3. Examine how skill-related components are utilized in a variety of activities and sports.
4. Use the Active Mind/Active Body activity on pages 112–113 to introduce students to the physical requirements of skill-related fitness.

Teach & Apply

Discussion

• Have students respond to the statement, "You have to be an athlete to be physically fit."
• Have students discuss which of the eleven physical fitness components are necessary to be a good athlete.
• Discuss Healthy People 2000, Objective 1.5.

Healthy People 2000

Objective 1.5—Reduce to no more than 15 percent the proportion of people aged 6 and older

ficiency in many of the skill-related components. This supports the belief that people tend to be involved in activities and games they do well. Unfortunately, too many adults do not participate in either skill- or health-related activities.

Being actively involved in leisure activities, such as sports and games, can contribute to the maintenance or improvement of physical fitness, a reduction in stress, and an enhancement of self-esteem. In fact, one of the main goals of the *Healthy People 2000* national health objectives is to get more people participating in physical activities during their leisure time.

Even though the skill-related fitness components can contribute greatly to your success in sports and games, they will not necessarily contribute to your health or to the reduction of health risk factors. However, a more complete understanding of each of the skill-related components can positively contribute to your personal fitness. Let's explore each of the skill-related fitness components in more detail.

Agility

The ability to change and control the direction and position of your body while maintaining a constant, rapid motion is **agility**. The soccer player, football running back, basketball player, and tennis player will all require agility. Other skill-related components of fitness, such as speed and coordination, may influence your level of agility.

• **Figure 4.2** *Skill-related Fitness.*

agility

the ability to change and control the direction and position of your body while maintaining a constant, rapid motion.

Enrichment   *This activity will allow you to provide a more challenging learning experience for some of your students.*

Have students complete the following activity: Conduct a survey of several athletes in a particular sport. Ask them to rate the contribution of each of the six components of skill-related fitness to success in their sport. Score each component by awarding six points to the highest-rated component, five for the next highest rated, four for the next highest rated, and so on. Add up the scores for each component to determine which one(s) contribute most to high performance in that sport. Repeat this process for several different sports. Write a report on your results.

• *Most people will never obtain the levels of skill-related fitness demonstrated by these athletes. Any Body Can, however, obtain good to better levels of health-related fitness.*

who engage in no leisure time physical activity.

The National Association of Sports and Physical Education (NASPE) developed a four-part definition for a physically educated person. The first criterion is to have learned skills necessary to perform a variety of physical activities. The second criteria is to be physically fit. Therefore, it is important for students to understand how the skill-related components of fitness can contribute to overall physical fitness.

Teaching Strategies

• Use the transparency/ master of Figure 4.1 to identify each of the physical fitness components.
• Use the transparency/ master of Figure 4.2 to identify each of the skill-related components.
• Use the transparency/ master of Figure 4.3 to discuss how each of the skill-related fitness components are utilized by a variety of activities and sports.
• Refer to specific figures in the chapter as you discuss each of the skill-related fitness components. (Agility— Figure 4.4, 4.18, and 4.20; Balance—Figure 4.5, 4.22, and 4.24; Coordination— Figure 4.6, 4.26, and 4.28; Power—Figure 4.7, 4.30, and 4.32; Speed—Figure 4.8, 4.34, and 4.36; Reaction Time—Figure 4.9 and 4.38.)

balance

the ability to control or stabilize your equilibrium while moving or staying still.

center of gravity

the area of your body that determines how your weight is distributed.

coordination

the ability to use your eyes and ears to determine and direct the smooth movement of your body.

Balance

The ability to control or stabilize your body while moving or staying still is **balance**. A simple act such as walking requires a great deal of balance. The gymnast, golfer, or ice skater all require well-developed balance.

Your **center of gravity** is the area of your body that determines how your weight is distributed. Your center of gravity is probably near your pelvic region (hips) and should stay over the base of support, which is your feet. You can improve your balance and biomechanics in many physical activities or exercises by shifting your center of gravity. For example, shifting your body weight while swinging a golf club would change your center of gravity and improve your golf shot.

Coordination

The ability to use your eyes and ears to determine and direct the smooth movement of your body (hands, feet, arms, head, and so on) is **coordination**. The jogger, soccer player, basketball player, and volleyball player, for example, all require coordination. Coordination requires using a combination of different muscle groups at once. Combining more than one set of muscle movements takes practice.

Across the Disciplines

Literature

Courage, self-reliance, endurance, physical skills, and survival are recurrent themes in literature for adolescents. Many of these books are award-winning classics that portray youth in conflict or overwhelmed by insurmountable environmental barriers. They are stories in which the young heroes and heroines must overcome fear, indecision, and self-doubt after they find themselves lost, stranded, or abandoned without adult supervision or guidance. A combi-

speed

the ability to move your body or parts of your body swiftly.

power

the ability to move your body parts swiftly while at the same time applying the maximum force of your muscles.

Other components of fitness, such as speed, reaction time, and agility, may influence your level of coordination.

Speed

The ability to move your body or parts of your body swiftly is **speed**. Foot speed is usually measured over a short and straight distance, usually less than 200 meters. Other speed evaluations might include hand or arm speed. The baseball pitcher, boxer, sprinter, and volleyball spiker all require specific kinds of speed. Certain types of muscle fibers (muscle cells), which are determined by hereditary factors, can influence your speed. Reaction time and muscular strength may also influence your speed.

Power

The ability to move your body parts swiftly (speed) while at the same time applying the maximum force of your muscles (strength) is **power**. The shot-putter, long jumper, power lifter, and swimmer all require high levels of power. Some degree of power is also important for everyday activities, such as lifting heavy items or making quick or sudden body movements. Strength is a fitness component that can be improved over time. As you increase your strength, you can increase your power. Biomechanical movement techniques can also affect your power, which means you can gain power by practicing your technique.

Stress Break

Many Americans regularly participate in games and sports in an effort to reduce their stress levels. However, you may find that the challenges of being a part of a competitive team, the intensity of competition, and the pressures of peer criticism often create stress instead of relieve it.

Competitive activities may be part of your personal fitness today, but you will find that as you age, health-related activities will become a bigger part of your personal fitness routine. Learn how to use your health-related fitness activities to help control daily stress. You will learn that these activities not only can help you get through today's problems but also can help you live a healthier, happier, and longer life.

• *These athletes possess extraordinary levels of speed and power.*

Discussion

• Have students identify what makes someone a great athlete. Ask, Why can't everyone who tries hard become a successful athlete? How important is practice?
• Discuss how possessing great speed or jumping ability is important to athletic performance but will provide little or no protection from heart disease and other chronic diseases.

Activity

Have students make posters of skill-related components.

Stress Break

Have students read the Stress Break and discuss how athletics can cause both positive and negative stress.

Teacher Readings

Kenney, W. L., Senior Editor, *ACSM Guidelines for Exercise Testing and Prescription,* American College of Sports Medicine, 4th Edition, Lea & Febiger, Philadelphia, PA: 1995.

nation of both skill-related and health-related fitness skills can be identified as either inhibitors or contributors to survival. You may wish to choose passages from some of these books to read aloud to the class and then discuss them with the students. Interesting adolescent literature featuring survival skills includes *Island of the Blue Dolphins,* by Scott O'Dell; *Lord of the Flies,* by William Golding; *Frozen Fire: A Tale of Courage,* by James Houston; *Sarah Bishop,* by Scott O'Dell; *Coming Back Alive,* by Dennis J. Reader; *In the Shadow of the Bear,* by Judith St. George; and *Almost Too Late,* by Elmo Wortman.

CNN® Health and Fitness Updates

You can update your coverage of health and fitness topics, as well as spark lively classroom discussion and deeper understanding, by using the **CNN Health and Fitness Updates.** These video updates are produced by Turner Educational Services, using the resources of CNN, the world's first 24-hour, all-news network.

With the introduction of the **CNN Health and Fitness Updates,** West Educational Publishing is proud to be the exclusive partner of CNN for textbook/video integration in high school fitness. By making use of the **CNN Health and Fitness Updates** you can bring the power of CNN, the network known for providing in-depth, live coverage and analysis of breaking news events, to your fitness class.

For assistance in using and incorporating the **CNN Health and Fitness Updates** into your classroom presentations, see the *Classroom Guide to the CNN Health and Fitness Updates.* The **CNN Health and Fitness Updates** are available with West Educational Publishing's *Foundations of Personal Fitness* by Don Rainey and Tinker Murray.

reaction time

the ability to react or respond quickly to what you hear, see, or feel.

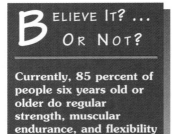

BELIEVE IT? ... OR NOT?

Currently, 85 percent of people six years old or older do regular strength, muscular endurance, and flexibility exercises.

See page 152 for answer.

• *Heredity is a major factor in determining your performance skills.*

Reaction Time

The ability to react or respond quickly to what you hear, see, or feel is **reaction time**. The more quickly you respond, the better your reaction time. Good reaction time is required for sprinters and swimmers, who must react to starts. The tennis player, boxer, and hockey goalie all require quick reaction times. Factors such as motivation, fatigue, and practice can influence reaction time.

Figure 4.3 lists the degree of benefits for skill-related fitness associated with different physical activities and sports. You can survey the figure and determine which of the physical activities you can participate in to improve or maintain your skill-related fitness.

Factors That Can Influence Skill-related Performance

Why are some individuals capable of outstanding physical performance? How can the marathoner run nonstop for 26 miles and average under five minutes per mile? What enables the Olympic weight lifter to lift incredible amounts of weight? Why aren't we all capable of such superhuman physical talents? Are there certain factors that determine these talents? Yes, there are!

Pick Your Parents Well.   Heredity is a major factor in determining performance potential. Your physical characteristics, such as height, weight, and body type, are generally similar to those of your parents. Your physical capabilities, such as speed and reaction time, are also inherited from your parents. Once you are fully grown, it is unlikely that you will ever see a drastic improvement in either of these components.

Practice, Practice, Practice.   Even if you have inherited a potential for great physical abilities, you still need to practice specific skills over and over to reach the level of performance exhibited by top athletes. Practice is important to anyone who wants to improve skills in a specific game or sport. Agility, coordination, power, and balance are skill-related components that can be improved through practice. How often and how specifically you practice will determine, to a great extent, how successful you will become. Later in the chapter you will conduct self-evaluations for skill-related fitness. You will notice that often one skill-related ability will also require the use of other skill-related components.

You can learn how to survey your skill-related fitness levels by completing the "Active Mind/Active Body" activities (pages 112 and 113) for each of the six skill-related fitness components. These activities are designed to introduce you to the skill-related fitness concepts.

Special Needs

The six skill-related components of fitness are areas of particular concern for the disabled population. Motor skill fitness levels that are low can be a result of many different factors that may inhibit efficient movement.

Balance is an area of major concern for special students. Since most motor activities rely on balance for successful performance, the disabled population is at a tremendous disadvantage when skill-related activities are involved. Maintaining a center of gravity is difficult for those students who have physical abnormali-

• *Soccer players must have high levels of both skill- and health-related fitness.*

Activity/Sport and Primary Emphasis*	Agility	Balance	Reaction Time	Power	Speed	Coordination
Archery S	*	***	*	*	*	****
Backpacking H	**	**	*	**	*	**
Badminton S	***	**	***	**	***	****
Ballet B	****	****	**	***	*	****
Baseball S	***	***	****	****	***	****
Basketball B	****	***	****	****	***	****
Bicycling H	*	****	**	*	**	**
Bowling S	**	***	*	**	**	****
Canoeing B	*	***	**	***	*	***
Circuit training H	**	**	*	***	**	**
Dance, aerobic H	***	**	**	*	*	****
Dance, line S	***	**	**	*	**	***
Dance, social H	***	**	**	*	**	***
Fitness calisthenics H	***	**	*	**	*	**
Football S	****	***	****	****	****	***
Golf (walking) B	**	**	*	***	*	****
Gymnastics B	****	****	***	****	**	****
Handball H	****	**	***	***	***	****
Hiking H	**	**	*	**	*	**
Horseback riding S	***	***	**	*	*	***
Interval training H	*	**	*	*	**	**
Jogging H	*	**	*	*	*	**
Judo S	****	***	****	****	****	****
Karate S	****	***	****	****	****	****
Mountain climbing H	***	****	**	***	*	****
Pool; billiards S	**	**	*	**	*	***
Racquetball; paddleball B	****	**	***	**	***	****
Rope jumping H	***	**	**	**	*	***
Rowing H	***	**	*	****	**	****
Sailing S	***	***	***	**	*	***
Skating, ice B	***	****	**	**	***	***
Skating, in-line B	***	****	*	**	***	***
Skiing, cross-country B	***	**	*	****	**	****
Skiing, downhill B	****	****	***	***	*	****
Soccer B	****	**	***	***	***	****
Softball (fast pitch) S	***	**	****	***	***	****
Softball (slow pitch) S	**	**	***	***	***	****
Surfing B	****	****	***	***	*	****
Swimming H	***	**	*	**	*	***
Table tennis S	**	**	***	**	**	***
Tennis B	***	**	***	***	***	****
Volleyball B	***	**	***	**	**	****
Walking H	*	**	*	*	*	**
Waterskiing S	***	***	*	**	*	***
Weight training H	*	**	*	**	*	**

*Primary Emphasis		Better – ****
S = Skill-related Fitness.		Good – ***
H = Health-related Fitness.		Fair – **
B = Both Skill- and Health-related Fitness.		Low – *

• **Figure 4.3** *Skill-related Benefits.*

Teacher Support Notes

Fitness tests can be a sensitive issue for many students. Many may be reluctant to do their best or even attempt these tests for fear they will be ridiculed by their classmates or, even worse, their instructor. It is important to establish a climate that will allow students to feel safe from embarrassment and that encourages them to put forth their best efforts on each evaluation. Tell students that they are not competing against any other classmate and that their scores will be used for development of their personal fitness profiles and to assess improvement over time.

Teacher Readings

Durstine, L. J., King, A. C., Painter, P. L., Roitman, J. L., Zwiren, L. D., and Kenney, W. L., Editors. *Resource Manual for Guidelines for Exercise Testing and Prescription,* 2nd Edition. Lea & Febiger, Philadelphia, PA: 1993.

ties that affect their posture.

The lack of coordination due to loss of vision or hearing can be expected. These students rely on other sensory input to sustain balance and perform skills that require coordination. Coordination is a central nervous system process, so if there is nervous system damage, performing activities requiring this component is difficult. Speed, agility, and reaction time are all products of central nervous system integration, so it can be expected that those disabled students will experience problems.

The Active Mind/Active Body activities on pp. 112–113 are not appropriate for the disabled population.

Active **Mind!**
Active **Body!**

Explain to the class that this activity is only designed to introduce them to the different parts of skill-related fitness. It is not a test for a grade nor is it a play activity. The activities should be conducted safely and responsibly. Have fun, but be serious about understanding the concepts.

- Divide the class into pairs.
- Demonstrate each of the activities to be performed.
- Provide a safe environment for conducting all activities.

Agility. Picking Up Lines
This activity may require some warm-up first. Use tape or markers to prepare the course. Try to avoid a slick surface. Have partners count out five seconds.

Balance. Blind One-Leg Stand
Make sure students are clear of any wall or obstacle that could be hit if they fall. Have partners count aloud for ten seconds. Students may attempt the activity more than once.

Coordination. Foot and Ball Volley
A variety of ball sizes may be used. Kicks should not be hard and students should be properly spaced to avoid being hit with a ball. Tell students that this is a test of foot-eye coordination.

Active **Mind!**
Active **Body!**

Exploring Skill-related Fitness

Picking Up Lines

One test of agility is an activity called *picking up lines.* Mark off two parallel lines 5 feet apart. Start at one line. Run to the other line and bend over to touch the line with your hand. Reverse your direction and return to the start, again bending over to touch the line. Go to the other line and back twice without stopping (Figure 4.4). Try to accomplish this in five seconds or less.

- *Figure 4.4*   Picking Up Lines (agility).

Blind One-Leg Stand

To test your balance, do the blind one-leg stand. Stand on one foot. Pull your other leg up and back. Close your eyes (Figure 4.5). Do not wobble or hop. Try to hold this position for ten seconds.

- *Figure 4.5*   Blind One-Leg Stand (balance).

- *Figure 4.6*   Foot and Ball Volley (coordination).

Foot and Ball Volley

Try the foot and ball volley to test your coordination (Figure 4.6). Drop a round ball (tennis ball size or bigger) over your dominant foot or the one you usually kick with. Try to bounce the ball off your foot three consecutive times. Now try it with your nondominant foot.

Wellness Connection

You might want to share the following with your students:

As a high school student you may feel that skill-related fitness is more important to you than health-related fitness. After all, skill-related aspects of physical fitness are what make you a better track

runner or basketball, volleyball, football, or softball player. But how long will these competitive activities stay important in your life? They might be important through high school or even several years beyond that. But soon you will be in your twenties and have a job, maybe

Standing Broad Jump

You can test your power with the standing broad jump (Figure 4.7). Lie on the floor. Mark off two lines, one at the top of your head and one at your feet. Now stand up and start at either end. Jump out toward the other line as far as possible. Try to jump past your height.

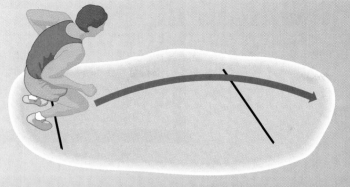

• **Figure 4.7** *Standing Broad Jump (power).*

 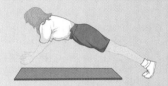 

• **Figure 4.8** *Push and Clap (speed).*

Push and Clap

To test your speed, do the push and clap (Figure 4.8). Lie face down on the floor in a push-up position. Place your hands to the sides of your chest. Push your body up in the air, and try to clap your hands twice before returning to the floor. Use a mat if one is available.

Hand Slap

Test your reaction time with the hand slap (Figure 4.9). Stand facing a partner. Have your partner place his or her hands palms up. Place your hands palms down over your partner's hands. Allow 4 inches of space between your hands and your partner's. Your partner will quickly attempt to touch the top of your hands. Try to remove your hands before being touched.

• **Figure 4.9** *Hand Slap (reaction time).*

Power. Standing Broad Jump

The activity area should be a smooth, nonslip surface. Students should wear shoes with a nonslip sole. Have students use their arms as well as their legs to propel their bodies. Partners should observe and mark the distance of the jumps. Repeated attempts are allowed.

Speed. Push and Clap

This activity is intended to introduce the concept of hand speed. Have students perform this activity on a mat. This activity will require adequate upper body strength, so you need to encourage students that one clap is good and two claps is great.

Reaction Time. Hand Slap

Many students are familiar with this activity. However, it is necessary to remind them that the activity is not intended for hitting someone hard, but only a touch.

Assess

Use the Active Mind/Active Body activities on pages 112–113 to assess student understanding of the different skill-related components of physical fitness. Then use the Section 1 Review questions to assess students' comprehension of the concepts presented in Section 1.

a family, a mortgage, and many new responsibilities. Now you no longer play football, run competitive track, or even consider being involved in those activities that seemed so important in high school. However, with the average life expectancy well in the seventies, you still have over 50 years of life ahead of you. At this stage of your life, health-related fitness, which puts an emphasis on your functional health, becomes much more meaningful than skill-related fitness.

ANSWERS TO SECTION 1 REVIEW

1. *Agility*—the ability to change and control the direction and position of your body while maintaining a constant, rapid motion. *Balance*—the ability to control or stabilize your body while moving or staying still. *Coordination*—the ability to use your eyes and ears to determine and direct the smooth movement of your body. *Speed*—the ability to move your body or parts of your body swiftly. *Power*—the ability to move your body parts swiftly while at the same time applying the maximum force of your muscles. *Reaction time*—the ability to react or respond quickly to what you hear, see, or feel.

2. Heredity is a major factor in determining your performance potential. Speed and reaction time are primarily inherited. Practicing a skill over and over can improve skills such as agility, coordination, and balance. How often and how specifically you train will determine some of your success.

SECTION 1 REVIEW

Answer the following questions on a separate sheet of paper:

1. List and define each of the six skill-related fitness components.

2. Identify and explain two factors that can influence your skill-related fitness levels.

SECTION 2 | Whats and Whys of Health-related Fitness

health-related fitness

physical fitness primarily associated with disease prevention and functional health. Health-related fitness has five components: cardiovascular fitness, body composition, flexibility, muscular strength, and muscular endurance.

cardiovascular fitness

the ability to work continuously for extended periods of time.

● *Figure 4.10*
Health-related Fitness.

Health-related fitness is a type of physical fitness that emphasizes physical activities and exercise that will improve or help you maintain your functional health. The five components of health-related fitness are cardiovascular fitness, flexibility, muscular strength, muscular endurance, and body composition (Figure 4.10). Let's explore each of the health-related components of physical fitness in more detail.

Cardiovascular Fitness

Cardiovascular fitness refers to your ability to work continuously for extended periods of time (for example, walking briskly for twenty to forty minutes, cycling 5 to 10 miles, or in-line skating for thirty minutes to an hour). Your level of cardiovascular fitness depends on the ability of your heart to pump large amounts of blood to the muscles and organs of your body. It also is related to how well your lungs function and how well your blood vessels can deliver blood (oxygen) to your body. Examples of cardiovascular fitness activities might include walking, hiking, jogging, dancing, skipping rope, rowing, swimming, skating, and endurance games or sports.

Moderate to high levels of cardiovascular fitness are associated with increased longevity and reduced risk for cardiovascular disease and other hypokinetic conditions (see Chapter 1). Moderate to high levels of cardiovascular fitness are also associated with improved functional health.

Cardiovascular fitness can be improved simply by accumulating several minutes per day of activity in play, games, sports, work, getting to school, recreation, or planned exercise. Your cardiovascular fitness level is also determined to some extent by other factors, such

CRITICAL THINKING

Have students keep a seven-day journal of activities, in which they record all types of physical activity they perform. You might want to devise a journal entry sheet for students to use. The entry sheet might contain columns for the date, time of day, type of activity, length of participation (in minutes), and a blank column. At the end of the seven-day period, have students examine the types of activities they performed and categorize them according to skill-related or health-related activities. (They can list this in the blank column.) After they have

flexibility

the range of motion that your joints have during movement.

• *Maintaining high levels of flexibility will help you prevent injuries.*

BELIEVE IT? ... OR NOT?

When males and females were surveyed about their exercise habits, it was found that men were more likely to jog and use exercise equipment, whereas females preferred to do more walking, swimming, biking, aerobics, and calisthenics.

See page 152 for answer.

as age, heredity, gender, activity level, and body composition. You will learn more about cardiovascular fitness in Chapter 5.

Flexibility

Flexibility refers to the range of motion that your joints have during movement. Skin and connective tissue (such as tendons and ligaments) can restrict normal flexibility if not used regularly. Injured joints and excessive body fat can also restrict normal flexibility. Adults often lose their normal levels of flexibility because of the aging process and decreased participation in physical activities and exercise. Poor flexibility is associated with the development of many types of injuries, including lower back problems, muscle pulls, and muscle strains.

Good functional health depends on your improving or maintaining the range of motion (varying degrees of motion allowed) of your joints. You can do this by engaging in stretching activities that increase your muscular strength and muscular endurance, as well as improve your flexibility.

A moderate to high level of flexibility is important to you for efficient daily physical movements and can help reduce your risks for muscle and bone injuries. Moderate to high levels of flexibility can improve performance fitness and reduce some types of muscle sore-

• *Not all of us can become as flexible as this diver, but we can all strive for our own maximum flexibility.*

determined whether the activity is skill or health related, they should determine which components are involved. Under skill-related activities, they should list agility, balance, coordination, speed, power, reaction time, or a combination of components. Under health-related activities, they should list cardiovascular fitness, muscular endurance, flexibility, muscular strength, body composition, or a combination of components. Students should then analyze their own lifestyles and create different ways to improve their levels of activity to increase health-related fitness.

Close

Divide the class into groups and have them list daily activities they do that involve skill-related fitness components. Then have them list which components are involved in each activity.

Focus

Outcomes

In **Section 2** students will learn:

1. To identify and explain components of health-related fitness.
2. Why health-related fitness is important to their health.
3. Which lifetime activities are most often used by active adults.
4. To demonstrate physical activities associated with components of health-related fitness.

Focus Activities

1. Identify and explore the five health-related fitness components.
2. Examine how each of the health-related components contributes to better daily functional health and increased longevity.
3. Examine Figure 4.11 to identify the most popular fitness activities that are health related.
4. Use the Active Mind/Active Body activities on pages 122–123 to introduce

students to the physical requirements of health-related fitness.

Teach & Apply

Discussion

- Ask, Why are health-related fitness components important to everyone?
- Discuss each of the five health-related fitness components.

Stress Break
· · · · · · · · · · · · · ·

Read the Stress Break on this page out loud and have students identify muscle stress and tension in their daily routines. Ask, What are ways to relax the tension?

---

muscular strength

the maximal force that you can exert when you contract your muscles.

---

energy cost

the amount of energy required for you to perform different physical activities or exercises.

Stress Break
· · · · · · · · · · · · · ·

Be aware of what your body is doing. Take time to notice if your hands are squeezed or your jaw and teeth are clinched. You may be exhibiting unnecessary muscle stress. Relax your face and neck muscles every chance you get.

It is not uncommon for people who sit at a desk all day to have headaches and neckaches. A little awareness and a few simple stretches can help reduce these problems. Look for ways throughout the day to relax. A quiet walk or a few minutes of deep breathing can make a big difference in how you reduce and cope with daily stress.

---

ness following physical activity or exercise. You will learn more about flexibility in Chapter 6.

Muscular Strength

Muscular strength refers to the maximal force that you can exert when you contract your muscles. Your muscular strength will vary according to several factors, such as your age, gender, genetic makeup, and conditioning level. A moderate to high level of muscular strength helps reduce your risk for muscle, bone, and joint injuries.

You can develop and maintain muscular strength in a variety of ways, such as doing weight training, calisthenics, or work that requires heavy lifting. Gains in muscular strength can occur rapidly, particularly if you have been very sedentary.

Muscular strength is also important to help you move efficiently and reduce your energy cost. **Energy cost** refers to the amount of

- *All people benefit in many ways from increased muscular strength.*

ABILITY LEVELS

Reteaching

Some students may need help mastering the concepts contained in this section. In your Teacher Resource Package, you will find the reproducible worksheet shown here. This worksheet should help students who have been absent and those needing additional help to improve their comprehension and retention of the content in this section.

• *Cross country skiing is an excellent activity for increasing your muscular endurance.*

energy required for you to perform different physical activities or exercise. You have heard the saying "If you don't use it, you lose it!" This saying especially applies to the elderly, who become sedentary and lose their muscular strength. When you lose muscular strength, it has negative effects on your functional health level. You will learn more about muscular strength in Chapters 7 and 8.

Muscular Endurance

muscular endurance

the ability to contract your muscles several times without excessive fatigue.

Muscular endurance refers to your ability to contract your muscles several times without excessive fatigue. Moderate to high levels of muscular endurance enhance your muscular strength and allow you to do more work without getting tired than you could if you led a sedentary lifestyle. Like muscular strength, muscular endurance is important to help you move efficiently and reduce your energy cost for physical activities or exercises. Physical activities such as doing sit-ups, push-ups, or work that requires repetitive heavy lifting can help increase your muscular endurance. You will learn more about muscular endurance in Chapters 7 and 8.

Body Composition

body composition

the ratio of water, bone, muscle, and fat in the body.

percentage of body fat

the percentage of your body weight that is fat.

The ratio of water, bone, muscle, and fat in your body is what determines your **body composition** (see Chapter 1). Your **percentage of body fat** in relation to your percentage of water, bone, and muscle is important to your functional health and risks for chronic disease. You should have a reasonable amount of body fat

Teaching Strategies

• Use the transparency for Figure 4.10 to identify each of the health-related fitness components.
• Refer to specific figures in the chapter as you discuss each of the health-related fitness components. (Cardiovascular—Figure 4.13, 4.40, 4.41; Flexibility—Figure 4.14, 4.43, 4.47; Muscular Strength—Figure 4.15, 4.49, 4.51, 4.52; Muscular Endurance—Figure 4.16, 4.53; Body Composition—Figure 4.17, 4.55.)

Healthy People 2000

Objective 1.3—**Increase to at least 30 percent the population of people aged 6 and older who engage regularly, preferably daily, in light to moderate activity for at least 30 minutes per day.**
Light to moderate physical activity requires sustained, rhythmic muscular movements, is at least equivalent to sustained walking, and is performed at less than 60 percent of maximum heart rate for age.

Enrichment

This activity will allow you to provide a more challenging learning experience for some of your students.

Have students complete the following activity: Several methods are used to estimate energy expenditure. The following questions show two different methods of estimating energy expenditure.
a. If a person burns 100 kilocalories for every mile run, how many kilocalories would be burned if the person ran 2.5 miles? (250 kilocalories)
b. If a person burns 100 kilocalories for every mile run, how many kilocalories would be burned if the person ran for 30 minutes at a pace of 10 minutes per mile? (300 kilocalories)

Discussion

• Ask students to identify daily activities that require muscular strength and muscular endurance. How can these two components be important to the elderly? How do these two components relate to your energy levels?
• Discuss the importance of maintaining a healthy body composition.

Teacher Support Notes

• Even though body composition is not an activity, it is related to how much activity an individual regularly obtains.
• Today's teens are heavier and have a higher percentage of body fat than teens 10 to 15 years ago. This is related to the increase of fat in their diets and a lack of physical activity.

Activity

• Use the transparency/master of Figure 4.11 to discuss the top ten lifetime activities in which adults participate. Have students suggest reasons why adults would be more likely to participate in health-related fitness activities than team games and sports. Some reasons might include: Convenience, expense, better for health, can be done alone, stress reducing, and related to improved physical appearance. Ask students if they are as likely to do these activities and why.

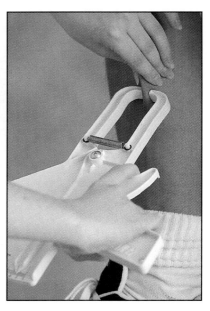

• *One of the many methods of determining your body composition is to measure a skinfold with skinfold calipers. Males should carry 7 to 19 percent body fat, females 12 to 24 percent. If your percentages are higher than these, you need to begin a program to reduce your body fat.*

kilocalorie

a unit used to measure energy; also called a *calorie*.

energy expenditure

the number of calories you burn each minute.

for good health (in other words, you should not be too fat or too lean).

By adopting a physically active lifestyle, you can help control your percentage of body fat. When you engage in physical activities or exercise, you burn or expend energy. When you expend energy, you are burning **kilocalories**. To control your weight, you need to balance the amount of calories you consume in your diet with the amount of calories you expend in daily living and physical activity. When you adopt an active lifestyle, your **energy expenditure** will be higher than if you are sedentary. You will learn more about body composition in Chapter 9.

Improving Your Personal Fitness Level

You can develop a moderate to high level of personal fitness without possessing an abundance of skill-related talents. Most adults who are active do not choose to participate in sports and games as their lifetime physical activities. Instead, they are more likely to choose health-related activities such as swimming, cycling, stair stepping,

Science and Technology

Many physical education teachers may feel that they don't have the time or expertise to develop a computer-generated training log for health-related fitness. This is no longer a problem with the increasing ease at which the Internet can be accessed. Before you access the

Internet, you will need to have a browser (software that connects to Internet sites).

With access to the Internet, physical education teachers are able to access shareware groups to find necessary software to address a multitude of health-related issues. The first place to look on

BELIEVE IT? ... OR NOT?

A basketball player who plays a full four-quarter game runs approximately 3 to 5 miles.

See page 152 for answer.

Rank	Activity
1	Swimming*
2	Fishing
3	Bicycling*
4	Bowling
5	Camping
6	Hiking*
7	Pool/billiards
8	Running/jogging*
9	Weight training*
10	Race cycling*
11	Softball
12	Volleyball
13	Motorboating
14	Dance exercising*
15	Golf
16	Basketball
17	Table tennis
18	Calisthenics*
19	Hunting
20	Baseball

*Denotes health-related activity or exercise

• ***Figure 4.11*** *Rankings of the Most Popular Lifetime Activities for Adults.*
Source: Data from *Gallup Poll,* George Gallup, Jr. (Wilmington, DE: Scholarly Resources Inc., 1991), 43.

BELIEVE IT? ... OR NOT?

The typical young adult (fourteen to seventeen years old) is about 5 to 7 pounds heavier today than the typical young adult in 1980.

See page 152 for answer.

jogging, or weight training. Figure 4.11 lists, in order of popularity, the lifetime activities that adults participate in the most. Notice that the majority of the top ten activities listed are not team sports or game related. In fact, six of the top ten are health-related activities (swimming, bicycling, hiking, running/jogging, weight training, and race cycling).

• Use the transparency/master of Figure 4.12 to discuss the health-related benefits associated with a variety of physical activities and sports. Compare these same activities to the skill-related benefits in Figure 4.3.

Activity

Have students make posters of the health-related fitness components.

Discussion

• Ask students, Did the health-related fitness activities require any skill-related fitness abilities?
• Stress again that these health-related components are important to life-long health and are not performance or athletic related.

Assess

Use the Active Mind/Active Body activities on pages 122–123 to assess student understanding of the different health-related components of physical fitness. Then use the Section 2 Review questions on the next page to assess students' comprehension of the concepts presented in Section 2.

the Internet for shareware software is: http://www.yahoo.com. This is a searchable database for everything on the Internet. Once you have accessed YAHOO, click your mouse on the text titled Recreation, or type the words "fitness software" in the search window. The results will give you a list of locations where fitness software is available for downloading.

Take the challenge: Access the YAHOO searchable index and "surf the pages" under recreation.

Remember: Add Internet pages that you like to your browser's bookmarks.

• *You need not train at high intensities and compete with others to achieve and maintain satisfactory levels of health-related fitness.*

Figure 4.12 shows the health-related benefits associated with different physical activities and sports. From the figure you can determine which of the physical activities can improve or maintain your health-related fitness.

You can learn how to survey your health-related fitness levels by completing the "Active Mind/Active Body" activities—one for each of the health-related fitness components—on the next few pages. These activities are designed to introduce you to the health-related fitness concepts.

BELIEVE IT? ... OR NOT?

Surveys in 1992 showed that less than 40 percent of high school students engaged in adequate amounts of vigorous exercise each week.

See page 152 for answer.

SECTION 2 REVIEW

Answer the following questions on a separate sheet of paper:

1. List and define each of the five health-related fitness components.
2. Why are the health-related fitness components more important to your functional health than the skill-related fitness components?

Close

Discuss this question: Can you improve and maintain the health-related fitness components by participating in a variety of skill-related fitness activities? The answer is yes. Activities like tennis, basketball, soccer, and water polo can improve or maintain good levels of health-related fitness.

Across the Disciplines

Social Studies

Historically, the ability to do well in sports and games has been highly valued in the United States. When President John F. Kennedy promoted youth physical fitness in 1961, the standardized test known as the Presidential Physical Fitness Test consisted of a battery of skill-related activities that identified and rewarded athletic performance. By comparing their scores with the national norms, students who took the test could determine how they ranked

BELIEVE IT? ...
OR NOT?

No real monetary bene-fits are associated with regular physical activity or exercise.

See page 152 for answer.

Activity/Sport and Primary Emphasis	Cardio-vascular fitness	Flexi-bility	Muscular strength	Muscular endurance	Body com-position
Archery **S**	*	*	**	*	*
Backpacking **H**	***	**	**	****	***
Badminton **S**	**	**	*	**	**
Ballet **B**	***	****	***	***	***
Baseball **S**	*	*	*	*	*
Basketball **B**	***	*	*	**	**
Bicycling **H**	****	**	**	****	***
Bowling **S**	*	*	*	*	*
Canoeing **S**	**	*	*	**	**
Circuit training **H**	**	***	***	****	**
Dance, aerobic **H**	****	***	**	***	****
Dance, line **S**	**	*	**	**	**
Dance, social **H**	**	*	**	**	**
Fitness calisthenics **H**	*	****	**	***	**
Football **S**	**	*	***	**	**
Golf (walking) **B**	**	**	*	*	**
Gymnastics **B**	**	****	****	****	**
Handball **H**	****	*	*	***	***
Hiking **H**	***	**	**	****	***
Horseback riding **S**	*	*	*	*	*
Interval training **H**	****	*	**	***	****
Jogging **H**	****	*	**	***	****
Judo **S**	*	**	**	**	*
Karate **S**	*	**	**	**	*
Mountain climbing **H**	****	**	****	****	****
Pool; billiards **S**	*	*	*	*	*
Racquetball; paddleball **B**	****	*	*	***	***
Rope jumping **H**	***	*	**	***	***
Rowing **H**	****	**	**	****	****
Sailing **S**	*	*	*	*	*
Skating, ice **B**	***	*	*	***	***
Skating, in-line **B**	***	**	*	***	***
Skiing, cross-country **B**	****	**	**	***	****
Skiing, downhill **B**	**	**	**	**	**
Soccer **B**	****	**	**	***	****
Softball (fast pitch) **S**	*	*	*	*	*
Softball (slow pitch) **S**	*	*	*	*	*
Surfing **B**	**	**	**	***	**
Swimming laps **H**	****	**	**	***	****
Table tennis **S**	*	*	*	*	*
Tennis **B**	***	*	*	**	**
Volleyball **B**	**	*	**	*	**
Walking **H**	***	*	*	**	***
Waterskiing **S**	**	**	**	**	**
Weight training **H**	*	**	****	***	***

Primary Emphasis
S = Skill-related fitness.
H = Health-related fitness.
B = Both Skill- and Health-related fitness.

Better – ****
Good – ***
Fair – **
Low – *

• **Figure 4.12**   *Health-related Benefits.*

Focus

Outcome

In **Section 3**, students will learn:

1. How to evaluate, inter-pret, and record their skill-related fitness levels.

Focus Activities

1. Evaluate skill-related fit-ness in each of the six skill-related fitness components, and interpret the results of each evaluation.
2. Use Figure 4.57 in the Active Mind/Active Body activity on pages 149–150 to determine your skill-related fitness profile.

Teach & Apply

Discussion

Because fitness has so many benefits, it is impor-tant for students to under-stand and pursue adequate levels of fitness. Students can improve their fitness levels, but they must first determine whether their fit-ness levels are acceptable or unacceptable. By testing their skill-related fitness lev-els and evaluating their rat-ings, they can begin to understand on which parts of fitness they need to con-centrate.

with their peers across the United States. Obtain a copy of the test and national norms used in the 1960s. Have students take as many of the tests as possible and compare their scores with the norms. In small-group discussions, have students reflect on how this one set of scores might have affected the self-image of the athlete, nonathlete, and all the other students who were consid-ered average. Have students brain-storm: (1) the reasons why learning the skills on this test might or might not have succeeded in raising fitness levels; and (2) in what ways the results of the test might or might not have predicted a person's potential in sports and games.

Active **Mind!**
Active *Body!*

Have students use the Active Mind/Active Body activity on these pages to experience the five components of health-related fitness.

Explain to the class that this activity is only designed to introduce students to the different parts of health-related fitness. It is not a test for a grade nor is it a play activity. These activities should be conducted safely and responsibly. Have some fun but be serious about understanding the concepts.

• Have students choose partners.
• Demonstrate to the class each of the activities to be performed.
• Be sure to provide a safe environment for conducting these activities.

Cardiovascular. Jumping Jacks

Have the students perform jumping jacks at the rate of one per second. Each partner should time the other while exercising, resting, and pulse taking for 30 seconds. Pulse may be taken at the carotid or radial artery.

Flexibility. Zipper Stretch

Clarify that this flexibility activity is for the shoulder

Active **Mind!**
Active **Body!**   **Exploring Health-related Fitness**

Jumping Jacks

You can assess your cardiovascular fitness level in a variety of ways. One simple way is to do thirty jumping jacks in thirty seconds, and then rest, standing in place, for thirty seconds (see Figure 4.13). After resting thirty seconds, take your pulse rate for thirty seconds. If your pulse rate is less than 60 beats in thirty seconds, you pass. If not, you may need to improve your cardiovascular fitness level.

a.   b.   c.

• **Figure 4.13**   *Jumping Jacks (cardiovascular fitness).*

Zipper Stretch

There is no single method to determine your flexibility level. Tests of flexibility usually focus on determining the range of motion of one or two joints. For example, one way to assess your shoulder flexibility is the arm stretch, or zipper stretch (see Figure 4.14). To begin this evaluation, raise your right arm, bend your elbow, and reach down behind your back as far as possible. Then, at the same time, bend your left elbow and reach around your back and try to clasp your right hand. Your goal is to touch or overlap your right hand. Now switch arms and repeat the test. You may find that you do better on one side than the other. This is common because many individuals are more flexible on one side than the other. If you touched your fingers or had some overlap, then you pass and are in the healthy zone for flexibility on this test. If you were unable to touch your fingers on one or both sides, you may need to work on improving your shoulder flexibility.

(Back)   (Front)

• **Figure 4.14**   *Zipper Stretch (flexibility).*

Wellness Connection

There are three basic categories of muscular exercises: isometric, isotonic, and isokinetic. Isometric exercises are carried out by pushing or pulling against a fixed or immovable object. Each muscle contraction should be held for five–ten seconds. These exercises are easy to do and require no special equipment or machines.

Isotonic exercises occur when a muscle moves a moderate load several times, such as in weight lifting. Flexibility, coordination, and endurance can best be achieved with low resistance and high

Push-Ups

A simple way to determine your muscular strength is to see if you can do a few push-ups (see Figure 4.15). Lie down so that you face the floor and put your hands under your shoulders. Keep your legs straight, and push off the floor until your arms are fully extended. To pass, boys should repeat this five times, and girls should complete three push-ups. If you cannot complete the appropriate number of push-ups, you may need to work on improving your muscular strength.

• **Figure 4.15**   *Push-ups (muscular strength).*

Wall Sit

You can survey your muscular endurance level by doing a wall sit (see Figure 4.16). Find a wall that you can lean back against comfortably and safely. Place your feet shoulders' width apart, and stand 1 to 1½ feet from the wall. Lean back against the wall so that your back is straight and your shoulder blades touch the wall. Now squat down until your knees are at a 90-degree angle. Try to hold this position for fifteen seconds. If you made fifteen seconds, you passed. If not, you may need to work on improving your muscular endurance.

• **Figure 4.16**   *Wall Sit (muscular endurance).*

Finger Pinch Test

To analyze your body composition, pinch a fold of skin on your thigh (see Figure 4.17). Place the end of your little finger on your kneecap. Spread out your hand, and extend your thumb on the same hand as far as possible up your thigh. With your other hand, pinch a fold of skin at the end of your thumb. If your skin pinch is wider than your thumb, you may need to work on improving your body composition.

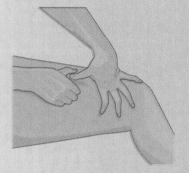

• **Figure 4.17**   *Finger Pinch Test (body composition).*

and that there are many other joints in the body that can be measured. Having good flexibility in one joint does not insure good flexibility in other joints.

Muscular Strength. Push Ups

Clarify that this muscular strength activity is specific to the chest and arms and that there are many other areas of the body in which muscular strength can be evaluated. Emphasize to students to keep their backs straight.

Muscular Endurance. Wall Sit

Clarify that this muscular endurance activity is specific to the legs and that there are many other areas of the body in which muscular endurance can be evaluated. Emphasize how the legs should be at a 90° angle. Have a partner count the fifteen seconds aloud. Students should not help themselves by applying pressure with their hands on their legs.

Body Composition. Finger Pinch Test

This is not an accurate test of body composition, but it can identify some concerns for being overfat. Chapter 9 will provide much more information about body composition. Some students may be very sensitive to this issue. Be sure to provide privacy if a student desires it.

repetitions, while muscular strength can best be achieved with high resistance and low repetitions. Examples of isotonic exercises would be done using free weights, such as barbells and dumbbells, or Nautilus or Universal equipment.

Isokinetic exercises are carried out with special machines that provide resistance to overload muscles throughout the entire range of motion. These exercises can be very effective at isolating and strengthening specific muscle groups, but the equipment is usually very expensive and available only at commercial fitness centers.

Assess

Use the Fitness Check Activities beginning on page 125 to assess student understanding of the different kinds of skill-related fitness evaluations. Then use the Section 3 Review questions to assess students' comprehension of the concepts presented in Section 3.

ANSWERS TO SECTION 3 REVIEW

1. Answers will vary. If students have specific goals for skill performance, then these evaluations could be important to them. However, if they are only concerned with fitness that can help them stay healthy and maintain functional health throughout their lives, these scores will have less importance.

2. These scores would indicate a potential for good abilities in sports and games.

SECTION 3   Skill-related Fitness Evaluations

In this section you will learn how to evaluate, record, and interpret your skill-related fitness levels by performing one or more evaluations for each of the skill-related fitness components. These evaluations are designed to assess skill-related fitness levels more accurately than the activities you did earlier in the chapter. The skill-related self-evaluations in this section can be administered with the help of a partner. Give your best effort on each skill-related component. If necessary, you may make additional attempts.

Score each skill-related evaluation as low, fair, average, or good to better. Record your best scores on a personal fitness profile chart like the one provided in the "Active Mind/Active Body" activity at the end of the chapter.

As you conduct these self-evaluations, concentrate on how each activity relates to each of the specific skill components of fitness. Remember, practice can improve your scores. However, high skill scores are not necessary for good fitness.

Be sure to consider the following safety tips before attempting any of the self-evaluations:

- Adequate stretching and warm-up should precede all evaluations.

- Correct instructions and demonstrations should precede all evaluations.

> "Whenever the urge to exercise comes upon me, I lie down for a while and it passes.
>
> —Robert Maynard Hutchins, quoted in Harry S. Ashmore, *The Life of Robert Maynard Hutchins* [Hutchins, who headed the University of Chicago from 1929 to 1951, enjoyed good health throughout his life; he died at age 78.]

BELIEVE IT? ... OR NOT?

At least 250,000 deaths per year in the United States are linked to a lack of regular physical activity.

See page 152 for answer.

SECTION 3 REVIEW

Answer the following questions on a separate sheet of paper:

1. After you have done the "Fitness Check" that begins on the next page, identify the skill-related fitness evaluations you completed. Explain their importance to your overall personal fitness level.

2. How can scores of "good to better" on your skill-related fitness evaluations influence your sports performance levels?

Close

Ask students to identify the test on which they performed the best and ask why they think they did well.

Equipment Options

At today's count, there are approximately 107 different shoe styles made for runners by seven major manufacturers. The number of shoe styles doubles when you separate men's shoes from women's shoes. So, what do you suggest as the best shoe for a student in a health-fitness course? The manufacturers might suggest the very best shoe (with a very high price) for the beginning runner. But shoes tend to wear out in six months or less under daily activities. Should you suggest that a student purchase a pair of $135 shoes, which have

Fitness Check

Evaluating Skill-related Fitness

Agility

Side Step Shuffle. *To evaluate your agility level, you can choose to use the side step shuffle, the agility run, or both. To do the side step shuffle, you'll need the following equipment: tape, chalk, or pens; a stopwatch; a smooth, flat surface 12 feet long; and a partner (to be a timer and counter). Use the following procedures:*

1. Make five parallel lines on the floor, each 2½ to 3 feet long. The lines should be three feet apart. (See Figure 4.18.)

2. Start the evaluation by standing astride the center line with one foot on the left and one on the right.

3. On the starting command of your partner, move to the right as quickly as possible. You must slide your feet. Do not allow them to cross over one another (any crossovers should be counted by your partner). Keep your center of gravity low by bending your knees.

4. Continue to the right until your right foot crosses the last line. You need only put one foot over the line. Then quickly change directions, and slide back to the left.

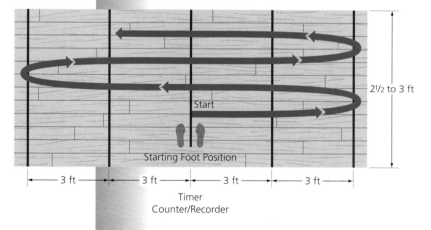

Start

2½ to 3 ft

Starting Foot Position

|← 3 ft →|← 3 ft →|← 3 ft →|← 3 ft →|

Timer
Counter/Recorder

• **Figure 4.18** *Side Step Shuffle (agility evaluation).*
Source: From *Essentials of Strength, Training, and Conditioning*, ed. T. R. Baechle (Champaign, IL: Human Kinetics Publishers, 1994), 269.

a life expectancy of four months, or should you suggest a lower quality, less expensive pair of shoes?

There are two things about which you should remind your students: price and quality are not the same, and shoes must be comfortable.

For better prices on superior shoes, look through the running magazines.

Shoes, like automobiles, have model years, and you can find some great deals on last year's model shoes if you look for them. **Take the challenge:** Look in the phone book to see if there is a discount or factory outlet shoe store in your town. **Remember:** Factory outlet stores may carry last year's model, but they have great prices.

Fitness Check

• Obtain necessary materials and equipment prior to each testing session. Have the areas marked off properly and be sure to conduct all tests in a safe manner.
• Demonstrate each test prior to student trials.
• You may want to create student testing teams. Assign each team a specific fitness component to measure. This student testing team will administer tests to all classmates, but will keep scores confidential.
• Allow for student warm-up prior to any test.
• Make copies of the Handout of Figure 4.57 (provided in your Teacher Resource Package) so students can record their scores.
Side Step Shuffle. Properly mark the testing area, and determine how time will be recorded (stopwatch, wall clock, etc.). Have testing team decide the command for starting. Allow for a trial run to ensure students' understanding of the test. Time keepers will start the time on the start command, and stop time at the ten-second mark. Score team will decide number of lines correctly crossed. Student record keeper will record scores for teacher. Each student should interpret his or her score using Figure 4.19 and record it on his or her fitness profile sheet (Figure 4.57).

Agility Run. Properly mark off the testing area and determine how time will be recorded (stopwatch, wall clock, etc.). Have testing team decide the command for starting. Allow for a trial run to ensure students' understanding of the test. It is recommended that the surface not be slick. Time keepers will start the time on the start command, and stop time at the completion of the test. Student record keeper will record scores for the teacher. Each student should interpret his or her score using Figure 4.21 and record it on his or her fitness profile sheet (Figure 4.57).

Skill Level	Males	Females
Good to better	More than 31	More than 28
Average	26 – 30	24 – 27
Fair	19 – 25	16 – 23
Low	Below 19	Below 16

• **Figure 4.19** *Agility Scores (number of lines crossed minus crossovers in side step shuffle).*
Source: From *Essentials of Strength, Training, and Conditioning,* ed. T. R. Baechle (Champaign, IL: Human Kinetics Publishers, 1994), 269.

5. Continue this procedure for ten seconds, at which time your partner will tell you to stop.
6. The objective is to cross as many lines as possible in ten seconds. Count your lines (include the starting line), and subtract one point for each time you crossed your feet. See Figure 4.19 to interpret your score. Record the score on your personal fitness profile chart like the one in the "Active Mind/Active Body" activity at the end of the chapter.

Agility Run. *Equipment needed for the agility run includes four chairs, boxes, or cones; measuring tape; a stopwatch; a smooth, flat surface 30 feet long; and a partner (timer). Follow these steps:*

1. Place four chairs (or boxes or cones) in a straight line, ten feet apart from each other (see Figure 4.20).
2. Lie on your back with your arms across your chest. Your head should be on the starting line and the rest of your body behind the line.

• **Figure 4.20** *Agility Run (agility evaluation).*

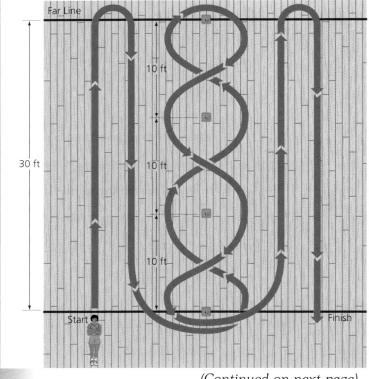

(Continued on next page)

Across the Disciplines

Environmental Science

The outdoor environment can make it difficult, unhealthy, and even dangerous to exercise. High ozone levels and overexposure to this gas can damage a person's lung tissue, which can reduce his or her ability to fight infection and make him or her more susceptible to colds, bronchitis, and pneumonia. If high levels of carbon monoxide are absorbed by a person's red blood cells, it can cause chest pain and heart trouble. A person who is trying to exercise in high levels of

Skill Level	Males	Females
Good to better	16.7 or less	18.4 or less
Average	16.8 – 18.6	18.5 – 22.3
Fair	18.7 – 18.8	23.4 – 22.4
Low	18.9 or Slower	23.5 or Slower

• **Figure 4.21** *Agility Scores (time in seconds in agility run).*
Source: Thomas K. Cureton, *Physical Fitness of Champion Athletes* (Urbana, IL: University of Illinois Press, 1951), 68.

• **Figure 4.22** *One-Foot Stand (balance evaluation).*

continued

3. On the starting command of your partner, stand up, and run through the course as quickly as possible (see Figure 4.20). Keep your turns close, and keep your center of gravity low.

4. Continue through the finish line, at which time your partner will record your time. Score your time to the nearest tenth of a second. See Figure 4.21 to evaluate your time. Record the score on your personal fitness profile chart like the one in the "Active Mind/Active Body" activity at the end of the chapter.

Balance

One-Foot Stand.   *Now evaluate your balance skills. You can choose the one-foot stand, the squat-stand, or both. To do the one-foot stand, gather the following equipment: a stopwatch, a flat surface, and a partner (timer). Here's the procedure:*

1. Start by removing your shoes and socks. Stand on your dominant foot (the one you typically kick with). Place the other foot flat on the inside of the supporting knee.

2. Place your hands on your waist. When your partner says "Start," raise the heel of your dominant foot off the floor. Hold this position for as long as possible (see Figure 4.22).

3. The evaluation is over when one of the following takes place: the support foot twists, hops, or shuffles; the heel contacts the floor; your hands lose contact from your waist; or sixty seconds expires.

4. The objective is to hold the position for a maximum of sixty seconds. Have your partner count your time out loud. Score your time to the nearest tenth of a second. See Figure 4.23 on the next page to evaluate your time. Record your score on your personal fitness profile chart like the one in the "Active Mind/Active Body" activity at the end of the chapter.

Squat-Stand.   *For the squat-stand, you'll need mats, a stopwatch, and a partner (timer). Follow these guidelines:*

1. Start by placing your feet shoulders' width apart. Bend your knees and back into a squat position. Go low enough to touch your hands on the floor. (It may be helpful to have mats *around* you, but it is not recommended to be *on* mats during this evaluation.)

2. Place your hands flat on the floor 8 to 12 inches in front of your feet. Spread your fingers. Your hands will require some adjusting.

One-Foot Stand. Determine how time will be recorded (stopwatch, wall clock, etc.). Have testing team decide the command for starting. Allow for a trial attempt to ensure students' understanding of the test. Time keeper will start the time on the start command, and stop when any of the test violations occur or 60 seconds expires. Student record keepers will record scores for the teacher. Each student should interpret his or her score using Figure 4.23 and record it on his or her fitness profile sheet (Figure 4.57).

Squat-Stand. Determine how time will be recorded (stopwatch, wall clock, etc.). Allow for a trial run to ensure students' understanding of the test. This test requires upper body strength that many students

carbon monoxide may experience impaired motor functions and coordination. High levels of molds, pollens, and other allergens can also impair a person's ability to exercise.

Have students research the weather and air quality conditions in various regions in the United States, including where they live, to determine regions that are the most beneficial for exercise and those that are the most detrimental. Students should investigate existing conditions that make physical activity dangerous. Arranging this information in a chart will assist students in making comparisons and drawing conclusions.

may not have. Be sure students are instructed on how to properly roll out of this position so as not to harm their necks. Time keepers will start the time when only the hands are touching the floor, and stop time when any other part of the body touches the floor, or 60 seconds expires. Student record keeper will record scores for the teacher. Each student should interpret his or her score using Figure 4.25 and record it on his or her fitness profile sheet (Figure 4.57).

Scarf Juggle. Emphasize that this test is for eye-hand coordination. Obtain plastic bags from the athletic training room. These bags are often used as ice packs. They may also be obtained from the produce department of your local grocery store. Allow for a trial attempt to ensure students' understanding of the test.

Skill Level	Males	Females
Good to better	37 or longer	23 or longer
Average	15 – 36	8 – 22
Fair	5 – 14	3 – 7
Low	0 – 4	0 – 2

• **Figure 4.23** *Balance Scores (time in seconds in one-foot stand).*
Source: Adapted with permission from Johnson and Nelson, *Practical Measurements for Evaluation in Physical Education,* 4th ed. (Edina, MN: Burgess Publishing, 1986), 238.

Skill Level	Males	Females
Good to better	50 or longer	40 or longer
Average	25 – 49	21 – 39
Fair	14 – 24	8 – 20
Low	0 – 13	0 – 7

• **Figure 4.25** *Balance Scores (time in seconds in squat-stand).*
Source: Adapted with permission from Barrow, *A Practical Approach to Measurement in Physical Education,* 2nd ed. (Philadelphia: Lea and Febiger, 1971), 237.

• **Figure 4.24**   *Squat-Stand (balance evaluation).*

3. Lean forward slowly while placing the inside of your knees on the outside of your elbows (see Figure 4.24). Continue to lean forward until all of your weight is supported on your hands and elbows. Time starts when both feet are off the ground.

4. Hold this position for sixty seconds, at which time your partner will stop you. Time also stops if any part of your body other than your hands touches the floor.

5. The objective is to stay balanced for as many seconds as possible up to sixty seconds. See Figure 4.25 to evaluate your time. Record the score on your personal fitness profile chart like the one in the "Active Mind/Active Body" activity at the end of the chapter.

Coordination

Scarf Juggle (Eye-Hand Coordination).   *The next two skill-related fitness evaluations test your coordination. The scarf juggle tests your eye-hand coordination. The soccer ball kick evaluates your eye-foot coordination. To do the scarf juggle, get two scarves, two plastic bags, or two pieces of tissue paper (12 to 18 inches square), and a partner to count for you. Follow these steps:*

1. Place both scarves into your dominant (writing) hand (see Figure 4.26 on the next page).

2. Raise your hand up swiftly, and release one of the scarves. Then quickly repeat the same movement with the other scarf.

3. As soon as you have released the second scarf, quickly *grab and toss* the first scarf again, immediately followed by a grab and toss of the second scarf. Try to keep the toss *up,* not out.

(Continued on next page)

Special Needs

The skill-related and health-related fitness evaluations in the Active Mind/Active Body activities on pages 112–113 and 122–123, as well as the fitness evaluations that follow, can be utilized with some of the disabled population if proper precautions and appropriate modifications are made (i.e. if the student experiences lower limb involvement, those tests need to be eliminated). Additional modifications might include: from a chair, either wheelchair or desk chair, the student can push on the sides of the seat to raise his body off the seat; in a wheel-

continued

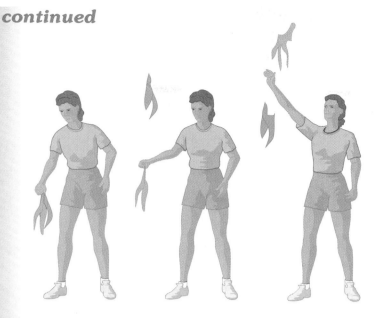

• *Figure 4.26*   *Scarf Juggle (evaluation of eye-hand coordination).*

Skill Level	Males and Females
Good to better	more than 13
Average	7 – 12
Fair	4 – 6
Low	0 – 3

• *Figure 4.27   Coordination Scores (number of caught tosses in scarf juggle).*

4. Keep both scarves in the air as long as you can by continuing to alternate tosses. Your partner should count each correct *grab and toss* as 1 point. (Do not count the first two tosses. Begin counting with your first grab.)

5. Repeat the process with your nondominant hand. Total the scores for both hands. See Figure 4.27 to evaluate your score. Record it on your personal fitness profile chart like the one in the "Active Mind/Active Body" activity at the end of the chapter.

Soccer Ball Kick (Eye-Foot Coordination).   *The soccer ball kick will assess your eye-foot coordination. You will need this equipment: three soccer balls or utility balls of similar size and weight, a standard gym wall (about 30 feet wide and 10 feet high), tape, a tape measure, a stopwatch, and a partner (timer and counter). Do the following:*

1. Place a piece of tape 9 feet from the wall. Place one ball on this line. The two spare balls are placed 9 feet behind the line.

2. Start the evaluation by standing behind the 9-foot line with one ball in front of you.

Have score keeper count the number of correct grabs in each hand. Remind students that the first two tosses do not count, only grabs count. The score is the total of both hands. Student record keeper will record scores for the teacher. Each student should interpret his or her score using Figure 4.27 and record it on his or her fitness profile sheet (Figure 4.57).

Teacher Readings

Johnson, B. L., and Nelson, J. K., *Practical Measurements for Evaluation in Physical Education*, 4th Edition, Burgess Publishing, Edina, MN: 1986.

Soccer Ball Kick. Emphasize that this test is for eye-foot coordination. Properly mark off the testing area and determine how time will be recorded (stopwatch, wall clock, etc.). Have testing team decide the command for starting. Allow for

chair (nonmotorized) the student can be timed propelling a set distance. (The Adapted Physical Education specialist assigned to the school campus can also help with evaluation modifications.) This approach does not always ensure diagnostic assessments, but the results can provide information to measure progress. If it is impossible to obtain any

meaningful measurements, then an alternative test might need to be used that will chart progress each time it is used. A possible evaluation source could be Winnick, J. and Short, F., *Physical Fitness Testing for the Disabled: Project UNIQUE*, Human Kinetics Publishers, Champaign, IL: 1985.

a trial run to ensure students' understanding of the test. Time keeper will start the time on the start command, and stop time when 30 seconds expires. The key point is to control the ball, not to hit it hard. If the ball gets out of control, students are better off grabbing a spare ball for continuation of the test. Testing team will decide the correct number of hits. Student record keeper will record scores for the teacher. Each student should interpret his or her score using Figure 4.29 and record it on his or her fitness profile sheet (Figure 4.57).

• **Figure 4.28**   *Soccer Ball Kick (test of eye-foot coordination).*

Skill Level	Males	Females
Good to better	20 and above	15 and above
Average	11 – 19	7 – 14
Fair	8 – 10	2 – 6
Low	0 – 7	0 – 1

• **Figure 4.29** *Coordination Scores (number of kicks in soccer ball kick). Source:* Adapted with permission from McDonald soccer test in Johnson and Nelson, *Practical Measurements for Evaluation in Physical Education,* 4th ed. (Burgess Publishing, 1986), 298.

3. On the starting command of your partner, begin kicking the ball against the wall as many times as possible in a thirty-second period. Note that how well you control the ball is more important than how hard you strike the ball. (See Figure 4.28.)

4. You may only kick the ball from behind the 9-foot line. If necessary, you may retrieve the ball with your hands and place it at the 9-foot line. If the ball is out of control, you may choose to retrieve one of the spare balls.

5. Continue to kick for thirty seconds. Your partner will stop you when your time is up. Record the highest number of legal kicks. See Figure 4.29 to evaluate your score, and record it on your personal fitness profile chart like the one in the "Active Mind/Active Body" activity at the end of the chapter.

Power

Vertical Jump.   *To assess your power level, use the vertical jump, standing broad jump, or both. The vertical jump test requires chalk, a wall 11 feet high or higher, measuring tape, and a partner to make measurements. Perform this test as follows:*

(Continued on next page)

Vertical Jump. There are special testing boards that allow for easy measurement of the vertical jump. If these are not available, it will be necessary to have students who are administering the

Wellness Connection

Tell students that at some time in our lives we are all likely to suffer some type of flexibility-related injury such as muscle pulls, muscle strains, or low back pain. There are a number of over-the-counter drugs and medicines that are considered analgesics, or pain relievers. However,

for flexibility-related injuries you will need to select a medicine that has an anti-inflammatory action. While acetaminophen may be fine for headache or fever, it does not have an anti-inflammatory property. A better choice would be plain aspirin (acetylsalicylic acid), or ibuprofen,

continued

1. Start the evaluation by standing with your dominant arm next to the wall. Place the chalk in your dominant hand. Start with both feet together and your body sideways to the wall. Raise your dominant hand, and mark the wall with the chalk (see Figure 4.30).

2. Step one step back from the start, and place both feet back together. In a smooth, quick motion, step forward, bend your knees and back, and then push upward with both feet. Raise your arm, and make a chalk mark on the wall at the highest point you can reach (see Figure 4.30). Be sure to stay as close to the wall as possible.

3. Your partner will measure the distance between the two marks and record the distance to the closest inch.

Skill Level	Males	Females
Good to better	22 and above	15 and above
Average	20 – 21	13 – 14
Fair	12 – 19	8 – 12
Low	0 – 11	0 – 7

• **Figure 4.31** *Power Scores (inches in vertical jump). Source:* Data from Johnson and Nelson, *Practical Measurements for Evaluation in Physical Education,* 4th ed. (1986) and Frierwood, *Annual Official Rules and Reference Guide of U.S. Volleyball Association* (U.S. Volleyball Association, 1967), 211.

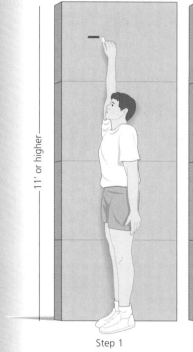
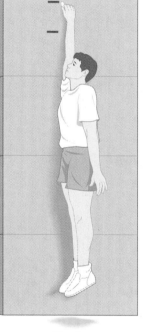

11' or higher

Step 1   Step 2

• **Figure 4.30** *Vertical Jump (power evaluation).*

test use a ruler while standing on a table or chair. The key point is to have students bend their knees prior to the jump and throw their arm up as high and close to the wall as possible. The distance between the two chalk marks is the vertical jump. Student record keeper will record scores for the teacher. Each student should interpret his or her score using Figure 4.31 and record it on his or her fitness profile sheet (Figure 4.57).

Teacher Readings

Morrow, J. R., Jackson, A. W., Disch, J. G., and Mood, D. P., *Measurement and Evaluation in Human Performance*, Human Kinetics, Champaign, IL: 1995.

naproxen, or ketoprofen.
For a stronger drug, you would need a doctor's prescription. In any case, if you

have concerns regarding the proper treatment for a flexibility-related injury, see your family doctor.

Standing Broad Jump.
Properly mark off the testing area. It is best to have a nonslip surface to both start and land. A slick take-off point will reduce student scores. Make sure the landing area is safe and free of any obstacles. Allow for trial attempts to ensure students' understanding of the test. Encourage students to bend their knees and thrust their arms forward as they jump. Testing team shall determine the distance of the best jump. Student record keeper will record scores for the teacher. Each student should interpret his or her score using Figure 4.33 and record it on his or her fitness profile sheet (Figure 4.57).

Teacher Readings

Morrow, J. R., Falls, H. B., and Kohl, H. W., Editors. *The Fitnessgram Technical Reference Manual*, The Cooper Institute for Aerobics Research, Dallas, TX: 1994.

4. The objective is to jump as high as possible above your standing reach mark. See Figure 4.31 to evaluate your score. Record it on your personal fitness profile chart like the one in the "Active Mind/Active Body" activity at the end of the chapter.

Standing Broad Jump.   *You can also test your power by performing the standing broad jump. You'll need chalk; measuring tape; and a smooth, flat area 10 feet long. Here's how to perform this evaluation:*

1. Mark a starting line. Then measure a distance of 9 feet from that line. The distance should be marked in 1-inch intervals.
2. Stand with both feet behind the starting line with your toes on the line (see Figure 4.32).
3. By combining the bending of your knees and the swinging of your arms, jump outward as far as possible. This movement must be done quickly. Be sure not to fall backward when landing, because measurements are taken from the closest point to the starting line.
4. Your partner will measure from the starting line to the closest point of your landing.

10 feet

• **Figure 4.32**   *Standing Broad Jump (power evaluation).*

(Continued on next page)

COOPERATIVE LEARNING

Here are a few strategies that might make your cooperative learning group work a little easier.
• Assign students specific *roles* to play within the groups. (This role is in addition to the individual tasks assigned to the students, which were discussed earlier.)

Some easily implemented roles are *reader*, who is responsible for reading all materials to the group; *recorder*, who writes out the best answers for any worksheets or questions the group must complete; and *materials handler*, who is responsible for getting and putting away

continued

5. The objective is to jump as far from the start as possible. See Figure 4.33 to evaluate your score. Record it on your personal fitness profile chart like the one in the "Active Mind/Active Body" activity at the end of the chapter.

Skill Level	Males (by age)				Females (by age)			
	14 yrs.	15 yrs.	16 yrs.	17+ yrs.	14 yrs.	15 yrs.	16 yrs.	17+ yrs.
Good to better	80 – 90	84 – 96	90 – 98	93 – 101	71 – 80	71 – 80	71 – 80	72 – 81
Average	74 – 79	80 – 83	84 – 89	86 – 92	64 – 70	65 – 70	65 – 70	65 – 71
Fair	66 – 73	73 – 79	78 – 83	78 – 85	58 – 63	59 – 64	59 – 64	59 – 64
Low	56 – 65	62 – 72	65 – 77	67 – 77	48 – 57	50 – 58	50 – 58	50 – 58

• **Figure 4.33**   *Power Scores (inches in standing broad jump). Source: Data from Johnson and Nelson, Practical Measurements for Evaluation in Physical Education, 4th ed. (1986) and AAHPERD Youth Fitness Test Manual (1976), 213.*

Speed

Four-Second Dash.   *You can evaluate your speed using the four-second dash or the 50-yard dash. Equipment for the four-second dash includes markers or tape, measuring tape, a whistle, a stopwatch, a flat running area 30 to 40 yards long, and a partner (starter and timer). To perform the four-second dash:*

1. Mark a starting line. Then mark a line 10 yards from the start. Mark nine additional lines that are each 2 yards apart (see Figure 4.34).

2. Where you begin is your choice. You may begin at the start line, or you may start 2 yards behind the start line. Regardless

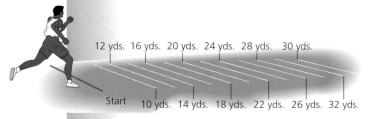

12 yds. 16 yds. 20 yds. 24 yds. 28 yds. 30 yds.

Start   10 yds. 14 yds. 18 yds. 22 yds. 26 yds. 32 yds.

• **Figure 4.34**   *Four-Second Dash (speed evaluation).*

Four-Second Dash. Properly mark off the testing area. It is best to have a flat, smooth area that does not require a sudden stop. Make sure students have conducted a proper warm-up with both stretching and cardiovascular activities. Have students positioned all along the running course. Their responsibility is to determine the exact distance completed in four seconds. A stopwatch is required for one member of the testing team. The timer will start the watch the moment the student being tested moves, and when four seconds has expired he or she will blow a whistle or yell, "mark." The other members of the testing team will determine the correct distance traveled. Student record keeper will

Teacher Readings

Baumgartner, T. A., and Jackson, A. S., *Measurement for Evaluation in Physical Education and Exercise Science.* 5th Edition, W. C. Brown, Dubuque, IA: 1994.

any materials needed by the group. These roles should be rotated so that each student gets a chance to play each role during different class periods.
• Another strategy that is easily implemented is that of *jigsawing* materials. To jigsaw a lesson, you must first distribute a set of materials to each group. The materials need to be divisible by the number of students in the group. Each group member is assigned a different part of the material to learn and then teach to the other group members. Each student in the group is responsible for learning and teaching a section of the material.

Skill Level	Males	Females
Good to better	31 and above	27 and above
Average	29–30	25–26
Fair	27–28	23–24
Low	Below 27	Below 23

• **Figure 4.35** *Speed Scores (yards in four-second dash).*
Source: Adapted with permission from Johnson and Nelson, *Practical Measurements for Evaluation in Physical Education,* 4th ed. (1986), 258.

record scores for the teacher. Each student should interpret his or her score using Figure 4.35 and record it on his or her fitness profile sheet (Figure 4.57).

50-Yard Dash. Properly mark off the testing area. It is best to have a flat, smooth area that does not require a sudden stop. Make sure students have conducted a proper warm-up with both stretching and cardiovascular activities. A stopwatch is required for one member of the testing team. The timer will stand at the finish line. The timer is also the starter. All students should understand how the start is conducted. The starter's hand and voice will start the test. Time is stopped as the student being tested crosses the finish. Student record keeper will record scores to

of where you start, your partner will begin your time as you cross the starting line. Four seconds from the beginning of your time, your partner will blow the whistle.

3. Continue to sprint until you hear the four-second whistle. Then slowly come to a stop.

4. Your partner will record the distance in (yards) that you reached at the four-second whistle.

5. The objective is to obtain the greatest distance in four seconds. See Figure 4.35 to evaluate your time. Record the score on your personal fitness profile chart like the one in the "Active Mind/ Active Body" activity at the end of the chapter.

50-Yard Dash. *The 50-yard dash is a second way you can assess your speed. You'll need the following equipment: measuring tape; a smooth, flat surface 70 yards or longer; a stopwatch; and a partner (starter and timer). Here is how to perform the 50-yard dash (see Figure 4.36):*

1. Mark off a safe course 50 yards long. Be sure to allow additional distance for a safe stopping zone.

2. Have the starter positioned at the finish line with a stopwatch. The starter/timer will raise an arm, shout the instruction "Ready," and then simultaneously drop his or her arm and shout the instruction "Go."

3. You will sprint as quickly as possible to the finish line. Be sure to stay on the balls of your feet, pump your arms, and lean forward slightly.

4. Continue to the finish line, and record your score to the nearest tenth of a second. See Figure 4.37 to evaluate your time. Record the score on your personal fitness profile chart like the one in the "Active Mind/Active Body" activity at the end of the chapter.

Start   50 yrds finish

• **Figure 4.36** *50-Yard Dash (speed evaluation).*

(Continued on next page)

Across the Disciplines

Technology

Computer programs such as Hypercard, Hyperstudio, or Powerpoint enable a user to design a computer-generated slide show implementing graphics, animation, sound, and text. Animation and graphics can be used as powerful illustrators of information. The computerized slide show can be an informative, interactive, and entertaining method of introducing material to students, providing tutoring to students who have been absent, and checking for understanding.

continued

Skill Level	Males (by age)			
	14 yrs.	15 yrs.	16 yrs.	17+ yrs.
Good to better	6.3–7.0	6.1–6.8	6.0–6.6	6.0–6.5
Average	7.1–7.5	6.9–7.1	6.7–6.9	6.6–6.9
Fair	7.6–8.5	7.2–8.0	7.0–7.7	7.0–7.6
Low	>8.5	>8.0	>7.7	>7.6

Skill Level	Females (by age)			
	14 yrs.	15 yrs.	16 yrs.	17+ yrs.
Good to better	7.0–7.9	7.1–8.0	7.1–8.1	7.1–8.1
Average	8.0–8.7	8.1–8.7	8.2–8.9	8.2–8.9
Fair	8.8–10.3	8.8–10.3	9.0–10.4	9.0–10.4
Low	>10.3	>10.3	>10.4	>10.4

• **Figure 4.37** *Speed Scores (seconds in 50-yard dash).*
Source: Data from Johnson and Nelson, *Practical Measurements for Evaluation in Physical Education,* 4th ed. (1986) and *AAHPERD Youth Fitness Test Manual* (1976), 260.

Reaction Time

Yardstick Drop. *You can assess your reaction time with a test called the* yardstick drop. *You'll need a yardstick, a table and chair, and a partner. Follow these steps:*

1. Start by sitting in a chair and resting your arm on a table. You may use another chair as a table, if necessary (see Figure 4.38).

2. Extend your fingers over the edge of the table 3 inches. Rest the heel of your hand on the table.

3. Have your partner place the yardstick over your fingers. The placement of the 0 point of the stick should be even with the top of your thumb. Your thumb and index finger should be 2 inches apart with the end of the yardstick centered between them. Your hand must remain still (see Figure 4.38).

4. You should look only at the bottom of the stick. Do not look at your partner's hand.

the nearest tenth of a second for the teacher. Students should be allowed to take additional trials. Each student should interpret his or her score using Figure 4.37 and record it on his or her fitness profile sheet (Figure 4.57).

Yardstick Drop. It is best to have a table on which students can rest their arms. An alternative is to have students kneel and rest their arm on the seat of a chair. Do not allow students to move their fingers before the ruler is dropped. Their eyes should remain fixed on their hand. Take a close look at the scoring of this test. There are five trials; discard the best and worst and average the other three. Extra trials are not necessary. Student record keeper will record scores for the teacher. Each student should interpret his or her score using Figure 4.39 on the next page and record it on his or her fitness profile sheet (Figure 4.57).

This computer technology also may give students the opportunity to synthesize course information and utilize higher-level thinking skills as they design and write their own programs. Assign specific chapters in this book to groups of three or four students and have them create a slide show or program. Their audience will be their classmates. They may choose to illustrate one of the physical activities, present critical information in an innovative format, or design an interactive self-evaluation for classmates to use. These student-generated products not only benefit the students who create them, they could also provide learning opportunities for future classes.

Focus

Outcomes

In **Section 4** students will learn:

1. How to evaluate, interpret, and record their health-related fitness levels.

Focus Activities

1. Evaluate health-related fitness in each of the five health-related components and interpret the results of each evaluation.
2. Use Figure 4.58 in the Active Mind/Active Body Activity on page 151 to determine their health-related fitness profiles.

Teach & Apply

Discussion

Because fitness has so many benefits, it is important for students to understand and pursue adequate levels of fitness. Students can improve their fitness levels, but they must first determine whether their levels are acceptable or unacceptable. By testing their health-related fitness levels and evaluating their scores, they can begin to understand the parts of fitness on which they need to concentrate.

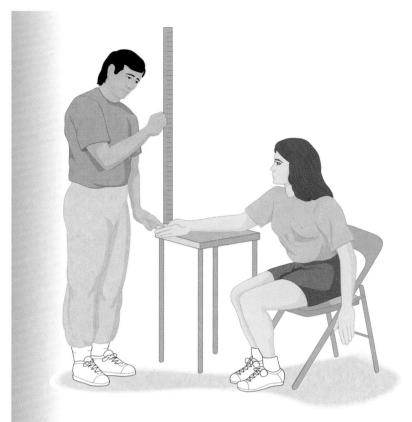

• **Figure 4.38**   *Yardstick Drop (evaluation of reaction time).*
Source: Data from Johnson and Nelson, *Practical Measurements for Evaluation in Physical Education,* 4th ed. (1986).

Skill Level	Males and Females
Good to better	1–2"
Average	3–4"
Fair	5–6"
Low	7" or more

• **Figure 4.39**   *Reaction Time Scores (average inches in yardstick drop).*

5. As your partner drops the stick at random times, try to catch it with your fingers as quickly as possible. Your partner will then record the measurement at the point on the yardstick that you caught it with your fingers. Each attempt is scored to the nearest half-inch. The reading is taken just above the thumb.

6. Do five trials. Your score is determined by discarding the best and worst scores. Add the remaining three scores, and divide by 3. See Figure 4.39 to evaluate your score. Record the score on your personal fitness profile chart like the one in the "Active Mind/Active Body" activity at the end of the chapter.

Special Needs

Certain factors must be considered when including disabled students in fitness programming. The fact that the student is disabled makes displaying correct biomechanics impossible. A student's walking pattern can be greatly impaired, yet he or she can still benefit from a fit-ness program that includes walking. The disabled person may need some form of assistance in order to ambulate, i.e. a prosthesis, AFOs (ankle-foot orthotics), a walker, forearm crutches, or a wheelchair. Evaluation of the student's biomechanics should take ambulation aids into

SECTION 4   Health-related Fitness Evaluations

You can evaluate, record, and interpret your own health-related fitness levels just as you did for the skill-related components. Many of the health-related tests in this section are based on the Prudential *Fitnessgram*.

To determine how you scored on an evaluation, refer to the figures for each health-related fitness evaluation. The figures show the healthy zone of fitness—scores that represent levels of personal fitness that are good to better. Scores that fall below the healthy fitness zone are considered to be lower than required for a reasonable level of personal fitness.

The following health-related self-evaluations can be administered with the help of a partner and your instructor. Give your best effort for each evaluation. If necessary, you may make additional attempts. Record your best scores on your personal fitness profile chart, like the sample provided in the "Active Mind/Active Body" activity at the end of the chapter. As you conduct these self-evaluations, concentrate on how each particular activity relates to each of the specific health-related components. Practice can improve your scores and your own level of personal fitness. Consider the following safety tips before attempting any of the self-evaluations:

- Adequate stretching and warm-up should precede all evaluations.
- Correct instructions and demonstrations should precede all evaluations.

It is important for you to learn to monitor your levels of both skill-related and health-related fitness throughout the rest of your life. This will help you gauge your personal fitness progress and allow you to make changes in your personal fitness goals.

BELIEVE IT? ... OR NOT?

Currently, all people six years old or older engage in leisure-time physical activity.

See page 152 for answer.

SECTION 4 REVIEW

Answer the following questions on a separate sheet of paper:

1. After you have done the "Fitness Check" that begins on the next page, identify health-related fitness evaluations you completed, and explain their importance to your overall personal fitness level.

2. List and explain the three health-related evaluations for flexibility.

Assess

Use the Fitness Check activities to assess student understanding of health-related fitness evaluations. Then use the Section 4 Review questions to assess students' comprehension of the concepts presented in Section 4.

ANSWERS TO SECTION 4 REVIEW

1. Answers will vary.
2. *a.* Trunk Lift—Answer should agree with information on pages 140–141.
   b. Arm Lift—Answer should agree with information on page 141.
   c. Back Saver Sit and Reach—Answer should agree with information on pages 141–142.

Close

Ask students to identify the test area on which they performed the best and have them discuss why they think they did well.

consideration.

Generally, students with disabilities display deviations from the norm in posture and have difficulty making correct postural adjustments. This can be due to muscle weakness, contractures, or misalignment of the skeletal system.

When the discussion turns to injury prevention, specific considerations with the disabled population must be taken into account. The following factors should be noted: medications may affect the student's alertness, sensory functions may be compromised, weakened muscle(s) may result in the student tiring more easily, or there may be increased chances for superficial injuries due to the addition of an ambulation aid.

CHAPTER 4
SECTION 4
138

Fitness Check

- Obtain necessary materials and equipment prior to each testing session. Have the areas marked off properly and be sure to conduct all tests in a safe manner.
- Demonstrate each test prior to student trials.
- You may want to use a video camera to record tests so students can view their results.
- You may want to create student testing teams.
- It is a good idea to have students warm-up prior to any test.
- Make copies of the Handout of Figure 4.58, which is provided in your Teacher Resource Package, so students can record their scores.

Three-Minute Step Test.
Often this test is best administered to large groups all at once. One suggestion is to use the bottom row of the gym bleachers; however, this step may be a little higher than twelve inches. It is also best to have a cadence of up-down commands equal to twenty-four counts per minute. This is important to ensure that students don't go too fast. Students should sit down immediately after the test and count their

Fitness Check

Evaluating Health-related Fitness

Cardiovascular Fitness

One way to evaluate your cardiovascular fitness level is by taking the three-minute step test. The other way is to complete the PACER 20-meter shuttle run. Choose one or both evaluations.

Three-Minute Step Test.   In the three-minute step test, you step up and down on a 12-inch step at 24 steps per minute. (See Figure 4.40.) You then measure your recovery pulse for one minute immediately upon stopping to determine your cardiovascular fitness level. If your recovery pulse rate is low (less than 85 beats per minute), you are in the high fitness zone. If your recovery pulse is between 85 and 95 beats per minute, you are in the healthy fitness zone (in other words, you have good to better levels of cardiovascular fitness). If your recovery pulse is high (120 beats per minute or higher), you have a low level of cardiovascular fitness.

• **Figure 4.40**   *Three-Minute Step Test (cardiovascular fitness evaluation).*

(Continued on next page)

Wellness Connection

Tell students that many people believe that they can determine a person's level of wellness solely on the basis of the person's external, physical traits. Give them the following scenario and then ask them if the individual in the story has truly obtained wellness: Billy Goodbody is the strongest student at Centerville High. He stands six feet tall and weighs just over 220 pounds. He lifts weights six days a week and takes all the nutritional supplements and vitamins that he reads about in the muscle magazines. He's a handsome boy with blond hair and blue eyes.

continued

PACER (Progressive Aerobic Cardiovascular Endurance Run) 20-Meter Shuttle Run. To perform the PACER 20-meter shuttle run, begin walking or jogging when you hear the beep on the PACER cassette tape. You need to get to the line that is 20 meters away before the next beep (Figure 4.41). Then turn around and return to the starting line, trying to beat the next beep. If you don't reach the line before the beep, join the observers on the sideline. You (or a partner on the sidelines) will count the number of times you make it to each line before the beep. (From start

pulse for a full minute. Teachers should record scores and students should interpret their scores using their pulse rates to determine their fitness levels. Students should record their scores on their fitness profile sheets (Figure 4.58). **PACER 20-Meter Shuttle Run.** Properly mark off the testing area. It is best to have a flat, smooth area. This test is best administered by the use of an audio tape that provides beeps that indicate proper pacing speed. Students should not leave any station before the next beep sounds. Students should try to pace themselves according to the beeps. Students should also be aware that the pace will increase as the test goes on. It is best to have a partner count the correctly completed laps. The PACER Test can be administered to more than one student at a time, but it is not recommended to have more than ten students complete it at a time. Teachers should record scores and students should interpret their scores using Figure 4.42 and record them on their fitness profile sheets (Figure 4.58). Note: Chapter 5 will provide additional cardiovascular evaluations.

• **Figure 4.41**
Schematic Diagram of the PACER Test (cardiovascular fitness evaluation).
Source: With permission from The Cooper Institute for Aerobics Research, *The Prudential Fitnessgram Test Administration Manual* (Dallas, TX: 1992).

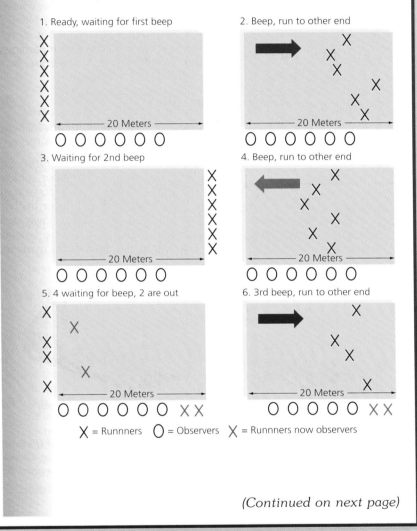

X = Runnners   O = Observers   X = Runnners now observers

(Continued on next page)

But there is more you should know about Billy. Because of his compulsive training schedule and strict diet, he seldom goes out with his friends from school. In fact, Billy has very few people he could actually call friends. His parents have encouraged him to get involved with clubs and groups at school, but he is just not interested. He does not even play on the Centerville High football team. He says that would mean depending on other people, and Billy has never been able to put trust in anyone but himself.

Ask the students to identify at least five problems in Billy's life. What kind of interventions would they suggest to help Billy Goodbody obtain true wellness?

(continued)

• **Figure 4.52**   *Flexed Arm Hang Test (muscular strength evaluation).*
Source: With permission from The Cooper Institute for Aerobics Research, *The Prudential Fitnessgram Test Administration Manual* (Dallas, TX: 1992), 52.

Flexed Arm Hang Test.   A third way you can assess your muscular strength is by performing the Prudential *Fitnessgram* flexed arm hang test. This test is similar to the pull-up test but does not require you to lift your body up and down. To begin this test, grasp a horizontal bar with an overhand grip, palms facing away from the body (see Figure 4.52). Then, with the assistance of a partner or two, raise your body off the ground so that your chin is above the bar and your arms are flexed. As soon as you reach this position, your partner should start a stopwatch and time how many seconds you can hang in this position. If you touch the bar with your chin or your chin falls below the level of the bar, the stopwatch should be stopped.

Record your results, and use Figure 4.50 to determine how well you did. For example, if Gary, a seventeen-year-old male, was able to hang for eighteen seconds, he would be in the healthy fitness zone for muscular strength. Once you have completed one or more of the muscular strength evaluations, record your scores on your personal fitness profile chart like the one in the "Active Mind/Active Body" activity at the end of the chapter.

Muscular Endurance

Curl-up Test.   *The curl-up evaluation can be used to assess your abdominal muscular endurance.* To begin this test you need two partners, a mat, and a measuring strip (such as a yardstick or tape measure) that is 30 inches long and 4.5 inches wide. Lie on your back on the mat with your knees bent at an angle of 140 degrees, feet flat on the floor, legs slightly apart, arms straight and parallel to your trunk, and palms resting on the mat. One partner

Flexed Arm Hang Test.
Not all students will be able to do a pull-up. It is well documented that many teen-age females have less upper body strength than their male counterparts. This is related to differences in body composition between genders. (See Chapter 9.) The Flexed Arm Hang may be a more suitable option for the evaluation of upper body strength and endurance for males and females who have trouble with the pull-up test.

The student testing team can be used to administer this test. Make sure the bar is high enough to prevent students' feet from touching the floor. Students may use a chair or have a partner assist them into the start position. Palms should be facing away from the body and the chin position should be above the bar (not touching). Timer should use a stopwatch to record the seconds. The time will stop when the chin touches the bar or the chin drops below the bar. Students do not need to exceed the maximum number of seconds recommended in Figure 4.50. Student record keeper will record scores for the teacher. Each student should interpret his or her score using Figure 4.50 and record it on his or her fitness profile sheet (Figure 4.58).

Special Needs

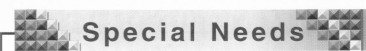

Congenital heart conditions are often defects in the structure of the heart that can be repaired by surgery. It is important that students with these types of congenital problems maintain a healthy, active lifestyle to avoid future problems. Generally, there are no minimal restrictions after successful surgery. Students with metabolic or chromosomal disorders (e.g., Down's Syndrome) have a 20% to 60% prevalence of congenital heart defects. Instructors should exercise caution when programming for these individuals.

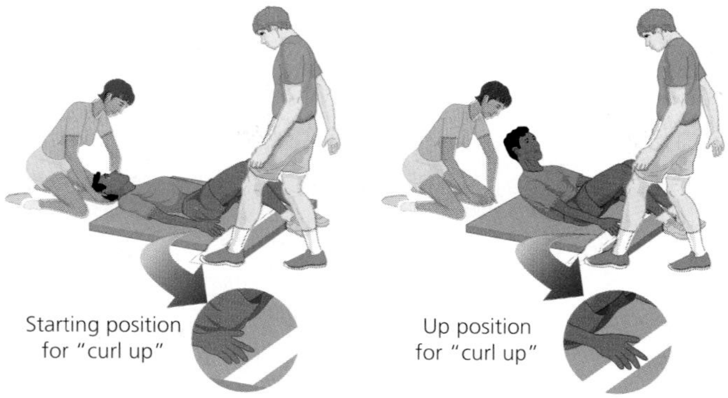

Starting position
for "curl up"

Up position
for "curl up"

• **Figure 4.53**   *Curl-up Test (muscular endurance evaluation).*
Source: With permission from The Cooper Institute for Aerobics
Research, *The Prudential Fitnessgram Test Administration Manual* (Dallas, TX: 1992), 19.

Age	Number of Curl-ups
	Males
13	21–40
14	24–45
15+	24–47
	Females
13	18–32
14	18–32
15+	18–35

Scores below the healthy zone are considered low.

• **Figure 4.54**   *Curl-up Scores (healthy zone).*
Source: With permission from The Cooper Institute for Aerobics Research, *The Prudential Fitnessgram Test Administration Manual* (Dallas, TX: 1992), 46–47.

should use his or her hands to make a resting place for your head. After you have assumed the correct position on the mat, have one of your partners place the measuring strip under your knees on the mat so that your fingertips are just resting on the edge of the measuring strip (see Figure 4.53). You may need a partner to secure the ends of the measuring strip. Start to curl up until your fingers reach the other side of the measuring strip, and keep your heels in contact with the mat. Then curl back down until your head touches your partner's hand. Do as many curl-ups as you can to a maximum of seventy-five. Pace yourself at a controlled rate of twenty curl-ups per minute, or about one curl-up every three seconds.

Record your results, and use Figure 4.54 to determine how well you did. For example, if Polly, a fourteen-year-old female, was able to do twenty-six curl-ups, she would be in the healthy fitness zone for muscular endurance. Once you have completed the muscular endurance evaluation, record your score on your personal fitness profile chart like the one in the "Active Mind/Active Body" activity at the end of the chapter.

Body Composition

You can use a body mass index to evaluate your body composition.

Body Mass Index (BMI).   The Prudential *Fitnessgram* Body Mass Index (BMI) evaluation gives you a description of your weight

(Continued on next page)

Curl-up Test. Discuss how strong, tight abdominal muscles can help prevent problems with low back injury. Strong abdominals prevent the pelvic girdle from tilting forward and placing additional strain on the lower back muscles.

Properly set up the testing area. Have partners assist anyone being tested. Mats are recommended. Have student partners place the measuring strip in the proper position. Students should raise their torsos up just high enough for their fingertips to cross over the measuring strip, then return to starting position. Students' hips must remain in contact with the mat at all times. Have students breathe out when they come up. It is also important to maintain proper pacing. Students do not need to exceed the maximum number of curl-ups recommended in Figure 4.54. Student record keeper should record scores for the teacher. Each student should interpret his or her scores using Figure 4.54 and record it on his or her fitness profile sheet (Figure 4.58).

Mild cardiac defects may not be corrected by surgery. Many times these types of defects go undetected, or if they are detected, surgery can be delayed until a certain age. These students will need to be restricted from any strenuous exercise.

Students with disabilities, particularly those whose disabilities affect large muscle groups, will experience restricted aerobic workload capacity. These students can benefit greatly from training that allows them to progress at their own rates. Even though a student may be limited in physical abilities, all training sessions should focus on the overload principle, with each session becoming increasingly more demanding.

Body Mass Index Test.
Discuss with students that there are ways other than the Body Mass Index Test to evaluate body composition. These ways will be discussed at length in Chapter 9.

This evaluation is not as accurate as skinfold testing or underwater weighing because it does not take into account body types such as short, stocky frames, which can carry more muscle mass.

Have students take off their shoes to weigh themselves. (It is helpful to have scales available throughout this course.) Make sure students have privacy when weighing. This is a sensitive issue and not for the student test team to know.

(continued)

Body Mass Index

Weight (pounds)	48	49	50	51	52	53	54	55	56	57	58	59	60	61	62	63
								Height (inches)								
80	24.5	23.5	22.5	21.7	20.8	20.1	19.3	18.6	18.0	17.3	16.8	16.2	15.7	15.1	14.7	14.2
85	26.0	24.9	24.0	23.0	22.1	21.3	20.5	19.8	19.1	18.4	17.8	17.2	16.6	16.1	15.6	15.1
90	27.5	26.4	25.4	24.4	23.5	22.6	21.7	21.0	20.2	19.5	18.8	18.2	17.6	17.0	16.5	16.0
95	29.1	27.9	26.8	25.7	24.8	23.8	23.0	22.1	21.3	20.6	19.9	19.2	18.6	18.0	17.4	16.9
100	30.6	29.3	28.2	27.1	26.1	25.1	24.2	23.3	22.5	21.7	20.9	20.2	19.6	18.9	18.3	17.8
105	32.1	30.8	29.6	28.4	27.4	26.3	25.4	24.5	23.6	22.8	22.0	21.3	20.5	19.9	19.2	18.6
110	33.6	32.3	31.0	29.8	28.7	27.6	26.6	25.6	24.7	23.9	23.0	22.3	21.5	20.8	20.2	19.5
115	35.2	33.7	32.4	31.2	30.0	28.8	27.8	26.8	25.8	24.9	24.1	23.3	22.5	21.8	21.1	20.4
120	36.7	35.2	33.8	32.5	31.3	30.1	29.0	27.9	27.0	26.0	25.1	24.3	23.5	22.7	22.0	21.3
125	38.2	36.7	35.2	33.9	32.6	31.4	30.2	29.1	28.1	27.1	26.2	25.3	24.5	23.7	22.9	22.2
130	39.8	38.1	36.6	35.2	33.9	32.6	31.4	30.3	29.2	28.2	27.2	26.3	25.4	24.6	23.8	23.1
135	41.3	39.6	38.0	36.6	35.2	33.9	32.6	31.4	30.3	29.3	28.3	27.3	26.4	25.6	24.7	24.0
140	42.8	41.1	39.5	37.9	36.5	35.1	33.8	32.6	31.5	30.4	29.3	28.3	27.4	26.5	25.7	24.9
145	44.3	42.5	40.9	39.3	37.8	36.4	35.0	33.8	32.6	31.4	30.4	29.3	28.4	27.5	26.6	25.7
150	45.9	44.0	42.3	40.6	39.1	37.6	36.2	34.9	33.7	32.5	31.4	30.4	29.4	28.4	27.5	26.6
155	47.4	45.5	43.7	42.0	40.4	38.9	37.5	36.1	34.8	33.6	32.5	31.4	30.3	29.3	28.4	27.5
160	48.9	47.0	45.1	43.3	41.7	40.1	38.7	37.3	35.9	34.7	33.5	32.4	31.3	30.3	29.3	28.4
165	50.5	48.4	46.5	44.7	43.0	41.4	39.9	38.4	37.1	35.8	34.6	33.4	32.3	31.2	30.2	29.3
170	52.0	49.9	47.9	46.6	44.3	42.6	41.1	39.6	38.2	36.9	35.6	34.4	33.3	32.2	31.2	30.2
175	53.5	51.4	49.3	47.4	45.6	43.9	42.3	40.8	39.3	37.9	36.7	35.4	34.2	33.1	32.1	31.1
180	55.0	52.8	50.7	48.8	46.9	45.1	43.5	41.9	40.4	39.0	37.7	36.4	35.2	34.1	33.0	32.0
185	56.6	54.3	52.1	50.1	48.2	46.4	44.7	43.1	41.6	40.1	38.7	37.4	36.2	35.0	33.9	32.8
190	58.1	55.8	53.5	51.5	49.5	47.7	45.9	44.3	42.7	41.2	39.8	38.5	37.2	36.0	34.8	33.7
195	59.6	57.2	55.0	52.8	50.8	48.9	47.1	45.4	43.8	42.3	40.8	39.5	38.2	36.9	35.7	34.6
200	61.2	58.7	56.4	54.2	52.1	50.2	48.3	46.6	44.9	43.4	41.9	40.5	39.1	37.9	36.7	35.5
205	62.7	60.2	57.8	55.5	53.4	51.4	49.5	47.7	46.1	44.5	42.9	41.5	40.1	38.8	37.6	36.4
210	64.2	61.6	59.2	56.9	54.7	52.7	50.7	48.9	47.2	45.5	44.0	42.5	41.1	39.8	38.5	37.3
215	65.7	63.1	60.6	58.2	56.0	53.9	51.9	50.1	48.3	46.6	45.0	43.5	42.1	40.7	39.4	38.2
220	67.3	64.6	62.0	59.6	57.3	55.2	53.2	51.2	49.4	47.7	46.1	44.5	43.1	41.7	40.3	39.1
225	68.8	66.0	63.4	60.9	58.6	56.4	54.4	52.4	50.5	48.8	47.1	45.5	44.0	42.6	41.2	39.9
230	70.3	67.5	64.8	62.3	59.9	57.7	55.6	53.6	51.7	49.9	48.2	46.6	45.0	43.5	42.2	40.8
235	71.9	69.0	66.2	63.7	61.2	58.9	56.8	54.7	52.8	51.0	49.2	47.6	46.0	44.5	43.1	41.7
240	73.4	70.4	67.6	65.0	62.5	60.2	58.0	55.9	53.9	52.0	50.3	48.6	47.0	45.4	44.0	42.6
245	74.9	71.9	69.0	66.4	63.8	61.5	59.2	57.1	55.0	53.1	51.3	49.6	47.9	46.4	44.9	43.5
250	76.4	73.4	70.5	67.7	65.1	62.7	60.4	58.2	56.2	54.2	52.4	50.6	48.9	47.3	45.8	44.4

• Figure 4.55 *BMI Chart.*

relative to your height. You can use Figure 4.55 to find your BMI. For example, if John, a fifteen-year-old male, weighed 125 pounds and were 68 inches tall, his BMI in Figure 4.55 would be 19. This would place John in the healthy fitness zone for body composition based on the values in Figure 4.56.

To determine your BMI, look up your weight and height in Figure 4.55. When you have completed the body composition evaluation, record your score on your personal fitness profile chart like the one in the "Active Mind/Active Body" activity at the end of the chapter.

Across the Disciplines

Geography

Establish one class period a week when the students will walk, run, or walk/run for thirty to forty minutes. Since walking around a track or jogging path can soon lose its appeal, illustrate how

equating the distance walked can be applied to a "virtual" journey. Explain to students that, as a group, they are going to "Walk Across … (a state or a country) using the collective mileage of all the students to make the journey possible. Students will need maps to mark their

Body Mass Index

Weight (pounds)	64	65	66	67	68	69	70	71	72	73	74	75	76	77	78
							Height (inches)								
80	13.8	13.3	12.9	12.6	12.2	11.8	11.5	11.2	10.9	10.6	10.3	10.0	9.8	9.5	9.3
85	14.6	14.2	13.7	13.3	13.0	12.6	12.2	11.9	11.6	11.2	10.9	10.6	10.4	10.1	9.8
90	15.5	15.0	14.6	14.1	13.7	13.3	12.9	12.6	12.2	11.9	11.6	11.3	11.0	10.7	10.4
95	16.3	15.8	15.4	14.9	14.5	14.1	13.7	13.3	12.9	12.6	12.2	11.9	11.6	11.3	11.0
100	17.2	16.7	16.2	15.7	15.2	14.8	14.4	14.0	13.6	13.2	12.9	12.5	12.2	11.9	11.6
105	18.1	17.5	17.0	16.5	16.0	15.5	15.1	14.7	14.3	13.9	13.5	13.2	12.8	12.5	12.2
110	18.9	18.3	17.8	17.3	16.8	16.3	15.8	15.4	14.9	14.5	14.2	13.8	13.4	13.1	12.7
115	19.8	19.2	18.6	18.0	17.5	17.0	16.5	16.1	15.6	15.2	14.8	14.4	14.0	13.7	13.3
120	20.6	20.0	19.4	18.8	18.3	17.8	17.3	16.8	16.3	15.9	15.4	15.0	14.6	14.3	13.9
125	21.5	20.8	20.2	19.6	19.0	18.5	18.0	17.5	17.0	16.5	16.1	15.7	15.2	14.9	14.5
130	22.4	21.7	21.0	20.4	19.8	19.2	18.7	18.2	17.7	17.2	16.7	16.3	15.9	15.4	15.1
135	23.2	22.5	21.8	21.2	20.6	20.0	19.4	18.9	18.3	17.8	17.4	16.9	16.5	16.0	15.6
140	24.1	23.3	22.6	22.0	21.3	20.7	20.1	19.6	19.0	18.5	18.0	17.5	17.1	16.6	16.2
145	24.9	24.2	23.5	22.8	22.1	21.5	20.8	20.3	19.7	19.2	18.7	18.2	17.7	17.2	16.8
150	25.8	25.0	24.3	23.5	22.9	22.2	21.6	21.0	20.4	19.8	19.3	18.8	18.3	17.8	17.4
155	26.7	25.8	25.1	24.3	23.6	22.9	22.3	21.7	21.1	20.5	19.9	19.4	18.9	18.4	17.9
160	27.5	26.7	25.9	25.1	24.4	23.7	23.0	22.4	21.7	21.2	20.6	20.0	19.5	19.0	18.5
165	28.4	27.5	26.7	25.9	25.1	24.4	23.7	23.1	22.4	21.8	21.2	20.7	20.1	19.6	19.1
170	29.2	28.3	27.5	26.7	25.9	25.2	24.4	23.8	23.1	22.5	21.9	21.3	20.7	20.2	19.7
175	30.1	29.2	28.3	27.5	26.7	25.9	25.2	24.5	23.8	23.1	22.5	21.9	21.3	20.8	20.3
180	31.0	30.0	29.1	28.3	27.4	26.6	25.9	25.2	24.5	23.8	23.2	22.5	22.0	21.4	20.8
185	31.8	30.8	29.9	29.0	28.2	27.4	26.6	25.9	25.1	24.5	23.8	23.2	22.6	22.0	21.4
190	32.7	31.7	30.7	29.8	28.9	28.1	27.3	26.6	25.8	25.1	24.4	23.8	23.2	22.6	22.0
195	33.5	32.5	31.5	30.6	29.7	28.9	28.0	27.3	26.5	25.8	25.1	24.4	23.8	23.2	22.6
200	34.4	33.4	32.3	31.4	30.5	29.6	28.8	28.0	27.2	26.4	25.7	25.1	24.4	23.8	23.2
205	35.3	34.2	33.2	32.2	31.2	30.3	29.5	28.7	27.9	27.1	26.4	25.7	25.0	24.4	23.7
210	36.1	35.0	34.0	33.0	32.0	31.1	30.2	29.4	28.5	27.8	27.0	26.3	25.6	25.0	24.3
215	37.0	35.9	34.8	33.7	32.8	31.3	30.9	30.0	29.2	28.4	27.7	26.9	26.2	25.5	24.9
220	37.8	36.7	35.6	34.5	33.5	32.6	31.6	30.7	29.9	29.1	28.3	27.6	26.8	26.1	25.5
225	38.7	37.5	36.4	35.3	34.3	33.3	32.4	31.4	30.6	29.7	28.9	28.2	27.4	26.7	26.1
230	39.6	38.4	37.2	36.1	35.0	34.0	33.1	32.1	31.3	30.4	29.6	28.8	28.1	27.3	26.6
235	40.4	39.2	38.0	36.9	35.8	34.8	33.8	32.8	31.9	31.1	30.2	29.4	28.7	27.9	27.2
240	41.3	40.0	38.8	37.7	36.6	35.5	34.5	33.5	32.6	31.7	30.9	30.1	29.3	28.5	27.8
245	42.1	40.9	39.6	38.5	37.3	36.3	35.2	34.2	33.3	32.4	31.5	30.7	29.9	29.1	28.4
250	43.0	41.7	40.4	39.2	38.1	37.0	35.9	34.9	34.0	33.1	32.2	31.3	30.5	29.7	29.0

Age	BMI Males	Age	BMI Females
13	23.0–16.6	13	24.5–17.5
14	24.5–17.5	14	25.0–17.5
15	25.0–18.1	15	25.0–17.5
16	26.5–18.5	16	25.0–17.5
17	27.0–18.8	17	26.0–17.5
17+	27.8–19.0	17+	27.3–18.0

Scores below the healthy zone are considered low.

• **Figure 4.56** *BMI Evaluation (healthy zone).*
Source: With permission from The Cooper Institute for Aerobics Research, *The Prudential Fitnessgram Test Administration Manual* (Dallas, TX: 1992), 46–47.

One way to measure height is to have tape on the wall that has height marked in inches. Have student test team measure the students.

Students should use Figure 4.55 to determine their BMI. Students should interpret their scores using Figure 4.56 and record them on their fitness profile sheets (Figure 4.58).

Teacher Readings

Prudential Fitnessgram Test Administration Manual, Cooper Institute for Aerobics Research, Dallas, TX: 1992.

place of embarkation, their route, and destination. Assign groups of three to research specific points of interest on their tours. As the class travels along its route, each group will discuss special historic landmarks, topography, climate, and the local industry or agriculture. As the class nears a destination, they will learn from their classmates what they might expect to eat that day, what language is spoken, what kind of currency they might need, and how their peers in that particular region might spend their time.

This activity can enable students to experience positive mental, emotional, and social rewards for physical exercise.

Any Body Can!

You may want to point out to students that women's sports were not as popular during Babe Didrikson's time as they are today. Ask them how this fact would have affected her popularity. Ask if students are aware of any other athletes who have continued to compete and be successful while dealing with a life-threatening disease.

Healthy People 2000

Objective 1.7—**Increase to at least 50 percent the proportion of overweight people age 12 and older who have adopted sound dietary practices combined with regular physical activity to attain an appropriate body weight.**

Overweight occurs when too few calories are expended and too many consumed for individual metabolic requirements. The results of weight-loss programs focused on dietary restrictions alone have not been encouraging. Physical activity burns calories, increases the proportion of lean to fat body mass, and raises the metabolic rate. Therefore, a combination of both caloric control and increased physical activity is important for attaining a healthy body weight.

Neither frequent fluctuations in body weight nor

Any Body Can!

"Babe" Didrikson Zaharias

Mildred "Babe" Didrikson Zaharias (1911–1956) was perhaps the greatest all-around woman athlete in American history. She had tremendous skills and, despite an early death, used them to maintain her health and fitness level.

Zaharias grew up in Port Arthur, Texas and earned the nickname "Babe" after baseball hero Babe Ruth because she could throw and hit baseballs harder than any boy in her neighborhood. In high school she played on every girls' team: volleyball, basketball, baseball, tennis, swimming, and golf. In one high school basketball game she scored 104 points.

While still in her teens, Babe became a two-time member of the All-American Women's basketball team. She helped her team win a national championship in 1931. At the 1932 Amateur Athletic Union National Track and Field Championships she won the shot put, baseball throw, long jump, 80-meter hurdles, and javelin throw. At the 1932 Olympics in Los Angeles, Babe won gold medals in the javelin throw and the hurdles, and finished second in the high jump.

After the Olympics, Babe became a national celebrity. She took up the game of golf in

earnest and won 17 amateur golf tournaments in a row, including both the U.S. and British National Championships. Babe joined the women's professional golf circuit in 1947 and won 31 Ladies Professional Golf Association (LPGA) victories.

At the height of her career, she was diagnosed with colon cancer. She underwent treatment, and returned to golf and won the 1954 U.S. Women's Open Golf Championship. After her victory, she told reporters, "This should show people not to be afraid of cancer."

Babe's commitment to her personal fitness made her the nation's leading female sports star for more than 30 years. The Associated Press named her Female Athlete of the year six times (1932, 1945, 1946, 1947, 1950, and 1954). She was elected to the LPGA Hall of Fame in 1951, the National Track and Field Hall of Fame in 1974, the International Women's Sports Hall of Fame in 1980, and the U.S. Olympic Hall of Fame in 1983. In 1950, the Associated Press named her the female Athlete of the Half Century.

Not everyone can be a world champion athlete like Babe Didrikson Zaharias, but Any Body Can learn to develop and maintain their skill- and health-related fitness. That's right, you can do it!

Wellness Connection

Tell students that you don't have to score a touchdown, dunk a basketball, or hit a home run to benefit from physical activity. A well-designed physical activity and exercise program can produce a number of wellness benefits. Physical activity and exercise programs can:

- Improve your mood
- Help relieve stress and tension
- Cause the release of endorphins and serotonin, which tend to promote a feeling of well-being
- Help prevent or control depression
- Increase your energy level

CONSUMER CORNER

Who Is the Expert?

At times you may need to seek out professional personal fitness advice. Where should you go for advice? Many people claim to be experts in the area of personal fitness. Unfortunately, many of these so-called experts are not really experts at all. How can you tell whether or not you're getting good advice?

Perhaps the smartest first step is to ask people you know—your parents, teachers, and friends—to make a recommendation. The physical education teachers at your school will be able to answer many of your questions. If they can't answer a particular question, they can probably recommend someone in your community who has developed a reputation for providing good, sound advice.

If someone has been recommended to you, ask about the person's education and training background. Does the person have a degree in physical fitness? What sort of training has

the person had? Be sure that the person's education and training are directly related to your fitness questions. A medical doctor, for example, would be very knowledgeable about your cardiovascular system, but unless the doctor has had special training, he or she would probably not be the best person to offer advice about a weight-training program to rehabilitate your injured knee.

Being a wise fitness consumer can help you protect your health, as well as save you time and money. A wise fitness consumer has a wealth of knowledge about fitness-related evaluations in order to be able to assess the advice of the professionals.

Most of the time, however, you should be able to solve your own personal fitness problems. Correctly administering self-evaluations can help you understand your own fitness needs and solve your own problems.

Active Mind! Active Body! Evaluating Fitness Levels

This "Active Mind/Active Body" activity is designed to help you learn to profile your personal fitness.

Use Figure 4.57 on page 150 as a sample to see how well you performed on the various skill-related fitness evaluations by checking off your score category on each test. Your personal fitness profile chart can be used to help you plot and identify your strengths and weaknesses on skill-related and health-related fitness components.

(Continued on next page)

extreme restrictions in food intake are desirable. Overweight people should increase their physical activity and should avoid calorie-dense foods, especially those high in fat. Diets that are lower in fat and higher in vegetables, fruits, and grains can facilitate weight reduction. Extremely low-calorie diets, cyclic weight reduction, and fad weight-loss regimes of unscientific merit should be avoided. Practices should be adopted that are safe and that lead to long-term maintenance of appropriate weight. Extreme behaviors as exhibited in bulimia or anorexia nervosa should be medically treated.

Self-help groups and programs that apply the principles of behavior modification (for example, goal setting, self-monitoring, stimulus control, reinforcement) may help overweight individuals to sustain the physical activity and dietary practices needed to reach an appropriate body weight.

- Reduce or maintain body weight
- Improve self-image
- Reduce your risk for heart disease
- Help you sleep better
- Make you more relaxed
- Help you live longer and better

Teacher Support Notes

• The health-related fitness test scores provided in this chapter are criterion referenced. That means they are developed and compared against a standard of what is considered good health and fitness. This is important to note because students are not being compared to other students but to scientific opinion as to what their fitness levels should be.

• The health-related scores are different from the skill-related scores. On the health-related evaluations, students will either be in the good-to-better range or fall in a fitness category that is below what is necessary for personal fitness.

• Students should be most concerned with their evaluation scores and should strive to improve any scores that are not in the good-to-better category.

Evaluating Fitness Levels *(continued)*

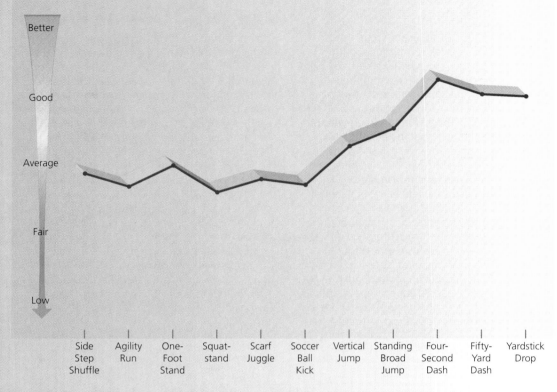

Figure 4.57   *Sample Skill-related Personal Fitness Profile Sheet.*

If you scored in the good to better zone on most of the skill-related evaluations, try to maintain your levels by practicing these skills in your personal fitness program. This is especially important if you are interested in performance fitness, which is primarily associated with your ability to perform successfully skills that are applied during games and sports. If your skill-related fitness scores were mostly low, you need to improve your skills so that you can engage in a variety of physical activities and influence your health-related fitness in a positive way. Even if you score low on every skill-related evaluation, you can still develop a personal fitness plan that can help you achieve a good to better level of health-related fitness.

Use Figure 4.58 on page 151 as a sample to rate yourself on the various health-related fitness evaluations you completed earlier in the chapter.

CRITICAL THINKING

Divide the class into cooperative learning groups of four students each. Assign a different city and state to each group. Cities should reflect areas where extreme weather and other environmental conditions can occur. For example:

Group 1	Buffalo, New York
Group 2	Atlanta, Georgia
Group 3	Seattle, Washington
Group 4	Austin, Texas
Group 5	Your city (or another of your choosing)

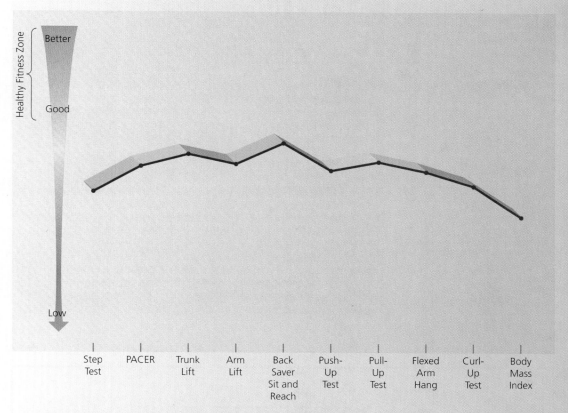

• **Figure 4.58** *Sample Health-related Personal Fitness Profile Sheet.*

REMEMBER This!

Your levels of health-related fitness determine your functional health. Therefore, you should do your best to develop and maintain good to better levels of health-related fitness throughout your life.

If you scored in the good to better zone on most of the health-related evaluations, try to maintain these levels by participating regularly in your personal fitness program. If you scored below the good to better zone on many or most of the health-related evaluations, try to improve these levels by developing and maintaining a personal fitness program. Be patient and recognize that participating in the process of living a physically active lifestyle is more important than the outcome of any one or two health-fitness evaluations.

Healthy People 2000

***Objective 1.8*—Increase to at least 50 percent the proportion of children and adolescents in first through twelfth grade who participate in daily school physical education.**

Participation in school physical education assures a minimum of physical activity for children. Presumably it also encourages extracurricular activity by children and continued physical activity into adulthood. Findings from the National Children and Youth Fitness Studies I and II suggest that the quantity, and in particular the quality, of school physical education programs have a significant positive effect on the

Have each group research weather conditions for its assigned city for each season of the year. The research should include average and extreme temperatures, humidity, precipitation, etc. Have groups use this information to develop a time line that shows the best and safest exercises for people who live in their assigned cities for each season of the

year. Students may add graphics to the time line.

Have students draw conclusions about the limitations to exercise that people who live in their assigned cities would face during each season of the year. Students can develop a second time line to show this information.

health-related fitness of children and youth. In addition, recent reports suggest that physical education programs in early childhood not only promote health and well-being, but also contribute to academic achievement.

Most children in the lower grades are enrolled in school physical education but many receive it fewer than five days per week. In the upper grades, fewer children are enrolled but those who are more often participate in daily physical education classes. Therefore, to achieve this objective, physical education needs to be more frequent for children in the lower grades, whereas enrollment needs to be increased for children in the upper grades.

Answers to
BELIEVE IT? ... OR NOT?

Pg. 110 False. The number of people six or older who regularly engage in these activities is unknown, but the goal of *Healthy People 2000* is 40 percent participation.
Pg. 115 True.
Pg. 119 True.
Pg. 119 True.
Pg. 120 True.
Pg. 121 False. It has been estimated that society could save $1,900 annually for each sedentary individual who begins a regular physical activity or exercise program. Savings would show up in such ways as fewer medical bills and less lost time at work.
Pg. 124 True.
Pg. 137 False. Of all people six years old or older, 24 percent do not participate in regular leisure-time physical activity. The goal of *Healthy People 2000* is to reduce this number to only 15 percent.

SUMMARY

Skill-related fitness, or performance fitness, has six parts. These parts are primarily associated with your ability to perform successfully skills that are applied during games and sports. Skill-related fitness includes agility, balance, coordination, speed, power, and reaction time. Health-related fitness has five parts, which are primarily associated with disease prevention and functional health. Health-related fitness includes cardiovascular fitness, flexibility, muscular strength, muscular endurance, and body composition. You need some degree of proficiency in both health-related and skill-related fitness because both kinds of fitness contribute to your performance in everyday life activities.

You can evaluate your skill-related and health-related fitness to determine your own levels of personal fitness. You can identify your strengths and weaknesses in skill-related and health-related fitness. You then can plot your results on a personal fitness profile chart and develop a method to monitor your personal fitness progress.

It is important for you to monitor your levels of both skill-related and health-related fitness throughout the rest of your life. By monitoring your personal fitness progress, you will be able to change your personal fitness goals as necessary and fine tune your personal fitness plan over time.

Special Needs

Students with disabilities often demonstrate various degrees of flexibility. Any flexibility program should be approached with extreme caution. A physician's permission should be obtained prior to beginning any flexibility program.

Down's Syndrome students typically exhibit laxity in all joints. Of particular concern is a condition called atlantoaxial instability, in which excessive mobility can occur in the cervical area of the spinal column. This condition exposes Down's Syndrome students to possible serious neck injuries if the neck is

Chapter 4 Review

True/False

On a separate sheet of paper, mark each question below either T for True or F for False.

1. Health-related fitness is primarily associated with disease prevention and functional health.
2. Both skill-related and health-related fitness can contribute to how we perform *everyday* life activities.
3. Power is a combination of speed and agility.
4. Improving your muscular endurance can improve your power.
5. The two factors that affect skill-related fitness components the most are heredity and practice.
6. *Cardiovascular fitness* refers to your ability to exercise at high intensity for short periods of time.
7. Poor flexibility can be associated with many injuries, including low back problems.
8. The ability to repeat the same task over and over is muscular endurance.
9. The amount of water, muscle, bone, and fat contained by our bodies is referred to as *body composition*.
10. The highly skilled athlete will have minimal needs for health-related fitness components.

Multiple Choice

1. Which of the following fitness components is not skill-related?
   a. power
   b. speed
   c. muscular strength
   d. balance

2. If you had to cross a bridge that was 10 feet long and 6 inches wide, which skill-related component would you most need?
   a. coordination
   b. power
   c. agility
   d. balance

3. Which of the following are associated with power?
   a. speed and reaction time
   b. strength and coordination
   c. speed and strength
   d. strength and reaction time

4. Which of the following has little or no influence on determining your foot speed?
   a. strength
   b. weight
   c. power
   d. heredity

5. Reaction time is best described by which of the following?
   a. the amount of time it takes you to respond to what you hear, see, or feel
   b. the amount of time it takes to cover a short distance
   c. the amount of time it takes to change the direction of your body
   d. none of the above

Answers

True/False

1. T
2. T
3. F
4. F
5. T
6. F
7. T
8. T
9. T
10. F

Multiple Choice

1. c
2. d
3. c
4. b
5. a

involved in a vertebral shift, causing the vertebrae to compress, and possibly causing spinal cord injury.

Flexibility is also compromised in students with spina bifida, muscular dystrophies, and cerebral palsy due to the configuration of the joints, muscles, and tendons. It is important for these students to include flexibility exercises to increase range of motion in their programs. It is important to remember that stretching programs should concentrate on slow, static stretches that move the body part to the extreme of available ROM. That position needs to be held for a specified number of seconds.

Chapter 4 Review

Multiple Choice
(continued)

6. d
7. d
8. d
9. b
10. d

Discussion

1. Answers may vary but should include the following information: Skill-related fitness is primarily associated with the ability to perform successfully during games and sports. Health-related fitness is primarily associated with disease prevention and functional health. Many skill-related fitness components are related to heredity.

2. Games such as soccer, basketball, hockey, tennis, and water polo require high levels of skill-related fitness. These games also require participants to have acceptable levels of cardiovascular, flexibility, muscular strength, and muscular endurance fitness.

3. Answers will vary depending on the specific evaluations the students chose. In general, health-related fitness evaluations can identify fitness weaknesses that will have an impact on your risk of disease and loss of functional health.

6. Which fitness component requires a great deal of oxygen over an extended period of time?
    a. agility
    b. coordination
    c. muscular endurance
    d. cardiovascular fitness

7. Which of the following statements is not true about flexibility?
    a. it can improve your performance fitness
    b. it can reduce your risk for injury
    c. it can reduce muscle soreness
    d. it can improve body composition

8. Your muscular strength is not influenced by which of the following?
    a. age

    b. gender
    c. heredity
    d. height

9. The vertical jump and standing broad jump are evaluations for which of the following?
    a. strength
    b. power
    c. agility
    d. coordination

10. Which of the following can be used as measures of flexibility?
    a. back saver sit and reach
    b. trunk lift
    c. arm lift
    d. all of the above

Discussion

1. List and explain three major differences between health-related fitness and skill-related fitness.

2. Explain how involvement in skill-related activities can contribute to the improvement or maintenance of health-related fitness.

3. Identify three of the health-related evaluations you used in this chapter, and explain how each can be of value to your fitness now and in the future.

 # Across the Disciplines

ART

A collage is a modern art form that may be used to integrate a series of images into one picture that reflects the artist's viewpoint. Discuss how students could use a collage as a form of expression of

how they react to the mixed messages they may receive from advertisements that target their age group. Have students brainstorm the most popular current commercials in magazines, on billboards, radio, and television for products that affect an individual's cardiovascular

Vocabulary Experience

Match the correct term in Column A to the definition in Column B by writing the appropriate number in each blank.

Column A	Column B
_____ health-related fitness	**1.** Your ability to contract your muscles several times without excessive fatigue.
_____ muscular endurance	**2.** Contains five components and is associated with disease prevention.
_____ balance	**3.** The ratio of water, bone, muscle, and fat in your body.
_____ skill-related fitness	**4.** Your ability to control or stabilize your equilibrium while moving or staying still.
_____ body composition	**5.** Your ability to react or respond quickly to what you hear, see, or feel.
_____ reaction time	**6.** Contains six components and is associated with performance fitness.

Critical Thinking

1. What criteria would you use to evaluate someone's skill-related and health-related fitness profile? Explain.

2. Compare muscular strength and muscular endurance. How can you evaluate each of them?

3. Discuss the accuracy of this statement: Health-related fitness is better for you than skill-related fitness.

Vocabulary Experience

_2_ health-related fitness
_1_ muscular endurance
_4_ balance
_6_ skill-related fitness
_3_ body composition
_5_ reaction time

Critical Thinking

1. Answers should include at least one test from each of the six skill-related components and at least one test from each of the five health-related components. These tests would provide a comprehensive test battery to determine an individual's physical fitness level.

2. Muscular strength refers to the maximal force that you can exert when you contract your muscles. This can be measured by doing pull-ups or push-ups. Muscular endurance refers to your ability to contract your muscles several times without excessive fatigue. This can be measured by doing curl-ups or the flexed arm hang.

3. The statement, "Health-related fitness is better for you than skill-related fitness," is a true statement.

fitness (snack foods, exercise equipment, smoking, alcohol, etc.). Have students identify items such as clothing, locations, music, humor, models, and sport activities, which are used to attract their attention in these advertisements. Examine the difference between real and perceived messages in the advertise-ments. Discuss whether the information in the advertisements conflicts with or supports what they understand about the development of cardiovascular health. Students will share, with their classmates, the collages they have created to express their points of view.

Chapter 5 is 32 pages long and divided into the five sections listed to the right. Major learning outcomes of the chapter are also listed to the right. Briefly, this chapter introduces students to the health-related fitness component of cardiovascular fitness. It emphasizes the importance of conditioning the circulatory system. It also provides students with examples of how to evaluate and improve their cardiovascular fitness.

Teacher
Resource
Material

In the Teacher Resource Package accompanying the textbook, you will find the following material to help you teach this chapter.

Activity Sheets

Reteaching Worksheets are provided in the Teacher Resource Package for each section of this chapter.

Chapter 5
Cardiovascular Fitness and You

156

PACING CHART

You could easily spend five to six days teaching this chapter if students read the entire chapter, do the Active Mind/Active Body activities, and complete several of the handouts from the Teacher Resource Package. However, you can cover the material in this chapter in four days. It is recommended that physical activity be a regular part of each class period (20 to 30 minutes minimum). The following are some examples of how to cover the main topics in the chapter if you are pressed for time.

Contents

1. Pump, Circulate, and Deliver
2. Preventing Cardiovascular Disease
3. Aerobic and Anaerobic Physical Activity and Exercise
4. Factors That Influence Your Cardiovascular Fitness Levels
5. Developing Cardiovascular Fitness

Outcomes

After reading and studying this chapter, you will be able to:

1. Explain how the heart, lungs, and blood vessels contribute to moderate to high levels of personal fitness.
2. Explain how moderate to high levels of cardiovascular fitness can reduce your risk for cardiovascular disease.
3. Identify examples of aerobic and anaerobic physical activities and exercises.
4. Describe the benefits of engaging in regular cardiovascular physical activity and exercise.
5. Identify and explain cardiovascular fitness evaluations that you could use to assess your cardiovascular fitness levels now and in the future.
6. Explain how you can develop moderate to high levels of cardiovascular fitness.

Key Terms

After reading and studying this chapter, you will be able to understand and provide practical definitions for the following terms:

recovery heart rate	vein	aerobic fitness level
diaphragm	muscle pump	interval training
intercostal	blood pressure	slow-twitch muscle fiber
abdominal	systolic blood pressure	fast-twitch muscle fiber
asthma	diastolic blood pressure	percentage of maximum
hemoglobin	atherosclerosis	heart rate
circulatory system	myocardial infarction (MI)	target heart rate zone
artery	aerobic	
capillary	anaerobic	

157

Transparencies/ Masters

A transparency or master is provided in the Teacher Resource Package for each of the following figures: 5.1, 5.2, 5.3, 5.4, 5.6, 5.7, 5.8, 5.9, 5.10, 5.11, 5.12, 5.13, 5.14, 5.15, 5.16, 5.17, 5.18, 5.19, and 5.20.

Discuss the Photo

Ask students to discuss in what ways the physical activities shown in the photos on these two pages are consistent with improving or maintaining cardiovascular fitness. Ask students what they do to maintain their cardiovascular fitness. Discuss with them some of the risk factors for cardiovascular disease. Emphasize that cardiovascular disease (heart disease, stroke, etc.) is the number one cause of death in the United States.

Time	Suggestions
Day 1	Assign students to read Section 1 prior to class. In class, do the Active Mind/Active Body activities on pages 161 and 166. Also include a variety of discussion about photos and figures.
Day 2	Assign students to read Sections 2 and 3 prior to class. In class, discuss ways of preventing cardiovascular disease. Also begin discussion about aerobic and anaerobic physical activity and exercise.
Day 3	Assign students to read Section 4 prior to class. Finish the discussion of Section 3. Discuss Section 4 and highlight the specific benefits of cardiovascular fitness conditioning.
Day 4	Assign students to read the Fitness Check and Section 5. Have them do at least one of the fitness evaluations. Discuss methods by which they can develop and/or maintain cardiovascular fitness.

CHAPTER 5
SECTION 1
158

Focus

Outcome

In **Section 1** students will learn:

1. To explain how the heart, lungs, and blood vessels contribute to moderate to high levels of personal fitness.

Focus Activities

1. Discuss the components that contribute to cardiovascular fitness, including the heart, the lungs, the blood and blood vessels, and blood pressure.
2. Use the Active Mind/ Active Body activities on pages 161 and 166 to have students determine maximum heart rate and their resting blood pressure.

INTRODUCTION

Of all the skill-related and health-related fitness components, cardiovascular fitness is the most important for maintaining your functional health throughout life. Cardiovascular fitness is the ability of the body to work continuously for extended periods of time. If you develop moderate to high levels of cardiovascular fitness, you can reduce your risks for cardiovascular disease, increase your predicted longevity, and help maintain your physical independence in living. Moderate to high levels of cardiovascular fitness will also increase your energy levels, make you look and feel better, reduce your stress levels, and help you control your weight and body composition. In this chapter, you will learn about the components that influence cardiovascular fitness, facts about cardiovascular disease, the specific benefits of cardiovascular fitness, and how you can develop moderate to high levels of cardiovascular fitness.

SECTION 1 Pump, Circulate, and Deliver

Cardiovascular fitness depends on a strong heart, an ability to deliver large amounts of blood to the muscles and organs of the body, and good lung function. In this section you will learn more about your heart, lungs, blood, blood vessels, and blood pressure.

Your Heart

Your heart is a muscle about the size and shape of your fist. It beats at the rate of about 50 to 80 (72, on average) beats per minute when your body is at rest, pumping about 5 liters of blood per minute (think of five 1-liter bottles of cola). See Figure 5.1. The heart is really two pumps in one. The right side of the heart pumps blood to the lungs, and the left side pumps blood to the upper and lower body (see Figure 5.2). During physical activity or exercise, your heart rate (pulse) increases (see Figure 5.3 on page 160) in response to your body's need for more blood. Your working muscles, tissues, and organs need blood to supply them with oxygen and other nutrients.

Your heart's ability to supply oxygen to your working muscles and organs is the major factor that determines your level of cardiovascular fitness. Oxygen, which is delivered by the blood, helps your cells produce the energy necessary for you to meet the demands of physical activities or exercise. As the demand for oxygen, and therefore blood, increases with increasing physical work, your heart must be able to meet this demand, or you quickly tire.

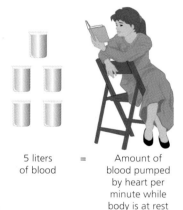

5 liters of blood = Amount of blood pumped by heart per minute while body is at rest

• **Figure 5.1** *Your heart pumps about 5 liters of blood every minute when your body is at rest.*

ABILITY LEVELS

Reteaching

Some students may need help mastering the concepts contained in this section. In your Teacher Resource Package, you will find the reproducible worksheet shown here. This worksheet should help students who have been absent and those needing additional help to improve their comprehension and retention of the content in this section.

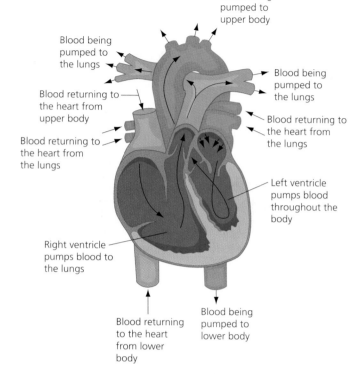

Blood being
pumped to
upper body

Blood being
pumped to
the lungs

Blood being
pumped to
the lungs

Blood returning to
the heart from
upper body

Blood returning to
the heart from
the lungs

Blood returning to
the heart from
the lungs

Left ventricle
pumps blood
throughout the
body

Right ventricle
pumps blood to
the lungs

Blood returning
to the heart
from lower
body

Blood being
pumped to
lower body

• **Figure 5.2**   *The heart acts as a pump, pumping blood to the
lungs and throughout the body.*

At maximal or exhaustive levels of exercise, your heart can beat at
a rate that can be estimated by subtracting your age from 220. For
example, if you are fifteen years old, your maximum heart rate is
approximately 220 – 15, or 205, beats per minute. (See the "Active
Mind/Active Body" activity on page 161.) Also, as you reach maximal levels of exercise, your heart beats more strongly. Therefore, you
can pump even more blood per minute (about 20 liters per minute).

Following a session of normal cardiovascular physical activity or
exercise, your heart rate gradually returns to resting levels. This is
called your **recovery heart rate** (see Figure 5.3). Your recovery heart
rate should drop back toward normal levels within 5 to 10 minutes of
finishing the exercise session. A general rule of thumb is that your
heart rate should be 120 beats per minute or lower within ten minutes
of cardiovascular conditioning. If it's higher than 120 beats, either you
are working too hard or your cardiovascular fitness level is low.

recovery heart rate

the gradual return of the heart
rate to resting levels within 5 to
10 minutes of a session of normal cardiovascular physical
activity or exercise.

Teach & Apply

Discussion

Ask students the following
questions: What do you
know about your heart?
How can you train your
heart to improve its efficiency? How fast does a
hummingbird's heart beat?
(about 1,000 beats per
minute) How fast does an
infant's heart beat? (varies,
around 100 beats per
minute) How fast does your
heart beat? (normal 50–80
beats per minute)

Teaching Strategies

Hold up two 1-liter bottles
(one bottle should be full of
water). Pour the water from
one bottle to the other at a
rate of five times per minute
to demonstrate how much
blood the heart pumps in a
minute. You can also use
Figure 5.1 to reinforce the
concept.

Enrichment   *This activity will allow you to provide a more challenging learning
experience for some of your students.*

**After the class has studied Fig-
ure 5.2, assign the students the
task of writing a paragraph describing the flow of
blood through the heart, arteries, capillaries, veins,
muscles, and lungs. Details should include an**

**explanation of the oxygen–carbon dioxide exchange
at the pulmonary level and muscle level as well as
the blood flow through the chambers of the heart.
Figure 5.5 will also be helpful for this activity.**

Activity

Check with the biology department of your school or the local library to locate a videotape that shows how the circulatory system works.

Discussion

• Use Figures 5.2 and 5.5 to show the circulatory system and the heart. Illustrate the four steps by which oxygen and carbon dioxide are handled by the body. Then, trace the flow of blood through the heart. You should emphasize that the heart is two pumps in one. The right side receives venous blood from the extremities in the right atrium and pumps it from the right ventricle to the lungs. Blood then returns from the lungs to the left atrium and is pumped to the upper and lower body by the left ventricle via the aorta.

• Use Figure 5.3 to illustrate how heart rate changes as one engages in a steady bout of exercise that can be carried on for several minutes at a time.

Teacher Support Notes

Cardiovascular conditioning for several weeks will lower resting heart rate significantly. Some highly trained endurance athletes have resting heart rates

REMEMBER This!

Someone who is usually sedentary often gets a side stitch during cardiovascular activity. This type of problem usually goes away after a few weeks of regular physical activity or exercise as the muscles that control breathing become conditioned.

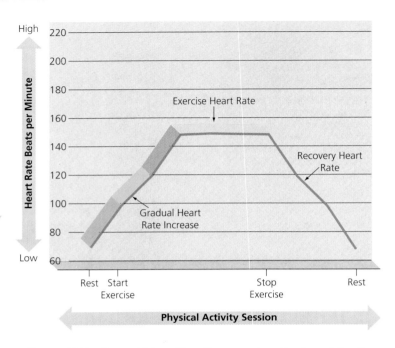

• **Figure 5.3** *Normal Heart Rate Response to a Session of Cardiovascular Physical Activity.*

By engaging in regular physical activity or exercise, you can condition your heart to become more efficient at rest, as well as during exercise. After 8 to 30 weeks of conditioning, your resting heart rate will be much lower than it was before conditioning. It could drop from 72 beats to 60 beats per minute. The extra conditioning causes the nerves that control your heart rate to adapt to make your heart more efficient. Your heart will also beat with greater force if you begin and maintain a conditioning program. Your heart will be able to pump with greater force both while you are at rest and during maximal exercise. This means that you can pump even more blood (oxygen) to your muscles and tissues—possibly as much as 5 liters more than your maximum before you began conditioning.

Your Lungs

Your lungs exchange oxygen and carbon dioxide during rest, as well as during physical activity and exercise. If your lungs are healthy, you can breathe about 6 liters of air per minute at rest and up to 100 liters of air per minute during vigorous exercise (see Figure 5.5).

Across the Disciplines

Physics

Any change in pressure applied to a fluid in a confined space is sent unchanged through that fluid (Pascal's principle.) Blood is a fluid that responds to pressure the ways other fluids do. The force of blood flowing through the circulatory system puts pressure on the walls of all the blood vessels (arteries, capillaries, and veins.) The pressure lessens as the blood travels from the aorta through the large arteries, small arteries, capillaries, small veins, and finally through the

Active Mind! Active Body!

What is Your Maximum Heart Rate?

Figure 5.4 lists estimated maximum heart rates for both boys and girls, ages 14 to 18 years. You can calculate this rate for yourself by subtracting your age from 220.

Age	Estimated Maximum Heart Rate
14	206
15	205
16	204
17	203
18	202

• **Figure 5.4** *Estimated Maximum Heart Rate.*

around 30 beats per minute. They also have very large resting stroke volume values. Parasympathetic nerves, which usually slow down bodily actions, and sympathetic nerves, which usually speed up bodily actions, control involuntary smooth muscle actions in the body. They comprise the autonomic nervous system. The decrease in resting heart rate is associated with greater control by the vagal nerves or parasympathetic nerves on the SA node (pacemaker tissue of the heart). This lowering of resting heart rate with conditioning has been called "increased vagal tone." With conditioning, maximal stroke volume will increase, but maximal heart rate will not increase and may even be reduced somewhat due to the increased stroke volume, because the heart can only pump so fast to empty effectively.

When you move more air through your lungs, you can get more oxygen into your blood and to your body. You can also remove carbon dioxide from your body more effectively. (See Figure 5–5 again.) If you are a chronic smoker, you will probably damage your lungs, reducing your ability to breathe large amounts of air. That is one rea-

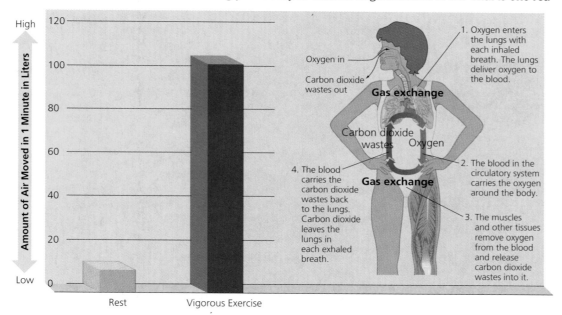

1. Oxygen enters the lungs with each inhaled breath. The lungs deliver oxygen to the blood.

Oxygen in

Carbon dioxide wastes out

Gas exchange

Carbon dioxide wastes   Oxygen

4. The blood carries the carbon dioxide wastes back to the lungs. Carbon dioxide leaves the lungs in each exhaled breath.

Gas exchange

2. The blood in the circulatory system carries the oxygen around the body.

3. The muscles and other tissues remove oxygen from the blood and release carbon dioxide wastes into it.

• **Figure 5.5** *The Circulatory System and a Comparison of Amount of Air You Breathe at Rest and During Vigorous Exercise.*

Discussion

• Use Figure 5.5 to discuss the changes in the amount of air that students might be able to breathe in moving from rest to maximal exercise. Have students think of a large balloon. Ask them how large the balloon would have to be to hold 100 liters of air (about 3 feet high and 3 feet around). Then tell them that this is the amount of air healthy lungs can move each minute during vigorous exercise.

large veins to the right atrium where the pressure is almost zero. Discuss with students the help blood receives from one-way valves in veins and skeletal muscles to move against gravity back to the heart.

Assign students, in groups of five, to demonstrate Pascal's principle—how the circulatory system is designed to move blood in a round-trip journey to and from the heart. Also have them demonstrate an example of how a cardiovascular disease can inhibit that process. Students may choose to design an experiment, write a dramatization using classmates to play the various parts, etc.

diaphragm

a muscle in the middle chest area that is used in breathing.

intercostal

a muscle around the ribs that is used in breathing.

abdominal

a muscle in the lower stomach area that is used in breathing.

asthma

restriction of the breathing passages due to dust, allergies, pollution, or even vigorous exercise.

son why chronic smokers usually have lower cardiovascular fitness levels than nonsmokers.

With cardiovascular conditioning, you improve your ability to breathe large amounts of air. Following several weeks of cardiovascular conditioning, the muscles that you use to breathe—such as the **diaphragm**, the **intercostals**, and the **abdominals**—do not fatigue as easily as they did when you were sedentary. (See Figure 5.6.)

During physical activity and exercise, the air passages in your lungs relax and open up so that you can move more air to meet the demands for oxygen in your muscles and tissues (Figure 5.7). When some people engage in physical activity or exercise, their air passages constrict instead of relax. These people often have trouble moving large amounts of air and may even get very short of breath.

Asthma is the most common condition causing the air passages to become restricted during physical activity or exercise. Several things can bring on asthma attacks, including dust, allergies, pollution, and even vigorous exercise. People with asthma should seek medical advice about their condition. They can usually engage in physical activity and exercise. However, they may need to spend more time warming up and need to work at more moderate levels of intensity to reduce the chances of an asthma attack. A doctor may also prescribe a "puffer," or inhaler, to use during workouts. Many people who have trouble with asthma when they are young have fewer problems with it as they age. Therefore, even if you have asthma, you can and should develop regular physical activity and exercise patterns that will help you later in life.

• *If you have asthma, you might benefit from the use of an inhaler, which will help you breathe during your workouts.*

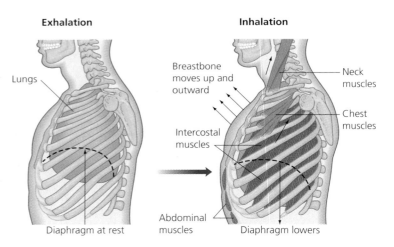

• **Figure 5.6** *Muscles Used in Breathing.*

• Use Figure 5.6 to discuss the major muscles involved with breathing. Point out that the diaphragm and the intercostals are involved mainly in breathing while sitting at rest. The abdominal muscles are recruited and used to a greater extent as you get into higher intensities of physical activity or exercise. Also draw attention to the Believe It Or Not on page 159. Ask how many students thought it was true.
• Use Figure 5.7 to introduce students to the respiratory problem of asthma. Ask students how many of them have had or currently suffer from asthma. Ask those that have asthma what causes it.

Activity

Have each student bring a straw to class (you may be able to get these in the school cafeteria). Have them sit at rest and breathe normally through the straw while pinching their noses shut. Then, have them walk briskly, still breathing through the straw (have them keep pinching their noses). Ask them how it felt. The sensation should be much like asthmatics have when they have vasoconstriction (restriction) of the air passages.

Discussion

Ask the students to name some of the substances in their blood. (Answers should include: hemoglobin, carbon dioxide, oxygen, etc.)

CRITICAL THINKING

After students have learned the meaning of blood pressure (including proper technique for measuring), resting and exercise heart rate, and target heart rate, divide the class into small "statistic gathering" groups. Assign a group to each of the following age groups: 20–30 years old, 31–40 years old, 41–50 years old, 51+ years old.

Have the groups collect the following information from people in each age group: resting heart rate, exercise heart rate, blood pressure.

Make sure the following are repre-

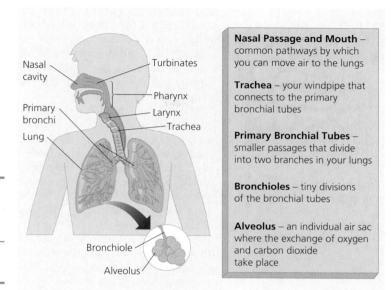

Nasal Passage and Mouth – common pathways by which you can move air to the lungs

Trachea – your windpipe that connects to the primary bronchial tubes

Primary Bronchial Tubes – smaller passages that divide into two branches in your lungs

Bronchioles – tiny divisions of the bronchial tubes

Alveolus – an individual air sac where the exchange of oxygen and carbon dioxide take place

• *Figure 5.7*   *Your Air Passageways.*

hemoglobin

an iron-rich compound in the blood that helps carry oxygen from the lungs to the muscles, tissues, and organs.

circulatory system

the heart and the system of blood vessels in the body, including the arteries, capillaries, and veins.

artery

a blood vessel that carries blood away from the heart and branches out to supply oxygen and other nutrients to the muscles, tissues, and organs of the body.

capillary

a small blood vessel that delivers oxygen and other nutrients to the individual muscle, tissue, and organ cells.

vein

a blood vessel that collects blood from the capillaries and carries it back to the heart.

Your Blood and Blood Vessels

Your blood and blood vessels are important to your cardiovascular fitness. **Hemoglobin** is an iron-rich compound in your blood that helps carry oxygen from your lungs to your muscles, tissues, and organs. Hemoglobin levels can increase with cardiovascular training, which results in more effective delivery of oxygen to your body. Your blood also carries carbon dioxide from the cells of your muscles, tissues, and organs back to the lungs so the carbon dioxide can be removed from your body. Your blood contains additional substances needed for good cardiovascular health (for example, the substances that help keep your blood from clotting inside your blood vessels). These substances are more efficient with good to better levels of cardiovascular fitness.

The arteries, capillaries, and veins are blood vessels that, along with the heart, make up the **circulatory system**. **Arteries** carry blood away from the heart (see Figure 5.2 again) and branch out to supply the muscles, tissues, and organs of the body with oxygen and other nutrients. Blood moves through the arteries to the **capillaries**, which are near the cells of the body. The small capillaries deliver oxygen and other nutrients to the individual muscle, tissue, and organ cells. The blood from the capillaries is then collected in the **veins** and carried back to the heart. (See Figure 5.8.)

sented: weight lifter, runner, walker, aerobic dancer, and someone who does not exercise.

Have the groups present the information they collect in graph and written form. Students will summarize and draw conclusions from the information relating to the factors listed above.

To personalize this activity, have students collect the same information on themselves three different times during the course of the semester. Students should then evaluate and draw conclusions about themselves and classmates as they relate to exercise.

Discussion

• Use Figure 5.8 to discuss the importance of having a closed circulatory system including the arteries, capillaries, and veins. If the system had a leak, like in a major artery puncture wound, blood flow would be seriously disrupted and blood pressure would fall.

• Remind students about the dangers of blood pooling by showing Figure 3.13 from Chapter 3. Discuss the term "muscle pump."

• Discuss the concept of redistribution of blood flow as one moves from rest to exercise.

Discussion

Use Figure 5.9 to discuss the measurement of systolic blood pressure. Ask students if they have ever had their blood pressure measured. If so, ask them what it is. Also ask them if it is normal. How do they know?

Teacher Support Notes

Figure 5.9 shows a simplified three-step process for measuring systolic blood pressure. In step one, the blood pressure cuff is applied to the student's right arm and the bulb is squeezed to increase the pressure surrounding the brachial artery, which constricts, temporarily cutting off blood flow to the forearm. In step two, with the

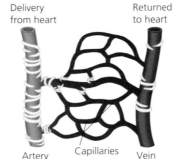

Delivery from heart
Returned to heart

Artery   Capillaries   Vein

• **Figure 5.8** *The blood travels from arteries, through the capillaries to deliver oxygen and nutrients, and then back to the heart through the veins.*

muscle pump

the contraction of the muscles in the body (especially the legs) as the muscles squeeze the veins to help blood move back to the right side of the heart.

blood pressure

the force by which blood is pushed against the walls of the arteries.

systolic blood pressure

the pressure on the arteries when the heart contracts.

diastolic blood pressure

the pressure on the arteries when the heart relaxes after contraction.

The veins have a series of one-way valves that cause blood to move back toward the heart (refer back to Figure 3.13 in Chapter 3). When the muscles in your body (especially your legs) contract, they squeeze the veins to help blood move back to the right side of your heart. This action is called the **muscle pump**. By doing your cardiovascular cool-down, you prevent blood from pooling by activating the muscle pump.

Your blood vessels are also important because they help you shift blood around in your body during exercise. When you are at rest, much of your blood is in the large veins of your lower stomach area and legs. During physical activity or exercise, you must be able to shift blood quickly from the large veins to the arteries that deliver blood to the muscles, tissues, and organs. You do this by increasing your heart rate, by constricting the blood vessels in some areas of your body, and by relaxing blood vessels elsewhere. This constricting and relaxing of blood vessels is controlled by nerve activity that your body does automatically—you do not even need to think about it. However, you can improve your ability to shift blood by constricting or relaxing your blood vessels. This ability comes with good to better cardiovascular fitness levels.

Blood Pressure

Blood pressure is defined as the force by which blood is pushed against the walls of your arteries. Blood pressure consists of two parts. Your **systolic blood pressure** is the pressure on your arteries when your heart contracts. Your **diastolic blood pressure** is

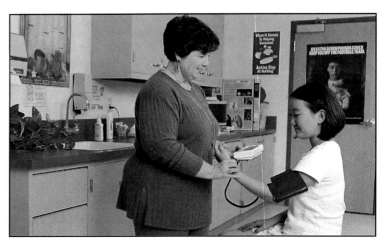

• *See your school nurse or another trained health professional to determine your blood pressure.*

Special Needs

Many disabled students exhibit very limited aerobic fitness. It is important to have as much information as possible about each student who may be prone to cardiopulmonary problems. Oxygen intake differs greatly depending on the disability. The greater the damage to the central nervous system, the less efficient oxygen transport can be. A 55% to 70% threshold level of the maximum heart rate is appropriate for the health impaired (i.e., 55% of 200 is 110). This is the approximate rate for a beginning program. It is better and safer to start too

Stress Break

Regular exercise can reduce or prevent high blood pressure. Exercise alone is not the answer, however. Two other parts of the puzzle are good nutrition and sound stress management strategies.

How you deal with your parents, teachers, and peers during irritating or emotional situations can raise your blood pressure. Therefore, having the ability to recognize stressful situations and then to deal with them in a positive way is vital to your health. Abilities that help you deal with stressful situations are called *coping strategies.*

You could use negative strategies such as drinking, smoking, yelling, screaming, or suppressing your emotions. However, positive coping strategies, such as eating well, exercising regularly, relaxing when possible, and learning to talk about your problems, are better for your health.

associated with the pressure on your arteries when your heart relaxes after contraction. Blood pressure is reported as two numbers, such as 120 over 80, which is written 120/80. Your systolic blood pressure is the top number. Your diastolic blood pressure is the bottom number. Normal blood pressure should fall below values of 140/90 on average, when measured on a regular basis. Blood pressure is easy to measure, but it should be determined by trained health professionals (see Figure 5.9). What is your blood pressure? See the "Active Mind/Active Body" activity on page 166 to find out.

Individuals with blood pressure above 140/90 may have hypertension (high blood pressure). Those with hypertension are at a higher risk for stroke and heart attack.

Individuals with hypertension may be told by their doctors to modify their diet and engage in regular physical activity or exercise. After several weeks of dieting and regular physical activity or exercise, a person can expect to reduce his or her blood pressure by about 10 units (for example, from 140/90 to maybe 130/80). This reduction is probably due to a lower resting heart rate and better nerve control of the blood vessels. If diet and regular physical activ-

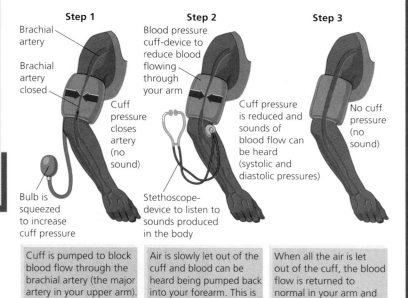

Step 1
Brachial artery
Brachial artery closed
Cuff pressure closes artery (no sound)
Bulb is squeezed to increase cuff pressure

Step 2
Blood pressure cuff-device to reduce blood flowing through your arm
Cuff pressure is reduced and sounds of blood flow can be heard (systolic and diastolic pressures)
Stethoscope-device to listen to sounds produced in the body

Step 3
No cuff pressure (no sound)

Cuff is pumped to block blood flow through the brachial artery (the major artery in your upper arm).

Air is slowly let out of the cuff and blood can be heard being pumped back into your forearm. This is called your systolic (or top) blood pressure.

When all the air is let out of the cuff, the blood flow is returned to normal in your arm and the sounds that can be heard disappear. This is called your diastolic blood pressure.

• *Figure 5.9* *Measuring Your Blood Pressure with a Blood Pressure Cuff.*

cuff still inflated to about 200 mmHg, the nurse (or other health professional) releases the pressure slowly from the cuff and listens with a stethoscope for a tapping sound. When blood flow returns to the forearm, the first tapping sound heard is the systolic pressure (for example 120 mmHg). When the tapping sounds muffle and disappear, the diastolic pressure is recorded (80 mmHg, for example). In step three, the cuff is then completely deflated and the student's blood pressure can be recorded.

Discussion

• Discuss with students whether they think that regular cardiovascular conditioning can help control a person's blood pressure. If they think so, ask them how this might work.
• Ask students if they have ever experienced dizziness when they change positions quickly. If they have, ask them if the experience scared them. Does it make them feel better to know that this is normal for the vast majority of people?

Assess

Use the Section 1 Review questions to assess students' comprehension of the concepts presented in Section 1.

low than too high with the disabled population. Some medically disabled students who have limited large muscle use may be unable to maintain their MHR for a time period long enough to improve cardiorespiratory endurance.

Exercise is critical to the maintenance of respiratory function in the disabled population. Students with spinal cord injuries or malformations (e.g., spina bifida) will have impaired respiratory mechanics. Students who are wheelchair bound often exhibit poor postural alignments that may compromise lung efficiency. Students who are diagnosed with asthma should only begin an exercise program with direct input from a physician.

What is Your Blood Pressure?

Have the school nurse measure your blood pressure. If the school nurse cannot measure your blood pressure, have it measured by your physician at your next medical checkup or at a health fair.

REMEMBER This!

Even if a person is on medication to control hypertension, regular physical activity or exercise habits usually allow the person to take less medication than if he or she were inactive. Taking a lower amount of medication is desirable, because it usually means fewer negative side effects from the medication.

ity or exercise do not return blood pressure to normal, the doctor may prescribe medication.

There is no such thing as low blood pressure unless a person has symptoms such as dizziness, feels tired all the time, or has had an accident that caused a substantial loss of blood. A person with any of these symptoms, along with low blood pressure, should consult a physician and get a checkup.

Some people experience dizziness or "see stars" if they change their posture rapidly. Have you ever jumped up quickly from the couch, perhaps when the doorbell rang? If so, you may have felt dizzy for a few seconds. This is because your heart rate and blood pressure levels were low while you were at rest, and it took a few seconds for your body to respond by pumping more blood to your brain when you jumped up. This kind of response is normal and happens at one time or another to everyone. If you ever have what seem to be abnormal symptoms involving your heart, lungs, blood, blood vessels, or blood pressure, however, see your physician immediately.

SECTION 1 REVIEW

Answer the following questions on a separate sheet of paper:

1. How does your heart change with cardiovascular conditioning to make it more efficient at rest, as well as during exercise?

2. What muscles do you use when you breathe?

3. What is blood pressure, and what numbers for it are considered normal?

Wellness Connection

Stroke Volume—How Does It Relate To Cardiovascular Fitness?

You may want to share the following with your students:

The term *stroke volume* refers to the amount of blood that is pumped each

time the heart beats. Since we know the heart is a muscle, and that muscles respond to training, we can make our hearts stronger by exercising them. The stronger our heart muscles are, the more blood they can pump with each beat.

Suzie is a senior on the cross-country

Any Body Can!

Flora "Flo" Hyman

Flora "Flo" Hyman (1954–1986) has been called the best female volleyball player the U.S. has ever produced. She helped the U.S. women's volleyball team move from obscurity to international prominence (fame).

Flo began playing volleyball in high school and immediately became one of the nation's top players. She went on to become a three-time All-American at Houston, and was named to the U.S. national volleyball team in 1974. In 1976, she was named the nation's outstanding collegiate volleyball player.

The U.S. national volleyball team did not qualify for the 1976 Olympics, but by 1978 the U.S. team ranked fifth in the world, and moved to second place in 1979. Much of the improved success was due to Flo Hyman's contributions. She had grown to 6 feet, 5 inches tall and became one of the best "hitters" in the world.

Flo became the leader of the U.S. national volleyball team, which gained international recognition between 1979 and 1984. She stayed with the team through the 1980 Moscow Olympics boycott. Then, in the 1984 Los Angeles Olympics, thirty-year-old Flo Hyman helped lead her teammates to a silver medal finish behind the first place Chinese women.

Following the 1984 Olympics, Flo joined a professional volleyball circuit in Japan. On January 24, 1986, she collapsed during a match and died suddenly from a ruptured aorta (artery carrying blood from the heart to the rest of the body). Her death was due to a genetic disorder called *Marfan's syndrome* that can cause the aortic wall to become weak and to burst. Although Marfan's syndrome is very difficult to diagnose, Flo Hyman's tragic sudden death stimulated medical study in the diagnosis and treatment of this cardiovascular disorder. Today physicians are much more aware of the need to screen for and treat Marfan's syndrome. Flo Hyman's accomplishments on the volleyball court helped make volleyball the most popular high school sport today for girls in the U.S. Her aggressive, dominating style of play also helped stimulate the promotion of women's professional outdoor beach volleyball. In 1987, the Women's Sports Foundation honored her memory by establishing the "Flo Hyman Award" for women who capture Flo's dignity, spirit, and commitment to excellence.

Not everone can be as good at volleyball as Flo Hyman, but Any Body Can learn to identify and control cardiovascular disease risks while developing and maintaining their cardiovascular fitness. That's right, you can do it!

---

track team at Midtown High School and has been involved with vigorous cardiovascular training for the past four years. Her resting heart rate is 52 beats per minute. Johnny is also a senior at Midtown High but has never participated in sports or engaged in a regular fitness program. His resting heart rate is 86 beats per minute. Suzie has a high stroke volume and can supply her body's demand for oxygen with only 52 heart beats per minute. Johnny has a lower stroke volume and it takes 86 beats per minute to satisfy his body's need for oxygen. With a good cardiovascular fitness program Johnny can increase his stroke volume and lower his resting heart rate.

Chapter 5 Section 2
167

Any Body Can!

Ask students if they are aware of other athletes who have died suddenly. What were the causes? Did those athletes die during an actual competition? Also ask if Flo Hyman's death was due to controllable or uncontrollable risk factors. Do they think her volleyball conditioning could have had any imput on how long she lived?

Close

Divide the class into groups of three to four students and have them develop a report about various medications for the treatment of hypertension. Have each group choose one type of medication and briefly explain to the class how it works and what its side effects are. Then ask them if they think exercise is similar to a medication for hypertension.

Teacher Readings

Kenney, W. L., Senior Editor, *ACSM Guidelines for Exercise Testing and Prescription*, American College of Sports Medicine, 4th Edition, Lea & Febiger, Philadelphia, PA: 1995.

Focus

Outcome

In **Section 2** students will learn:

1. To explain how moderate to high levels of cardiovascular fitness can reduce their risk for cardiovascular disease.

Focus Activity

1. Discuss the process of atherosclerosis and the cardiovascular complications of heart attacks, strokes, and hypertension.

SECTION 2

Preventing Cardiovascular Disease

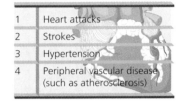

1	Heart attacks
2	Strokes
3	Hypertension
4	Peripheral vascular disease (such as atherosclerosis)

- **Figure 5.10** *Major Cardiovascular Diseases.*

Cardiovascular disease affects the heart and blood vessels of the body. There are a variety of cardiovascular diseases, such as heart attacks, strokes, hypertension, and peripheral vascular diseases (diseases of the arteries and veins of the extremities). See Figure 5.10. Cardiovascular diseases continue to be the leading cause of death in the United States. Most forms of cardiovascular disease are preventable. Whether or not you get them usually depends on how well you can modify or lower your health risk factors. You may want to go back to the "Active Mind/Active Body" activity on page 22 to review your risk factors.

Atherosclerosis

atherosclerosis

a disease process that causes substances to build up inside arteries, reducing or blocking blood flow.

The most common cause of cardiovascular disease can be traced to the development of **atherosclerosis**, a disease process that makes substances build up inside arteries, reducing or blocking blood flow. The cause of atherosclerosis is not known for sure. Experts believe that atherosclerosis probably occurs because the walls of arteries become damaged from hypertension, substances in cigarette smoke, or other causes. When the artery walls are damaged, cholesterol and other blood fats attach to the artery walls as the arteries try to repair themselves. (This process is more likely to occur when the blood fat levels are too high.) The process usually begins in childhood or young adulthood and continues for many years before cardiovascular disease is recognized. In Figure 5.11 you can see the process of atherosclerosis beginning and eventually almost blocking an artery.

Although atherosclerosis is treatable, it is much easier, safer, and less costly for you to try to prevent the process by developing a healthy lifestyle and controlling all the risk factors you can. For example, you have learned that HDL cholesterol is "good cholesterol," and higher levels of HDL in the blood help lower the risk of developing atherosclerosis. Regular cardiovascular physical activity and exercise have been shown to raise HDL cholesterol levels and to reduce the risk of developing cardiovascular diseases. Also, regular cardiovascular physical activity and exercise lower LDL cholesterol (or "bad cholesterol") levels and thereby lower cardiovascular disease risk. You will learn more about cholesterol in Chapter 10.

BELIEVE IT? ... OR NOT?

People who die suddenly while exercising always have advanced cases of atherosclerosis.

See page 183 for answer.

Reteaching

ABILITY **L**EVELS

Reteaching

Some students may need help mastering the concepts contained in this section. In your Teacher Resource Package, you will find the reproducible worksheet shown here. This worksheet should help students who have been absent and those needing additional help to improve their comprehension and retention of the content in this section.

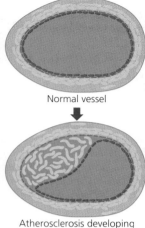

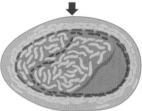

Normal vessel

Atherosclerosis developing

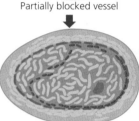

Partially blocked vessel

Totally blocked vessel

A healthy artery provides an open passageway for the flow of blood

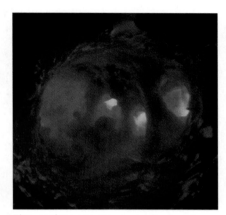

Plaques along an artery narrow its diameter and interfere with blood flow. Clots can form, making the problem worse.

- **Figure 5.11**   *The Stages in Atherosclerosis.*

Heart Attacks

myocardial infarction (MI)

a heart attack; a blockage of a vessel that feeds the heart muscle.

Myocardial infarction (MI) is the medical term for *heart attack*. A heart attack is a blockage of a vessel that feeds the heart muscle (see Figure 5.12). People having a heart attack may have tightness in the chest, sweating, nausea, and shortness of breath. Anyone with these symptoms should get to a doctor or hospital quickly.

Myocardial infarctions can be minor or major, depending on which artery or arteries become blocked. A person who has a heart attack

Teach & Apply

Discussion

• Use Figure 5.10 to discuss with students the various cardiovascular diseases. Ask them to recall what their individual cardiovascular risk factors were from the Chapter 1 Active Mind/Active Body activity.
• Use Figure 5.11 to discuss the process of atherosclerosis, which is the most common cause of cardiovascular disease. Discuss the illustration and the actual photos that show the plaque or narrowing of the artery.

Teacher Support Notes

• It is important that students understand that the development of atherosclerosis is a very complex process, and that it is not completely understood. It involves the interaction of many factors that change over time within the arterial wall. It is naive to believe

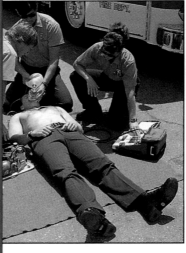

that it is high levels of cholesterol and other blood fats by themselves that just plug up an artery. Atherosclerosis begins for many individuals in childhood and adolescence, and therefore, it is important to control the cardiovascular risks that one has, if possible.

• HDL cholesterol can be raised about 5 units in many individuals by jogging for about 10 to 12 miles per week (at a pace of approximately 10 to 12 minutes per mile). The best way to lower LDL cholesterol levels is to lose weight if one is overweight.

Discussion

Use Figure 5.12 to illustrate a myocardial infarction to students. Ask them whether they think the blockage highlighted would cause a major or minor heart attack. Ask if they know someone who had a heart attack and lived. Is he or she taking better care of himself or herself since the heart attack?

Teacher Support Notes

The blocked artery pictured in Figure 5.12 is the left anterior descending (or LAD) coronary artery. It supplies blood to the left ventricle and the septum of the heart. A blockage of this nature would probably cause serious damage to the heart and limit its ability to pump blood. In fact, a blockage such as this one very likely would cause

• *Participating in a regular cardiovascular fitness program will significantly decrease your risks for having a heart attack.*

and lives can often resume a normal lifestyle, particularly if the person modifies his or her health risks and follows medical advice. Many fatal heart attacks could have been prevented. If you perform regular cardiovascular physical activity or exercise, your risk for having a heart attack will be reduced. Regular exercise will also reduce your risk of dying from a heart attack if you do have one.

Strokes

Strokes occur when there is a blockage or partial blockage of an artery supplying blood to the brain. Strokes, like heart attacks, can be minor or more major, depending upon which artery or arteries become narrowed or blocked. Strokes usually damage the brain and can leave a person partially or almost totally paralyzed. Sometimes when the damage from a stroke is minor, a person may only be paralyzed temporarily. However, a major stroke often results in death. If you perform regular cardiovascular physical activity or exercise, you will significantly reduce your risk for strokes. Figure 5.13 shows the affected sites of cardiovascular disease, along with the complications that result.

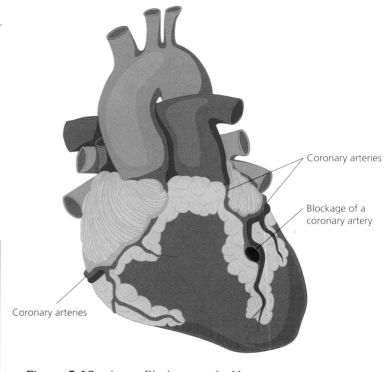

Coronary arteries

Blockage of a coronary artery

Coronary arteries

• **Figure 5.12**   *Artery Blockage on the Heart.*

Science and Technology

When describing the cardiovascular system, teachers rely on overhead transparencies and slides to show students the related organs. With a computer and access to the Internet, the teacher can now access interactive software that will give students a true understanding of

this complex system. The site on the Internet that has the best information for discussing the cardiovascular system is located at http://www.adam.com.

A.D.A.M. software is an interactive software package that allows students to view any anatomical system found in

Stress Break

People are usually classified as having Type A or Type B behavior. Type A individuals have been described as aggressive, concerned with time, tense, and competitive. Type B individuals are relaxed and generally do not get overstressed about things that would upset a Type A person.

Until recently, experts thought that all Type A individuals were at a higher risk for cardiovascular disease than Type B individuals. The experts reasoned that distress can cause increases in heart rate, blood pressure, and other important cardiovascular functions over time. However, most experts now agree that Type A individuals who can lower their stress levels with physical activity, exercise, or other methods are at no more risk for cardiovascular disease than Type B individuals. Type A individuals who do not reduce their stress levels effectively, however, have a higher than normal risk for developing cardiovascular disease.

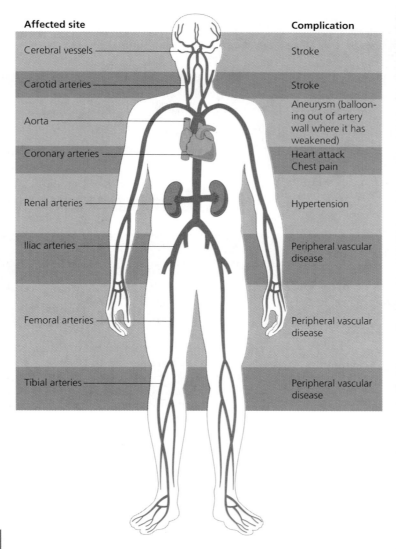

Affected site	Complication
Cerebral vessels	Stroke
Carotid arteries	Stroke
Aorta	Aneurysm (ballooning out of artery wall where it has weakened)
Coronary arteries	Heart attack Chest pain
Renal arteries	Hypertension
Iliac arteries	Peripheral vascular disease
Femoral arteries	Peripheral vascular disease
Tibial arteries	Peripheral vascular disease

• **Figure 5.13** *Sites Where Atherosclerosis Can Occur.*

Hypertension

Hypertension is the number-one risk factor increasing the likelihood of strokes. Hypertension is also a major risk factor in heart attacks. As you have learned, we all can and should know what our blood pressure is. If you have hypertension or develop it in the future, you can treat it effectively and safely under a doctor's super-

death. A blockage to a smaller branch of a right coronary artery would probably be less serious.

Stress Break

Have students make a list of things that might cause them to rate themselves as a Type A or Type B individual. Ask them to determine whether they feel as though they handle daily stress effectively most of the time.

Healthy People 2000

***Objective 1.1*—Reduce coronary heart disease deaths to no more than 100 per 100,000 people.** (Incidence was 135 per 100,000 people in 1987.)
Write this objective on the board or on an overhead transparency and create a discussion about why this goal is important.

Discussion

Use Figure 5.13 to discuss the sites where strokes and other cardiovascular diseases might occur. Ask students if they know someone who has had a stroke or has peripheral vascular disease.

Assess

Use the Section 2 Review questions to assess students' comprehension of the concepts presented in Section 2.

humans. The pictures are photo-quality diagrams showing muscles, heart, lungs, and the vascular system. The software allows students to trace blood flow from the muscle, through the heart and lungs, and back to the muscle. The pictures are printable and can be copied for use in tests or help guides.

Other interesting sites that will link the

teacher to the world of cardiovascular fitness are located at http:/www.yahoo.com/health. **Take the challenge:** Access ADAM and play with the software demonstrations. **Remember:** The Internet has hundreds of links to help the physical educator.

ANSWERS TO SECTION 2 REVIEW

1. It is a disease process that causes substances to build up inside arteries, reducing or blocking blood flow.
2. It is a blockage of a coronary artery supplying blood to the heart, and is often associated with atherosclerosis.
3. A stroke is a blockage of an artery supplying blood to the brain. The blockage is often associated with atherosclerosis.

Close

Use the "**A**ny **B**ody **C**an" feature about Flo Hyman to stimulate a discussion about famous athletes who have died suddenly due to cardiovascular diseases.

BELIEVE IT? ... OR NOT?

Over 60 million American adults and youth have high blood pressure.

See page 183 for answer.

vision. Your commitment to regular cardiovascular physical activity or exercise will reduce your risk for developing hypertension or help you manage it.

SECTION 2 REVIEW

Answer the following questions on a separate sheet of paper:
1. What is atherosclerosis and how does it occur?
2. What is a heart attack and what causes it?
3. What is a stroke and what causes it?

SECTION 3

Aerobic and Anaerobic Physical Activity and Exercise

aerobic

with oxygen.

anaerobic

without oxygen.

aerobic fitness level

cardiovascular fitness level.

Cardiovascular fitness is developed by engaging in aerobic activities. **Aerobic** means "with oxygen." Aerobic activities require you to work in a rhythmic, continuous manner using the large muscle groups of your body for several minutes at a time. **Anaerobic** means "without oxygen." Anaerobic activities require high levels of energy, are done at high intensity, and last only a few seconds or minutes.

Aerobic Work

When you work aerobically, you can supply large amounts of blood (and oxygen) to your muscles, tissues, and organs to meet their demands. Regular participation in aerobic activities is essential for good to better levels of health-related fitness. The term **aerobic fitness level** is often used to mean *cardiovascular fitness level.* Examples of aerobic activities include walking, hiking, jogging/running, swimming, cycling, cross-country skiing, dancing, skipping rope, rowing, stair climbing, in-line skating, and endurance games.

Anaerobic Work

Anaerobic activities are often, but not always, associated with developing skill-related fitness. Participation in anaerobic activities leads to moderate to high levels of muscular strength, muscular endurance, and flexibility. Examples of anaerobic activities include running up two flights of stairs, sprinting 40 yards, doing a fast break

Reteaching

Name _____ Date _____ Period _____

Chapter 5
Section 3

Aerobic and Anaerobic Physical Activity and Exercise

Directions: Answer the questions in the blanks provided.

In front of each of the following statements, write *Aerobic* or *Anaerobic,* according to the condition each one describes.

Aerobic	1. means "with oxygen"
Aerobic	2. activities including walking, swimming, cycling, rowing, skipping rope, and jogging
Anaerobic	3. associated with developing skill-related fitness
Aerobic	4. you can supply large amounts of blood and oxygen to your muscles, tissues, and organs
Anaerobic	5. activities require high levels of energy
Aerobic	6. requires you to work in a rhythmic, continuous manner
Anaerobic	7. activities are done at a high intensity
Anaerobic	8. leads to moderate to high levels of muscular strength, muscular endurance, and flexibility
Aerobic	9. activities require you to use the large muscle groups of your body for several minutes at a time
Aerobic	10. participation is essential for good to better levels of health-related fitness
Aerobic	11. you can meet your energy needs by supplying larger amounts of oxygen to your body.
Anaerobic	12. activities last only a few seconds or minutes
Anaerobic	13. you cannot meet the oxygen demands of a high-intensity physical activity
Aerobic	14. you can carry on a conversation while working steadily

Reteaching Worksheets   43   © 1997 West Publishing Co.

ABILITY LEVELS

Reteaching

Some students may need help mastering the concepts contained in this section. In your Teacher Resource Package, you will find the reproducible worksheet shown here. This worksheet should help students who have been absent and those needing additional help to improve their comprehension and retention of the content in this section.

• *Jumping rope continuously for several minutes is an example of aerobic activity. Sprinting over hurdles is an example of anaerobic activity.*

Focus

Outcome

In **Section 3** students will learn:

1. To identify examples of aerobic and anaerobic physical activities and exercises.

Focus Activities

1. Discuss aerobic and anaerobic work.
2. Use Figure 5.14 to discuss the difference between aerobic and anaerobic activities or exercises.

Teach & Apply

Activity

Have students make posters with two columns. In one column, students should list about fifteen aerobic physical activities. In the second column, have students list about fifteen anaerobic physical activities.

BELIEVE IT? ...
OR NOT?

When you engage in physical activity or exercise, it is best to breathe in through your nose and out through your mouth.

See page 183 for answer.

Aerobic Activity
Supply of Oxygen = Body's Demand for Oxygen

Anaerobic Activity
Body's Demand for Oxygen Exceeds Body's Ability to Supply Oxygen

• **Figure 5.14** *Aerobic versus Anaerobic Activities.*

in basketball, or swimming 100 meters as fast as you can. These activities require large amounts of energy—a requirement that your body cannot meet for very long, because you cannot supply enough blood (oxygen) to your muscles, tissues, and organs to meet the high demand. Therefore, your ability to work anaerobically depends on the ability of your muscles, tissues, and organs to work with limited amounts of oxygen.

Aerobic versus Anaerobic Work

When you can meet your energy needs by supplying large amounts of oxygen to your body, you are working primarily in an aerobic mode (see Figure 5.14). If you cannot meet the oxygen demands of a high-intensity physical activity, you are working in a more anaerobic mode. You learned about the talk test in Chapter 3. If you can pass the talk test by carrying on a conversation while working steadily, you are working aerobically. If you can't pass the talk test because you are breathless at a high work intensity, you are working more anaerobically.

Many of the physical activities you enjoy may be part aerobic and part anaerobic. For example, in tennis you might play for one full hour (aerobic component). You might also do quick sprinting and hit the ball hard (anaerobic components), then take short rest periods. If you sprinted the straightaways on a track and walked/jogged the curves for several laps, you would be working both aerobically and anaerobically. The short sprints would be anaerobic, but because you

Enrichment   *This activity will allow you to provide a more challenging learning experience for some of your students.*

Have the students interview a coach or athletic trainer. The interview should include questions related to the benefits of aerobic activities and anaerobic activi- **ties in conditioning programs. The students should write a report on the responses to the questions, and be ready to share their information with the rest of the class.**

Assess

Use the Section 3 Review Questions to assess students' comprehension of the concepts presented in Section 3.

ANSWERS TO SECTION 3 REVIEW

1. Answers will vary but might include: walking, hiking, or bicycling.
2. Answers will vary but might include: sprinting 40 yards all out, doing a fast break in basketball, lifting your maximum weight in the bench press.
3. Generally, if you can pass the talk test while doing a physical activity or exercise, you are working aerobically. If you can't pass the talk test, you are working more anaerobically.

Close

Discuss with students how interval training can be used by athletes in training as well as by individuals with injuries undergoing rehabilitation. Ask students how the two programs might differ in terms of FIT. Have them develop examples of the two different programs for homework.

BELIEVE IT? ... OR NOT?

One of the *Healthy People 2000* goals is to increase the amount of time that physical education classes in schools spend being physically active. Most students are active during less than 30 percent of their physical education classes. The *Healthy People 2000* goal is to increase the active time to at least 50 percent.

See page 183 for answer.

• *These students are engaging in interval training. What clues tell you that they are working aerobically rather than anaerobically?*

interval training

alternating higher-intensity physical activities or exercises with lower-intensity recovery bouts for several minutes at a time.

did several laps over a period of several minutes, the activity would also be aerobic.

Alternating higher-intensity physical activities or exercises with lower-intensity recovery bouts for several minutes at a time is called **interval training**. (A slower version of this kind of conditioning was presented to you in Figure 3.11 in Chapter 3.) Interval training allows you to work at higher intensities for longer periods of time than you could work in a continuous manner.

By engaging in specific aerobic or anaerobic physical activities or exercises, you can improve your ability to perform work in both modes for improved skill- and health-related fitness. Developing cardiovascular fitness by engaging in aerobic activities will be discussed in Section 6, later in this chapter. Examples of other anaerobic activities will be discussed in Chapters 7 and 8.

SECTION 3 REVIEW

Answer the following questions on a separate sheet of paper:

1. List and describe three aerobic activities.
2. Name and describe three anaerobic activities.
3. How can you determine if you are working aerobically or anaerobically?

Equipment Options

In previous years, teachers have taught students to take their pulses by feeling their wrists or necks. However, two new types of cardio-pulse monitors are rapidly becoming accessible to the P.E. teacher.

The first type of pulse monitor is called a telemetry system. These types of monitors consist of a radio transmitter attached via an elastic strap across the chest of the student, and a radio receiver that looks like a watch. Pulse monitors in this category transmit the heart rate of the individual by radio fre-

SECTION 4

Factors That Influence Your Cardiovascular Fitness Levels

Factors such as age, gender, genetics, body composition, and level of conditioning all help determine how much cardiovascular fitness you can achieve. In this section you will learn about these factors and the typical cardiovascular benefits that **A**ny **B**ody **C**an achieve.

Age

As you age, you lose cardiovascular fitness. You will lose less cardiovascular fitness, however, if you remain active. Remember, most people can develop and maintain their cardiovascular fitness at levels in the good to better range no matter what their ages.

Gender

After puberty, males (on average) have higher cardiovascular fitness levels than females. The higher levels for males are because males usually have higher hemoglobin levels than females and carry less body fat. A higher level of hemoglobin allows an individual to carry more oxygen in his or her blood, which would improve performance in cardiovascular activities. Carrying lower levels of body fat also improves cardiovascular performance as long as an individual does not get too lean (see Chapter 9 for more details). However, some conditioned females have higher levels of cardiovascular fitness than some unconditioned or even moderately conditioned males.

Genetics

Genetics can determine both your initial levels of cardiovascular fitness and your ability to improve your cardiovascular fitness. Some people have, and can develop, higher levels of cardiovascular fitness because they have higher numbers of slow-twitch muscle fibers (or muscle cells) than do other people. **Slow-twitch muscle fibers** are associated with a high ability to do aerobic work. **Fast-twitch muscle fibers** are better suited to help you perform anaerobic work.

Young adults, on average, have about 50 percent slow-twitch fibers and 50 percent fast-twitch fibers in their skeletal muscles (muscles that move joints and help support your body structure). Young adults who are good at aerobic activity and have high to very high levels of cardiovascular fitness have closer to 70 to 80 percent slow-twitch

slow-twitch muscle fiber

a muscle cell that is associated with a high ability to do aerobic work.

fast-twitch muscle fiber

a muscle cell that is suited to anaerobic work.

quency to the receiver, which can be placed on the wrist of the student or held by the teacher.

A less expensive and more versatile pulse monitor is found in the form of a fingertip attachment. Finger-attached monitors have a two-foot lead that quickly clips to the student's finger, and gives a pulse rate via an LED readout.

The finger-attached monitors are less accurate. **Take the challenge:** Determine if it is feasible to use a pulse monitor to teach your students about their heart rates. **Remember:** As with any piece of equipment, cost can vary depending on brand name, features, and place purchased. So, shop around.

Focus

Outcomes

In **Section 4** students will learn:

1. To describe the benefits of regular cardiovascular physical activity/exercise.
2. To identify and explain cardiovascular fitness evaluations used to assess cardiovascular fitness now and in the future.

Focus Activities

1. Discuss the effects of age, gender, genetics, body composition, and level of conditioning on cardiovascular fitness.
2. Have students complete one of the additional cardiovascular fitness evaluations in the Fitness Check activity on page 177.

Teach & Apply

Discussion

Ask students what kind of cardiovascular conditioning their parents and grandparents have. Ask if they think it has decreased with age. Then, ask them if they know someone older than 40 or 50 who can do as much work as they can. If so, ask them why they think this is so.

Assess

Use the Section 4 Review questions to assess students' comprehension of the concepts presented in Section 4.

ANSWERS TO SECTION 4 REVIEW

1. Genetics influence your trainability, as learned in Chapter 3. Genetics also influence cardiovascular fitness because of the percentage of slow-twitch and fast-twitch fibers with which a person is born. People with higher percentages of slow-twitch fibers (70 to 90%) have higher cardiovascular fitness levels than individuals with more fast-twitch fibers.

BELIEVE IT? ... OR NOT?

Research has shown that adolescent boys are more physically active than adolescent girls. About two-thirds of adolescent boys and one-half of adolescent girls participate in moderate to vigorous activity for twenty minutes three or more days per week.

See page 183 for answer.

fibers. The ratio of fibers you have is determined mainly by genetics. You will learn more about slow- and fast-twitch muscle fibers in Chapter 7.

Body Composition

Your percentage of body fat can also influence your cardiovascular fitness level. Generally, the lower or higher your body fat percentage is compared with normal levels (see the skinfold evaluation in Chapter 9), the worse your cardiovascular fitness. By increasing your percentage of body fat (if it is too low, like in starvation), or decreasing it (if it is too high, like in obesity), you can improve your cardiovascular fitness level. After all, if you have abnormal fat levels, you will not be as efficient at moving about as you would if you had normal levels of body fat.

Level of Conditioning

Your level of conditioning can influence your cardiovascular fitness level. If you are currently doing no aerobic activities, you can certainly improve your cardiovascular fitness level if you begin a personal fitness program that includes aerobic exercises. Your potential for cardiovascular fitness depends not only on your initial fitness level but also on genetics, trainability, your FIT, and your specific goals.

In Chapter 1 you learned about personal fitness and the positive outcomes of living an active lifestyle. The more specific benefits of participation in regular cardiovascular physical activities or exercise for 8 to 30 weeks are summarized in Figure 5.15.

For additional methods of measuring your cardiovascular fitness, see the "Fitness Check" on the next page.

SECTION 4 REVIEW

Answer the following questions on a separate sheet of paper:

1. How does your genetic makeup influence your cardiovascular fitness level?
2. How does your body composition influence your cardiovascular fitness level?
3. List and describe five benefits of cardiovascular physical activity and exercise.

Reteaching

Name _____ Date _____ Period _____

Chapter 5 Section 4
Factors That Influence Your Cardiovascular Fitness Levels

Directions: Answer the questions in the blanks provided.

1. As you age, you ___lose___ cardiovascular fitness over time.
2. In front of each statement below, write *Males* if the description concerns males' cardiovascular fitness, and *Females* if the description concerns females' cardiovascular fitness.

   Males   higher cardiovascular fitness levels after puberty
   Females lower hemoglobin levels
   Females higher levels of body fat
   Males   higher hemoglobin levels
   Males   lower levels of body fat
3. Which muscle fibers are associated with a high ability to do aerobic work?
   Slow-twitch muscle fibers
4. Which muscle fibers are better suited to help you perform anaerobic work?
   Fast-twitch muscle fibers
5. Young adults, on average, have about what percent slow-twitch fibers?
   _50%_
6. What percent of slow-twitch fibers do young adults have who are good at aerobic activity and have high to very high levels of cardiovascular fitness?
   _70 - 90%_
7. The ratio of fibers you have is determined mainly by ___genetics___.

Reteaching Worksheets   45   © 1997 West Publishing Co.

ABILITY LEVELS

Reteaching

Some students may need help mastering the concepts contained in this section. In your Teacher Resource Package, you will find the reproducible worksheet shown here. This worksheet should help students who have been absent and those needing additional help to improve their comprehension and retention of the content in this section.

Healthy Heart	• Lower resting heart rate • More blood pumped per beat • Lower blood pressure at moderate physical activity or exercise activities
Healthy Lungs	• Better ability to maintain high breathing rates for longer periods of time
Healthy Blood	• Higher HDL cholesterol • Lower LDL cholesterol and other "bad" blood fats • Higher hemoglobin levels
Healthy Arteries	• Less atherosclerosis • Better blood flow • Lower blood pressure at rest • Improved ability to deliver oxygen to muscles, tissues, and organs
Healthy Cells	• Cells become better at using oxygen that is delivered
Healthy Emotions	• Reduced stress levels
Healthy Image	• Improved self-esteem • Improved personal appearance with weight control
Healthy Lifestyle	• Increased functional health and predicted longevity

• **Figure 5.15** *Typical Benefits Following Cardiovascular Condi-tioning in a Previously Inactive Young Adult after 8 to 30 Weeks.*

Fitness Check

Additional Cardiovascular Fitness Evaluations

In Chapter 4 you performed jumping jacks and one or two car-diovascular "Fitness Checks" to assess your cardiovascular fit-ness level. In this section you will learn additional ways to evaluate your cardiovascular fitness level now and in the future. You should perform one or more of the evaluations described in this section.

Endurance Walk/Run Evaluations

You can evaluate your cardiovascular fitness level by perform-ing an endurance walk/run assessment for time or for distance. The 1-mile assessment requires you to walk/run as fast as you can to cover the distance. The 12-minute assessment requires you to cover as much distance as possible in the time requirement. The 20-minute assessment requires you to pace yourself steadily as you walk/run for specific distances. If you perform one of these evalua-

(Continued on next page)

2. Carrying excess body fat reduces your car-diovascular fitness performance. It is like carrying a backpack of dead weight.
3. Answers will vary but might include the fol-lowing: lower resting heart rate, higher HDL levels, lower blood pressure at rest, reduced stress levels, and increased func-tional health and pre-dicted longevity.

Close

Use the Fitness Check on this page to evaluate the cardiovascular fitness of the students.

Read to your students the follow-ing paragraphs describing Robert and his lifestyle. Then have them list the controllable and noncontrollable factors that influ-ence Robert's cardiovascular fitness.

Robert is a 46-year-old office worker who finds his job stressful and hectic. To ease his stress, Robert smokes more than a pack of cigarettes throughout the day. He rushes lunch at fast-food restaurants where he typically eats pizza, cheeseburgers, French fries, and soft drinks.

Robert's height is 5'7" and his weight has bal-looned to well over 200 pounds. As a result, Robert has decided to eliminate dinner.

Robert's leisure-time activities include watching television and working in his flower garden.

Fitness Check

Make sure students have the opportunity to adhere to the five criteria listed in the text prior to any administration of an evaluation. You should determine ahead of time whether you need to record each student's distance or time. Then, have students complete at least one of the cardiovascular evaluations.

The authors prefer administering the 20-minute steady-state walk/run or the Walker (30, 35, or 40 minute) cardiovascular evaluations. We feel that students must prepare for these evaluations over time and that they encourage students to practice working continuously for several minutes. These evaluations help students experience what it is like to meet guidelines 1 and 2 for adolescents (see Chapter 1) as well as adult recommendations for developing and maintaining cardiovascular fitness. Many students may want to walk only for their cardiovascular conditioning and for the evaluation. But, if they walk briskly and try to meet the recommenda-

• *The endurance walk/run is a great way for beginners to improve their cardiovascular fitness.*

	Male (min:sec)	Female (min:sec)
Age	**Good-Better**	**Good-Better**
13	10:00-7:30*	11:30-9:00
14	9:30-7:00	11:00-8:30
15	9:00-7:00	10:30-8:00
16	8:30-7:00	10:00-8:00
17	8:30-7:00	10:00-8:00
17+	8:30-7:00	10:00-8:00

* Scores below the healthy zone are considered low.

• **Figure 5.16**   *1-Mile Walk/Run (healthy fitness zone).*
Source: From The Cooper Institute for Aerobics Research with permission, *The Prudential Fitnessgram Test Administration Manual* (Dallas, TX: 1992), 46–47 for standards in figures.

Additional Cardiovascular Fitness Evaluations (*continued*)

tions, consider the following factors to accurately assess your cardiovascular fitness level:

1. It is recommended that you workout five to eight weeks before the test.
2. Practice walking/running the distance once or twice before the day of the actual test.
3. Learn to pace yourself through the whole distance or for the full amount of time.
4. Evaluate yourself only when the weather conditions are reasonable (not too hot, not too cold, and not too windy).
5. Make sure the distance you walk/run is accurate. It is best to use a regulation track, which is usually about 440 yards or 400 meters in circumference.

Use Figure 5.16 to evaluate your 1-mile cardiovascular performance. For example, if Lisa, a fifteen-year-old girl, can walk/run 1 mile in 10 minutes and 30 seconds, she is at a good level of cardiovascular fitness. A time of 8 minutes would put her in the better or higher range.

Use Figure 5.17 to evaluate your 12-minute walk/run cardiovascular performance. For example, if Lisa completed the 12-minute walk/run and covered 1,900 yards, she would be at a good level of cardiovascular fitness. A distance of 2,100 yards would put her in the better or higher range.

Use Figure 5.18 to evaluate your 20-minute walk/run cardiovascular performance. For example, if Lisa covered 1.5 miles in the 20-minute walk/run, she would be at a good level of cardiovascular fitness. A distance of 1.8 miles for her would be better or higher.

The Walker Evaluation

If you cannot run because of injury, because of poor biomechanics, or because your joints cannot handle the stress, you can assess your cardiovascular fitness by taking a walking test. The walk evaluation is designed to help you assess your cardiovascular fitness while you walk briskly at a steady pace for 30, 35, or 40 minutes. This evaluation is based on the concept that to expend the same amount of energy as you do running, you must walk for a longer period of time, because your intensity of work is lower when you walk.

Use Figure 5.19 to evaluate your walking cardiovascular performance. For example, if Lisa completed the 30-minute walk and

CULTURAL DIVERSITY

Australia

Australians love competition and pride themselves on being a nation of athletes. About one-third of the population participates actively in sports.

Because 75 percent of Australians live within 50 miles of the shore, surfing, swimming, water skiing, windsurfing, scuba diving, and snorkeling are popular. Sailing is a national passion—nearly one million families own some sort of boat.

Long-distance bicycling enthusiasts appreciate the miles of flat terrain,

covered 1.85 miles, she would be at a good level of cardiovascular fitness. A distance of 2.0 miles for her would be better.

Figure 5.20 on the next page provides you with an example of a six-week walking conditioning program designed to help you walk 2.0 to 2.2 miles (for boys) or 1.85 to 2.0 miles (for girls) in 30 minutes. This program is similar to the 20-minute walk/jog conditioning program you learned about in Chapter 3.

tions in Figure 5.19, the majority of them will be working at moderate to higher intensities for at least 30 minutes. This is a behavior that is currently encouraged throughout the extensive body of health/ fitness research literature. We also realize that some teachers will prefer to administer the 1-mile walk/run or 12-minute walk/run evaluations. We have included them for your convenience.

Use Figure 5.16 to help students evaluate their 1-mile walk/run cardiovascular performance. Use Figure 5.17 to help students evaluate their 12-minute walk/run cardiovascular performance. Use Figure 5.18 to help students evaluate their 20-minute walk/run cardiovascular performance. Use Figure 5.19 to help students evaluate their 30, 35, or 40-minute walk/run cardiovascular performance. You can use Figure 5.20 to provide students an alternative conditioning protocol for walking, as opposed to the walk/jog conditioning protocol presented in Figure 3.11 in Chapter 3.

Age	Male distance (yards) Good-Better	Female distance (yards) Good-Better
13	2500-2650*	1800-1900
14	2600-2800	1900-2100
15	2600-2800	1900-2100
16	2600-2800	1900-2100
17	2800-3000	2000-2300
17+	2800-3000	2000-2300

* Scores below the healthy zone are considered low.

• **Figure 5.17**
Twelve-Minute Walk/Run Evaluation (healthy fitness zone).

Male Distance (miles)

Age	Good–Better
14	1.8–2.0*
15	1.8–2.0
16	1.8–2.0
17	1.8–2.0
17+	1.8–2.0

Female Distance (miles)

Age	Good–Better
14	1.5–1.8
15	1.5–1.8
16	1.5–1.8
17	1.5–1.8
17+	1.5–1.8

• **Figure 5.18**   *Twenty-Minute Walk/Run Evaluation (healthy fitness zone).*

Walking Time	Miles—Males Good	Miles—Males Better	Miles—Females Good	Miles—Females Better
Thirty minutes	2.0–2.2 or farther		1.85–2.0 or farther	
Thirty-five minutes	2.13–2.25 or farther		1.95–2.13 or farther	
Forty minutes	2.23–2.4 or farther		2.0–2.23 or farther	

• **Figure 5.19**   *Walk Evaluations (healthy fitness zone, age fourteen and older).*

(Continued on next page)

golfers use more than 1,400 courses, and tennis courts abound. Skiers can enjoy downhill or cross-country skiing during a season that runs from late June through September!

Cricket, similar to baseball, is Australia's only national sport. Millions of people play it in fields, backyards, and on sporting ovals. Rugby, soccer, and Australian Rules football, invented in the Australian goldfields in the 1880s, also attract numerous competitors and fans. Unlike American football players, Australian Rules players wear no protective clothing and must rely on their fitness, wits, and luck to guard themselves against injury.

CNN® Health and Fitness Updates

You can update your coverage of health and fitness topics, as well as spark lively classroom discussion and deeper understanding, by using the **CNN Health and Fitness Updates.** These video updates are produced by Turner Educational Services, using the resources of CNN, the world's first 24-hour, all-news network.

With the introduction of the **CNN Health and Fitness Updates,** West Educational Publishing is proud to be the exclusive partner of CNN for textbook/video integration in high school fitness. By making use of the **CNN Health and Fitness Updates** you can bring the power of CNN, the network known for providing in-depth, live coverage and analysis of breaking news events, to your fitness class.

For assistance in using and incorporating the **CNN Health and Fitness Updates** into your classroom presentations, see the *Classroom Guide to the CNN Health and Fitness Updates.* The **CNN Health and Fitness Updates** are available with West Educational Publishing's *Foundations of Personal Fitness* by Don Rainey and Tinker Murray.

BELIEVE IT? ... OR NOT?

The resting heart rates of highly conditioned endurance athletes have been found to be as low as 28 beats per minute. Their hearts can also pump more than twice as much each beat as the hearts of inactive people.

See page 183 for answer.

If you are at a high risk for cardiovascular disease, your physician may recommend a treadmill stress test.

continued

	30 Minute Walking Conditioning Program
Week 1	
Day 1	3/1—3/1—3/1
	(3 min. brisk walk/1 min. slow walk—3 min. brisk walk/1 min. slow walk—3 min. brisk walk/1 min. slow walk)
Day 2	3/1—3/1—3/1
Day 3	4/1—3/1—3/1
Week 2	
Day 1	5/1—5/1—4/1
Day 2	5/1—5/1—5/1
Day 3	9/1—9/1 or 15 min. nonstop brisk walk
Week 3	
Day 1	10/1—10/1 or 17 min. nonstop brisk walk
Day 2	11/1—10/1 or 18 min. nonstop brisk walk
Day 3	12/1—11/1 or 19 min. nonstop brisk walk
Week 4	
Day 1	14/1—9/1 or 20 min. nonstop brisk walk
Day 2	15/1—10/1 or 22 min. nonstop brisk walk
Day 3	18/1—9/1 or 24 min. nonstop brisk walk
Week 5	
Day 1	20 min. brisk walk or 30 min. brisk walk — Test (optional) (Boys should try to go 2.0 to 2.2 miles; Girls 1.85 to 2.0 miles) Those who completed the goals in 30 minutes on day one can move to a maintenance program. All others should continue on this program for 2 more weeks.
Day 2	22/1—8/1 or 26 min. nonstop brisk walk
Day 3	24/1—8/1 or 25 min. nonstop brisk walk
Week 6	
Day 1	25/1—6/1 or 26 min. nonstop brisk walk
Day 2	26/1—6/1 or 28 min. nonstop brisk walk
Day 3	30 min. brisk walk evaluation

• **Figure 5.20**   *Thirty-Minute Walking Conditioning Program.*

Medical or Laboratory Evaluation

A final way to determine your cardiovascular fitness level is to have it evaluated by trained medical professionals during a treadmill or bicycle exercise stress test. This method would usually be used only if you needed special followup after a medical screening, before you began your personal fitness program. However, adults with serious health risks may require this type of testing before they begin vigorous exercise programs.

CRITICAL THINKING

Cholesterol is a key factor in the development of heart disease, even in young adults. Since the American diet is dangerously high in fat, which turns to cholesterol in the body, it is important for students to internalize information relating to cholesterol, diet, heart disease, and exercise.

Have students keep a seven-day diary of everything they eat. Encourage them to also involve a parent in this activity. Arrange, where possible, to have students' cholesterol levels measured.

Divide the class into these groups:

SECTION 5 Developing Cardiovascular Fitness

REMEMBER This!

Your FIT is the frequency, intensity, and time/ duration of your workout program. Your FIT is based on your goals and individual needs for developing and maintaining personal fitness.

To develop cardiovascular fitness, you need to design your personal fitness plan to include physical activities or exercises that are primarily aerobic. Remember, aerobic activities are rhythmic and continuous, and they force you to use the large muscle groups of your body for several minutes at a time. Aerobic activities include walking, hiking, jogging/running, swimming, cycling, cross-country skiing, dancing, skipping rope, rowing, stair climbing, in-line skating, and endurance games. Always include gradual warm-up and cool-down with your aerobic activities in your personal fitness plan.

In designing your personal fitness plan to develop or maintain cardiovascular fitness, use the scientific principles you learned in Chapter 3. The recommendations that follow are based on these principles.

Overload Principle

To improve your cardiovascular fitness, you need to determine your FIT. Use the results from your cardiovascular fitness evaluations to help you determine your FIT.

CONSUMER CORNER

Misleading Cardiovascular Consumer Claims

Promoters and advertisers make many false or misleading claims, saying that you can develop the benefits of cardiovascular fitness without engaging in moderate to vigorous physical activity or exercise. The truth is, however, that there are no shortcuts to achieving or maintaining good to better levels of cardiovascular fitness. You need to develop a FIT plan, including aerobic activities or exercises, to improve or maintain your cardiovascular fitness levels. Cardiovascular fitness products such as motorized exercise machines that do most of the work for you, vibrators, or massagers, do not overload your heart, lungs, or blood vessels enough to improve your cardiovascular fitness.

Someone who claims you can skip working out and instead simply take a pill or read a book to develop or maintain good cardiovascular fitness levels is guilty of false advertising. Be aware of people who suggest that you will see immediate results (results in less than one or two weeks, for example) from a cardiovascular fitness product or special workout that they want to sell you. Remember, it usually takes 8 to 30 weeks to see significant benefits in your cardiovascular fitness levels, unless you already have good to better levels.

Focus

Outcome

In **Section 5** students will learn:

1. To explain how to develop moderate to high levels of cardiovascular fitness.

Focus Activities

1. To discuss how students can develop and maintain good to better levels of cardiovascular fitness.
2. To use Figure 5.21 to discuss the concept of determining each student's target heart rate zone.

Consumer Corner

Have students read the "Consumer Corner" and bring to class clippings or copies of current events related to misleading consumer claims about cardiovascular products.

Teacher Readings

Durstine, L. J., King, A. C., Painter, P. L., Roitman, J. L., Zwiren, L. D., & Kenney, W. L., Editors, *Resource Manual for Guidelines for Exercise Testing and Prescription*, 2nd Edition, Lea & Febiger, Philadelphia, PA: 1993.

1. Those already on exercise programs.
2. Those who are basically sedentary.
3. Those who would be willing to adhere to a diet of fresh fruits and vegetables, while omitting foods high in fat.
4. Those students who will begin an exercise program for the first time.

Every Friday, evaluate and share progress. At the end of the semester, have cholesterol levels checked again. Analyze results and draw conclusions.

Note for the instructor: It is difficult for teenagers to involve parents. However, encourage them to do so in activities such as this. Besides good PR for your profession, it can personally help many adults who need help with their current state of wellness.

Teach & Apply

Discussion

Use Figure 5.21 to discuss how the target heart rate zone is calculated. Discuss with students the fact that the range of heart rates presented in the figure are related to the intensities they should work at in cardiovascular activities to achieve best results.

Teacher Support Notes

The method presented in the text for determining target heart rate zone is the easiest method for students to learn. There are other ways to determine the target heart rate zone, which provide slightly different

percentage of maximum heart rate

a method of calculating an exercise intensity; 60 to 90 percent of your maximum heart rate.

target heart rate zone

the recommended intensity for aerobic conditioning; estimated to be between 60 and 90 percent of one's predicted maximum heart rate.

• *You can monitor the intensity of your workout by checking your pulse to see if you are in your target heart rate zone.*

Frequency

How frequently should you exercise? A minimum of three days per week is recommended, and four to six days a week is better. If you are just starting out, begin with three days per week. Then, during the improvement stage, add more days per week.

Intensity

You can set the intensity of your aerobic conditioning at a **percentage of maximum heart rate**. This simple method of determining intensity is good to use if you are just starting out or if you need to lose weight before you can do more vigorous physical activity or exercise. With this method you determine your aerobic intensity according to a straight percentage of your maximum heart rate. It is recommended that you work at between 60 and 90 percent of your predicted maximum heart rate, which is called your **target heart rate zone** (Figure 5.21).

In some cases (for example, if you have been very sedentary), you may have to start out at lower intensities (40 to 50 percent of your predicted maximum heart rate) and gradually progress to 60 to 90 percent. To calculate your target heart rate zone for training if you are fifteen years old, first determine your predicted maximum heart rate (220 – age = 205). Then determine 60 percent of 205 (205 × 0.6 = 123). Finally, determine 90 percent of 205 (205 × 0.9 = 184). Thus, your target heart rate zone for training is between 123 and 184 beats per minute using this method.

On days when you feel like doing lighter aerobic activity, you might work at about 123 beats per minute. On days you do more vigorous aerobic activity, you could work at a heart rate of about 184 beats per minute. If you work at levels lower than your target heart rate, your health can still benefit, but you may not see much change in your personal fitness levels. If you work at levels above your target heart rate zone, you may place yourself at higher risk for injury, especially if you work too hard, too often. Remember, you can also use the perceived exertion scale in Figure 3.5 or the talk test to monitor your aerobic intensity.

Time/Duration

At the start of your personal fitness program, your goal should be twenty to thirty minutes of aerobic activity per physical activity or exercise session. If you are deconditioned, however, you may have to accumulate 20 or 30 minutes each day in two or three separate aerobic sessions of 10 to 15 minutes each. You could also do an interval workout at low intensity to accumulate your 20 or 30 minutes. For example, you might jog for two minutes at 60 percent of your maximum heart rate and then walk for a minute to recover.

ABILITY LEVELS

Reteaching

Some students may need help mastering the concepts contained in this section. In your Teacher Resource Package, you will find the reproducible worksheet shown here. This worksheet should help students who have been absent and those needing additional help to improve their comprehension and retention of the content in this section.

Answers to
BELIEVE IT? ...
OR NOT?

Pg. 159 True.
Pg. 168 False. Individuals under age thirty-five who exercise suddenly during exercise usually are found to have had genetic cardiovascular problems that caused their deaths. Therefore, we should all know our cardiovascular risk factors and try to modify them.
Pg. 169 True.
Pg. 170 True.
Pg. 172 True.
Pg. 173 False. Unless you are an animal whose nostrils can flare out (a horse, for example), you should breathe through your nose and mouth during physical activity or exercise to move large amounts of air (oxygen).
Pg. 174 True.
Pg. 176 True.
Pg. 177 False. Although it is true that people with Type A behavior who do nothing to reduce their daily stress levels are at high risk for cardiovascular disease, Type A people who do reduce their daily stress levels with physical activity and exercise are at a much lower cardiovascular risk.
Pg. 180 True.

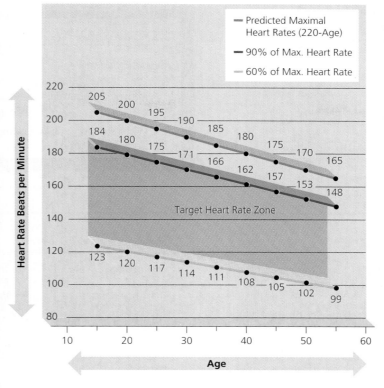

● **Figure 5.21** *Determining Your Target Heart Rate Zone for Training.*

You would repeat this ten times to accumulate your 20 or 30 minutes (review Figure 3.11 in Chapter 3). As your aerobic fitness level improves, or if you have good to better aerobic fitness already, increase your workout time/duration to 40 to 60 minutes.

Progression Principle

The rate at which you modify your FIT should be based on your personal fitness goals and your changing levels of aerobic fitness. Remember, never change your frequency, intensity, or time/duration all at the same time or too quickly. Be patient, and allow for gradual improvements. It is easier on your body to work at a lower intensity and to work longer. However, to achieve higher goals of personal fitness, you will need to work more frequently, harder, or for longer periods of time.

results. You may want to present to students other methods with which you are familiar. For more information about these methods, see Ross, R. M. and Jackson, A. S., *Understanding Exercise: Concepts, Calculations, and Computers,* MacJR/CSI Publishing, Houston: 1990.

Discussion

Remind students that if they can't accumulate 20 to 30 minutes of continuous cardiovascular activity, they can break up their activity or exercise sessions throughout the day. They can still get health benefits by walking briskly three times a day for 10 minutes at a time, for example. Encourage students to use the walking and jogging conditioning protocol (see Figure 3.11) or the walking conditioning protocol (see Figure 5.20) if they have not tried them. These protocols were developed by the authors for adolescents in an actual high school setting. They have worked effectively for the vast majority of students.

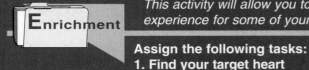

This activity will allow you to provide a more challenging learning experience for some of your students.

Assign the following tasks:
1. Find your target heart rate zone.
2. Perform the following exercise bouts:
   a. Walk for 4 minutes at a brisk pace
   b. Jog for 4 minutes at a slow pace
   c. Jog for 4 minutes at a pace that you think will elevate your heart rate into the target zone.

3. **After each exercise bout, measure your heart rate. Record the heart rates.**
4. **After each exercise bout, rate and record the intensity of the exercise using the Rate of Perceived Exertion Scale in Figure 3.5.**
5. **Follow the 4-minute jog at target zone pace with another more intense 4-minute jog. Measure your heart rate and make a rating of perceived exertion.**

CHAPTER 5
SECTION 5
184

Assess

Use the Section 5 Review questions to assess students' comprehension of the concepts presented in Section 5.

ANSWERS TO SECTION 5 REVIEW

1. The minimum frequency should be three days per week.
2. The target heart rate zone for a 20-year-old is between 120 and 180 beats per minute.
3. Your beginning time/duration goal should be 20 to 30 minutes per session. You may have to achieve this goal by accumulating your time by doing shorter sessions more than one time per day.

Close

Have students discuss the cartoons in the chapter (pages 159 and 175). Ask them what message is being expressed and why.

SECTION 5 REVIEW

Answer the following questions on a separate sheet of paper:

1. What is the minimum number of days recommended for improving your cardiovascular fitness?
2. What is the target heart rate zone for a 20-year old?
3. What should your beginning time/duration goal be for personal fitness?

SUMMARY

Cardiovascular fitness refers to your ability to work continuously for extended periods of time. Your level of cardiovascular fitness depends on the ability of your heart to pump large amounts of blood to the muscles and organs of the body. It also is related to how well your lungs function and how well your blood vessels can deliver blood (oxygen) to your body.

Moderate to high levels of cardiovascular fitness or aerobic fitness are associated with increased longevity and reduced risk for cardiovascular disease. Moderate to high levels of cardiovascular fitness can help prevent atherosclerosis, which is the most common disease process causing heart attacks and strokes. Your commitment to regular cardiovascular activity can also reduce your risk for hypertension.

Cardiovascular fitness or aerobic activities might include walking, hiking, jogging, dancing, skipping rope, rowing, swimming, skating, and endurance games or sports. Anaerobic activities are different from aerobic activities because they are done at very high intensities and last only a few seconds or a few minutes.

Your cardiovascular fitness level will be influenced to some extent by factors such as your age, gender, genetics, body composition, and level of conditioning. You can expect to see many specific improvements such as a lower resting heart rate, higher HDL cholesterol, and improved self-esteem levels following 8–30 weeks of cardiovascular conditioning.

You can use a variety of walking and running cardiovascular fitness evaluations to help you determine your cardiovascular fitness. You can then improve or maintain your cardiovascular fitness simply by accumulating 20 to 30 minutes of activity several times a week in play, games, sports, work, getting to school, recreation, or planned exercise.

COOPERATIVE LEARNING

Here are some ideas for using cooperative learning in your class:
• When groups have been given a problem to solve, each student in the group must contribute to the solution of the problem. Group members can determine who does what in reaching the solution.

• Students work in pairs on an assignment. One student acts as reader, the other as recorder. Both students must agree on the recorded answer.
• Students work in groups to research a topic. Each group member must check at least one resource and write information

Chapter 5 Review

True/False

On a separate sheet of paper, mark each question below either T for True or F for False.

1. Muscular fitness is the most important of all the skill-related and health-related fitness components in relation to your functional health.

2. Healthy lungs breathe between 6 (at rest) and 150 (during exercise) liters of air per minute.

3. The resting heart rate usually falls between 50 and 80 beats per minute.

4. A twenty-year-old female has a predicted maximum heart rate of 180 beats per minute, on average.

5. Atherosclerosis is the most common cause of cardiovascular disease.

6. Regular aerobic exercise is associated with increases in HDL cholesterol.

7. Strokes are caused by restriction of blood flow to the heart.

8. Systolic blood pressure is the pressure on the arteries when the heart contracts.

9. Slow-twitch muscle fibers are associated with your ability to do anaerobic work.

10. A male who can complete 2 miles of walking/running in 20 minutes has a good level of cardiovascular fitness.

Multiple Choice

1. Which of the following are not muscles associated with deep breathing?
   a. abdominals
   b. intercostals
   c. tongue
   d. diaphragm

2. Which of the following conditions is associated with asthma for many people?
   a. dust
   b. allergies
   c. exercise
   d. all of the above

3. Which of the following is caused by a blockage of a coronary artery?
   a. atherosclerosis
   b. muscle pump
   c. stroke
   d. myocardial infarction

4. Which of the following is an example of an anaerobic physical activity?
   a. walking 2 miles

   b. swimming 1 mile
   c. sprinting 40 yards
   d. in-line skating for 30 minutes

5. Which of the following will not have a major influence on your cardiovascular fitness?
   a. genetics
   b. conditioning level
   c. strength
   d. gender

6. Following twenty weeks of cardiovascular fitness conditioning, your resting heart rate would most likely do which of the following?
   a. be slower
   b. be faster
   c. stay the same
   d. none of the above

7. Which of the following would not be a benefit you would expect to see after 8 to 30 weeks of cardiovascular conditioning?
   a. decreased resting blood pressure
   b. lower HDL cholesterol levels

on it. Group members then write the report together, making sure all researched information is included. Each group member must participate in the presentation if an oral report is given.
• When a reading assignment is given, have students work in pairs, with one student reading orally and the other student summarizing what has been read.

Students should relate what they're reading to what they have already learned about the subject. The reader and summarizer should reverse roles every paragraph or two.
• Have students work in twos or threes to quiz each other on the material for an upcoming quiz or test.

Discussion

1. Answers will vary but might include: walking for 30 minutes, doing 10 repetitions of alternating intervals of jogging for 2 minutes followed by walking briskly for 1 minute, swimming laps for 20 minutes, riding a stationary cycle for 40 minutes, or doing stair-stepping exercise for 30 minutes.
2. Answers will vary but might include: lower resting heart rate, more blood pumped per beat, better ability to maintain high breathing rates, lower LDL cholesterol, reduced stress.
3. Regular cardiovascular physical activity and exercise are associated with reducing the risks for cardiovascular disease. As per question 2, the benefits of cardiovascular conditioning reduce one's risk.

Vocabulary Experience

_6_ hemoglobin
_4_ interval training
_5_ muscle pump
_2_ recovery heart rate
_3_ circulatory system
_1_ asthma

Critical Thinking

1. You can reduce your risk by developing and maintaining an active cardiovascular activity or exercise lifestyle and controlling the cardiovascular risk factors that are controllable.
2. It probably would be best for this person to condition himself or herself first by following the walking condi-

Chapter 5 Review

c. greater self-esteem
d. decreased stress levels

8. Which of the following is a good time for a fifteen-year-old female who evaluates her cardiovascular fitness by completing the Prudential *Fitnessgram* 1-mile walk/run?

a. 10 minutes, 30 seconds
b. 12 minutes flat
c. 14 minutes, 30 seconds
d. 20 minutes flat

9. Which of the following methods should you use to determine your intensity for cardiovascular physical activity or exercise?

a. target heart rate zone
b. talk test
c. rating of perceived exertion
d. all of the above

10. The target heart rate zone for a sixteen-year-old female should be in what range?

a. 104 and 124 beats per minute
b. 112 and 123 beats per minute
c. 118 and 147 beats per minute
d. 123 and 184 beats per minute

Discussion

1. List and identify five different physical activities or exercises that will help you improve or maintain your cardiovascular fitness level.

2. List and describe five typical benefits of cardiovascular conditioning in a previously inactive young adult after 8 to 30 weeks of training.

3. How can you reduce your own risk of having a heart attack, a stroke, or hypertension by engaging in regular cardiovascular conditioning?

Vocabulary Experience

Match the correct term in Column A to the definition in Column B by writing the appropriate number in each blank.

Column A	Column B
_____ hemoglobin	**1.** Restriction of your breathing passages due to dust, allergies, pollution, or even vigorous exercise.
_____ interval training	**2.** Should be less than 120 within 10 minutes of cardiovascular activity or exercise.
_____ muscle pump	**3.** Arteries, veins, and capillaries.
_____ recovery heart rate	**4.** Sprinting the straightaways on a track and walking/jogging the curves for several laps.
_____ circulatory system	**5.** Helps squeeze the veins to help blood move back to the right side of the heart.
_____ asthma	**6.** An iron-rich compound that carries oxygen in blood.

Wellness Connection

Hypertension: The Silent Killer

In many cases the cause of hypertension is unknown. Excessive elevated blood pressure can damage arteries, which can contribute to heart attack, stroke, congestive heart failure, vision problems, and kidney disease. While there may be some symptoms of hypertension in some people, in many cases there are no obvious physical indications of the problem. In fact, for some, the first symptom of hypertension may be death, and that is *not* a good first symptom.

Critical Thinking

1. How can you help reduce your risk of cardio-vascular disease? Explain your answer.

2. What cardiovascular evaluation would you recommend to a friend who was very sedentary and 20 pounds overweight? Explain your answer.

3. How can you use interval training in your personal cardiovascular fitness plan? Give an example.

Case Study — Diane's Fitness Level

Diane is a seventeen-year-old. She was very active when she was fourteen through sixteen years old. However, in the past year she has become very inactive because she took a part-time job after school and does not take physical education in school (it is not required for her to graduate). Diane has noticed that her aerobic fitness level has dropped. She gets tired almost every day and feels she has low levels of energy. Although Diane used to participate regularly in aerobic dance, walking, and swimming, she has never had a class that educated her about personal fitness. Therefore, she needs the help of someone knowledgeable about designing and implementing fitness programs—someone like you!

Here is your assignment:

Assume you are Diane's friend, and she asks you for some help with her plans for returning to an active lifestyle. Organize a list of things Diane should consider and do before beginning a moderate to vigorous personal cardiovascular fitness program. Then list the recommendations you would give to Diane for the first 2 weeks of her conditioning. Use the following keys to help you:

KEYS TO HELP YOU

- Consider Diane's history of personal aerobic activity and exercise.
- Consider how she should evaluate her current cardiovascular fitness level.
- Consider her needs and goals (for example, how she will find time to do physical activity or exercise).
- Determine a reasonable plan to give Diane that covers the concepts of overload, frequency, intensity, time/duration, and progression.

Because of this fact, it is very important to have regular checks for hypertension. Hypertension can be identified by measuring the body's blood pressure using a device called a sphygmomanometer. This procedure is quick, painless, cheap, easy, and quite accurate. You can have your blood pressure taken in a matter of a few minutes at the doctor's office, the school nurse's office, a health fair, or anywhere you have a sphygmomanometer and someone who knows how to properly operate it. If a problem is found with elevated blood pressure, it should be brought to the attention of your family doctor. Your doctor may recommend controlling the problem by diet, exercise, or medication.

---

tioning protocol in the text. Then, the person could try to meet the standards for either the 30, 35, or 40 minute walk.

3. Interval training can be designed so that you are combining moderate to vigorous exercise periods with short recovery periods. It can be used by athletes, students in personal fitness classes, or by individuals in rehabilitation programs.

KEYS TO CASE STUDY

Answers will vary but might include something like the following: Diane should complete the PAR-Q questionnaire in Chapter 2 before beginning her program, just to be safe. If she can answer "no" to the seven questions, she can begin conditioning by following the protocol of her choice in Figure 3.11 (Chapter 3) or Figure 5.20 (Chapter 5). Following an initial conditioning period, she can assess her progress by taking the cardiovascular fitness evaluation of her choice in Chapter 5.

RESOURCES

HANDOUTS A chapter test is available for Chapter 5 in your Teacher Resource Package.

Chapter Overview

Chapter 6 is 28 pages long and divided into four sections listed to the right. Major learning outcomes of the chapter are also listed to the right. Briefly, this chapter introduces students to the health-related fitness component of flexibility. It emphasizes the importance of developing and maintaining good to better levels of flexibility.

Teacher Resource Material

In the Teacher Resource Package accompanying the textbook, you will find the following material to help you teach this chapter.

Activity Sheets

One Reteaching Worksheet is provided in the Teacher Resource Package for each section of this chapter.

Chapter 6

Your Flexibility

188

PACING CHART

You could easily spend five days teaching this chapter if students read the entire chapter, do the Active Mind/Active Body activities, and complete several of the handouts from the Teacher Resource Package. However, you can cover the material in this chapter in three days. It is recommended that physical activity be a regular part of each class period (20 to 30 minutes minimum). Following are some examples of how to cover the main topics in the chapter if you are pressed for time.

Contents

Outcomes

After reading and studying this chapter, you will be able to:

1. Explain why flexibility is important and how it contributes to the development and maintenance of moderate to high levels of personal fitness.
2. Explain how moderate to high levels of flexibility fitness can reduce your risk for functional health problems.
3. Discuss the benefits of developing and maintaining good to better levels of flexibility.
4. Give examples of the types of stretching that can positively influence your flexibility.
5. Explain how you can develop moderate to high levels of flexibility.

Key Terms

After reading and studying this chapter, you will be able to understand and provide practical definitions for the following terms:

range of motion (ROM)
hyperflexibilitiy
muscle imbalance
low back injury

elasticity
static stretching
ballistic stretching
reflex

reflex-assisted stretching
plyometric training
passive stretching

189

Transparencies/ Masters

A transparency or master is provided in the Teacher Resource Package for each of the following figures: 6.1, 6.2, 6.3, 6.4, 6.5, 6.6, 6.7, 6.8, 6.9, 6.10, 6.11, 6.12, 6.13.

Discuss the Photo

Ask students to discuss why good to better levels of flexibility are important to their functional health. Ask students to discuss the photos and explain why flexibility is important to each of the physical activities shown. Ask them what types of problems they might encounter daily if they lost their normal flexibility levels. Ask students what will happen to their flexibility as they age if they become inactive.

Teacher Readings

Arnheim, D., *Modern Principles of Athletic Training,* 8th Edition, Times Mirror/Mosby, St. Louis, MO: 1989.

Time	Suggestions
Day 1	Assign students to read Sections 1 and 2 prior to class. In class, do the Fitness Check activity on page 198 in Section 2. Also include a variety of discussion about photos and figures.
Day 2	Assign students to read Sections 3 and 4 prior to class. In class, discuss the different types of stretching that students can do. Also discuss how to develop and maintain good to better levels of flexibility.
Day 3	Demonstrate and have the students do the stretches in the Active Mind/Active Body activity on page 205.

Focus

Outcomes

In **Section 1** students will learn:

1. To explain why flexibility is important and contributes to the development and maintenance of moderate to high levels of personal fitness.

2. To explain how moderate to high levels of flexibility fitness can reduce their risk for functional health problems.

Focus Activities

1. Discuss the concepts of hyperflexibility and muscle imbalances.

2. Discuss the health-related implications of low back problems.

INTRODUCTION

lexibility *refers to the* range of motion (ROM) *that your joints have during movement.* Range of motion *is the varying degrees of motion allowed around a joint (see Figure 6.1).* Your flexibility levels can influence your functional health. Poor flexibility of one or more of your body parts could restrict your ability to carry on normal, daily physical activities, which would reduce your quality of life. Many adults lose their normal levels of flexibility due to the aging process and decreased participation in physical activity and exercise. Poor flexibility can contribute to many types of injuries, including low back pain, muscle pulls, muscle strains, and muscle cramps. In this chapter you will learn about the relationship between flexibility and your functional health, different types of stretching and flexibility activities, the specific benefits of flexibility, and how to develop your flexibility fitness.

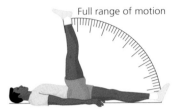

Full range of motion

• **Figure 6.1**   *Full Range of Motion.*

SECTION 1   Flexibility and Functional Health

range of motion (ROM)

varying degrees of motion allowed around a joint.

Your body has many types of joints (places where bones meet and move) that allow for varying **range of motion (ROM)**. Joints like those in your shoulders and hips are ball-and-socket joints, which allow a wide ROM. Joints such as those in your knees are hingelike, and allow you to move forward and backward. Your neck joints allow you to pivot and rotate through a wide ROM. Your wrist and ankle joints allow your bones to glide over one another. (See Figure 6.2.)

Hyperflexibility and Muscle Imbalances

You might think that the more flexibility a person has, the better. This is not necessarily true. A joint with too much flexibility around it (**hyperflexibility**) can become injured easily.

hyperflexibility

the condition of having too much flexibility.

Hyperflexibility can occur when a joint has been stretched beyond its normal ROM, or when weak muscles surround a joint (as can happen following a muscle injury). Hyperflexibility can also occur because of genetic tendencies for "loose joints." A person with a hyperflexible shoulder joint may have stretched ligaments or tendons that cause the shoulder to dislocate easily.

Reteaching

ABILITY LEVELS

Reteaching

Some students may need help mastering the concepts contained in this section. In your Teacher Resource Package, you will find the reproducible worksheet shown here. This worksheet should help students who have been absent and those needing additional help to improve their comprehension and retention of the content in this section.

Pivot

Ball and Socket

Pivot

Gliding

Hinge

• **Figure 6.2**   *Joints of the Human Body.*

By strengthening the muscles that control the movement of the shoulders, you can help improve the stability of your shoulders. These muscles are the rotator cuff (the muscles that surround the shoulder joint) and the biceps (the muscles in the front of your upper arm).

When you strengthen your muscles for improved flexibility, make sure you work the muscles that oppose one another in movements. This will help you avoid a **muscle imbalance**. Muscle imbalances occur when one muscle group, such as the quadriceps (the muscles in the front of your thigh), is too strong in relation to a complementary set of muscles, such as the hamstrings (the muscles in the back of your thigh). Biomechanically it is normal for your quadriceps to be stronger than your hamstrings. However, overdeveloping your quadriceps in relation to your hamstrings puts you at risk for a hamstring injury. An imbalance can also reduce your normal ROM.

muscle imbalance

an imbalance that occurs when one muscle group that controls a joint is too strong in relation to a complementary set of muscles (another set of muscles that helps control the same joint).

Teach & Apply

Discussion

Direct students' attention to Figure 6.1 and ask them what "range of motion" means to them. Discuss with them what "within normal limits" (WNL) means. (See Believe It Or Not on page 194 for an explanation.)

Teaching Strategies

Use a protractor or a goniometer to measure the range of motion of the wrist and ankle on a student volunteer. (See an athletic trainer to borrow a goniometer.) Have the student extend his or her wrist upwards as far as possible. Align the protractor or goniometer with the student's forearm. Then, measure the difference between the forearm angle and the wrist extension angle. Do the same for the ankle in extension and flexion.

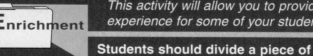

Enrichment   *This activity will allow you to provide a more challenging learning experience for some of your students.*

Students should divide a piece of paper into three columns. In the first column, have the students compile a list of joints found in the human body. In the second column, they should indicate a possible accident that could diminish the range of motion in a particular joint. In a third column, have them list preventive measures. Ask students to share the results of an injury they or someone they know has experienced. Did the injury result in loss of range of motion? Does the person experience pain in the joint area? What measures will the person need to take in order to maintain the maximum range of motion possible?

Activity

Have students develop posters on the topic of flexibility. They should use either an A, B, C concept or Any Body Can to develop their posters.

Discussion

Use Figure 6.2 to discuss the types of joints found in the body. Ask students if they have ever had a joint injury. If they have, ask them what their doctors did or recommended that they do to regain the range of motion (ROM) around the injured joint. Ask students if they know anyone who has had a knee injury that required surgery. Ask them how the doctors tested the knee before and after surgery. Did the doctor or a physical therapist have them strengthen the muscles surrounding the knee to help improve ROM and stabilize the knee? How long did it take to rehabilitate the knee?

Activity

Use a leg extension and leg flexion machine to demonstrate to students the differences in muscle strength of the quadriceps and hamstrings. Show students that they can lift more weight in extension than in flexion. Tell them that this is normal. However, if there is too much imbalance between muscle groups it may reduce flexibility, ROM, and increase the risk of injury.

• *Improving or maintaining your flexibility can reduce your risk for low back pain.*

low back injury

injury to the muscles, ligaments, tendons, or joints of the lower back.

Low Back Pain

Functional health depends upon good to better levels of flexibility and strength. For example, there is a relationship between **low back injuries** and poor flexibility.

Low back pain is a major health problem in industrial societies like the United States. It has been estimated that 80 percent of all people on Earth will suffer from low back pain at one time or another in their lives. You probably know of at least one or two adults who suffer from low back pain or injuries.

People with low back pain often end up with more chronic problems, such as low back injuries. Figure 6.3 illustrates the major causes of low back injuries in American workers. As the figure shows, the leading cause of low back injuries is lifting. Twisting, bending, and pulling can also cause you to hurt your back if you are not careful.

Low back injuries are associated with inflexible and weak muscles that support the spine and pelvic girdle. Your risk of back injuries can be decreased if you develop and maintain the muscular strength and ROM of your low back.

You can also help prevent low back injuries by learning to lift and carry heavy objects according to biomechanical principles. You probably have lifted a heavy box or other object like the one shown in Figure 6.4. Did you lean over at the waist and lift upward to move the object? If so, you may have hurt your back. Figure 6.4 shows the preferred lifting technique. You should bend your knees, lift mainly with your quadriceps, and keep the weight close to your body.

When you are carrying heavy objects, try to balance the load so that there is an equal amount of weight stressing your joints. For example, when you carry two sacks of groceries, carry one in each hand, not both in one hand. Avoid excessive twisting, pulling, or pushing movements that could strain your low back. Use proper foot movements when you have to turn while lifting a heavy object. Do

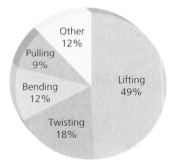

• **Figure 6.3**   *Most Common Reasons for Low Back Injuries.*

Across the Disciplines

Science

Technological advances in the field of medicine enable surgeons to use artificial body parts to replace hearts, legs, or arms. In the 1960s, an artificial knee joint with a range of movement wide enough to replace the knee was developed. The knee joint connects the bones in the upper and lower leg. The most common contemporary knee is made of a hard, lightweight metal. A plastic material is used to create a durable weight-bearing surface. A complex procedure

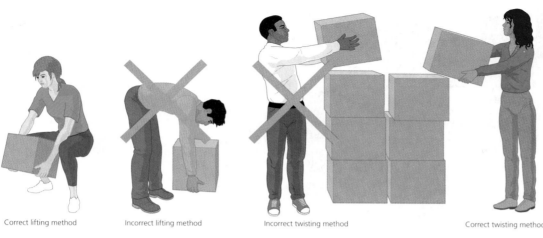

Correct lifting method   Incorrect lifting method   Incorrect twisting method   Correct twisting method

• **Figure 6.4**   *The Right Way and Wrong Way to Lift.*

Discussion

Ask students if they can tell you the proper way to lift heavy objects. Have them discuss what they have heard or know. Use Figure 6.4 to show students general recommendations for safe lifting. Emphasize that proper lifting depends on using proper biomechanical principles.

not twist with the load, as shown in Figure 6.4 unless you move your feet in the direction that you turn. See Figure 6.5 for additional tips on how you can prevent low back injuries and maintain your low back functional health.

REMEMBER This!

If you are in doubt about whether an object is too heavy for you to lift, don't be afraid to ask for help when trying to lift it. There is no reason to risk your functional health to injury because you are too scared or embarrassed to ask for help.

SECTION 1 REVIEW

Answer the following questions on a separate sheet of paper:

1. Define *flexibility.*
2. What are the top three causes of low back injuries in American workers?

Assess

Use the Section 1 Review questions to assess students' comprehension of the concepts presented in Section 1.

ANSWERS TO SECTION 1 REVIEW

1. Flexibility refers to the range of motion that your joints have during movement.
2. The top three causes are lifting, twisting, and bending.

SECTION 2   Factors That Influence Your Flexibility

The total ROM that you have around a joint varies from one joint to another and usually differs from one individual to the next. Your muscular flexibility depends on several factors, such as genetics, gender, age, body temperature, injuries, excessive body fat, and lifestyle activity levels.

Close

enables surgeons to restore mobility, range of motion, and stability to some joints that have failed due to injury or other reasons. Discuss with students how knee and hip replacement surgery could benefit an older person as well as a younger one (restores mobility, including restored range of motion to the joint; increases independence; provides

opportunity to return to active lifestyle; etc.). Have students research current advances in artificial joint replacement and compare the improvements that have been made for the recipient, what limitations there are, and what kind of physical therapy might be needed to restore range of motion to the joint.

Have students evaluate the occupations of their community's two or three major industries to determine the types of jobs that would place one at high risk for a back injury. Ask them to observe how many workers they notice wearing back support devices while they work.

Focus

Outcome

In **Section 2** students will learn:

1. The benefits of developing and maintaining good to better levels of flexibility.

Focus Activities

1. Discuss the factors that affect flexibility and the benefits of flexibility conditioning.

2. Use the Fitness Check activity on page 198 to have students examine the flexibility ratings of various physical activities and sports.

BELIEVE IT? ... OR NOT?

The term *within normal limits*, or *WNL*, indicates that there is a range of normal values for a certain personal fitness component. For example, if you are lying on your back on the floor and you can move your leg from the floor straight up in the air (to a 90-degree angle), your range of motion is WNL. (See Figure 6.1.) If you cannot move through this range, you may have abnormal range of motion.

See page 203 for answer.

Don't

Do

Sleeping

Do not lie flat on your back: this arches the spine too much.

Lie on your back and support your knees.

Do not use a high pillow.

Lie on your side with knees bent and pillow just high enough to keep your neck straight.

Do not sleep face down.

Sitting

Do not leave your lower back unsupported when not upright.

Sit straight with back support, knees higher than hips.

Standing

Do not let your back bend out of its natural curve.

Stand upright, hips tucked, knees slightly bent.

Walking

Do not lean forward or wear high heels.

Lead with chest, toes forward.

● **Figure 6.5**   *Care of the Spine. Source:* Reprinted from F. S. Sizer, E. N. Whitney, and L. K. DeBruyne, *Making Life Choices: Health Skills and Concepts* (St. Paul: West Publishing, 1994), 287.

ABILITY LEVELS

Reteaching

Some students may need help mastering the concepts contained in this section. In your Teacher Resource Package, you will find the reproducible worksheet shown here. This worksheet should help students who have been absent and those needing additional help to improve their comprehension and retention of the content in this section.

Any Body Can!

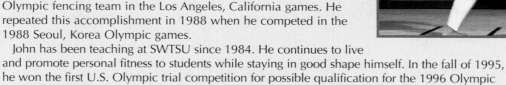

John Moreau and Dann Baker

John Moreau and Dann Baker are international competitors who teach physical activity courses that require good to better levels of flexibility at Southwest Texas State University (SWTSU) in San Marcos, TX. John specializes in teaching fencing, weight training, jogging, self-defense, and personal fitness classes, while Dann specializes in teaching wrestling, karate, and jogging classes.

Following his junior year in college, John joined the U.S. Army to train and compete in the modern pentathlon (one-day event including pistol shooting, fencing, swimming 300 meters, horseback riding over barriers, and running 4,000 meters). In 1981, John competed in the World Military Modern Pentathlon Championships where the U.S. team finished third. In 1984 John was on the U.S. Olympic fencing team in the Los Angeles, California games. He repeated this accomplishment in 1988 when he competed in the 1988 Seoul, Korea Olympic games.

John has been teaching at SWTSU since 1984. He continues to live and promote personal fitness to students while staying in good shape himself. In the fall of 1995, he won the first U.S. Olympic trial competition for possible qualification for the 1996 Olympic games in Atlanta, Georgia.

Dann earned a college scholarship to Minot College in Minot, North Dakota for his wrestling and football talents. Following a year at Minot, Dann joined the U.S. Air Force. While in the Air Force, Dann won the interservice wrestling championship and was the Pacific Air Command judo champion. He learned karate (Kenpo style) starting at the age of 10 and later applied his skills in the U.S. Special Forces as a trainer in martial arts. Dann served in Viet Nam in 1968 where he was "missing in action".

In 1973 Dann went to SWTSU to finish his college education, and he has been there ever since. He helped found and has coached the SWT wrestling teams to numerous state championships. Dann also continues to live and promote personal fitness. In 1992, he came out of competition retirement and finished second in the World Black Belt Karate Championships. He repeated his second place finishes in 1993 and 1994. In 1995, Dann became the oldest (48) individual to win the World Black Belt Self-Defense Karate Championship. He was also elected to the Karate Hall of Fame as the Most Outstanding Competitor in the U.S. in 1995.

Not everyone can be as versatile as John and Dann, but Any Body Can learn to develop and maintain their own good levels of flexibility. That's right, you can do it!

Any Body Can!

You might want to provide students with the following background information on these two men.

John Moreau was born on April 10, 1951 in Kansas City, Missouri. He went to high school in Endicott, New York where he ran cross country and track at Union-Endicott High School. He went to college at the State University of Binghamton (New York) where he ran cross country and track and first competed in fencing and swimming.

Dann Baker was born September 21, 1947 on the Turtle Mountain Indian Reservation in Belcourt, North Dakota. He is one-half Chippewa Indian. Dann went to high school at Flandreau Indian School in South Dakota where he competed in all sports. He was a two-time state wrestling champion and first team all-state in football.

Ask students what they think has motivated John and Dann to accomplish these achievements. Ask students if they know anyone who is similarly motivated.

Enrichment

This activity will allow you to provide a more challenging learning experience for some of your students.

Have the students experience a reduction in range of motion by restricting the movement of a joint. This may be accomplished by improvising a splint for the fingers, wrist, elbow, knee, or ankle. Materials for splints might include bandages, heavy cardboard, and athletic tape. Instruct the students not to place tape directly on the skin, nor to restrict circulation by placing the splint on too tightly. The splints may be worn for the school day. Ask the students to share their experiences. What activities were restricted by not having a full ROM? Did the students feel frustration in their inability to complete their daily routines with normal ease? If the loss of ROM was a permanent condition, what limitations would the students experience during their lifetimes?

Teach & Apply

Discussion

Ask students if they have noticed whether they are more or less flexible than people they know. Ask them why they think this is.

Activity

• Have students gather clippings of current sports events from magazines and other sources to make a bulletin board showing examples of the extremes of flexibility (from poor to excellent).

• Have students visit a nursing home and interview some of the people who live there. Have them observe whether the residents struggle to do their daily activities. Have them ask the residents if they feel that physical activities or exercise improve their flexibility and ROM.

Stress Break
. . . .

Ask the students to respond to the content of the "Stress Break" feature. Ask them if they have ever felt their muscles getting tight while just sitting in class. What did they do about it?

elasticity

the rubberband-like flexibility of the muscles, tendons, and other connective tissues.

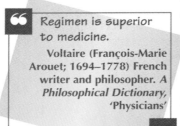

> Regimen is superior to medicine.
>
> **Voltaire (François-Marie Arouet; 1694–1778) French writer and philosopher.** *A Philosophical Dictionary,* 'Physicians'

Stress Break
. . . .

Stretching is an effective way to reduce stress. Stretching reduces muscle tension and allows you to feel more relaxed. Stretching also allows you to get in touch with your body and helps you sense which areas are tighter than others. Without regular stretching, your muscles tend to become tighter and feel tense, creating more distress.

What Affects Flexibility?

Some people have more flexible joints, tendons, and ligaments than others because of their genetic makeup. In general, females are slightly more flexible than males, at least in some movements (for example, the movements included in the back saver sit and reach evaluation described in Chapter 4). Younger people are usually more flexible than older people, because some elasticity loss occurs with aging and sedentary living. **Elasticity** refers to the rubberband-like flexibility of your muscles, tendons, and other connective tissues. You can maintain your elasticity at higher levels as you age if you stretch regularly.

Flexibility can change by as much as 20 percent with increases or decreases in muscular temperature. If you are properly warmed up, you will have better flexibility than if you are not warmed up. Cold temperatures in your physical activity or exercise environment will probably decrease your flexibility until you warm up.

Injuries to your muscles, skin, or connective tissues may result in the loss of some flexibility. Scar tissue that forms when your body heals itself can limit your ROM. Flexibility exercises can help you regain your normal ROM after an injury.

Excessive body fat can also limit your ROM. The excess fat restricts movement because of extra bulk around your joints. Losing excess body fat (see Chapter 9) can improve your flexibility by allowing joints to move through their full ROM.

The most significant negative influence on your flexibility level is an inactive lifestyle. As you decrease your physical activity or exercise levels, your muscles lose elasticity, and your tendons and ligaments get tighter and shorter. If you remain inactive for long periods of time, you will also probably add body fat, which will limit your flexibility even further.

Typical Benefits of Flexibility Conditioning

The typical benefits of participating in a regular flexibility stretching program are summarized in Figure 6.6. Flexibility conditioning usually includes a stretching program like the one described for warm-up in Chapter 3. Other flexibility activities and exercises will be illustrated and explained for you later in this chapter.

Participation in some types of physical activities and exercises will help you develop flexibility more than will participation in other types of activities and exercises. Figure 6.7 shows the flexibility benefits of a variety of physical activities and exercises.

CRITICAL THINKING

For this activity, have students involve parents and school staff members to insure that all different age groups are represented (as much as possible). Students should select people that represent as many different occupations/lifestyles as possible.

Using three or four basic tests, have students measure the flexibility of these adults. Several simple tests are available. However, it is important to measure the flexibility of several areas of the body. Three suggested tests are:

BELIEVE IT? ...
OR NOT?

If you lift weights regularly, you will get muscle bound or bulky and develop muscle imbalances that reduce your flexibility.

See page 203 for answer.

Healthy Joints:	• Increases ROM for the joints conditioned • Promotes more flexible muscles and tendons • Decreases risk of joint injury
Healthy Muscles:	• Increases stability for your joints • Increases ROM for strength development
Fewer Health-related Injuries:	• Helps control instability • Reduces risk for various chronic muscle/skeletal pain like low back pain
Reduced Stiffness and Soreness:	• Increases blood flow with warm-up stretching, increases ROM • After physical activities ROM can be regained with stretching resulting in reduced stiffness and muscular soreness the next day • Stretching after physical activity reduces risk for blood pooling and muscle cramping
Healthy Emotions:	• Reduced tension and stress levels
Healthy Image:	• Increased functional health and future opportunities to participate in a variety of physical activity and exercise

• **Figure 6.6** *Typical Benefits Following Flexibility Conditioning in a Previously Inactive Young Adult after 8 to 30 Weeks.*

Sport or Activity	Flexibility Benefits	Sport or Activity	Flexibility Benefits	Sport or Activity	Flexibility Benefits
Aerobics	***	Dance cont.		Skating; Ice, Roller, or In-line	*
Archery	*	Ballet	****	Skiing	
Backpacking	**	Line	**	Cross-Country	*
Badminton	**	Social	*	Downhill	*
Baseball	*	Fencing	**	Soccer	**
Basketball (half court)		Football	*	Softball (fast pitch)	*
(vigorous)	*	Golf (walking)	**	(slow pitch)	*
Bicycling	**	Gymnastics	****	Surfing	**
Bowling	*	Hiking	**	Swimming	**
Calisthenics	****	Horseback Riding	*	Table Tennis	*
Canoeing	*	Jogging	*	Tennis	*
Circuit Training	***	Martial Arts	*	Volleyball	*
Continuous Rhythmical		Mountain Climbing	*	Walking	*
Excercise	***	Racquetball/Handball	*	Water Polo	**
Dance		Rope Jumping	*	Waterskiing	*
Aerobic	***	Rowing	*	Weight Training	*
		Sailing	*		

Better ****   Good ***   Fair **   Low *

• **Figure 6.7** *Flexibility Benefits of Various Sports and Activities.*

Discussion

Use Figure 6.6 to discuss with students the benefits of participating in a regular flexibility conditioning program.

Activity

Use Figure 6.7 to have students examine how the physical activities or sports in which they participate rate in terms of promoting good to better levels of flexibility.

Assess

Use the Fitness Check on page 198 to assess student progress. Then, use the Section 2 Review questions to assess students' comprehension of the concepts presented in Section 2.

Teacher Readings

Baumgartner, T. A., and Jackson, A. S., *Measurement for Evaluation in Physical Education and Exercise Science*, 5th Edition, W. C. Brown, Dubuque, IA: 1994.

1. Back saver sit and reach
2. Trunk lift
3. Arm lift
(See pages 140–142.)

Have students draw conclusions relating occupation and lifestyle to flexibility (overall and specific).

ANSWERS TO SECTION 2 REVIEW

1. Answers will vary, but may include the following: Females are more flexible than males, at least in some movements like the back saver sit and reach. Flexibility generally decreases with age. Excessive fat can limit flexibility and ROM.
2. Answers will vary, but can be found in Figure 6.6.

Close

Ask students to discuss the implications of the cartoon that shows stretching for the cookies. (See page 201.)

Teacher Readings

Johnson, B. L., and Nelson, J. K., *Practical Measurements for Evaluation in Physical Education,* 4th Edition, Burgess Publishing, Edina, MN: 1986.

Fitness Check

Fitness Evaluation

Examine Figure 6.7 on the preceding page to determine whether you engage in activities or sports that help maintain or increase your flexibility levels. If you are not participating in activities or sports that are rated at least fair (**) at positively influencing your flexibility levels, you should add activities or sports to your daily activity routine that are rated fair, good, or excellent.

SECTION 2 REVIEW

Answer the following questions on a separate sheet of paper:

1. List and explain three factors that influence your flexibility.
2. Which two flexibility conditioning benefits are the most important to you, and why?

CONSUMER CORNER

Flexibility and Consumer Issues

Many commercial stretching devices to help increase your flexibility are advertised. Some of these devices are designed to stretch your lower leg and Achilles' tendon (heel cord). Others work your hamstrings and quadriceps. Although these devices may provide a convenient way to stretch, they are not necessary and can be costly.

For example, an exercise bicycle will improve your lower body flexibility, while at the same time building your cardiovascular endurance. Most people can work out on an exercise bike without much difficulty so it is a good choice for people just beginning an exercise program. A wide variety of exercise bikes are available at a wide range of prices so be sure to check sources such as *Consumer Reports* before making a purchase.

Good flexibility levels are important, of course. They help avoid lost time from work, costly medical bills, and needless pain and suffering. By learning a variety of stretches for each of your body parts, you will always be able to practice proper stretching and thus prevent injuries.

Special Needs

In the disabled population, both active and passive stretching is beneficial. Static stretching should only be performed to the point of pain—not beyond. Severely limited individuals may need to be actively manipulated through passive stretching. In this type of stretching, the joint and/or muscles are actually manipulated through a limited range of motion using one hand to stabilize the body or joint while the other hand moves the limb.

Ballistic stretching should be avoided with the disabled population.

Often the best plan of attack for the

SECTION 3 — Types of Stretching and Your Flexibility

To improve your flexibility, you must overload your muscles. This is done by stretching them beyond their normal resting length. Four basic stretching techniques can help improve your flexibility level. These include static stretching, ballistic stretching, reflex-assisted stretching, and passive stretching.

Static Stretching

In **static stretching**, you assume a stretch position slowly and then hold it for several seconds (10 to 60), until you feel slight discomfort but no real pain (see Figure 6.8). Variations include slow movements like arm circles or slow neck stretches side-to-side.

Static stretching, when done regularly, is safe and effective at increasing the ROM of the joints you work. Everyone should do some static stretching to help maintain or improve flexibility.

Ballistic Stretching

Ballistic stretching involves quick up-and-down bobbing movements that are held very briefly (Figure 6.9). You may have seen athletes doing ballistic stretches in their warm-ups before a game.

For health-related personal fitness, ballistic stretches are not necessary. In fact, they are not recommended, because they can increase your risk for injury, particularly if you are not warmed up properly before you do them. However, if you are interested in high-performance levels of fitness, you may need to include ballistic stretching in your personal fitness program. Ballistic stretching challenges your reflexes and increases your flexibility, which can help you improve your skill-related fitness.

static stretching

exercises in which you assume a stretch position slowly and then hold it for several seconds (10 to 60 seconds), until you feel slight discomfort but no real pain.

ballistic stretching

exercises that involve quick up-and-down bobbing movements that are held very briefly.

BELIEVE IT? ... OR NOT?

Back problems are the most common reason for decreased work capacity and reduced leisure-time activity in Americans below the age of forty-five. The average American typically experiences his or her first back problems by the age of thirty-two.

See page 203 for answer.

• **Figure 6.8** Static Stretching.

• **Figure 6.9** Ballistic Stretching.

Focus

Outcome

In **Section 3** students will learn:

1. To give examples of the types of stretching that can positively influence their flexibility.

Focus Activity

1. Give examples of the different types of flexibility, including static stretching, ballistic stretching, reflex-assisted stretching, and passive stretching. Discuss with students.

Teach & Apply

Discussion

Ask students about the types of stretching they have seen athletes doing before they compete. Ask them if the same stretches are safe for the average person (nonathlete). Have them try to explain their answers.

disabled student is to combat contractures that result from the imbalance located between the flexor and extensor muscles. Caution needs to be exercised when utilizing passive stretching, since the student is not the one controlling the movement or the amount of force used.

Flexibility programs for the disabled student need to be designed for each individual with limitations in range of motion being the basis for programming. A student's physician or physical therapist should be consulted before any flexibility program is implemented. Such programs can actually be contraindicated for some disabled students.

Activities

• Use Figure 6.8 to show students how to do static stretching, then have them practice the stretch shown.
• Use Figure 6.9 to show students how to do safe ballistic stretching, then have them practice the stretch shown.
• Use Figure 6.10 to show students how to do a plyometric bound. Have them practice the stretch shown.

Teacher Support Notes

In recent years some fitness experts have recommended that ballistic stretches should always be avoided. This is probably true for the average person. However, there is a body of physiological evidence that shows that high performance power movements are enhanced following ballistic and plyometric conditioning. Safe ballistic

reflex

a response that the nerves and muscles provide to various movements.

reflex-assisted stretching

exercises that challenge the reflexes to adapt so that they allow the joints to move at faster speeds and with more explosive power.

plyometric training

exercises such as bounding and jumping movements that increase your ability to develop force more quickly in explosive movements; a kind of reflex-assisted stretching.

Reflex-assisted Stretching

Your **reflexes** are the responses that your nerves and muscles provide to various movements. An example of a reflex is the simple knee jerk, when you involuntarily extend your knee after your doctor taps your knee tendon with a rubber hammer. Your body performs a variety of reflex actions daily, such as reflexes that keep us from falling and help us maintain balance. Reflexes can be very sensitive or dull. Your reflexes can become dull as you age if you have an inactive lifestyle. A regular stretching program can help you maintain or improve many of your normal reflex actions as you age.

Reflex-assisted stretching includes a variety of different stretching movements that will challenge your reflexes to adapt to these movements, allowing your joints to move at faster speeds and with more explosive power. Reflex-assisted stretching is usually not recommended for a general personal fitness program unless you are interested in performance fitness.

An example of reflex-assisted stretching is **plyometric training** (Figure 6.10). Plyometric training includes bounding and jumping exercises. Plyometric training increases your ability to develop force quicker in explosive movements, which is important in sport events that require you to jump at maximal levels. If you are interested in doing plyometric training, seek out a certified strength and conditioning coach to help you develop a safe and effective program for yourself.

BELIEVE IT? ...
OR NOT?

It is easier for shorter people to touch their toes than taller people because they have shorter legs and a shorter trunk.

See page 203 for answer.

Lunge position   Vertical jump   Lunge position with legs switched

• **Figure 6.10** Plyometric Training (a kind of reflex-assisted stretching).

ABILITY LEVELS

Reteaching

Some students may need help mastering the concepts contained in this section. In your Teacher Resource Package, you will find the reproducible worksheet shown here. This worksheet should help students who have been absent and those needing additional help to improve their comprehension and retention of the content in this section.

Passive Stretching

passive stretching

exercises in which a partner or device provides the force for a stretch.

Passive stretching is a type of stretching in which a partner or device provides the force for your stretch (Figure 6.11). For example, once you have done a static stretch, a partner can push you a bit further to increase your ROM for the joint worked. A device such as a towel can also be used for passive stretching. For example, sit on the floor and place a towel under your heel. Hold the towel with both hands, and pull it toward you. In this way you can passively stretch your hamstring muscles. If you pull too hard you might overstretch your hamstrings, however. Passive stretching can be dangerous if your device or partner pushes you too far and causes muscle pulls or tears. Be careful if you include passive stretching in your personal fitness plan.

All four types of stretching just discussed can help you maintain or improve your flexibility levels. Everyone should do some static stretching regularly. Do some ballistic and reflex-assisted stretching if you want to improve your performance fitness. Finally, passive stretching can improve your ROM but should be done with caution to avoid overstretching your muscles.

The flexibility evaluations discussed in Chapter 4 can help you determine your flexibility levels. Design a plan for maintaining or improving your flexibility according to the results of these evaluations.

If you ever have a serious injury or chronic bone or joint problems, consult an athletic trainer, physical therapist, or physician. These specialists can help evaluate any limitations on your flexibility levels. They may want to conduct more in-depth evaluations to help you improve your flexibility levels or to assist you in returning to your previous level of flexibility.

Stretching Benefits

stretching and plyometric training improves the way in which nerves activate the muscles to contract.

Discussion

Ask students if they have ever done or seen stretching techniques using partners or rubber band (flexible tubing) devices. If not, ask them if they have seen people using this kind of stretching in rehabilitation.

Activity

Use Figure 6.11 to show students how to do a passive stretch. Have them practice the stretches shown. Try to acquire some rubber bands (flexible tubing) of varying tensions and have students practice stretching with them.

Assess

Use the Section 3 Review questions to assess students' comprehension of the concepts presented in Section 3.

BELIEVE IT? ... OR NOT?

While sitting on the floor, if you are unable to touch your toes after two or three tries, you probably need to work on your flexibility.

See page 203 for answer.

• **Figure 6.11** *Passive Stretching Examples.*

Enrichment

This activity will allow you to provide a more challenging learning experience for some of your students.

Ask the students to scan magazines for pictures that demonstrate the four basic stretching techniques (static stretching, ballistic stretching, reflex-assisted stretching, and passive stretching). These examples may be found in exercise articles, advertisements, or pictures of people doing everyday activities. Have the students bring their selected pictures and present an analysis of the movement. The analysis should include the joint involved, how the stretch is classified, and the amount of effort or energy that the muscle must produce.

SECTION 3 REVIEW

Answer the following questions on a separate sheet of paper:

1. What is ballistic stretching, and why is it potentially dangerous?
2. What is the difference between reflex-assisted stretching and passive stretching?

ANSWERS TO SECTION 3 REVIEW

1. Ballistic stretching involves quick up-and-down bobbing movements that are held very briefly. This type of stretching is potentially dangerous because you can overstretch or tear a muscle group, particularly if you aren't warmed up.
2. Reflex-assisted stretches, like bounding exercises, cause your reflexes to adapt to move at greater speeds. Passive stretching is a type of stretching done with a partner or device that provides the force for the stretch.

Close

Have students discuss the "Any Body Can" feature on page 195, which highlights two multi-talented athletes and instructors of fitness. Ask them how high levels of flexibility fitness are important to John's and Dann's performances. Have students design two to three static stretches.

SECTION 4 Developing Your Flexibility Fitness

To develop flexibility fitness, you need to design your personal fitness plan to include physical activities or exercises that will maintain or improve your ROM. An easy way to maintain or develop your flexibility level is to include a stretching program in your warm-up and cool-down routines. Use the scientific principles you learned in Chapter 3 and your personal fitness goals to develop your own flexibility program. The recommendations that follow are based on these principles.

Overload Principle

Determine your FIT by using the results from your flexibility fitness evaluations. If you have good to better levels of flexibility, design a stretching program to help you maintain your flexibility. If you have low levels of flexibility, you need a program of stretching that increases your FIT to help you develop good to better levels of flexibility.

Specificity Principle

To improve the flexibility of a particular joint or body area, do stretches that affect the nerves, muscles, and connective tissues that control movement around that joint or body part. To maintain or improve your overall flexibility levels, do a variety of stretches that influence all your major body parts.

Frequency

How often should you do your stretches? A minimum of three days per week is recommended, but doing some stretching daily is best. If

REMEMBER This!

Never change the frequency, intensity, and time/duration of your exercise all at the same time or too quickly. Be patient, and allow for gradual improvements.

Equipment Options

Prior to the 1980s, flexibility was measured as a pass or fail event. If you could touch the palms of your hands to the floor while bending over straight legged, you were flexible, and if you couldn't, you were like 98% of the population. Now that flexibility is considered an integral part of fitness, manufacturers are developing new equipment to improve and measure flexibility. However, the most responsive and safe equipment for increasing flexibility is a workout partner. Partners can increase the pressure of a stretching exercise,

you are just starting out, begin with three days per week. Then, during the improvement stage of progression, add more days per week.

Intensity

The intensity of your stretching is determined by the points where muscles are stretched beyond their normal resting lengths. You have reached that point if you stretch enough to feel slight discomfort but no real pain during the stretch. Be careful to avoid injuries if you do ballistic, reflex-assisted, or passive stretching techniques. Too much bouncing, jerking, or other sudden movements can increase your risk for injuries.

Time/Duration

How do you determine the time/duration of your stretches? For static stretching, begin by holding each stretch for 10 to 15 seconds at a time, repeating this three times for each static stretch you do. As your ROM increases, work toward holding each stretch for 30 to 60 seconds, repeating this three times per stretch.

If you are doing ballistic, reflex-assisted, or passive stretching, do five to fifteen slow and gentle movements, repeating this three times per stretch. You may want to increase the number or sets of stretches over time, based on your own performance fitness needs. Remember, ballistic, reflex-assisted, and passive stretching are more hazardous than static stretching in regard to injury risk and, therefore, should be done with caution.

Progression Principle

The rate at which you modify your FIT should be based on your personal fitness goals and your changing levels of flexibility fitness. In Chapter 3 you learned twelve basic stretches that you could include in the warm-up and cool-down portions of your personal fitness routine. Figure 6.12 shows you several other stretches that you should be able to perform safely and effectively.

SECTION 4 REVIEW

Answer the following questions on a separate sheet of paper:

1. What is the minimum frequency recommended for stretching in order to improve flexibility?
2. What time/duration is recommended for the different kinds of stretching to improve flexibility?

Focus

Outcome

In **Section 4** students will learn:

1. To explain how they can develop moderate to high levels of flexibility.

Focus Activities

1. Discuss the FIT for the development and maintenance of good to better levels of flexibility.
2. Use Figure 6.12 to teach students how to perform stretches in addition to those taught in Chapter 3.
3. Use Figures 6.13 and 6.14 in the Active Mind/ Active Body activity on page 205 to teach students about appropriate ways to stretch.

Note: Answers to Section 4 Review are on page 206.

Teacher Readings

Ross, R. M. and Jackson, A. S., *Understanding Exercise: Concepts, Calculations, and Computers.* MacJR/CSI Publishing, Houston, TX: 1990.

---

and respond immediately to voice commands.

New equipment is available to determine baseline flexibility and increases in flexibility. The most popular piece of equipment is the sit and reach device. Another piece of equipment that can be used to measure flexibility is a carpenter's angle. Carpenter's angles can be used to measure the angle of joint mobility. To use a carpenter's angle, adjust the angle to mimic the angle of stretch, and read the degrees of the angle. **Take the challenge:** Try to find a stretching device that doesn't look like it could cause an injury. **Remember:** Safety is essential with any equipment.

Teach & Apply

Discussion

Ask students what kind of stretches they like to do as part of their warm-up and cool-down activities in class. Ask them to discuss if they have noticed whether the stretching they have been doing in class has had any effects on their flexibility.

Healthy People 2000

Objective 1.6—**Increase to at least 40 percent the proportion of people aged 6 or older who regularly perform physical activities that enhance and maintain muscular strength, muscular endurance, and flexibility.**

Whole-body stretch

Neck stretches

Lower back stretch

Lower back stretches

Calf muscle stretch

Buttocks stretch

Hamstring stretch

Inner thigh stretch

Upper body stretches

Upper back and side stretch

• *Figure 6.12*   *Recommended Stretches to Help You Meet Flexibility Goals Safely. Source:* Adapted from F. S. Sizer, E. N. Whitney, and L. K. DeBruyne, *Making Life Choices: Health Skills and Concepts* (St. Paul: West Publishing, 1994), 251.

Reteaching

ABILITY LEVELS

Reteaching

Some students may need help mastering the concepts contained in this section. In your Teacher Resource Package, you will find the reproducible worksheet shown here. This worksheet should help students who have been absent and those needing additional help to improve their comprehension and retention of the content in this section.

Active **Mind!**
Active **Body!**

Stretches You Can Use in Your Flexibility Plan for Personal Fitness

Choose and safely demonstrate to your instructor one stretch for each of the following parts of your body: your neck, shoulders, abdominals (stomach muscles), low back, quadriceps, hamstrings, groin muscles, and lower leg (calf muscles). Figures 6.13 and 6.14 illustrate and describe more specifically how to perform a variety of stretches for maintaining and developing good to better levels of flexibility. You may need to avoid certain stretching activities because they may increase your risk for injury. Figure 6.14 shows several of the more hazardous stretches, along with suggestions on how you can modify them to make them safer.

• **Figure 6.13** *General Flexibility Routine–Additional Recommended Stretches.*
Source: Adapted from Dintiman et al., *Discovering Lifetime Fitness* (St. Paul: West Publishing, 1989): 113–122.

• *Shoulder shrug*

• *Shoulder blade pull*

(Continued on next page)

Place Objective 1.6 on the board or overhead projector and discuss with students whether they think this is an important and reasonable goal.

Activity

Use Figure 6.12 to teach the stretches shown. Demonstrate the stretches to students and then have students practice them.

Classroom Management

Be sure to spread students out for stretching activities. Use gym mats if they are available for floor stretches. Solicit student volunteers to help demonstrate stretches you cannot do. Allow enough time so that you can observe each student stretching and provide feedback about their techniques.

Activity

Use Figures 6.13 and 6.14 in the Active Mind/Active Body activity on this page to teach students about proper and improper ways to stretch.

Enrichment

This activity will allow you to provide a more challenging learning experience for some of your students.

Have the students bring an item from home that can be useful in the improvement of flexibility. The equipment should be a common household item. Have the students demonstrate how the item can be used in a stretching exercise. Discuss how everyday activities can be modified to include opportunities for an increase in ROM.

Assess

Use the Active Mind/Active Body activity on page 205 to assess students' progress. Then use the Section 4 Review questions to assess students' comprehension of the concepts presented in Section 4.

ANSWERS TO SECTION 4 REVIEW

1. Stretches should be done a minimum of three days per week to improve and maintain flexibility.
2. For static stretching, hold each stretch for ten to fifteen seconds at a time, repeating this three times for each static stretch done. For ballistic, reflex-assisted, or passive stretching, do five to fifteen slow and gentle movements, repeating this three times per stretch.

Close

Divide the class into groups of four or five students and have them develop a stretching routine. Have each group choose a different physical activity or sport for which to prepare. Have groups share their routines with the class.

Figure 6.13 (continued)

• *Shoulder pull*

• *Upper torso dangle*

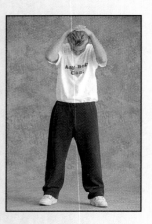

• *Toe touch*

• *Head pull down*

(Continued on next page)

Wellness Connection

If joints become injured or diseased, there will be a loss of range of motion. In extreme conditions there are various surgical procedures that may help relieve pain and increase range of motion. Some of these surgical procedures include the following:

• *Arthroplasty*—the reconstruction of a damaged joint using the patient's own tissue.
• *Osteotomy*—separation or cutting of a joint that has become fused or has shifted to an abnormal position.
• *Arthrodesis*—fusion of a damaged joint,

(Continued from previous page)

• *Opposite toe pull*

• *Side benders*

• *Knee hug*

• *Lower calf stretches*

• *Modified lotus*

Teacher Readings

Morrow, J. R., Jackson, A. W., Disch, J. G., and Mood, D. P., *Measurement and Evaluation in Human Performance,* Human Kinetics, Champaign, IL: 1995.

Teacher Readings

Dintiman, G. B., Davis, R. G., Pennington, J. C., and Stone, S. E., *Discovering Lifetime Fitness: Concepts of Exercise and Weight Control,* West Publishing, St. Paul, MN: 1989.

usually done to relieve pain. This procedure will result in a loss of range of motion.

• *Joint replacement*—the replacement or rebuilding of severely damaged joints. Synthetic materials such as Teflon or stainless steel may be used in this procedure. Hip replacement with various ball-and-socket structures is very common. Other joints that may be replaced include the knees, ankles, hands, wrists, and elbows.

Healthy People 2000

Objective 2.5—Reduce dietary fat intake to an average of 30 percent of calories or less and average saturated fat intake to less than 10 percent of calories among people aged 2 and older.

Considerable evidence associates diets high in fat with increased risk of obesity, some types of cancer, and possibly gallbladder disease. There is strong and consistent evidence for the relationship between saturated fat intake, high blood cholesterol, and increased risk for coronary heart disease. Lowering saturated fat intake can help to reduce total and LDL cholesterol levels, and thus coronary heart disease.

Figure 6.14   *General Flexibility Routine–Hazardous Stretches and Recommended Modifications.* **Do not** *do the exercises shown in the photos on the left. These exercises can cause various strains and sprains, put too much pressure on disks in your back, over stress ligaments and muscles, or in some other way lead to an unnecessary injury. The modifications shown on the right are safe ways to stretch.*

Hazardous	**Modifications**

• *Stretch neck roll*

• *Trunk roll*

(Continued on next page)

Science and Technology

Increasing range of motion and preventing muscular injury should be a top priority while participating in physical activity. Increasing your students' knowledge about flexibility and, at the same time, learning new stretching techniques and exercises is as easy as a "mouse" click on your computer. Among the many accessible sites on the Internet, the Stretching and Flexibility page is a must for the physical education teacher. Here you can learn about new scientific advancements concerning flexibility and proven stretching techniques.

• *Toe touch*

Hazardous

Modifications

• *Bar stretch*

• *Quadricep stretch*

(Continued on next page)

The objective recommends that healthy children follow the recommended eating patterns that are lower in fat and saturated fat as they begin to eat with the family, usually at age 2 or older. Because eating habits developed during childhood can influence lifetime eating practices, it is considered prudent to move toward these recommended eating patterns. However, as food intake varies from day to day, these recommendations are meant to represent an average of nutrient intake over several days. Implementation activities should recognize that this objective applies to the diet for a day or more, not to a single meal or a single food.

Teacher Readings

Anderson, B., *Stretching*, Shelter Publications, Inc., Bolinas, CA: 1980.

Included among these pages are descriptions of different stretching exercises and flexibility measures for different muscle groups. To locate the Flexibility page, use your Internet browser to open http://www.yahoo.com/health/fitness. If you are having trouble accessing this page, go to the YAHOO searchable index and type "flexibility" in the search window. You will be amazed at the many different pages available on the topics of muscle flexibility and stretching activities. Learning new stretching exercises from the Internet will keep students from becoming bored and will introduce them to less routine exercises. **Take the challenge:** Try to find as many Internet flexibility sites as you can.

(Continued from previous page)

Healthy People 2000

Objective 2.6—**Increase carbohydrate and fiber-containing foods in the diets of adults to five or more daily servings for vegetables (including legumes) and fruits, and to six or more daily servings for grain products.**

Vegetables (including legumes such as beans and peas), fruits, and grains are good sources of complex carbohydrates and dietary fiber, as well as several vitamins and minerals. These foods are also generally low in fat and can be substitutes for foods high in fat. Dietary patterns with higher intakes of vegetables (including legumes), fruits, and grains are asso-

Teacher Readings

Morrow, J. R., Falls, H. B., and Kohl, H. W., Editors. *The Fitnessgram Technical Reference Manual,* The Cooper Institute for Aerobics Research, Dallas, TX: 1994.

Hazardous   **Modifications**

• *Hurdler's stretch*

• *Deep knee bend*

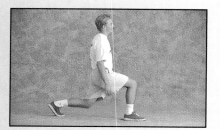

• *Yoga plow*

CULTURAL DIVERSITY

China

Traditionally, the Chinese use massage and gymnastics to strengthen the body. At dawn every day throughout China, people of all ages gather in a public park to practice *tai-chi,* also called *Tai-Chi Chuan* or *taijiquan.* This fitness routine is comprised of fluid, yet precise movements, which demand both breath and muscle control. Elements of tai-chi can also be used for self-defense.

One-fourth of all the people in the world live in China, so space is a luxury. For

• *Straight-leg sit-ups*

Hazardous **Modifications**

• *Double leg raise*

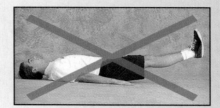 

• *Prone arch*

• *Back bend (there is no recommended alternative for the back bend)*

ciated with a variety of health benefits, including a decreased risk for some types of cancer.

Populations consuming diets rich in vegetables, fruits, and grain products have significantly lower rates of cancer of the colon, breast, lung, oral cavity, larynx, esophagus, stomach, bladder, uterine cervix, and pancreas. The strongest support for a protective effect from fiber-rich foods is for colon cancer, the second leading cause of cancer death in the United States. A fiber-rich diet is advocated in the management of constipation, and may be related to lower rates of hemorrhoids, diverticulosis/diverticulitis, and colon cancer.

Teacher Readings

Prudential Fitnessgram Test Administration Manual, Cooper Institute for Aerobics Research, Dallas, TX: 1992.

this reason table tennis, badminton, basketball, and gymnastics are popular. Bicycles are essential for transportation and provide good exercise.

In southern China, the subtropical weather and big rivers make swimming and diving frequent pastimes. There are more than 2,000 swimming pools in China, some of them Olympic sized. The country has a history of running state sports schools in the cities to develop the talents of promising young athletes, who may go on to compete internationally. In recent years, Chinese Olympic competitors have excelled in diving, gymnastics, and Ping-Pong.

CNN® Health and Fitness Updates

You can update your coverage of health and fitness topics, as well as spark lively classroom discussion and deeper understanding, by using the **CNN Health and Fitness Updates.** These video updates are produced by Turner Educational Services, using the resources of CNN, the world's first 24-hour, all-news network.

With the introduction of the **CNN Health and Fitness Updates,** West Educational Publishing is proud to be the exclusive partner of CNN for textbook/video integration in high school fitness. By making use of the **CNN Health and Fitness Updates** you can bring the power of CNN, the network known for providing in-depth, live coverage and analysis of breaking news events, to your fitness class.

For assistance in using and incorporating the **CNN Health and Fitness Updates** into your classroom presentations, see the *Classroom Guide to the CNN Health and Fitness Updates.* The **CNN Health and Fitness Updates** are available with West Educational Publishing's *Foundations of Personal Fitness* by Don Rainey and Tinker Murray.

SUMMARY

A moderate to high level of flexibility is important for efficient daily physical movements and to help reduce risks for muscle and bone injuries. Moderate to high levels of flexibility can improve performance fitness and reduce some types of muscle soreness following physical activity or exercise. You can help maintain your good, functional health by maintaining or improving your flexibility. For example, you can help reduce your risk for low back pain and low back injuries by developing flexible and strong muscles that support your spine and pelvic girdle.

Your flexibility levels are influenced by several factors, including your gender, age, genetic makeup, joint structure (connective tissue, such as tendons and ligaments), body temperature, injured joints, excessive body fat, and how active you are. Regular, specific stretching exercises can positively influence your flexibility.

Static stretching, ballistic stretching, reflex-assisted stretching, and passive stretching are all types of stretching that can increase your range of motion (ROM). Static stretching methods are the safest, but the other three types may be important for you to do if you are interested in performance fitness. The easiest strategy for including flexibility exercises in your personal fitness program is to make them part of your regular warm-up and cool-down routines.

COOPERATIVE LEARNING

When students are put into cooperative learning situations their behavior, at times, is anything but cooperative. You might have students who will not involve themselves with the group, those who are involved (but not with the current assignment), those who insist on working independently, or those who "take over" in the group. Talking with the groups that are experiencing problems and encouraging them to work things out among themselves can be effective in eliminating unwanted behaviors.

Ideas for developing cooperative learn-

Chapter 6 Review

True/False

On a separate sheet of paper, mark each question below either T for True or F for False.

1. When someone tells you that your ROM is within normal limits, it means your flexibility is poor.
2. Hingelike joints allow you to move forward and backward.
3. Your risk of back injuries is increased if you have inflexible and weak muscles that support your spine and pelvic girdle.
4. Lifting movements account for about 50 percent of all low back injuries.
5. The amount of body fat you carry has no effect on how flexible you are.
6. Flexibility can change as much as 80 percent with changes in muscular temperature.
7. Flexibility exercises can reduce the amount of muscle stiffness and soreness you have after exercising.
8. Your flexibility will improve significantly if you go bowling regularly.
9. Ballistic stretching is done very slowly without bouncing up and down.
10. Your reflexes cannot be influenced by a regular stretching program.

Multiple Choice

1. The condition of hyperflexibility is associated with which of the following?
   a. loose joints
   b. tight connective tissue
   c. strong muscles
   d. strong ligaments
2. What percentage of the people on Earth are estimated to have low back pain at one time or another in their lives?
   a. 20 percent
   b. 40 percent
   c. 60 percent
   d. 80 percent
3. Your flexibility is not influenced by which of the following?
   a. genetics
   b. age
   c. height
   d. physical activity level
4. Which of the following factors is the most significant in negatively influencing your flexibility levels?
   a. lack of physical activity
   b. excess body fat
   c. injured joints
   d. your gender
5. Which of the following is not a typical benefit of flexibility conditioning?
   a. increased ROM
   b. increased risk of joint injury
   c. reduced tension and stress levels
   d. increased functional health
6. Plyometric training is a type of _____ stretching.
   a. static
   b. ballistic
   c. reflex-assisted
   d. passive

Answers

True/False

1. F
2. T
3. T
4. T
5. F
6. F
7. T
8. F
9. F
10. F

Multiple Choice

1. a.
2. d.
3. c.
4. a.
5. b.
6. c.
7. d.
8. c.
9. a.
10. d.

ing activities for your class are limited only by your imagination. Here are a few ideas to get you started thinking. Cooperative learning groups can be used to help students learn vocabulary words and for developing large projects such as research papers. Cooperative groups can work together to solve problems such as the Case Studies that are in some of the Chapter Review materials, and equations such as the one used for determining relative muscular strength.

It takes time for both the teacher and the students to become familiar with the idea of cooperative learning. It's not easy to suddenly depend on others when you're used to depending only on yourself.

Discussion

1. Answers might include: Learn to lift and carry objects properly. Strengthen the muscles of the low back. Avoid excessive movements while lifting.

2. Answers will vary but should include benefits listed in Figure 6.6.

3. Answers will vary but might include any of the stretches from Figures 6.12 and 6.13.

Vocabulary Experience

_6_ elasticity
_2_ plyometrics
_1_ muscle imbalance
_5_ ROM
_3_ low back injury
_4_ reflex-assisted stretching

Critical Thinking

1. Some individuals can get hyperflexible joints due to injuries, and thus, too much flexibility can sometimes be detrimental.

2. Doing regular physical activity and exercise stimulates healthy changes to and adaptations in the muscles, tendons, and ligaments. See Figure 6.6.

3. When doing static stretching, you assume a stretch position slowly and then hold it for several seconds (10 to 60) until you feel slight discomfort, but no real pain. Static stretching would be ideal for someone just beginning a personal fitness program because it is the safest form of stretching.

Chapter 6 Review

7. Which of the following types of stretching requires a partner or device to help you complete a stretch?

  a. static
  b. ballistic
  c. reflex-assisted
  d. passive

8. What is the minimum number of days per week that you should do your stretching program to maintain or improve your flexibility levels?

  a. one
  b. two
  c. three
  d. four

9. To improve your flexibility, how must you overload your muscles?

  a. by stretching them beyond their normal resting length
  b. by shortening them below their normal resting length
  c. by lifting, twisting, bending, and pulling
  d. none of the above

10. Which of the following stretches may be hazardous to you and needs to be modified in order for you to do it safely?

  a. knee hug
  b. calf stretch
  c. groin stretch
  d. neck roll

Discussion

1. List and describe five ways you can help reduce your risk for low back pain and low back injuries.

2. Give five benefits that typically follow flexibility conditioning in a previously inactive young adult after 8 to 30 weeks.

3. Identify five stretches that are safe and effective for increasing or maintaining your flexibility levels.

Vocabulary Experience

Match the correct term in Column A to the definition in Column B by writing the appropriate number in each blank.

Column A		Column B
_____ elasticity	**1.**	When one muscle group that controls a joint is too strong in relation to another muscle group that also helps control the joint.
_____ plyometrics	**2.**	Bounding and jumping exercises.
_____ muscle imbalance	**3.**	Injury to the muscles, ligaments, tendons, or joints of the lower back.
_____ ROM	**4.**	The type of stretching that increases the rate at which you develop speed and explosive power.
_____ low back injury	**5.**	Range of motion or varying degrees of movement.
_____ reflex-assisted stretching	**6.**	Rubberband-like flexibility.

CRITICAL THINKING

The average age for the development of low back pain is 32 years. There are numerous causes for low back pain, but it is often related to daily lifting activities at school or work. Researchers have identified several variables that are associated with the incidence of low back pain. These variables include occupation (higher incidence with the more one lifts at work), age (the older one is, the higher the incidence), history of back injury (if someone has had a back injury, he or she is at higher risk), low levels of muscular strength (the weaker one is,

Critical Thinking

1. Respond to this statement: You can never have enough flexibility.

2. How does maintaining an active lifestyle contribute to the maintenance of the flexibility of your muscles, tendons, and ligaments?

3. Discuss static stretching and why you would recommend this technique to someone just starting a personal fitness program.

Case Study — Bob's Injury

Bob is a fifteen-year-old who is very active and enjoys jogging 3 to 5 miles daily. However, in the past year he has noticed that his muscles feel very tight, his lower back hurts occasionally, and he feels like he has lost some of his flexibility. Bob does not like to stretch and really sees no benefit in it. In fact, he thinks it is a waste of time. However, he is concerned about his loss of flexibility, because he thinks it may increase his risk for injuries during jogging. He would like to improve his flexibility levels back to what is normal for him, but he is not sure how to do so. Therefore, he needs the help of someone knowledgeable about designing and implementing fitness programs—SOMEONE LIKE YOU!

Here is your assignment:

Assume you are Bob's friend, and he asks you for some assistance with his plans for improving his flexibility. Organize a list of things Bob should consider and do before beginning flexibility conditioning. Then list the recommendations you would give Bob for his first two weeks of flexibility conditioning. Use these suggestions as a guide:

KEYS TO HELP YOU

- Consider Bob's history of flexibility conditioning.
- Consider how he should evaluate his current flexibility levels.
- Consider his needs and goals. (For example, how will he find time to do flexibility exercises?)
- Determine a reasonable plan to give Bob that covers the concepts of overload, frequency, intensity, time/duration, and progression.

KEYS TO CASE STUDY

Answers will vary but might include something like the following: Bob should complete the PAR-Q in Chapter 2 before beginning his program. If he can answer "no" to the seven questions in the PAR-Q, he can begin a general personal fitness program. In his first two weeks, Bob should begin by doing static stretching three times a week. He needs to do about 10 stretches in each session. He can choose a variety of stretches from Figures 6.12 and 6.13. He needs to choose stretching activities that he likes and ones he will continue to do. He also needs to follow the tips for controlling low back problems highlighted in Figure 6.5. He must recognize that he needs to be involved in personal fitness for the long haul. He needs to emphasize flexibility as part of his plan to control and prevent further back problems if possible.

---

the higher his or her risk), participation in sports (participants have a higher incidence than nonparticipants), as well as psychological factors (boring, repetitive jobs may increase the incidence).

Use Figure 6.3 on page 192 to discuss the most common causes of back

injuries among American workers. Have students roleplay correct and incorrect lifting techniques. (Be sure students don't injure themselves when demonstrating incorrect techniques.) Have students explain what is wrong with the incorrect techniques.

RESOURCES **HANDOUTS** A chapter test is provided for Chapter 6 in your Teacher Resource Package.

Chapter Overview

Chapter 7 is 28 pages long and divided into the five sections listed to the right. Major learning outcomes of the chapter are also listed to the right. Briefly, this chapter introduces students to progressive resistance and weight training. It emphasizes muscle growth benefits and other health- and fitness-related benefits associated with weight training. Students will discuss the negative physiological and psychological effects of steroids. The chapter explains and clarifies many of the myths that surround the image of weight training, while allowing students to become familiar with the equipment and facilities associated with progressive resistance.

Teacher Resource Material

In the Teacher Resource Package accompanying the textbook, you will find the following materials to help you teach this chapter.

Chapter 7

Developing Muscular Strength and Endurance through the Science of Weight Training

216

PACING CHART

It is recommended that Chapter 7 be taught in conjunction with Chapter 8 in order for students to fully experience and understand the values of weight training. The combinations of the two chapters (including activity time) could be taught over a four- to five-week unit. However, you can cover the material in Chapter 7 in four days. It is recommended that physical activity be a regular part of each class period (20 to 30 minutes minimum). Following are some examples of how to cover the main topics in the chapter if you are pressed for time.

Contents

Outcomes

After reading and studying this chapter, you will be able to:

1. Discuss the benefits of weight training.
2. Explain how muscular strength and muscular endurance can contribute to good fitness and health.
3. Explain progressive resistance and weight training.
4. Explain how muscles work and grow.
5. Identify the negative effects of steroids.
6. Give examples of weight training myths, and tell why they are incorrect.
7. Describe weight-training equipment and facilities, and discuss how they are used.

Key Terms

After reading and studying this chapter, you will be able to understand and provide practical definitions for the following terms:

relative muscular strength
relative muscular endurance
progressive resistance
weight training
cardiac muscle
smooth muscle
skeletal muscle
contract

muscle fiber (muscle cell)
connective tissue
nerve
blood vessel
concentric contraction
eccentric contraction
isotonic progressive resistance
isometric contraction

hypertrophy
atrophy
hyperplasia
genetic potential
microtear
testosterone
free weights
weight machines

217

Activity Sheets

One Reteaching Worksheet is provided in the Teacher Resource Package for each section of this chapter. A handout is also provided for the Active Mind/Active Body activity on page 239.

Transparencies/Masters

A transparency or master is provided in the Teacher Resource Package for each of the following figures and exhibits: The Many Benefits of Weight Training, 7.1, 7.2, 7.3, 7.4, 7.5, 7.6, 7.7, 7.8, 7.9, and Calculating Relative Muscular Strength.

Discuss the Photo

Ask students to discuss their opinions of body-builders, power lifters, and athletes using weights. Ask about any past experiences they have had with weight training.

CHAPTER 7

Time	Suggestions
Day 1	Assign students to read Sections 1 and 2. Discuss the opinions about weight training. Discuss and calculate relative strength. Discuss the forms and benefits of progressive resistance.
Day 2	Assign students to read Section 3. Use transparencies to discuss how muscles grow and become stronger. Have students move light weights to simulate muscle contractions. Discuss steroids.
Day 3	Have the class go through a circuit made of isometric exercises. Discuss the "Stress Break" and the "Consumer Corner." Review the benefits of weight training. Explain why muscles become sore.
Day 4	Assign students to read Sections 4 and 5. Discuss. Have students use weight training equipment to experience its effects. Use the Active Mind/Active Body on page 239.

CHAPTER 7
SECTION 1
218

Focus

Outcomes

In **Section 1** students will learn:

1. To explain how muscular strength and muscular endurance can contribute to good fitness and health.
2. The importance of relative muscular strength and endurance.
3. How to determine relative muscular strength.

Focus Activities

1. Discuss how opinions about weight training have changed over the years.
2. Learn to calculate relative strength.
3. Discuss the difference between muscular strength and muscular endurance.

INTRODUCTION

*N*ever before have the benefits of muscular strength and muscular endurance been so accepted and so frequently recommended by experts as being an important part of your physical fitness plan. Experts today have concluded that building muscular strength and endurance, through the use of weight training, is an integral part of good health and fitness for all ages and sexes. Simple, everyday life practices such as climbing a flight of stairs, lifting a backpack full of books, practicing good posture, or any number of running and jumping activities, can become easier and more efficient if weight training is a part of your fitness plan. You should also realize that weight training can have toning, firming, and shaping benefits on our personal appearance.

Years ago lifting weights was thought to be an activity reserved for only a few unusual people, such as the strong man at the circus. It was only a few years ago that professional athletes were not allowed to lift weights for fear it might reduce their speed or limit their abilities to perform. There was even a time when few, if any, exercise and fitness professionals considered lifting weights to be a valuable part of a personal fitness program. In fact, experts considered lifting weights to be potentially harmful to health and fitness.

In the past 15 to 20 years, however, weight training has evolved from the Dark Ages into the Scientific Age—an age that understands its benefits and encourages its use. As a result, students and adults of all ages are going to health clubs, spas, and gyms all across the country to participate in weight training.

This chapter will focus on the benefits of weight training, the different kinds of weight training, and the different kinds of muscles and how they work. You will learn about the many myths that still surround this fitness activity and the equipment associated with weight lifting. Remember, you do not have to be a high-performance athlete to be involved in weight training. **A**ny **B**ody **C**an participate in weight training. All you need is desire.

SECTION 1
How You and Your Muscles Can Benefit from Weight Training

Good levels of physical fitness require adequate levels of both muscular strength and muscular endurance. Even though strength and endurance are closely related, there are some important differences.

Muscular Strength

As you learned in Chapter 4, muscular strength is the amount of force (muscular contraction) a muscle or muscle group can exert against a resistance in one maximum effort. A person who can lift 100 pounds one time during a weight-training exercise is stronger

Reteaching

ABILITY LEVELS

Reteaching

Some students may need help mastering the concepts contained in this section. In your Teacher Resource Package, you will find the reproducible worksheet shown here. This worksheet should help students who have been absent and those needing additional help to improve their comprehension and retention of the content in this section.

• *Weight training is a popular physical activity for developing personal fitness.*

relative muscular strength

how much weight you can lift one time in relation to your body weight and gender.

REMEMBER This!

The strongest person may not be the fittest. You do not have to have superhuman strength to be fit and healthy. Although your muscular strength can improve your athletic or performance fitness, your relative muscular strength is more relevant to your functional health. It is important for you to develop and maintain enough strength to carry your body weight efficiently throughout your day-to-day routines. Participation in a regular weight-lifting program can help you achieve this goal.

than a person who can lift 80 pounds one time in the same exercise, regardless of the individual's size, age, or weight.

However, it is important to note that good health and fitness depend more on **relative muscular strength** than on absolute muscular strength. Relative muscular strength is how much weight you can lift in relation to your body weight and gender. For example, Jim weighs 125 pounds and can lift 130 pounds during a weight-training exercise. Wilbur weighs 160 pounds and can lift 150 pounds during the same exercise. Wilbur clearly has the greatest amount of strength, but who is the strongest pound for pound? You can determine this by dividing the amount of weight lifted by the body weight of the individual. The individual with the higher number is exerting more strength per pound of body weight. In this example, Jim has the best *relative* muscular strength:

$$\frac{\text{Bench Press}}{\text{Body Weight}} = \frac{\text{Relative Muscular}}{\text{Strength}}$$

Jim $\quad \dfrac{\text{Bench Press 130 lbs}}{\text{Body Weight 125 lbs}} = 1.04$

Wilbur $\quad \dfrac{\text{Bench Press 150 lbs}}{\text{Body Weight 160 lbs}} = .93$

Jim's ratio of weight lifted in comparison with his body weight is higher than Wilbur's. In Chapter 8 you will be asked to determine your absolute muscular strength and your relative muscular strength for a variety of weight-lifting exercises.

Assess

Use the Section 1 Review questions to assess students' comprehension of the concepts presented in Section 1.

ANSWERS TO SECTION 1 REVIEW

1. Muscular endurance is the ability of the same muscle or muscle group to contract repeatedly for an extended period of time without undue fatigue. Muscle strength is the amount of force a muscle or muscle group can exert against a resistance in one maximum effort.

2. Relative muscular strength pertains to how much weight you can lift in relation to your body weight and gender. To possess enough muscular strength to adequately handle your body weight is an important part of physical fitness.

Muscular Endurance

Muscular endurance, you will recall, is the ability of the same muscle or muscle group to contract for an extended period of time without undue fatigue. The ability to lift 75 pounds on the bench press fifteen times is an example of muscular endurance. Good health and fitness, however, depend more on **relative muscular endurance**. This is measured by how many times you can lift a given weight in relation to your body weight and gender. For example, Jane has a maximum lift of 65 pounds on the shoulder press (an exercise that pushes weight over your head). Susan has a maximum lift of 50 pounds on the shoulder press. If they are asked to do 50 percent of their maximum shoulder press as many times as possible, Susan might do more lifts than Jane. In this case, even though Susan is not the strongest, she has higher relative muscular endurance than does Jane.

If you are interested in improving either your muscular strength or muscular endurance, you might want to experience any of the suggested activities in this chapter. One of the best and most popular ways to improve muscular strength and muscular endurance is to start a weight-training program now!

relative muscular endurance

how many times you can lift a given weight in relation to your body weight and gender.

SECTION 1 REVIEW

Answer the following questions on a separate sheet of paper:

1. Explain the difference between muscular endurance and muscular strength.

2. Why is relative muscular strength more important to physical fitness than just absolute muscular strength?

SECTION 2 Progressive Resistance

To increase a muscle's strength or endurance, you must first overload that muscle. The overload principle is based on putting a greater amount of stress (weight or resistance) on your muscle than the muscle is accustomed to. As your muscle adapts to this stress by becoming stronger, you again increase the amount of stress (more weight or resistance) so that the muscle will continue to grow and become stronger. The continued systematic increase of muscle stress through

Close

Ask students to consider if their muscular strength and endurance are at acceptable physical fitness levels.

Wellness Connection

If a person takes steroids, the reason is usually to get bigger, stronger, or faster. However, steroid use during adolescence can result in permanent stunting of growth due to the premature closure of the epiphyseal plates of the bones.

Steroid use in competitive sports is banned and drug testing is carried out to enforce this ban. It was big news in 1988 when Ben Johnson, a Canadian sprinter, was stripped of his Olympic medal and world record for the 100-meter sprint after traces of the anabolic steroid stanolozol were detected in his system.

progressive resistance

the continued, systematic increase of muscle stress through the use of weights or other forms of resistance.

weight training

the use of such equipment as barbells, dumbbells, and machines to improve fitness, health, and appearance.

the use of weights or other forms of resistance is called **progressive resistance**. **Weight training** (the use of equipment such as barbells, dumbbells, and machines to improve fitness, health, and appearance) has become a very popular and effective way to apply progressive resistance.

The Range of Possibilities

The popularity of weight training has grown tremendously. Weight training is becoming more and more important as science and medicine discover its potential health and fitness benefits. However, the term *weight training* is often misused to describe all forms of progressive resistance. The following is a list of names and descriptions for all forms of progressive resistance training:

- *Weight training.* A general description referring to the use of such equipment as barbells, dumbbells, and machines to improve general fitness, health, and appearance, which **A**ny **B**ody **C**an do.
- *Weight lifting.* Competitive sport lifting performed by athletes who have genetic advantages and who follow very specific programs to build power and strength. For example, an Olympic lifter might perform the clean and jerk or the snatch. A power lifter could do a squat, bench press, and dead lift.
- *Body building.* A competitive sport in which muscle size and shape are more important than muscle strength. Body builders

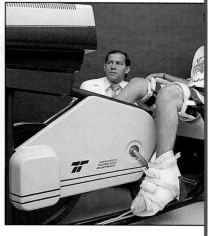

• *Examples of progressive resistance training: To the Left: Body Building; Center: Olympic Lifting; To the Right: Rehabilitation.*

But losing a medal or being disqualified from competition is a small penalty compared to the health risks involved. Some of the side effects and adverse reactions of anabolic steroid use include liver and other forms of cancer, heart disease, high blood pressure, high blood cholesterol, depression, hostility, mood swings, suicidal tendencies, baldness, acne, testicular atrophy, impotence, breast enlargement in males, and masculinizing effects in females. The former actor and NFL lineman Lyle Alzado blamed his brain cancer, from which he died in 1992, to his steroid abuse. If injectable anabolic steroids are abused, there is the additional risk of HIV infection and AIDS from the sharing of needles.

CHAPTER 7
SECTION 2
221

Focus

Outcomes

In **Section 2** students will learn:

1. To explain progressive resistance and weight training.
2. To explain the different forms of progressive resistance.
3. To identify and explain the benefits of weight training.

Focus Activities

1. Define and discuss progressive resistance and weight training.
2. Discuss the different forms of progressive resistance and the purpose of each.
3. Identify and discuss the primary and secondary benefits of weight training.

Teach & Apply

Discussion

- Review the overload principle and then explain how the use of weights or other resistance would be considered overload.
- Review the progression principle and then explain how progressive resistance is a form of progression.

Discussion

• Discuss and explain each form of resistance training.
• Discuss the photos of resistance training.

RESOURCES Use the color transparency, The Many Benefits of Weight Training to discuss the primary and secondary benefits.

Stress Break

Discuss the Stress Break. Ask students, How can weight training make some positive changes in your self-esteem and self-concept? Is weight training a good way to ventilate your daily stress?

Stress Break

Participating in physical activities that improve your self-esteem is a great way to deal with or avoid stressful situations in your life. The better you feel about yourself, the less likely you are to be overly sensitive to someone else's opinion of you. A few simple changes in your personal appearance, such as increased muscle tone, loss of weight, and improved posture, can have a huge positive impact on your self-esteem. Do something good for yourself. Start a regular weight-training program. Positive physical changes will soon occur, and you may see a pleasant change in your attitude.

have genetic advantages and follow very specific programs utilizing many different exercises.

• *Strength training or muscle conditioning.* Training done by competitive sport athletes. The goal is to improve performance in a particular sport and to reduce the chance of injury. The programs of these athletes are specific to their sports.

• *Rehabilitation.* The use of resistance exercises to recover from a muscle or bone injury.

The Many Benefits of Weight Training

There are many reasons why a well-planned weight-training program should be a part of your life. Millions of people are training with weights every day, each for his or her own reasons.

Primary Benefits. Weight training leads to several primary benefits as listed below, which are directly related to strength gains in both muscles and bones:

Primary Benefits	• Increased size of muscle fibers (bigger muscle) • Increased strength of muscles (stronger muscle) • Increased strength and density of bones (this can prevent a bone disease called osteoporosis) • Increased strength in ligaments and tendons (these connect bones to bones and muscles to bones)

Secondary Benefits	• Increases muscular endurance, which can improve your work capacity (do more work)
	• Helps reduce injury
	  a. serve as shock absorbers for your internal organs when you fall or bump into objects
	  b. protect you from back injuries
	  c. prevent sports injuries
	• Improves personal appearance
	  a. tones, tightens, and shapes muscles
	  b. burns calories, speeds up metabolism, and burns fat (the more muscle you have, the more calories you can burn)
	  c. contributes to good posture
	  d. contributes to good self-esteem and self-concept
	• Improves flexibility if done properly (full range of motion)
	• Enhances sports performance (strength and coordination)
	• Reduces stress in a positive way
	• Can slow down the aging process

As we get older, our bodies shrink in size and strength. Scientists today believe that much of this loss of size and strength is a result of inactivity, not age. Use it or lose it! **A**ny **B**ody **C**an use it!

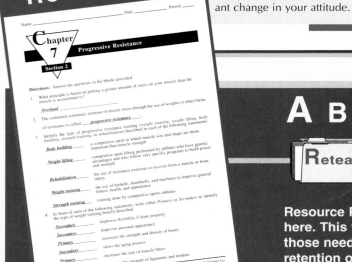

Reteaching

ABILITY LEVELS

Reteaching

Some students may need help mastering the concepts contained in this section. In your Teacher Resource Package, you will find the reproducible worksheet shown here. This worksheet should help students who have been absent and those needing additional help to improve their comprehension and retention of the content in this section.

SECTION 2 REVIEW

Answer the following questions on a separate sheet of paper:

1. Explain the relationship between weight training and progressive resistance.
2. Explain the difference between weight lifting and weight training.
3. In your opinion, which is the most important primary benefit of weight training? Why do you think so?

SECTION 3 — The Muscle and How It Works (Physiology)

The muscle is the organ that creates the movement of our bodies. It must contract for movement to occur (Figure 7.1). Understanding how this movement is created can help you better understand and appreciate the many benefits that can be obtained from a weight-training program, now and throughout your life.

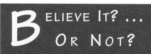

BELIEVE IT? ... OR NOT?

Twenty-eight percent of men and 65 percent of women over age seventy-four cannot lift 20 pounds; however, reasonable amounts of weight training can help older adults regain their strength and functional independence, which allows them to care for themselves.

See page 240 for answer.

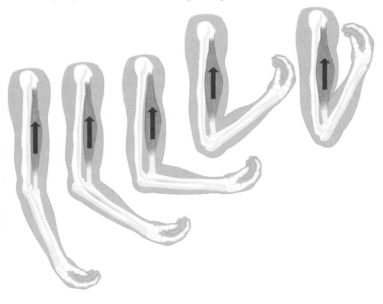

• **Figure 7.1** *Muscles Become Shorter as They Contract.*

Assess

Use the Section 2 Review questions to assess students' comprehension.

ANSWERS TO SECTION 2 REVIEW

1. By using barbells, dumbbells, and machines (weight training) to apply stress to the muscle over a period of time, you are performing progressive resistance.
2. Weight training refers to the use of a barbell, dumbbells, etc. to improve general fitness, health, and appearance. Weight lifting refers to competitive sports that have maximal strength attainment as the primary goal.
3. Answers will vary.

Close

Have students respond to the statement, "Use it or lose it."

Enrichment — *This activity will allow you to provide a more challenging learning experience for some of your students.*

Have students use the list of primary and secondary benefits of weight training on page 222 to develop a survey. The survey should ask participants whether the benefits are being experienced. Students should distribute the survey at a local health or fitness club. They should try to find people participating in at least one of the following forms of progressive resistance training: weight training, weight lifting, and bodybuilding. Students should compile the results of their survey and share them with the class.

Focus

Outcomes

In **Section 3** students will learn:

1. To explain the components of muscles and how they work.
2. To explain how and why muscles grow.
3. To identify and explain the negative effects of steroids.
4. Why muscles become sore.

Focus Activities

1. Use transparencies/ masters of Figures 7.2, 7.3, 7.4, and 7.5 to explain the components of muscles and how they work and grow.
2. Have students do weight training exercises that demonstrate concentric, eccentric, and isometric contractions.
3. Explain muscle hypertrophy. Discuss the reasons why hypertrophy occurs differently in individuals.
4. Discuss factors associated with the development of muscular strength.
5. Define the term "steroids" and identify the negative effects associated with their use.
6. Explain how weight training activities can cause muscle soreness.

---

cardiac muscle

muscle in the heart and arteries.

smooth muscle

muscle located around internal organs that automatically controls many functions of the body.

skeletal muscle

muscle located around bones and joints that controls movement.

contract

to shorten.

muscle fibers (muscle cells)

long, thin structures the size of human hairs that contract to create movement. They run the entire length of a muscle.

connective tissue

the "glue" for the body tissue that binds muscles and bones together while still allowing them to move more efficiently.

nerve

in a muscle, the part that delivers the messages from the brain to direct each individual muscle fiber to contract.

blood vessel

in a muscle, the structure that provides oxygen, energy, and a waste removal system for each muscle fiber.

Your body has hundreds of muscles. They are grouped into one of three categories, depending on their function (see Figure 7.2). **Cardiac muscles** are located in the heart. **Smooth muscles** are located around internal organs and arteries, and automatically control many functions of the body. **Skeletal muscles** are located around bones and joints and control movement. Since weight training has little or no effect on cardiac and smooth muscles, the remainder of the chapter will focus mainly on skeletal muscles and how weight training influences them.

Skeletal Muscles: The Movers and Shakers

There are over 430 skeletal muscles in the human body (Figure 7.3). Even though skeletal muscles are usually grouped together, they are also capable of working independently as a highly organized team of movement. Each skeletal muscle has a primary job, which is to **contract** (shorten). When muscles contract, they force bones and joints to move.

Each skeletal muscle contains muscle fibers, connective tissue, nerves, and blood vessels. **Muscle fibers** (**muscle cells**) are long, thin structures the size of a human hair that contract to produce movement (see Figure 7.4). They run the entire length of the muscle. **Connective tissues** bind the muscles and bones together while still allowing them to move efficiently. Connective tissues include tendons (which connect muscle to bone), ligaments (which connect bone to bone), and cartilage (which is the material located in the joints that serves as a cushion between two bones). (See Figure 7.4.) **Nerves** deliver the messages from the brain that direct each individual muscle fiber to contract. **Blood vessels** provide oxygen, energy, and a waste removal system for each muscle fiber.

The skeletal muscle is capable of three kinds of contraction. Each contraction is unique and is capable of stimulating both muscle growth and muscle strength.

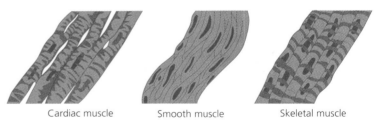

Cardiac muscle   Smooth muscle   Skeletal muscle

• **Figure 7.2**   *Categories of Muscle Tissue.*

CRITICAL THINKING

Students should have a thorough understanding of muscular fitness and its importance and relationship to a person's overall wellness. Have students interview adults who represent many different occupations. Include:

a. Professionals
b. Homemakers
c. Construction workers
d. Salespeople
e. School staff
f. All types of blue-collar workers

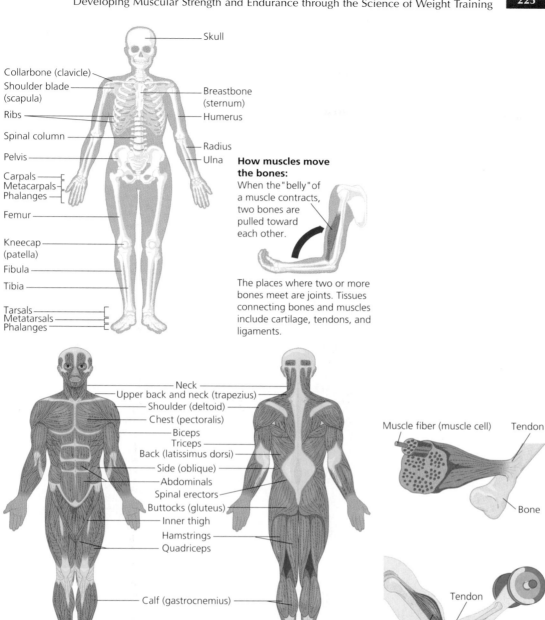

How muscles move the bones:

When the "belly" of a muscle contracts, two bones are pulled toward each other.

The places where two or more bones meet are joints. Tissues connecting bones and muscles include cartilage, tendons, and ligaments.

• **Figure 7.3**   *The Skeletal and Muscular Systems.*

• **Figure 7.4**   *Tendons and How They Attach to the Bone.*

Teach & Apply

Discussion

Discuss the three types of muscle tissue. Explain to students that this section deals with the components of and development of skeletal muscle tissue.

Teaching Strategies

RESOURCES   **TRANSPARENCIES**   Use transparency/master of Figure 7.2 to give students an idea of how the three different muscle tissues look.
• Use transparencies/masters of Figures 7.3 and 7.4 to discuss how bones and muscles are attached to one another.

Discussion

Discuss the concept of muscle contraction. Ask, Why is this the main job of the muscles? Describe the three types of muscle contraction.

Teaching Strategy

Use the transparency/master of Figure 7.5 to explain the three types of muscle contraction.

During the interviews, students should gather information about actual physical movement relating to the job. You can prepare a list of survey questions or challenge the students to do so.

Once information has been gathered, students should analyze opportunities within the occupations that help individuals in maintaining a certain level of muscular fitness. Then have students develop creative techniques and opportunities that the person could use to help improve his or her basic muscular fitness within the occupations. Force students to think critically about how muscular fitness relates directly to one's ability to perform tasks in certain occupations at the best possible level.

Activity

• Have students use a light dumbbell to do an arm curl to feel the concentric and eccentric contractions.

• Have students put their left palms in their right palms. Instruct them to push with the left hand and pull with the right hand. They should perform this activity as hard as they can. This activity will represent an isometric contraction.

Teaching Strategies

• Prepare an isometric workout using a variety of stations. Include the use of towels, ropes, doorways, partners, and different parts of their bodies.

• The authors strongly suggest that students should begin, as early as possible, their introduction to weight training safety and proper exercise techniques. Stu-

---

concentric contraction

the contraction and shortening of a muscle, which results in the movement of bones and joints; also called *positive work*.

---

eccentric contraction

a muscle's slow release of a contraction as it becomes longer; also called *negative work*.

---

isotonic progressive resistance

a combination of concentric and eccentric muscle contractions.

---

isometric contraction

a muscle's pushing against an immovable object and having no movement occur as it attempts to contract. The muscle does not become shorter or longer but creates tension.

Concentric Contraction. When a muscle contracts and becomes shorter, it is undergoing **concentric contraction** (Figure 7.5). The result is a movement of bones and joints. This type of contraction is often referred to as *positive work*.

Eccentric Contraction. When the muscle slowly releases its contraction and becomes longer, it is undergoing **eccentric contraction** (Figure 7.5). The muscle must control the speed of the lengthening process. The muscle should lengthen slowly and smoothly. Eccentric contraction is often referred to as *negative work*.

If the muscle were to simply relax rather than contract, gravity would quickly pull the arm down. This would not allow for any muscle work to be done during the eccentric contraction. Muscle work during the eccentric contractions is necessary for development of muscle strength and growth. It is believed that eccentric movements cause most of the muscle soreness we experience after weight training sessions.

Most weight-training techniques and equipment combine both concentric and eccentric muscle contractions. This combination of concentric and eccentric muscle contractions is called **isotonic progressive resistance**. It is by far the most popular form of weight training.

Isometric and Static Contractions. When a muscle pushes against an immovable object, it attempts to contract and create movement, but no movement occurs. This kind of contraction is an **isometric contraction**. The muscle does not become shorter or longer but creates tension (Figure 7.5).

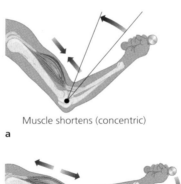

Muscle shortens (concentric)

a

Muscle lengthens (eccentric)

b

Muscle pushes against immovable object (isometric)

c

• **Figure 7.5**   *Different Kinds of Muscle Contraction.*

ABILITY LEVELS

Reteaching

Some students may need help mastering the concepts contained in this section. In your Teacher Resource Package, you will find the reproducible worksheet shown here. This worksheet should help students who have been absent and those needing additional help to improve their comprehension and retention of the content in this section.

How and Why Muscles Grow

Even with all of today's scientific technology and equipment, we are still unable to understand exactly how and why muscles grow. However, we do know that weight training, if used over an extended period of time, can and will increase muscle mass.

Hypertrophy—Getting Bigger. Most experts believe that the number of muscle fibers you have at birth will remain the same throughout your life. These experts believe that muscle growth is due to an enlargement (thickening) of each existing muscle fiber, not to an increase in the number of fibers. This muscle enlargement is called **hypertrophy**.

Most of your muscle growth is caused by the normal growth process that you experience during growth spurts. After your normal growth process stops, however, your muscles are still capable of growth. During weight training, each time you perform a resistance exercise, a chemical is produced that can cause muscle fibers to grow thicker. If each of the thousands of muscle fibers within a muscle slightly increases in size, the entire muscle will become larger.

The exact opposite occurs when you fail to use a muscle. The muscle fibers become smaller, resulting in a smaller muscle. This loss of muscle size is called **atrophy**. For example, the muscles around a broken bone atrophy because the cast around the bone prevents the muscles from being used. They lose some of their size because of lack of use, but this loss is only temporary. The muscles will regain their size after a short time with regular use.

Hyperplasia. Some experts believe that muscles grow when muscle fibers split and create additional fibers. This process is called **hyperplasia**. The additional fibers, they believe, account for the increase in muscle size. As yet, however, hyperplasia has been seen only in some animals (dogs, cats, and rats).

How and Why Muscles Get Stronger

Increased strength is usually the main goal of individuals who begin a weight-training program. Fortunately, all the primary and secondary benefits listed earlier in this chapter are acquired at the same time. With proper training and good nutrition, weight training can and will improve muscle strength. However, many other factors such as genetic potential, muscle mass, and nerves also affect muscle strength.

Genetic Potential. Each of us inherits a set number and percentage of different muscle fibers. The individual born with the most muscle fibers has the greatest **genetic potential** for muscle growth.

hypertrophy

muscle enlargement due to the thickening of each existing muscle fiber.

atrophy

a loss of muscle size and strength because of lack of use.

hyperplasia

a theory of muscle enlargement that says muscle growth is due to muscle fibers splitting and creating additional fibers.

genetic potential

inherited muscle characteristics that determine the percentage, type, and number of our muscle fibers.

CHAPTER 7
SECTION 3
227

dents will be asked to perform both pre- and post-strength evaluations. We feel that students must prepare for these evaluations over a reasonable period of time. These daily experiences and evaluations will allow students to perform their best as well as meet Guidelines 1 and 2 for adolescents (Chapter 1). Continue to combine the contents of Chapters 7 and 8, but be sure the students are actively involved in weight training exercises at least three times per week.

Discussion

• Ask, What is muscle hypertrophy? What is muscle atrophy?
• Discuss the two theories of muscle growth: hypertrophy and hyperplasia.

Teacher Support Notes

Research supports the belief that weight training can cause muscles to become larger because each individual muscle fiber increases in size. The question remains: Is all of this growth attributed to individ-

Enrichment

This activity will allow you to provide a more challenging learning experience for some of your students.

Ask the students to read an article on anabolic steroids in a newspaper, magazine, or encyclopedia. The students should then write answers to the following questions.

1. What might schools do to reduce steroid use among their students?
2. Do you agree with the idea that the use of steroids gives the athlete an unfair advantage? Explain your answer.

ual cell growth or to an increase in the total number of muscle cells? Hyperplasia is very difficult to prove in humans because of hereditary factors. It has been found to occur in animals, but as yet there is no conclusive evidence showing that a muscle fiber can split and become two functioning muscle fibers.

Teaching Strategies

RESOURCES Use transparency/ master of Figure 7.4 to **TRANSPARENCIES** show what an individual muscle fiber looks like. Describe how this relates to hypertrophy.

Discussion

Discuss the statement, "Anybody can become a world-class bodybuilder or power lifter if they work hard enough and long enough."

Teacher Support Notes

Somatotype will determine to a large part how much potential a person has to become a world-class weight trainer or bodybuilder. Your somatotype is inherited from your parents and you can do little to alter or change your basic shape. See Chapter 9 for more information regarding this issue.

REMEMBER This!

Do not be overly concerned with your genetic potential. Your goal should be to design and implement a program that meets your needs and desires for personal fitness.

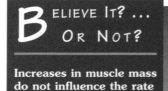

BELIEVE IT? ... OR NOT?

Increases in muscle mass do not influence the rate at which you burn calories at rest.

See page 240 for answer.

Hard work in the weight room can help you reach your genetic potential for muscle mass and strength. This does not mean that all individuals can or will obtain the profile of someone like Arnold Schwarzenegger. Very few people are born with the genetic potential to develop muscles with a mass like Schwarzenegger's muscles, no matter how hard they train.

Another genetic factor that influences skeletal muscle growth is the percentage of different types of muscle fibers. As described in an earlier chapter, there are two main types of muscle fibers: fast-twitch and slow-twitch muscle fibers. Fast-twitch fibers are also called *white fibers,* because they are not supplied with much blood. They have a greater capacity to increase in size. They also fatigue very rapidly because they are used more for anaerobic work. Athletic events such as shot put, javelin throw, and football require the use of fast-twitch fibers because these are anaerobic events that require little oxygen.

Slow-twitch fibers are also called *red fibers* because they are richly supplied with blood. These fibers do not grow fast, and they do not have the same capacity for size as the fast-twitch fibers. The slow-twitch fibers do not fatigue as rapidly as fast-twitch fibers and are used more for aerobic work. Activities like cycling, swimming, and running require slow-twitch fibers. Figure 7.6 summarizes the involvement of fast- and slow-twitch fibers in different sports events.

Each of us has both fast-twitch and slow-twitch fibers. The amounts of fast-twitch and slow-twitch fibers we have are determined largely by genetics. However, each of us can realize some degree of muscle growth regardless of our dominant muscle fiber type.

Muscle Mass. The larger the muscle, the greater its potential for strength. As you train, each muscle fiber continues to grow (get

Event	Involvement of Fast-Twitch Fibers	Involvement of Slow-Twitch Fibers
100-yard dash	High	Low
Marathon	Low	High
Olympic weight lifting	High	Low
Barbell squat	High	High
Soccer	High	High
Basketball	High	Low
Distance cycling	Low	High

• **Figure 7.6** *Relative Involvement of Fast-Twitch and Slow-Twitch Skeletal Muscles in Sport Events.*

Across the Disciplines

Language Arts

The English language has been influenced by many other languages (Latin, German, French, etc.). Have students list words that have their origins in another country. Historical events, peo-

ple, and industry have all increased the vocabulary of the language as new words have been coined to describe an event or mechanism. Have students list words that have been introduced by the technological revolution and computer industry, i.e., byte, RAM, ROM, laser, etc.

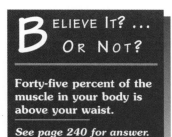

thicker). As the size of the muscle increases, so does its ability to exert force (strength).

Nerves and Muscles (Messages from the Brain). Before a muscle can contract, it must receive a message from the brain. That message is carried by specialized nerves (Figure 7.7). Regular weight-training sessions can improve the ability of nerves to carry messages to a muscle. The messages will then arrive faster and cause more muscle fibers to contract. The result is improved strength.

The beginning weight trainer can attribute most early gains in strength (that is, in the first one to two months) to the nerves' ability to get a better response from the muscle fibers. Continued strength gains will then come from muscle hypertrophy (muscle mass increase).

Other Factors Associated with Muscle Strength.   Several other factors can influence the development of muscular strength. Consistent training habits (working out regularly) are important. Your current level of strength is another factor in how fast you'll gain muscular strength. Beginning lifters will see a more rapid strength improvement than experienced weight trainers. Strength will also improve at a rate based on your training intensity. Intensity includes how hard you work and the kind of program (strength versus endurance) you follow. Intensity is also based on the number of sets and repetitions, as well as which muscles are being worked. Finally, strength gain depends on the length of the training program (weeks, months, or years). The longer you work, the more you can improve your strength.

> A feeble body weakens the mind.
> Jean Jacques Rousseau

Messages to and from brain

Nerve

Muscle fibers

• *Figure 7.7*   *Nerves–Connecting Muscles to the Brain.*

Teaching Strategies

RESOURCES TRANSPARENCIES Use transparency/master of Figure 7.6 to identify how fast-twitch fibers can have an effect on a person's potential to perform specific athletic events.

Activity

Have students use their fitness profile sheets from Chapter 4 to assess their potential to have either high levels of slow-twitch fiber or high levels of fast-twitch fiber.

Discussion

Discuss how the muscles and the nerves of the body are related to skeletal and muscle movement.

Teaching Strategies

RESOURCES TRANSPARENCIES Use transparency/master of Figure 7.7 to show how messages are sent from the brain to the individual muscle fiber.

Teacher Readings

Baechle, T. R., and Groves, B. R., *Weight Training: Steps to Success*, Human Kinetics, Champaign, IL: 1992.

In some situations, existing words acquire an entirely different meaning depending on the context in which they are used. Have students brainstorm the vocabulary contributions of the fitness industry (e.g., aerobics, couch potato, spud dud, pumped up, etc.). Discuss the problems a visitor to this country might encounter if he or she has a limited understanding of the English language. Older generations of Americans might not understand the new terminology. Have students develop a list of words that have a different connotation when used in the fitness context. Ask them to predict future trends that might influence the language they speak.

Activities

• Have students make posters about the negative effects of steroids.
• Read and discuss the "Wellness Connection" on pages 220–221 of the Teacher's Wraparound.

Discussion

Discuss steroids and their illegal use. Have students suggest reasons why someone might want to risk the use of steroids.

Assess

Use the Section 3 Review questions to assess students' comprehension of the concepts presented in Section 1.

ANSWERS TO SECTION 3 REVIEW

1. Concentric contraction—the shortening of a muscle during contraction. Eccentric contraction—when the muscle slowly releases its contraction and becomes longer. Isometric contraction—when a muscle pushes against an immovable object and no movement occurs in the muscle, but tension is created.

The Dangers of Steroids

Steroids are drugs that are illegal and very hazardous to your health. However, many people still use these drugs. Why? People use steroids because they think steroids will give them a performance advantage.

There is no place for the use of steroids in the world of health and fitness. Steroids, health, and fitness simply do not go together. The following is a list of both the long-term and short-term effects of steroids.

Long-term effects	• Increased risk of developing coronary heart disease. • Higher levels of cholesterol. • Elevated blood pressure. • Kidney and liver damage. • Sexual dysfunction. • Increased risk of cancer.
Short-term effects	• Acne. • Loss of hair in males, and facial hair growth in females. • Nausea, diarrhea, fever, and nosebleeds. • Increased appetite. • Psychological symptoms, including aggressive behavior (Roid Rage). • Reduction of hormone secretion.

Why Are My Muscles Sore?

We have all experienced some muscle soreness at one time or another, usually after an active or vigorous session of muscle use. The beginning stages of weight training will also produce a certain amount of muscle soreness. This soreness is usually delayed twenty-four to forty-eight hours after the workout. Don't let this discourage you. It is normal. Everyone has it. With proper training technique and time, the soreness will go away.

There are two main theories about why muscles get sore. The first theory is that **microtears**, or small tears, occur when parts of the muscle fibers and connective tissue actually tear due to the greater-than-usual resistance. These tears are not a serious problem, however. With rest and good nutrition, muscles quickly repair themselves, and you are ready for the next workout.

The second theory of muscle soreness suggests that during intense exercise, a muscle may not receive all the oxygen it needs (anaerobic exercise). Even though this oxygen deficiency is temporary, it may still contribute to soreness. As mentioned earlier, it is during the eccentric (lengthening) movement that most muscle soreness is acquired.

microtear

a small tear in a part of a muscle fiber or connective tissue because of greater-than-usual resistance; causes muscle soreness.

Special Needs

Among some disabled students are disorders that directly affect muscular strength and endurance. These conditions may result from actual involvement of the muscles (e.g., muscular dystrophy) or may be a result of faulty nerve transmission (e.g., myasthenia gravis).

In either case, care must be taken when developing weight training programs for these individuals. Muscular strength and endurance in the mentally retarded population is generally poor due to inactivity. However, weight training is an excellent activity for the higher-functioning men-

Treatments for Muscle Soreness

There are several strategies for helping alleviate muscle soreness. First, let time heal the muscles. After three days most soreness is usually gone. Be sure to stretch before and after workouts. Reduce the amount of weight you lift, and do a light workout. Finally, drink plenty of water, and eat a sensible diet.

BELIEVE IT? ...
OR NOT?

Beginning weight trainers can increase their strength 35 to 50 percent after two months of weight training.

See page 240 for answer.

SECTION 3 REVIEW

Answer the following questions on a separate sheet of paper:

1. List and explain the three kinds of muscular contraction.
2. Explain the difference between hypertrophy and atrophy, and discuss how each occurs.
3. How is muscular strength influenced by genetic potential?
4. Explain the theory of muscle soreness associated with microtears.

SECTION 4   Weight Training and Its Many Myths

For years people did not include weight-training sessions in their personal fitness programs. Their decisions to avoid weight training were based on misinformation and the belief that weight training was not healthy. Today, however, people all over the world are participating in and enjoying the many benefits of weight training. This section will explain the differences between the muscles of males and females, identify many of the myths associated with women and weight training, and discuss other myths surrounding weight training.

Myths Associated with Women and Weight Training

Myth 1: Females Who Lift Weights Will Develop Big, Bulky Muscles Like Those of Males.   The average female compared with the average male has a smaller and lighter skeleton, has narrower shoulders, has about 8 percent more body fat, and is 30 to 40 pounds lighter. She also has less muscle mass. The quality

2. Hypertrophy is the increased size of a muscle. It is an expected result of weight lifting. Each muscle fiber increases in size and causes an increase in total muscle size. Atrophy is a decrease in the size of a muscle. It is an expected result of muscle disuse. Each muscle fiber decreases in size and causes a decrease in total muscle size.

3. We are born with a certain number of muscle fibers and a percentage of a specific kind of muscle fiber. The person born with more muscle fibers has the greatest potential for strength.

4. The microtear theory suggests that a greater than usual resistance will cause a small tear in the muscle fiber. This small tear can cause temporary pain or discomfort. With proper rest, nutrition, and fluid replacement, these tears will repair themselves.

tally retarded student.

The overload principle needs to be carefully studied and modified for those students with neuromuscular disorders. Overloading already weak muscles can cause permanent loss of muscle fiber and function. Progressive resistance programs often need to be conducted at a slower rate of progression than the rate used with able-bodied students.

The value of weight training for disabled students with muscular weakness disorders needs to be carefully reviewed. No weight training program should be developed for any student with muscular disorders without input from a physician.

Close

Discuss how weight training has evolved over the years into a vital part of any sound fitness program.

Focus

Outcomes

In **Section 4** students will learn:

1. Why the myths associated with females and weight lifting are not true.
2. Why the myths associated with weight lifting information are not true.

Focus Activity

1. Discuss each of the ten myths and explain why they are not true.

Teacher Readings

Pauletto, B., *Strength Training for Coaches*, Human Kinetics, Champaign, IL: 1991.

testosterone

a male hormone that plays an important role in building muscles.

of her muscles is the same as the male's. The woman, however, possesses fewer muscle fibers, and those muscle fibers are thinner. (This is determined by genetic potential.) Males, in contrast, generally have considerably more muscle mass and therefore are able to develop bigger and stronger muscles. These differences become much more obvious during the adolescent years and the onset of puberty.

A major reason for the strength and size differences between males and females is the male hormone **testosterone**. Testosterone plays an important role in building muscles. Women do possess testosterone, but at much lower levels than do men.

In summary, females have fewer muscle fibers than males, their muscle fibers are thinner in size, and their levels of testosterone are lower. Some hypertrophy will occur in females, but it is very unlikely that their muscles will become as large as men's muscles.

Myth 2: Female Muscles Will Not Develop Strength. The average female has less strength than the average male, especially upper body strength. This does not mean females are incapable of obtaining strength, however. When males and females are placed in similar weight-training programs, their strength improvements are similar. In fact, females may improve more because of the lower level at which they started.

In summary, females can develop very beneficial levels of strength in all parts of their bodies. Often females and males have equal relative muscle strength (strength in relation to their body weight).

Myth 3: Weight Training Has Few Benefits for Women and Will Only Detract from Their Personal Appearance ("Defeminize" Them). Thousands of females concerned about their health and fitness are utilizing weight-training rooms. They now realize the muscle toning, muscle shaping, and weight-control benefits of weight training. In addition, females who follow weight-training programs have stronger muscles and a greater capacity to handle daily tasks, as well as unexpected emergencies. Properly designed programs can help females reach their personal appearance goals and improve their self-esteem. Tight, firm muscles have nothing to do with looking less feminine.

In summary, females can obtain the same weight-training benefits as males. A well-designed program can help females look feminine, but with better-toned muscles and less fat.

Other Weight-training Myths

Myth 4: With Enough Time and Effort, Anyone Can Be a World-Class Bodybuilder or Power Weight Lifter. You can expect strength and mass improvements as a result of weight training, but you are always limited to your genetic potential. Not everyone can obtain the same results.

Reteaching

Name _____ Date _____ Period _____

Chapter 7
Section 4
Weight Training and Its Many Myths

Directions: Answer the questions in the blanks provided.

Identify each of the following statements as *Fact* or *Myth*.

Myth	1. Females' muscles will not develop strength.
Fact	2. Women have lower levels of testosterone than men.
Fact	3. Females have fewer muscle fibers than males.
Myth	4. Weight training will make you slower and less coordinated.
Fact	5. Most people who lift properly will increase their flexibility.
Fact	6. The average female has less strength, especially upper body strength, than the average male.
Myth	7. Weight training is a good way to improve cardiovascular fitness.
Fact	8. Females can obtain the same weight-training benefits as males.
Myth	9. Muscle can turn to fat if a person stops lifting weights.
Myth	10. Weight training is harmful to the growth and development of adolescents.
Fact	11. It is very unlikely that women's muscles will become as large as men's muscles.
Myth	12. Elderly people should avoid weight training.
Fact	13. Weight training is an anaerobic activity that will do little to improve cardiovascular fitness.
Myth	14. Weight training has few benefits for women and will only detract from their personal appearance.
Myth	15. With enough time and effort, anyone can be a world-class bodybuilder or power weight lifter.

Reading Worksheets   56   © 1997 West Publishing Co.

ABILITY LEVELS

Reteaching

Some students may need help mastering the concepts contained in this section. In your Teacher Resource Package, you will find the reproducible worksheet shown here. This worksheet should help students who have been absent and those needing additional help to improve their comprehension and retention of the content in this section.

BELIEVE IT? ... OR NOT?

Twenty-five million Americans have osteoporosis (a bone disease); of these, 50 percent are women.

See page 240 for answer.

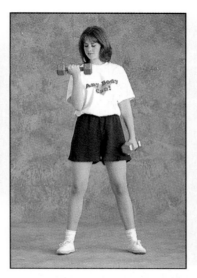
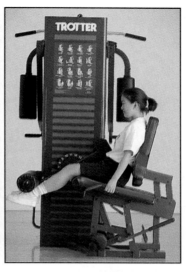

• *More and more women are finding out first hand about the benefits of weight training.*

Myth 5: Muscle Can Turn to Fat if a Person Stops Lifting Weights. Muscle and fat are actually separate kinds of tissue and do not change from one to the other. If you stop lifting, however, you will see a decrease in your muscle size (atrophy). If you continue to eat the same amount and do not exercise, you will gain weight in the form of fat.

Myth 6: Weight Training Reduces Flexibility. Most people who lift properly will actually increase their flexibility. The key is

Teach & Apply

Discussion

• Discuss Myth 1 and list the reasons why the females in your class are not going to develop large muscles during the next five to six weeks of weight lifting.
• Your list should include the following: Their testosterone levels are 10 times lower than that of males. Their intensity and duration will not be high enough. Their diets are probably not strict enough. They do not have as many muscle fibers as males. Their muscle fibers are thinner. Their body fat is, on average, 8% higher than males. Their body weight is less than males.

Enrichment

This activity will allow you to provide a more challenging learning experience for some of your students.

Have students conduct a survey of adults in the community to determine the extent to which the "10 Myths" are thought to be true. Compile the results of the survey along with recommendations on how the myths can be corrected.

CHAPTER 7
SECTION 4
234

Teacher Support Notes

Females do possess testosterone but not at the levels of males. However, males' testosterone levels begin to drop during middle age and continue to drop with continual age. The female hormone, estrogen, declines with age, while the female's testosterone level stays the same. This creates a higher percentage of testosterone overall as females age. These changes in hormone levels are often characterized by older men losing much of their aggression and females developing some male characteristics, such as facial hair and aggressive behavior.

Discussion

Discuss how females can gain strength at faster rates than males. Remember to consider how much relative strength applies to body weight and strength.

Teacher Readings

Baechle, T. R., Editor. *Essentials of Strength Training and Conditioning*, National Strength and Conditioning Association, Human Kinetics, Champaign, IL: 1994.

BELIEVE IT? ... OR NOT?

Males have ten to twenty times more testosterone than females.

See page 240 for answer.

• *Weight training is just as popular and beneficial for women as men.*

to lift weights through a full range of motion, which keeps the muscles stretched.

Myth 7: Weight Training Will Make You Slower and Less Coordinated. Weight training can actually improve your strength. That means you can better coordinate your body movements and slightly increase your speed.

> Exercise and temperance can preserve something of our early strength even in old age.
>
> **Cicero**
> (106 BC–43 BC) Roman orator and statesman. *An Old Age, X*

Myth 8: Elderly People Should Avoid Weight Training. Today doctors are actually encouraging older people to use weight training to improve or maintain their ability to walk, lift things, climb stairs, and stay active and healthy.

Myth 9: Weight Training Is a Good Way to Improve Cardiovascular Fitness. Weight training is an anaerobic activity that will do little to improve cardiovascular fitness. Other activities such as jogging, cycling, and swimming, must be used to improve cardiovascular fitness.

Myth 10: Weight Training Is Harmful to the Growth and Development of Adolescents. Most adolescents are able to participate in safe, well-organized, and supervised weight-lifting programs. Weight training can help adolescents obtain many of the same weight-training benefits adults get from this training. In fact, as you go through your adolescent growth spurt, weight training can be very beneficial to you because it can help you maximize the development of your bones.

Science and Technology

In today's world, students become easily bored with filmstrips and colored drawings about the muscle groups. Teachers need to remember that, as technology advances, so must teaching techniques and tools. One tool that is available to the teacher is the color scanner. A scanner is similar to the copy machine. However, instead of putting the image on paper, the scanner converts it to an electronic file. Once an image is scanned, the electronic file can be viewed on a computer screen.

One use of this technology is to scan

Any Body Can!

Kevin Saunders

Kevin Saunders is a world-class wheelchair Paralympic champion. He is the first person with a disability to serve on the President's Council on Physical Fitness.

Kevin Saunders was born on December 8, 1955 in Downs, Kansas and grew up on a farm where he learned to work hard from dawn to dusk. In high school he played football and participated in track. As a senior he played quarterback in football and participated in the state tournament in the discus. Following high school, Kevin attended two different community colleges where he played soccer and football. He later transferred to Kansas State University and participated in the club sport of rugby.

Kevin graduated from Kansas State in 1978 and began a job as a federal inspector for the United States Department of Agriculture. His first assignment was in Corpus Christi, Texas. On April 7, 1981, Kevin was at the Port of Corpus Christi Public Elevator to check on grain dust collection, which is highly flammable. At 3:10 P.M. that day an explosion ripped through the area of the elevator where Kevin was working. The explosion threw Kevin 300 feet into the air and over a two-story building into a parking lot, fracturing his skull, collapsing one lung, breaking his shoulder blade, and paralyzing him from the chest down. Doctors said he would not survive, but he did.

After two weeks in intensive care and living in a coma-like state, Kevin accepted what he'd suspected—he would never walk again. His doctor told him, "you'll be confined to a wheelchair the rest of your life." Kevin screamed, "No way! That can't be right!"

Kevin was mad about the accident and his condition (which is understandable). When he was released from the hospital, it took him several months of frustrating rehabilitation to regain his work ethic and motivation to get on with his life.

In 1983 Kevin became motivated to train to rehabilitate his body, because he was very weak. He read and learned how to train scientifically, and began lifting weights and "running" (in his wheelchair). In 1984 he won a bronze medal (3rd place) in the pentathlon (a one-day muscular strength and endurance competition that includes the shot put, the javelin, the 200 meters, the discus, and the 1500 meters) at the National Wheelchair Track and Field Championships.

In 1988 he competed in the Olympic Games in Seoul, Korea where he earned a bronze medal in the pentathlon. In 1992, Kevin competed in the Olympic Games again in Barcelona, Spain. He was able to bring home another bronze medal in the pentathlon event. Later in 1992, Kevin was appointed to the President's Council on Physical Fitness, which was a dream come true for him.

Kevin spends his time now training and lecturing to groups about physical fitness all over the U.S. He has become a hero to young and old, abled and disabled. His autobiography, "There's Always A Way," written with Bob Darden is highly motivating.

Fortunately not everyone has to overcome the personal challenges that Kevin Saunders did to become a champion athlete, but Any Body Can learn to develop and maintain muscular strength and endurance. That's right, you can do it!

Any Body Can!

If possible, have students attend a wheelchair sporting event or watch a film/video of an event.

Discuss with students the diffferent ways these athletes must compensate for their disabilities. Ask students how they think the disabilities might affect the athletes' personal fitness programs.

Teacher Readings

Kraemer, W. J., and Fleck, S. J., *Strength Training for Young Athletes*, Human Kinetics, Champaign, IL: 1993.

Teacher Readings

Hatfield, F. C., *Bodybuilding: A Scientific Approach*, Contemporary Books, Inc., Chicago, IL: 1984.

different pictures of muscle groups and copy them into a viewing file using Adobe Photoshop or similar software packages. With the proper programming software (Hypercard or Coursebuilder), a teacher can design a complete self-paced computerized instructional program about the muscular system. Many people think that this is too hard or work intensive. It isn't if you use basic designs. This is why it is suggested that you use Hypercard as a beginner's programming software. **Take the challenge**: Check out the book *Hypercard for Dummies*. **Remember**: Once you become at ease using scanning and programming software, you may begin to enjoy using it as a teaching tool.

CHAPTER 7
SECTION 4
236

Assess

Use the Section 4 Review questions to assess students' comprehension.

ANSWERS TO SECTION 4 REVIEW

1. Females have smaller muscles, smaller muscle fibers, weigh less, have higher body fat, lower levels of testosterone, workout intensity will not be high enough, and their diets are not strict enough.
2. Weight training is primarily an anaerobic activity that will do little to improve cardiovascular fitness.

Close

Show an appropriate video on weight training.

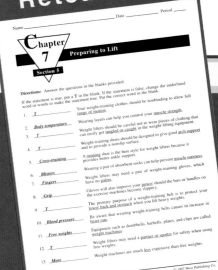

SECTION 4 REVIEW

Answer the following questions on a separate sheet of paper:

1. Explain why females are unlikely to develop large, bulky muscles.
2. Explain why weight training is not a good activity for the development of cardiovascular fitness.

SECTION 5 Preparing to Lift

Before you ever push up a barbell or curl a dumbbell, you need to know some important facts. You need to consider such things as proper clothing, footwear, equipment, and facilities—all of which are important to your continued success. How you prepare now can determine your future success and safety.

Clothing and Equipment

The following are some tips for choosing proper clothing and equipment.

Clothes. A variety of styles, colors, and sizes of clothing can be worn in the weight room. Weight-training clothing is designed to enhance your comfort, performance, and safety in the weight room. Your clothes should be nonbinding to allow full range of motion. They should also keep you warm or cool, depending on the temperature of your workout facility. Wearing layers can help you control your body temperature. Be careful not to wear pieces of clothing that can easily get tangled or caught on the equipment.

Footwear. You should always wear properly fitted shoes. They should be designed to give you good arch support and to provide a nonslip surface. A cross-training shoe is probably the best style, because it provides better ankle support. Wearing a pair of absorbent socks can help prevent blisters.

Gloves. You may need a pair of weight-training gloves, which have no fingers. They cover your palms, where most of the blisters and calluses form on your hands. If you have sensitive skin on your hands or you want to avoid rough hands, wear gloves. Gloves will

> ## BELIEVE IT? ... OR NOT?
>
> A pound of fat is 18 percent bigger than a pound of muscle, which means more inches for you to carry.
>
> *See page 240 for answer.*

ABILITY LEVELS

Reteaching

Some students may need help mastering the concepts contained in this section. In your Teacher Resource Package, you will find the reproducible worksheet shown here. This worksheet should help students who have been absent and those needing additional help to improve their comprehension and retention of the content in this section.

• *Examples of weight training equipment: Straps, gloves, belts, weight plates, collars, and dumbbells.*

Focus

Outcomes

In **Section 5** students will learn:

1. To determine the proper kinds of clothing and footwear to be worn in the weight room.
2. To identify and use the proper kinds of equipment in the weight room.
3. The differences between free weights and machines.

Focus Activities

1. Explain and demonstrate the use of gloves, weight training belts, straps, and wraps.
2. Discuss the advantages and disadvantages of both free weights and machines.
3. Use Figure 7.8 in the Active Mind/Active Body activity on page 239 to help students learn about their weight room facility.

also improve your grip, should the bars or handles on the exercise machines become slippery.

Weight-training Belts. The primary purpose of a weight-training belt is to protect your lower back and stomach when you lift heavy weights. The belt gives the stomach muscles something to push against and, as a result, causes pressure to build up in the abdomen. This pressure pushes against and stabilizes the lower spine, which protects the lower back.

Be aware that wearing belts causes an increase in blood pressure. For this reason, belts should be worn only during lifting exercises. Loosen or remove your belt when you rest between lifting exercises. Belts come in all sizes and are made of leather or synthetic fabrics.

Enrichment

This activity will allow you to provide a more challenging learning experience for some of your students.

Ask the students to visit a sporting goods store or health club. Discuss the variety of weight training clothing and equipment with a salesperson or an employee. The students should prepare a list of clothing and equipment that was recommended through the interview, including a justification for each item listed.

Teach & Apply

Discussion

Ask students, What are the kinds of clothing commonly worn in gyms and health clubs? Tell them that they will find all types of colors, sizes, and styles. Clothes usually support the individual's personality and/or mood.

Discussion

Discuss the purpose of gloves, weight belts, straps, and wraps and when they should be used.

Teacher Support Notes

• Gloves—They come in a variety of colors, styles, and fabrics, such as leather or nylon. They prevent callous buildup and prevent grips from slipping. They can also serve as a kind of hygiene when using equipment shared with others. Cost is $10 and up.
• Belts—They are the most popular piece of equipment used. Their main purpose is to increase back support. They need to be cinched tight. They come in a variety of sizes, shapes, and materials. The most common are made from leather and nylon mesh. Cost is $20 and up.

Straps and Wraps. Straps are 1-½ inch wide strips of canvaslike material that are wrapped around your wrist and then twisted around a bar. They are used for very heavy lifts when your grip cannot support the weight. Wraps or elastic bandages are used to give additional support to joints. They are most often used during heavy leg exercises. They can provide support, but they also restrict your range of motion.

Free Weights or Weight Machines?

Weight training can be performed using a variety of equipment. Most weight-training facilities have a variety of both free weights and weight machines.

Equipment such as dumbbells, barbells, plates, and clips is called **free weights**. The name *free weight* describes the unlimited direction and movement capacity of this equipment. This freedom of movement also creates a greater potential for accidents, however, because more balance and coordination is needed than is required when using machines. Thus, you may need a partner or spotter for your safety when you use free weights. Free weights do provide the

free weights

objects of varied weights that can be moved without restriction and used for weight lifting; examples are barbells and dumbbells.

CONSUMER CORNER
Buying Weight-Training Equipment

If you are interested in starting a weight-lifting program, you have a number of options. You could join a health club and use its equipment. This can become expensive, however, because you are usually required to pay monthly fees.

You may be able to use the weight room facilities at your school, but you may run into conflicts caused by time and supervision schedules. If you can find a time to work out at your school, this will probably be your best choice because of convenience and lack of expense.

One other option is to purchase your own equipment to use at home. Free weights (dumbbells, barbells, plates, clips, and so

on), are often a consumer's first choice for use at home, because they are less expensive and take up less room than other equipment. If you purchase free weights, be aware that the cheapest product may not be the wisest consumer choice. For example, plastic weights filled with sand do not last as long as metal weights.

Exercising at home with weight machines has become popular. Many different models are available. If you choose to purchase a weight machine for home use, you first need to consider how much you can afford to spend, your space limitations, how durable the machine is, and if it is appropriate for your personal needs and goals.

Wellness Connection

Tell students the following:
There are two concepts that are important to understand with regard to muscular strength and weight training. These two concepts are specificity and symmetry. The principle of specificity states that a weight training program can focus on a

particular muscle or group of muscles. If you are weight training to improve performance in a particular sport or activity, then your weight training program should exercise the muscle groups actually used in the specific sport or activity for which you are training. For example, if

What Is in Your Weight Room?

Use the equipment checklist in Figure 7.8 to identify all the equipment in your school's weight-training facility. You may also want to use this checklist at the local health club or YMCA facility. Include specific details when you describe equipment.

Free weight	Description
Type of bar:	
Olympic	
standard	
cambered	
Dumbbells:	
type and weight	
Benches and weight racks:	
Weight plates:	
type and weight	

Machines

Name of machine and specific muscle to be used:
1. _____
2. _____
3. _____
4. _____
5. _____
6. _____

Other Equipment:
weight belts _____
mats _____
jump ropes _____
scales _____

Other Concerns:
temperature _____
sound system _____
lighting _____

• **Figure 7.8**   *What Is in Your School's Weight Room?*

---

advantage of being more versatile and less expensive than other weight-training equipment.

Weight-training equipment designed to move weights up and down using a system of cables and pulleys is called **weight machines**. Most machines are designed to work only one muscle area and require little or no balance. They do not require spotters because the weights are connected to the machine and have a predetermined path of movement. With weight machines it is easy to vary the resistance. You simply move a pin to the new weight selection. Weight

weight machines

a system of cables and pulleys designed for the movement of weights as used in weight-training exercises.

---

you are training for bodybuilding and really want to develop size and definition of the lower leg, you would focus your efforts on the gastrocnemius, soleus, and tibialis anterior muscles.

Symmetry, on the other hand, refers to the interrelation of muscles to form an aesthetically pleasing and properly functioning whole. It is important to maintain

a degree of symmetry within the muscle groups. If one particular muscle group becomes hypertrophied, there may be an increased likelihood of injury due to this muscle imbalance. In addition to the injury potential, a body that is extremely asymmetrical in muscular development is not particularly attractive.

• Straps—They can help speed up the muscle and strength gains by allowing the arms to act as hooks to lift the weight. There are straps that have hooks that do not require the strap to be wrapped on the bar. Cost is $6 and up.
• Wraps—These are for maximal or near maximal lifts. They should not be used as a crutch during regular workouts. The best ones are thick and tightly elastic. Cost is $18 and up.

You might want to divide the class into pairs or small groups and assign each group to use the checklist at a different health club facility in your area, so that all facilities are covered. After data have been collected, compile a list that shows all of the different weight-lifting equipment available for use in your area.

Activity

• Have each student properly put on the correct size belt and cinch it up tight. Have them use the belt any time they do squats or any exercise that needs additional support for the back.
• Have students try lifting with and without gloves to feel the difference.
• Demonstrate how to put straps on the wrist and the bars. Have students practice this procedure.

- Demonstrate how to properly place wraps on the knee. Have students use wraps during maximal lifts if they feel they need to do so.
- Explain and discuss the advantages and disadvantages of free weights and machines.

Teaching Strategies

RESOURCES Use the transparency/master of Figure 7.9 to **TRANSPARENCIES** discuss free weights and machines.

- Have students experience a variety of machines and free weights to better understand the difference between the two types of equipment.
- Use the Active Mind/Active Body activity on page 239 to determine what type of equipment is in your weight lifting facility.

Classroom Management

Put students in groups and have them walk through the facility while using the checklist in Figure 7.8. Have students write a detailed explanation of the equipment and the other concerns in the weight room.

Answers to
BELIEVE IT? ... OR NOT?

Pg. 223 True.
Pg. 228 False. For every additional pound of muscle mass, you burn 50 to 100 more calories per day.
Pg. 229 False. Sixty-five percent of the muscle in your body is above your waist.
Pg. 231 True.
Pg. 233 False. Actually, 80 percent of those with osteoporosis are women. If you do weight training regularly, you can help reduce your risk for osteoporosis.
Pg. 234 True.
Pg. 236 True.

machines are much more expensive, however, than free weights and take up large amounts of space. Do the Active Mind/Active Body activity on the preceding page to identify the types of weights in your school's weight room.

Both free weights and weight machines are capable of producing strength and mass improvements through isotonic progressive resistance training. Understanding the advantages and disadvantages of each type of equipment can help you decide which is best for you. Figure 7.9 compares the advantages and disadvantages of free weights and weight machines.

Factor	Free Weights	Machines	Advantage
Cost	Much less expensive, $200 can acquire all you need, one size fits all	Very costly to purchase, maintenance cost, need a variety of machines or pay membership to a club	Free weights
Space	Takes minimal space and may be moved easily	Big, bulky, and heavy; difficult to move	Free weights
Safety	Spotters are required, balance is required, greater chance of injury, weights get left laying around which can cause accidents	Weights cannot fall on you, requires no balance or spotters to lift	Machine
Variety	Allows for many different exercises with the same equipment, helps prevent boredom, works all parts of the body	Usually only one exercise can be done on a machine, need many machines to provide variety, can be boring	Free weights
Technique/ Balance	Harder to learn, much more complicated technique, balance is a necessity	Much easier to learn, no balance required	Machine
Time	Requires partner, takes more time to change weight plates	Less total time, can do alone, easier to change amount of resistance	Machine
Beginning lifter	Need a partner, harder technique to learn, balance	Safer, quicker, no need for spotter, easier to learn technique	Machine
Athletic Power and Coordination	Requires coordination and balance of many muscles at same time—more like actual sport activity	Isolates single muscle and reduces need for balance	Free weights
Motivation	Easier to determine and see strength improvement	Harder to understand strength improvement	Free weights

- ***Figure 7.9*** *Comparison of Free Weights and Weight Machines.*

▐▌▌▬▬▐▌▌ Equipment Options

What do you look for when it's time to purchase new weight lifting equipment, and how do you decide what you need? These are two questions often pondered by the P.E. teacher. There are three major categories for weight lifting equipment: free weights, universal systems, and hydraulic systems. The most durable equipment is found with free weights. Free weights are virtually indestructible because they have few breakable parts and are forged from steel. The problem with this system is safety. Free weights need to be used under

SECTION 5 REVIEW

Answer the following questions on a separate sheet of paper:

1. Explain how weight-training gloves, weight-training belts, and straps can be of use in the weight room.

2. List what you feel are the three most important advantages of free weights and the three most important advantages of weight machines.

Activity

Have students visit their local YMCA, community recreation center, or private facility to examine the equipment available.

Assess

Use the Section 5 Review questions to assess students' comprehension of the concepts presented in Section 5.

SUMMARY

Muscular strength and endurance are health-related fitness components that everyone should consider vital to good health and fitness. The benefits of muscular strength and endurance are important to you now and throughout your adult life. The sooner you get started, the more protection you will give your body against future problems associated with poor strength and endurance. Weight training is a safe and popular way to incorporate strength and endurance into your life. Understanding how and why your muscles become bigger and stronger can help you consistently participate in progressive resistance activities.

For years, weight training was surrounded by myths that led people to believe that it should be avoided. Fortunately, medical and fitness experts today see weight training as a needed and valued part of a total fitness program.

The existence of many different kinds of weight-training machines and free weights makes it necessary for you to understand the advantages and disadvantages of each so you can be a wise consumer. Weight training can be an enjoyable and beneficial activity that **A**ny **B**ody **C**an do.

ANSWERS TO SECTION 5 REVIEW

1. Gloves can prevent callous buildup and prevent the grip from slipping, weight training belts give support to the back, and straps allow wrist and arm muscles to handle more weight.

2. Answers will vary but should include any advantages or disadvantages listed in Figure 7.9.

Close

Have someone from a local weight training facility visit the class to describe his or her facilities and services.

supervision.

Universal systems will fit in tight areas and are designed for the most popular exercises. These systems are much safer than free weight systems, however, the range of motion for given exercises is limited.

Hydraulic machines are the safest to use because they react to force rather than creating force. The discouraging factors are their cost and repair rates. **Take the challenge**: Determine the exact space available for weight lifting equipment. **Remember**: Space will be your most limiting factor.

Chapter 7 Review

True/False

On a separate sheet of paper, mark each question below either T for True or F for False.

1. The maximum amount of force a muscle can exert against a resistance is muscular strength.
2. Relative muscular strength takes into consideration your body weight and your strength.
3. Putting greater stress on a muscle than it is accustomed to is the principle of specificity.
4. Body builders, athletes, and power lifters use the same kind of weight-training programs.
5. A primary benefit of weight training is the prevention of a bone disease called osteoporosis.
6. Tendons and ligaments are forms of connective tissue.
7. Eccentric muscle contractions are called *positive work*.
8. Isometric contractions start by lengthening and then get shorter.
9. The term *hypertrophy* is used to describe how muscle fibers get thicker and cause muscles to grow.
10. Most experts believe that heavy weight training and good nutrition will increase the number of muscle fibers a person was born with.
11. Slow-twitch muscle fibers contribute more to muscle endurance, while fast-twitch muscle fibers contribute more to muscle mass and strength.

Multiple Choice

1. Which of the following is an example of muscular endurance?
   a. five arm curl reps with 20 pounds
   b. fifteen bench press reps with 75 pounds
   c. ten sit-ups
   d. a fifteen-second isometric contraction
2. When Bob started weight lifting six months ago, he was able to shoulder press 50 pounds, eight times. Later, he was able to press the same weight twelve times. He then increased the weight to 60 pounds and pressed it eight times. Which of the following exercise principles is Bob using?
   a. overload
   b. specificity
   b. intensity
   d. progressive resistance
3. What term describes the use of barbells, dumbbells, and machines to improve fitness, health, and appearance?
   a. body building
   b. strength and conditioning
   c. weight training
   d. weight lifting
4. Which of the following is not a benefit of weight training?
   a. significant increase in cardiovascular efficiency
   b. increased bone strength and density
   c. slowing of the aging process and reduction in stress
   d. faster metabolism and better self-esteem
5. Skeletal muscle does which of the following?
   a. moves bones and joints
   b. protects against injury
   c. burns up calories
   d. all of the above
   e. a and b only
6. Which of the following is *not* a part of each skeletal muscle?
   a. nerves
   b. blood vessels
   c. muscle fibers
   d. cartilage

CHAPTER 7 REVIEW 242

Answers

True/False

1. T
2. F
3. F
4. F
5. T
6. T
7. F
8. F
9. T
10. F
11. T

Multiple Choice

1. b
2. d
3. c
4. a
5. d
6. d
7. b
8. c
9. b
10. c

Discussion

1. Relative muscular endurance is how many times you can lift a given weight in relation to your body weight and gender. Example: Jane has a maximum lift of 65 pounds on the shoulder press. Susan has a lift of 50 pounds on the shoulder press. If they are asked to do 50% of their maximum shoulder press as many times as possible, Susan might do more lifts than Jane. Even though Susan is not the strongest, she has higher relative muscular endurance than Jane.

⚫ CULTURAL DIVERSITY 🌐

Bangladesh

Students in Bangladesh exercise daily in their school physical training classes. They run relay races and play organized games including volleyball, cricket, tennis, and soccer.

Soccer is the most popular team sport, particularly in the cities.

Bangladesh was once an Indian state, and so several of the games that are still frequently enjoyed by adults and young people came from India. *Kabaddi*, also called *ha-do-do*, is one of these. A little

7. When the muscle becomes shorter, what kind of a contraction is it?

a. eccentric
b. concentric
c. isometric
d. isotonic

8. Which of the following is not a result of steroid use?

a. coronary heart disease
b. kidney damage
c. decreased appetite
d. loss of hair in men

9. What is the main reason that females do not grow muscles as large as males do?

a. Females do not lift hard enough.
b. Females do not have as much testosterone as men.
c. The female body is not capable of lifting heavy weights.
d. Females do not spend enough time in the weight room.

10. Free weights are common in most weight rooms. Which one of the following is *not* an advantage of free weights?

a. They cost less.
b. They take up less space.
c. They are less dangerous.
d. They require more balance.

Discussion

1. Define and give an example of relative muscular endurance.

2. Discuss the ways in which weight training can improve your personal appearance.

3. Define and give examples of isotonic progressive resistance.

4. Identify and explain five myths associated with weight training.

Vocabulary Experience

Match the correct term in Column A to the definition in Column B by writing the appropriate number in each blank.

Column A

____ relative muscular strength

____ overload principle

____ hypertrophy

____ genetic potential

____ muscular strength

Column B

1. The amount of force a muscle or muscle group can exert in one maximum effort.
2. Applying greater stress to a muscle than it is normally accustomed to.
3. Your strength in relation to your weight.
4. An increase in the size of a muscle.
5. An inherited limitation.

Critical Thinking

1. Explain the differences between weight training and body building.

2. Respond to the following statement: I'm an athlete, and if steroids can make me be the best I can be, I'm going to use them.

3. List and explain reasons why females can benefit from weight training.

2. Answers should include: Tones and shapes muscles, burns calories, speeds up metabolism, burns fat, contributes to good posture, and contributes to self-esteem and self-concept.
3. Concentric contractions result when a muscle contracts and becomes shorter; eccentric contractions result when a muscle slowly releases its contraction and becomes longer. Most weight training techniques combine these movements, which result in isotonic progressive resistance.
4. Answers will vary but should include any 5 of the 10 myths in Section 4.

Vocabulary Experience

3 relative muscular strength
2 overload principle
4 hypertrophy
5 genetic potential
1 muscular strength

Critical Thinking

1. Weight training is the use of barbells, dumbbells, machines, etc. to improve general fitness, health, and appearance. Bodybuilding is a competitive sport in which muscle size and shape are more important than muscle strength.
2. Answers should include a discussion of the risks of steroid use.
3. Benefits include: muscle toning, muscle shaping, weight control, stronger muscles, and a greater capacity to handle daily tasks.

like "Red Rover" played on American playgrounds, kabaddi is a unique team sport because it requires no equipment and is the only field game in the world that has categories for age and weight. Each team has 12 members, but only seven play at once. Men play the game in two 20-minute halves; women and children play 15-minute halves. A "raider" from one team crosses a line drawn in the center of a large court, over into "anti-raider" territory. As he runs, he calls out "kabaddi, kabaddi" repeatedly, loudly, and without taking a breath. The raider attempts to touch as many of his opponents as possible, without being caught, and return to his side before losing his breath.

Chapter 8 is 56 pages long and divided into the six sections listed to the right. Major learning outcomes of this chapter are also listed to the right. Briefly, this chapter identifies the considerations associated with planning and implementing a weight training workout. After establishing goals and learning safety techniques, students will experience a variety of weight training exercises and programs, all of which will prepare students to design weight training programs to meet their goals and needs.

Teacher Resource Material

In the Teacher Resource Package accompanying the textbook, you will find the following material to help you teach this chapter.

Chapter 8

Start Lifting—Safely and Correctly

244

PACING CHART

It is recommended that Chapter 8 be taught in conjunction with Chapter 7 in order for students to fully experience and understand the values of weight training. The combination of the two chapters (including activity time) could be taught over a four- to five-week unit. However, you can cover the material in this chapter in seven days. Following are some examples of how to cover the main topics in the chapter if you are pressed for time.

Contents

1. Setting Obtainable Goals
2. Weight-lifting Safety
3. Considerations for Your First Workout
4. Developing and Maintaining Muscular Fitness
5. Programs for Strength and Hypertrophy
6. Exercises, Muscles, and Proper Technique

Outcomes

After reading and studying this chapter, you will be able to:

1. Identify and explain obtainable goals for weight training.
2. Demonstrate and explain correct safety practices for a weight lifter.
3. Demonstrate and discuss safety practices for a spotter.
4. List and discuss all the components of a weight-training workout and how they are interrelated.
5. Discuss how frequency, intensity, and time/duration are used in developing weight-training programs.
6. Explain the purposes of strength testing and how you can evaluate your own strength.
7. Explain the differences among a variety of weight-training programs.
8. Demonstrate and explain the correct lifting technique for a variety of weight-training exercises.
9. Design a suitable weight-training program to meet your personal goals, and explain it.

Key Terms

After reading and studying this chapter, you will be able to understand and provide practical definitions for the following terms:

spotters	small muscle group	multiple set method
wraparound thumb grip (closed grip)	muscle intensity	negative workout method
repetition (rep)	training load	superset method
set	recovery time	antagonistic muscles
weight-training circuit	weight-training cycle	compound set method
large muscle group	split workout	
	pyramid training	

245

CHAPTER 8

Time	Suggestions
Day 1	Read Sections 1 and 2. Discuss. Have students demonstrate spotting techniques and proper grips.
Day 2	Assign students to read pp. 251–253, 277–280. Demonstrate each exercise and have students demonstrate. Homework: Active Mind/Active Body, page 254.
Day 3	Assign students to read pp. 253–261, 283, 285, 287, 289. Discuss and demonstrate.
Day 4	Read pp. 262, 265–266, 267–269, 284–285, 291–293. Discuss and demonstrate.
Day 5	Assign students to read Section 5 and pp. 286, 287, 289–291. Discuss and demonstrate.
Day 6	Assign students to read Fitness Check, pp. 263, 269–271, 293. Have students attempt estimated one-rep maximums on a variety of exercises.
Day 7	Have students do the Active Mind/Active Body on page 295.

Focus

Outcomes

In **Section 1** students will learn:

1. To identify obtainable goals for weight training.
2. The rules for writing obtainable goals.

Focus Activity

Discuss the importance of goals. Have students write obtainable goals.

Teach & Apply

Discussion

Discuss the factors that should be considered when writing goals.

INTRODUCTION

*H*aving completed Chapter 7, you now know the benefits of weight training and how your muscles grow and become stronger. You may have acquired clothing and equipment suitable for weight training. As soon as you have established your goals, you will be ready to "pump some iron."

This chapter will teach you about the safety practices associated with every aspect of weight training. You will also learn how to evaluate your strength and design a personal weight-training program to meet your needs. In addition, you will learn how to perform properly many different weight-training exercises and other strength-building activities.

SECTION 1   Setting Obtainable Goals

Setting realistic and challenging strength goals is closely connected with your continued success in weight training. A properly planned program can help keep you motivated even through difficult times, when progress is not as fast as you would like it to be. If you keep in mind that you are working toward progress and self-improvement, you will have a better chance at being successful.

Why and How to Set Goals

You are more likely to realize the benefits of a weight-training program if you have a desired goal. Having a well-designed personal goal can help you achieve any task. People who set goals tend to accomplish more than those who don't set goals.

Goals also help keep you motivated. Each time you realize a goal, you feel good about yourself. You are then more likely to establish an even more challenging goal.

Before you set any goal, consider each of the following:

- *Your age.* Adolescents may want strength and muscle mass, whereas older adults may want more endurance and less body fat.
- *Your gender.* Males and females may or may not have the same goals.

ABILITY LEVELS

Reteaching

Some students may need help mastering the concepts contained in this section. In your Teacher Resource Package, you will find the reproducible worksheet shown here. This worksheet should help students who have been absent and those needing additional help to improve their comprehension and retention of the content in this section.

BELIEVE IT? ...
OR NOT?

If you work out, you will reach your peak muscular strength by age sixteen.

See page 270 for answer.

* *Your physical maturation.* How much growth and development you already have can determine reasonable and obtainable goals for you.
* *Your current level of strength.* Beginners can expect rapid gains, whereas advanced and intermediate lifters will have slower progress. Strength pretests can be used to determine strength improvements.
* *Your physical limitations or past injuries.* Your goals may need to be modified if you realize that you are not capable of certain tasks.
* *Your work habits.* How much time you have affects your workout.

Rules for Writing Goals

You should write down your weight-training goals on a sheet of paper, a technique that increases the chances that you will stick to your plan. Here are some important rules to follow as you write your goals:

1. Make the goals reasonable and obtainable, but not too easy.
2. Establish long- and short-term goals. The short-term goals act as motivators to keep you going. For example, suppose you can lift 100 pounds on the bench press now, and you would like to be able to do 135 pounds. Thus, your long-term goal is to lift 135 pounds. Your short-term goals could be to lift 110 pounds, then 120 pounds, then 130 pounds, and finally 135 pounds. Give yourself a reasonable amount of time between each short-term goal.
3. Have a variety of short-term goals, such as controlling your body weight and percentage of body fat, improving your eating habits, and having regular workout attendance. These short-term goals can help you reach your long-term goals.
4. If you have an injury or become ill, it may be necessary to revise your goals.

REMEMBER This!

Goals are personal. They represent your desires. If goals are reasonable and obtainable, Any Body Can improve.

SECTION 1 REVIEW

Answer the following questions on a separate sheet of paper:

1. List and explain four things to consider before setting goals for weight training.
2. Why is it important to develop short-term goals?

SECTION 2   Weight-lifting Safety

Safety should always be a foremost consideration when lifting weights. If you don't observe basic safety guidelines at all times, your risk of injury can be great. The following is a list of basic guidelines that can help reduce the possibility of an accident when you lift weights:

1. Have a partner when lifting free weights.
2. Make sure you are familiar with the proper use of all weight equipment prior to using it. Also be familiar with the weight-training area.
3. A brief heart and muscle warm-up combined with specific stretching may be helpful.
4. Never hold your breath. Exhale during the concentric (positive) stage. This can prevent dizziness or fainting.
5. Never sacrifice proper technique to lift extra weight. Cheating can lead to injury.
6. Wear safety belts when doing heavy exercises that require the use of abdominal and back muscles.
7. Use collars for all free weights.
8. Control the speed of the weights at all times.
9. Progress slowly over a period of time.
10. Allow for rest between training days (usually forty-eight hours).
11. Return all equipment to its proper place after using it.
12. Be alert at all times!
13. Act responsibly. The weight-lifting area is no place for irresponsible behavior.

Are Spotters Necessary?

Spotters are classmates or friends who assist you with weight room safety. Their responsibilities are very important and should not be taken lightly. How well they perform their duties can make the difference between your having a successful, safe workout or an injury. Spotters should be required for free-weight lifts, such as the bench press, the overhead press, and squats. They may not be necessary for other lifts, but it is always a good idea to have a partner, just in case.

spotters

individuals who assist you with weight-room safety.

Focus

Outcomes

In **Section 2** students will learn:

1. To explain general weight training safety guidelines.
2. To explain correct safety practices for spotters.
3. To explain general lifting guidelines.
4. To use the proper grips for weight training.

Focus Activities

1. Discuss and demonstrate correct weight training safety guidelines.
2. Demonstrate and practice proper spotting techniques.
3. Demonstrate and practice all the lifting guidelines.
4. Demonstrate and practice all three grips.

Reteaching

Name _____ Date _____ Period _____

Chapter 8 Weight-lifting Safety
Section 2

Directions: Answer the questions in the blanks provided. Before each statement write *Yes* if a safety guideline is described, and *No* if it is not.

1. **No** — Hold your breath or exhale during the eccentric stage.
2. **Yes** — Use collars for all free weights.
3. **No** — Progress rapidly over a period of time.
4. **Yes** — Have a partner when lifting free weights.
5. **Yes** — Control the speed of the weights at all times.
6. **No** — Sacrifice proper technique to lift extra weight.
7. **Yes** — Return all equipment to its proper place after using it.
8. **Yes** — Wear safety belts when doing heavy exercises that require the use of abdominal and back muscles.
9. **No** — Do not rest between training days.
10. **Spotters** _____ are classmates or friends who assist you with weight room safety.
11. List three (3) free weight lifts that require spotters.
   Bench press
   Overhead press
   Squats
12. List the three (3) main jobs of the spotter.
   Assist the lifter when help is needed to keep the weight moving in a smooth, steady motion
   Observe and point out any improper technique being used by the lifter
   Be a motivator

Reteaching Worksheets

ABILITY LEVELS

Reteaching

Some students may need help mastering the concepts contained in this section. In your Teacher Resource Package, you will find the reproducible worksheet shown here. This worksheet should help students who have been absent and those needing additional help to improve their comprehension and retention of the content in this section.

• *Proper spotting techniques should be used at all times in the weight room to maximize safety.*

Teach & Apply

Discussion

Discuss the importance of each of the weight training safety guidelines.

Teaching Strategies

• Give some suggested activities that would be appropriate warm-up activities. Have the class determine two or three activities that each class member should use prior to lifting.
• Combine the demonstration of safety collars, weight belts, bars, and weights with the Active Mind/Active Body activity on page 239 in Chapter 7.
• You should identify your rules and the consequences for anyone not following these rules.
• Have posters in the weight room that list all of the safety guidelines.

Stress Break
••••••••••••••••

By now you are aware of the many benefits associated with exercise and stress reduction. There is no question that the two go hand in hand. Having a good friend to talk with and share your feelings with can also be a great way to deal with stress. A true, honest friend can help you make decisions, as well as provide you with a feeling of being needed and appreciated. Everyone needs to know that someone cares. A good fitness partner or spotting partner could be just that kind of person. After all, you two already have something in common, and you spend lots of time together. If someone spots for you, you had better trust him or her, too.

The spotter has three main jobs:

1. Assist the lifter when help is needed to keep the weight moving in a smooth, steady motion. (The spotter should stay ready at all times.)
2. Observe and point out any improper technique being used by the lifter.
3. Be a motivator. Encourage the partner to maintain an acceptable level of intensity.

In addition to the three primary jobs just described, the spotter should do the following:

• Keep the lifting area free of weights or other equipment that could get in the way.
• Put the proper amount of weight on the bar, and have it evenly spaced.
• Keep body and hands in a ready position at all times.
• Communicate with the lifter. Make sure the commands are understood. Know how many repetitions will be attempted.
• Know how to properly apply enough help without jerking the bar.
• Be ready to assume all the weight, if necessary.
• Be alert at all times!

Lifting—The Right Way

Each weight-training exercise has a specific lifting technique. Later in this chapter, you will learn a variety of weight-training exercises and their proper techniques.

Enrichment

This activity will allow you to provide a more challenging learning experience for some of your students.

Divide the class into groups of three or four students. Ask each group to rank, from most important to least important, the safety guidelines listed on page 248. Compile the results from all groups to show how different items were ranked. Then have groups defend the rankings.

Activity

Give students a short quiz over the safety guidelines. Require them to meet minimum criteria before they are given permission to lift.

Teacher Support Notes

You may want to tell students:

• Progress in both strength and hypertrophy are quicker and safer when proper lifting technique is strictly adhered to. Cheating on your form is only working muscles that the exercise was not intended to use.
• Controlled speed of both concentric and eccentric movements will also produce results more quickly and safely.

Activities

• Have students take weights off the racks and put them back on the racks to experience the strength and balance required to manipulate the weight plates.
• Have them place all the equipment in its proper place.

Discussion

Discuss the role of the spotters and their importance.

(a)

(b)

(c)

 Figure 8.1 Bar grips: (a) Overhand, (b) Underhand, and (c) Alternated.

wraparound thumb grip (closed grip)

a grip used in lifting in which the fingers and thumb go in opposite directions around the bar to help keep the bar from rolling out of the hand.

General Lifting Guidelines.   You should follow some guidelines for all weight-training exercises. It is important that you learn and apply these guidelines, especially when using free weights.

• Practice all techniques with a very light weight before attempting heavier resistance.
• Know how to use the correct grip for each exercise.
• Communicate with your spotter. Make sure you understand each other's verbal and nonverbal commands.
• Keep your back straight at all times, whether you are lying down or standing.
• When performing standing lifts, be sure to have a wide, stable base with your feet flat on the floor.
• When lifting objects from the floor, use your legs, not your back.
• Keep the weight close to your body.
• All lifts should be done through a full range of motion. This means that muscles should be flexed and extended completely when you lift.
• Concentrate on the muscles that should be doing the work.
• Breathe out (exhale) during the exertion (concentric) phase.
• Breathe in (inhale) during the relaxing (eccentric) phase.
• Never hold your breath, as this can reduce the flow of blood and oxygen to your brain. A lack of oxygen can cause you to pass out while you are lifting.
• Do not hyperventilate (breathe rapidly). Control your breathing at all times.
• Make sure you keep your hands on the bar and maintain pressure until all weights are put safely back on the racks.

Proper Grips and Grip Placement.   There are three kinds of grips: the overhand, underhand, and alternated. Their use is determined by the specific exercise to be done. Each of these grips should be done with a **wraparound thumb grip (closed grip)**. In this grip, the fingers and thumb go in opposite directions around the bar, which helps keep the bar from rolling out of the hand (see Figure 8.1).

In the overhand grip, your palms face away from you as you grab the bar. In the underhand grip, your palms face you as you grab the bar. In the alternated grip, one palm faces away from you, and one palm faces you.

There are three widths of grip placement. Their use is determined by the exercise (see Figure 8.2). In the common grip, your hands are evenly spaced, about shoulders' width apart. In the narrow grip, your hands are evenly spaced, but close together. In the wide grip, your hands are evenly spaced, but wider than shoulders' width apart.

Across the Disciplines

Language Arts

As students begin their weight lifting programs, they may find articles in magazines that are factual, as well as inaccurate and motivational, as well as sensational. Discuss the publication industry by examining the difference between articles that appear in scholarly publications and articles in commercial magazines. Although many of the articles in commercial magazines are excellent, well-researched, factual commentaries, students should learn to

• **Figure 8.2** *Grip Placement. From left to right: Wide, Common, and Narrow.*

SECTION 2 REVIEW

Answer the following questions on a separate sheet of paper:

1. List and explain four reasons why spotters are necessary in the weight room.
2. Why is it important to use proper breathing techniques when lifting weights?
3. Explain the difference between overhand and underhand weight-lifting grips.

Assess

Use short quizzes and physical demonstrations to assess student progress. Then use the Section 2 Review questions to assess students' comprehension of the concepts presented in Section 2.

ANSWERS TO SECTION 2 REVIEW

1. To assist the lifter in the smooth movement of the bar, if necessary; critique lifting technique; motivate partners; keep lifting area safe; assist with the placement of weights on the bar; and communicate with the lifter.
2. Holding your breath can reduce blood flow and oxygen to the brain. This could cause fainting.
3. For an overhand grip, place the palms downward, away from you, and for an underhand grip, place the palms upward, facing you.

SECTION 3

Considerations for Your First Workout

There are several different ways you can vary your weight-training program. Before you design and begin a personal program, make sure you clearly understand each of the following components of weight-training routines: the repetition, the set, the exercises you can choose from, the muscle groups being worked, and the order of exercise (Figure 8.3).

The Repetition

Each time you lift a weight, do a push-up, or do a chin-up, you have completed a **repetition**, or **rep**. If you do ten push-ups, you have completed ten reps. A person who does a squat twice with 150 pounds has completed two reps with 150 pounds. Reps are the basic unit of any workout plan. The number of reps will vary, depending on your goals.

repetition (rep)

the completed execution of an exercise one time.

Close

Discuss the "Stress Break" on page 249. Can weight training with a friend reduce stress?

carefully appraise what they read.

Have students suggest criteria by which they would evaluate weight training articles. After students have selected and evaluated weight training articles from fitness magazines, have them prepare a report for the class. Encourage students to scrutinize what they read in print, measure it against the knowledge they currently have, and be willing to investigate further when what they read does not support the information they believe to be correct. Some magazines students might find interesting to evaluate are: *Muscular, Mr. Health, Mr. Health Fitness, Muscle and Fitness, Exercise and Health, Muscle,* and *Shape.*

Focus

Outcomes

In **Section 3** students will learn:

1. To identify and explain components of a weight training workout.
2. To explain how workout components are interrelated.
3. To identify weight training exercises and the muscles that are worked.
4. To identify and explain a variety of weight training exercise circuits.

Focus Activities

1. Discuss the different components of the workout including the rep, set, exercises, muscle groups, and order of exercises.
2. Demonstrate how to correctly apply the concept of reps and sets to an exercise.

set

a group of consecutive reps for an exercise.

• **Figure 8.3**   *The Workout Plan. The Complete Weight-training Program Includes All the Parts of a Workout Shown Here.*

B ELIEVE IT? ... OR NOT?

Over 1 million people regularly participate in weight-training programs.

See page 270 for answer.

The Set

Each time you complete a group of consecutive reps for any exercise, you have completed a **set**. If you do ten reps of push-ups consecutively, you have done one set of ten reps. If you repeat the process (ten more push-ups) after a short rest, you have completed a total of two sets of ten reps. The number of sets in each workout can vary. The number of sets, like the number of repetitions, will be determined by your goals.

You can describe your workout using numbers to indicate sets and reps. The first number will always indicate sets; the second number, reps. For example, Renée has decided to lift three sets of twelve reps, which she can indicate by writing 3×12 (the $\times$ means "times"). 4×5 will indicate four sets of five reps.

The Exercises

Just as there are special exercises for cardiovascular endurance and flexibility, there are exercises developed especially for weight-

• *Keeping a log of your weight training goals and workout information can help you keep track of your progress.*

Reteaching

ABILITY LEVELS

Reteaching

Some students may need help mastering the concepts contained in this section. In your Teacher Resource Package, you will find the reproducible worksheet shown here. This worksheet should help students who have been absent and those needing additional help to improve their comprehension and retention of the content in this section.

training. All of the weight-training exercises involve the use of equipment—either free weights, such as barbells and dumbbells, or weight machines. Some of the more common weight training exercises are *bench press, arm curl,* and *squats.* You'll learn how to do these exercises and many more in this chapter. You will also learn which parts of your body benefit from each type of exercise. This knowledge will enable you to choose the most appropriate exercises for each muscle group that you want to develop.

Muscle Groups

The Six Major Body Areas

The Chest
The Back
The Legs
The Shoulders
The Arms
The Abdominals

For weight-training purposes, your body has six major areas: chest, back, legs, shoulders, arms, and abdominals. In each of these areas of the body there are different muscle groups, such as the triceps and biceps in the arms.

As a beginning weight trainer you will want to develop a well designed weight-training program for each area of the body. To do this you will need to learn which exercises work which body areas and muscle groups. The "Active Mind/Active Body" activity on the next page will help you match weight-training exercises with specific body areas and muscle groups.

The Order of Exercises— "The Circuit"

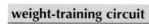

weight-training circuit

a specific sequence of weight-training exercises.

Each time you prepare for a weight-training session, you must have a plan that arranges your exercises in an efficient, sensible sequence. The **weight-training circuit** is a plan that organizes weight-training exercises in a specific sequence to best meet the needs of each individual. Weight-training circuits will help you maintain proper intensity for each muscle group, as well as maximize your workout time. You can schedule the order of the exercises in your workout circuit in a variety of ways. The following discussion contains suggestions that will help you develop a circuit to meet your needs and goals.

large muscle group

muscles of large size or a large number of muscles being used at one time.

Large Muscle Groups versus Small Muscle Groups. One way to order the exercises in your workout is by size of muscle groups (large versus small). The term **large muscle group** refers both to groups of muscles of large size and to a large number of muscles being used at one time. Examples of large muscle groups include the legs, chest, and back.

Large muscle group exercises require more strength, energy, and mental concentration than do small muscle group exercises. For any particular area of your body, it is important to do the large muscle group exercises first.

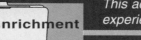

Exercise = Organs (a more complex combination)

Body parts = Body systems (separate functioning parts)

Workout = Living body (the complete product)

Each component is vital to the end product. If any part is left out, then the product is less than complete and becomes weakened.

Active Mind!
Active Body!

Have students do the Active Mind/Active Body activity on this page to determine the location and name of the muscles that are worked by specific exercises.

This activity will require students to do a variety of exercises. It is suggested that these exercises be divided into four or five subgroups. These subgroups may then be utilized throughout the unit to introduce students to new exercises.

Active Mind! *Active* Body!

Which Muscle Am I Working?

The purpose of this activity is to help you learn which weight-training exercises you'll need to select to improve strength or endurance in specific areas of your body.

First you need to identify the major muscle groups in the different areas of the body. (See Figures 8.4 and 8.5 on the following pages.)

Next, look at the table below, which lists some of the more common weight-training exercises. For each exercise, on a separate sheet of paper, write the muscle group and body area that is developed by that exercise. You may want to refer to Figures 8.4, 8.5, and 8.6 (on page 258), as you complete the table.

You should actually attempt each of the exercises so you can feel in your own body where the work is being done. The Exercise Technique Checklist at the end of this chapter will guide you and help you prevent injuries. For the purposes of this activity it is not necessary for you to use additional weight—the bar alone will enable you to feel which muscles are working.

Exercise	Muscle group	Body Area
1. bench press	pectoralis	middle chest
2. squat		
3. military press		
4. incline press		
5. shrugs		
6. upright row		
7. dumbbell flys		
8. front, lateral, and back shoulder-raises		
9. lat pull down		
10. bent-over row		
11. good morning		
12. leg curl		
13. leg extension		
14. lunge		
15. heel raises		
16. arm curls		
17. French press		
18. bent knee sit-ups		

Source: Figure 8.6 Adapted with permission from "Exercise Selection" by D. Wathen in *Essentials of Strength Training and Conditioning,* ed. T. R. Baechle (Human Kinetics Publishers, 1994): 419–420.

Teacher Readings

Baechle, T. R. and Groves, B. R. *Weight Training: Steps to Success,* Human Kinetics, Champaign, IL: 1992.

Special Needs

It is important to stress that weight training may be contraindicated for students with certain disabilities, while others may benefit from such a program.

Some students who have disabilities that cause muscular weakness are likely to demonstrate some apathy or resis-tance to a weight training program because their disorder can restrict movement.

Any strength training program must be consistent with the student's capacities. With the disabled population, it is important to first establish the focus of any

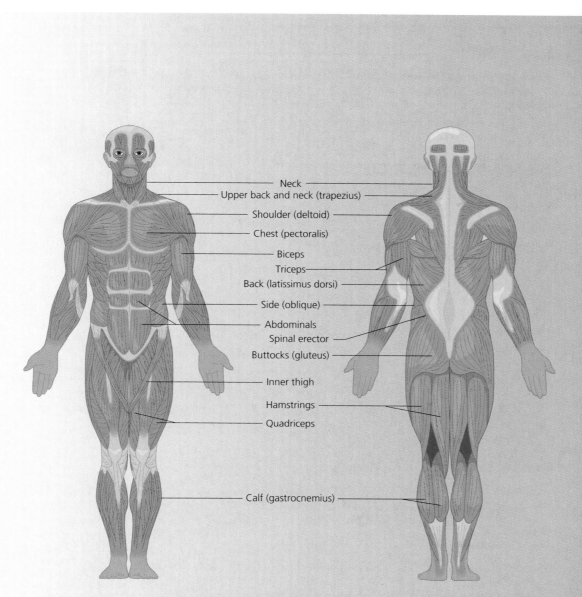

Neck
Upper back and neck (trapezius)
Shoulder (deltoid)
Chest (pectoralis)
Biceps
Triceps
Back (latissimus dorsi)
Side (oblique)
Abdominals
Spinal erector
Buttocks (gluteus)
Inner thigh
Hamstrings
Quadriceps
Calf (gastrocnemius)

• **Figure 8.4** *The Muscular System.*

(Continued on next page)

Teaching Strategies

• Use transparencies/ masters 8.4 and 8.6 to introduce students to the Active Mind/Active Body activity.
• Point out to students that often an exercise can require the use of more than one muscle.
• Have students physically demonstrate the weight lifting exercise you have assigned. This will require them to use the exercise technique checklist in Section 6. Use checklist handouts from the Teacher Resource Package. It is suggested that students use only the bars with no added weight to perform these exercises. It may be appropriate for some students to use broomsticks if they cannot handle the weight of the bar.
• Constantly monitor the progress of each student and teach or reteach as needed.

Teacher Readings

Pauletto, B., *Strength Training for Coaches,* Human Kinetics, Champaign, IL: 1991.

weight training program (i.e. improve power, increase and/or maintain strength, etc.). Goals need to focus on simple, specific short objectives with consideration given to the time within which the goal can be accomplished.

Some basic safety considerations for weight training for the disabled are as follows: Medical evaluations and assessments are essential before any weight training program is started. Student and instructor must be aware of when muscle exhaustion sets in and cease training at that time. A warm-up period is essential. Any program must be slow and well monitored. Constant supervision of the disabled student is essential.

Activity

Have students do two sets of five reps using both the bench press and squat stations. This activity could be combined with the introduction to spotting techniques.

Discussion

• Discuss the six areas of the body that are considered important to your workouts. They include chest, back, legs, shoulders, arms, and abdominals.
• Discuss the importance of knowing which muscles are involved during each exercise.

Teacher Readings

Kraemer, W. J. and Fleck, S. J. *Strength Training for Young Athletes,* Human Kinetics, Champaign, IL: 1993.

Which Muscle Am I Working? *(continued)*

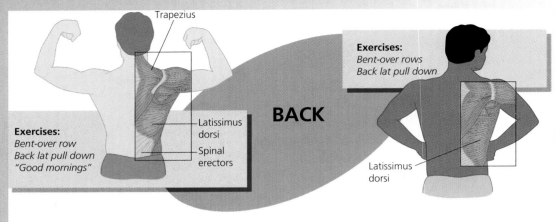

BACK

Trapezius

Latissimus dorsi

Spinal erectors

Exercises:
Bent-over row
Back lat pull down
"Good mornings"

Exercises:
Bent-over rows
Back lat pull down

Latissimus dorsi

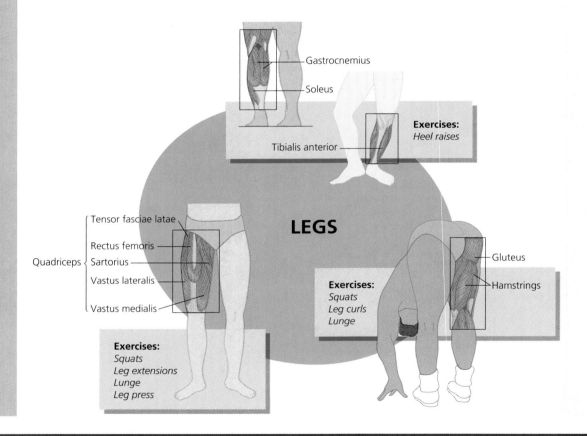

LEGS

Gastrocnemius

Soleus

Tibialis anterior

Exercises:
Heel raises

Tensor fasciae latae
Rectus femoris
Quadriceps { Sartorius
Vastus lateralis
Vastus medialis

Gluteus

Hamstrings

Exercises:
Squats
Leg curls
Lunge

Exercises:
Squats
Leg extensions
Lunge
Leg press

CRITICAL THINKING

Students need a thorough understanding of the different types of weight training programs prior to examining individual program design.

Divide the class into groups of three or four, depending upon the size of the class. Each group will design a strength training routine for one type of program.

1. Pyramid training
2. Multiple set
3. Negative method
4. Supersets
5. Compound sets
6. Multiple sets

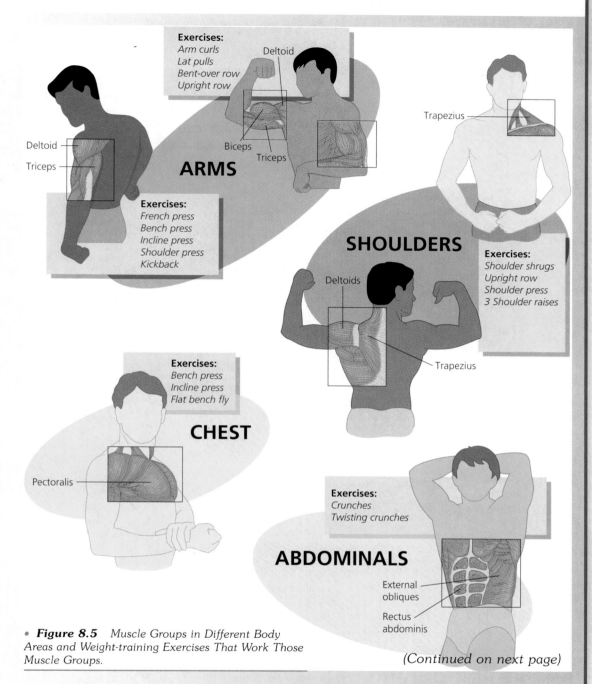

ARMS

Exercises:
Arm curls
Lat pulls
Bent-over row
Upright row

Deltoid

Biceps

Triceps

Deltoid

Triceps

Exercises:
French press
Bench press
Incline press
Shoulder press
Kickback

Trapezius

SHOULDERS

Deltoids

Trapezius

Exercises:
Shoulder shrugs
Upright row
Shoulder press
3 Shoulder raises

Exercises:
Bench press
Incline press
Flat bench fly

CHEST

Pectoralis

Exercises:
Crunches
Twisting crunches

ABDOMINALS

External
obliques

Rectus
abdominis

• ***Figure 8.5*** *Muscle Groups in Different Body Areas and Weight-training Exercises That Work Those Muscle Groups.*

(Continued on next page)

Teaching Strategies

• Have the day's circuit written on the board or have a handout of the day's circuit ready for individual groups as they enter the weight room.
• Over the course of the units, provide students with workouts that utilize all of the circuit examples.
• It is suggested that you prepare student workout record sheets and introduce them as soon as students begin their workouts. See Figure 8.22 on page 271 for a sample of a record sheet.
• The record sheet should be used to note exercises, reps, sets, and amount of weight used in each of the circuits.

Teacher Readings

Hatfield, F. C., *Bodybuilding: A Scientific Approach,* Contemporary Books, Inc., Chicago, IL: 1984.

List the six programs and the following statement on the board:

You have decided that you are a physical wreck. Tomorrow, you are determined to do something about it. Select one of the six methods listed and develop your own routine. Once this is completed, summarize the rationale behind the method selected and the benefits to be realized.

Discussion

• Discuss how the order of your exercises can affect your workout intensity, time, and individual goals. The order of exercise is referred to as a circuit.
• Use transparencies/masters 8.7, 8.8, 8.9, and 8.10 to discuss the more common circuits.

Activity

Have students experience examples of the large versus small circuit, push versus pull circuit, and the upper body versus lower body circuit.

Teacher Readings

Blimkie, C. J. R., and Bar-Or, O., Editors. *New Horizons in Pediatric Exercise Science*, Human Kinetics, Champaign, IL: 1995.

Exercise	Primary muscle group	Secondary muscle group	Equipment	Sports in which performance is enhanced
Leg extension	Quadriceps	—	Machine	All activities or sports
Leg curl	Hamstrings	Gastrocnemius	Machine	All activities or sports
Heel raise	Gastrocnemius, soleus	—	Machine, barbell	All activities or sports
Leg press	Quadriceps, gluteals	Hamstring	Machine	All activities or sports
Lunge	Quadriceps, gluteals	Hamstring	Barbell, dumbbells	All activities or sports
Squat	Quadriceps, gluteals	Hamstring	Barbell	All activities or sports
Sit-ups	Iliopsoas	Abdominals	Floor machine	All activities or sports
Bench press	Pectoralis major, anterior triceps, deltoid	Spinal erectors	Barbell, bench, machine, dumbbells	Football, basketball, wrestling, shot put, hockey, rowing, boxing, gymnastics
Dip	Pectoralis major, triceps	Anterior deltoid	Parallel bars	Football, basketball, wrestling, shot put, hockey, rowing, boxing, gymnastics
Incline press	Anterior pectoralis major, deltoid, triceps	—	Barbell, dumbbells, incline bench, machine	Football, basketball, wrestling, shot put, hockey, rowing, boxing, gymnastics
Fly (supine)	Pectoralis major	Deltoid	Dumbbells, machine	Football, tennis, discus throw, baseball, softball, wrestling, backstroke
Overhead press	Deltoid, triceps	Trapezius	Barbell, dumbbells, machine	Gymnastics, shot put
Behind-neck press	Deltoid, triceps	Trapezius	Barbell	Gymnastics, shot put
Bent-over rowing	Latissimus dorsi, rhomboids	Deltoid, biceps	Barbell, dumbbells, pulley machine	Wrestling, rowing, baseball, basketball, bowling
Upright rowing	Trapezius	Deltoid, biceps	Barbell, dumbbells, pulley machine	All activities or sports
Lat pull-down	Latissimus dorsi	Biceps	Pulley machine	Basketball, baseball, swimming, tennis, volleyball, wrestling
Good morning	Spinal erector	—	Barbell	All activities or sports
Internal/external shoulder rotation	Rotator cuff	—	Barbell, dumbbells, machine	All activities or sports
Front shoulder raise	Anterior deltoid	—	Barbell, dumbbells	All activities or sports
Bent-over lateral raise	Posterior deltoid	Rhomboids, Latissimus	Dumbbells, machine	All activities or sports
Lateral shoulder raise	Deltoid	Trapezius	Dumbbells, machine	All activities or sports
Shoulder shrug	Trapezius	—	Barbell, dumbbells, machine	All activities or sports
Arm curl	Bicep	Forearm muscles	Barbell, dumbbells, pulley machine	All activities or sports
French press	Triceps	—	Barbell, dumbbells, pulley machine	All activities or sports

Figure 8.6 *Weight-training Exercises, Primary and Secondary Muscles, Equipment, and Their Relationships to Activities and Sports.*

Wellness Connection

One of the potential problems of starting a weight training program may be muscle soreness. This usually occurs from beginning a new type of exercise or engaging in one in which you have not participated for a long time.

There are really two kinds of muscle soreness. One type occurs immediately after exercise as a result of a reduced blood supply to the muscles. This type of soreness usually goes away on its own after a short time. The second type of muscle soreness is felt anywhere from 24 to 48 hours after exercise.

small muscle group

muscles of small size or a small number of muscles being used at one time.

A **small muscle group** refers both to groups of muscles of small size and to a small number of muscles, usually one or two, being used at one time. Examples of small muscle groups include upper arms, forearms, and lower legs.

Small muscle groups are often involved with the movement of larger muscle group exercises. For this reason it is important not to exercise or fatigue small muscle groups before the large muscle exercises for the same body area have been completed. These small muscle groups are best worked individually at the end of the workouts. For example, if you do a bench press (a large muscle group exercise), you use the large pectoralis muscle (chest) and deltoid muscle (shoulder), as well as the small tricep muscle (arm). You will also need to include an individual tricep exercise, such as a tricep extension, but only after you have completed the bench press work. Figure 8.7 shows an example of how to organize the workout of large and small muscle groups in different muscle areas during your workout.

Push Exercises versus Pull Exercises.   Another suggestion for sequencing your exercises is to alternate pulling motions (flexing) with pushing motions (extension). Alternating pushes and pulls gives your muscles more recovery time because the same muscle is not worked two or more times in succession (see Figure 8.8). Figure 8.9 shows an example of how to organize push and pull exercises in your workout.

Upper Body versus Lower Body.   You might choose to alternate an exercise for the upper body (waist and above) with an

Exercise Order	Muscle Type	Muscle Group
1. Squat	Large	Thigh and hips (quadriceps)
2. Heel raise	Small	Calf (gastrocnemius)
3. Bench press	Large	Chest (pectoralis)
4. Tricep extension	Small	Upper arm–back (triceps)
5. Bent-over row	Large	Back (lattissimus dorsi)
6. Arm curl	Small	Upper arm–front (biceps)

• **Figure 8.7** *Organizing the Work of Large and Small Muscle Groups in a Workout.*

BELIEVE IT? ... OR NOT?

A 3- to 4-pound increase in muscle mass in a year, as a result of weight training, will increase the amount of calories you burn in one day by 150 to 200 calories.

See page 270 for answer.

There are several theories on why we may experience muscle soreness after exercise. One theory says that very tiny tears may occur in the muscle during muscle contraction. Another theory says that during muscular contraction there is a local muscle spasm, which reduces the blood supply to the muscle. Localized lack of blood produces muscle pain, pain produces more spasms, and the cycle continues.

Stretching exercises may help to reduce muscle soreness due to exercise. You may also help avoid muscle soreness by doing warm-up and cooldown exercises, progressing slowly on your muscle training program, and avoiding jerky, intense movements.

CNN® **Health and Fitness Updates**

You can update your coverage of health and fitness topics, as well as spark lively classroom discussion and deeper understanding, by using the **CNN Health and Fitness Updates.** These video updates are produced by Turner Educational Services, using the resources of CNN, the world's first 24-hour, all-news network.

With the introduction of the **CNN Health and Fitness Updates,** West Educational Publishing is proud to be the exclusive partner of CNN for textbook/video integration in high school fitness. By making use of the **CNN Health and Fitness Updates** you can bring the power of CNN, the network known for providing in-depth, live coverage and analysis of breaking news events, to your fitness class.

For assistance in using and incorporating the **CNN Health and Fitness Updates** into your classroom presentations, see the *Classroom Guide to the CNN Health and Fitness Updates.* The **CNN Health and Fitness Updates** are available with West Educational Publishing's *Foundations of Personal Fitness* by Don Rainey and Tinker Murray.

Assess

Use the Active Mind/Active Body activities on page 254 to assess student progress. Then use the Section 3 Review questions to assess students' comprehension of the concepts presented in Section 3.

ANSWERS TO SECTION 3 REVIEW

1. The term rep is short for repetition. Reps are the basic unit of any weight training workout. Each time an exercise is done, it is referred to as a rep. A group of consecutive reps for an exercise is called a set. Each time you repeat the process of consecutive reps, you have completed another set. Reps and sets help to determine the intensity and variation of weight training workouts.

2. *a.* Large muscle groups versus small muscle groups. This type of circuit will use the large muscles of the leg first and then do specific exercises that work the small muscles of the leg. This ensures that the large muscles will not be fatigued first when most of the energy is needed.

REMEMBER This!

You need to apply the principles of overload, specificity, and progression in your weight-training program. You should increase your muscle intensity gradually over time by overloading your muscles to achieve your muscular fitness goals. You can apply the specificity principle by correctly organizing weight-training exercises to work specific muscle groups. The progression principle applies to weight training just as it applies to the other components of personal fitness: never change your frequency, intensity, or time/duration all at the same time or too quickly. Be patient, and allow for gradual improvements.

BELIEVE IT? ... OR NOT?

The largest muscle in your body is the latissimus dorsi, which is a large muscle in the middle and lower back.

See page 270 for answer.

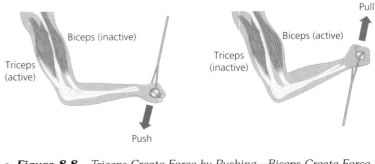

• **Figure 8.8** *Triceps Create Force by Pushing—Biceps Create Force by Pulling.*

Exercise Order	Exercise Type	Muscle Groups
1. Leg press	Push	Thigh–front (quadriceps)
2. Leg curl	Pull	Thigh–back (hamstring)
3. Bench press	Push	Chest (pectoralis)
4. Bent-over row	Pull	Back (lattissimus dorsi)
5. Military press	Push	Shoulder (deltoid)
6. Arm curl	Pull	Upper arm–front (biceps)

• **Figure 8.9** *Organizing Push Exercises and Pull Exercises in Your Workout to Maximize Recovery Time.*

exercise for the lower body (hips and below). This method allows muscles more recovery time but is more difficult than the two previous ways of ordering workouts.

Workouts alternating upper and lower body muscles require an equal number of upper and lower body exercises. This means you would be doing two to three more leg exercises than you would have done in the two previous types of workouts. These additional leg exercises would require you to use more energy, thus making your workout more difficult. This type of alternating plan is, however, a suitable plan for the individual wanting to perform a higher intensity leg workout. Figure 8.10 shows an example of how to organize upper and lower body exercises in your workout.

Science and Technology

New technological advancements in weight lifting equipment include the advent of adjustable, hydraulic counter-resistant weight lifting machines. These machines resemble a Universal weight lifting system, except the weight plates are replaced with hydraulic cylinders and the resistance exerted by the cylinders is controlled by an adjustable flow valve. These machines create a resistant force, but the force is unidirectional instead of constant. These machines were designed to increase safety, which they have done.

Exercise Order	Exercise Type	Muscle Groups
1. Military press	Upper	Shoulder (deltoid)
2. Leg extension	Lower	Thigh (quadriceps)
3. Back lat pull	Upper	Back (lattissimus dorsi)
4. Lunge	Lower	Thigh and hip (quadriceps/gluteals)
5. Arm curl	Upper	Upper arm–front (biceps)
6. Leg press	Lower	Thigh–front (quadriceps)

• **Figure 8.10** *Organizing Upper and Lower Body Exercises in a Workout to Maximize Recovery Time.*

Strongest Muscle versus Weakest Muscle.   A final way to order your exercises is to work the weakest muscle first. For example, if your back muscles are your weakest area, exercise your back muscles first, while you have the most energy and can work at higher intensities.

SECTION 3 REVIEW

Answer the following questions on a separate piece of paper:

1. Define sets and reps and explain the relationship between them.
2. List and explain three ways to arrange the weight-training exercises in your workout.

SECTION 4 Developing and Maintaining Muscular Fitness

To develop and maintain your muscular fitness, your personal fitness plan must include weight-training exercises. To improve your muscular fitness, you need to determine your FIT (frequency, intensity, and time/duration) by estimating or determining exactly the

b. Push exercises versus pull exercises. This type of circuit alternates exercises that require push movements (bench press, shoulder press, French press, etc.) with exercises that require pull movements (lat pull, bent-over row, arm curl, etc.). The advantage of this circuit is to allow muscle recovery time between push exercises and pull exercises.
c. Upper body exercises versus lower body exercises. This type of circuit alternates exercises that require upper body muscles (above the waist) with exercises that require lower body muscles (below the waist). The advantage of this circuit is to allow muscle recovery time between upper or lower body exercises.

Close

Have students develop a circuit of exercises that will be used by the class during the next workout session.

The disadvantage of this new technology is twofold. The cost of these new machines is high, because each machine is designed for a specific muscle workout. The second disadvantage of this technology is the change in muscle dynamics. Because of the unidirectional resistive force, ordinary weight training exercises will not get the results as seen with conventional weight sets. Before the physical education teacher decides to purchase this new equipment, he or she should first learn more about it. **Take the challenge:** Use your Internet browser and connect to news:misc.fitness.weights. This is an excellent resource to learn about the newer weight training technologies.

Focus

Outcomes

In **Section 4** students will learn:

1. To identify and explain the factors that determine the intensity of a workout.
2. How to determine their estimated one-rep maximums.
3. To identify and explain ways to vary the frequency of workouts.
4. To explain and demonstrate different strength tests.
5. To explain why record keeping is important.

Focus Activities

1. Discuss how intensity can be determined in weight training.
2. Use the Fitness Check on pages 263–264 to have

muscle intensity

the amount of tension or stress placed on a muscle.

REMEMBER This!

Keep in mind that you are not finding your one-rep maximum so that you can lift that amount. The amount you will lift on a regular basis will be a percentage (from 60% to 95%) of your maximum. You are only determining your maximum so that you can safely train at a lesser weight.

maximum amount of weight you can lift. Use the scientific principles you learned in Chapter 3 and your personal fitness goals to develop your specific muscular fitness plan.

Determining your FIT for weight training is more complicated than it is for cardiovascular fitness, because frequency, intensity, and time/duration for weight training overlap and are not as easily separated into different components. It is very difficult to determine your intensity without considering your recovery time/duration and the frequency of your workouts at the same time. Therefore, in the following discussion, intensity and recovery time/duration for weight training will be explained before frequency.

Weight-training Intensity

Muscles get stronger and bigger only if you continue to overload them with tension or stress. The amount of tension or stress placed on a muscle is called **muscle intensity**. You can determine the intensity of a workout in a variety of ways.

Your specific weight-training goals will guide your intensity plan. Do you want strength and power, or do you want toning and endurance? Maybe you are only interested in good overall muscle fitness. Knowing how much and the kind of intensity to put into your workout can make a big difference in how successful you will be. When designing the intensity of your workout, consider the amount of weight you will lift, the number of reps and sets, and how many different exercises per body part you will do.

The Amount of Weight. One of the first questions you have to answer in determining your workout intensity is, "How much weight should I lift?" The answer to this question is often determined by a maximum strength test.

A maximum strength test determines the maximum amount of weight a person can lift one time (one rep) for a particular exercise. A simple way of doing this type of test is to keep increasing the amount of weight you try to lift until you cannot lift any more. The maximum amount you can lift one time is often referred to as your *one-rep maximum.*

Beginning weight lifters are advised not to do one-rep maximums to determine their maximum strength. Until they become more experienced, they can estimate their maximum by doing multiple reps with a weight less than their maximum.

As you participate in a regular weight-training program, your maximum strength will increase. You will need to periodically test your maximum so that you can continue to increase your intensity. As you become more experienced, you may choose to do actual one-rep maximums rather than estimating your maximum. The "Fitness Check" activity on the next page will help you determine your personal maximum for a variety of exercises.

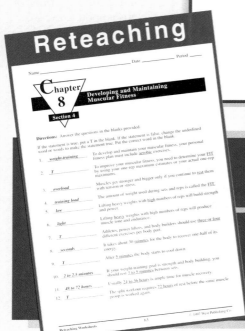

Reteaching

ABILITY LEVELS

Reteaching

Some students may need help mastering the concepts contained in this section. In your Teacher Resource Package, you will find the reproducible worksheet shown here. This worksheet should help students who have been absent and those needing additional help to improve their comprehension and retention of the content in this section.

Fitness Check ✓

Determining Your Maximum Strength (One-Rep Maximums)

Determine your estimated one-rep maximum for each of the following exercises: bench press, squat, military press, biceps curl, and bent-over row. As you work to determine these maximums, it is very important that you use the proper technique for each exercise. (See Section 6 later in this chapter.)

Be sure to use the estimated maximum method. To use this method, choose a weight for which you can do 6 to 10 reps. Do the reps, then look at Figure 8.11 to find your one-rep maximum.

For example, Julie can squat 105 pounds seven times. She would find the column for seven reps in Figure 8.11 and then, in that column, find the amount of weight she lifted (105 pounds). She would then read across from 105 to the far-right column to obtain her estimated one-rep maximum (130 pounds).

Pounds Lifted (70% of Max., 9–10 Reps.)	Pounds Lifted (80% of Max., 7–8 Reps.)	Pounds Lifted (85% of Max., 6 Reps.)	Pounds Lifted (100% of Max., 1 Rep.)
40	45	50	60
50	55	60	70
55	65	70	80
65	70	75	90
70	80	85	100
75	90	95	110
85	95	100	120
90	105	110	130
100	115	120	140
105	120	130	150
110	130	135	160
120	135	145	170
125	145	155	180
135	150	160	190
140	160	170	200
150	170	180	210
155	175	185	220
160	185	195	230
170	190	205	240
175	200	210	250

- **Figure 8.11** *Estimate Your Maximum Strength with 6 to 10 Reps (weights rounded off to the nearest 5 pounds).*

(Continued on next page)

students determine their estimated one-rep maximums for a variety of exercises.
3. Demonstrate an ability to interpret and apply the training load determination chart (Figure 8.13).
4. Discuss and experience a variety of recovery time periods between sets.
5. Discuss and experience three-day total body workouts and split-week workouts.
6. Discuss how to test and reasons for strength testing.

Fitness Check

- Using Figures 8.11 and 8.12, have students perform the Fitness Check activity on this page.
- Have students use the lifting technique checklist in the Active Mind/Active Body activity on page 277 to ensure correct technique for each of the estimated one-rep maximum exercises.

Enrichment

This activity will allow you to provide a more challenging learning experience for some of your students.

The student should respond to the following situation: What would happen if, while taking a muscular fitness test, the person:
1. did not warm-up before testing began?

2. took more than one strength test on the same day?
3. attempted a maximum lift more than three times with the same weight?
4. took a test on the day following a hard workout?

- All students should have ample practice with these exercises before attempting the estimated one-rep maximums.
- Encourage students to focus on improvement and to not be overly concerned with the scores of other students.

Teacher Readings

Fleck, S. J. and Kraemer, W. J. *Designing Resistance Training Programs,* Human Kinetics, Champaign, IL: 1987.

Determining Your Maximum Strength (One-Rep Maximums) *(continued)*

Record your results, as described on the preceding page, for each exercise. You can use these results to determine the amount of weight you will use in workouts. You will also use the results to assess your improvement in later tests.

Once you have obtained your estimated one-rep maximum for the five exercises, use Figure 8.12 to determine your pound-for-pound relative strength. Do this for all five exercises, and record how you performed. For example, in Chapter 7, Jim's estimated one-rep maximum for the bench press was 130 pounds, and he weighed 125 pounds. His relative strength was calculated by dividing 130 by 125, which told us that Jim's relative strength was 1.04. To determine Jim's relative performance rates, look at Figure 8.12, and find 1.04 under "bench press." Then read across to the left. Jim's bench press performance would rate as moderate, or average.

Men

Relative Strength Rating	Biceps Curl	Military Press	Bench Press	Squat	Bent-over Row
Outstanding	> .64	> .99	> 1.29	> 1.84	> .94
	.55–.64	.90–.99	1.15–1.29	1.65–1.84	.85–.94
Moderate	.45–.54	.75–.89	1.0–1.14	1.30–1.64	.75–.84
	.35–.44	.60–.74	.85–.99	1.0–1.29	.65–.74
Unacceptable	< .34	< .60	< .85	< 1.0	< .64

Women

Relative Strength Rating	Biceps Curl	Overhead Press	Bench Press	Squat	Bent-over Row
Outstanding	> .45	> .50	> .85	> 1.45	> .55
	.38–.44	.42–.49	.70–.84	1.30–1.44	.45–.54
Moderate	.32–.37	.32–.41	.60–.69	1.0–1.29	.35–.44
	.25–.31	.25–.31	.50–.59	.80–.99	.25–.34
Unacceptable	< .25	< .25	< .50	< .80	< .25

Figure 8.12 *One-Rep Maximums Can Be Used to Determine Relative Strength and Strength Range for Specific Exercises.*

Across the Disciplines

Sociology

Sport as a social institution is a relatively recent development. Some sociologists view sport as serving two important functions for society: social integration and the reinforcement of important social standards and values. Others view sport as a mechanism to promote social inequality.

A consequence of the popularity of sport in American secondary schools is its generation of male status within the high school's social system. Traditionally,

training load

the amount of weight a weight trainer lifts during his or her workout.

Once you have determined your maximum for a specific exercise, you can then take a percentage of your maximum to determine how much weight you should lift for each exercise. The amount of weight used during sets and reps is called the **training load**.

See Figure 8.13 to determine your training load. Suppose your maximum lift on the bench press is 100 pounds. Beginners should

1 Rep. Maximum	Training load percentages							
	50%	60%	70%	75%	80%	85%	90%	95%
30	15	18	21	23	24	26	27	29
40	20	24	28	30	32	34	36	38
50	25	30	35	38	40	43	45	48
60	30	36	42	45	48	51	54	57
70	35	42	49	52	56	60	63	67
80	40	48	56	60	64	68	72	76
90	45	54	63	68	72	77	81	86
100	50	60	70	75	80	85	90	95
110	55	66	77	83	88	94	99	105
120	60	72	84	90	96	102	108	114
130	65	78	91	98	104	111	117	124
140	70	84	98	105	112	119	125	133
150	75	90	105	113	120	128	135	143
160	80	96	112	120	128	136	144	152
170	85	102	119	128	136	145	153	162
180	90	108	126	135	144	153	162	171
190	95	114	133	143	152	162	171	181
200	100	120	140	150	160	170	180	190
210	105	126	147	158	168	179	189	200
220	110	132	154	165	176	187	198	209
230	115	138	161	173	184	196	207	219
240	120	144	168	180	192	204	216	228
250	125	150	175	188	200	213	225	238
260	130	156	182	195	208	221	234	247
270	135	162	189	203	216	230	243	257
280	140	168	196	210	224	238	252	266
290	145	174	203	218	232	247	261	276
300	150	180	210	225	240	255	270	285
310	155	186	217	233	248	264	279	295
320	160	192	224	240	256	272	288	304
330	165	198	231	248	264	281	297	314
340	170	204	238	255	272	289	306	323
350	175	210	245	263	280	298	316	333
360	180	216	252	278	288	306	324	342
370	185	222	259	280	296	315	333	352
380	190	228	266	285	304	323	342	361
390	195	234	273	293	312	332	351	371
400	200	240	280	300	320	340	360	380

• **Figure 8.13** *If You are a Beginner, You Should Work at 50 to 60 Percent of Your One-rep Maximum.*

Teach & Apply

Discussion

Discuss the different factors that can determine the intensity of a workout.

Activities

• Have students use their estimated one-rep maximums to determine what 60% of their training load will be for each of the maximums.

 **RESOURCES** **TRANSPARENCIES** Use transparency/master 8.13 to explain training loads.

male athletes are favored over nonathletes. Studies have shown that participation does not generate the same popularity for women.

Golf, tennis, volleyball, figure skating, swimming, diving, and track have been classified by adolescents as gender-appropriate sports for women. Basketball and softball have been classified as gender-inappropriate sports for women.

Discuss with students the ideas that have limited female participation in vigorous, competitive sports as well as weight training. Based on current trends in the fitness industry and society's endorsement of personal fitness, have students predict future trends in the social institution of sport.

Discussion

Compare the effects of lifting a heavy weight for a low number of reps with lifting a lighter weight for a high number of reps.

Teacher Support Notes

Research strongly supports the use of a repetition continuum. The continuum will help lifters determine the number of repetitions and weight necessary to achieve strength gains. Resistance that can be lifted six times seems to result in the greatest amount of strength improvement. Research suggests that repetitions beyond twenty RM (rep maximum) will show diminishing strength gains and improvement in muscle endurance.

BELIEVE IT? ... OR NOT?

A good way to build up your leg strength is to wear ankle weights strapped to your lower legs while you walk or run.

See page 270 for answer.

Fitness and Health:
2-3 Sets of 8-12 Reps.
Toning and Endurance:
2-3 Sets of 12-20 Reps.
Strength and Power:
3-5 Sets of 4-6 Reps.
Body Building:
Combination of All Three.

• **Figure 8.15** *Sets and Reps to Meet Your Goals.*

use 50 to 60 percent of their maximums, whereas conditioned weight trainers may want to use 75 to 85 percent of their maximum. Let's suppose you feel you are somewhere between a beginner and a conditioned weight trainer so you decide to work at 70 percent of your maximum. You would use 70 pounds for a prescribed number of reps.

The Number of Reps and Sets.   In general, lifting heavy weights with low numbers of reps will build strength and power. Lifting light weights with high numbers of reps will produce muscle tone and endurance (Figure 8.14). Figure 8.15 suggests the numbers of reps and sets you should do for various weight-training goals.

Number of Different Exercises per Body Part. The greater the number of different exercises you use to work a body part, the greater your intensity. One or two different exercises for each of your body parts is sufficient to improve and maintain health and fitness. Athletes, power lifters, and body builders should use three or four different exercises per body part. When you increase the number of exercises, you also increase the number of sets used per body part. This will increase the intensity of your workout, as well as your total workout time.

> Look to your health; and if you have it, praise God, and value it next to a good conscience; for health is the second blessing that we mortals are capable of; a blessing that money cannot buy.
>
> **Izaak Walton (1593–1683)**
> **English writer. *The Compleat Angler*, Pt. 1, Ch. 21**

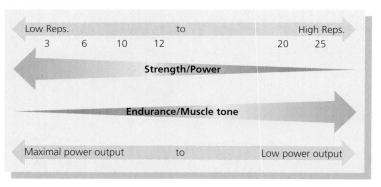

• **Figure 8.14**   *Repetition Continuum. Strength/Power versus Endurance/Muscle Tone.*

Special Needs

For the disabled population, the training sequence in which exercises are performed is critical to ensuring that maximum benefit is gained from the workout. Lifts that work multiple muscle groups and joints should be utilized before work is done involving individual muscles and joints. It should also be emphasized that each muscle group worked should be given sufficient rest between each set.

Testing to determine muscular fitness of a disabled student is important so that his or her specific physical needs can be addressed. Tests that can be used to

Recovery Time/Duration

recovery time

time or rest between exercises.

Your **recovery time**—time or rest between exercises—plays a big role in the intensity, and outcome of your workout. Therefore, you must decide how long to rest between sets, between different exercises, and between different workouts. Too much time between sets of different exercises can cause you to cool down, which increases your risk of injury. Too little time prevents your muscles from recovering and does not allow for proper intensity. It takes about thirty seconds for the body to recover one-half of its energy and about three minutes for full recovery. After five minutes the body starts to cool down. Here are some recovery time guidelines.

Between Reps.   You should not rest between reps. Reps should be continuous and controlled.

Between Sets.   How long you rest between sets depends on your weight-training goals:

- *Fitness and health* . . . . .Rest 1½ to 2 minutes.
- *Strength and body building* . . . .Rest 2 to 2½ minutes.
- *Toning and endurance* . . . . . . .Rest 30 to 60 seconds.
- *Power (very heavy weights)* . . . .Rest 3 to 5 minutes.

Between Exercises.   You will determine the amount of rest between exercises when you choose the order of exercises in your workout. The push-pull method and the upper body-lower body method require 1½ to 2 minutes between exercises. The large muscle-small muscle method requires 2 to 2½ minutes between exercises.

weight-training cycle

a change in your weight-training programs over a period of time.

Between Cycles.   Athletes or competitive lifters do not train the same way year-round. They must regularly modify their programs to meet the needs of off-season, pre-season, and in-season. Each modified program is called a **weight-training cycle**. Your personal health and fitness weight-training routine will also require modifications (cycles) throughout the year. You should change your exercises, sets, and workout days to prevent boredom. It may even be good to get away from the weights for a few weeks and do some other exercises, such as push-ups, bar dips, chin-ups, or isometrics. See Figures 8.16, 8.17, and 8.18 on the next page. Keep your workouts fresh. Don't be afraid to throw in some variety.

Weight-training Frequency

With weight training there are no shortcuts to success. The frequency and consistency of your workouts is very important. Decide which days of the week are best for you, and then avoid missing sessions.

Teaching Strategies

RESOURCES Use transparencies/masters 8.14 and 8.15 to teach the concept of rep numbers and the amount of resistance.

TRANSPARENCIES

- Plan your circuit of exercises, the number of sets, and the percentage of workload to show a variety of intensities to students.
- It is not recommended to have students participate in more than four sets per body part. This intensity is high and it will make it difficult for the entire class to complete the workout.

Discussion

- Discuss how recovery time is important in determining intensity and how it can be a factor in achieving your specific goals.
- Discuss the variety of ways recovery time can be implemented.
- Discuss why rest is important to muscle growth. Refer to Chapter 7.

Teaching Strategies

Prepare a musical tape that has specific recovery periods timed out. Students are instructed to rotate sets or stations while the music has stopped and to lift while the music plays.

assess muscular fitness will vary, depending on the specific disability.

Developing strength for the disabled student is of utmost importance for those who need increased muscle endurance to perform daily activities. Functional, independent living is emphasized in other aspects of the disabled student's school program and this should carry over to their fitness training as well. The strength and endurance necessary to be mobile should be a primary goal.

Teacher reference: *Conditioning with Physical Disabilities,* Kevin F. Lockette and Ann M. Keyes in cooperation with the Rehabilitation Institute of Chicago, Human Kinetics, Champaign, IL, 1994.

Discussion

- Discuss the three photos on this page and how these exercises can be used when weights are not available or when cycle changes are occurring in your program.
- Discuss the reasons for doing strength testing and how it should be conducted.
- Remind the class that one-rep maximums will be checked at the end of the unit.
- Discuss record keeping and how it can be an important part of accomplishing the students' goals.

● **Figure 8.16** *Starting and Finishing Position for Push-ups.*

● **Figure 8.17** *Starting and Finishing Position for Bar Dip.*

● **Figure 8.18** *Starting and Finishing Position for Chin-ups.*

Monday (workout)

Tuesday (off)

Wednesday (workout)

Thursday (off)

Friday (workout)

Sat. & Sun. (off)

● **Figure 8.19** *Sample Workout Week—Three Days, Total Body.*

split workout

a weight-training workout schedule in which you do not work each muscle group at each workout session but, instead, exercise one-half of your body at each session.

A well-designed plan can help you maintain consistency and workout intensity. Each workout should provide enough stress on the muscles to stimulate the muscle growth process. After this stimulation occurs, the muscle must have time to recover and grow. Usually 48 to 72 hours is ample time for muscle recovery. For example, if Jessie completes a chest, shoulder, and tricep workout on Monday afternoon, he should not work the same muscle groups again until Wednesday afternoon (after a total recovery time of 48 hours).

Three-Days-a-Week, Total-Body Workout. You may decide to work all muscle groups (total body) three times a week, with at least one day off between workouts. This is the most popular plan for beginners. It allows for all muscles to receive ample work, while at the same time allowing for ample rest. See Figure 8.19.

Four-Days-a-Week, Split Workout. Those in more advanced weight-training programs may decide to use a split workout schedule, which requires more intensity and frequency (four days a week). In a **split workout**, you do not work every muscle group at every session. Instead, you only exercise one-half of your body at each session. This means that each body part can be worked at a much greater intensity. You do three or four different exercises per body part and three or four sets for each different exercise. Because

CRITICAL THINKING

Introduce students to the 15–20 major muscles and muscle groups that are used in exercise. These areas of the human body should be represented:
1. Shoulders
2. Chest
3. Abdominals
4. Upper back
5. Lower back
6. Upper legs
7. Lower legs
8. Arms
9. Forearms
10. Buttocks

• *Testing Your Strength. Top Left: Bench Press; Top Right: Squat; Bottom: Seated Military Press.*

Monday:
Chest, Shoulders, Triceps
Tuesday:
Back, Legs, Biceps, Abs.
Wednesday:
Rest!
Thursday:
Repeat Monday's workout
Friday:
Repeat Tuesday's workout
Saturday/Sunday:
Rest!

• **Figure 8.20** *Sample Workout Week—Four Days, Split Workout.*

this workout requires a greater intensity, your muscles need greater recovery time. The split workout requires 72 hours of rest before the same muscle group is again worked. (See Figure 8.20.)

Testing Your Muscular Fitness

Muscular fitness is tested for many reasons. This testing should be done on a regular basis.

Reasons for Testing.   How can you benefit from muscular fitness tests? First, pretests can be used to determine how much weight you should lift in your workouts. Second, muscular fitness tests help identify your weak points, which you can then take into consideration when designing your weight-training program. Finally, these tests will help you keep track of your progress, which becomes a great motivator for your future workouts. Post-tests are used for this purpose.

Identification of muscle groups used during exercise enhances a student's ability to select proper strength training exercises and routines.

As an assignment, have students list their favorite sport on a sheet of paper. Have them take one of the skills needed for that sport and do the following:

1. Analyze the skill and list the muscles involved.
2. Develop a simple routine of two or three exercises that could be used to strengthen those muscles.

Two good examples to use for explaining this assignment: forearm tennis stroke, and throwing a baseball.

CNN® Health and Fitness Updates

You can update your coverage of health and fitness topics, as well as spark lively classroom discussion and deeper understanding, by using the **CNN Health and Fitness Updates.** These video updates are produced by Turner Educational Services, using the resources of CNN, the world's first 24-hour, all-news network.

With the introduction of the **CNN Health and Fitness Updates,** West Educational Publishing is proud to be the exclusive partner of CNN for textbook/video integration in high school fitness. By making use of the **CNN Health and Fitness Updates** you can bring the power of CNN, the network known for providing in-depth, live coverage and analysis of breaking news events, to your fitness class.

For assistance in using and incorporating the **CNN Health and Fitness Updates** into your classroom presentations, see the *Classroom Guide to the CNN Health and Fitness Updates.* The **CNN Health and Fitness Updates** are available with West Educational Publishing's *Foundations of Personal Fitness* by Don Rainey and Tinker Murray.

Teaching Strategies

• Have folders prepared for student groups of three. These folders should contain record sheets similar to Figure 8.22. The record sheets should contain all the exercises and muscles the class will be responsible for knowing during the unit.
• Have students complete the record sheets each time they have a workout.
• Folders should be placed in a box or tray at the end of the period. Instructors should check to see if they are completed accurately.

Assess

Use the Active Mind/Active Body activities beginning on page 277 to assess student progress. Student demonstrations and record-keeping charts may also provide student assessment. Then use the Section 4 Review questions to assess students' comprehension of the concepts presented in Section 4.

Answers to

Believe It? ... Or Not?

Pg. 247 False. Most people reach their peak muscular strength between the ages of twenty and thirty. You can also maintain moderate to high levels of strength into your forties and fifties by remaining active.
Pg. 248 False. You can get seriously injured if you lift without spotters, particularly if you are lifting at high intensities with free weights. Exercises like the bench press, squats, and military press are some of the most potentially dangerous lifts for you if you don't use spotters.
Pg. 252 True.
Pg. 259 True.
Pg. 260 False. The largest muscle in your body is the gluteus maximus, which is your buttock muscle.
Pg. 261 True.
Pg. 266 False. Although you might get a bit stronger if you wear ankle weights, you will also significantly increase your risk for lower body injuries. Ankle weights increase the forces acting on your ankles, knees, and hips.
Pg. 275 True.

How to Test.   Keep the following tips in mind when taking a muscular fitness test:

• Be sure to warm up before any testing. This prevents injury and will help you achieve your best performance.
• Use correct technique at all times.
• Have spotters assist all lifts.
• Do not take more than one strength test on the same day.
• Do not attempt a maximum lift more than three times with the same weight.
• Do not test on days following a hard workout. Allow for proper rest.
• Test any body part you desire.

Record Keeping

Keeping good records is an important part of your weight-training program. Records provide information from the past that can help you make decisions about the future. Figure 8.21 shows parts of your workout routine that you should keep track of. Figure 8.22 shows a sample record-keeping chart.

Part of the Workout	Example of Record Keeping
Days of the week/date	Monday the 23rd Split week
Body part and sets, repetitions, and amount of weight lifted	Chest: bench press 3 × 10 at 100 pounds Legs: squats 3 × 12 at 165 pounds
Body weight, body composition	September 10, 1995: 150 pounds 18 percent body fat
Absences, illnesses	Missed Tuesday, October 10, and Wednesday, October 11, due to a cold.
Personal best	Maximum on bench press = 135 pounds Maximum on squats = 210 pounds
Eating habits	Started eating better breakfast on Monday; missed lunch on Thursday
Total workout time	Workouts lasted 40 minutes

• *Figure 8.21*   *Elements of Record Keeping for Weight-training Programs.*

Wellness Connection

Back pain is a common problem seen in many people today. Back pain, backache, or low-back pain is frequently associated with a weakness or an imbalance in the muscles associated with the back. The four key muscle groups that are referred to as back or trunk muscles include:
• rectus abdomens (stomach muscles)
• erector spinae (back muscles)
• hip flexor muscles (sling muscles)
• abdominal oblique muscles (side and hip muscles)
    If any of these muscle groups are

S = Sets
R = Reps.
WT = Weight

Exercises for the Chest Area (Pectoralis)	Date: _____																	
	Record:	S	R	WT	S	R	WT	S	R	WT	S	R	WT	S	R	WT	S	R	WT
1 **Bench Press**																			
2 Dumbbell Press																			
3 Flys																			
4 Close Grip Press																			
5 **Incline Press**																			
6 Dumbbell Press																			
7 Flys																			
8 Close Grip																			
9 **Decline Press**																			
10 Dumbbell Press																			
11 Flys																			
12 Close Grip Press																			
13 **Dips**																			
14																			

• **Figure 8.22** *Sample Record-keeping Chart.*

SECTION 4 REVIEW

Answer the following questions on a separate sheet of paper:

1. Identify three factors that can help you determine the intensity of your weight-training workouts.
2. List three ways to adjust the intensity of your weight-training workout.
3. Why should your total recovery time between workouts of the same body parts be at least forty-eight hours?
4. Identify three reasons for testing your muscular fitness.

SECTION 5 Programs for Strength and Hypertrophy

You can choose from several different methods to increase your strength and hypertrophy. This section will look at ways to improve strength first. It then will examine methods for building muscle mass.

weak, there is an increased likelihood of backache. Persons who carry a lot of extra body fat in their abdominal areas may also experience back problems. If muscles become stretched and are unable to provide necessary support, the other sets of back muscles are forced to take on extra work to make up the difference. Appropriate back exercises recommended by your doctor, physical therapist, or other qualified professionals may help relieve problems due to weakness in one or more sets of back-related muscles.

ANSWERS TO SECTION 4 REVIEW

1. Answers will vary but may include: amount of weight; number of sets, reps, exercises per body part, and workout days per week; recovery time.
2. Answers will vary but may include: the use of heavy weight with low reps or light weight with a higher number of reps, using more sets per exercise, using more exercises per body part, changing the amount of time between sets, using full body workouts or split workouts.
3. Muscles need this amount of time to recover. The recovery time is when muscle growth and repair occurs.
4. Answers will vary but may include: to determine how much weight to lift during workouts, to identify weak points, to keep track of progress.

Close

Ask students to describe the feeling that occurs at the end of their sets when they are straining on the last few reps. How long does that feeling last?

Focus

Outcomes

In **Section 5** students will learn:

1. To explain the effects of a variety of specific weight training programs.
2. To explain how these specific programs are conducted.

Focus Activities

1. Discuss how to design programs for which strength is the primary goal.
2. Participate in weight training workouts designed primarily to acquire strength.
3. Discuss how to design programs for which hypertrophy is the primary goal.
4. Participate in weight training workouts designed primarily to acquire hypertrophy.

pyramid training

a weight-training strength program for the large muscle groups that starts by using light weights during the first set and then increases the amount of weight and decreases the number of reps with each following set.

REMEMBER This!

All methods of weight training will increase your strength and muscle mass to some degree. However, certain programs will produce greater increases in strength than in muscle mass, and other programs will produce greater increases in muscle mass than in strength. These differences are due to the way your muscle cells respond to different types of weight training and to the specificity principle. Your muscles will adapt specifically to the challenges you give them as you lift weights.

Strength Programs (Strength Is the Primary Goal)

If your primary goal in weight training is to gain strength, you might want to consider the following strength programs. These programs can help you optimize intensity and time as you try to reach your strength potential.

All three of the strength programs require the use of higher percentages of your maximum lifts than is recommended for beginners. Make sure you have been lifting for several (six to eight) weeks before attempting workouts that require you to exceed 80 percent of your maximum. This can help prevent muscle damage or injury.

Pyramid Training. **Pyramid training** starts by using light weights during the first set. It then increases the amount of weight and decreases the number of reps with each following set. The amount of weight increase can be determined by increasing the percentage of your own rep maximum. (See Figure 8.23.) No other exercise is done until all pyramid sets are completed. There should be a two- to three-minute rest between each set. Pyramid training is recommended for larger muscle groups, such as those in the chest, back, legs, and shoulders.

For example, John has a bench press maximum of 130 pounds. He might follow this schedule for a pyramid-training session (weights are rounded to the nearest 5 pounds):

First set: 1 × 10–12, 90 pounds (70 percent of 130 pounds).
Second set: 1 × 6–8, 105 pounds (80 percent of 130 pounds).
Third set: 1 × 4–7, 110 pounds (85 percent of 130 pounds).
Fourth set: 1 × 2–3, 115 pounds (90 percent of 130 pounds).
Fifth set: 1 × 1–2, 125 pounds (95 percent of 130 pounds).

The fourth and fifth sets should be used only by more advanced lifters since they involve lifting near-maximum weight.

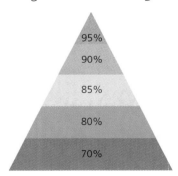

• *Figure 8.23* *Pyramid Training.*

ABILITY LEVELS

Reteaching

Some students may need help mastering the concepts contained in this section. In your Teacher Resource Package, you will find the reproducible worksheet shown here. This worksheet should help students who have been absent and those needing additional help to improve their comprehension and retention of the content in this section.

Any Body Can!

Mark Henry

Mark Henry is a 24-year-old African American male, originally from Silsbee, Texas. Mark is one of the strongest people in the world, and he is proud to promote the fact that he is a lifetime drug-free championship weight and power lifter.

Mark began getting serious about weight training and power lifting in high school. He was the three-time power lifting champion (super heavyweight division) in Texas.

Mark is currently 6 feet, 3 inches tall, weighs over 400 pounds, and wears a size 16 E shoe. Yet, he can slam dunk a basketball and earned third place in the 1994 Slamfest sponsored by Footlocker Sporting Goods.

In 1995, Mark became the first individual in decades to earn and hold the simultaneous titles of U.S. national champion in weight and power lifting in the super heavyweight division. His weight lifting and power lifting achievements at the 1995 national meets include the following:

National Weight Lifting Championship—	Snatch Lift	392 pounds
	Clean and Jerk	<u>485</u> pounds
	Total	**977** pounds
National Power Lifting Championship—	Squat Lift	954 pounds
	Dead Lift	903 pounds
	Bench Press	<u>483</u> pounds
	Total	**2,340** pounds

Mark's lift total of 3,317 pounds on the combined five lifts is the most anyone in the U.S. has ever lifted, on or off drugs (for example, anabolic steroids).

Some of Mark's other outstanding weight lifting honors include being a member of the 1992 and 1996 Olympic weight lifting teams. He also won a gold medal in the super heavyweight division at the 1995 Pan American Games in Argentina.

Mark is often asked why he doesn't use anabolic steroids or other drugs to enhance his performance. His standard answer to this question is, "To be honest, I never have thought about using drugs to improve my performances, but I have thought a lot about what others might be able to lift without taking drugs." Mark has drug tested negative over 30 times for national and international competitions and is an excellent role model for those who want to achieve high levels of personal fitness naturally, without drug influences.

Not everyone can be a weight and power lifting champion like Mark Henry, but Any Body Can learn to lift weights for personal fitness and have success while remaining drug free. That's right, you can do it!

Teach & Apply

Discussion

• Discuss the reasons why muscles get stronger. Refer to Chapter 7, Section 3.
• Review information that explains why most of the early strength gains are due to improvements in neural factors, confidence, and technique.

Teaching Strategies

RESOURCES

TRANSPARENCIES

Use transparency/master of Figure 8.23 to explain pyramid training.

• You may want to adjust the percentages of load for each level of the pyramid.
• Include a pyramid workout in the latter part of the unit.
• Tell students that the beginning sets start at the bottom of the pyramid and go upward.

Enrichment

This activity will allow you to provide a more challenging learning experience for some of your students.

Assign the students the task of comparing the "Intensity" part of the FIT formula when determining weight training and cardiovascular training work loads. Include in the comparison the similarities and the differences.

Discussion

- Define and explain how multiple sets may be used specifically for strength gains.
- Point out the high percentage of workload that is required for strength.
- Define negative sets and explain how they may be used to develop strength. It is not recommended that beginning classes use this method. It increases the chance of injury and should only be used by experienced lifters.
- Discuss why muscle hypertrophy occurs. See Chapter 7, Section 3.
- Discuss how the development of hypertrophy differs from strength development. Identify the specific differences in each workout.
- Discuss how muscle growth begins to occur after five to six weeks of training.
- Define and explain superset training.
- Define and explain antagonistic muscles.
- Define and explain a compound set.

multiple set method

a weight-training strength program that uses the same amount of weight (a percentage of your maximum) for each set until you are fatigued.

negative workout method

a weight-training strength program that uses very heavy weights at the end of a prescribed number of sets and repetitions.

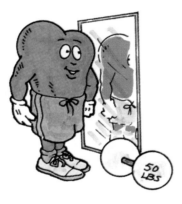

superset method

a weight-training hypertrophy program that uses two different exercises that train opposing muscles, without allowing for rest between sets.

Multiple Sets.   In the **multiple set method,** you use the same amount of weight for each set. You decide which percentage of your maximum to use (85, 90, or 95 percent) and then do reps until you are fatigued. The number of reps should range from three to seven. Rest two to three minutes between each set. As with the pyramid program, the fourth and fifth sets are for more advanced lifters.

For example, Joe has a bench press maximum of 130 pounds. Here is a suggested multiple set program for his training:

First set: 1×4–7, 110 pounds (85 percent of 130 pounds).
Second set: 1×4–7, 110 pounds (same as above).
Third set: 1×4–7, 110 pounds (same as above).

Note that unless you have been lifting for several weeks (six to eight), you should not use these higher maximum percentages.

Negative Method.   In the **negative workout method** you use very heavy weights. You usually use this method at the end of a prescribed number of sets and reps, adding 10 to 15 percent more weight than you usually use. Your spotters, who are required for safety, help place the bar into position. You then slowly control the bar as it comes down. When it gets to your chest (in the bench press), your spotters help raise the bar back to the starting position for another negative (eccentric) rep. Because this method can cause excessive soreness, don't use it often.

Say Fred uses 110 pounds during his normal bench press sets of four to five reps. His negative set would be 1×3, 125 pounds (about a 15 percent increase from 110 pounds). Note that three to four reps per set is the maximum recommended.

Hypertrophy Programs (Muscle Mass Is the Primary Goal)

If your primary goal is hypertrophy (muscle enlargement), you might want to consider some programs that can help you optimize intensity and time as you pursue your hypertrophy potential. Two of the three programs (supersets and compound sets) require high intensities with short rest periods. The third program (multiple sets) requires a greater percentage of your maximum. To prevent possible muscle damage or injury, make sure you have been lifting for several weeks (six to eight weeks) before attempting these workouts.

Supersets.   The **superset method** requires you to use two different exercises that train opposing muscles, without allowing for rest between the sets. For example, do a set of ten biceps curls immediately followed by a set of ten triceps extensions. (These exercises are illustrated in the next section). This is a good way to keep opposite

▐▊▌▬▬ ▐▊▌Equipment Options

How do you determine the quality of free weights? Most free weight discs are made from cast iron, and it is impossible to determine the differences in the discs and dumbbells without X rays.

The bar is the most essential item in free weights. Always choose bars that

are categorized as Olympic sets. A forged bar is stronger than a cast bar, and every bar should have a maximum design weight stamped on its ends. If a bar does not have a maximum design weight stamp, *do not* purchase it.

When purchasing benches, remember

• *An example of the superset weight training method is illustrated above: To the left, leg extensions; to the right, leg curls.*

BELIEVE IT? ...
OR NOT?

The average male will lose 50 percent of his muscle mass between the ages of eighteen and sixty-five. Weight training can prevent much of this muscle loss.

See page 270 for answer.

CONSUMER CORNER

Are Supplements Necessary?

With the increased popularity of weight training, many fitness enthusiasts are looking for ways to obtain the "hard body" look that many professional bodybuilders have. Many people are attracted to television, magazine, and book ads that claim supplements can guarantee significant gains in muscle strength and mass. According to the advertisers, these protein powders, amino acids, vitamins, and minerals can enhance the results you can gain from a regular weight-training program.

The truth is that few, if any, of these supplements are beneficial to most fitness enthusiasts. A physician might prescribe a supplement to treat a specific medical problem. However, a healthy diet will provide all the protein, vitamins, and minerals you need for muscle strength and mass gains. Supplements taken above your daily needs are costly and are excreted from your body as waste materials. Some can even be harmful to your health.

that the diameter and wall thickness of the tubing used for the frame design determines the strength of the bench. Benches with adjustable weight stands should be avoided because the pins that hold the adjustable arms tend to break under repeated use.

The final inspection should be given to the welded areas of the equipment. If a piece of equipment has visible, lumpy, or cracked welds at the joints, don't buy it. The best piece of equipment will look as if it was forged from one piece of metal. **Take the challenge:** Inspect your present equipment and see if it meets the standards discussed.

Teacher Support Notes

Supersets are primarily used for single joint exercises (elbow and knee). They should not be done with the same amount of weight used in regular sets. Less weight is recommended.

Teacher Support Notes

• Compound sets may be used on single or multiple joint exercises. For example, do a set of bench press followed by a set of flat bench fly. Less weight is recommended for this training technique.
• A giant set is three consecutive sets of different exercises that work the same muscle. It is not recommended for beginners.

Discussion

Discuss how the multiple sets method used for hypertrophy requires lower percentages of weight and less recovery time.

Assess

Student demonstration and record-keeping charts may be used to provide assessment of student progress. Then use the Section 5 Review questions to assess students' comprehension of the concepts presented in Section 5.

CHAPTER 8
SECTION 5
276

antagonistic muscles

opposing muscles.

compound set method

a weight-training hypertrophy program that requires you to do two different exercises that use the same muscle group, without allowing for rest between the sets.

muscles balanced in strength. Another name for these opposing muscles is **antagonistic muscles**.

Compound Sets.   The **compound set method** requires you to do two different exercises that use the same muscle group, without allowing for rest between the sets. For example, do a set of ten reps of bench press, immediately followed by a set of ten reps of flat bench fly.

Multiple Sets.   With the multiple set method, you use the same amount of weight for each set. The amount of weight should be 70 to 80 percent of your maximum. Do three to five sets of eight to ten reps. Rest thirty to ninety seconds between sets. This is the recommended progression for beginners after they've done six weeks of weight training with 50 to 60 percent of their maximum.

REMEMBER This!

A muscle actually grows and becomes stronger between workouts, not during workouts. Never work the same muscle group two days in a row.

SECTION 5 REVIEW

Answer the following questions on a separate sheet of paper:

1. Explain the difference between muscular strength programs and muscular hypertrophy programs.
2. Define and explain pyramid training.
3. Explain the difference between supersets and compound sets.

SECTION 6   Exercises, Muscles, and Proper Technique

Knowing how to lift a weight properly is important, especially when using free weights. Correct lifting technique reduces the possibility of injury, and produces the desired results more quickly. This section provides a detailed checklist to help you learn a variety of weight-training exercises. Go through each part of the exercise checklist to develop good lifting techniques. Practice these lifts with spotters and light weights until you are certain you can correctly execute the lift. To get started, use the "Active Mind/Active Body" activity beginning on the next page.

ANSWERS TO SECTION 5 REVIEW

1. Muscular strength programs are designed to optimize your intensity and time in order to reach your strength potential. They require the use of heavier weight with greater recovery time. Muscular hypertrophy programs are designed to optimize your intensity and time to reach your muscle growth potential (mass). They require the use of weight 70–80% of your maximum and reduce the amount of recovery time.
2. It is a strength training–specific program that progresses from light weights, high reps to heavy weights, low reps.
3. Supersets require the use of two different exercises that train opposing muscles. Compound sets require the use of two different exercises that train the same muscle.

Close

Have students discuss the Consumer Corner on page 275. What are supplements? What are some reasons for using supplements?

Across the Disciplines

Sociology

In 1991, nonmedical steroid distribution became a federal offense. However, steroid abuse still continues to flourish among male adolescents. Sociologists and medical experts report there is a

growing adolescent subculture that is driven by an obsession with body size and bodybuilding drugs. The death of former professional football player Lyle Alzado in 1992 has seemed to make relatively little impact on teenagers, who not only want to have phenomenal

Active Mind! Active Body!

Lifting Technique Checklist

Study the correct lifting technique for each of the following weight-training exercises. Demonstrate the bench press, military press, bent-over row, squat, arm curl, and French press. Use only an empty bar or broomstick, not weights, for demonstration. Have your instructor or partners use the Exercise Technique Checklist to evaluate you.

The following weight-training exercises are grouped together according to the areas of the body (chest, shoulders, back, legs, arms, abdominals) that they work.

Chest

Bench Press Body area: middle chest.
Muscles: pectoralis, deltoid, triceps.
Variations: Dumbbells.
Caution: Spotters recommended.

- Lie face up on a bench. Position your back and buttocks flat on the bench.
- Position your eyes directly under the bar. Keep your head down.
- Position your feet flat on the floor. If the bench is too high, use a chair or the end of the bench to lift your feet. (This prevents your back from arching.) Your legs should remain relaxed.
- Grasp the bar with hands slightly farther apart than shoulders' width.
- Your hands should be evenly spaced on each side from the center of the bar; use a wraparound thumb grip, and lock your wrists.
- Move the bar off the rack, and position it over your chest. (Spotters can assist.)

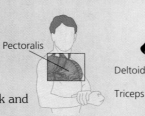
Pectoralis

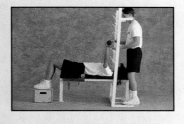
Deltoid
Triceps

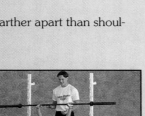

• ***Figure 8.24*** *Bench Press.*

(Continued on next page)

Focus

Outcomes

In **Section 6** students will learn:

1. To demonstrate and explain the correct lifting technique for a variety of weight training exercises.
2. To design and explain a weight training program to meet personal goals and needs.

Focus Activities

1. Use the Active Mind/Active Body activity on this page to have students demonstrate correct lifting technique for a variety of weight training exercises.
2. Have students do the Active Mind/Active Body on page 295.

Teach & Apply

Teacher Support Notes

• The bench press is one of the most popular weight training exercises. It is recommended that you use this exercise as one of the pre-post exercises to demonstrate strength improvement.

physiques and extraordinary strength, but who are willing to take any risk to reach their goals. Trust, reliable information, and communication are significant factors in educating teenagers about the hazards of steroids.

Conduct an on-line search in the library to find appropriate current articles on steroid use. Prepare several readings for the class that illustrate both the physical and psychological effects of using steroids. Discuss the articles with the students. Have the students write a short essay explaining why they believe steroid abuse is a problem and what steps should be taken to prevent its use among adolescents.

Teaching Strategies

Keys to instructing the incline bench press (two-joint exercise):

• Consider the same concerns that were listed for the bench press.
• Also, the bar should come closer to the chin and touch the upper part of the chest.

Teacher Support Notes

• Students will not be as strong on the incline bench press as they are on the bench press. The increased angle of the bench does not allow for the use of all the chest muscles. The upper pectoralis is primarily involved.

Lifting Technique Checklist *(continued)*

• Keep your elbows out, parallel to the bar.
• Stabilize the bar before lowering it. (Spotters should release the bar.)
• Lower the bar slowly to the middle of your chest. Maintain control and speed; touch, do not bounce the bar off your chest.
• Push upward to the starting position. Go through the full range of motion. (Spotters hands should be in the ready position.)
• Breathe out (exhale) during the push stage. Do not hold your breath.
• Keep your back, head, and buttocks in contact with the bench at all times.
• At the completion of the reps, replace the bar on the rack. Never release your grip until the bar is safely in the rack. (Spotters should assist to replace the bar.)

Variation of Bench Press—Flat bench dumbbell press.

Incline Bench Press   Body area: upper chest.
Muscles: upper pectoralis, deltoid, triceps.
Variations: dumbbells.
Caution: Spotters recommended.

• Lie face up on an incline bench. Position your back and buttocks flat on the bench.
• Position your feet flat on the floor. If the bench is too high, use a chair or the end of the bench to lift your feet. Do not use your feet to lift your body. Your legs should remain relaxed.
• Grasp the bar with hands slightly farther apart than shoulders' width.
• Your grip should be evenly spaced. Use a wraparound thumb grip, and lock your wrists.
• Move the bar off the rack, and position it over your chest. (Spotters can assist.)
• Keep your elbows out and parallel to the bar.

Pectoralis

Deltoid

Triceps

Enrichment

This activity will allow you to provide a more challenging learning experience for some of your students.

Have students keep a training log that records the activities in their personal fitness program. For cardiovascular conditioning, they should record their exercise heart rate for each workout. For weight training, they should record the amount of weight they have lifted for each exercise. After each week, they should average their heart rate or weight lifted. Has there been an increase or decrease in either heart rate or weight lifted?

Remind students that for cardiovascular conditioning, a beginner should exercise at 60 to 70 percent of their maximum heart rate. A beginning weight trainer should exercise at 60 to 70 percent of the maximum weight he or she can lift one time. Has students' training met these guidelines?

- Lower the bar slowly to the top of your chest, near your chin. Maintain control and speed. Touch the bar to your chest. Do not bounce it off your chest.
- Push the bar upward to the starting position. Go through the full range of motion. (Spotters hands should be in a ready position.)
- Breathe out (exhale) during the push stage. Do not hold your breath.
- Your back, head, and buttocks must remain in contact with the bench at all times.
- At the completion of the reps, replace the bar on the rack. Never release your grip until the bar is safely in the rack. (Spotters should assist to replace the bar in the rack.)

Figure 8.25   *Incline Bench Press.*

Variation of Incline Bench Press (dumbbells).

Flat Bench Fly   Body area: chest.
Muscles: pectoralis.
Variations: incline or decline bench.

- Lie face up on a bench. Position your back and buttocks flat on the bench.
- Position your feet flat on the floor. If the bench is too high, use a chair or the end of the bench to lift your feet. Do not use your feet to lift your body. Your legs should remain relaxed.
- Grasp a dumbbell in each hand. Use a wraparound thumb grip.
- Raise your arms and hands to position the dumbbells together over your chest. Your arms should be extended, and your palms should face each other.

Pectoralis

(Continued on next page)

• Incline benches can be set at a variety of angles. For the best results, it is suggested that the bench angle be between 15 and 30 degrees.
• The use of the dumbbells in this exercise will require more balance.

Teaching Strategies

Keys to instructing the flat bench fly (one-joint exercise):

• Body position on the bench.
• Minimal movement of the elbow joint.
• Depth of the dumbbells at the bottom of the exercise.
• Placement of spotters' hands on the lifter's elbows if assistance is needed.
• Identification of the muscle used.

Enrichment

This activity will allow you to provide a more challenging learning experience for some of your students.

Have the students write answers to the following question: Would you, or would you not, be willing to follow an exercise program designed to develop muscle strength and/or muscle mass? Defend your decision. Have students categorize their answers according to physical appearance, fear of injury, etc. Determine the top three reasons students would not want to follow a program for developing muscle strength/mass and the top three reasons students would want to follow a program.

Teacher Support Notes

The flat bench fly is primarily used to isolate the pectorals. There is very little biceps required and no triceps. It is not a choice for strength development. It is great for defining the pectorals. This exercise should be done after the completion of the two-joint exercises for the chest.

Teaching Strategies

Keys to instructing the seated "back" shoulder press (two-joint exercise):

• Position of back (belts recommended).
• Grip and grip placement.
• Head up.
• Elbows parallel to the bar.
• Placement of spotters' hands if assistance is needed.
• Identification of the muscles used.

Lifting Technique Checklist *(continued)*

• Before you lower the dumbbells, slightly bend both elbows.
• Lower the dumbbells in a wide arc.
• Your elbows should remain slightly bent. Keep your arms in line with your shoulders and chest.
• Lower the dumbbells slowly, controlling their speed until they are level with your shoulders.
• Return the dumbbells to the starting position. Keep your elbows slightly bent until you reach the top of the lift. Continue the reps.
• Breathe out (exhale) during the push stage; do not hold your breath.

Figure 8.26   *Flat Bench Fly.*

Shoulders

Seated "Back" Shoulder (military) Press
Body area: shoulders.
Muscles: deltoid, triceps, trapezius.
Variation: front of the neck, dumbbell press (standing or sitting), machine.
Caution: Spotters and weight belts recommended.

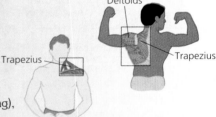

• Sit on a bench or chair. Place your feet flat on the floor.
• Grasp the bar with hands slightly farther apart than shoulders' width.
• Your grip should be evenly spaced. Use a wraparound thumb grip, and lock your wrists.
• Your elbows should be under the bar and parallel to the bar.
• Your back should be straight (not arched) and your head up.
• The starting position for the bar is at shoulder height and close to the body. (Spotters can assist.)

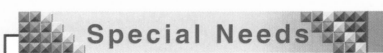

Special Needs

There are a number of disorders that affect muscles directly, but there are other conditions that should be noted. Myasthenia gravis (MG) results when nerve impulses are hindered—interfering with the muscle's ability to contract.

Students who experience neuromuscu-lar disorders should avoid training that uses eccentric contraction because of possible muscle trauma that can occur. Isometric training can be beneficial to students with arthritis or other conditions where joint movement is limited.

The most common form of muscular

- The bar is pushed upward to full arm extension.
- Breathe out (exhale) during the push stage; do not hold your breath.
- Your elbows should remain under, and parallel to, the bar at all times, with your back flat.
- Lower the bar slowly to the back of the neck. Maintain control and speed. Do not let the bar bounce off of your neck or shoulder.
- At the completion of the reps, replace the bar on the rack. (Spotters can assist.)

Figure 8.27 *Seated "Back" Shoulder (military) Press.*

Variation "A"—Standing Dumbbell Overhead (military) Press.

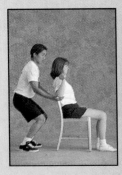

Variation "B"—Seated Military Dumbbell Press.

Variation "C"—Seated Shoulder Press (machine).

Variation "D" Incline Shoulder Press (machine).

(Continued on next page)

Teacher Support Notes

- A popular variation of the seated "back" shoulder press is to use dumbbells either in a standing or seated position.
- The use of a free bar or machine can also allow for the seated "back" shoulder press to be performed in front of the head. By using a variation of front and back presses, the three different heads of the deltoid muscle are better worked.

dystrophy—Duchenne—causes the student to become progressively incapacitated as the muscles gradually weaken and eventually atrophy. The muscles increasingly lose protein and are replaced with fat.

Students with spinal cord injuries (particularly lower cord lesions) generally develop large-diameter muscle fibers in their arms due to constant propulsion of a wheelchair.

Multiple sclerosis results from the degeneration of the myelin sheath in random areas of the brain and spinal cord. As the myelin sheath degenerates, the function of the nerves is affected. The more areas that deteriorate, the greater the loss of muscle function.

Teaching Strategies

Keys to instructing the shoulder shrug (two-joint exercise):

• Correct technique for picking up the bar from the floor.
• Grip and grip placement.
• Stance.
• Controlled speed of movement.
• Shoulders should rotate slightly to the rear.

Teacher Support Notes

The trapezius muscle is subdivided into four different heads. The shoulder shrug effectively works two of the muscle heads. The other two heads are better worked by doing the bent-over row.

Lifting Technique Checklist *(continued)*

Shoulder Shrug Body area: shoulders.
Muscles: trapezius.
Variations: dumbbell.

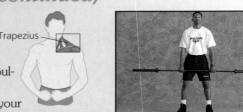

Trapezius

• To pick up the bar from the floor, assume shoulders'-width stance, with your feet flat.
• Bend your knees, not your waist. To place your hands on the bar, fully extend your arms.
• Your grip should be slightly wider than your shoulders and outside your knees.
• Your grip should be evenly spaced. Use a wraparound thumb grip.
• The bar should be close to your shins.
• Position your shoulders over the bar.
• Your back must stay flat. Keep your head up. Pull your shoulder blades together. Do not bend at the waist.
• Begin lifting by extending your legs, not your back.
• Move your hips forward, and raise your shoulders.
• Keep the bar close to your body, with your back and feet flat.
• Raise the bar until your knees are slightly bent and your arms are fully extended.
• Breathe out (exhale) during the lifting stage.
• Lift the bar by raising your shoulders toward your ears. Do not bend or pull with your arms.
• Hold this "shrug" position for 2 counts.
• Breathe out (exhale) during the lifting stage.
• Lower the bar slowly to your waist. Maintain control and speed. Keep your feet flat and your knees slightly bent.
• At the completion of the reps, return the bar to the floor. To protect your back, be sure that you use the same technique you used to pick up the bar to return the bar to the floor.

• **Figure 8.28** *Shoulder Shrug (barbell).*

Variation of Shoulder Shrug (dumbbell).

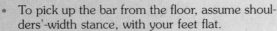

CRITICAL THINKING

Prior to this critical thinking activity, make sure students understand these two points:
1. How specific flexibility is to each joint.
2. Flexibility relates not only to activity levels but to lifestyle in general.
Divide the class into three groups:

1. Athletes,
2. Sedentary students,
3. Students who will volunteer to work on their flexibility each day for four weeks.
Test students before and at the end of the flexibility period, using three or four

Upright Row Body area: shoulders.
Muscles: deltoids, trapezius, biceps.
Variations: dumbbells.

Trapezius   Deltoids

Trapezius

- To pick up the bar from the floor, assume shoulders'-width stance, with feet flat.
- Bend your knees, not your waist. To place your hands on the bar, fully extend your arms.
- Your hands will grip 8 to 10 inches apart and be placed inside your legs.
- Your hands should be evenly spaced in the grip. Use a wraparound thumb grip.
- The bar should be close to your shins.
- Position your shoulders over the bar.
- Your back must stay flat. Keep your head up. Pull your shoulder blades together. Do not bend at the waist.
- Begin lifting by extending your legs, not your back.
- Move your hips forward, and raise your shoulders.
- Keep the bar close to your body, with your back and feet flat.
- Raise the bar until your knees are slightly bent and your arms are fully extended.
- Breathe out (exhale) during the lifting stage.
- Pull the bar upward along your stomach and chest toward your chin. Keep the bar close to your body.
- Continue to raise the bar until it is under your chin.
- Your elbows should be higher than your wrist and shoulders.
- Breathe out (exhale) during the lifting stage.
- Lower the bar slowly to your waist. Maintain control and speed. Keep your feet flat, with knees slightly bent.
- At the completion of the reps, return the bar to the floor. To protect your back, be sure to use the same technique you used to pick up the bar to return the bar to the floor.

- *Figure 8.29*
Upright Row (barbell).

- *Variation—Upright Row (dumbbells).*

(Continued on next page)

Teaching Strategies

Keys to instructing the upright row (two-joint exercise):

- Correct technique for picking up the bar from the floor.
- Grip and grip placement.
- Stance.
- Distance of the bar from the body.
- Height of bar at the top of the lift.
- Position of elbows.
- Avoid leaning backward at the top of the lift.
- Identify the muscles used.

basic tests such as sit and reach back saver, prone trunk lift, and shoulder extension. Tests need to measure the flexibility of several areas of the body.

Also, gather lifestyle information from students. Have students analyze their test results and draw conclusions.

Teaching Strategies

Keys to instructing the front dumbbell shoulder raise (one-joint exercise):

• Stance, if done from a standing position.
• Position of back.
• Speed of movement.
• Direction of dumbbell.
• Adequate room to lift the arms.
• Height of dumbbell.
• Specific part of muscle being used.

Teacher Support Notes

The front dumbbell shoulder raise is primarily used to isolate the front (anterior) head of the deltoid muscle.

Teaching Strategies

Keys to instructing the side (lateral) dumbbell shoulder raise (one-joint exercise):

• Consider the same concerns that were listed for the front dumbbell shoulder raise.

Teacher Support Notes

The side (lateral) dumbbell shoulder raise is primarily used to isolate the middle (medial) head of the deltoid muscle.

Lifting Technique Checklist *(continued)*

Front Dumbbell Shoulder Raise Body area: shoulders.
Muscles: front part of deltoids.
Variations: standing or sitting.

• Start in a standing position with feet shoulders'-width apart and head up.
• Hold a dumbbell in each hand, with arms hanging on each side of your body and elbows slightly bent.
• Slowly raise your arms in front of your body. Continue to raise your arms until your hands are level with your shoulders. Your arms must stay in front. (The exercise can be done by alternating arms or raising both arms at the same time.)
• Breathe out (exhale) during the lifting stage.
• Hold this position for 2 counts.
• Lower your arms slowly to the starting position. Maintain control and speed. Continue the reps.

• **Figure 8.30** *Front Dumbbell Shoulder Raise.*

Side (lateral) Dumbbell Shoulder Raise Body area: shoulders.
Muscles: middle part of deltoids.
Variations: standing or sitting.

• Start in a standing position, with feet shoulders'-width apart and head up.
• Hold a dumbbell in each hand, with arms hanging on each side of your body and elbows slightly bent.
• Slowly raise your arms to the side of your body. Continue to raise your arms until your hands are level with your shoulders. Keep your elbows level with your hands.
• As you raise your arms, rotate your wrists down and elbows up, as if you were pouring water out of a glass. (This exercise may be done by alternating arms or raising both at the same time.)

• **Figure 8.31** *Side (lateral) Dumbbell Shoulder Raise.*

Wellness Connection

Tell students that physical activity and exercise can have many health benefits. However, some exercises may be harmful and should be avoided. In the chart to the right are listed some potentially dangerous exercises with a suggested alternative exercise.

- Breathe out (exhale) during the lifting stage.
- Hold the position for 2 counts.
- Lower your arms slowly to the starting position. Maintain control and speed. Continue the reps.

Bent-over Dumbbell Shoulder Raise

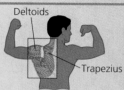

Body area: shoulders.
Muscle: back part of deltoid.
Variations: standing or sitting.

- Start in a standing position with feet shoulders'-width apart, knees slightly bent and head up.
- Hold a dumbbell in each hand with arms hanging on each side of your body.
- Bend your torso at the waist. Your arms should be hanging straight down.
- Slowly raise your arms upward, continue to raise your arms until your hands are almost level with your shoulders.
- Breathe out (exhale) during the lifting stage.
- Hold this position for 2 counts.
- Lower your arms slowly to a starting position. Maintain control and speed. Continue the reps.

• **Figure 8.32**   *Bent-over Dumbbell Shoulder Raise.*

Back

Bent-over Row Body area: upper back.
Muscles: latissimus dorsi, trapezius, biceps.
Caution: Weight belts may be necessary during maximum lifts.

- To pick up the bar from the floor, assume shoulders'-width stance, with feet flat.
- Bend your knees and waist to place your hands on the bar. Fully extend your arms.
- Your grip should be slightly wider than your shoulders and outside your knees.

(Continued on next page)

Potentially Dangerous	Alternative Exercise
1. Straight-leg sit-ups	1. Bent-leg sit-ups
2. Locked-knee toe touch	2. Bent-knee hang downs
3. Double leg lifts	3. Raised leg crunches
4. Full squats	4. Partial squats
5. Ballistic stretching	5. Passive stretching
6. Neck circling	6. Side neck stretches
7. Hands behind the head sit-up	7. Hands crossed on chest sit-up

Teaching Strategies

Keys to instructing the bent-over dumbbell shoulder raise (one-joint exercise):

- Consider the same concerns listed for front and side raises.
- Position of the back when torso is bent at waist.
- Position of head.

Teacher Support Notes

The bent-over dumbbell shoulder raise is primarily used to isolate the back (posterior) head of the deltoid. Parts of the trapezius muscle are also used.

Activity

Put the names of each exercise that have been taught in class on separate pieces of paper and put them into a container. Have students pick one exercise from the container and have them demonstrate the correct technique for that exercise. The rest of the class should determine if the correct technique was used and what muscles are involved.

Teaching Strategies

Keys to instructing the bent-over row (two-joint exercise):

Teacher Support Notes

The bent-over row can be performed with a side or narrow grip. With a narrow grip and the elbows close to the body, the latissimus dorsi muscle receives much of the stress. When the grip is wide and the elbows stay out, the trapezius and rear deltoids receive most of the stress.

This exercise requires the back to remain flat and in nearly a parallel position; therefore, it is recommended to use a belt.

A good variation of the exercise is the one-arm dumbbell bent-over row. This variation will allow for additional range of motion.

Teaching Strategies

Keys to instructing the back lat pulldown (two-joint exercise):

- Grip and grip placement.
- Position of head.
- Use of back muscles, not biceps.
- Position of bar at the bottom of the exercise.
- Speed of movement.
- Identification of the muscles used.

- Correct technique for picking up the weight from the floor.
- Position of back and head.
- Grip and grip placement.
- Stance and flex of knees.
- Speed of movement.
- Identification of the muscles used.

Lifting Technique Checklist *(continued)*

- Your hands should be evenly spaced in the grip. Use a wrap-around thumb grip.
- The bar should be close to your shins.
- Position your shoulders over the bar.
- Your back must stay flat. Keep your head up, and pull your shoulder blades together.
- Begin lifting by extending your legs until your back is slightly above a parallel position in relation to the floor. Keep your knees flexed and your back flat. Hold this position.
- With arms fully extended, pull the bar up and touch your lower chest or upper abdomen. Keep your elbows out.
- Breathe out (exhale) during the lifting stage.
- Keep your upper body and legs in a set position.
- Lower the bar slowly to the starting position. Maintain control and speed.
- At the completion of the reps, return the bar to the floor. Be sure to use the same technique you used to pick up the bar.

Figure 8.33 *Bent-over Row (free weight).*

Back Lat Pulldown Body area: midback.
Muscles: latissimus dorsi, trapezius, biceps.
Variations: Pull bar to front of chest (this exercise requires special apparatus).

- Grasp the bar with hands 7 to 8 inches wider apart than shoulders' width.
- Your hands should be evenly spaced in the grip. Use the wraparound thumb grip, with arms fully extended.
- Pull the bar straight down until you reach a kneeling position or sit in a chair.
- Your head and torso should remain in an upright position.
- Begin to pull the bar downward toward the back of the neck. Your back muscles, not your arms, should start the motion.

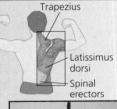
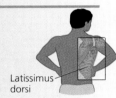

Trapezius
Latissimus dorsi
Spinal erectors
Latissimus dorsi

Figure 8.34 *Back Lat Pulldown (machine).*

COOPERATIVE LEARNING

Peer tutoring is a cooperative learning strategy that can have very positive results in the classroom. In peer tutoring, two students of differing ability levels are paired to work together. This strategy allows the more able student to give individualized instruction to the less able student, which benefits both students. Peer tutoring allows students opportunity for discussion, questioning, and interaction with peers.

In the strategy of paired reading, two students of differing ability levels are paired together to complete reading

- Continue to pull the bar downward until it touches the base of your neck. Keep your head and torso up. (In a variation, the bar would go to the front.)
- Breathe out (exhale) during the lifting stage.
- Allow the bar to return slowly to the starting position. Maintain control and speed. Continue the reps.

Straight-back Good Morning Body area: lower back.
Muscles: spinal erectors.
Caution: Spotters and light weights recommended.

- Assume shoulders'-width stance, with feet flat and head and shoulders up.
- Spotters will lift and place the bar across the back of your shoulders, not your neck. (The lifter could use a weight rack to position the bar.)
- Grasp the bar with hands slightly wider apart than shoulders' width.
- Your hands should be evenly spaced in the grip. Use a wraparound thumb grip.
- Slightly bend your knees. Lean forward by bending at the waist.
- Continue downward. Bend until your back is parallel to the floor. Keep your back and feet flat.
- Slowly return to the starting position. Maintain control and speed.
- Continue the reps. Have spotters remove the bar at the completion of the reps.

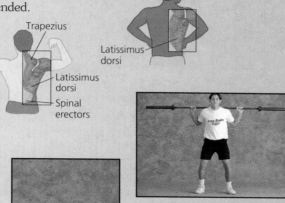

Figure 8.35 Straight-Back Good Morning.

Legs

Back Squat
Body area: front upper leg.
Muscles: quadriceps, gluteals, hamstrings.
Variations: Machine leg press.
Caution: Spotters and squat rack recommended; weight belt required.

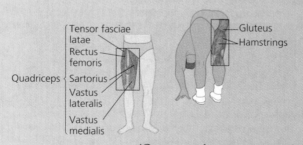

(Continued on next page)

(Continued on next page)

Teacher Support Notes

- There are many variations of the back lat pulldown. The bar may be pulled to the front with either a wide or narrow grip. Another variation is to slightly lean back.
- Wide and narrow grip chins can produce many of the same effects.
- The wider grip will reduce the stress of the biceps and isolate the lats better.

Teaching Strategies

Keys to instructing the straight-back good morning:

- Correct technique for picking up the weight from the floor.
- Placement of the weight on the shoulders.
- Flat back and parallel to floor.
- Flexed knees.
- Speed of movement.
- Identification of the muscles used.

Teacher Support Notes

- Good mornings require the weight to rest on the cervical area of the neck. For this reason, it is advised to place a towel or pad on the bar to cushion the neck.
- Because good mornings work the muscles of the lower back, it is strongly recommended that light weight be used to begin with. All movements should be done smoothly and slowly.

assignments. The higher-ability student is able to work individually with the lower-ability student in pronouncing words and comprehending the material read. Students might discuss the concepts or vocabulary in the selection read. Care needs to be taken in the pairing of students for this strategy. At times, higher-achieving students don't want to help lower-achieving students.

Dyad reading is another cooperative learning strategy that pairs students to complete a reading assignment. For this strategy, each student in the pair reads the material silently and then the pair spends time summarizing the material aloud, one partner at a time.

Teaching Strategies

Keys to instructing the back squat (multi-joint exercise):

- Belt on properly.
- Position of bar on shoulders.
- Straight back.
- Head position.
- Heels on the floor.
- Depth of knee bend.
- Breathing.
- Balance.
- Identification of the muscles used.

Teacher Support Notes

- The squat is one of the more popular exercises in the weight room. It is also one of the more dangerous exercises because of the heavier weight being used, and also for the often incorrect technique used.
- The weight belt is always required to provide support for the back. (See "Weight training Belts" in Section 5 of Chapter 7.)
- It is suggested that students do not go below a parallel squat, as they will put additional stress on the knees. Some students may be advised to do half squats.
- This might be a good exercise to have pre- and post-one-rep maximum to show improvement.
- It is not recommended that benches or chairs be used to determine the depth

Lifting Technique Checklist (continued)

- The bar should be positioned on the rack about shoulder high.
- Your hands should be slightly wider apart than your shoulders.
- Your hands should be evenly spaced. Use a wraparound thumb grip.
- Position your shoulders, hips, and feet under the bar.
- Place the bar across your shoulders (not on your neck).
- Pull your shoulders back. Straighten up your back and raise your chest, with your head up.
- Begin the lift by straightening your legs. (Spotters assist in removing the weight.)
- Take one step away from the rack, and assume shoulders'-width stance.
- Your feet should be lined up evenly and your toes slightly turned out. Your weight should be evenly distributed on your feet.
- Stabilize the bar before starting the downward motion. (Spotters should release the bar.)
- Slowly bend your knees and lower your hips. Keep your back flat. Do not lean forward.
- Continue to lower the bar until your thighs (quadriceps) are parallel to the floor. Do not bounce or hesitate at the bottom.
- Your knees must stay lined up with your feet. Do not let them point in or out.
- Your heels must stay on the floor. Do not lean forward on your toes.
- The bar is lifted by straightening your legs and hips.
- Your head and eyes are up, and your knees are aligned with your toes, and back is flat.
- Your feet are flat, with weight slightly more on the heels.
- Breathe out (exhale) during the lifting stage near the top of the lift.
- Slowly return to the starting position. Maintain control and speed.
- Continue the reps. Replace the bar on the rack. Never release your grip until the bar is safely in the rack. (Spotters should assist in replacing the bar.)

- **Figure 8.36**   Back Squat.

Leg Press (machine)—Works Quadriceps.

Across the Disciplines

World Cultures

There are thousands of arts and styles within the classical martial arts. The major martial arts dynasties originated in China, Japan, and Korea. Both armed and unarmed styles of martial arts required ancient warriors to possess both flexibility and strength.

China has a 2,000-year martial arts history. Chinese martial arts were practiced in secrecy for many centuries. That practice still exists to some extent.

In Japan, the hundreds of martial arts

Lunge Body area: leg.
Muscles: quadriceps, gluteals, hamstrings.
Variations: straight bar.
Caution: Spotters recommended.

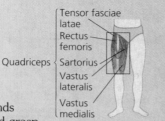
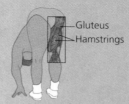

- Assume shoulders'-width stance, with feet flat on the floor and back straight.
- Bend your knees and waist to place your hands on the dumbbells. Fully extend your arms and grasp the dumbbells with a wraparound grip.
- Your hands should be slightly wider apart than your shoulders.
- Return to a standing position.
- Take one big step directly forward with your left leg.
- Your left foot should hit heel first and go to a flat position.
- Bend your left knee slowly to a parallel position. Your left knee should not go beyond your toes.
- Your right knee should slightly bend, but not touch the floor.
- Your back should remain straight. Do not lean forward at the waist.
- Return to the starting position by pushing back with your left leg.
- Breathe out (exhale) during the push stage. Do not hold your breath.
- Hesitate at the starting position. Then repeat the same task with your right leg.
- At the completion of the reps, return the dumbbells to the floor or rack.

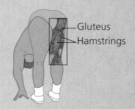

Figure 8.37 *Lunge (free weight).*

Leg Curl (machine) Body area: upper back leg.
Muscles: hamstring.

- Lie face down on the bench (machine).
- Keep your hips, legs, and chest flat on the bench.
- Your kneecaps should be past the end of the bench.
- Your hands should grasp the bench handles.

(Continued on next page)

of the squat. This can cause dangerous compression of the spine should the lifter hit the chair too hard.

- It may be advantageous for some students to place their heels on a raised board 1"–2" high. This may help their balance as they conduct a squat.

Teaching Strategies

Keys to instructing the lunge (multi-joint exercise):

- Correct technique for picking up the weight from the floor.
- Stance.
- Length of stride.
- Foot strike.
- Alternating legs.
- Depth of knee bend and position of front knee.
- Position of back.
- Balance.
- Identification of the muscles used.

Teacher Support Notes

- The lunge may be conducted with either a straight bar or dumbbells.
- Lunges may be used in conjunction with squats to develop the same muscles. The longer your stride, the greater the stress on the gluteus maximus. Shorter strides direct stress to the quads.
- Variations of the lunge done to either side are called side lunges.
- Be certain that this exercise is conducted on a non-slip surface.

and styles fall into two categories, the ancient Bujutsu (jitsu) and the 20th-century category, the Budo (do). The secrets of the feudal martial systems were zealously guarded by the ancient warriors, the Samurai.

The *forms* practiced in martial arts are known as *kata* (formal exercises) requiring strength, flexibility, agility, and endurance. Students may know these kata as karate, tae kwon do, and kung-fu.

Discuss with students their understanding of the formal exercises of martial arts in relation to strength, flexibility, and agility. Assign groups of students to research some of the movements to demonstrate to the class.

Teaching Strategies

Keys to instructing the leg curl (one-joint exercise):

• Position of body on the bench, kneecaps and heels on pads.
• Hip movement.
• Range of motion.
• Speed of movement.
• Identification of the muscles used.

Teacher Support Notes

• The leg curl will require the use of a special apparatus. Most versions are the prone style, but the standing variation is effective.
• The hamstring muscles are usually much weaker than the quadriceps. Students will need to use less weight for these muscles.

Teaching Strategies

Keys to instructing the leg extension (one-joint exercise):

• Position of upper body and pad on ankle.
• Range of motion.
• Speed of motion.
• Identification of the muscles used.

Teacher Support Notes

The leg extension is a great quadriceps isolation exercise. It is used by many lifters to provide muscle separation in the quads.

Lifting Technique Checklist (continued)

• Position the back of your ankle on the roller pads.
• Begin the lift by flexing your knees. Raise the pads to your buttocks.
• Your hips must remain in contact with the bench.
• Breathe out (exhale) during the pull stage. Do not hold your breath.
• Slowly lower the roller pad to the starting position and continue the reps.

• **Figure 8.38**   *Leg Curl (machine).*

Leg Extension (machine) Body area: front upper leg. Muscles: quadriceps.

• Sit in an upright position on the bench with your head up.
• Your back is flat, and your grip is on the handles.
• Place your upper ankle under the roller pad.
• Raise the roller pad by extending your legs at the knee.
• Extend your legs completely, and hold for 2 counts.
• Breathe out (exhale) during the push stage. Do not hold your breath.
• Slowly lower the pad to the starting position.
• Your back and buttocks must stay in contact with the bench.
• Continue the reps.

Tensor fasciae latae
Rectus femoris
Sartorius
Vastus lateralis
Vastus medialis

Quadriceps

• **Figure 8.39**   *Leg Extension (machine).*

CRITICAL THINKING

Developing muscular strength and/or endurance can be a costly venture whether you intend to purchase free weights or one of the new exercise devices on the market. And not everyone can afford membership in a health club. What options are open to an individual?

There are several options if a person chooses to be creative.

Give students a list of common items found around the house (or in someone's junk pile!). Have them create strength training exercises using these items. Items can include:

Standing Heel Raise Body area: lower leg.
Muscle: gastrocnemius.

- The bar should be positioned on the rack about shoulder high.
- Your grip width should be slightly wider than your shoulders' width.
- Your hands should be evenly spaced in the grip. Use a wraparound thumb grip.
- Place the bar across your shoulders (not on your neck).
- Your feet should be 8 to 10 inches apart. Place the balls of your feet on a raised surface 1½ to 2 inches high.
- Lock out your knees (straight not flexed).
- Push up on your toes to raise your heels to their highest position.
- Breathe out (exhale) during the push stage. Do not hold your breath.
- Slowly lower your heels until they touch the floor, and continue the reps.
- Replace the bar in the rack.

• *Figure 8.40* *Standing Heel Raise (free weight).*

Arms

Arm Curl Body area: front of upper arm.
Muscles: biceps.
Variation: dumbbells.

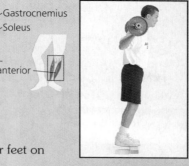

- Assume shoulders'-width stance, with feet flat on the floor.
- Bend your knees, not your waist, to place your hands on the bar.
- Your grip should be the width of your hips.
- Your grip should be evenly spaced. Use a wraparound thumb grip, with palms up.
- Keep your back flat, and straighten your legs to stand up.
- In your starting position, your knees should be slightly bent and your arms fully extended in front.
- Keep your elbows in a stationary position at your side.
- Raise the bar by flexing your arm at the elbow. Raise the bar until your upper and lower arms are squeezed together.

(Continued on next page)

1. milk jugs/cartons
2. jump rope
3. paint cans
4. bat
5. balls
6. gardening tools
7. pieces of wood
8. chain
9. rubber tires/inner tubes

Then have each student bring in two items from around the house or neighborhood that could be used to create an exercise device. Once these items are brought, divide the class into four groups. Give each group several items. Each group must develop an exercise routine using those items. Then groups must share with the class.

Teaching Strategies

Keys to instructing the standing heel raise (one-joint exercise):

- Position of feet on platform.
- Balance.
- Speed of movement.
- Identification of the muscles used.

Teacher Support Notes

- Variations of the standing heel raise can be accomplished by changing the direction of the toes. They may be pointed out, straight, or in.
- It is also suggested that a large amount of reps be done for this muscle.

Teaching Strategies

Keys to instructing the arm curl (one-joint exercise):

- Correct technique for picking up the weight from the floor.
- Stance.
- Grip and grip position.
- Position of elbows.
- Back movement.
- Range of motion.
- Speed of movement.
- Identification of the muscle used.

Teacher Support Notes

• The E-Z curl bar has bends in it that allow for a more comfortable grip and muscle contraction.

• The biceps curl is one of the most popular exercises in the weight room and has many variations. Variations include the use of dumbbells in a variety of ways, such as alternating curls, concentration curls, hammer curls, and preacher curls.

Teaching Strategies

Keys to instructing the French press (one-joint exercise):

• Correct technique for picking up weight from the floor.
• Stance.
• Movement of the shoulder.
• Position of elbows.
• Speed of movement.
• Identification of the muscle used.

Teacher Support Notes

• If the elbows are allowed to move away from their position near the ears during the French press, the result will be an increase in the stress on the deltoid instead of the intended triceps.
• A specially designed bar is often used in this exercise to provide comfort and the ability to use both arms at once.

Lifting Technique Checklist (continued)

• Keep your back flat and straight. Do not swing your body.
• Breathe out (exhale) during the lifting stage. Do not hold your breath.
• Slowly lower the bar to the starting position. Continue the reps.

• **Figure 8.41**   *Arm Curl.*

French Press Body area: back of upper arm.
Muscle: triceps.
Variation: dumbbells.

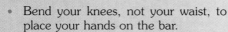

• Assume shoulders'-width stance, with feet flat on the floor.
• Bend your knees, not your waist, to place your hands on the bar.
• Your grip should be 6 inches apart in the middle of the bar. Use a wraparound thumb grip.
• Keep your back flat, and straighten your legs to stand up.
• Raise the bar over your head, with arms fully extended and knees slightly bent.
• The area from the shoulder to the elbow should stay in this position throughout the exercise.
• Slowly lower the bar to the back of your neck by bending your arm at the elbow.
• Keep your elbows close to your head and near your ears.
• When the bar touches the back of your neck, return the bar to the overhead position by straightening your arms.
• Do not allow your elbows to move away from your ears.
• Breathe out (exhale) during the pushing stage; do not hold your breath.
• Continue the reps.

• **Figure 8.42**   *French Press.*

• *Variation of French Press (dumbbells).*

Wellness Connection

There are a number of health concerns that are associated with obesity. Heart disease, high blood pressure, atherosclerosis, and stroke are more common in obese persons. Liver disorders, gallbladder disease, respiratory problems, and diabetes are also seen in a higher incidence.

The burden of extra fat puts a strain on the skeletal system. Arthritis is more common, particularly in the hips, knees, and lower spine. The more weight a person carries, the greater the wear and tear on the joints. This wear and tear

Dumbbell Kickback Body area: back of upper arm.
Muscle: triceps.

- Assume shoulders'-width stance, with feet flat on the floor and knees slightly bent.
- Bend over at the waist until your upper body is parallel to the floor.
- Extend one arm, and place your hand on a bench or chair for balance.
- Place the dumbbell in your other hand. Use a wraparound thumb grip, with your palm facing your leg.
- Raise the dumbbell to your waist. Bend your arm at the elbow so that your upper arm is parallel to the floor and your lower arm is perpendicular to the floor.
- Straighten your elbow until your arm is straight. Do not move the position of your elbow in relation to your waist.
- Breathe out (exhale) during the lifting stage; do not hold your breath.
- Slowly lower the dumbbell to the starting position. Do not swing your arm.
- Continue the reps, and then switch arms.

Deltoid
Triceps

• **Figure 8.43**
Dumbbell Kickback.

Abdominals

Abdominal Crunch Body area: stomach.
Muscles: abdominals.
Variations: incline bench, raised feet, machines.

- Lie face up on a mat or carpet floor. Your back and buttocks should be flat on the surface.
- Your knees should be bent. Position your feet flat on the floor with your heels twelve to eighteen inches from your buttocks.
- Place your hands and arms across your chest. Your hands should be placed near the opposite shoulders.
- Position your chin in a tucked position which allows your chin to touch your chest.
- Contract your abdominal muscles and raise your torso until your elbows contact your upper thigh.

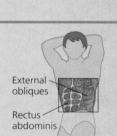

External
obliques

Rectus
abdominis

(Continued on next page)

Teaching Strategies

Keys to instructing the dumbbell kickback:

- Stance.
- Back parallel to floor.
- Position of elbow.
- Movement of shoulder.
- Arm extension.
- Speed of movement.
- Identification of the muscle used.

Keys to instructing the abdominal crunch:

- Provide a safe surface for this exercise.
- Knees bent.
- Position of hands.
- Range of motion.
- Identification of the muscles used.

Teacher Support Notes

There are many exercises that can be used to work the abdominal area. These exercises may be targeted for specific areas of the abdominals, such as upper or lower abs.

can cause pain that results in even less physical activity and the risk of additional weight gain. Low-back pain is also more common in people who are obese.

Surgical procedures on obese persons involve an increased risk, and postsurgical complications such as infection are also increased. In addition, anesthetic risk is increased due to obesity.

Overweight mothers tend to have a higher infant and maternal mortality rate.

Finally, cancer is more prevalent in obese persons. Men who are obese tend to have a higher incidence of cancer in the colon, rectum, and prostate. In women who are obese, there is a higher incidence of cancer in the ovaries, uterus, cervix, and breasts.

Teaching Strategies

Keys to instructing the twisting abdominal crunch:

• Consider the same concerns listed for the abdominal crunch.
• Range of motion during twist.

Activities

• Prepare questions on note cards. The note cards should include questions about exercises, equipment, muscles, and rules for the weight room. Place these questions throughout the weight room and have students go to each question station to answer the questions. This can serve as either an introductory quiz or an end-of-course evaluation.
• Students will use the Active Mind/Active Body on page 295 to design a three-week personal workout schedule.

Lifting Technique Checklist *(continued)*

• Breathe out (exhale) when your elbows contact your thighs.
• Slowly return to the starting position. Do not let your chin lose contact with your chest. Your head should not touch the floor.
• Repeat the process until the reps are completed.

• *Figure 8.44*   *Abdominal Crunch.*

Twisting Abdominal Crunch Body area: stomach.
Muscles: abdominals, obliques.
Variations: incline bench, raised feet.

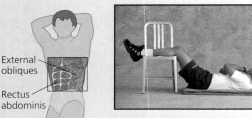
External obliques
Rectus abdominis

• Lie face up on a mat or carpet floor. Your back and buttocks should be flat on the surface.
• Your knees should be bent. Position your feet flat on the floor with your heels twelve to eighteen inches from your buttocks.
• Place your hands and arms across your chest. Your hands should be placed near the opposite shoulders.
• Keep your chin in a tucked position, which allows your chin to touch your chest.
• Contract your abdominal muscles and raise your torso from the floor. Continue to raise your torso until your elbows are near your thighs.

• *Figure 8.45*   *Twisting Abdominal Crunch.*

• Twist your torso to the left and touch your right elbow to your left thigh. If possible, extend your right elbow past the left thigh.
• Breathe out (exhale) when your elbow contacts your thigh.
• Slowly return to the starting position. Do not let your chin lose contact with your chest. Your head should not touch the floor.
• Start the process again, but twist the torso to the right side touching your left elbow to your right thigh.
• Slowly return to the starting position.
• Repeat the process until the reps are completed.

CULTURAL DIVERSITY

Scotland

Scots have a long tradition of sports, going back to the 12th century when golf was invented. Today, Scotland boasts more than 400 courses, many of them hilly and located along scenic coastlines.

Strenuous walking is required, but golf is inexpensive to play here and open to anyone who is interested.

Soccer is sometimes called Scotland's true religion. Professional teams have ardent fans who follow the season from October through May. Amateur teams

Designing Your Personal Weight-training Program

This activity will guide you in designing a program geared to your own needs and goals. Using the following list of program components and the record keeping chart in Figure 8.46, create a three-week workout schedule that will meet your weight-training goals.

Program Components:

1. Your goals (hypertrophy, strength, endurance, and so on).

2. Which days of the week (three days or four days).

3. Which exercises (upper or lower body; big or small muscles).

4. The order of exercises (push-pull or big-small).

5. The weight arrangement (pyramid or same load).

6. Number of reps (based on intensity, such as 60, 75, or 85 percent of maximum).

7. Number of sets (1 to 3 or 4 to 5).

8. Length of rest periods between sets (20 to 30 seconds, 30 to 90 seconds, or 2 to 3 minutes).

9. How to vary the program from week to week.

Weight Training: Daily Workout Design Chart

Day of the Week _____ Week # _____

Body Part	Set x Rep. x Weight	Exercise
Chest		
Shoulder		
Triceps		
Legs		
Back		
Biceps		
Abdominals		

• **Figure 8.46** *Weight Training: Daily Workout Design Chart.*

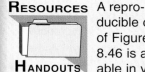

• Have students use their record sheets, their maximum scores, and their goals to design their workouts.

• Students should use each of the suggested components listed in the Active Mind/Active Body activity.

RESOURCES A reproducible copy of Figure 8.46 is available in your Teacher Resource Package.

HANDOUTS

Assess

Use the Active Mind/Active Body activities on page 277 and this page to assess students' progress. Physical demonstrations and lab activities may also be used to assess students' progress. Then use the Section 6 Review questions on the next page to assess students' comprehension of the concepts presented in Section 6.

---

are plentiful, and most children play soccer at school. Rugby football is not quite as popular and is primarily an amateur sport, yet many boys aspire to be famous players.

Two uniquely Scottish sports are curling and shinty. Curling is played on an ice rink and involves sliding round, flat, polished granite stones toward a target.

Each player has a long-handled broom to sweep the ice clean in front of the stones as they travel. Rarely played outside of Scotland, shinty is a rough game similar to field hockey and is often called the fastest game in the world. It has survived centuries of play without discernible rules and is noted for the allowed free use of the stick, or *caman*.

Close

Have students discuss what their favorite exercises are and why.

SECTION 6 REVIEW

Answer the following questions on a separate sheet of paper:

1. List seven upper body weight-training exercises.
2. List six lower body weight-training exercises.

SUMMARY

Weight training is a great way to improve and maintain your muscular strength and endurance. Once you have learned how to design reasonable and obtainable goals you can begin your workouts. Properly designed long- and short-term goals can also help you stick to your workout plans.

Your choice of a weight-training partner is an important consideration. This person should be a friend, a motivator, and a spotter. Your partner's interest and attitude can have an effect on your success. You and your partner need to know safety and correct technique in the weight room.

Because weight training is directed at the muscles of your body, you should be able to identify and explain which muscles are being exercised during your workouts. How the exercises are organized is an important consideration for your muscle development. Organizing your exercises in a variety of ways can keep your workouts intense and prevent workout boredom. Properly designed workouts will allow adequate recovery time between sets, exercises, and workouts.

You should occasionally conduct strength evaluations on a variety of your muscles. These evaluations should be conducted safely and correctly. Your strength evaluations can both motivate you and help you determine your workout training loads.

As you become more experienced with weight training, you may want to try more advanced programs. Specific programs like supersets, pyramids, and compound sets are designed for specific results. Your goals and desires will help you determine which program to use and how often you should use each one.

Which program you use is subject to change, but correct lifting technique is not. There is only one correct way to lift weights. Never sacrifice correct form while attempting to lift heavy weights. Not everyone has the same type of equipment; therefore, it is necessary that you clearly understand how to conduct a variety of exercises with a variety of equipment.

Weight training is an activity that you can do the rest of your life. The skills and knowledge that you have gained in this chapter and Chapter 7 should provide you with the confidence and ability to establish and revise your own program to fit your changing needs and goals.

Across the Disciplines

Literature

Overweight adolescents may believe that they are the only teenagers who are teased by their peers about their physical appearance or abilities. The obese or overweight teenager is often negatively portrayed in films. The character is often ridiculed for gluttonous behavior in the cafeteria, excluded from peer groups because of their physical appearance, and taunted by athletes as well as the coach during gym class. Changing students' misconceptions about obesity,

Chapter 8 Review

True/False

On a separate sheet of paper, mark each question below either T for True or F for False.

1. Setting realistic goals can determine the success of your weight-training workouts.
2. Safety is always the most important factor in the weight room.
3. It is not necessary to use a wraparound thumb grip on all lifts.
4. Reps are the basic unit of any workout plan.
5. It is usually a good idea to work your smaller muscles first so that you will be warmed up when you go to the large muscles.
6. Pretesting your maximum strength can help you plan your goals and workouts.
7. Muscle strength can best be developed with heavy weights and low numbers of repetitions.
8. Muscles should recover during twenty-four hours of rest before they are worked again in the weight room.
9. Negative workouts are for strength development, but they should not be used often.
10. Supersets should work antagonistic muscles.

Multiple Choice

1. Christen is considering a weight-training program. Which of the following should she consider before developing her goals?
   a. her current level of strength
   b. her daily schedule
   c. past injuries
   d. all of the above
   e. a and c only

2. Which of the following muscle combinations are not considered main muscle areas of the body?
   a. neck and back
   b. chest and shoulder
   c. legs and arms
   d. abdominals and arms

3. Pat has designed a workout with the following order of exercises: bench press, lunge, shoulder press, squat, bent-over row, leg extension. Which of the following best describes this order of exercises?
   a. push versus pull
   b. strongest muscles versus weakest muscles
   c. upper body versus lower body
   d. large muscles versus small muscles

4. Weight room safety includes which of the following rules?
   a. do not hold your breath
   b. control the speed of weights at all times
   c. use proper technique at all times
   d. all of the above
   e. a and c only

5. Which of the following is *not* a responsibility of the spotter?
   a. stay in a ready position at all times
   b. motivate your partner
   c. correct improper technique
   d. determine how much weight your partner should use

6. Paige is interested in improving her muscle tone and endurance. Which of the following plans should she put in her program?
   a. 2 to 3 sets of 12 to 20 reps
   b. 2 to 3 sets of 8 to 12 reps
   c. 3 to 5 sets of 4 to 6 reps
   d. 1 to 2 sets of 7 to 10 reps

Answers

True/False

1. T
2. T
3. F
4. T
5. F
6. T
7. T
8. F
9. T
10. T

Multiple Choice

1. d
2. a
3. c
4. d
5. d
6. a
7. d
8. a
9. d
10. b

learning what is an acceptable body composition level for an individual, and acquiring compassion for the overweight or obese teenager can begin in this personal fitness course.

The subjects of obesity and weight are addressed in some entertaining and well-written books for adolescents. Readers are encouraged to discover all of the potential and abilities others may possess by looking beyond their exteriors. You may wish to choose passages or chapters from some of these books to read to the class or to suggest as supplemental reading: *Weight: A Teenage Concern,* by Elaine Landau, and *Underneath I'm Different,* by Ellan Rabinowich.

Discussion

1. Specific weights will vary but should show an increase of weight and a reduction in reps at each level of the five-stage pyramid. Specific weights will vary but should show two antagonistic muscles being worked for 8–10 reps with no rest between the sets. An example could be French press for 8–10 reps followed by arm curls for 8–10 reps with no rest between sets. This process would be conducted three times.

2. Answers will vary but may include any of the following for common grip exercises: arm curls, bench press, incline press, bent-over row, front shoulder press, back shoulder press, and shrugs.

Answers will vary but may include any of the following for the narrow grip: upright row, arm curls, and French press.

3. *a.* Assist the lifters with the weight if needed.

b. Correct incorrect lifting technique.

c. Be a motivator.

d. Keep weights put away for safety.

e. Communicate with the lifter about the number of reps.

f. Be alert at all times. All of these enhance safety and success in the weight room.

Chapter 8 Review

7. Recovery time for muscles is important at which of the following times?

  a. between sets

  b. between exercises

  c. between workouts

  d. all of the above

  e. a and c only

8. A split-week workout would use which of the following routines?

  a. Monday, Tuesday, Thursday, Friday (off Wednesday, Saturday, and Sunday)

  b. Monday, Wednesday, and Friday (off Tuesday, Thursday, Saturday, and Sunday)

  c. Sunday, Tuesday, and Thursday (off Monday, Wednesday, Saturday, and Sunday)

  d. Monday, Wednesday, Friday, and Sunday (off Tuesday, Thursday, and Saturday)

9. Tony wants to use the compound set program for more muscle mass. Which routine would he choose?

  a. bench press, no rest, bench press

  b. arm curls, no rest, french press

  c. squats, no rest, arm curls

  d. any of the above

10. Which of the following exercises does not work the chest?

  a. bench press

  b. french press

  c. incline press

  d. flat bench fly

Discussion

1. Design and explain a five-set pyramid workout for the bench press. Choose your own weight. Then design and explain a three-set superset workout for the arms. Choose your own weight.

2. Identify three weight-training exercises that require the use of the common grip and three that require the use of the narrow grip.

3. Identify and explain six techniques used by spotters. Why are these techniques necessary in the weight room?

CRITICAL THINKING

Body composition, especially the amount of fat tissue a person has, is more of a concern now than ever before. Obviously, this is more of a concern for adults than for teens, as statistics show the average American gains weight as he or she ages.

Have students interview their parents and at least one other adult. They should gather the following information regarding weight:

a. how it has changed with age.

b. health problems they have had associated with weight gain.

Vocabulary Experience

Match the correct term in Column A to the definition in Column B by writing the appropriate number in each blank.

Column A

_____ repetition

_____ split workout

_____ superset method

_____ recovery time

_____ negative workout method

_____ set

Column B

1. Using very heavy weights at the end of a prescribed number of sets and repetitions.

2. A group of consecutive repetitions for any exercise.

3. Time or rest between exercises.

4. Workout requiring you to use two different exercises that train opposing muscles without rest between sets.

5. Completed execution of an exercise one time.

6. High intensity workout that exercises one half of your body at each workout session.

Critical Thinking

1. Identify five components of record keeping, and explain why keeping records is important to your weight-training program.

2. Explain how you can determine your estimated one-repetition maximum.

3. Explain how you can apply each of the following plans when arranging the order of exercises in your workout:
   a. Large muscles versus small muscles.
   b. Push versus pull.
   c. Upper body versus lower body.
   d. Strong muscles versus weak muscles.

Vocabulary Experience

_5_ repetition
_6_ split workout
_4_ superset method
_3_ recovery time
_1_ negative workout method
_2_ set

Critical Thinking

1. *a.* Frequency of workouts—How often do you work out in a week?
   b. How many sets, reps, and the amount of weight.
   c. Specific exercises.
   d. Duration of workout—How long did the workout last?
   e. Eating habits.
   f. Personal best.
   g. Illnesses.
   Weight training records can show improvement, and can help you plan future workouts.
2. You can estimate your maximum strength by doing multiple reps with a predetermined amount of weight. Then use the chart in Figure 8.11 to estimate your maximum strength.
3. *a.* Do a set of bench press, followed by a set of bench fly.
   b. Do a set of shoulder press, followed by a set of arm curl, followed by a set of French press.
   c. Do a set of bent-over row, followed by a set of squats, followed by a set of lat pull.
   d. If you have weak back muscles, you would need to work the back first while you have the most energy.

It would also be helpful in this activity if each student could interview someone who has lost a considerable amount of weight and what impact that loss has had on his or her overall wellness. Have all age groups represented:
a. 20–30 years old
b. 31–40 years old
c. 41–50 years old
d. 51+ years old
Students should do two things with the information gathered:
1. Chart/graph the incidence of health problems with age and weight gain.
2. Summarize and draw conclusions from information collected.

Chapter Overview

Chapter 9 is 30 pages long and divided into the five sections listed to the right. Major learning outcomes of the chapter are also listed to the right. Briefly, this chapter introduces students to the basics of body composition. It emphasizes the scientific principles of exercise that students should learn to use in developing and maintaining a healthy body composition. It also provides students with additional methods to evaluate their body composition.

Teacher Resource Material

In the Teacher Resource Package accompanying the textbook, you will find the following materials to help you teach this chapter.

Activity Sheets

One Reteaching Worksheet is provided in the Teacher Resource Package for each section of this chapter. A handout is also provided for the Fitness Check activity on page 316.

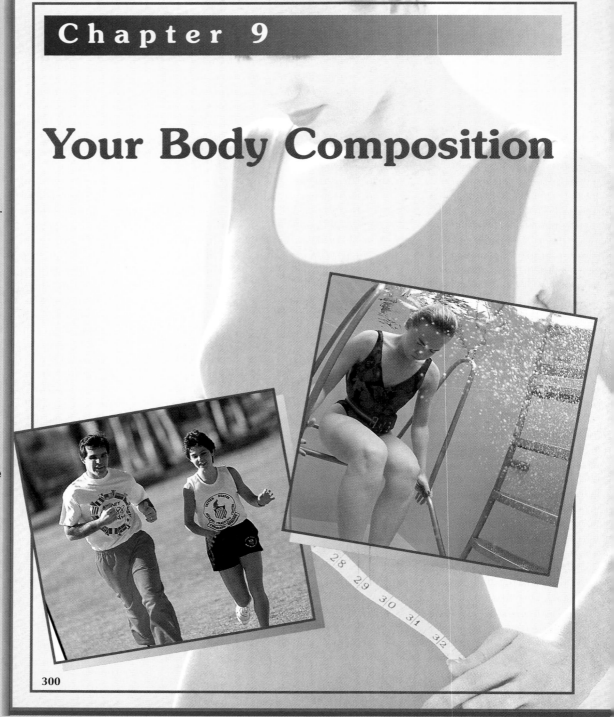

Chapter 9

Your Body Composition

300

PACING CHART

You could easily spend five days teaching this chapter if students read the entire chapter, do the Active Mind/Active Body and Fitness Check activities and complete several of the handouts from the Teacher Recource Package. However, you can cover the material in this chapter in three days. It is recommended that physical activity be a regular part of each class period (20 to 30 minutes minimum). Following are some examples of how to cover the main topics in the chapter if you are pressed for time.

Contents

1. The Basics of Body Composition
2. Factors That Influence Your Body Composition
3. Body Composition Evaluations
4. Developing and Maintaining a Healthy Body Composition
5. Controlling Your Weight and Body Composition Safely

Outcomes

After reading and studying this chapter, you will be able to:

1. Explain how body composition is important and contributes to the development and maintenance of moderate to high levels of personal fitness.
2. Discuss how developing and maintaining acceptable levels of lean and fat body tissue can reduce your risk for functional health problems.
3. List and describe body composition evaluations that you could use to assess your body composition now and in the future.
4. Identify and explain strategies you can use to influence your body composition in a positive way.
5. Identify and explain how to control your body weight and body composition safely.

Key Terms

After reading and studying this chapter, you will be able to understand and provide practical definitions for the following terms:

somatotype	lean body weight	metabolic rate
ectomorph	underfat	resting metabolic rate
mesomorph	overfat	(RMR)
endomorph	ideal body weight	eating disorders
essential fat	energy balance	anorexia nervosa
excessive leanness	caloric input	bulimia
diabetes mellitus	caloric expenditure	

Transparencies/Masters

A transparency or master is provided in the Teacher Resource Package for each of the following figures: 9.1, 9.2, 9.3, 9.4, 9.5, 9.6, 9.7, 9.8, 9.9, 9.10, 9.11, 9.12, 9.13, 9.14, 9.15, 9.16.

Discuss the Photo

Ask students what they think of when they look at the photo on this page. How many of their answers reflect a concern with body composition? Ask how students feel about their own body composition and what pressure society puts on them in this area. Also ask students if they can guess how the photo of the girl under water is related to a chapter about body composition.

CHAPTER 9

Time	Suggestions
Day 1	Assign students to read Sections 1 and 2 prior to class. In class, discuss the basis of body composition and factors that influence it. Also include a variety of discussion about photos and figures.
Day 2	Have students do the Fitness Check activity on page 316. Then have them interpret their body composition using Figure 9.11.
Day 3	Assign students to read Sections 3 and 4 prior to class. Discuss with students how to develop and maintain a healthy body composition and how to recognize and avoid behaviors associated with eating disorders.

Focus

Outcome

In **Section 1** students will learn:

1. To explain how body composition is important and how it contributes to the development and maintenance of moderate to high levels of personal fitness.

Focus Activities

1. Discuss the concepts of body type and body composition.

2. Discuss how body composition is related to functional health.

INTRODUCTION

In Chapter 1 you learned that body composition is determined by the ratio of water, bone, muscle, and fat in your body. When you look around your personal world, you have probably noticed that "thin is in." The images we see in media advertisements emphasize lean, attractive people. Have you noticed that thin people, not overweight people, are the ones typically trying to sell us all types of products, from toothpaste to exercise equipment?

Physical appearance is important to us all, but it is important that you learn about factors that can influence your own body composition and how you can have an impact on it as you age. It is very difficult, and sometimes unhealthy, for you to try to look as lean and attractive as many of the celebrities that you might idolize. Therefore, it is important for you to learn how participation in regular physical activity or exercise, along with the development of proper nutrition behaviors, can help you make significant changes in your body composition. By learning more about body composition, you will be able to develop realistic mental and physical images of what your body composition can and should be.

In this chapter you will learn about the basics of body composition and the factors that influence body composition. You will study examples of body composition self-evaluations, learn how to develop and maintain healthy body composition levels, and understand the facts about controlling your weight and your body composition safely.

SECTION 1   The Basics of Body Composition

somatotype

the type of body you have in terms of your body composition related to heredity.

If you look around your school, you will notice students and teachers of all sizes and shapes, or body types. Everybody's body type is based, at least in part, on genetics. When you grow to adulthood, you will probably look very similar to your parents. However, you will still have some ability to control your body composition as you age.

Your Body Type

ectomorph

a slender, lean somatotype.

Your body type is determined by the mixture of your bones, muscles, connective tissues, and the amount of body fat you carry. Your **somatotype** is the type of body you have in terms of your body composition related to heredity. You are either small, medium, or large in size. You are also slender and lean (**ectomorph**), muscular (**mesomorph**), or heavier and rounder (**endomorph**). See Figure 9.1. Your somatotype provides a general description of your body composition, although most people are a combination of body types.

mesomorph

a muscular somatotype.

ABILITY LEVELS

BELIEVE IT? ...
OR **N**OT?

It is estimated that over 33 percent of the adult population is obese, and the numbers are increasing.

See page 318 for answer.

endomorph

a heavier, rounder somatotype.

essential fat

the minimum amount of body fat necessary for good health.

excessive leanness

a percentage of body fat that is too low for good health.

diabetes mellitus

a chronic disease affecting the blood sugar.

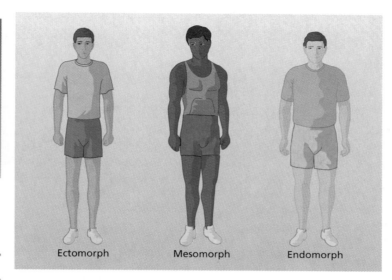

| Ectomorph | Mesomorph | Endomorph |

• **Figure 9.1**   *General Body Types: Ectomorph, Mesomorph, and Endomorph.*

It is important that you have an essential amount of fat without having too much fat. **Essential fat** is the minimum amount of body fat necessary for good health. Adolescent males need at least 7 percent body fat. Adolescent females need about 12 percent.

Essential fat helps insulate your body against cold weather and helps cushion your internal organs to protect them from injury. Essential fat also provides you with a valuable source of stored energy so that you can meet your body's need for fuel. Having a percentage of body fat that is too low (**excessive leanness**) or too high (obesity), can be unhealthy.

Body Composition and Your Functional Health

Figure 9.2 illustrates the relationship between carrying too little or too much body weight (and fat) and the risk for developing chronic diseases for adults. The *J* shape of the curve means that those who weigh the least and are excessively lean (those with low essential body fat), as well as those who weigh the most and who are obese (those with excessive body fat) have the greatest risks for developing chronic diseases such as hypertension, heart disease, colon cancer, and **diabetes mellitus**.

Although your weight can influence your functional health, too many people are overly concerned about how much they weigh.

Teach & Apply

Discussion

• Ask students how they feel about the quote, "Thin is in." Is it true or false?
• Use Figure 9.1 to discuss with students the concept of somatotype. Ask them if they can generally categorize body shapes and types. Explain to them that body composition is related, at least in part, to genetics. You can set the tone for the class to control the teasing of others because of their body types or sizes. You can promote acceptance of a variety of body shapes by educating students about these concepts.

Teacher Support Notes

The amounts of essential fat recommended for adolescents are greater than that for adults. Adolescents are still growing and developing and need to maintain

Enrichment

This activity will allow you to provide a more challenging learning experience for some of your students.

Have the students present evidence that the following statement is valid: "Overfat is more important than overweight in determining a person's level of health and personal fitness." You may want to have students do this activity early in their study of the chapter, and then again after they have completed the chapter. They can, of course, use the information in this text to support the statement. It is suggested that you require them to provide evidence from at least one outside source.

these levels for good health. As you well know, they can experience significant changes in height and weight in a single semester. The recommended amounts of 7% (for adolescent males) and 12% (for adolescent females) essential fat are based on the research conducted by Dr. Timothy Lohman from the University of Arizona.

Teaching Strategies

The x-axis showing percentages of normal weight in Figure 9.2 may be hard for students to understand. If so, simply tell them that if they are 20–30 pounds *lighter or heavier* than normal, they may be at higher risk for chronic disease late in life. (The concept of percent of normal weight on the x-axis is used frequently by epidemiologists.)

Teacher Support Notes

In mature adults, ideal body weight can be calculated and is a useful way to provide adults with goals for reducing their body fat levels. However, it is too difficult to predict ideal weight in adolescents to be useful for setting realistic goals. The authors have included the concept for educational purposes. Students can then apply the concepts later in adulthood.

BELIEVE IT? ... OR NOT?

You can lose weight most effectively by going on a diet of less than 1,000 calories per day.

See page 318 for answer.

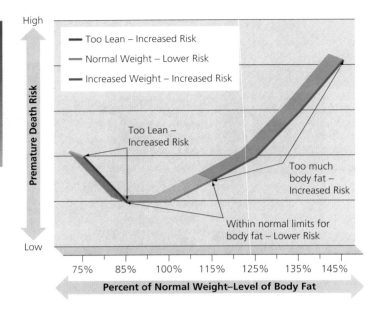

• *Figure 9.2*   *Body Composition and Risk for Chronic Diseases.*

lean body weight

the weight of the bones, muscles, and connective tissue.

underfat

carrying too little body fat.

overfat

carrying too much body fat.

Weight is a poor indicator of your total body composition and really tells you nothing about how lean or fat you are. In reality, when you compare two people of the same size, one may simply weigh more because he or she has more bone, muscle, and connective tissue weight (**lean body weight**) than the other person.

It is more important for you to be concerned about your body composition—particularly the ratio of your lean body weight to your percentage of body fat—than about how much you weigh. Your percentage of body fat can be calculated by using the following equations:

Your body fat weight = Your total body weight − Your lean body weight.

$$\text{Your percentage of body fat} = \frac{\text{Your body fat weight}}{\text{Your total body weight}}.$$

By monitoring your body composition on a regular basis (every 3 to 6 months), you can determine whether your body composition is *within normal limits* (WNL) for good health. For example, adolescent males should carry between 7 and 19 percent body fat, and adolescent females should carry between 12 and 24 percent body fat to be WNL for healthy body composition. If you carry too little body fat, you are **underfat**. If you carry too much body fat, you are **overfat**.

Excessive leanness is associated with being too underfat. Obesity is associated with being too overfat. Adolescent males are considered

Across the Disciplines

Science

Archimedes (c. 287–c. 212 B.C.) is credited with many discoveries and inventions. He calculated the approximate value of the mathematical figure known as *pi* and also invented the

Archimedes screw, which was used to lift water up from one level to another. He is most famous, though, for Archimedes' Principle. This principle explains that an object put into a fluid such as water will appear to lose an amount of weight equal to the weight, or volume, of the

ideal body weight

the perfect weight for good health.

• *You can be either too thin for good health, or too heavy.*

*...ot everyone can be as lean and glam-
...s as the media often portrays people.*

to be overfat when their body fat is greater than 20 percent and obese when their body fat exceeds 25 percent. Adolescent females are considered to be overfat when their body fat is greater than 25 percent and obese when their body fat exceeds 32 percent.

There is no single **ideal body weight** or ideal percentage of body fat for you. Ideal body weight can be calculated for adults. However, the methods used to do so do not apply as effectively for young adults, whose bodies are still growing and developing.

SECTION 1 REVIEW

Answer the following questions on a separate sheet of paper:

1. Define *somatotype*.
2. What is the *J*-shaped relationship between body composition and the risk for developing chronic diseases?
3. How can you calculate your percentage of body fat?

Assess

Use the Section 1 Review questions to assess students' comprehension of the concepts presented in Section 1.

**ANSWERS TO
SECTION 1 REVIEW**

1. Somatotype is the type of body you have in terms of your body composition, related to heredity.
2. The "J" relationship refers to the fact that if you are too lean or weigh too much, you will be at greater risk for premature death from chronic disease.
3. You can calculate your percentage of body fat if you know your total body weight and your lean body weight. Your percentage of body fat equals your body fat weight divided by your total body weight.

Close

fluid it displaces.

Have students design an experiment that demonstrates Archimedes' Principle and present it to the class. Students should be able to discuss the implications of their experiments as related to body composition evaluation.

Have students review the three personal fitness assessments discussed in the chapter—skinfold evaluations, body mass index, and body circumference measurements—and create a chart that illustrates the six methods they have learned in terms of accuracy, effort, cost, and availability.

If possible, film the students' experiments and post students' charts to use as teaching tools.

Have students write a one- or two-page report about the chronic diseases (heart disease, hypertension, diabetes mellitus, and so on) associated with being too lean or weighing too much. Have students explain the relationships.

CHAPTER 9
SECTION 2
306

Focus

Outcome

In **Section 2** students will learn:

1. How developing and maintaining acceptable levels of lean and fat tissue can reduce your risk for functional health problems.

Focus Activities

1. Discuss the factors that influence body composition (for example, energy balance, caloric input, and caloric expenditure).
2. Do the Active Mind/Active Body activity on page 312.

SECTION 2

Factors That Influence Your Body Composition

• *Your body composition is influenced by genetics, growth and development, diet, and your physical activity level.*

energy balance

the balance between calories consumed in the diet and the amount of calories burned in daily physical activity.

caloric input

the number of calories consumed in the diet.

caloric expenditure

the number of calories expended or burned in daily physical activity.

Other factors besides genetics can influence your body composition. These factors include your growth and development, diet (the food you consume), and activity level. As you grow, your body increases both the number and size of your fat cells. If you are fatter when you are younger, you tend to develop more fat cells than if you are leaner. Extra fat cells can make it more difficult for you to control your weight and percentage of body fat as you age. The number of fat cells that you will eventually have will be established when you reach your early twenties. However, the size of your fat cells can continue to increase unless you control your diet and adopt an active lifestyle. Fortunately, even individuals with extra fat cells have some control over their body composition and can maintain their body fat levels within normal limits.

Your diet and activity level can also significantly affect your energy balance and body composition. In fact, eating a healthy diet and maintaining an active lifestyle are the two most important steps you can take to help control your body composition now and as you get older.

Energy Balance

Energy balance is the balance between how many calories you *consume* in your diet (**caloric input**) and the amount of calories you *expend* or *burn* in daily physical activity (**caloric expenditure**). If you eat fewer calories in your diet than you expend (or burn) daily, you will lower your percentage of body fat. A simple energy balance equation that illustrates this example might look like the following:

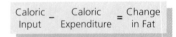

$$\text{Caloric Input} - \text{Caloric Expenditure} = \text{Change in Fat}$$

Caloric Input

Your caloric input is determined by the types and amounts of food you consume. The foods that provide you with calories in your diet are carbohydrates, fats, and proteins. Each of these foods supplies different amounts of calories. For example, 1 gram of carbohydrate provides 4 calories of energy; 1 gram of fat provides 9 calories of energy; and 1 gram of protein provides 4 calories of energy (Figure 9.3). If you know these equivalents and the number of grams of these nutri-

---

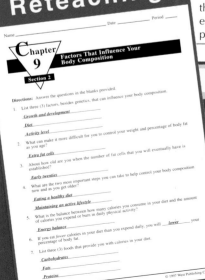

Reteaching

Name _____ Date _____ Period _____

Chapter 9 Factors That Influence Your Body Composition

Section 2

Directions: Answer the questions in the blanks provided.

1. List three (3) factors, besides genetics, that can influence your body composition.
   Growth and development
   Diet
   Activity level
2. What can make it more difficult for you to control your weight and percentage of body fat as you age?
   Extra fat cells
3. About how old are you when the number of fat cells that you will eventually have is established?
   Early twenties
4. What are the two most important steps you can take to help control your body composition now and as you get older?
   Eating a healthy diet
   Maintaining an active lifestyle
5. What is the balance between how many calories you consume in your diet and the amount of calories you expend or burn in daily physical activity?
   Energy balance
6. If you eat *fewer* calories in your diet than you expend daily, you will _____*lower*_____ your percentage of body fat.
7. List three (3) foods that provide you with calories in your diet.
   Carbohydrates
   Fats
   Proteins

© 1997 West Publishing Co.

Reteaching Worksheets   66

ABILITY LEVELS

Reteaching

Some students may need help mastering the concepts contained in this section. In your Teacher Resource Package, you will find the reproducible worksheet shown here. This worksheet should help students who have been absent and those needing additional help to improve their comprehension and retention of the content in this section.

• *It is important for you to be aware of the number of calories that you are consuming each day in order to control your body composition.*

---

1 gram carbohydrates = 4 calories

1 gram fat = 9 calories

1 gram protein = 4 calories

• **Figure 9.3** *Calories per Gram of Nutrient.*

---

metabolic rate

the number of calories that is burned or expended as heat.

---

resting metabolic rate (RMR)

the amount of calories you need and expend while sitting comfortably at rest.

---

ents in the food you consume, you can calculate the amount of calories you consume at each meal and for each day. You can then use this information to determine if your daily caloric intake is appropriate for your energy needs. (Chapter 10 will tell you more about this.)

It is recommended that adolescent males consume between 2,500 and 3,000 calories per day. Adolescent females should consume 2,000 to 2,500 calories per day. These recommendations are based on the average energy needs for adolescents. Females typically need fewer calories than males because males, on average, are larger than females and carry more muscle mass.

The recommended amounts of calories for adolescents are higher than for adults. The reason is that adolescents, who are growing and developing rapidly, need more energy than adults, who are fully grown. If you are a very active person, you will need to consume even more calories than is recommended to meet your energy needs.

Caloric Expenditure

Your **metabolic rate** is the number of calories that you burn or expend as heat. For example you burn calories at rest and during physical activity. Your caloric expenditure is determined by your resting metabolic rate and how physically active you are daily. Your **resting metabolic rate (RMR)** is the amount of calories you need and expend while sitting comfortably at rest.

that they are often not in energy balance. In fact, many overtrained athletes are glycogen (stored glucose or sugar) depleted and experiencing staleness from low carbohydrate intake (see Chapter 10). Students need to understand that they not only need to be concerned with caloric intake but caloric expenditure as well.

Discussion

• Use Figure 9.3 to discuss with students the calories associated with each gram of carbohydrate, fat, and protein consumed.
• Discuss the photo on page 321 showing power walking. Ask students if power walking with hand weights will expend more calories than walking without hand weights.
• Discuss with students whether their body composition is more related to their lifestyle habits or to genetics.

Teacher Support Notes

Dr. Claude Bouchard and his colleagues have studied the relationship between weight gain and genetics. They had 12 pairs of identical twins live in a controlled experimental environment for over 100 days. During the 100 days, they were overfed each day by 1,000 calories more than they needed. By the end of the study there was a wide variation in weight gain among twin pairs. But each individual gained similar amounts

• *Your resting metabolic rate is at its highest during infancy; it slows as you age.*

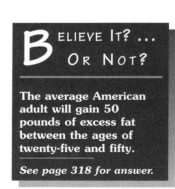

BELIEVE **I**T? ... **O**R **N**OT?

The average American adult will gain 50 pounds of excess fat between the ages of twenty-five and fifty.

See page 318 for answer.

Resting Metabolic Rate (RMR). Your RMR represents the energy needed for your heart to beat, for blood to be delivered to the tissues, for your muscles to contract, and so on. For most young adults, this amounts to about 1 to 1.5 calories per minute. In other words, even if all you did was sit perfectly still twenty-four hours a day, you would still need to consume between 1,440 and 2,160 calories just to keep your body functioning.

Your RMR can be affected by several factors, including genetics, age, gender, diet, and activity level. Some people have much higher RMRs than others because of genetic differences. This fact explains why some people tend to be able to eat just about anything and everything they want and not gain weight, whereas others eat in a similar way and gain lots of weight. It may also help explain, at least in part, why some people have a much easier time losing weight and body fat than others.

Figure 9.4 illustrates the relationship between RMR, gender, and age. The figure shows that males, on average, have higher RMRs than females, and also that RMR decreases as you age. This decrease with age is very important, because it suggests that as you age, you will not need to consume as many calories to meet your daily energy needs. If you do not reduce your caloric intake or increase your energy expenditure levels as you age, you will typically see a weight and fat gain.

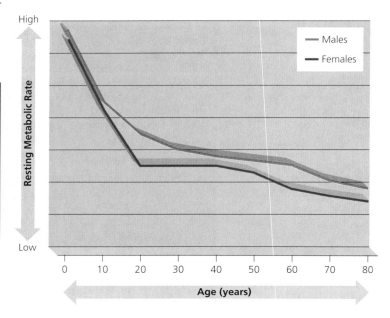

• **Figure 9.4** *Your Metabolic Rate as You Age.*

Special Needs

Students with disabilities often experience difficulty with self-esteem because their physical appearance may be affected by their conditions. They may not physically fit within the norm, thus making it awkward to discuss body composition.

Endomorphic students will have a tendency to experience difficulty with endurance activities. Mesomorphic students tend to have high energy levels and may sometimes be hyperactive. Ectomorphs tend to do well with endurance-type activities. A student's

The decrease in RMR helps explain the "creeping" effect of weight and fat gains as people age. Even by consuming just a few more calories than needed, aging adults tend to slowly gain weight and fat over time. Thus, the excess weight and fat that many middle-aged people have "creeps" up on them. For example, a woman might be expected to gain 10 pounds in a year if she consumed about 100 calories (a 2-inch wedge of angel food cake) a day more than she burned.

The number of calories you consume in your diet and the way you eat can stimulate or slow your RMR. For example, if you eat regularly (three to six times) throughout the day, you tend to stimulate your RMR, because digesting your food requires extra energy. However, if you eat only one meal per day (as many busy people do), you actually slow your RMR. This can cause you to gain weight and increase your body fat.

Restricting the number of calories in your daily diet can also significantly slow your RMR. For example, if you went on a diet of 500 calories per day (well below daily recommendations) for several days, you could cause your RMR to drop as much as 75 percent. This would only produce negative results for you. For example, you would always be hungry. You would be tired, because you would have low levels of energy. Finally, you would not see as much weight loss as you had hoped for because your RMR would be lower than normal.

It is thought that by participating in regular physical activity or exercise, you can stimulate your metabolic rate, not only during work but also to some degree following your workout. Because technology (remote controls, dishwashers, garage door openers, and so on) has made it so easy for all of us to remain fairly inactive and comfortable, it only makes sense that we all need to develop and maintain more active lifestyles to achieve energy balance.

Burning Calories with Physical Activity and Exercise. In addition to your RMR, the number of calories you burn in voluntary activities daily also helps determine your total caloric expenditure. You probably have noticed that people have lifestyles that are either very active, very inactive, or somewhere in between. People who are always on the go burn lots of calories, whereas people who just sit around burn few calories.

The number of calories you burn in voluntary activities depends on the number and size of muscles that you work, the weight of the body parts you move, the intensity of your work, and the time/duration of your activities. If you work with your legs (walking) versus your arms (lifting), you will burn more calories, because the larger the active muscle mass (legs versus arms), the more energy needed.

If you weighed 200 pounds and your friend weighed 150 pounds, you would use more energy than your friend if you both did the same

• *You will burn more calories if you are physically active than if you are sedentary.*

somatotype tends to have a direct effect on postural deviations and alignment.

Amputations, atrophy of muscles, or compromised limb development will restrict lean muscle mass, thus making it difficult to assess body mass in individuals with disabilities. Often those students who exhibit atrophy begin to show an increase in body fat and subsequent

weight gain as deteriorating muscle begins to be replaced by connective tissue that is filled with fat and water. These students also experience slower body metabolism as working muscle mass decreases. It is well documented that increased activity among the disabled will improve metabolism.

adulthood, which can negatively influence their ability to control their body composition.

Discussion

Have students guess at how many calories they expended the last time they engaged in physical activity or exercise. Ask them which factors might help determine how many calories they will expend during physical activity or exercise.

Teaching Strategies

Give students examples of how to expend or burn 100 calories by being physically active. Use some of the following ideas from *Men's Health* magazine (article by P. Myatt Murphy, December, 1995):

• Shoot 207 basketball foul shots at 12 shots per minute.
• Hum the theme to *Rocky* as you skip rope for 9-1/2 minutes.
• Chop wood continuously for four minutes, 22 seconds.
• Ride a stationary bike at 20 mph for four minutes, 52 seconds.
• Play racquetball for seven minutes, 17 seconds.
• Play Michael Jordan on the basketball court for nine minutes.
• Use a stationary rower for 11 minutes.

REMEMBER This!

You have a choice about how active you are. When your voluntary activity levels are higher, you will burn more calories. The most effective way to control your body composition is by controlling the number of calories in your diet and your voluntary activity level.

Stress Break
• • • • • • • • • • • • •

It's not enough that your life is full of all kinds of stressors. Now you have pressure to compete with Madison Avenue's or Hollywood's idea of what is thin. Don't get caught up in their unrealistic expectation for thin bodies. In fact, many models are practicing unhealthy behaviors (such as fad diets, diet pills, and so on) to maintain their weight and appearance.

Know what are healthy and reasonable goals for your body composition, and do not allow yourself to fall prey to these unrealistic expectations. After all, working toward a healthy, fit body should make you feel better about yourself, not create undue stress.

activity with equal effort. Moving the heavier body parts requires more energy than moving the smaller body parts.

The longer you engage in physical activity or exercise, the more calories you will burn. You will also burn more calories if you work at a higher intensity, because harder work requires more fuel.

If you engage in daily voluntary activities, you will burn more calories than someone else who lives a sedentary lifestyle. For example, say two individuals have the same resting metabolic rate. One is moderately active, and the other is sedentary. The more active person will burn more calories than the sedentary person. Figure 9.5 shows a typical breakdown of the total energy that these two individuals would spend in one day. The active person burns 500 calories more than the sedentary person. In one week's time, the active person would burn 3,500 calories (7 days × 500 calories) more than the sedentary person.

A pound of fat contains 3,500 calories. If you consume 3,500 calories more than you burn, you will gain a pound of fat. If you want to lose a pound of fat, you need to eat 3,500 fewer calories than you burn. For example, if you wanted to lose a pound of fat in a week, you might use several different strategies. If you were to try to lose the 3,500 calories by just controlling your diet, and you were not active, you would have to reduce your daily caloric intake by 500 calories per day (3,500 calories/7 days = 500 calories/day), which might be difficult. If you tried to lose the 3,500 calories by keeping your diet the same but getting more exercise, you would have to burn an additional 500 calories per day. This would be equivalent to walking an additional 5 miles daily. (Walking 1 mile burns about 100 calories.)

You may have guessed by now that the smartest approach to losing a pound of fat in a week might be to combine the two approaches just described. For example, you could reduce your daily caloric intake by 250 calories and burn an additional 250 calories per day. With this method, you would lose a pound of fat in one week without needing to become too extreme with your diet or activity plan. By combining a proper diet and activity level, you can con-

Energy Needs	Sedentary Person	Active Person
Energy for resting metabolic rate	1,600 calories	1,600 calories
Energy for voluntary activities	100 calories	600 calories
Total energy needs	1,700 calories	2,200 calories

Figure 9.5   *Energy Expenditure of Sedentary versus Active Persons.*

CRITICAL THINKING

Eating disorders are critical problems in the United States, especially among teenage girls. Discuss with students why this is the case. How has society and our culture influenced people in such a way as to "pressure" them into experiencing eating disorders?

Have students write letters to the editor of the local newspaper describing what they think it would be like to be trapped in the destructive behaviors associated with anorexia and bulimia.

Share several of the best letters with the class. Have students write another

trol your lean muscle mass and percentage of body fat much more efficiently than if you work on only one side of the energy balance equation.

Figure 9.6 lists selected physical activities and exercises. The list can give you ideas on how to increase your caloric expenditure. You can then use the "Active Mind/Active Body" activity on the next page to analyze your own caloric expenditure through exercise.

This figure shows how many calories per minute are spent in activities for people at five different body weights. The calories per pound per minute (Cal/Lb/Min) number makes it possible for you to calculate the number of calories for your own body weight, if it is not exactly one of the five weights listed here.

Activity	Cal/Lb/Min[a]	Calories Spent per Minute (for 5 body weights, in pounds)				
		110	125	150	175	200
Aerobic dance (vigorous)	0.062	6.8	7.8	9.3	10.9	12.4
Basketball (vigorous, full court)	0.097	10.7	12.1	14.6	17.0	19.4
Bicycling						
13 miles per hour	0.045	5.0	5.6	6.8	7.9	9.0
19 miles per hour	0.076	8.4	9.5	11.4	13.3	15.2
Canoeing (flat water, moderate pace)	0.045	5.0	5.6	6.8	7.9	9.0
Cross-country skiing (8 miles per hour)	0.104	11.4	13.0	15.6	18.2	20.8
Golf (carrying clubs)	0.045	5.0	5.6	6.8	7.9	9.0
Handball	0.078	8.6	9.8	11.7	13.7	15.6
Horseback riding (trot)	0.052	5.7	6.5	7.8	9.1	10.4
Rowing (vigorous)	0.097	10.7	12.1	14.6	17.0	19.4
Running						
5 miles per hour	0.061	6.7	7.6	9.2	10.7	12.2
7.5 miles per hour	0.094	10.3	11.8	14.1	16.4	18.8
10 miles per hour	0.114	12.5	14.3	17.1	20.0	22.9
Soccer (vigorous)	0.097	10.7	12.1	14.6	17.0	19.4
Studying	0.011	1.2	1.4	1.7	1.9	2.2
Swimming						
20 yards per minute	0.032	3.5	4.0	4.8	5.6	6.4
45 yards per minute	0.058	6.4	7.3	8.7	10.2	11.6
Tennis (beginner)	0.032	3.5	4.0	4.8	5.6	6.4
Walking (brisk pace)						
3.5 miles per hour	0.035	3.9	4.4	5.2	6.1	7.0

[a]Cal/Lb/Min is an abbreviation for calories (Cal) per pound (Lb) of body weight per minute (Min). You can use it to calculate the number of calories you use at your body weight for a minute of activity. To calculate the total number of calories you spend for a longer time, multiply the Cal/Lb/Min factor by your exact weight and then multiply your answer by the number of minutes you spend on the activity. For example, if you weight 142 pounds, and you want to know how many calories you spend doing 30 minutes of vigorous aerobic dance: 0.062 Cal/Lb/Min × 142 lb = 8.8 calories per minute. 8.8 Cal/Min × 30 Minutes = 264 Total Calories Spent.

Source: Values for swimming, bicycling, and running have been adapted with permission of Ross Laboratories, Columbus, Ohio 43216, from G.P. Town and K.B. Wheeler, Nutrition Concerns for the Endurance Athlete, Dietetic Currents 13(1986):7-12. Copyright 1986 Ross Laboratories. Values for all other activities: Copyright 1983 by Consumers Union of the United States, Inc., Yonkers, N.Y. 10703-1057. Adapted with permission from CONSUMER REPORTS BOOKS,1983.

Figure 9.6   *Energy Demands of Activities.*

- Lift weights for 13 minutes.
- Walk uphill for 13 minutes.

You can also use some of the following points from the same article to educate students about how easy it is to consume 500 calories:

- Eat 5 hard pretzels.
- Eat 3 ounces of pecans.
- Eat 40 fat-free saltines.
- Eat 3 or 4 cubes of cheddar cheese.
- Eat 2 cups of sherbet.

Discussion

- Use Figure 9.5 to discuss with students the total amount of energy (in calories) that two individuals might consume in a typical day.
- Use Figure 9.6 to discuss with students the energy demands of various activities and exercises.

Activities

- Have students make a large poster of Figure 9.6 or another similar caloric expenditure chart that they can find in current periodicals.
- Have students do the Active Mind/Active Body activity on the next page to analyze their own caloric expenditures during physical activity and exercise.

letter to the editor in answer to the first letter they wrote. Emphasis should be on encouraging the person to accept himself or herself as he or she is and on ways to maintain or achieve a healthy weight and outlook.

Encourage students to personalize this activity to help them really understand:

1. the dangers of eating disorders.
2. how threatening eating disorders are.
3. how to help people trapped by these disorders.

Students will read about eating disorders later in this chapter.

Assess

Use the Active Mind/Active Body activity on this page to assess student progress. Use the Section 2 Review questions to assess students' comprehension of the concepts presented in Section 2.

ANSWERS TO SECTION 2 REVIEW

1. Caloric input − caloric expenditure = changes in fat level.
2. RMR stands for resting metabolic rate. It is the amount of calories you need and expend while sitting comfortably at rest.
3. The more active you are, the more calories you will expend. The number of calories you burn in voluntary activities depends on the intensity, frequency, and time/duration in which you engage in them.

Calculating Caloric Expenditure

Review Figure 9.6, and pick two activities or exercises that you do somewhat regularly. Calculate how many calories you would expend for one week if you did each exercise or activity three times a week for twenty minutes, forty minutes, or one hour.

SECTION 2 REVIEW

Answer the following questions on a separate sheet of paper:

1. Give a simple energy balance equation.
2. What is RMR, and what factors influence it?
3. How can voluntary activities increase the number of calories you burn?

SECTION 3   Body Composition Evaluations

In Chapter 4, you performed a simple body composition evaluation by pinching your thigh. You also performed the *Prudential Fitnessgram* Body Mass Index (BMI) Fitness Check in that chapter. In this section you will learn some additional ways to evaluate your body composition. You should perform one or more of the self-evaluations described here.

Height/Weight Chart Fitness Check

Height and weight charts provide average weight ranges based on your height, age, and gender. These charts provide only a very rough measure of body composition. You can use Figure 9.7 to compare your weight with that of others of your same height, age, and gender.

Close

Discuss the "Stress Break" feature on page 310 with students. Have they been aware of the pressures produced by advertising agencies? Do they think they have been influenced by the ads, or have they been able to resist the pressure to be "beautiful"?

Wellness Connection

You might want to tell students about some questionable and dangerous methods people use to lose body fat:
• Stomach stapling (gastroplasty)—reduction of the stomach size by stapling off a part of it.
• Gastric balloon—small plastic balloon

is inserted through the mouth down into the stomach in an attempt to create the feeling of fullness.
• Intestinal or gastric bypass surgery—surgical technique to remove or disconnect parts of the digestive tract.
• Liposuction (suction lipectomy)—surgi-

Height (in inches)	Females Weight Range (in pounds)					
	12	13	14	15	16	17
53–54.9	58 – 78	—	—	—	—	—
55–56.9	76 – 101	74 – 98	—	—	—	—
57–58.9	79 – 106	84 – 112	84 – 112	95 – 127	104 – 139	86 – 115
59–60.9	87 – 116	88 – 118	95 – 127	99 – 132	103 – 137	99 – 132
61–62.9	96 – 128	99 – 132	102 – 136	103 – 137	105 – 140	109 – 145
63–64.9	105 – 140	105 – 140	108 – 144	113 – 151	114 – 152	114 – 152
65–66.9	109 – 145	115 – 154	116 – 155	121 – 161	122 – 163	121 – 161
67–68.9	126 – 168	115 – 154	128 – 170	130 – 173	126 – 168	123 – 164
69–70.9	—	—	121 – 162	126 – 168	144 – 192	130 – 174

Height (in inches)	Males Weight Range (in pounds)					
	12	13	14	15	16	17
53–54.9	65 – 86	65 – 86	—	—	—	—
55–56.9	68 – 91	73 – 97	—	—	—	—
57–58.9	78 – 104	77 – 103	80 – 107	—	—	—
59–60.9	85 – 114	85 – 113	91 – 121	—	—	—
61–62.9	94 – 125	94 – 125	94 – 126	104 – 139	99 – 132	108 – 144
63–64.9	101 – 134	105 – 140	103 – 138	105 – 140	105 – 140	114 – 152
65–66.9	111 – 148	111 – 148	115 – 154	114 – 152	118 – 157	124 – 166
67–68.9	124 – 166	123 – 164	124 – 166	125 – 167	124 – 166	133 – 178
69–70.9	—	135 – 180	130 – 173	130 – 174	133 – 178	136 – 181
71–72.9	—	—	144 – 192	143 – 191	144 – 192	146 – 194
73–74.9	—	—	—	148 – 197	161 – 215	151 – 202
75–76.9	—	—	—	166 – 221	—	162 – 216

The numbers in these columns may surprise you. Some older teens weigh less than some younger teens the same height, because gains in weight often don't keep up with gains in height.
Note: The lower number in each weight range was derived by calculating 10 percent below, and the higher number was derived by calculating 20 percent above, the expected weight for height and age of youths 12 to 17 years old.

• **Figure 9.7** *Expected Weight Ranges for Teenagers (based on height and age).*

Remember, however, that your weight in comparison with that of others does not really provide you with information about how lean or fat you are. You should use height and weight charts only in a general way to get an idea about your weight in relation to that of others.

Body Circumference Fitness Check

Another way to evaluate your body composition is to take body circumference measurements to help you estimate your percentage of body fat. When you measure circumferences or girths (measurements around a body), you need to use a tape measure (Figure 9.8).

cal insertion of a tube into fat pockets of the body in order to suck out and remove localized fat deposits.
• Wiring the jaws shut—medical/dental procedure of wiring the jaws shut (as you would do for a broken jaw) so the patient cannot eat solid foods.
• Efforts to lose body fluids—the use of saunas, steam rooms, rubber or plastic perspiration outfits, or diuretic drugs, which result primarily in a temporary water weight or body fluid loss.
• Passive weight loss devices—the use of belts, rollers, electrical stimulators, or other devices that supposedly burn up calories without having to exert any type of effort.

Focus

Outcome

In **Section 3** students will learn:

1. To list and describe evaluations that they could use to assess their body composition now and in the future.

Focus Activities

1. Use Figure 9.7 to discuss and demonstrate weight in relation to height.
2. Use Figures 9.9 and 9.10 to discuss and demonstrate the Fitness Check on page 316.
3. Discuss and demonstrate how to determine and evaluate students' body composition using Figure 9.11.
4. Discuss and demonstrate the Fitness Check on page 316 using Figures 9.12, 9.13, and 9.14.
5. Discuss medical and laboratory evaluations.

Teach & Apply

Activity

Use Figure 9.7 to have students check their weight in relation to their height.

- *Record your body circumference measures and use either your weight (males) or height (females) to determine your body composition as described in the text.*

Teacher Support Notes

Remind students that height and weight charts are one of the poorest ways to assess body composition, but they are a good way to get students to think about how they should measure their body composition. Have a weight scale available so that students can measure their weight in privacy. Allow them to keep their records confidential between themselves and you.

Activity

Use Figure 9.8 to demonstrate how to do body circumference measures. Then have students use either Figure 9.9 or 9.10 to assess their body circumference measures and percentages of body fat. Then have them use Figure 9.11 to evaluate their body fat scores.

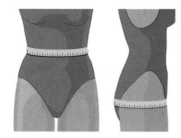

- **Figure 9.8** *Anatomic Landmarks for Measuring Various Girths.*

Two different methods are used for males and females to estimate percentage of body fat from body circumference measurements.

For Males. Males can estimate their percentage of body fat by measuring weight in pounds and then measuring the circumference of the waist at the navel level. To do this estimate, weigh yourself without your shoes on, but dressed in your exercise clothing. Measure your waist circumference with the tape measure pulled snugly, but not too tight. Measure to the nearest half-inch. Once you have obtained your measurements, Figure 9.9 will help you determine your percentage of body fat. Using a ruler, connect the points from your body weight to your waist circumference. The point where the line intersects the middle scale tells you your approximate percentage of body fat.

For Females. Females can estimate their percentage of body fat by measuring their height and the circumference at the widest point of their hips. To do this, measure your height, without your shoes on, to the nearest half-inch. The hip circumference measurement should be taken with the tape measure pulled snugly, but not too tight, and to the nearest half-inch. Once you have obtained your measurements, you can use Figure 9.10 to determine your percentage of body fat. Using a ruler, connect the points from your body height to your hip circumference. The point where the line intersects the middle scale tells you your approximate percentage of body fat.

For Both Males and Females. Whether you are male or female, once you have determined your percentage of body fat, you

ABILITY LEVELS

Reteaching

Some students may need help mastering the concepts contained in this section. In your Teacher Resource Package, you will find the reproducible worksheet shown here. This worksheet should help students who have been absent and those needing additional help to improve their comprehension and retention of the content in this section.

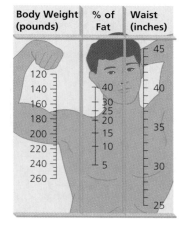

• **Figure 9.9** *Percentage of Body Fat for Males from Weight and Waist Circumference Measurements.*

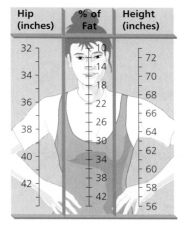

• **Figure 9.10** *Percentage of Body Fat for Females from Hip Circumference and Height Measurements. Source:* Figures 9.9 and 9.10 adapted with permission from J. H. Wilmore, *Sensible Fitness* (Champaign, IL: Human Kinetics, 1986).

can use Figure 9.11 to evaluate your body fat score. For good to better health, males should carry 7 to 19 percent body fat. Females should carry 12 to 24 percent body fat. If you do not score in the *good* to *better* healthy zones, you should try to improve your body composition.

Skinfold Evaluation Fitness Check

The most commonly used method to evaluate body composition is skinfold measurements. Skinfold measurements are good indicators of body composition because 50 percent of all body fat is between the muscles and skin, and the other 50 percent is inside the body. Skinfold measurements are taken with skinfold calipers, which are devices used to pinch the fat between the muscles and skin to measure skinfold thickness in millimeters. For adolescents, two skinfold measurements are typically taken: the back of the upper arm (triceps) and the inside of the calf at its widest part. You can use the "Fitness Check" activity on the next page to determine your skinfold measurements.

Medical or Laboratory Evaluations

Other methods to evaluate body composition are used by medical professionals or laboratory technicians. These methods include underwater weighing, bioelectrical impedance, and magnetic resonance imaging (MRI) scans. The techniques are usually used only in research or for special follow-up after medical screening.

Underwater weighing is based on the concept that people who have lower levels of body fat sink when they try to float in water,

Fitness Rating	% Fat (Males)	Fitness Rating	% Fat (Females)
Too Lean	6 or less	Too Lean	11 or less
Healthy Lean	7–9	Healthy Lean	12–14
Healthy	10–19	Healthy	15–24
Borderline High	20–24	Borderline High	25–29
Overfat	25 or more	Overfat	30 or more

• **Figure 9.11** *Rating Body Fatness.*

surements to check that they are evaluating each other accurately.

• It is a good idea to know what your triceps and thigh measures are so that if students are having trouble they can take your measures for additional practice. That way you will know if they understand the technique.

• Tell students that when assessing body composition, they should not expect to see quick changes. Generally speaking, if one is monitoring body composition changes, they should only have it checked about every three months or so.

Teacher Support Notes

The authors believe that the skinfold evaluation is the most accurate assessment of body composition that can be done in most school settings. When skinfold measures are accurately made, they provide an excellent way to educate students about body composition. Taking skinfold measures also provides teachers with a one-on-one opportunity to teach students that there are ways for them to control their

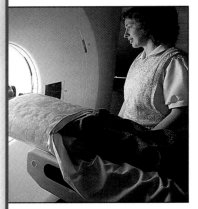

• *MRI scans are the most accurate way to determine body composition levels but cost at least $1,000 a scan.*

whereas people with excess fat float easily in water. This body composition measurement technique involves weighing a person in a submerged chair, which is attached to a scale.

Bioelectrical impedance is a body composition measurement procedure during which harmless electrical current is transmitted between two electrodes attached to your body while you are lying down. A person who is fatter will have a greater resistance to the current flow than a leaner person. Mathematical equations are then used to determine body composition.

MRI scans use the technology of medical imaging techniques, radio waves, and computers to assess body composition. This method is considered to be the most accurate way to assess body composition. However, it is also the most expensive (about $1,000 a scan).

For your own personal fitness assessments, skinfold evaluations provide the most accurate measure of your body composition. Measures of your body mass index (BMI) are the next best way to determine your body composition (see Chapter 4). Body circumference measurements are less accurate, but they are better than just measuring your height and weight.

Fitness Check — Body Fat Measurements

Use the following guidelines to determine skinfold measurements accurately. To measure your skinfolds you should work with a partner and take each other's measurements with a set of calipers.

1. Use your left hand to grasp each skinfold. Avoid grasping the muscle or pinching too tight.

2. For the triceps, use your thumb and index finger to pick up a skinfold in the middle of your partner's right arm exactly half way between the shoulder and the elbow (Figure 9.12). Have your partner keep his or her arm relaxed at the side of the body.

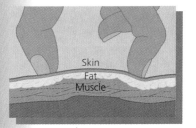 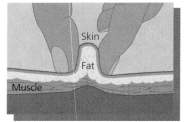

• **Figure 9.12** *Under-the-Skin View of Skinfold Test.*

Science and Technology

Determining the body composition of an individual was once an intense process. It required immersing an individual in a tank of water and measuring the exact displacement of water created by the addition of the individual. Today, technology has created machines that use electrical impedance to determine body fat percentages. Statistical tests, which predict the percentage of fat from skinfold measurements, are also available.

Advancements in computer technology now allow for programs to estimate the body composition of an individual using

3. For the calf, have your partner stand up and place his or her right foot on a bench or chair. Use your thumb and index finger to pick up a skinfold in the middle of the inside part of the lower leg at its widest part (Figure 9.13).

4. With your right hand, place the opened caliper one half inch below the skinfold grasp and directly below the pinch, with the scale of the caliper visible.

5. Close the calipers on the skinfold and hold it for two to three seconds. Read and record the measurement to the nearest millimeter. Repeat this two more times.

6. Use the middle of the three readings as your skinfold score. For example, if the three readings are 18, 16, and 15 mm, use 16 as your score.

7. Add up your tricep and calf skinfold scores and use Figure 9.14 to determine your percentage of body fat. Read straight down from your sum of skinfolds to the "% of Fat" reading. Keep track of your findings as follows:

Triceps skinfold   ____ mm

Calf skinfold   + ____ mm   % body fat ____ %

Sum of skinfolds   = ____ mm

(Continued on next page)

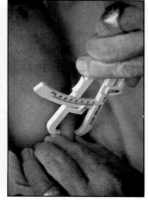

• **Figure 9.13**   *Skinfold Test for Calf and Tricep.*

body composition. In order for you to feel comfortable doing skinfold testing (if you have not done this before), you should attend a workshop or obtain a videotape to get appropriate training and practice in measuring skinfolds accurately. Your goal should not be to just assess students' body composition, more importantly, you should teach students the technique so that they can understand and use the process as adults. Also included in the text are several methods besides skinfolds for you to use in assessing body composition. It is recommended that you use BMI measures (see Chapter 4) as your first alternative, if you do not have students do the skinfold evaluation.

Discussion

Discuss with students the photo of the MRI scan as a method to assess body composition. Ask if students know anyone who has done an MRI scan to assess body composition. Then ask students if they have ever seen or heard of someone getting weighed underwater. Would they consider either of these methods if they could afford them?

different body measurements. These computer-aided programs can also estimate the areas of fat distribution, allowing for specific targeting for weight loss. With these programs, a teacher can estimate a student's body fat and report with a printout approximate areas of fat distribution. A body composition estimate, as described, can be a helpful teaching instrument when discussing weight loss and obesity. **Take the challenge**: Connect to http://www.yahoo.com/health/weight. and search the indices for helpful body composition programs and guides. **Remember**: Not all body composition programs are accurate; you may want to go to a newsgroup on the Internet and ask for the opinions of others.

Teacher Support Notes

Underwater weighing and bioelectrical impedance measures are often used in physical education and exercise sciences laboratories to asess body composition. As good as these methods can be, they are not without error. For example, in the underwater (or hydrostatic) weighing technique, large errors can occur if residual volume (amount of air that cannot be exhaled from the lungs) is not measured. This is because fat not only causes one to float, but so does air. In the bioelectrical impedance method, large errors can occur if measures are taken when subjects are dehydrated, or if they have eaten too close to the time of assessment.

Assess

Use the Fitness Check on page 316 to assess student progress. Use the Section 3 Review questions on the next page to assess students' comprehension of the concepts presented in Section 3.

Body Fat Measurements *(continued)*

Answers to BELIEVE IT? ... OR NOT?

Pg. 303 True.
Pg. 304 False. Your resting metabolic rate (RMR) will actually drop by as much as 75 percent when you consume less than 1,000 calories a day. Your hypothalamus (the lower part of your brain), which regulates your RMR, will sense that you are starving your body and will reset or lower your RMR. Not only will you feel hungry on this type of diet but you also will not lose as much weight as expected due to your lowered RMR.
Pg. 308 True.
Pg. 322 False. Researchers have found that people who carry excess fat around their abdomens ("apple-shaped" people) are at increased health risk compared with people who carry excess fat on their hips or thighs ("pear-shaped" people).
Pg. 323 False. Only 5 percent of people who are overfat have hormonal problems related to their RMR. Most people just need to eat less and become more active to reduce their weight and body fat.

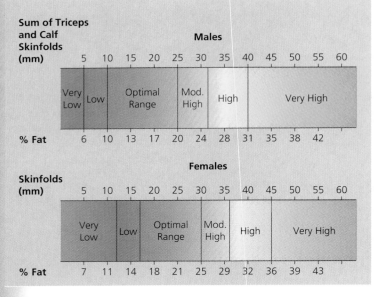

• *Figure 9.14* *Skinfold Measurements (sum of triceps and calf skinfolds) and Body Fat Percentages. Source:* Adapted with permission from: T. G. Lohman, *Measuring Body Fat Using Skinfolds* (videotape) Champaign, IL: Human Kinetics, 1982.

8. Calculate your body fat weight by multiplying your weight by your percentage of body fat:

Weight _____ pounds
% Body fat × _____
Body fat weight = _____ pounds

9. Calculate your lean body weight by subtracting your fat weight from your weight:

Weight _____ pounds
Body fat weight − _____ pounds
Lean body weight = _____ pounds

10. Determine your range of ideal body weight by dividing 0.76 and 0.88 (for females) or 0.81 and 0.93 (for males) into your lean weight. These numbers represent calculations based on good to better levels for body composition. (Males should carry 7 to 19 percent body fat, and females should carry 12 to 24 percent body fat.)

🏋 Equipment Options

Research scientists suggest that you use a specific brand of skinfold calipers, depending on what fatness chart you may be using. As a P.E. teacher, you will find that many of the calipers on the market can cost up to $1,000. What should you do? Don't panic; the scientists' suggestions are for clinical research studies. For your purposes, any set of skinfold calipers will work when used properly.

The least expensive skinfold calipers are made of plastic and cost approximately $2 to $4, depending on where

Females:

Ideal minimum (12%) = Your lean body weight ÷ 0.88 = _____ lbs.

Ideal maximum (24%) = Your lean body weight ÷ 0.76 = _____ lbs.

Males:

Ideal minimum (7%) = Your lean body weight ÷ 0.93 = _____ lbs.

Ideal maximum (19%) = Your lean body weight ÷ 0.81 = _____ lbs.

11. Refer to Table 9.11 to evaluate your body fat score. For good to better health, males should carry 7 to 19 percent body fat and females should carry 12 to 24 percent body fat. If you did not score in the good to better zones, you should try to improve your body composition by getting closer to your ideal body weight range.

SECTION 3 REVIEW

Answer the following questions on a separate sheet of paper:

1. How do you determine your body composition by using body circumference measures?

2. How do you determine your body composition by using skinfold measures?

3. What are two medical or laboratory techniques of measuring body composition?

SECTION 4 Developing and Maintaining a Healthy Body Composition

To develop and maintain a healthy body composition, you need to design a personal fitness plan to control your caloric intake and caloric expenditure. By adjusting your diet, your physical activity, and your exercise level, you can make positive changes in your body composition. You will also need to determine your FIT by using the results from your body composition evaluations. Apply the scientific principles you learned in Chapter 3 and your personal fitness goals to develop your own body composition improvement plan. The recommendations that follow can help you develop your plan.

**ANSWERS TO
SECTION 3 REVIEW**

1. For males, measure your weight and the circumference of your waist at the navel level. Then use Figure 9.9 to determine your percentage of body fat. For females, measure your height and the circumference of your hips at their widest point. Then use Figure 9.10 to determine your percentage of body fat. Figure 9.11 can be used to evaluate your percentage of body fat.

2. Males and females can measure their skinfolds at the triceps and calf. Add the measures together and then you can use Figure 9.14 to find your percentage of body fat. Figure 9.11 can be used to evaluate your percentage of body fat.

3. Underwater weighing, bioelectrical impedance, and MRI scans are used.

Close

you purchase them. Some of the professional organizations, such as AAPHERD, have calipers and charts available. Other good suppliers of inexpensive calipers are HEALTHEDCO and EDUCORP. These two companies usually mail catalogs to every school in the United States; you may have one in a desk drawer.

After purchasing the calipers, be sure to read the instructions on their use. **Take the challenge**: Get a set of calipers and begin practicing your skinfold readings. **Remember**: In visibly obese children, the plastic skinfold calipers may not have a large enough opening to measure the fold. Don't try to spread them apart—they *will* break.

Have students compare their body circumferences and skinfold results for body composition. Were the results consistent for percentage of body fat? Ask them, Why or why not?

Any Body Can!

After students have read the Christy Henrich feature, ask them if they know of any young athletes who have overtrained or developed eating disorders. Did this problem lead to serious complications or was it solved before it caused an injury or illness? You could also prompt discussion by asking students if they think obsessions such as Christy's result from people being too competitive or from other psychological causes.

Any Body Can!

Christy Henrich

Christy Henrich (1972–1994) was at one time one of America's best gymnasts at 4 feet, 10 inches tall, and 95 pounds. She was a world-class competitor. As competitive as she was, however, she could not beat the eating disorder bulimia. When she died at age 22, she weighed 61 pounds.

Christy grew up just outside Independence, Missouri. She started in gymnastics at the age of four. By the time Christy was in high school she was training seven days a week to become an Olympic gymnast.

In 1986, at the age of 14, Christy finished fifth at the national junior (under 18) championships. In 1988, Christy finished tenth at the senior national championships and set her sights on making the 1988 U.S. Olympic gymnastic team. She missed earning a spot on that Olympic team by 0.118 of a point in a vault performance at the Olympic trials.

Christy regrouped somewhat from her Olympic trials disappointment and continued to train harder than ever. In 1989 she finished second in the all-around gymnastic competition at the U.S. championships. She also finished fourth in the world championships in the uneven parallel bars event. Unfortunately, for Christy, at the same time she was having such great success in competition, she developed a serious eating disorder.

She began eating less and less because she felt that she was "too fat," although she only weighed 90 pounds. She also became bulimic. Christy felt that the leaner she could become the better she would perform. Unfortunately, this is not true. The pressure to be thin is, however, one that athletes (for example gymnasts, dancers, runners, and figure skaters) and models face daily. This pressure is even harder on high performance individuals who strive for perfection in everything they do in life.

Christy entered counseling to control her eating disorder once others helped her recognize her problem. She had some moderate success fighting her addiction in the early 1990s. But she had a relapse in June of 1994, and in late July she went into a coma for three days and died. Her body shut down because it did not have enough fuel. In a sense, Christy died of malnutrition.

Christy Henrich was an outstanding athlete, but she was not perfect. She became obsessed with perfection in her sport. This obsession contributed to the development of a fatal eating disorder, that ironically, she thought would improve her performances.

Not everyone can be a world champion athlete like Christy Henrich, but Any Body Can develop a sound nutrition and personal fitness plan. You can also learn to recognize the early signs of eating disorders and understand how to prevent them (see page 323 for more information).

Reteaching

ABILITY LEVELS

Reteaching

Some students may need help mastering the concepts contained in this section. In your Teacher Resource Package, you will find the reproducible worksheet shown here. This worksheet should help students who have been absent and those needing additional help to improve their comprehension and retention of the content in this section.

Specificity Principle

To improve your body composition, you need to control the number of calories in your diet and your caloric expenditure in relation to how active your lifestyle is. Aerobic activities are especially important in your plan, because they cause you to expend several calories per minute in each session. Muscular strength and endurance activities are also important to include, because they will help you improve or maintain your muscle mass while helping you control fat weight.

Frequency

The first component of FIT, of course, is *frequency*. The rule for frequency in your diet should be to eat at regular intervals three times per day, plus one or two planned snacks. In this way you will avoid hunger and impulse eating. Snacks should not be potato chips, cookies, and other fattening foods. Carrot sticks, apples, and other fresh fruits and vegetables make nutritious, good-tasting snacks.

As for frequency of physical activity or exercise, try to achieve the goals of Guidelines 1 and 2 in Chapter 1 (see "Remember This!" below). Be active daily, and include aerobic work as well as muscular strength and endurance work regularly.

Intensity

The second component of FIT, *intensity,* also applies both to diet and physical activity or exercise. To lose a pound of fat, you need to reduce your dietary intake by 3,500 calories below what's normal for you over a set period of time. If you want to gain weight, you need to increase your caloric intake above what's normal for you over a set period of time. If you maintain your caloric intake at the same level and do not vary your physical activity levels, you will maintain your weight and percentage of body fat.

As for physical activity or exercise, to lose a pound of fat, you need to expend 3,500 more calories than what's normal for you over a set period of time. If you want to gain weight, you need to decrease your caloric expenditure below what's normal for you over a set period of time. If you maintain your caloric expenditure at the same level and do not vary your caloric intake, you will maintain your weight and percentage of body fat (Figure 9.15). The following equations summarize the intensity relationships:

Weight maintenance:	Caloric input	=	Caloric expenditure.
Weight loss:	Caloric input	<	Caloric expenditure.
Weight gain:	Caloric input	>	Caloric expenditure.

• It is very difficult to improve or maintain healthy body composition levels without burning calories.

REMEMBER **This!**

Guideline 1. All adolescents should be physically active daily, or nearly every day, as part of play, games, sports, work, transportation, recreation, physical education, or planned exercise, in the context of family, school, or community activities.

Guideline 2. Adolescents should engage in three or more sessions per week of activities that last 20 minutes or more at a time and that require moderate to vigorous levels of exertion.

Focus

Outcome

In **Section 4** students will learn:

1. To identify and explain strategies they can use to influence their body composition now and in the future.

Focus Activity

1. Discuss the recommended FIT for developing and maintaining a healthy body composition.

Teach & Apply

Discussion

Ask students if they have thought about trying to control their body weight and body composition now or as they get older. How do they plan to do it?

Enrichment

This activity will allow you to provide a more challenging learning experience for some of your students.

Ask students to respond to the following questions:

1. Is your body composition (percentage of body fat) what you would like it to be?

2. What do you think you will need to do in the future to obtain or maintain a desirable level of body composition (percentage of body fat)?

Have students write their answers to these questions with full explanations, not just simple "yes" or "no" answers. The quality of their responses should be determined by the amount of detailed description provided. They should write at least one page in response to each question.

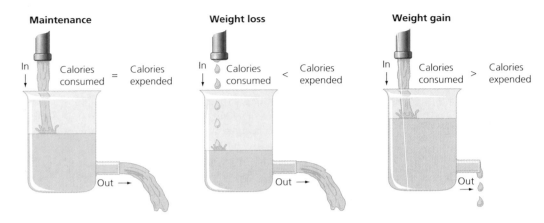

Maintenance

In ↓   Calories consumed = Calories expended

Out →

Weight loss

In ↓   Calories consumed < Calories expended

Out →

Weight gain

In ↓   Calories consumed > Calories expended

Out →

• **Figure 9.15** *Example of Weight Loss, Weight Gain, and Weight Maintenance in Relation to Exercise Intensity.*

Discussion

Have students discuss Figure 9.15 in relation to weight maintenance, weight loss, and weight gain. Ask students how many of them want to maintain their weight, lose weight, or gain weight. Ask them to share with you how they will try to do this successfully.

Teacher Support Notes

Many adolescents aren't concerned with weight loss or maintenance. They want to gain weight and get bigger. In Chapter 10, there are dietary recommendations for gaining weight and muscle mass. In terms of exercise, it is important that you tell students who if they want to gain weight, they should increase their caloric intake while doing more weight training and doing less aerobic activity. Remember, instruct those students who are trying to gain weight to continue doing the minimum amount (3 days per week for 20–30 minutes) of aerobic activity to maintain good to better levels of cardiovascular fitness.

BELIEVE IT? ... OR NOT?

Carrying excess fat around your abdomen places you at the same increased risk for chronic diseases and premature death as does carrying excess fat around your thighs.

See page 318 for answer.

REMEMBER This!

Never change your frequency, intensity, or time/duration all at the same time or too quickly. Be patient, and allow for gradual improvements.

Time/Duration

You have seen that you should work both sides of the energy balance equation to control your body composition. Reduce or increase your caloric intake and caloric expenditure as necessary. In doing so, keep in mind that body composition changes usually occur more slowly than changes in other aspects of personal fitness, such as cardiovascular fitness or muscular strength and endurance.

How can this knowledge be applied to the third component in FIT, *time/duration?* You need to be persistent and patient in working toward your goals. Physical activities or exercises that cause you to work for more than several minutes (45 to 60 minutes) at moderate to vigorous intensity are the most effective at burning fat and excess calories. If you are trying to lose weight and body fat, try to lose no more than 1 to 2 pounds per week for safe, effective results. If you are after weight gain, you should expect slow gains of no more than 1/2 pound per week. By gaining weight slowly and steadily, you add less body fat and more lean muscle. Remember, your ability to change your body composition is related to your genetic potential, so try to develop reasonable and obtainable goals for yourself for the long haul.

Progression Principle

The rate at which you modify your FIT should be based on your personal fitness goals and your changing levels of body composition. Keep in mind that while you are young and growing, your body composition can change fairly quickly. As you get older, however, you wouldn't expect much change for at least 3 to 6 months in most cases.

Assess

Use the Section 4 Review questions to assess students' comprehension of the concepts presented in Section 4.

COOPERATIVE LEARNING

While students are working together in groups, you should be observing the groups and the interactions going on within them. Which students are participating? Which aren't? Is one student "taking over"?

You should observe the groups and encourage all students to participate equally in contributing ideas, expressing their feelings, asking questions, and offering positive expressions of encouragement to fellow group members. You need to make sure groups are on task and actually doing the work assigned.

BELIEVE IT? ... OR NOT?

Most individuals who have difficulty losing weight and reducing their body fat have gland (or hormonal) problems that slow their RMR.

See page 318 for answer.

SECTION 4 REVIEW

Answer the following questions on a separate sheet of paper:

1. What should your frequency of eating be each day to control your body fat percentage?
2. How many calories does a pound of fat have?
3. What equations describe weight maintenance, weight loss, and weight gain?

ANSWERS TO SECTION 4 REVIEW

1. Eat at regular intervals three times per day, plus one or two planned snacks.
2. A pound of fat has 3,500 calories.
3. Weight maintenance—caloric intake equals caloric expenditure; weight loss—caloric input is less than caloric expenditure; weight gain—caloric input is greater than caloric expenditure.

SECTION 5 — Controlling Your Weight and Body Composition Safely

To control their body composition, young adults sometimes experiment with various quick-fix methods or behaviors such as fad diets, diet pills, and weight-gain powders and pills. These strategies lead to only partial success at best and often lead to dangerous eating disorders.

Eating Disorders

eating disorders

behaviors that cause a person to overeat, undereat, or practice extreme unhealthy actions to control their weight.

Eating disorders are behaviors that cause people to overeat, undereat, or practice extremely unhealthy actions to control their weight. Eating disorders can include a person's eating too much or too little for his or her needs, which is particularly dangerous if the person is still growing and developing. Two eating disorders that are common among young adults are anorexia nervosa and bulimia.

anorexia nervosa

an eating disorder in which people abnormally restrict their caloric intake.

Anorexia nervosa is an eating disorder in which a person abnormally restricts his or her caloric intake. More females than males have anorexia nervosa. People with this disorder believe that they are overweight, even though they appear very lean. People with anorexia nervosa can develop serious malnutrition and have a significant loss of important body fluids. Because they can develop these and other serious health problems, people with this disorder need to seek medical help. In extreme cases, the disease can result in death.

Some common signs or symptoms of a person who is at risk for developing anorexia nervosa are as follows:

- Sudden large weight loss.
- Preoccupation with food, calories, and weight.

Close

Have students write plans for how they will control their body composition in the future. Have students do this activity in class and have them turn it in.

Focus

Outcome

In **Section 5** students will learn:

1. To identify and explain how to control their body weight and body composition safely.

Focus Activity

1. Discuss the eating disorders and strategies for controlling weight and body composition.

You may need to offer assistance to groups that are struggling with the assignment or with personality conflicts within the group. Teaching students the skills they need to work well within groups is an important part of the teacher's task. Students must learn to be tolerant and accepting of fellow group members.

You may find your students are already skilled at working together and won't need a lot of help from the teacher. On the other hand, you may find yourself working harder than ever (at least at the beginning) to implement cooperative learning in your classroom. Give it enough time to work, and you should have some positive results.

Teach & Apply

Discussion

• Ask students if they know someone who has an eating disorder. What was the problem? How was it identified and treated?

• Have students discuss the strategies listed in the text for controlling weight and body composition. Which ones do they think are most effective?

bulimia

an eating disorder in which people overeat and then force themselves to vomit afterward or purposely overuse laxatives to eliminate food from their bodies.

• *You should and can develop effective personal strategies for controlling your weight and body composition.*

• Choice of baggy or layered clothing.
• Behaviors of the exercise zealot.
• Mood swings.
• Consumption of minimal amounts of food in front of others.

Bulimia is an eating disorder in which people overeat and then force themselves to vomit afterward (called "bingeing and purging"), or they purposely overuse laxatives to eliminate food from their bodies. Like anorexia nervosa, bulimia is more common among females than males. Bulimics are usually not extremely underweight. In fact, they often have normal body composition. However, they have an addictive behavior that causes them to be obsessed with food and to hide their actions. Bulimia can cause serious negative long-term health effects. Although bulimics need to seek out professional medical help for their problem, they are often reluctant to do so.

Some common signs or symptoms of a person who is at risk for developing bulimia are as follows:

• Noticeable weight loss or gain.
• Excessive concern about weight.
• Habit of visiting the bathroom immediately after meals (to induce vomiting).
• Depressed moods.
• Strict dieting followed by eating binges.
• Very critical attitude toward own body size.

Strategies for Controlling Weight and Body Composition

Poor dietary habits or behaviors and lack of regular physical activity or exercise are the main causes of excessive leanness or obesity. You can use several effective strategies to modify your caloric intake and caloric expenditure habits safely and effectively:

• Eat regularly. Always eat breakfast. Do not starve yourself or fast to lose weight.
• Keep a record of what, where, when, and how much you are eating. (You will learn more about this in Chapter 10.) Cut back on foods that provide empty calories (for example, sodas, candy bars, chips, and cookies). Eat foods that are low in fat.
• Avoid the yo-yo effect of dieting, in which you try to lose weight by dieting without being active (Figure 9.16). If you follow a diet that restricts your caloric intake too much, you tend to lose not only fat but also lean body mass. When you resume normal eating, you also gain back more fat weight than you lost.

Reteaching

Name _____ Date _____ Period _____

Chapter 9 Controlling Your Weight and Body Composition Safely

Section 5

Directions: Answer the questions in the blanks provided.

1. In front of each statement, write either *Anorexia nervosa* or *Bulimia*, to identify the type of eating disorder described.

  Bulimia People who overeat and then force themselves to vomit afterwards.
  Bulimia A person has a habit of visiting the bathroom immediately after meals.
  Anorexia A person believes that he or she is overweight, even though he or she appears very lean.
  Anorexia A person wears baggy or layered clothing.
  Bulimia A person follows strict dieting followed by eating binges.
  Anorexia A person abnormally restricts his or her caloric intake.
  Anorexia A person can develop serious malnutrition and have a significant loss of important body fluids.

2. In front of each statement, write *Yes* if an appropriate strategy for controlling weight and body composition is described, and *No* if it is not.

  _No_ Reward yourself with food when you accomplish new positive behaviors or habits and achieve goals.
  Yes Do not starve yourself or fast to lose weight.
  Yes Keep a record of what, where, when, and how much you are eating.
  _No_ Try to lose weight by dieting without being active.
  Yes Cut back on foods that provide empty calories.
  _No_ Eat foods that are high in fat.
  Yes Keep a physical activity and exercise log or journal to help you chart your progress.
  Yes Eat regularly, and always eat breakfast.

© 1997 West Publishing Co.

Reteaching Worksheets   70

ABILITY LEVELS

Reteaching

Some students may need help mastering the concepts contained in this section. In your Teacher Resource Package, you will find the reproducible worksheet shown here. This worksheet should help students who have been absent and those needing additional help to improve their comprehension and retention of the content in this section.

"Do you really think five minutes on the skip rope can balance five hours at the trough?"

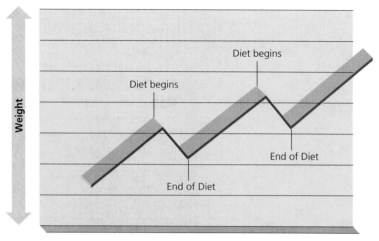

Weight

Diet begins

Diet begins

End of Diet

End of Diet

• **Figure 9.16** *The Yo-Yo Effect of Dieting.*

• Reward yourself when you accomplish new positive behaviors or habits and achieve your goals. Appropriate rewards should not include food but might be something like some new clothes to fit your new shape.

CONSUMER CORNER   Shortcuts Don't Work

Excessive weight loss over a short period of time can be a serious health concern. If you are considering a diet plan that promises huge, fast weight loss, you should follow this plan only under the direction of a physician who specializes in weight-loss medicine. However, choose your health care provider carefully. Many unqualified individuals claim they have a wealth of knowledge about weight-loss procedures when they do not. They only want to charge you for their advice.

Do not accept the opinion of someone who is not professionally trained and certified in nutrition and weight control. Trusting someone who is not professionally trained in nutrition and weight control can be dangerous to your health, as well as a good way to get "ripped off." The best way to control your body weight and body composition is to combine exercise and diet in a sound personal fitness plan.

Teacher Support Notes

The strategies listed in the text for controlling weight and body composition are based on concepts promoted by Dr. John Foreyt from the Baylor College of Medicine in Houston, Texas. Dr. Foreyt is a dietary behavioral expert who has helped many individuals lose 100 pounds or more and successfully keep the weight off.

Discussion

Use Figure 9.16 to illustrate the concept of why yo-yo dieting does not work in the long haul. Discuss the concept with students.

Consumer Corner

Have students discuss the Consumer Corner. Ask them to share examples they have seen of false quick-weight-loss advertising or marketing schemes.

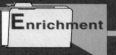

Enrichment

This activity will allow you to provide a more challenging learning experience for some of your students.

Assign students the task of reading newspaper or magazine articles on one or more of the following issues related to controlling body weight/composition.
• Fad diets
• Diet pills
• Weight gain supplements

• Anorexia nervosa
• Bulimia
• Yo-Yo dieting
Have students write a summary report of their articles. They should focus on any recommendations included in the articles that will assist people in dealing with these issues.

Assess

Use the Section 5 Review questions to assess students' comprehension of the concepts presented.

ANSWERS TO SECTION 5 REVIEW

1. An eating disorder in which a person abnormally restricts his or her caloric intake.

2. An eating disorder in which people overeat and then force themselves to vomit afterward or purposely overuse laxatives to eliminate food from their bodies.

3. Answers will vary but should include two of the following: eat regularly; keep a record of what, where, when, and how much you eat; avoid yo-yo dieting; reward yourself when positive behaviors and goals are achieved; get active.

Close

Use the Any Body Can feature highlighting Christy Henrich to discuss the extreme behaviors that are associated with eating disorders. Ask students to think of other famous people they have heard about who have struggled with eating disorders.

- Get active. Keep a physical activity and exercise log or journal to help you chart your progress and allow you to reevaluate your goals over time. Chapter 3 has recommendations for keeping a journal.

SECTION 5 REVIEW

Answer the following questions on a separate sheet of paper:

1. What is anorexia nervosa?
2. What is bulimia?
3. List two recommendations for safely modifying your caloric intake and expenditure.

SUMMARY

Physical appearance is important to us all. It is often very difficult and unhealthy, however, to try to be as lean and attractive as many celebrities and models. Many young adults have unrealistic expectations about what their bodies should look like and how much they should weigh.

Each person needs an essential amount of body fat for good health. Excessive leanness and obesity, however, are associated with an increased risk for the development of chronic diseases and premature death. Lean muscle weight includes bone, muscle, and connective tissue weight. Assessing your body composition provides more information than just knowing what you weigh. Your body composition is the ratio of lean body weight to percentage of fat in your body.

Factors that influence your body composition include genetics, growth and development, diet, and activity level. Your resting metabolic rate (RMR) is the amount of calories you need and expend while sitting at rest. Your RMR decreases with age. You can maintain your body composition, however, by balancing your energy input and energy expenditure as you age. You can do this most effectively by monitoring your diet and engaging in voluntary physical activities.

You can evaluate your body composition using a variety of different methods. Skinfold measures are the most accurate, followed in order of accuracy by body mass index (BMI) measures, body circumference measurements, and height/weight charts.

To improve or maintain your good functional health, it is important to develop and maintain an acceptable body composition level. The best way to control your body composition level safely is to modify your diet, if necessary, and adopt an active lifestyle.

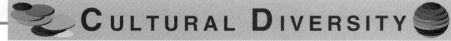

CULTURAL DIVERSITY

Africa

Africa is a country of contrasts in geography and its people. European and Arab influences are evident all over the continent in the architecture, the foods, and even in the games and sports Africans enjoy. Soccer, originally brought to Africa by English colonists, is by far the most popular sport. Horse and camel riding are pursued in the northern mountains of Tunisia. Camel races are popular, too!

In Morocco, village children play soc-

Chapter 9 Review

True/False

On a separate sheet of paper, mark each question below either T for True or F for False.

1. Your body type is called your *somatotype*.
2. The graph showing the relationship between body weight and the risk for premature death is *J* shaped.
3. Lean body weight equals body fat weight divided by total body weight.
4. The size of your fat cells will not increase after you reach the age of twenty-five.
5. The energy balance includes energy input and energy expenditure.
6. RMR increases as you age and is higher for females than males.
7. Adopting a diet of less than 1,000 calories is a good way to lose weight.
8. One pound of fat is equivalent to 3,500 calories.
9. Height and weight charts really do not provide information about how lean or fat you are.
10. Anorexia nervosa is associated with disordered eating and excessive exercise disorder.

Multiple Choice

1. What is the minimum recommended amount of essential fat for young adult males?
   a. 1 percent
   b. 7 percent
   c. 12 percent
   d. 18 percent
2. What is the minimum daily recommended caloric intake for young adult females?
   a. 500 calories per day
   b. 1,000 calories per day
   c. 1,500 calories per day
   d. 2,000 calories per day
3. Your body composition is influenced by which of the following?
   a. genetics
   b. age
   c. gender
   d. all of the above
4. Your RMR is not influenced by which of the following?
   a. age
   b. height
   c. gender
   d. physical activity level
5. If you want to lose a pound of fat in a week, how many calories should you lose per day to be successful?
   a. 100
   b. 250
   c. 375
   d. 500
6. What percentage of your body fat is between your muscles and skin?
   a. 25 percent
   b. 50 percent
   c. 75 percent
   d. 100 percent
7. The body composition evaluation method of underwater weighing is based on what concept?
   a. fat floats
   b. fat sinks
   c. fat neither sinks nor floats
   d. none of the above

Answers

True/False

1. T
2. T
3. F
4. F
5. T
6. F
7. F
8. T
9. T
10. T

Multiple Choice

1. b.
2. d.
3. d.
4. b.
5. d.
6. b.
7. a.

cer, but also swim and learn gymnastics. Casablanca residents are enthusiastic about rugby, bicycle racing, horse racing, and camel racing. Near Marrakech, acrobats train at a tumbling school, while wealthy Moroccans ski in the Atlas mountains.

Further southeast in Ghana, students play rugby and tag at recess. Here the national sport is soccer, too, but athletes also compete and excel in boxing and track and field events, especially sprints, relays, the long jump, and the triple jump. Toward the southernmost end of the continent in Zimbabwe, European-style sports like cricket, lawn bowling, golf, tennis, and polo are primarily enjoyed by the white population.

Chapter 9 Review

Multiple Choice
continued

8. c.
9. a.
10. b.

8. What type of high-calorie burning activity is especially important for you to include in your body composition improvement plan?

  a. flexibility
  b. plyometric
  c. aerobic
  d. anaerobic

9. If you want to gain weight, how many pounds per week would be healthy and effective?

  a. ½
  b. 1
  c. 2
  d. 5

10. Which of the following signs or symptoms is not characteristic of bulimia?

  a. noticeable weight loss or gain
  b. lack of concern about weight
  c. habit of visiting the bathroom immediately after meals
  d. depressed moods

Discussion

1. Answers may vary but could include: genetics, gender, RMR, caloric intake, and caloric expenditure.

2. Answers may vary but could include: measuring BMI, using height/weight charts, using body circumference measures, skinfold measures, underwater weighing, bioelectrical impedance, and MRI scans.

3. Modify your caloric intake and caloric expenditure by following the example in Figure 9.15. For weight maintenance, caloric intake needs to equal caloric expenditure. For weight loss, caloric input needs to be less than caloric expenditure. For weight gain, caloric input needs to be greater than caloric expenditure.

Discussion

1. List and describe five factors that influence your body composition.

2. List and describe five methods to evaluate your body composition.

3. Explain how you can safely reduce your body weight, increase your body weight, or maintain your body weight.

Vocabulary Experience

4 caloric input
1 anorexia nervosa
5 caloric expenditure
3 essential fat
2 lean muscle weight
6 resting metabolic rate

Vocabulary Experience

Match the correct term in Column A to the definition in Column B by writing the appropriate number in each blank.

Column A	Column B
____ caloric input	**1.** An eating disorder in which people abnormally restrict their caloric intake.
____ anorexia nervosa	**2.** Bone, muscle, and connective tissue weight.
____ caloric expenditure	**3.** Needed to insulate your body against the cold and to help cushion your internal organs and protect them from injury.
____ essential fat	**4.** The number of calories you consume.
____ lean muscle weight	**5.** The amount of calories you expend or burn in daily physical activity.
____ resting metabolic rate	**6.** The amount of calories you need and expend while sitting comfortably at rest.

Critical Thinking

1. Body weight does not take into consideration your body type or changes that occur with body composition due to growth and development.

Special Needs

Traditional tests and evaluations used to determine body composition are usually not of much use when trying to utilize them with the disabled population. Unlike the able-bodied population, in which standards for assessing body composition exist, there are no standards specifically for disabled students. Skinfold measurements do not provide valid indications of an individual's body composition if that individual's disability is such that a great deal of atrophy has occurred. When atrophy occurs, lean body mass decreases.

Critical Thinking

1. Why is body weight a poor indicator of total body composition? Explain your answer.
2. What behaviors will slow down or speed up your resting metabolic rate?
3. Respond to this statement: *I don't care if I do look thin in the mirror; I still want to lose more weight.*

Case Study — Jackie's Activity Level

Jackie is a sixteen-year-old inactive female who has 32 percent body fat and would like to lose 20 pounds. However, she is unsure about how to lose the weight safely and effectively, reduce her body fat to 25 percent, and begin a regular physical activity or exercise program. Therefore, Jackie needs the help of someone knowledgeable about designing and implementing fitness programs—someone like you!

Here is your assignment:

Assume you are Jackie's friend. She asks you for some assistance with her plans for improving her body composition. Make a list of things Jackie should consider and do before beginning a program to control her body composition. Then list

the recommendations that you would give to Jackie for the first two weeks of her program.

The following will help you guide Jackie:

KEYS TO HELP YOU

- Consider Jackie's current body composition and percentage of body fat.
- Think about how she should evaluate her current body composition.
- Analyze her needs and goals. (For example, how should she go about controlling her body composition?)
- Determine a reasonable plan for Jackie that covers the concepts of specificity, frequency, intensity, time/duration, and progression.

Anorexia nervosa can be an extremely serious disorder that can lead to hypertension, slower heart rate, dehydration, hypothermia, cardiac arrest, and in some cases, death. Bulimia sufferers also face the same risk of developing serious side effects as those who are anorexic. In addition, bulimics are at risk of developing ulcers, gastrointestinal disturbances, and cardiac problems associated with potassium and sodium levels.

2. Your resting metabolic rate (RMR) will drop if you restrict the calories in your diet. It will be increased if you participate regularly in physical activity.
3. This may indicate that the individual has a false sense of self-image and be overly concerned with appearance.

KEYS TO CASE STUDY

Jackie should complete the PAR-Q in Chapter 2 before beginning her program. If she can answer "no" to the seven questions, she can begin a general personal fitness program. Jackie should set a goal of trying to lose weight gradually over time at about 1 pound per week. She should have her body composition checked about every 3 months. She should start an aerobic fitness program 3–5 days per week, and begin lifting weights 3 times per week. In the first two weeks of her program, she should begin slowly (3 aerobic workouts and 2 weight training workouts per week) and work up to a point where she can expend 250 more calories per day than usual.

Chapter Overview

Chapter 10 is 34 pages long and divided into the four sections listed to the right. Major learning outcomes of the chapter are also listed to the right. Briefly, this chapter introduces students to basic food nutrients and to ways in which the body uses these nutrients to produce energy for personal fitness. It gives students valuable information that will help them make good decisions when considering a weight control or weight gain program. It also gives students the knowledge to evaluate diet plans according to national guidelines.

Teacher Resource Material

In the Teacher Resource Package you will find the following materials to help you teach this chapter.

Activity Sheets

One Reteaching Worksheet is provided for each section of this chapter. A handout is also provided for the Active Mind/Active Body activity on page 352.

Chapter 10

Nutrition and Your Personal Fitness

330

PACING CHART

You could easily spend five to six days teaching this chapter if students read the entire chapter, do the Active Mind/Active Body activities, and complete several of the handouts from the Teacher Resource Package. However, you can cover the material in this chapter in four days. It is recommended that physical activity be a regular part of each class period (20 to 30 minutes minimum). Following is an example of how to cover the main topics in the chapter in a limited amount of time.

Time	Suggestions
Day 1	Assign Section 1 for students to read prior to class. In class, discuss the six classes of food nutrients, and foods that con-

Contents

Outcomes

After reading and studying this chapter, you will be able to:

1. Identify the basic food nutrients, and explain how developing and maintaining a healthy diet can positively influence your functional health.
2. Explain how good nutrition contributes to the development and maintenance of moderate to high levels of personal fitness.
3. Give examples of appropriate choices for developing a healthy diet.
4. Discuss ways to evaluate your current and future nutrition.
5. Identify strategies for improving your nutrition choices and making you a smarter food consumer.
6. Identify and explain ways you can make food choices that will improve your performance fitness.

Key Terms

After reading and studying this chapter, you will be able to understand and provide practical definitions for the following terms:

nutrient	fat	water-soluble vitamin
carbohydrate	saturated fat	antioxidant
glucose	unsaturated fat	mineral
hypoglycemic	protein	electrolyte
glycogen	amino acid	Food Guide Pyramid
simple carbohydrate	vegetarian	Recommended Daily
complex carbohydrate	vitamin	Allowance (RDA)
fiber	fat-soluble vitamin	caffeine

Transparencies/Masters

A transparency or master is provided in the Teacher Resource Package for each of the following figures: 10.1, 10.2, 10.3, 10.4, 10.5, 10.6, 10.7, 10.8, 10.9, 10.10, 10.11, 10.12, 10.13, 10.14, 10.15, 10.16, and 10.17.

Software

Diet Analysis Plus (Version 2.0) West Publishing.

Discuss the Photo

Ask students what their favorite foods are. Then ask, Why is it important for you to try different types of foods? How do you think learning about nutrition can affect your personal fitness? Do you ever help do the family shopping? If so, do you read labels for nutrition information?

331

	tain each nutrient and/or combinations of nutrients.
Day 2	Assign Section 2 for students to read prior to class. In class, discuss the Dietary Guidelines for Americans in relation to the Food Guide Pyramid and nutrition labeling.
Day 3	Assign Section 3 for students to read prior to class. In class, discuss the FIT concept in relation to healthy nutrition. Also, use Figures 10.12, 10.13, and 10.14 to show and discuss weight maintenance, loss, and gain. Have students begin the Active Mind/Active Body activity on page 352.
Day 4	Assign Section 4 for students to read prior to class. Have students finish, if necessary, the Active Mind/Active Body activity on page 352; in class, discuss which menu they found to be the most nutritious. Why do they think so? Also, discuss nutrition in regard to performance fitness, using the appropriate photos and figures.

CHAPTER 10

CHAPTER 10
SECTION 1
332

Focus

Outcome

In **Section 1** students will learn:

1. To identify the basic food nutrients.
2. To explain how developing and maintaining a healthy diet can positively influence their functional health.

Focus Activities

1. Use transparencies/masters of Figures 10.1, 10.2, 10.3, 10.4, and 10.5 to discuss the six basic food nutrients.
2. Use figures and photos in this chapter to give examples of the basic food nutrients.
3. Give a pre-test to determine how much students already know about nutrition.

INTRODUCTION

*M*aking sure you get proper nutrition involves understanding what nutrients are available in foods and how your body uses them. Nutrients are substances in foods that your body needs for proper growth, development, and functioning. Proper nutrition is closely associated with good health and freedom from disease. You have already learned about the benefits of adopting a physically active lifestyle. You also need to learn about proper nutrition so that you will be able to meet your nutrient needs for regular physical activity and exercise.

The field of nutrition is filled with fallacies, misconceptions, fads, and misinterpretations. It is often difficult, even for experts in the field of nutrition, to determine the difference between fact and fiction in regard to various nutrition claims that we all see in the media. By gaining an understanding about the basic principles of sound nutrition, however, you will become a wiser and better consumer.

A great deal more nutrition information is available to the public today than ever before. This means it is easier than ever to develop and maintain a sound nutrition plan for yourself. In this chapter you will learn about the basic food nutrients, how to balance your dietary needs, how to read food labels, how to evaluate your nutrition, how to develop and maintain healthy nutrition now and in your future, and how to eat to improve your performance fitness.

SECTION 1   The Basic Food Nutrients

nutrient

a substance in foods that the body needs for proper growth, development, and functioning.

carbohydrate

a nutrient that includes sugars and starches (like pasta).

glucose

sugar; the basic form of carbohydrate and a valuable source of energy.

Meeting your dietary requirements involves eating the right proportion of nutrients daily. Adequate intake of all the **nutrients** contributes to your feeling good, looking good, and performing well both mentally and physically. Your body grows and renews itself daily. You develop new tissues every day to build and repair bone, muscle, skin, and blood. What you eat today will influence your growth and development tomorrow.

The best foods for you to consume are those that will meet your daily nutrition needs to maintain and improve your functional health. The nutrients that supply your body with its daily nutrition requirements fall into six classes: carbohydrate, fat, protein, vitamins, minerals, and water.

Carbohydrate

Carbohydrates (which include sugars and starches) is one of the most important nutrients you consume in your diet. **Glucose**, the basic form of carbohydrate, is a valuable source of energy. If your

ABILITY LEVELS

Reteaching

Some students may need help mastering the concepts contained in this section. In your Teacher Resource Package, you will find the reproducible worksheet shown here. This worksheet should help students who have been absent and those needing additional help to improve their comprehension and retention of the content in this section.

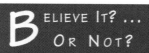

BELIEVE IT? ... OR NOT?

Of the current ten leading causes of death of Americans, eight have been associated with improper diet and excessive alcohol consumption.

See page 359 for answer.

hypoglycemic

having a condition in which the blood glucose level drops and the person feels dizzy, tired, and irritable.

glycogen

the stored form of glucose in the liver and skeletal muscle.

simple carbohydrate

simple sugar; a carbohydrate that is absorbed quickly into the bloodstream and that provides a quick form of energy.

complex carbohydrate

a carbohydrate that is starchy and broken down more slowly in the body than a simple carbohydrate.

• *You probably first learned about nutrition at an early age. It is now time for you to learn more and put your nutrition knowledge into practice.*

blood glucose levels drop significantly, you can become **hypoglycemic** and feel dizzy, tired, and irritable.

Glucose can be stored to a limited extent in your body in the form of **glycogen** in the liver and skeletal muscle. People who engage in ultraendurance training or competition lasting two hours or longer often deplete their glycogen stores. People who are regularly glycogen depleted are at higher risk for overtraining and staleness (poor physical performance). To maintain normal glucose and glycogen levels, you must regularly replenish your carbohydrate stores. Carbohydrates come mainly from plant foods and are classified as either simple or complex.

Simple carbohydrates are called *simple sugars,* and they taste sweet. They are absorbed quickly into your bloodstream and provide a quick form of energy. Examples of simple sugars are milk, fruits, candy, cookies, and soda. **Complex carbohydrates** are starchy—for example, potatoes and corn. They are broken down more slowly by your body than are simple carbohydrates. Other examples of complex carbohydrates are breads, cereals, pasta, and rice.

Teach & Apply

Discussion

Ask students, What are nutrients? What nutrient do you think is the most important to functional health?

Activity

On the board or overhead projector, have students list the six groups of nutrients. Under each nutrient, write foods that they have eaten in the past 24 hours that contain each specific nutrient. (Hint: Some foods could have more than one nutrient.)

Healthy People 2000

Objective 2.5—Reduce dietary fat intake to an average of 30 percent of calories or less and average saturated fat intake to less than 10 percent of calories among people aged two and older.

Enrichment

This activity will allow you to provide a more challenging learning experience for some of your students.

Have the students collect pictures of food items they enjoy eating. The collection of pictures may be obtained from magazines, newspapers, and advertisements. In order to better represent the Food Guide Pyramid, you may wish to assign a certain number of pictures to be collected in each food group. Once the pictures have been collected, have the students make flash cards. On the front of the card students should glue a picture of one food item. On the back of the card, the students are to write the number of kilocalories and the number of fat grams for the food item. "The Calorie Game" may then be played by participants who guess or state the number of kilocalories and/or fat grams in the food item.

Healthy People 2000

Objective 2.6—**Increase complex carbohydrate and fiber-containing foods in the diets of adults to five or more daily servings for vegetables (including legumes) and fruits, and to six or more daily servings for grain products.**

Teacher Support Notes

• The average American consumes 130 pounds of fat per year. This amount of fat would be equal to eating more than one full stick of butter each day.
• Practically all foods contain mixtures of three energy-yielding nutrients. Foods are sometimes classified, however, by the predominant nutrient. It is incorrect to call meat a protein; it is a protein-rich food. Beef, for example, contains fat as well as protein.

Discussion

• Discuss the the combinations of nutrients in foods. Ask students to give examples of these foods.
• Discuss the energy demands of the body and how the types of carbohydrates contribute to the functioning of the body.

• *Peas and beans are rich in carbohydrate. They are also good sources of fiber.*

fiber

a type of carbohydrate that is not digestible by humans and provides no energy.

BELIEVE IT? ... OR NOT?

The best way to get all the vitamins and minerals that you need daily is to take supplements.

See page 359 for answer.

The total amount of carbohydrates in your diet should be 50 to 60 percent of all the calories that you consume daily. Figure 10.1 provides a list of carbohydrates from various food groups.

Both complex and simple carbohydrates are important for your energy needs, but most of your calories should come from complex carbohydrate sources. Simple carbohydrates supply energy. However, they lack important vitamins (such as B vitamins) and minerals (such as iron) and are associated with producing cavities. Because simple carbohydrates lack essential vitamins and minerals, calories from simple carbohydrates are often called *empty calories*.

Fiber is another type of carbohydrate. It aids in proper digestion. Fiber is not digestible by humans and provides no energy. However, it helps eliminate waste products from the body and provides bulk (volume or size) to the diet. Some foods high in fiber include grains, stems, roots, nuts, seeds, and fruit coverings.

Dietary fiber is associated with reducing your risk for certain cancers, such as colon cancer. Your dietary intake of fiber is important and should be about 30 grams per day. However, you should also avoid too much fiber in your diet. Too much fiber can reduce your absorption of valuable minerals and cause lower digestive tract distress. You can learn to monitor your fiber intake, as well as your intake of other nutrients, by reading the nutrition labels on packaged foods. You will learn more about this in a later section of this chapter.

Bread, Cereal, Rice, and Pasta Group	Fruit Group	Vegetable Group	Milk, Yogurt, and Cheese Group
Bagels	Apples	Broccoli	Milk (2% or skim)
Breads	Bananas	Carrots	Pudding
Cereals	Fruit juices	Corn	Sherbet
Crackers	Nectarines	Peppers	Yogurt
English muffins	Oranges	(green, red)	Yogurt, frozen
Graham crackers	Pears	Potatoes	
Pasta (spaghetti,		Potatoes, sweet	
macaroni)		Tomatoes	
Popcorn			
Pretzels			
Rice			

It is important to choose foods from all the food groups to get the appropriate nutrients your body needs daily.

• **Figure 10.1** *Sources of Carbohydrates. Source:* Adapted with permission from D. S. Jennings and S. N. Steen, *Play Hard, Eat Hard,* American Dietary Association (Minneapolis: Chronimed Publishing, 1995).

⌐ Across the Disciplines

Geography

Have students record the number of meals that would qualify as fast food that they have had over the last week at home, school, or while dining out. Generate a class list of the different restau-

rants, such as Kentucky Fried Chicken, Taco Bell, Subway, or Pizza Hut, that they frequent. Have each student research a specific restaurant and collect the following information: the founder, location of the first restaurant and date it opened, ethnicity of region, type of food

• *Pastas and bread are excellent sources of complex carbohydrates.*

Fat

fat

a type of nutrient that is high in
energy; found in animal tissues,
nuts, seeds, and oils of some
plants.

Fats are nutrients that provide a valuable source of energy for your
body. Fats supply twice as much energy per gram as carbohydrates
or proteins. Unfortunately, we all can store too much fat, especially
if we do not balance our caloric intake and caloric expenditure.

Fats come primarily from animal products, but they also come
from the nuts and oils of some plants. Fats help absorb and carry the
vitamins A, D, E, and K in your body. Fats can also be stored as
triglycerides in your adipose (or fat) tissues. These triglycerides supply energy for exercise, especially as time/durations increase to
thirty minutes or longer. Fats also make foods taste good and
decrease hunger, because they take longer to digest than the other
nutrients.

Saturated Fat. Fats can be classified as saturated or unsaturated. **Saturated fats** are usually solid at room temperature and
come mainly from animal fats. Examples include lard, butter, milk,
and meat fats. Some oils, such as palm oil, peanut oil, and coconut
oil, are also high in saturated fat.

saturated fat

a fat that is usually solid at
room temperature, comes
mainly from animal fat, and typically contains high levels of
cholesterol.

Saturated fats typically contain high levels of cholesterol. Your body
always produces some cholesterol, and cholesterol is important to
the normal function of your body's cells. However, consuming a diet
high in saturated fats can cause your liver to produce excess cholesterol. Cholesterol levels above normal—especially over time—significantly increase a person's risk for heart disease and atherosclerosis
(see Chapter 5). To help you control your cholesterol levels, the

Activity

Divide the class into six groups. Give each group food composition charts for certain types of foods and have students investigate the differences in fat content of the foods. Examples of foods could be: milk (whole, 2%, skim), cheese (processed, hard, skim), frozen treats (ice cream, frozen yogurt, popsicles), and chips (regular, low fat, baked). Have them present their findings.

Discussion

• Discuss the following with students: Too much saturated fat, as well as total fat, in one's diet can put one at risk for heart disease. To reduce the amount of saturated fat in your diet, substitute nonmeat sources of protein for meat sources occasionally; substitute margarine for butter, or skim milk for whole milk.

• Ask students to describe foods that are normally low in fat but have been altered in such a way so as to make them high in fat. (Baked potato with sour cream, cheese, or butter or salad with cheese and dressing).

• *French fries may taste good, but they contain high levels of saturated fat when cooked in lard.*

unsaturated fat

a fat that is usually liquid at room temperature, comes mainly from plant sources, and does not contain cholesterol.

protein

a type of nutrient that is the basic building block of the body.

amino acid

a class of compounds that are the basic building blocks for proteins.

National Cholesterol Education Program recommends that you eat no more than 300 milligrams of cholesterol per day.

Unsaturated Fat. **Unsaturated fats** are usually liquid at room temperature, come mainly from plant sources, and do not contain cholesterol. Examples of unsaturated fats include corn oil, soybean oil, olive oil, sunflower oil, and some fish oils.

The total amount of fat in your diet should be no more than 30 percent of the total calories that you consume daily. Your saturated fat intake should be no more than 10 percent of your total daily fat consumption. Individuals who are trying to lose weight may reduce their fat intake to less than 30 percent of their total daily calories. However, excessive fat restriction (less than 20 percent) may be difficult to achieve, take the joy out of eating, and perhaps lead to eating disorders.

Protein

Proteins are nutrients that provide the basic building blocks of your body. They help you repair hair, skin, muscles, hemoglobin, hormones, and other proteins in your blood. Protein is very important for your normal growth and development.

Amino acids are compounds that can combine in different ways to form proteins. Your body can produce some protein (nonessential amino acids), but you must also consume a balanced diet to get the other protein (essential amino acids) that you need. The protein that you consume daily should include low-fat animal foods, as well as a

• *You have a choice when you are eating on the run. Try to make wise nutritional selections.*

Special Needs

Many students with disabilities take medications for various reasons. Medications can affect the body's nutritional balance. Students taking medications should always check with their physicians regarding any side effects and/or any necessary nutritional supplements. Also, it should be noted that certain health conditions may require supplements.

No matter what the disability is, the nutritional principles presented in this chapter apply to everyone. They should be emphasized with all students in mind.

Water is essential, especially for the

wide variety of plant foods. Some foods that are high in protein are meats, fish, poultry, eggs, cheese, and milk.

The total amount of protein in your diet should be 15 to 20 percent of the calories that you consume daily. Figure 10.2 provides a list of foods high in protein and examples of serving sizes.

Protein that comes from animal foods is complete. In other words, it has all the essential amino acids. Protein from plant foods is incomplete, or missing some of the essential amino acids. This fact is important for **vegetarians**, people who eliminate meat, fish, and poultry from their diets. (Some vegetarians also eliminate eggs and milk products from their diets.) Those who adopt a vegetarian diet need to eat a wide variety of plant proteins to get a combination of all the essential amino acids.

Although protein is important for healthy nutrition, eating excessive amounts of protein can do more harm than good. When you consume more protein than your body can use, it is stored as fat. Most people do not need or want to store excess fat. As you have learned throughout this text, excess fat reduces functional health.

Some people think that if they take protein supplements, they can rapidly increase the size of their muscles (hypertrophy). However, you learned in Chapters 7 and 8 that you will only get stronger and develop larger muscles if you lift weights at greater intensities and if your hormone levels (testosterone) increase.

vegetarian

a person who eliminates meat, fish, and poultry (and sometimes eggs and milk products) from their diet.

REMEMBER This!

Although very active people (for example, strength athletes) may need more protein daily because they are expending more calories than normal, they can get all the protein they need by taking in more calories in a balanced diet. Therefore, it is unnecessary and costly to use protein supplements. Advertisements that suggest that their protein supplements will enhance your performance are misleading and often one-sided.

Protein in Various Foods		
Food	Protein (grams)	Serving Size
Milk (2% or less)	8	8 ounces (1 cup)
Yogurt	8	8 ounces (1 cup)
Cheese	13	2 ounces (processed)
Fish	21	3 ounces (tuna sandwich)
Poultry	21	3 ounces (grilled chicken)
Meat (beef)	21	3 ounces (hamburger or roast beef sandwich)
Peanut butter	8	2 tablespoons
Nuts	5–7	1 ounce (1 handful)
Eggs	7	1

● **Figure 10.2** *Protein in Various Foods. Source:* Adapted with permission from D. S. Jennings and S. N. Steen, *Play Hard, Eat Hard,* American Dietetic Association (Minneapolis: Chronimed Publishing, 1995).

Teaching Strategies

Invite a nutritionist or spokesperson from either the American Heart Association or the American Cancer Society to talk to the class about eating for good health and fitness.

Discussion

• Discuss in class what is meant by "complete" proteins. (They contain all the essential amino acids.)
• Discuss a vegetarian diet and reasons people might choose this type of diet. Explain the combinations of foods that are needed for their bodies to receive the protein they need.

Teacher Support Notes

You may want to tell students the following: There are two types of vegetarians. Lacto-ovo-vegetarians avoid only meat, poultry, and fish. They get complete protein from eggs, milk, cheese, and yogurt. Lacto means milk and ovo means eggs. Other individuals,

disabled student, because it serves as a regulator of body temperature. This is particularly important for students with spinal cord injuries and other disabilities involving the central nervous system, since temperature regulation is often compromised. Water intake must be emphasized with these students.

One of the keys to helping monitor caloric intake and, therefore, weight control, is to be aware of the food that is being consumed by the individual. This involves the ability to read labels and analyze nutritional qualities of food in the diet. This may be a difficult task for students with cognitive disabilities who may have difficulty reading and/or processing such information.

called vegans, eliminate all animal sources of food. Unless they combine foods carefully, they will not have the protein they need. Three equations can help vegetarians plan meals with complete protein:

- Legumes + grains = complete protein
- Legumes + nuts or seeds = complete protein
- Any plant protein + eggs or dairy products = complete protein.

In addition to growth and maintenance of cells, enzymes, and hormones, protein aids in the production of antibodies and maintains an electrolyte balance by regulating the quantity of fluids in the body.

Discussion

Use Figure 10.3 to discuss with students the difference between fat-soluble and water-soluble vitamins. Include reasons why taking excess vitamins can be harmful.

- *Seafood, poultry, and lean red meats are examples of foods that are high in protein content.*

vitamin

a nutrient that helps control growth and helps the body release energy to do work.

fat-soluble vitamin

a vitamin that dissolves in the body's fat tissues and can be stored in the body; the vitamins A, D, E and K.

water-soluble vitamin

a vitamin that is not stored in the body and needs to be replaced regularly; vitamin C and the B vitamins.

antioxidant

a vitamin or mineral that may help protect the body from various types of cell damage.

Vitamins

Vitamins are nutrients that help control growth and help your body release energy to do work. Vitamins do not contain calories and do not provide your body with energy themselves. Vitamins are classified as fat soluble or water soluble.

Fat-soluble vitamins dissolve in your body's fat tissues and can be stored in the body. The fat-soluble vitamins are vitamins A, D, E, and K. **Water-soluble vitamins** are not stored to any real extent in your body and need to be replaced regularly by eating a healthy diet. Vitamin C and the B vitamins (B_1, B_2, B_{12}) are examples of water-soluble vitamins. Figure 10.3 lists the major roles and sources of vitamins.

Many Americans believe that they do not get enough vitamins in their diet because they eat on the run all the time. They respond by taking vitamin supplements. However, supplements are usually not necessary. Although people can develop a vitamin deficiency over time, it is rare. It happens only in extreme situations, such as starvation or certain disease conditions.

Excessive use of vitamin supplements can actually damage your body. Therefore, you should seek medical advice before taking vitamin supplements. A simple multiple vitamin, if needed, is often all that is recommended by physicians or professional dietitians.

Recently, scientists have found that the regular consumption of some vitamins and minerals called **antioxidants** may help protect the body from various types of cell damage. Antioxidants stabilize cells, helping prevent damage to them from cancer, atherosclerosis, overtraining, and premature aging. Vitamin C, vitamin E, and beta-

CRITICAL THINKING

Have the students bring in:
1. Some type of diet plan (from a magazine, book, computer search, one that parents have used, and so on)
2. An advertisement for some type of weight loss plan, the more unusual the better

First, discuss diet plans in general, using good plans and poor ones to make key points. Students need to be able to examine any diet plan critically, as statistics show that the majority of Americans will diet during their lifetimes.

Have students take two of the diet

Fat-soluble

Vitamin	What it Does in the Body	Major Food and Other Sources
A	Maintains normal vision and healthy bones, skin, internal linings, and reproductive system; strengthens resistance to infection	Vitamin A-fortified milk and dairy products; margarine; liver; dark green vegetables (broccoli, spinach, greens); deep orange fruits and vegetables (cantaloupe, apricots, sweet potatoes, carrots)
D	Promotes growth and health of bones	Vitamin D-fortified milk; eggs; liver; sardines; sunlight on the skin
E	Protects the body's cells from attack by oxygen	Vegetable oils and shortening; green, leafy vegetables; whole grains; nuts and seeds
K	Helps with blood clotting and bone growth	Normal bacteria in the digestive tract; liver; dark green, leafy vegetables; milk

Note: The names given here are the official names. Other names still commonly used and seen on labels are *alpha-tocopherol* for vitamin E, *vitamin B_1* for thiamin, *vitamin B_2* for riboflavin, *pyridoxine* for vitamin B_6, *folic acid* and *folacin* for folate, and *ascorbic acid* for vitamin C.

Water-soluble

Vitamin	What It Does in the Body	Major Food and Other Sources
C	Acts as the "glue" that holds cells together; strengthens blood vessel walls; helps wounds heal; helps bones grow; strengthens resistance to infection	Citrus fruits; dark green vegetables; cabbage-like vegetables; strawberries; peppers; potatoes
Thiamin	Helps the body use nutrients for energy	Small amounts in all nutritious foods
Riboflavin	Helps the body use nutrients for energy; supports normal vision; helps keep skin healthy	Milk; yogurt; cottage cheese; dark green vegetables; whole-grain products
Niacin	Helps the body use nutrients for energy; supports normal nervous system functions	Milk; eggs; poultry; fish; whole-grain products; all protein-containing foods
B_6	Helps the body use protein and form red blood cells	Green, leafy vegetables; meats; fish; poultry; whole-grain products; beans
B_{12}	Helps form new cells	Meat; fish; poultry; shellfish; eggs; milk; cheese
Folate	Helps form new cells	Dark green, leafy vegetables; beans; liver
Biotin and pantothenic acid	Helps the body use nutrients for energy	Widespread in foods

• **Figure 10.3**   *Major Roles and Sources of the Vitamins. Source:* Reprinted from F. S. Sizer, E. N. Whitney, and L. K. DeBruyne, *Making Life Choices: Health Skills and Concepts* (St. Paul: West Publishing, 1994).

Teacher Support Notes

You may want to tell students the following: Health habits change a person's need for vitamins. Smokers need more vitamin C, because one cigarette destroys about 25 mg of this vitamin. People living in smoggy cities do not get the same amount of vitamin D as people living in the country because smog absorbs the sun's ultraviolet rays.

Activity

Supply students with magazines that have pictures of food. Have students create a collage of foods representing all vitamins needed in a healthy diet.

plans students in the class have submitted and summarize positive and negative benefits of each plan in relation to proper nutrients, food pyramid, caloric intake compared to caloric needs of individuals, and so on.

Second, have students analyze the advertisements presented in class according to:

1. Claims made
2. Common denominators in the advertisements
3. Positive benefits
4. Negative aspects (especially if a drug is involved)
5. Nutritional value
6. Whether exercise is recommended as part of the plan

Any Body Can!

After students have read the feature on Oprah Winfrey, ask them if they think she will be able to keep her weight down. Ask them why they think she will or won't be able to maintain her weight loss. Then ask if they think Oprah is an exceptional person, or do they believe that **A**ny **B**ody **C**an apply himself or herself and do what Oprah did.

Any Body Can!

Oprah Winfrey

Oprah Winfrey in a well-known television talk-show host and actress. Oprah is also famous for her personal battles with weight gain and loss.

Oprah won a scholarship to Tennessee State University and graduated in 1976. She began her television career during college and became a reporter and news anchor for WTVF-TV in Nashville, Tennessee.

Oprah became the first African American woman to host a successful, nationally syndicated weekday talk show, The Oprah Winfrey Show. She is also the first African American female to own a production company for film and television (Harpo Studios) in the U.S.

Although Oprah has had great professional success, she has struggled for the past several years to control her weight. She has often shared her "yo-yoing" weight loss problems with her television audience. She repeatedly went through periods of rapid weight loss as she tried the latest "quick-fix diet," only to see all the weight, and then some, come back.

In March of 1993, Oprah weighed 222 pounds. She decided to contact a nationally known personal trainer to help her achieve and maintain healthy weight loss. Based on her personal goals and desires, Oprah developed a sensible dietary plan and began to exercise regularly. To achieve her weight loss goals, she would rise at 5:00 AM and run 4 miles on a treadmill. She also added weight lifting into her personal exercise plan.

Oprah progressed steadily in her personal fitness program. After the initial phase (8 weeks), she was able to lose 8 to 10 pounds each month. By July of 1993, she was running 5 to 6 miles per day at a 10 to 11 minute per mile pace. In August of that same year she completed a half-marathon (13.1 miles) in 2 hours and 16 minutes, and on November 10, 1993, she reached her goal weight of 150 pounds. Oprah lost 72 pounds in about 7 months, which is as much as anyone could realistically lose in that time (about 2 pounds per week) and *maintain the weight loss.*

In 1994 Oprah decided to train for a full marathon (26.2 miles). She concentrated on increasing her running mileage, and also intensified her strength and muscular conditioning. In 1994, she successfully completed the Marine Corps Marathon without walking a step. Since the marathon Oprah has cut back on her intensive training, but she is still eating sensibly and exercising regularly, to achieve even better levels of body composition.

Not everyone can be a television talk-show host, actress, and marathon runner like Oprah Winfrey, but Any Body Can learn to eat sensibly and live an active lifestyle to control their body composition. That's right, you can do it!

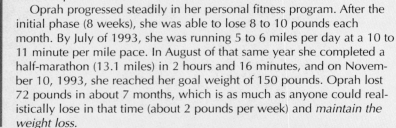

Wellness Connection

Health Foods, Natural Foods, and Organic Foods

Health food is a term often used to imply that a food is special and can benefit people's health. This term, however, is inherently misleading due to the fact that almost all foods are healthy when eaten in moderation and can be unhealthy when eaten in excess. Any food that has caloric value (a measurement of energy) would contribute to your health. By this definition, Ding Dongs, Dove Bars, and Dr. Pepper would all fit

carotene (associated with vitamin A) are examples of antioxidants. You will probably be reading and learning more about antioxidants in the near future.

Minerals

mineral

a chemical element that is important for the body's structure and function and for regulating metabolism.

Minerals are chemical elements that are important for your body's structure and function and for regulating metabolism. Like vitamins, minerals do not contain calories and do not supply your body with energy. Minerals are classified as either major minerals (your body needs more of these) or trace minerals (your body needs less of these). Examples of major minerals include calcium, phosphorus, magnesium, sodium, potassium, chloride, and sulfur. Examples of trace minerals are iron, manganese, copper, iodine, zinc, cobalt, fluoride, and selenium. Figure 10.4 on the next page lists the major roles and sources of minerals.

Four minerals that are particularly important in relation to your personal fitness are calcium, iron, potassium, and sodium. A diet rich in these and other minerals, along with an active lifestyle, can help you reduce your risk for chronic problems and diseases.

If you do not consume enough calcium in your diet or have problems absorbing what you do eat, you may be at a higher risk for

BELIEVE IT? ... OR NOT?

A person who is lifting weights regularly, and who wants to increase muscle mass, needs to consume four to five times the protein consumed by the average person.

See page 359 for answer.

● *Dairy products are rich in minerals and vitamins.*

Discussion

Use Figure 10.4 on the next page to discuss minerals. For each mineral, have students list a food they eat that supplies that mineral. Then have them list a function of each mineral.

Activity

Divide the class into four groups. Assign each group one of these minerals: calcium, iron, potassium, and sodium. Have each group prepare a presentation (skit, lecture, or poster) about the mineral and its importance to personal fitness.

into the category of health foods!

Natural foods are promoted as those foods produced and marketed with a minimum of processing and without the use of additives or artificial ingredients. This really applies only to meat and poultry. There is no legal meaning for "natural" when used with baked goods, processed foods, or beverages.

Organic foods are said to be foods grown without pesticides or synthetic fertilizers. This term is also misleading because in scientific usage, "organic" refers to compounds that contain carbon, which virtually all foods contain. Like the word "natural," "organic" has no legal meaning, and the term organic cannot be used to describe meat or poultry.

Discussion

Ask students if they think they drink enough water. Try to determine the range with regard to the amount of water that the students drink. Why do they think some drink so much more than others? Discuss how an individual might find opportunities throughout the day to drink water.

Teacher Support Notes

You may want to tell students the following: Foods containing water are a main source of the large quantity of water needed by the human body. Lettuce is about 96% water, eggs 75%, and white bread about 30%.

Mineral	What It Does in the Body	Major Food Sources
Calcium	Structural material of bones and teeth; helps muscles contract and relax; helps nerves communicate; helps blood to clot	Milk and milk products; small fish with bones; dark green vegetables; beans
Phosphorus	Structural material of bones and teeth; supports energy processes; part of cells' genetic material	All foods that come from animals
Magnesium	Helps build bones and teeth; helps build protein; helps muscles contract and relax; helps nerves communicate	Nuts; beans; dark green vegetables; seafood; whole grains; chocolate
Sodium	Maintains cell fluids; helps nerves communicate	Salt; soy sauce; processed foods; celery; milk
Potassium	Helps build protein; maintains fluid balance; helps nerves communicate; helps muscles contract	All nutritious foods; meats; milk and milk products; fruits; vegetables; whole grains; beans
Iron	Helps red blood cells carry oxygen; helps tissues use oxygen to release energy; supports normal immunity	Red meats; fish; poultry; shellfish; eggs; beans; dried fruits
Zinc	Helps build genetic material and protein; supports normal immunity; supports growth; helps make sperm; helps wounds heal	Protein-rich foods; meats; fish; poultry; whole grains
Iodine	Part of thyroid hormone needed for growth	Iodized salt; seafood
Selenium	Helps vitamin E protect cells from attack by oxygen	Seafood; meats; vegetables
Copper	Helps make red blood cells; helps build protein; helps the body use iron	Organ meats such as liver; seafood; nuts
Chromium	Helps the body use carbohydrates and fats	Liver; nuts; whole grains; cheese
Fluoride	Helps strengthen bones and teeth	Water; seafood
Manganese	Helps with many processes	Whole grains; fruits; vegetables
Molybdenum	Helps with many processes	Milk; beans

• **Figure 10.4** *Major Roles and Sources of the Minerals. Source:* Reprinted from F. S. Sizer, E. N. Whitney, and L. K. DeBruyne, *Making Life Choices: Health Skills and Concepts* (St. Paul: West Publishing, 1994).

osteoporosis (or brittle bones) as you age. You can significantly reduce your risk for osteoporosis by eating foods rich in calcium (see Figure 10.4) and by doing regular weight-bearing exercises, along with some weight training.

Iron is important for the formation of hemoglobin, which helps the blood carry oxygen (see Chapter 5). If your iron levels drop below normal, you may develop iron-deficiency anemia. This condition reduces your ability to carry oxygen and decreases your aerobic

Science and Technology

Technology is the best friend a P.E. teacher can have at his or her disposal. With electronic mail (e-mail) and Internet access, teachers have an unlimited set of nutrition resources available to them. The first place to locate information regarding nutrition is at http://www.dgsy.com/~trnutr/. This Internet address connects the physical education teacher to the world of training nutrition. Here, links are available to various newsgroups, companies, and individuals related to the field of nutrition. To review other nutrition sites, connect to http://www.yahoo.com

working ability. Vegetarians are at high risk for developing iron deficiencies because they do not eat meats, which are high in iron. However, vegetarians can reduce their risk for iron deficiency by eating a variety of plant foods rich in iron (beets and green leafy vegetables).

Potassium is a mineral that, in combination with sodium and calcium, helps maintain normal heart rhythm and control fluid balance. Sodium (Na^+), calcium (CA^{++}), and potassium (K^+) are often called **electrolytes**, because their electrical charges help control the body's fluid balance. *Fluid balance* refers to the body's ability to balance the amounts of water and electrolytes that are consumed with the amounts that are lost or excreted daily.

Potassium also aids in normal muscle contractions and in the conduction of nerve impulses that control the movement of your muscles. If your potassium levels drop low enough, such as when you exercise and sweat profusely, you may develop muscle cramps or problems with the conduction of nerve impulses. You can help maintain normal potassium levels by drinking plenty of fruit juices (like orange and tomato juices) or commercial sports drinks.

Many foods you eat (especially fast foods) are high in sodium. When you eat high levels of sodium, you tend to retain water. People with hypertension are often placed on low-sodium diets, which can help control their blood pressure by reducing fluid retention. Are you at high risk for developing hypertension? You may be at a higher risk for becoming hypertensive if your mother, father, grandmother, or grandfather has hypertension. If you are at high risk, you probably need to lower your sodium intake. It is a good idea to limit your sodium intake by not adding additional salt to your food. Participation in regular physical activity and exercise can also help control hypertension.

Water

From 60 to 70 percent of your body weight is water. Water is an essential nutrient for life. Without water, death would occur within six to seven days. Water helps regulate your body temperature, carries nutrients to cells, helps with digestion, and is important for chemical reactions in your body. It is recommended that you consume eight 8-ounce glasses of water or other fluids (milk, juices, and so on) daily to maintain your normal fluid balance.

As you learned in Chapter 2, it is especially important to drink adequate fluids when exercising in warm or hot environments. It is often impossible to "catch up" on your fluid balance if you wait until you are actually thirsty before you begin to drink. Thus, it is important to hydrate (drink fluids) before, during, and after moderate to vigorous physical activity or exercise. Figure 10.5 gives some general guidelines for drinking water or other fluids when you are active. Although water is the best and cheapest fluid to rehydrate with, you may pre-

electrolyte

a mineral whose electrical charge helps control the body's fluid balance.

• *Drink plenty of water to maintain your body's fluid balance.*

Healthy People 2000

Objective 2.19—**Increase to at least 75 percent the proportion of the Nation's schools that provide nutrition education from preschool through 12th grade, preferably as part of quality school health education.**

Most food preferences and many dietary habits are established during childhood. Providing nutrition education from preschool through 12th grade will reach children during the years when they are beginning to make their own decisions and to eat more food away from home.

Many students understand that there is a connection between good nutrition and good health, but a large number do not understand that a diet high in fat, sugars, or salt may increase the risk for certain chronic diseases. Although the majority know that a nutritious diet leads to good health, this knowledge is not reflected in their food-buying and meal patterns.

Assess

Use the Section 1 Review questions on the next page to assess the students' comprehension of the concepts presented in Section 1. Also, have students develop a food nutrient chart that explains at least two things they learned about each nutrient.

and type "nutrition" in the search index. Yahoo will return approximately 300 sites related to nutrition. This should be more than enough resources for the physical educator.

If physical education teachers are searching for nutritional software, they need to connect to http://mindlink.net/sasquatch or http://www.yahoo.com/

health/nutrition/ software. These two sites will allow the teacher access to software that can be downloaded and is designed to help calculate the percentage of calories from fat for given food sources. **Take the challenge:** Search the 300 resources returned by Yahoo. **Remember:** New Internet sites are added daily.

ANSWERS TO SECTION 1 REVIEW

1. *a.* Carbohydrate: a nutrient that includes sugars, starches, and fiber.
b. Fat: a nutrient that is high in energy and found in animal tissues, nuts, seeds, and fruits of plants. Two types are saturated and unsaturated.
c. Protein: a nutrient that is the basic building block of the body. It is made up of amino acids.
d. Vitamin: a nutrient that helps control growth and helps the body release energy to do work. Vitamins are fat soluble and water soluble.
e. Mineral: a chemical element that is important for the body's structure and function, and for regulating metabolism.
f. Water: a nutrient essential for life. Water regulates the body temperature, carries nutrients, helps digestion, and is important in chemical reactions in your body.
2. Grains, stems, roots, nuts, seeds, and/or fruit coverings.
3. Saturated fats are usually solid at room temperature; unsaturated fats are usually liquid.

• *Make sure you drink before, during, and after physical activity or exercise.*

Before	During	After
Drink 10 to 14 ounces of cold water one to two hours before the activity or exercise.	Drink 3 to 4 ounces of cold water every fifteen minutes.	Drink 2 cups (16 ounces) of cold water for every pound of weight loss.

• ***Figure 10.5*** *Guidelines for Fluid Replacement Before, During, and After Physical Activity or Exercise. Source:* Adapted with permission from D. S. Jennings and S. N. Steen, *Play Hard, Eat Hard,* American Dietary Association (Minneapolis: Chronimed Publishing, 1995).

fer a sports drink because of the taste. If you replenish your fluids during physical activity with something other than water, follow the guidelines for these drinks in Chapter 2.

SECTION 1 REVIEW

Answer the following questions on a separate sheet of paper:
1. List and describe the six classes of nutrients.
2. Name three foods that are high in fiber.
3. What is the difference between saturated and unsaturated fat?

SECTION 2

Choosing What You Should Eat: The Food Guide Pyramid

What should you eat? Do you enjoy what you eat? Do you get all the nutrients from your diet that you need to be healthy? These questions are all important for determining or choosing what you should eat.

The U.S. Department of Health and Human Services and the U.S. Department of Agriculture have published the *Dietary Guidelines for Americans,* which provide recommendations for a healthy way to eat. The *Dietary Guidelines* are designed to help you eat sensi-

Equipment Options

When trying to determine the fat content of a food, reading the new food labels can be very confusing. To help in this matter, a fat-gram calculator may be necessary. A fat-gram calculator is not the latest in laptop or palm-sized computer technology, although it will fit in a shirt pocket or purse. A fat-gram calculator is a simple slide rule that allows the user to compute the percentage of calories from fat for a given food source. To use a fat-gram calculator: Read the food label and determine the total grams of fat per serving. Locate the grams of fat

BELIEVE IT? ...
OR NOT?

It is a good idea to take salt tablets to help maintain your fluid balance if you are working out in the heat.

See page 359 for answer.

• *Nutrition professionals, such as these dietitians, analyze foods and counsel people about sensible eating.*

bly and help reduce your risk for heart disease, high blood pressure, stroke, certain cancers, and diabetes mellitus. The recommendations are as follows:

- Eat a variety of foods.
- Maintain a healthy weight.
- Choose a diet low in fat, saturated fat, and cholesterol.
- Choose a diet with plenty of vegetables, fruits, and grain products.
- Use salt and sodium only in moderation.
- Use sugars only in moderation.

Food Guide Pyramid

a visual outline of what people should eat each day.

Recommended Daily Allowance (RDA)

the amount of nutrients recommended daily for individuals by the U.S. Department of Agriculture.

The **Food Guide Pyramid** (see Figure 10.6 on the following page) was also developed by the U.S. Department of Health and Human Services and the U.S. Department of Agriculture to present a visual outline of what to eat each day based on the *Dietary Guidelines*. The Food Guide Pyramid is based on the **Recommended Daily Allowance (RDA)**, the amount of nutrients recommended daily for individuals by the U.S. Department of Agriculture.

Use the Food Guide Pyramid to develop a healthful diet that is right for you. The Food Guide Pyramid emphasizes foods from the five major food groups, which are shown in the lower three sections of the pyramid. Each of the food groups provides some, but not all, of the nutrients you need daily. Foods in one food group can't replace those in another. It is important to choose from all the food groups

on the slide rule; directly next to it will be the fat calories. Once you know the fat calories, you may slide the rule so that the fat calories align with the total calories of the food source. In a small box in the center of the rule, the percentage of calories from fat will show.

To locate a fat-gram calculator, contact your American Cancer Society or American Heart Association representative. They usually have a fat-gram calculator for a nominal cost, or for free. A fat-gram calculator may also be purchased from HEALTHEDCO. **Take the challenge:** Contact your local ACS and AHA representatives. **Remember:** These groups also carry other teaching aids related to nutrition.

Close

Divide the class into groups of four. Display pictures of a variety of nutritious foods and foods that are not nutritious. Have groups write down three foods with good nutritional value and three with poor nutritional value. Each group should share what foods its members chose and why they chose them.

Focus

Outcomes

In **Section 2** students will learn:

1. To explain how nutrition contributes to the development and maintenance of moderate to high levels of personal fitness.
2. To give examples of appropriate choices for developing a healthy diet.

Focus Activities

1. Using a transparency of Figure 10.6, analyze the Food Guide Pyramid.
2. Using a transparency of Figure 10.10, discuss and evaluate a food label.
3. Using the Active Mind/Active Body activity on page 352, calculate the total calories and percentages of nutrients of a sample meal.
4. Using the Active Mind/Active Body activity on page 352, decide if your meals in the past 24 hours were nutritious.

Teach & Apply

Discussion

• Discuss the recommendations for healthy eating supplied in the Dietary Guidelines for Americans.

RESOURCES Use the transparency in your Teacher **TRANSPARENCIES** Resource Package to discuss the Food Guide Pyramid (Figure 10.6). Ask students to give examples from each of the five major food groups.

Key
• Fat (naturally occurring and added)
▼ Sugars (added)

These symbols show fat and added sugars in foods. They come mostly from the fats, oils, and sweets group, but foods in other groups—such as cheese or ice cream from the milk group or french fries from the vegetable group—can also provide fat and added sugars.

Fats, Oils, and Sweets
Use sparingly

Milk, Yogurt, and Cheese Group
2-3 servings

Meat, Poultry, Fish, Dry Beans, Eggs, and Nuts Group
2-3 servings

Vegetable Group
3-5 servings

Fruit Group
2-4 servings

Bread, Cereal, Rice, and Pasta Group
6-11 servings

• *Figure 10.6*   *The Food Guide Pyramid: A Guide to Daily Food Choices. Source:* Reprinted from U.S. Department of Agriculture, Human Nutritional Information Service, 6505 Belcrest Rd., Hyattsville, MD 20782.

to get all the nutrients your body needs on a daily basis. Thus, the pyramid illustrates the need to eat a variety of foods to get the proper amounts of all the nutrients you need.

The Food Guide Pyramid shows that you need to eat more servings from foods located at the base of the pyramid than from foods located near the top. For example, the bread, cereal, rice, and pasta group provides you with the high percentage (50 to 60 percent) of carbohydrates your body needs. The fat, oils, and sweets should be consumed sparingly, because you do not need as much of these nutrients.

Reteaching

Name _____ Date _____ Period _____

Chapter 10 Section 2   **Choosing What You Should Eat: The Food Guide Pyramid**

Directions: Answer the questions in the blanks provided.

1. List five (5) recommendations from *The Dietary Guidelines*, designed to help you eat sensibly.
   Eat a variety of foods
   Maintain a healthy weight
   Choose a diet low in fat, saturated fat, and cholesterol
   Choose a diet with vegetables, fruits, and grains
   Use salt and sodium only in moderation

2. What was developed by the U.S. Department of Health and Human Services and the U.S. Department of Agriculture to present a visual outline of what to eat each day based on *The Dietary Guidelines*?
   Food Guide Pyramid

3. The Food Guide Pyramid emphasizes foods from how many major food groups?   *5*

4. The Food Guide Pyramid shows that you need to eat more servings from foods located in what part of the pyramid?
   Base

5. What group provides you with the high percentage (50 to 60%) of carbohydrates your body needs?
   Bread, cereal, rice, and pasta

6. Why does the Food Guide Pyramid give no specific serving size for the fats, oils, and sweets group?
   They are to be consumed sparingly

7. Food label ingredient lists contain ingredients by weight, in what order?
   Descending

72   © 1997 West Publishing Co.

Reteaching Worksheets

ABILITY LEVELS

Reteaching

Some students may need help mastering the concepts contained in this section. In your Teacher Resource Package, you will find the reproducible worksheet shown here. This worksheet should help students who have been absent and those needing additional help to improve their comprehension and retention of the content in this section.

BELIEVE IT? ...
OR NOT?

You cannot get nutritious meals at fast-food restaurants.

See page 359 for answer.

• *Breads are in the group of foods that forms the base of the Food Pyramid.*

Energy Balance

You can apply the Food Guide Pyramid to what you already know about energy balance. Your goal is to maintain a balance in your diet of energy and nutrients (carbohydrates, fat, protein, vitamins, minerals, and water). You studied energy balance in Chapter 9, primarily with regard to energy expenditure. However, you also need to pay attention to energy input (calories) in order to control the energy balance equation.

The Food Guide Pyramid shows a range of servings for each major food group. The number of servings that you need depends on how many calories you need—which, if you recall, depends on your age, gender, size, and activity level. Almost everyone should have at least the lowest number of servings in the ranges. Figure 10.7 shows how many servings you need each day to help maintain energy balance.

Examples of the amount of food that counts as one serving are listed in Figure 10.8. If you eat a larger portion, count it as more than one serving. For example, a dinner portion of spaghetti would count as two to three servings of pasta. Be sure to eat *at least* the lowest number of servings from each of the five food groups listed in Figure 10.8. You need all these servings for the vitamins, minerals, carbohydrates, and protein they provide. Just try to pick the choices with the lowest fat content. No specific serving size is given for the fats, oils, and sweets group because they are to be consumed sparingly. Figure 10.9 shows how you can cut down on your fat calories.

Activities

• Using Figure 10.7 on the next page as a guide, have students cut from magazines pictures that represent each food group. Have students draw a pyramid and attach the pictures in the appropriate places. The number of pictures should correspond to the number of servings for teenagers. For example, there should be nine pictures attached to the area for the bread group.

Enrichment   *This activity will allow you to provide a more challenging learning experience for some of your students.*

Share with the students the "Be Here Now" theory, developed by Dave Ellis, which implies that we can become more effective in all of our activities by choosing where to focus our attention. Be where you are when you are there. When you read a book, read the book. And when you eat, concentrate on eating. This includes focusing on the texture, color, and the sense of taste and mood that the food elicits. Have students select three food items while at home in order to experience "Be Here Now." Have the students list the food items on a sheet of paper with columns for texture, color, sense of taste, and mood. The mood column will represent how the student felt at the time he or she tasted the food item. Ask the students to present their findings in class.

- Have students write down foods they have eaten in the past 24-hour period. Have students indicate, by a show of hands, foods eaten in each food group. Record answers on the board or overhead projector.
- Supply food from each major food group to your class. Give real-life samples to show serving size or have students guess serving sizes for each food by serving themselves what they feel is the right portion of the food of their choice. Students may use Figures 10.8 for examples.

Stress Break

Explain that caffeine can cause some people to be overstimulated. Remind students that caffeine is found not only in tea and coffee, but also in colas and chocolate.

Teacher Support Notes

You may want to tell students the following:

- If you were to take away just one tablespoon of fat

Stress Break

Have you ever noticed that drinking beverages that contain caffeine, such as tea, cola, or coffee, gives you a quick pick-me-up, energy boost, or jolt? **Caffeine** is a mild stimulant of the central nervous system. The average adolescent drinks at least two to three beverages a day containing caffeine. Caffeine increases your heart rate, can make you feel less tired, increases your alertness, and improves your reaction time. However, caffeine also produces signs of distress. Too much caffeine can cause headaches, upset stomach, nervousness, sleeplessness, irritability, and diarrhea. The side effects of caffeine consumption can make your stressful situations even more stressful. Some people may even have anxiety or panic attacks from consuming too much caffeine.

Is it necessary to eliminate caffeine completely from your diet? Probably not. The equivalent of one or two caffeinated beverages per day is safe. However, you should monitor your caffeine intake. You can consume beverages that have low amounts of caffeine or that are caffeine-free. This will help you deal with or eliminate distress in your daily life.

- *Eating a variety of foods in the proper proportions is the key to sound nutrition.*

Food Group	Servings		
	Many Women and Older Adults (About 1,600 calories)	Children, Teen Girls, Active Women, and Most Men (About 2,200 calories)	Teen Boys and Active Men (About 2,800 calories)
Bread	6	9	11
Vegetable	3	4	5
Fruit	2	3	4
Milk	2–3†	2–3†	2–3†
Meat	2, for a total of 5 ounces	2, for a total of 6 ounces	3, for a total of 7 ounces

- **Figure 10.7** *Examples of Servings (and calories) to Maintain Energy Balance.* * These are the calorie levels if you choose low-fat, lean foods from the five major food groups and use foods from fats, oils, and sweets sparingly. †Women who are pregnant or breastfeeding, teenagers, and young adults to age twenty-four need three servings.

COOPERATIVE LEARNING

Evaluation of students' work in cooperative learning groups is essential. Teachers must evaluate the learning that has taken place, as well as the group's functioning. Both aspects of evaluation are necessary for successful cooperative learning group work.

In cooperative learning groups, students will produce one product (one worksheet, report, etc., that can be evaluated by a criterion-referenced system). This means that each student in the group will receive the same grade for the product no matter how much work he or

Milk, Yogurt, and Cheese	Meat, Poultry, Fish, Dry Beans, Eggs, and Nuts	Vegetables	Fruit	Bread, Cereal, Rice, and Pasta
I cup of yogurt or milk (2% or less)	2-3 ounces of cooked lean meat, poultry, or fish	1 cup of raw, leafy vegetables	1 medium apple, banana, or orange	1 slice of bread
1-1/2 ounces of natural cheese	1/2 cup of dry beans, 1 egg, or two tablespoons of peanut butter count as 1 ounce of lean meat	1/2 cup of other vegetables, cooked or chopped raw	1/2 cup of chopped, cooked, or canned fruit	1 ounce of ready-to-eat cereal
2 ounces of processed cheese		3/4 cup of vegetable juice	3/4 cup of fruit juice	1/2 cup of cooked cereal, rice, or pasta

• **Figure 10.8** *Examples of Serving Sizes for Each Food Group. Source:* Adapted from U.S. Department of Agriculture, Human Nutritional Information Service, 6505 Belcrest Rd., Hyattsville, MD 20782.

Fat hides calories in food. When you trim fat, you trim calories.

Large pork chop with ½ inch fat (352 calories).

Large potato with 1 tablespoon butter and 1 tablespoon sour cream (350 calories).

Whole milk, 1 cup (150 calories).

Large pork chop with fat trimmed off (265 calories).

Plain large potato (220 calories).

Nonfat milk, 1 cup (90 calories).

• **Figure 10.9** *Fat and Calories. Source:* Adapted with permission from F. S. Sizer, E. N. Whitney, and L. K. DeBruyne, *Making Life Choices* (St. Paul: West Publishing, 1994, page 176).

from your daily diet, you could lose as much as 10 pounds in a year.
• Bananas are the most popular fruit in the United States. They are followed in popularity by apples.
• In a lifetime, the average American eats about 50 tons of food.
• Many fast-food restaurants use a quarter-pound of beef (four ounces) in their hamburgers. This is considered two servings in the meat group of the Food Guide Pyramid.
• Only 9% of Americans eat the recommended three servings of vegetables and two servings of fruit a day.
• Here's a rough idea of your daily caloric needs to maintain your present weight: Extremely inactive = 12 calories per pound of weight; light activity = 15 calories per pound; and moderate activity = 20 calories per pound. Example: A moderately active 140-pound person would need 2,800 calories a day to maintain his or her weight (140 x 20 = 2,800).

she actually did. Because of this, it is important for the teacher to structure accountability within the group. Students must feel that the group depends on them to do their part.

During this evaluation time, students should discuss the "ups and downs" of their group work and how they handled any problems that may have come up.

Students should not be allowed to blame or put down other group members.

You should also be ready to share your observations of the group. You might find it helpful to have a list of behaviors you're looking for when observing groups. Then you will have something specific to share with group members.

Healthy People 2000

*Objective 2.13—*Increase to at least 85 percent the proportion of people aged 18 and older who use food labels to make nutritious food selections.

Food labeling provides information to people about food content and can facilitate dietary choices most conducive to health. Currently, adults report using label information to select foods that have been reduced in sodium, fat, and cholesterol. Sales figures show a shift toward products with such characteristics. As consumers become more aware of the importance to their health of dietary factors such as saturated fat, it is reasonable to anticipate that they will increasingly use label information in selecting food items for purchase.

Reading Food Labels and Evaluating Your Nutrition

Virtually all the food products that you purchase today have a label entitled "Nutrition Facts" on the package or container. Therefore, it is easy for you to determine what and how much you are consuming. If you begin to pay closer attention to food labeling, you will get even better at balancing your caloric intake and caloric expenditure. Figure 10.10 provides a sample food label and highlights factors you should look for to learn about what is in the foods you eat.

Food labels like the one in Figure 10.10 contain nutrition information about the following items:

- Serving size.
- Calories that the food contains per serving.
- Total amount of carbohydrate.
- Total amount of dietary fiber.
- Total amount of protein.
- Vitamins and minerals in each serving.
- Total amount of fat, saturated fat, and cholesterol.
- Total amount of sodium per serving.
- Percentage of calories supplied based on daily needs per serving.

Food labels also have a list of ingredients. The ingredient list contains ingredients by weight, in descending order. The ingredient that is listed first is found in the greatest amount. You can better balance your diet by analyzing what you eat for one to three days or by analyzing sample diets such as the ones in the "Active Mind/Active Body" activities on the next page.

- *You should read the "nutrition facts" on packages and containers of food products before you buy them.*

CULTURAL DIVERSITY

Switzerland

Sports are a way of life for the Swiss. The physical activity keeps them fit, yet they view sports as hobbies and are not, in general, as competitive as Americans. As soon as children can walk, they go to the mountains to hike or ski with their families. When they first start school, children begin a gymnastics program, which includes all kinds of physical exercise. As a result, the Swiss are strong hikers and good skiers who participate in these activities throughout their lifetimes. Most

Serving Size

Is your serving the same serving size as the one on the label? If you eat double the serving size listed, you need to double the nutrient and calorie values. If you eat one-half the serving size shown here, cut the nutrient and calorie values in half.

Calories

Are you overweight? Cut back a little on calories! Look here to see how a serving of the food adds to the daily total. A 5'4", 130-lb. active woman needs about 2,200 calories each day. A 5' 10" 174-lb. active man needs about 2,900. How about you?

Total Carbohydrate

When you cut down on fat, you can eat more carbohydrates. Carbohydrates are in foods like bread, potatoes, fruits, and vegetables. Choose these often! They give you more nutrients than sugars like soda pop and candy.

Dietary Fiber

Grandmother called it "roughage," but her advice to eat more is still up-to-date! That goes for both soluble and insoluble kinds of dietary fiber. Fruits, vegetables, whole-grain foods, beans, and peas are all good sources and can help reduce the risk of heart disease and cancer.

Protein

Most Americans get more protein than they need. Where there is animal protein, there is also fat and cholesterol. Eat small servings of lean meat, fish, and poultry. Use skim or low-fat milk, yogurt, and cheese. Try vegetable proteins like beans, grains, and cereals.

Vitamins and Minerals

Your goal here is 100% of each for the day. Don't count on one food to do it all. Let a combination of foods add up to a winning score.

Nutrition Facts
Serving Size ½ cup (114g)
Servings Per Container 4

Amount Per Serving

Calories 90   Calories from Fat 30

	% Daily Value*
Total Fat 3g	5%
Saturated Fat 0g	0%
Cholesterol 0mg	0%
Sodium 300mg	13%
Total Carbohydrate 13g	4%
Dietary Fiber 3g	12%
Sugars 3g	
Protein 3g	

| Vitamin A | 80% | • | Vitamin C | 60% |
| Calcium | 4% | • | Iron | 4% |

* Percent Daily Values are based on a 2,000 calorie diet. Your daily values may be higher or lower depending on your calorie needs:

	Calories:	2,000	2,500
Total Fat	Less than	65g	80g
Sat Fat	Less than	20g	25g
Cholesterol	Less than	300mg	300mg
Sodium	Less than	2,400mg	2,400mg
Total Carbohydrate		300g	375g
Fiber		25g	30g

Calories per gram:
Fat 9 • Carbohydrate 4 • Protein 4

More nutrients may be listed on some labels.

Total Fat

Aim low: most people need to cut back on fat. Too much fat may contribute to heart disease and cancer. Try to limit your calories from fat. For a healthy heart, choose foods with a big difference between the total number of calories and the number of calories from fat.

Saturated Fat

A new kind of fat? No—saturated fat is part of the total fat in food. It is listed separately, because it's the key player in raising blood cholesterol and your risk of heart disease. Eat less!

Cholesterol

Too much cholesterol—a second cousin to fat—can lead to heart disease. Challenge yourself to eat less than 300 mg each day.

Sodium

You call it "salt", the label calls it "sodium". Either way, it may add up to high blood pressure in some people. So, keep your sodium intake low—2,400 to 3,000 mg or less each day. The American Heart Association recommends no more than 3,000 mg sodium per day for healthy adults.

Daily Value

Feel like you're drowning in numbers? Let the Daily Value be your guide. Daily Values are listed for people who eat 2,000 or 2,500 calories each day. If you eat more, your personal daily value may be higher than what's listed on the label. If you eat less, your personal daily value may be lower.

For fat, saturated fat, cholesterol, and sodium, choose foods with a low % Daily Value. For total carbohydrate, dietary fiber, vitamins, and minerals, your daily value goal is to reach 100% of each.

g = grams (about 28 g = 1 ounce).
mg = milligrams (1,000 mg = 1 gram).

• *Figure 10.10* *Sample Food Label.*

Active Mind! Active Body!

Calculating Calories from an Example

Calculate the number of calories in your meal if you consume the following: 10 grams of carbohydrate, 5 grams of fat, and 4 grams of protein. (Remember from Chapter 9 that 1 gram of carbohydrate = 4 calories; 1 gram of fat = 9 calories; and 1 gram of protein = 4 calories.)

Now calculate what percentage of calories comes from carbohydrate, fat, and protein in the same example. *Hint:* Divide the number of calories for each nutrient by the total number of calories from all the nutrients.

Discussion

Use Figure 10.10 to discuss each type of information included on the nutritional food label and how to use each piece of information to make wise choices when selecting food.

Activities

• Provide students with menus from fast-food restaurants. Have them choose what they normally would eat for a meal at one restaurant. After choosing, students should figure total calories, fat, carbohydrates, protein, sodium, and cholesterol consumed in their meals. Discuss their choices. What alternate choices can be made at these restaurants?

• On one side of a 4-by-6-inch index card, have students copy a food label and ingredients from a food found at home. Have students write the name of the food on the other side of the index card. Play "guess my food" by having each student describe his or her food by using what he or she has listed on the card. Discuss the difference in what students may think is in a food and the actual nutrients and ingredients.

• Have students complete the Active Mind/Active Body activity on this page. Give the students additional problems if they are having trouble.

retired people still spend several hours a week exercising at their local gyms.

Schoolchildren play a variety of team games; the ones they play depend upon where in the country they live. Some students enjoy *Schlagball,* similar to American softball, but there are four bases, not three, and no catcher or pitcher.

Instead, the batter stands between first and fourth base, throws the ball up, and hits it. *Völkerball* is like team dodge ball. Teams line up facing one another and attempt to throw a ball and hit an opposing player below the waist before someone on that team can catch it and throw it back.

RESOURCES Have students use the Diet Analysis 2.0 **SOFTWARE** software to analyze their diets. Students will find the software extremely easy to use.

Teacher Support Notes

Remind students that fruits and vegetables do not come with nutrition labels. Stores often place the nutrition labels for these items above or below them for consumers to read as they shop.

Assess

Use the Section 2 Review questions to assess students' comprehension of the concepts presented in Section 2.

Active **Mind!** *Active* Body!

Calculating the Calories in Your Diet and Sample Menus

Perform one or both of the following:

1. Use the West Diet Analysis Computer Software that your teacher will provide you with to analyze either one, two, or three days of your food consumption. The form asks you to list the foods that you have consumed. It is best if you can analyze three days of your diet, particularly for two weekdays and one weekend day. Most people have different eating habits during the week and the weekend. Determine how your diet compares with the dietary guidelines that you have learned so far. For example, how many calories did you consume? What percentages of carbohydrate, fat, and protein did you get? Did you meet the RDAs for various nutrients? How many servings did you have for each food group section in the Food Guide Pyramid? Do you need to adjust your diet to achieve healthier nutrition? If so, how will you do this?

2. Analyze the five menus shown below using the calorie chart provided by your teacher to determine which of the five menus is the most nutritious. You will need to use what you know about the Food Guide Pyramid, serving information, caloric content, and balanced nutrition.

Menu 1
3 ounces baked chicken
1 small baked potato
1/3 cup corn
1 cup broccoli
2 slices pineapple
1 tablespoon margarine

Menu 2
2 ounces link sausage
10 french fries
1/2 cup marinated vegetables
1 slice apple pie
1 cup whole milk

Menu 3
2 slices whole-wheat bread
1 tablespoon mayonnaise
2 ounces deli turkey
1 leaf of lettuce
1 slice tomato
1 slice American cheese
1-ounce pack of corn chips
8 ounces cola

Menu 4
3 ounces baked flounder
1/2 cup zucchini
4 florets of cauliflower
1/4 cantaloupe
8 ounces water

Menu 5
8 ounces yogurt
1 plain bagel
1 teaspoon cream cheese
1 small apple
6 ounces orange juice

• **Figure 10.11** *Sample Menus to Analyze.*

Across the Disciplines

Economics

Since 1962, when President Kennedy sent the first consumer protection message to Congress, legislation has been passed that is directed at product safety and protection against fraud.

Nutrition is a big consumer concern and, therefore, big business. Have students brainstorm a list of items that have been advertised as nutritional aids or healthy choices. Identify the topics that are of the most concern or interest to the students.

SECTION 2 REVIEW

Answer the following questions on a separate sheet of paper:

1. Give three recommendations to follow in order to eat sensibly and reduce your risk for chronic diseases.
2. List the five major food groups represented in the Food Guide Pyramid, and give the recommended number of servings for each group.
3. Identify three items that are included in nutrition information labeling.

SECTION 3 — Developing and Maintaining Healthy Nutrition

To develop and maintain healthy nutrition, you need to become more aware of your caloric intake and the types of food that you are consuming. Remember, by adjusting your diet and your physical activity and exercise levels, you can make positive changes in your body composition. To improve your nutrition, you need to determine your FIT by using the results from the "Active Mind/Active Body" activity you did on page 352. Use the scientific principles you learned in Chapter 3 and your personal fitness goals to develop your own specific nutrition plan. To do this, use the recommendations that follow.

Specificity Principle

To apply the specificity principle in an attempt to improve your nutrition, keep a record of what, where, when, and how much you are eating. Learn to analyze your diet for unnecessary excess calories, low RDA values, and foods that provide empty calories (such as sodas, candy bars, chips, and cookies). Read the "Nutrition Facts" labels before you consume. If necessary, change your eating habits gradually so that you eat foods that are low in fat and are nutritious.

REMEMBER This!

Caffeinated beverages are often carbonated and contain high amounts of sugar and sodium. These additional ingredients are detrimental to maintaining normal blood sugar levels (they can make you hypoglycemic). They also can interfere with maintaining electrolyte and fluid balances. Therefore, keep your caffeinated drink consumption to a minimum. Make healthier choices, such as fruit juices, water, or sports drinks, whenever possible.

ANSWERS TO SECTION 2 REVIEW

1. Answers will vary but should include at least three of the following: eat a variety of foods; maintain a healthy weight; choose a diet low in fat, saturated fat, and cholesterol; choose a diet with plenty of vegetables, fruit, and grain products; use salt and sodium in moderation.
2. Bread, cereal, rice, and pasta: 6–11 servings; Fruit: 2–4 servings; Vegetables: 3–5 servings; Meat, poultry, fish, dry beans, eggs, and nuts: 2–3 servings; Milk, yogurt, and cheese: 2–3 servings.
3. Answers will vary but should include at least three of the following: serving size, calories, total carbohydrates, dietary fiber, protein, vitamins, minerals, total fat, saturated fat, cholesterol, sodium, daily values.

Close

Pair students, then have each pair plan a nutritious menu for breakfast, lunch, or dinner using food labels you provide.

Then, assign groups to find out the number of different products there are within a topic, their availability, cost range, merits, negative qualities, and how they compare to competitive products. Groups might choose to develop charts that report their research and consumer recommendations in a clear and informative way. The information provided should assist classmates in making rational choices.

Encourage the class to evaluate the reports and determine if the data provided would make them better consumers or if there is additional information they would need to make an informed decision. As a class, recommend helpful consumer resources.

Focus

Outcomes

In **Section 3** students will learn:

1. Ways to evaluate their current and future nutrition.
2. To identify strategies for improving their nutrition choices and helping them become smarter food consumers.

Focus Activities

1. Use transparencies of Figures 10.12, 10.13, and 10.14 to discuss the specificity and progression principles, along with frequency, intensity, and time (FIT), in relation to weight maintenance, loss, and/or gain.
2. Have students apply the specificity and progression principles along with FIT by using the results obtained in

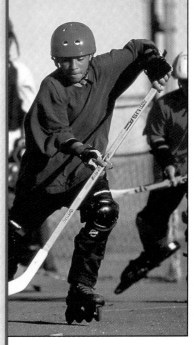

• *Eating sensibly can enhance your physical activity and exercise performance.*

REMEMBER This!

Never change the frequency, intensity, or time/duration of your nutrition plan all at the same time or too quickly. Healthy weight loss should not exceed 2 pounds per week. Weight gain should not exceed ½ pound per week. Be patient, and allow for gradual progress.

Frequency

The first component of FIT, as you remember, is *frequency*. To apply it to your nutrition plan, eat at regular intervals, three times per day, plus one or two planned snacks to avoid hunger and impulse eating.

Intensity

How does *intensity,* the second component of FIT, apply to your nutrition plan? To lose a pound of fat, you need to reduce your caloric intake by 3,500 calories below what's normal for you over a set period of time (for example, one or two weeks). You also need to include aerobic conditioning and weight training in your plan to maintain your lean body weight while you lose mostly fat weight. If you want to gain weight, you need to increase your caloric intake. You will also want to include weight training as part of your weight-gain plan so that you will mainly increase your lean body weight, not your fat weight. If you maintain your caloric intake at the same level and do not vary your physical activity levels, you will maintain your weight and percentage of body fat.

Time/Duration

As for the *time/duration* component of FIT, you should work both sides of the energy balance equation to control your caloric intake and caloric expenditure as necessary. If you are trying to lose weight and body fat, you should try to lose no more than 1 to 2 pounds per week for safe, effective results. If you are seeking weight gain, you should expect slow gains of no more than ½ pound per week. By gaining weight slowly and steadily, you add less body fat and more lean muscle. Your ability to improve your nutrition will depend on how you use your new knowledge and how you develop reasonable and obtainable goals for yourself over the long haul.

Progression Principle

The rate at which you modify your FIT (your progression) should be based on your personal fitness goals and your nutritional goals. Few people eat as well as they can all the time. (Holidays and celebrations are always challenges to good nutrition.) You will undoubtedly experience unwanted weight changes at some time in your life. However, you do have a choice about what and how you eat over time. Therefore, it is important that you establish sound nutritional patterns now that can last you for life.

Reteaching

Name _____ Date _____ Period _____

Chapter **10** Developing and Maintaining Healthy Nutrition

Section 3

Directions: Answer the questions in the blanks provided.

1. What two (2) things do you need to become more aware of in order to develop and maintain healthy nutrition?

Your caloric intake

The types of food that you are consuming

Identify the nutrition principle described by writing either *Specificity, Frequency, Intensity, Time,* or *Progression* in front of each statement.

Time
Frequency
Specificity
Intensity
Time
Progression
Specificity
Intensity
Progression

2. Work both sides of the energy balance equation to control your caloric intake and caloric expenditure as necessary.
3. Eat at regular intervals three times per day, plus one or two planned snacks to avoid hunger or impulse eating.
4. Keep a record of what, where, when, and how much you are eating.
5. Include aerobic conditioning and weight training in your plan to maintain your lean body weight while you lose mostly fat weight.
6. Try to lose no more than 1 to 2 pounds per week for safe, effective results.
7. Establish sound nutritional patterns now that can last you for life.
8. If necessary, change your eating habits gradually so that you eat foods that are nutritious and low in fat.
9. If you maintain your caloric intake at the same level and do not vary your physical activity levels, you will maintain your weight and percentage of body fat.
10. The rate at which you modify your FIT or your progression should be based on your personal fitness goals and your nutritional goals.

73   © 1997 West Publishing Co.

Reteaching Worksheets

ABILITY LEVELS

Reteaching

Some students may need help mastering the concepts contained in this section. In your Teacher Resource Package, you will find the reproducible worksheet shown here. This worksheet should help students who have been absent and those needing additional help to improve their comprehension and retention of the content in this section.

Examples of Healthy Nutrition

The sample menu in Figure 10.12 provides an example of healthy nutrition for a young adult who wants to consume 2,500 calories. About 55 percent of the calories come from carbohydrate; 25 to 30 percent, from fat; and 15 to 20 percent, from protein.

In Chapter 9 you learned about developing and controlling your body composition at healthy levels. Figures 10.13 and 10.14 provide sample menus that you can either use for effective weight control (loss or maintenance) or for weight gain, depending on your goal.

BELIEVE IT? ... OR NOT?

Forty percent of the calories in the average American diet come from fats. This figure is too high and is associated with an increased risk for heart disease, cancer, and diabetes.

See page 359 for answer.

Breakfast	2 pancakes
	Syrup
	1 cup 2% milk
Snack	1 bagel
	Jam or jelly
	6 ounces orange juice
Lunch	1 slice vegetable pizza
	Carrot and celery sticks
	2 graham crackers
	1 cup 2% milk
Snack (Before physical activity or exercise)	2 fig bars
	16 ounces of water
Snack (Afterward)	1 box fruit juice
	1 packet raisins
Dinner	3 ounces roasted chicken breast
	1/2 cup rice
	1 slice bread
	Lettuce and tomato
	1 tablespoon dressing
	1 cup 2% milk
Snack	1 cup frozen yogurt
	1 cup lemonade
	1 sandwich (2 slices multigrain bread, 3 ounces lean turkey, lettuce, tomato, and mustard)

• ***Figure 10.12*** *Sample Menu for Good Nutrition. Source:* Adapted with permission from D. S. Jennings and S. N. Steen, *Play Hard, Eat Hard,* American Dietary Association (Minneapolis: Chronimed Publishing, 1995).

the Active Mind/Active Body activity on page 352.

Teach & Apply

Discussion

Discuss how the scientific principles learned in Chapter 3 relate to nutrition.

Activity

Have students compare their diet analyses from the Active Mind/Active Body activity on page 352 with the sample menu in Figure 10.12. Then ask them what is missing in their own diets. What foods do they eat too much of? Too little?

Discussion

Discuss the effects of healthy and unhealthy weight loss and weight gain. Remind students about the body composition information learned in Chapter 9.

 **Enrichment**

This activity will allow you to provide a more challenging learning experience for some of your students.

Assign students the task of writing a "response letter" to an imaginary former student who, feeling very poorly about his or her state of health, has asked for help. The "imaginary student" has stated that he/she was very active in high school. The student maintained a healthy weight and could eat "anything!" However, during the freshman year at college, the student gained 15 pounds! Clothes that were once comfortable could not even be buttoned. The student also complained of having little energy and an inability to sleep well at night. Have your students write a letter to the imaginary student sharing information they have learned along with some possible problem-solving techniques.

Figure 10.13 *Sample Menu for Weight Control.* *Source:* Adapted with permission from D. S. Jennings and S. N. Steen, *Play Hard, Eat Hard,* American Dietary Association (Minneapolis: Chronimed Publishing, 1995).

Breakfast	3/4 cup orange juice
	3/4 cup raisin bran (1 teaspoon sugar optional)
	1 slice whole-wheat toast
	1 tablespoon jam or jelly
	1 cup low-fat (2%) milk
Lunch	1 turkey sandwich (3 ounces turkey breast, 2 slices whole-wheat bread, mustard, sliced tomato, and lettuce)
Snack	1 banana
Dinner	3 ounces lean beef
	1 medium baked potato
	1 cup plain nonfat yogurt
	1/2 cup green beans
	1 cup low-fat (2%) milk
	1/2 cup ice milk
Snack	3/4 cup tomato juice
	1 ounce pretzels
	1/4 cup raisins

Activity

Have groups compare the menus in Figures 10.13 and 10.14. Have them make a chart that lists the elements that make each menu a weight control or weight gain menu.

Teacher Support Notes

You may want to tell students the following:

• If both of a person's biological parents are overweight, his or her chances of also being overweight are 80%. However, people whose genes may be "weighted" against them can lower their risk of obesity by healthful eating and exercise.
• According to a federal study, 34% of high school females and 15% of high school males in the United States perceive themselves as overweight, though many of them are not.

Consumer Corner

Have students bring in the packaging for food they purchased from vending machines. Have them analyze the foods for nutrient content. Discuss why people eat these foods.

CONSUMER CORNER

Nutrition and Consumer Choices

If you are like most Americans, you are finding that you are eating more meals away from home than ever before. We have all come to depend on fast-food restaurants, cafeterias, and vending machines for our daily nutrition needs.

As a wise consumer, you can make smart choices to guarantee that you get all the nutrients you require when you eat out, while avoiding foods high in calories, fat, and sodium. Most fast-food restaurants and cafeterias provide customers with healthy food choice menus that are low in calories, fat, and sodium. For example, you can choose grilled chicken (less fat) instead of fried chicken (high fat). You can enjoy the salad bar with fruits and vegetables instead of eating french fries (high fat and sodium). You can also choose to avoid overloading on sauces, sour cream, and butter. When making a beverage choice, you can replace high-sugar sodas with low-fat milk or water. Finally, if you learn to read the "Nutrition Facts" labeling on vending machine foods, you can make better consumer choices.

Special Needs

An individual's mechanical efficiency has a direct correlation to the way that the energy of food is translated into "work." Therefore, many disabled individuals who exhibit poor mechanical efficiency because of their disability require

Breakfast	1 cup orange juice
	6 pancakes
	1/4 cup syrup
	2 pats margarine
	1-1/2 cups low-fat (2%) milk
Snack	1 soft pretzel
	1-1/2 cups tomato juice
Lunch	1 turkey sandwich (4-5 ounces turkey breast,
	7-inch pita bread pocket, 2 tablespoons light
	mayonnaise, chopped tomato, and lettuce)
Snack	1 package powdered breakfast mix
	1 cup low-fat (2%) milk
Dinner	1 medium vegetable-cheese pizza
	2 cups low-fat (2%) milk
	1/4 cup raisins
Snack	1 peanut butter and jelly sandwich (3 tablepoons
	peanut butter, 3 tablespoons jelly, 2 slices whole-
	grain bread)
	1 cup low-fat (2%) milk

• **Figure 10.14** *Sample Menu for Weight Gain. Source:* Adapted with permission from D. S. Jennings and S. N. Steen, *Play Hard, Eat Hard,* American Dietary Association (Minneapolis: Chronimed Publishing, 1995).

SECTION 3 REVIEW

Answer the following questions on a separate sheet of paper:

1. How many times per day should you eat?
2. How many calories do you need to cut from your caloric intake to lose a pound of fat?
3. If you are trying to gain weight, how much should you realistically expect to gain each week?

Assess

Use the Section 3 Review questions to assess the students' comprehension of the concepts presented in Section 3.

ANSWERS TO SECTION 3 REVIEW

1. Three times per day, plus one or two planned snacks.
2. 3,500 calories.
3. No more than one-half pound per week.

Close

Have students make a chart that is divided in half. One half should be labeled "Weight Control" (maintenance and/or loss); the other half should be labeled "Weight Gain." Under the appropriate category, students should list the information they have learned about the scientific principles relating to weight control and weight gain.

a closely monitored diet. Those particularly at risk of compromised metabolic functioning are those individuals who are obese, have reduced sensory input, cerebral palsy, muscular dystrophy, and/or any individual that experiences compromised muscle tone.

CHAPTER 10
SECTION 4

358

Focus

Outcome

In **Section 4** students will learn:

1. To identify and explain ways they can eat to improve their performance fitness.

Focus Activity

1. Discuss how students should eat to improve their performance fitness.

Teach & Apply

Teacher Support Notes

You may want to tell stu-

Reteaching

Name_____ Date_____ Period_____

Chapter 10 Section 4
Eating to Improve Your Performance Fitness

Directions: Answer the questions in the blanks provided.

1. Your last pre-event meal should be eaten at least how long before the practice or competition?

   One to three hours.

2. Why do you want a relatively empty stomach prior to the practice or competition?

   To avoid nausea or potential stomach cramps.

3. Eat foods high in carbohydrates, and avoid foods high in _____ *protein or fat* which take longer to digest.

4. What types of sugars should be avoided immediately before competition, because they only provide quick energy and may even hamper your performance in the the long run?

   Simple.

5. The energy you need for a hard workout or competition comes from foods eaten how long before?

   Several hours and days.

6. List seven (7) foods or drinks that you may consume immediately after the competition to help recover your energy stores.

   Medium bagel   *Pretzels*

   Fruit yogurt   *Large banana*

   Cranberry-apple juice *Apple juice*

   Orange juice

7. How many hours after competition should you eat a meal high in carbohydrates?

   2 hours.

Reteaching Worksheet   © 1997 West Publishing Co.

SECTION 4   Eating to Improve Your Performance Fitness

Many young adults are interested in competing in various physical activities or sports, at least occasionally. Others aim for a high-performance personal fitness and are willing to work harder than they would have to just for good health. People in both of these categories need to pay close attention to their diets before and after competition.

If you are one of these people, make sure you have plenty of energy to compete and are well hydrated prior to competition (pre-event). Your last pre-event meal is important, but it's even more important to eat a healthy diet for several weeks before your competition. This is necessary to maintain satisfactory energy levels.

Your last pre-event meal should be eaten at least one to three hours before the practice or competition. You want a relatively empty stomach prior to the practice or competition to avoid nausea or potential stomach cramps. Each person digests food at different rates. Therefore, you may want to be cautious and allow more time (three hours, for example) for digestion of the pre-event meal.

Eat foods high in carbohydrate. Avoid foods high in protein or fat, because they take longer to digest. Also avoid eating foods high in simple sugars (candy bars, honey, and so on) immediately before competition, because they provide only quick energy and may even hamper your performance in the long run. The energy you need for a hard workout or competition comes from foods eaten several hours and days before. You can use the recommendations in Figures 10.15 and 10.16 to help guide your pre-event meal planning.

You may sometimes participate in all-day competitions or a series of physical activities such as track meets, basketball tournaments, tennis tournaments, or wrestling meets. At these times, you need to make wise food choices throughout the day to maintain your energy levels. You also need to prevent dehydration, which would have a negative effect on your performance. Try to consume fluids, particularly water, throughout the day. Avoid foods that take longer to digest (fat, protein, and fiber), especially if you have to perform several times throughout the day. (See Figure 10.17 on page 360.)

Following competition, you must restore your glucose and glycogen stores in order to recover effectively for your next workout or competition. You also need to replace the fluids (as you learned in Chapter 2 and Section 1 earlier in this chapter) that you have lost from sweating during physical activity. Immediately after the competition, you should consume one of the following foods or drinks to

REMEMBER This!

Before an athletic event, eat as follows:
- **Complex carbohydrates.**
- **Water.**
- **Moderate portions.**
- **3 to 4 hours before the event.**

Be sure to avoid large amounts of these nutrients:
- **Fat.**
- **Protein.**
- **Fiber.**
- **Last-minute sweets.**

ABILITY LEVELS

Reteaching

Some students may need help mastering the concepts contained in this section. In your Teacher Resource Package, you will find the reproducible worksheet shown here. This worksheet should help students who have been absent and those needing additional help to improve their comprehension and retention of the content in this section.

1 to 2 Hours Before	2 to 3 Hours Before	3 or More Hours Before
Fruit or vegetable juice	Fruit or vegetable juice	Fruit or vegetable juice
Fresh fruit (low fiber, such as plums, melon, cherries, or peaches)	Fresh fruit	Fresh fruit
	Breads, bagels, English muffins (no margarine or cream cheese)	Breads, bagels, English muffins
		Peanut butter, lean meat, low-fat cheese
		Low-fat yogurt
		Baked Potato
		Cereal with low-fat milk (2%)
		Pasta with tomato sauce

• **Figure 10.15**   *Eating Before the Event. Source:* Adapted with permission from D. S. Jennings and S. N. Steen, *Play Hard, Eat Hard,* American Dietary Association (Minneapolis: Chronimed Publishing, 1995).

A.M.	P.M.
1 cup orange juice	1 cup vegetable soup
Bagel	2 ounces skinless chicken
2 tablespoons peanut butter	2 slices wheat bread
2 tablespoons honey	2 slices tomato
Or	1 cup low-fat frozen yogurt
1 cup orange juice	1 cup apple juice
3/4 cup corn flakes	**Or**
Medium banana	Large baked potato
Wheat toast and jelly	1 teaspoon margarine
1 cup low-fat (2%) milk	Carrot sticks
Or	1/2 cup fruit salad
1 cup orange juice	1 cup low-fat (2%) milk
Pancakes and syrup	**Or**
English muffin and jelly	Salad: lettuce, 1 ounce ham, 1 ounce turkey, 2 slices tomato, 2 tablespoons dressing
1 cup low-fat yogurt	1/2 cup pudding
Or	**Or**
1 cup orange juice	2 cups spaghetti
Waffles and strawberries	2/3 cup tomato sauce with mushrooms
1 cup low-fat yogurt	French bread
	1 cup lemon sherbet
	1 cup low-fat (2%) milk

• **Figure 10.16**   *Sample Meals Prior (three to four hours) to Physical Activity or Exercise. Source:* Adapted with permission from D. S. Jennings and S. N. Steen, *Play Hard, Eat Hard,* American Dietary Association (Minneapolis: Chronimed Publishing, 1995).

dents that in recent years exercise scientists have discovered a variety of ways in which modifying one's nutritional regimen can enhance performance. For example, Dr. Mike Sherman from Ohio State University has reported that endurance athletes can enhance their performances by reducing training volume 6–7 days prior to competition and by eating a diet consisting of 55% carbohydrates. Using this plan, athletes can increase their resting glycogen stores and exercise longer prior to exhaustion. For sports performance, students should also pay close attention to becoming well hydrated several days prior to the event as well as trying to stay hydrated during the event. This can help them reduce the risk for heat injuries.

Assess

Use the Section 4 Review questions to assess students' comprehension of the concepts presented in Section 4.

Enrichment

This activity will allow you to provide a more challenging learning experience for some of your students.

Ask students to consider what they have discovered about their eating habits and behaviors. Have the students fold a sheet of paper to create three columns. Label the columns with the following headings: *Ineffective Eating Habits*; *Discovery*; and *Intention*. Have the students list their ineffective eating habits; what they discovered about the effects of their eating habits; and what they intend to do to bring about change. The intention statements may be kept on file, allowing the students to periodically review their statements in order to measure their progress or regain their focus.

Close

Good Foods	Foods to Avoid
Bagels	Candy bars
Bananas	Doughnuts
Fruit juice	French fries
Muffins	Hot dogs
Pretzels (hard or soft)	Nachos or potato chips
Sports drinks (6-8% carbohydrate)	Soda

• **Figure 10.17** *Foods for All-Day Competitions. Source:* Adapted with permission from D. S. Jennings and S. N. Steen, *Play Hard, Eat Hard,* American Dietary Association (Minneapolis: Chronimed Publishing, 1995).

help recover your energy stores:

• Medium bagel (50 grams carbohydrate).
• Pretzels (23 grams carbohydrate per ounce).
• Fruit yogurt (40 grams carbohydrate per 8 ounces).
• Large banana (40 grams carbohydrate).
• Cranberry-apple juice (43 grams carbohydrate per 8 ounces).
• Apple juice (30 grams carbohydrate per 8 ounces).
• Orange juice (28 grams carbohydrate per 8 ounces).

Two hours after competition, eat a meal rich in carbohydrates, similar to the meals in Figure 10.16. You can add a bit more protein and fat in the post-event meal for calories and taste.

SECTION 4 REVIEW

Answer the following questions on a separate sheet of paper:

1. For performance fitness, when should you eat your last meal before practice or competition?

2. Why should your pre-event meal be high in carbohydrate and low in fat?

SUMMARY

Proper nutrition is important for good health. If you eat sensibly, you can reduce your risks for developing heart disease, high blood pressure, stroke, certain cancers, and diabetes mellitus. Balancing your diet by paying attention to your personal needs for calories, nutrients, vitamins, minerals, and fluids is the best way to optimize your nutrition. Most Americans eat too much fat and not enough carbohydrates for their nutrition needs. In your diet, 50 to 60 percent of the total calories should come from carbohydrate; 30 percent from fat (with only 10 percent being saturated fat); and 15 to 20 percent from protein. To develop and maintain healthy nutrition habits, use the Food Guide Pyramid to help you meet your daily RDA nutrition needs.

If you learn to read food labels, you can become a better consumer and become skilled at matching your daily caloric intake needs with your daily caloric expenditure. You should regularly evaluate your nutrition habits and your diet to control your body weight and body composition.

If you are involved in high-performance fitness or competitive sports or physical activities, you have special dietary needs. You should develop a nutrition plan that covers the time before the event, during the event, and immediately following the event. By eating right to compete or work out, you can improve your performance and speed your recovery time.

 ## CRITICAL THINKING

hapter 10 Review

True/False

On a separate sheet of paper, mark each question below either T for True or F for False.

1. When you are hypoglycemic, you are full of energy and pep.

2. Fiber is easily digestible and is high in calories.

3. Of your total calories, 30 percent should come from fat, with no more than 10 percent from saturated fat.

4. Vitamin K is an example of a water-soluble vitamin.

5. Antioxidants may help prevent cancer, atherosclerosis, overtraining, and premature aging.

6. The RDA is the Recommended Daily Allowance for calories, vitamins, minerals, and other nutrients.

7. An example of the size of one serving is one medium apple.

8. Teenage girls should consume two to three servings of milk daily.

9. "Nutrition Facts" are part of the food labeling that you can find on food containers or packages.

10. If you are eating to compete, you should consume simple sugars for quick energy right before the contest.

Multiple Choice

1. What is the basic form of carbohydrate?
   a. fiber
   b. glucose
   c. glycogen
   d. electrolytes

2. What kind of nutrients are candy bars, honey, and fruits?
   a. simple carbohydrates
   b. fiber
   c. complex carbohydrates
   d. fat

3. Cholesterol is found in which of the following?
   a. unsaturated fats
   b. vegetables
   c. saturated fats
   d. corn and olive oil

4. Which of the following vitamins is not fat soluble?
   a. vitamin A
   b. vitamin C
   c. vitamin D
   d. vitamin E

5. Too much sodium in your diet may increase your risk for which of the following medical problems?
   a. hypertension
   b. elevated cholesterol
   c. osteoporosis
   d. none of the above

6. How many 8-ounce glasses of water should you consume every day to maintain a fluid balance (not counting days when you exercise in hot environments)?
   a. two
   b. four
   c. six
   d. eight

7. Which of the following items should be consumed at the highest percentage in your diet?
   a. carbohydrate
   b. fat
   c. protein
   d. saturated fat

Answers

True/False

1. F
2. F
3. T
4. F
5. T
6. T
7. T
8. T
9. T
10. F

Multiple Choice

1. b.
2. a.
3. c.
4. b.
5. a.
6. d.
7. a.
8. d.
9. a.
10. d.

Discussion

1. Answers may vary but could include: The Food Guide Pyramid illustrates that you should eat more servings from the base of the pyramid than from the top. This can help you get the nutrients you need daily.

2. Answers may vary but could include: By reading the food labels on containers and packages of food, you can determine how many calories you are consuming as well as whether you are getting enough carbohydrates, proteins, fats, vitamins, and minerals.

3. Answers may vary but could include: You would

may need to supply calorie books and charts for students to use in completing the seven-day records.

Have them exchange records with another student. Analyze and draw conclusions about:
1. Daily caloric expenditure versus needs

2. Snacks eaten (amount and kind)
3. Fat content of diet
4. Nutritional value
5. Representation of food pyramid
6. Overall assessment
7. Changes needed for a healthier diet

want to use the information in Section 4 of this chapter and the information contained in Figures 10.15, 10.16, and 10.17. You should eat foods high in carbohydrates, but don't overeat. Avoid foods high in protein and fat, because they take longer to digest. Also avoid eating foods high in simple sugars before competition, because they provide only quick energy and may even hamper your performance in the long run.

Vocabulary Experience

1 electrolytes
6 vegetarian
5 hypoglycemic
3 unsaturated fat
2 protein
4 mineral

Critical Thinking

1. We all learn behaviors about eating at an early age. Family and cultural values may encourage us to eat too many calories or not enough of some valuable nutrients we need. You may need to change your eating behaviors to meet your personal fitness goals.
2. Electrolytes and water work together to help maintain fluid balance. Maintaining fluid balance helps one avoid heat injuries because it helps prevent or delays dehydration.
3. Answers will vary.

Chapter 10 Review

8. Which of the following recommendations are part of the U.S. Department of Health and Human Services and the U.S. Department of Agriculture *Dietary Guidelines for Americans*?
 a. eat a variety of foods
 b. maintain a healthy weight
 c. use salt and sodium only in moderation
 d. all of the above

9. Which of the following food groups should be consumed sparingly?
 a. fats, oils, and sweets
 b. fruits
 c. vegetables
 d. milk, yogurt, and cheese

10. How many servings should you eat each day from the bread, cereal, rice, and pasta food group?
 a. one
 b. two to three
 c. four to five
 d. six to eleven

Discussion

1. Discuss how you can make the Food Guide Pyramid work for you in developing a plan for sound nutrition.
2. Explain how you can read and understand food labeling so that you can improve or maintain sound nutrition.

3. If you were to train and compete in a 10-kilometer walk/run in your community, how could you modify your nutrition plan to optimize your performance?

Vocabulary Experience

Match the correct term in Column A to the definition in Column B by writing the appropriate number in each blank.

Column A	Column B
_____ electrolytes	**1.** A mineral such as Ca^{++} or Na^+ that helps control the body's fluid balance.
_____ vegetarian	**2.** A nutrient that is the basic building block of the body.
_____ hypoglycemic	**3.** A substance that is usually liquid at room temperature and that comes mainly from plant sources.
_____ unsaturated fat	**4.** A chemical element that is important for the body's structure and function and that regulates the body's metabolism.
_____ protein	**5.** Having low blood glucose (or sugar) levels.
_____ mineral	**6.** A person who eliminates meat, fish, and poultry from the diet.

Wellness Connection

Is Vitamin C a Mircle Drug?

As you have learned, vitamins are nutrients that help control growth and help your body release energy to do work. Vitamin C is a water-soluble vitamin that needs to be consumed on a regular basis. In the early 1700s, the British navy found that sailors could not take voyages longer than about three months because the crew would develop the vitamin C deficiency called scurvy.

While vitamin C is an important vitamin and critical to good health, it has not

Critical Thinking

1. Respond to this statement: Family and culture do not influence what you eat.

2. How is fluid balance influenced by electrolytes and water? How can the maintenance of fluid balance help you prevent heat injuries?

3. Compare your eating habits with those of a family member. Which one of you is making wiser food choices?

RESOURCES

HANDOUTS

A chapter test is provided for Chapter 10 in your Teacher Resource Package.

KEYS TO CASE STUDY

Answers will vary, but might include something like the following: Since Javier wants to gain weight, he should increase his caloric intake while doing more weight training and less aerobic activity. He should still continue doing the minimum amount (three days per week for 20–30 minutes) of aerobic activity to maintain good to better levels of cardiovascular fitness. He also needs to follow a menu similar to the one illustrated in Figure 10.14, which is designed for weight gain. He should start his first two weeks of the program by increasing his frequency of weight training to three days per week. He should also set a goal to gain no more than a half pound per week to be successful. It would also be wise for him to assess his body composition every three months to monitor his percentage of body fat.

Case Study — Gaining Weight

Javier is a fifteen-year-old active male. He lifts weights two times a week. Javier is interested in gaining weight, particularly muscle mass. However, he is unsure about how to gain the weight safely and effectively, get stronger, and not increase his percentage of body fat. Therefore, he needs the help of someone knowledgeable about designing and implementing fitness programs—someone like you!

Here is your assignment:

Assume you are Javier's friend, and he asks you for some assistance with his plans for gaining weight by adjusting his nutrition and physical activity routine. Make a list of things Javier should consider and do before beginning his program. Then list the recommendations you would give to Javier for the first two weeks of his program.

The following suggestions may help you:

KEYS TO HELP YOU

- Consider Javier's current diet and nutrition habits.
- Decide how he should evaluate his current diet. Think about his needs and goals. For example, how should he go about changing his diet?
- Determine a reasonable plan to give Javier that covers the concepts of specificity, frequency, intensity, time/duration, and progression.

been shown to be a miracle vitamin. A deficiency of vitamin C can result in disease; however, the presence of vitamin C or extremely large amounts of the vitamin do not enhance your health or guarantee freedom from disease. In fact, very large doses of vitamin C can cause health problems such as diarrhea, kidney stones, damage to growing bone, gout, and a burning sensation during urination. A healthy and balanced diet should provide all the vitamin C needed for most people. If you take vitamin supplements, be careful not to exceed the established dietary allowances established by the Food and Nutrition Board of the National Academy of Sciences/ National Research Council.

Chapter 11 is 30 pages long and divided into the three sections listed to the right. Major learning outcomes of the chapter are also listed to the right. Briefly, this chapter exposes students to a wide variety of activities, exercises, and sports in which they can participate for a lifetime of personal fitness. It provides students with information about the aging process, and how they can control some factors associated with aging. It also provides students with information to make them wiser personal fitness consumers.

Teacher Resource Material

In the Teacher Resource Package accompanying the textbook, you will find the following material to help you teach this chapter.

Activity Sheets

One Reteaching Worksheet is provided in the Teacher Resource Package for each section of this chapter.

Chapter 11

Shaping Your Current and Future Personal Fitness Program

364

PACING CHART

You could easily spend five days teaching this chapter if students read the entire chapter, do the Active Mind/Active Body activities, and complete several of the handouts from the Teacher Resource Package. However, you can cover the material in this chapter in three days. It is recommended that physical activity be a regular part of each class period (20 to 30 minutes minimum). Following are some examples of how to cover the main topics in the chapter if you are pressed for time.

Contents

1. The Aging Process
2. The Physical Activity, Exercise, and Sports Spectrum
3. Becoming a Better Health and Personal Fitness Consumer

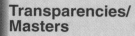

Outcomes

After reading and studying this chapter, you will be able to:

1. Explain how you can use what you have learned about developing personal fitness to help you control the aging process.
2. Discuss why and how you may have to adjust your personal fitness plan as you age.
3. Identify examples of leisure activities from the physical activity spectrum.
4. Explain how to find professional personal fitness advice.
5. Explain strategies for becoming a more informed and wiser personal fitness consumer.
6. Evaluate health and fitness centers to identify those that are reputable.

Key Terms

After reading and studying this chapter, you will be able to understand and provide practical definitions for the following terms:

aging process
leisure
leisure activity
lifetime activity
family physician
physical therapist
athletic trainer
podiatrist
dietitian
exercise physiologist

professional health and
  fitness certification
health educator
physical educator
personal trainer
aerobic dance instructor
fitness specialist
commercial gym
commercial fitness center
commercial dance studio

hospital-based wellness
  center
corporate fitness center
community recreational
  center
college- or university-
  based fitness center
sports medicine clinic
  center

365

Transparencies/Masters

A transparency or master is provided in the Teacher Resource Package for each of the following figures: 11.1, 11.2, 11.3, 11.4, and 11.5.

Discuss the Photos

Ask students to discuss what they think about the photos that show older individuals living active lifestyles. Ask students if they are concerned about how they will look and feel as they get older. Ask them how they can maintain personal fitness as they age. This should get them to think about the future and the functional abilities that their parents and grandparents have. It should also provide opportunities to let students express their perceptions of the physical abilities of the elderly.

Teacher Readings:

Powers, S. K. and Howley, E. T., *Exercise Physiology: Theory and Application to Fitness and Performance,* 2nd Edition, Brown & Benchmark, Madison, WI: 1994.

Time	Suggestions
Day 1	Assign students to read Section 1 prior to class. In class, discuss the aging process and how it can be controlled to some extent. Discuss in depth the concepts contained in Figures 11.1, 11.2, 11.3, and 11.4.
Day 2	Assign students to read Section 2 prior to class. In class, discuss the physical activity, exercise, and sports spectrum. Have students do the Active Mind/Active Body activity on page 377. Also include a variety of discussion about the photos.
Day 3	Assign students to read Section 3 prior to class. Discuss with students how to become a better health and personal fitness consumer. Have students do the Active Mind/Active Body activity on page 381.

CHAPTER 11
SECTION 1
366

Focus

Outcomes

In **Section 1** students will learn:

1. To explain how they can use what they have learned about developing personal fitness to help control the aging process.
2. To discuss why and how they may have to adjust their personal fitness plans as they age.

Focus Activities

1. Discuss the example of preventing or slowing aging of bone mass.
2. Discuss how students can control the aging process, at least to some degree.

INTRODUCTION

*I*f you are like most adolescents, you haven't given much thought to how you will look and feel as you age. How healthy and fit will you be by the year 2000? By 2010? By 2050? How old do you think you will live to be?

Life expectancy has increased dramatically in the United States since 1900. People who live to the age of sixty-five have very good odds of living into their eighties. However, these people won't be satisfied just to be alive. They will want to feel good and be healthy. They will want to be able to take care of themselves and live independently.

As you learned in Chapter 1, a healthy, active lifestyle can add years to your life and help you maintain your physical independence. In previous chapters you explored the many aspects of personal fitness. It is now time for you to use what you have learned to shape your current and future fitness.

You are at a critical age for making decisions about how healthy and active you will be in the future. Research has shown that young adults who do not develop positive attitudes and behaviors toward health and physical activity often become sedentary and inactive adults. You know what happens to sedentary people. Sedentary living and poor health behaviors can expose you to increased risk for chronic disease, disability, and even death. This means that the personal fitness habits you develop and maintain now can help you age more gracefully and reduce your risks for health problems throughout your life.

In this chapter you will learn more about the aging process and how you can control some of the mental and physical factors related to aging. You will learn more about a variety of physical activities, exercises, and sports that can help you stay active throughout your life. You will design your personal fitness program for now and the future. You will also learn more about becoming a better and wiser personal fitness consumer.

SECTION 1   The Aging Process

aging process

how the body changes as a person gets older.

The **aging process** is how your body changes as you get older. Figure 11.1 illustrates four physical functions and how they change with age. Notice that not all of the functions illustrated change at the same rate or to the same amount. For example, the speed at which nerve impulses travel in your body decreases only by about 10 to 15 percent from age 30 to 90, but maximum breathing capacity decreases 50 to 60 percent in the same amount of time. As you might guess, decreases in physical functions depend to a large extent on how healthy and active you remain. That is why it is said that a healthy, active lifestyle can slow the aging process.

ABILITY LEVELS

Reteaching

Some students may need help mastering the concepts contained in this section. In your Teacher Resource Package, you will find the reproducible worksheet shown here. This worksheet should help students who have been absent and those needing additional help to improve their comprehension and retention of the content in this section.

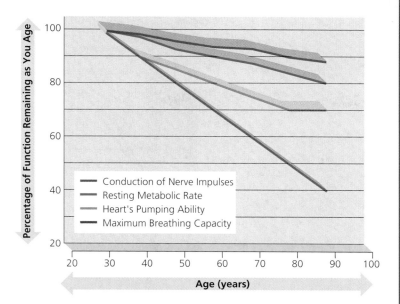

• **Figure 11.1**   *Effects of Aging on Selected Physical Functions.*

Preventing or Slowing Aging of Bone Mass

Figure 11.2 shows one strategy to prevent or slow the aging process. Researchers have been studying bone mass and the development of osteoporosis to see if there is a relationship between being physically active and reducing bone mass loss with aging. Typically, as people grow and develop, they reach their peak bone mass between the ages of 27 and 32. After bone mass levels peak, they then decrease with age.

More active people have greater bone mass than inactive people as they age. This means that as active people age, they will be at a lower risk for osteoporosis than inactive people. If you are active now, you can increase your peak bone mass. If you stay active as you age, you may be able to maintain a higher bone mass than if you are inactive. Instead of getting brittle bones by age 65, you may still have strong bones into your eighties.

Controlling the Aging Process

The sum of all your mental and physical functions determines your functional health (see Chapter 1). As you age, you will be able to slow down the rate and the amount of change for many, but not all, men-

Discussion

Use Figure 11.2 to discuss the theoretical strategy of how to increase peak bone mass and prevent osteoporosis.

Teacher Support Notes

Figure 11.2 emphasizes the importance of having adolescents live an active lifestyle in order to lay down as much bone mass as possible before their mid-20s. If they adopt an inactive lifestyle as adolescents, they will not develop as much bone mass and they will be at a higher risk to develop osteoporosis sooner than if they had been active. This is particularly important for adolescent females, as they will face increased risk of osteoporosis beginning at postmenopausal age.

Healthy People 2000

Objective 9.4—Reduce deaths from falls and fall-related injuries to no more than 2.3 per 100,000 people. (Age-adjusted baseline: 2.7 per 100,000 in 1987.)

Write this objective on the chalkboard or place it on

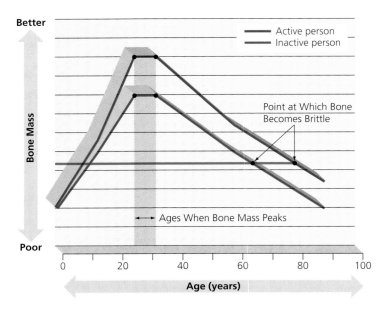

● **Figure 11.2** *Increasing Peak Bone Mass and Preventing Osteoporosis. Source:* Adapted with permission from H. C. G. Kemper and Niemeyer, "The Importance of a Physically Active Lifestyle during Youth for Peak Bone Mass," in *New Horizons in Pediatric Exercise Science,* ed. C. J. R. Blimkie and B. Oded (Champaign, IL.: Human Kinetics, 1995).

● *Participation in regular physical activity and exercise can help you increase your bone mass and maintain it longer than if you remain sedentary.*

Across the Disciplines

Language Arts

Motivational statements may be effective in reconnecting or refocusing people to a previously set goal. Have students brainstorm where they may find examples of motivational messages (e.g., on buildings, clothing, and so on). Discuss the power of word association with commercial statements such as "Just Do It—Nike", "There's an athlete in all of us—Reebok", etc.

Examine the power of insignias or symbols as well as music recognition in con-

BELIEVE IT? ...
OR NOT?

You can lose 6 inches around your waist in two weeks; you can lose 10 pounds of fat in a week; you can make your stomach washboard hard and trim in six weeks; you can run a 26-mile marathon after conditioning for only five weeks.

See page 389 for answer.

tal and physical functions. Figure 11.3 indicates whether or not a physically active lifestyle and healthy eating can have a positive impact on various body functions as you age. As you can see, an active lifestyle and healthy eating will not necessarily keep you from getting gray hair or going bald. However, being active and eating well can help you stay mentally and physically young relative to your age. You probably know some people who look and feel much younger than most people their age. You may know people in their fifties, sixties, and seventies who are able to do more physical work than other, much younger people. Staying active and eating right can keep you in the younger-looking, more productive group.

Body Function	You Can Make a Positive Impact	You Cannot Make an Impact
Graying of hair		X
Balding		X
Resting energy metabolism	X	
Increased body fat	X	
Increased blood presssure	X	
Increased resting pulse	X	
Elevated cholesterol levels	X	
Decreased functional health	X	
Inherited diseases		X
Hypokinetic diseases	X	
Loss of elasticity of joints*		X
Loss of flexibility of joints**	X	
Bone loss	X	
Mental confusion	X	
Reduced self-esteem	X	
Depression	X	

 * elasticity = ability to return immediately to its original size, shape, etc.
** flexibility = ability to bend without breaking

• **Figure 11.3** *Controlling the Aging Process by Being Physically Active and Eating a Healthy Diet. Source:* Adapted with permission from F. S. Sizer, E. N. Whitney, and L. K. DeBruyne, *Making Life Choices: Health Skills and Concepts* (St. Paul: West Publishing, 1994).

the overhead projector and discuss with students why it is important. Point out that falls are often related to osteoporosis (bones such as the hip break, causing a fall), low levels of muscular strength and endurance contribute to the fall or lack of muscular strength and endurance.

Discussion

• Use Figure 11.3 to ask students which factors they can or cannot control by being physically active and eating a healthy diet as they age. Ask them if they can think of other factors besides those in Figure 11.3.
• Ask students what they think about the statement, "If you don't use it, you'll lose it!"
• Use Figure 11.4 to discuss the Activity Pyramid for promoting physical activity and exercise. Ask students how this pyramid relates to the Food Guide Pyramid in Chapter 10 (see Figure 10.6 in Chapter 10).

nection with their association with an organization, product, message, etc. Mascots, the gesture for "number 1" or "champions," and music such as "We Will Rock You," or the school fight song are used to motivate both athletes and spectators. Discuss the various personal motivational responses people may have to these factors and why these occur.

Have students select a musical theme, quotation, poem, or self-authored passage that they will use for motivation to continue their commitment to achieving and maintaining personal fitness. Have students write a short essay explaining choices of motivational theme, how they are implementing them, and what they plan to do if they begin to weaken or fail.

Teacher Support Notes

The Activity Pyramid and the Food Guide Pyramid encourage students to concentrate on engaging in behaviors (consuming more carbohydrates and fresh fruits and vegetables, and living an active lifestyle) at the bottom of the pyramids. The behaviors (consuming more fats, oils, and sweets, and physical inactivity) at the top of both pyramids should be limited. The Activity Pyramid provides suggestions to all types of students in terms of physical activity or exercise habits (inactive, sporadic, or consistent). The Activity Pyramid reinforces the concepts supported by the *Healthy People 2000* Objectives, the National Institutes of Health (NIH), and the Surgeon General's Report (Spring, 1996) that encourages all Americans to pursue active lifestyles.

Assess

Use the Section 1 Review questions to assess students' comprehension of the concepts presented in Section 1.

• *Regular physical activity and exercise are important to people of all ages.*

The aging process also depends on a person's state of mind. Some people think and act much older than they actually are in terms of their health and activity levels. They practice poor health habits and adopt sedentary lifestyles. These habits and lifestyles, in turn, cause them to become depressed, lose self-esteem, and prematurely lose their physical independence. Thus, many older people will tell you, "If you don't use it, you'll lose it!"

Of course, it is normal to lose some mental and physical functioning as you age. You will probably have to adjust your personal fitness program as you age to meet your changing needs. For example, you may have to adjust your FIT for selected activities so that you can recover more completely between workouts. You may find that you need to select different physical activities as you age to keep yourself from getting bored and thus help maintain your adherence. You may find that you can adjust your personal fitness program by cross-training (see Chapter 3). In that way you can recover effectively from day to day and minimize your risk for an overuse injury.

As you age, you will need to pay even closer attention to your body. You will need to understand your mental and physical limitations. You then will be able to meet special situations and needs more effectively and maintain a healthy, active, and productive lifestyle until the end of your years.

Figure 11.4 shows you an activity pyramid that can help you develop and maintain regular physical activity patterns that will help you reduce your risks for chronic diseases as you age. The pyramid illustrates a sensible, step-by-step, daily and weekly plan to help you become and stay active.

Notice that "everyday" physical activities form the base of the pyramid. The next step, or level, of the pyramid includes exercise and recreational activities. The third level promotes leisure activities and the development and maintenance of strength and flexibility. The top step reminds you to cut down on your sedentary habits so that you sit less and move more.

SECTION 1 REVIEW

Answer the following questions on a separate sheet of paper:

1. List and explain three examples of how your body will change as you get older.
2. How can living a physically active lifestyle influence your bone mass?
3. Why is the aging process related to state of mind?

CRITICAL THINKING

Research indicates that exercise and proper diet play a significant role in the aging process. While young people believe they will live forever, they need to understand:
1. They will grow old.
2. Their lifestyles will affect both the

quality and quantity of life.
3. The physiology of aging.
This critical thinking activity involves two parts:
A. Have students interview someone age 40+ who has exercised faithfully over the years. The focus should be on:

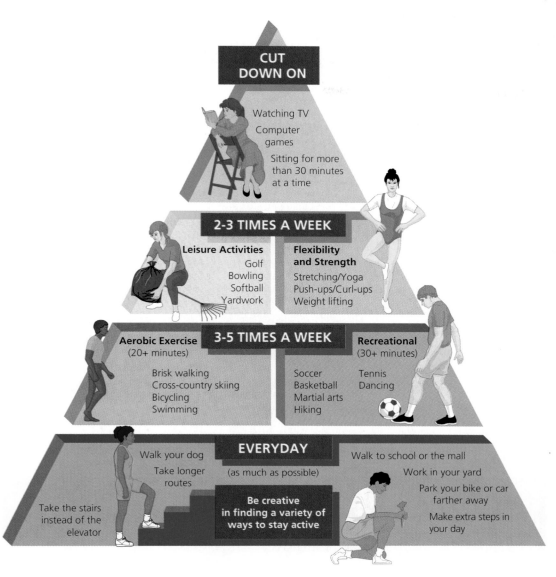

CUT
DOWN ON

Watching TV

Computer
games

Sitting for more
than 30 minutes
at a time

2-3 TIMES A WEEK

Leisure Activities
Golf
Bowling
Softball
Yardwork

**Flexibility
and Strength**
Stretching/Yoga
Push-ups/Curl-ups
Weight lifting

3-5 TIMES A WEEK

Aerobic Exercise
(20+ minutes)

Brisk walking
Cross-country skiing
Bicycling
Swimming

Recreational
(30+ minutes)

Soccer   Tennis
Basketball   Dancing
Martial arts
Hiking

EVERYDAY

Walk your dog   Walk to school or the mall

Take longer   (as much as possible)   Work in your yard
routes
                                         Park your bike or car
                Be creative   farther away
          in finding a variety of
Take the stairs **ways to stay active**   Make extra steps in
instead of the   your day
elevator

• **Figure 11.4**   *Use your "Active Mind" to think of a variety of ways to have an
"Active Body." This Activity Pyramid provides a plan for developing a physically
active lifestyle.*

Adapted with permission from Park Nicollett Medical Foundation, 1995.

Close

a. how exercise and proper diet have
made the person's life more productive.
b. how exercise and proper diet have
helped the person maintain himself/
herself physically (overall wellness).
B. Create four posters representing four
age groups:
• age 18   • age 50
• age 35   • age 65

Using photographs, drawings, pictures,
and/or statements, create profiles of two
different people at each age:
1. One living a sedentary lifestyle.
2. Another living/having lived an active
lifestyle.
    Emphasis and focus is on the aging
process and how it should be viewed.

Stress Break

Have students read and discuss the Stress Break Feature. Ask them if they have ever used some of the stress management techniques discussed.

Focus

Outcome

In **Section 2** students will learn:

1. To identify examples of leisure activities from the physical activity spectrum.

Focus Activities

1. Discuss the concepts of leisure and lifetime activities.
2. Discuss with students the activities presented in the text.

BELIEVE IT? ... OR NOT?

"Physical activity is a key ingredient to healthy aging"

See page 389 for answer.

Stress Break

As you age, you will have to deal with new and different stressors daily. To reduce and deal effectively with stress, you can use various stress-relieving strategies. Some effective stress-relieving strategies are relaxation techniques, breathing exercises, meditation, distraction or imagery, yoga, slowing down, cutting back, physical activity, and exercise. The strategies that last the longest and are most effective in reducing heart rate, blood pressure, and other physical markers of stress are physical activity and exercise.

In addition to using appropriate stress relievers, you should learn to practice common stress management techniques. Some keys to stress-relieving strategies and relaxation techniques that you can practice now and in the future include the following:

- Accept some lack of ability in controlling everything in your life. You can't control everything that happens to you daily.
- Keep in mind that your own perceptions can create stress. Try to have a variety of viewpoints to understand other individuals' perceptions and attitudes.
- Realize that happiness is a by-product of what you do. It isn't something that is given to you.
- Focus on the entire process of your activities, not so much on how you are doing them each second.
- Find a sense of purpose (family, friends, ideas, and so on).
- Learn to forgive others.
- Don't live in the past. You can't undo what happened yesterday or the day before.
- Remember that laziness, procrastination, and sloppiness usually create more stress than they relieve.

SECTION 2 — The Physical Activity, Exercise, and Sports Spectrum

Throughout this text you have been encouraged to develop and maintain an active lifestyle. You have learned that some physical activities are aerobic, and others are anaerobic. Some activities will improve your flexibility, whereas others are better designed to improve your cardiovascular fitness. There is a spectrum (a wide variety and range) of physical activities, exercises, and sports that can

---

Reteaching

Name _____ Date _____ Period _____

Chapter 11
Section 2
The Physical Activity, Exercise, and Sports Spectrum

Directions: Answer the questions in the blanks provided.

1. What activities include any and all physical activities, exercises, sports, and leisure-time activities that you can participate in for long periods of time?

   Lifetime

Identify the type of lifetime activity described in each statement.

Tennis   2. Requires high levels of coordination and can help you develop and maintain your aerobic fitness if you play with partners of ability similar to yours.

Volleyball   3. Can be played recreationally or as a competitive sport. Many communities are building sand courts to promote participation.

Tai Chi   4. A physical activity of Chinese origin that includes various movements, including light calisthenic activities with controlled breathing.

Triathlons   5. Endurance competitions that include swimming, cycling, and running for various distances.

Aerobic Dance   6. Originally developed by Jacki Sorenson in 1969 as a way of combining music and dance movements to achieve fitness.

Skiing   7. The safest way to participate is to take lessons and purchase or rent quality equipment.

Circuit Training   8. Involves lifting weights and doing calisthenics at different stations for several seconds, followed by periods of brief rest.

Martial Arts   9. Karate and judo are two popular forms. A good teacher can help you develop skills.

Basketball   10. You can get an excellent cardiovascular and muscular endurance workout if you play half-court or full-court games for several minutes.

© 1997 West Publishing Co.

Reteaching Worksheets   76

ABILITY LEVELS

Reteaching

Some students may need help mastering the concepts contained in this section. In your Teacher Resource Package, you will find the reproducible worksheet shown here. This worksheet should help students who have been absent and those needing additional help to improve their comprehension and retention of the content in this section.

• *Whatever physical activities or exercises you decide to do, you should strive to improve or maintain good to better levels of functional health.*

leisure

free (nonwork) time.

leisure activity

an activity, sport, or other experience that people participate in during their free (nonwork) time.

help you improve or maintain your functional health. Some are better suited than others to the development of certain aspects of your healthy, active lifestyle.

Leisure Activities

Figures 4.3 and 4.12 in Chapter 4 rated several different physical activities, exercises, and sports on how well they would help you develop the skill- and health-related components of your personal fitness. Notice that many activities (for example, golf) were rated low in terms of helping develop health-related fitness. However, playing golf recreationally does improve some skill-related fitness components (coordination and power) and is a good way to spend your **leisure** time.

Golf is just one example of a leisure activity. **Leisure activities** are the activities, sports, and other experiences that people participate in during their free (nonwork) time. Leisure activities do not necessarily help develop either your health- or skill-related fitness, but they do provide other benefits. By engaging in leisure activities, you can reduce your stress levels, have fun with others socially, burn calories, develop and maintain self-esteem, and pursue an active lifestyle.

As you continue to develop and refine your personal fitness program, you should experiment and try a wide variety of physical activities, exercises, and sports. You then can select the ones you like to do, as well as choose ones that will help you meet your personal fitness goals.

• *Golf is an example of a popular leisure activity.*

Teach & Apply

Discussion

Ask students to respond to the following questions: How healthy and fit will you be by the year 2000? By 2010? By 2050? How old do you think you will live to be?

Teacher Support Notes

You may want to tell students the following:
The average life expectancy for adults in the United States is 75 years. On average, men live to be 72 to 73 years old, while women live to be 78 to 80. By the year 2000, the U.S. population of the "oldest old"—those over age 85—will have increased by about 30% to a total of 4.6 million.

Discussion

Review Figures 4.3 and 4.12 from Chapter 4 with

Enrichment   *This activity will allow you to provide a more challenging learning experience for some of your students.*

Have the students review and list the lifetime activities found on pages 374–380. Have them indicate, beside each activity, their current level of participation, if they would like to participate in the future, or if they have no interest in participating. How many students indicate a desire to participate in a completely new activity? How many expressed no interest in participating in an activity outside of a familiar one? Are there activities in which no one desired to participate?

students. Have them evaluate the activity of golf in terms of how it rates for improving health- and skill-related fitness. Discuss the concept of leisure activities. Have students also look at and identify the activities and sports that emphasize the development and maintenance of health-related fitness.

Teacher Support Notes

It is important to point out to students that one of the best ways to improve their adherence to physical activity and exercise is to have them engage in leisure activities with family or friends. This can make their experiences even more pleasurable. It provides them with opportunities to talk about things in their lives that may be producing stress. They may not resolve these issues, but they can forget them for a while or perhaps develop new strategies to deal with them.

Activity

Have students make a list of activities, exercises, and sports in which they are already engaging. Then have them make a chart that helps them analyze lifetime activities according to considerations such as cost, personality and attitude, equipment and facilities, etc.

lifetime activity

a physical activity, exercise, or sport that a person can participate in for long periods of time (years to decades).

• *Volleyball is a lifetime activity that can be played at the recreational or competitive level.*

As you create your personal fitness program, you should focus first on developing and maintaining your health-related fitness. If you then want to participate in sports, your moderate to high levels of health-related fitness will make you better prepared physically to compete, reduce your risks for injuries, and improve your overall performance. Having moderate to high levels of health-related fitness will also help you enjoy leisure activities even more than if you had a low level of personal fitness.

Lifetime Activities

Your ultimate goal should be to engage in lifetime activities. **Lifetime activities** include any and all physical activities, exercises, sports, and leisure-time activities that you can participate in for long periods of time (years to decades). It is only natural that your choice of lifetime activities will change as you age. Your interests in personal fitness now are different than they will be in ten, twenty, or thirty years.

The following are descriptions of just a few of the many lifetime activities you may find that you enjoy. Learn to analyze your lifetime activities to make sure they help you meet your personal needs for health-related fitness, skill-related fitness, stress reduction, and worthwhile leisure pursuits. Also, determine which lifetime activities are realistic for you based on the following:

• *Cost.* Can you afford to participate in the activity?
• *Your personality and attitude.* Does the activity fit your style?
• *Availability of equipment and facilities.* Where can you find equipment or facilities for the activity?
• *Your social needs.* Will you do the activity alone or with friends?
• *Environmental hazards.* Can you engage in the activity safely?

Lap Swimming. Swimming laps is a great way to develop and maintain coordination and agility. If you swim for several minutes, you can also develop or maintain your cardiovascular fitness and help control your body composition. You can use all kinds of strokes in lap swimming and vary your routine to help you with your fitness adherence.

Aqua Activities. In recent years many people have discovered that they enjoy working out in the pool by doing exercises against the resistance provided by the water. For example, when you stand in a pool with water at chest level and move your arms back and forth through the water, you can feel the resistance of the water. Aqua activities reduce the pounding that your body takes in weight-bearing activities (for example, walking or jogging) and can be modified in intensity by working in the shallow or deep ends of the pool. You can use aqua activities to develop and maintain good to better levels of aerobic fitness, muscular endurance, and body composition.

Special Needs

It can sometimes be difficult to develop a fitness program for disabled students that is both safe and effective. It takes a great deal of input from various sources (i.e. parents, physician, physical therapist, adapted physical education specialist) as well as sufficient knowledge of disabling conditions.

Disabled students have the same need for recreation and leisure activities as do their nondisabled peers. Often the need is even greater for the disabled population, since they tend to have more free time. Participation in leisure activities,

Cycling (touring, mountain biking, and stationary cycling).   Cycling is a very popular form of exercise with all age groups. Tour cycling is usually done on roads with a light-framed bike that has thin tires. Mountain biking is designed to be done on trails with a bike having a heavier frame and wider tires for better traction. For safety, always wear a helmet for tour or mountain bike cycling. Stationary cycling can be done at home or at a health and fitness club. Cycling is excellent for developing and maintaining balance and cardiovascular fitness and for helping you control your body composition.

Skating (in-line skating, rollerskating, and street hockey).   In-line skating and street hockey have become extremely popular in the last few years. To be safe in these activities, you need to wear safety gear. In-line skating activities are excellent for developing and maintaining balance and are moderately good for improving cardiovascular endurance and body composition.

Rock Climbing.   Rock climbing is a challenging anaerobic activity that requires high levels of muscular strength and endurance, as well as excellent balance and coordination. Rock climbing will also stress you aerobically on longer climbs. You should practice safe

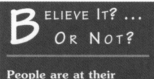

REMEMBER This!

Experiment to find the lifetime activities that will work for you. Seek out new lifetime activities if you get bored with the old ones, but *get active and stay active!* If you become inactive again for a period of time, regroup and *get active again.*

BELIEVE IT? ... OR NOT?

People are at their physical peak for performance at age twenty. From that point on, people go "downhill."

See page 389 for answer.

• *Lap swimming and rock climbing are both popular lifetime activities.*

Teacher Support Notes

Another concept that is important to share with students is that of self-discipline. Participation in regular physical activity and exercise requires some degree of self-discipline on the part of students. Students owe it to themselves to make time in their daily schedules to pursue and maintain personal fitness. Obviously, some days are better than others in terms of scheduling and participating in physical activities and exercise. But a little bit of self-discipline can help students get back to regular physical activity and exercise if they miss a day or two due to scheduling conflicts.

Discussion

Discuss the descriptions of the lifetime activities presented in the text. Ask students if they have specific questions about any of the activities.

Teaching Strategies

When possible, demonstrate (or seek outside help for demonstrations) the activities presented in Section 2 to students. In some cases you might want student volunteers to demonstrate these activities, particularly if they have had experience doing them.

particularly within the community, tends to contribute to social acceptance of the disabled in the sports setting. In addition, positive gains can be seen in the development of fitness, mobility, and self-image. It is often through recreational activities that disabled students are able to experience the success that they may not experience in other areas.

Almost any leisure activity can be adapted or modified so that disabled students can successfully participate in it.
Teacher source for recreational activities for the disabled populations: *I CAN: Sport, Leisure, and Recreation Skills Program,* by J. Wessel, Hubbard Press, Glenview, IL: 1979.

CHAPTER 11
SECTION 2
376

Teacher Support Notes

• If you ask adolescents if they swim regularly (particularly in the summer), most will say that they do. However, a majority of them jump in the water to cool off for just a few moments at a time. For students to get the most out of a swimming personal fitness program, it is best if they learn several strokes and swim for several minutes at a time. Swimming will not increase the heart rate of students (if they are efficient swimmers) as high as if they jogged. For example, maximal heart rates average about 15 beats per minute lower during swimming than running. This is probably due to the horizontal body position for swimming versus running and the cooling effect of the water.

• Aqua aerobics have become very popular for individuals who are overweight and who have had injuries and are in pain while doing weight-bearing activities. Aqua activities are also excellent for injury rehabilitation. For example, injured competitive runners have popularized pool running (with a supportive flotation belt) in recent years to maintain cardiovascular conditioning until their injuries heal.

• *Downhill skiing requires good to better levels of coordination and power.*

• *Ballet dancers usually have high levels of balance, coordination, and agility.*

climbing skills by always climbing with a partner and using your safety gear.

Tennis.   Tennis is a popular lifetime activity. It requires high levels of coordination and can help you develop and maintain your aerobic fitness if you play with partners of ability similar to yours. Many city parks, city recreation departments, and private tennis clubs offer lessons for people of all ages and abilities.

Water or Snow Skiing.   Whether you're on the water or the snow, skiing allows you to enjoy the great outdoors. The safest way to participate in skiing is to take lessons and purchase or rent quality equipment. Skiing of any type requires excellent coordination and power. Cross-country skiing is an excellent way to develop and maintain your cardiovascular fitness and body composition.

Racquetball.   Racquetball requires excellent coordination and agility. It is one of the most popular indoor lifetime activities. It is an excellent sport to help you develop and maintain your cardiovascular fitness and body composition. If you like to compete, racquetball tournaments are regularly held at many fitness clubs and are designed to challenge players of all ages and abilities.

Aerobic Dance (step aerobics).   Aerobic dance and step aerobics classes are held in just about every community in the United States. Aerobic dance develops coordination and is excellent for aerobic conditioning and controlling body composition. Aerobic dance or step aerobics classes are usually designed for people of all levels, from beginners (low impact or lower intensity, less bouncing and jarring movements), to those at intermediate and advanced conditioning levels. If you participate in aerobic dance or step aerobics, make sure you purchase a pair of shoes with good cushioning and support to help prevent overuse injuries.

Aerobic dance was originally developed by Jacki Sorenson in 1969 as a way of combining music and dance movements to achieve physical fitness. Although there are many variations of aerobic dance routines, the basic formula for an aerobics dance routine includes the following: warm-up, cardiovascular work (aerobic exercise), muscular strength, muscular endurance, flexibility components, and a cooldown. Use the instructions in the "Active Mind/Active Body" activity on the next page to design an aerobics dance exercise routine for yourself to present to your classmates (as an option, you can do this as a group project, with three or four other students).

Dance (ballet, line dancing, square dancing, and country-and-western dancing).   Many popular types of dance are easy to do, once you've had a few lessons. Dancing is good for developing your balance, coordination, and agility. Many forms of dance are also good for aerobic conditioning and weight

Wellness Connection

T'ai Chi

The Chinese physical activity called t'ai chi is a set of slow, stylized movements and controlled, focused breathing, which can contribute to improved circulation, flexibility, and stress reduction. While millions of Chinese practice the 128 postures or movements of t'ai chi, it is also beginning to gain popularity in the United States. The postures usually follow the same order, which makes it easy for strangers to meet and carry out the movements together in perfect unison.

Active Mind! Active Body!

Designing an Aerobic Dance Exercise Routine

Watch and critique four or five aerobic dance exercise routine videotapes. Examine the videos to determine the types of music used, intensities of the exercises done (low, moderate, and high intensity), the types of warm-up and cool-down done, and the types of dance movements performed. Then, design your own aerobic dance exercise routine by following these guidelines:

1. Develop a routine that lasts 12–15 minutes.
2. Select music that is appropriate for school use and that matches your routine.
3. Vary the routine intensity with low-impact and high-impact exercises.
4. Set the routine cadence to an 8 count.
5. If you use a group to develop the routine, make sure each group member contributes equally to the routine or exercise leadership.
6. Develop smooth transitions from one exercise to the next.
7. Use correct exercise technique at all times.
8. Make sure your routine includes these components: warm-up, activities for arms and shoulders, aerobic activities, abdominal exercises, activities for leg work, and a cool-down.
9. Practice your routine with music several times before your presentation.

control, if you dance regularly and for long enough periods of time. (As you have learned, health-related fitness results depend on your FIT.) Dancing is an excellent way to interact socially with others. In fact, many people would say that dance, in its many forms, is both a social grace and a skill.

Volleyball. Volleyball helps develop your coordination. It is an activity that can be played recreationally or as a competitive sport. Recently, two-person sand volleyball has become very popular. More and more communities are building sand courts to promote participation. If you want to play volleyball at levels above the recreational level, make sure you have developed good to better levels of health- and skill-related fitness to minimize your risks for injuries.

A typical round of t'ai chi lasts about 20 minutes, during which the arms and legs are in constant motion. The activity can be enjoyed by both young and old. The components of physical health, mental health, and social health can all be enhanced through the practice of t'ai chi.

It's interesting to note that t'ai chi is also a form of self-defense. The words t'ai chi chuan mean "supreme ultimate boxing." T'ai chi does not rely on strength or power, but on leverage. By leaning away from an attack, a skilled practitioner can throw an aggressor off balance, therefore making him vulnerable.

Active Mind! Active Body!

This activity could be started in Chapter 10 and continued with Chapter 11 material and extended over a seven-day period. The Active Mind/Active Body activity on this page should be preceded by preparation activities. For two to three days, students should view a variety of aerobic dance videos. The next two class periods can be allocated to designing and practicing the routines. Then, take two days to have student groups make presentations. In the preparation phase, make sure students turn in a daily report of their progress, identifying how long each part of their routines will take. Finally, it is a good idea to videotape each group presentation and then encourage students to critique their performances.

Teacher Readings

Wilmore, J. H., and Costill, D. L., *Physiology of Sport and Exercise,* Human Kinetics, Champaign, IL: 1994.

Teacher Support Notes

- Country-western line dancing has become one of the most popular forms of dance in the '90s. It is often demonstrated on cable television networks.
- Use the **A**ny **B**ody **C**an feature spotlighting Gabrielle Reece to discuss the popularity of volleyball with students. Sand volleyball courts are a type of facility that is being commonly built by communities throughout the country.
- The National Basketball Association (NBA) has popularized the game of basketball to new heights (no pun intended) in the '90s. Many adolescents enjoy playing basketball; in fact, that is all many want to do in physical education class. It is important to encourage student enthusiasm for basketball while also encouraging them to learn the skills to participate in a variety of activities. However, remind them that most of them won't be able to play basketball forever.
- Calisthenics often can be used as part of the students' personal fitness warm-up and/or cool-down periods. They should never be used (as too often in the past in physical education class) as punishment for students. This will only make students perceive physical activity and exercise as negative experiences.

• *Basketball is a lifetime activity you can engage in either by yourself or with friends.*

• *Circuit weight training is a great way to emphasize aerobic and anaerobic work together.*

Basketball.   Basketball is excellent for developing your coordination, reaction time, and power. It can also be fun just to shoot the ball in a game of "HORSE." You can also get an excellent cardiovascular and muscular endurance workout in basketball if you play half-court or full-court games for several minutes. Playing half-court or full-court basketball is not an activity that most people can do for a lifetime, but you probably can participate in it well into middle age if you maintain good to better fitness levels.

Calisthenics.   Doing regular calisthenics (push-ups, curl-ups, jumping jacks, and so on) can help you improve your muscular endurance and flexibility. If you do calisthenics in a continuous, rhythmic manner, you can also develop and maintain your aerobic fitness and control your body composition.

Circuit Weight Training.   Circuit weight training involves lifting weights and doing calisthenics at different stations for several seconds, followed by periods of brief rest while moving to the next station. For example, you might lift 50 percent of your maximum on leg extensions for thirty seconds and then rest fifteen seconds. You then would move to the next station, which might be push-ups, and do as many as you could in thirty seconds. Your circuit should include at least eight to ten different exercise stations. You should gradually increase your workout time in the circuit from twenty to thirty minutes.

Circuit training is excellent for developing a combination of muscular strength, muscular endurance, and cardiovascular endurance, all in one workout. By lifting weights and doing calisthenics for thirty seconds to a minute at several (about eight to ten) stations, for several minutes, you optimize the time you have to develop and maintain your health-related fitness.

Kayaking and Canoeing.   Kayaking and canoeing can be done recreationally or at competitive levels. These activities help develop your power. When done for long periods of time per session, they are good for aerobic fitness, muscular strength, and muscular endurance. These activities are also great ways to get outside, explore new areas, and help control stress levels.

Rowing (crew and stationary).   Rowing in all its different forms is an excellent activity to develop your coordination, power, aerobic fitness, and muscular endurance. It is also a great way to control your body composition. Rowing in a crew can be a great way to meet other people and be part of a team, even if it's just for recreation. Stationary rowing can be lots of fun, particularly if you can get access to a rowing machine with interactive video feedback to enhance your workout.

T´ai Chi.   T´ai chi is a Chinese physical activity that includes various movements, including light calisthenic activities with controlled

Science and Technology

Educators should never be afraid of technology; they should welcome it. Technology can open different avenues to teaching styles, and decrease day-to-day redundancies.

The changes occurring in education due to technological advances are staggering. With Internet access and the advent of the telecomputing age, physical education teachers will find that an infinite set of resources will be at their fingertips. This should excite and intrigue most physical education teachers. With the increasing accessibility of electronic

• Canoeing is a good way to get outside, enjoy nature, and reduce your stress levels. Working out regularly on a rowing machine can build your muscular strength, muscular endurance, and cardiovascular endurance.

• You can increase your self-confidence and self-esteem by participating in the martial arts.

breathing. T'ai chi exercises are excellent for improving flexibility and are helpful in stress reduction.

Martial Arts.   You might want to participate in one of the various martial arts. Karate and judo are two popular forms. A good teacher can help you develop martial art skills. All the martial arts are excellent ways to develop skill-related fitness and to control emotional stress. They can also help you develop self-confidence and self-esteem. However, the martial arts are not very effective at helping you develop or maintain health-related fitness levels.

Hiking and Backpacking.   Hiking and backpacking are excellent ways to get outside and enjoy nature while developing your muscular endurance and cardiovascular fitness. You probably won't have to go very far from where you live to find a county, state, or national park in which you can do some hiking. For safety, you should hike on well-marked trails and carry a water supply to prevent dehydration. If you hike in an area you're not familiar with, make sure you carry a map and compass to keep from getting lost.

Backpacking requires more planning than does just a half-day or full day of hiking. Before backpacking, you need to plan what supplies you will carry in your backpack (for example, tents, foods, and fluids), particularly if you will be gone for several days. You also have

mail and electronic newsgroups, physical education teachers are able to discuss fitness trends with colleagues across the globe. With these new resources, P.E. teachers will be able to find the means and programs necessary to motivate even the most stubborn student. As teachers rely more and more on comput-

ers, they will accept the computer as "teaching partner," and will find new and innovative ways to teach even the most basic of principles. **Take the challenge:** Find a beginner's book on programming and read it. **Remember:** You can't succeed unless you try.

BELIEVE IT? ... OR NOT?

In 1987, 13 percent of all deaths for people older than age eighty-five were fall-related injuries. The maintenance of muscular strength and endurance can reduce an older person's risks for fall-related injuries.

See page 389 for answer.

to decide how much weight you can carry for extended periods of time (perhaps an hour or two).

Hiking and backpacking can help you develop or maintain your personal fitness levels. However, you need to do some muscular endurance and cardiovascular conditioning prior to going on a long hike or backpacking trip. You should also make sure you purchase good hiking shoes or boots and break them in before participating regularly in hiking or backpacking.

Walking and Jogging.   Walking is one of the most popular activities that people of all ages engage in to develop and maintain muscular endurance and cardiovascular fitness. Jogging is not as popular as walking but has the same benefits. Chapters 3 and 5 gave examples of walking and jogging conditioning programs to help you reach good to better levels of cardiovascular fitness. You also know from Chapter 2 that it is important for you to wear proper shoes when you walk or jog.

Triathlons, Biathlons, and Marathons.   Triathlons (for example, the Ironman Triathlon in Hawaii) are endurance competitions that include swimming, cycling, and running for various distances. Biathlons are endurance events that usually combine two activities—for example, running and cycling, swimming and running, or cross-country skiing and rifle shooting. Marathons are endurance competitions that usually include running distances of at least 26.2 miles. Triathlons, biathlons, and marathons all require high levels of performance fitness.

Most people will never try to complete a triathlon, biathlon, or marathon. However, you may find that you want to challenge yourself to complete one of these events just for your own self-satisfaction. If you decide to attempt one of these activities, make sure you seek out professional advice from your physical education teacher, school coach, or other expert and also condition yourself properly for several months before the event.

SECTION 2 REVIEW

Answer the following questions on a separate sheet of paper:

1. List three benefits of participating in leisure activities.
2. What five factors should you consider before choosing lifetime activities that are realistic for you?
3. Why is circuit weight training a good way to develop and maintain health-related fitness?

Equipment Options

Deciding on what equipment teachers will need for a well-rounded fitness program encompasses research, pricing, and visual comparisons. To make sound decisions in acquiring the different fitness equipment needed, a teacher must learn about certain types of equipment and the differences in manufacturers. *Consumer Reports* and *Consumer Digest* are good resources for comparing fitness equipment. Other resources include local fitness clubs and community organizations and professional organizations such as AAPHERD.

Active Mind! Active Body!

Designing Your Personal Fitness Program

You have learned all about personal fitness in Chapters 1 through 10. Now take some time and write out a plan for your personal fitness program. Use the "Active Mind/Active Body" activities and "Fitness Checks" you have done throughout the text, as well as the exercise science principles and the FIT recommendations you have learned, to write a personal fitness prescription for good health and an active lifestyle. Focus on the health-related components of personal fitness (cardiovascular fitness, flexibility, muscular strength and endurance, body composition, and nutrition). Reviewing the Case Studies you completed will also help you develop an appropriate program.

List your goals and how you expect to accomplish them. Don't forget to describe in detail the healthy nutrition practices you intend to follow. If you are interested in high-performance fitness, you can use some of the activities described in this chapter to develop a program for yourself that focuses on skill-related fitness (agility, balance, coordination, power, speed, and reaction time). After you complete your plan, explain how you might need to modify your program when you are thirty, fifty, and seventy years old.

SECTION 3

Becoming a Better Health and Personal Fitness Consumer

Throughout the text you have read the "Consumer Corner" features. It is important for you to become a better health and personal fitness consumer. Now, more than ever before, a large number of health and fitness products and services are being marketed and sold to the public. Many of these products and services are not effective or produce only partial positive results, leaving consumers frustrated and angry about their purchases and the money that they wasted.

In this section you will learn how to find qualified and knowledgeable health and fitness experts who can help you get accurate, professional, personal fitness advice. You will learn how to identify and

Focus

Outcomes

In **Section 3** students will learn:

1. To explain how to find professional fitness advice.
2. To explain strategies for becoming a more informed and wiser personal fitness consumer.
3. To evaluate health and fitness centers to identify those that are reputable.

Focus Activities

1. Discuss how to find a qualified fitness expert.
2. Discuss how to evaluate consumer health and fitness information.
3. Discuss how to choose a reputable health and fitness facility.

Teacher Readings

McArdle, W. D., Katch, F. I., and Katch, V. L., *Exercise Physiology: Energy, Nutrition, and Human Performance*, 4th Edition, Lea & Febiger, Philadelphia, PA: 1996.

The limiting factors that will affect equipment decisions will be budget constraints and adequate space for the equipment. The knowledgeable P.E. teacher will be able to overcome many of the budget constraints by shopping wisely; however, the limitations due to space will dampen enthusiasm for some equipment purchases. The P.E. teacher should thoroughly assess what his or her goals are for a fitness program, and what the immediate needs are. **Take the challenge:** Assess your fitness goals and develop a long-range plan for the acquisition of equipment. **Remember:** All equipment is not alike, and you don't have to pay premium prices for premium equipment.

Any Body Can!

Discuss with students any obstacles they feel Gabrielle had to overcome in her life. (Loss of father at an early age; being raised by freinds.) Ask students to think about obstacles they have had to overcome or are trying to overcome. What advice would they give to others who may be struggling with similar obstacles?

Teacher Readings

Blimkie, C. J. R., and Bar-Or, O., Editors. *New Horizons in Pediatric Exercise Science*, Human Kinetics, Champaign, IL: 1995.

Any Body Can!

Gabrielle Reece

Gabrielle Reece is a 6'3", 172-pound professional four-woman circuit beach volleyball player and a super model. She has become a role model for women's fitness for the 1990s and the future.

Gabrielle (who prefers to be called "Gabby" or "Gab") was born in 1970. In her junior year of high school, she began playing volleyball and was discovered by a modeling scout. She did well at both modeling and volleyball, and by her senior year she had earned a volleyball scholarship to Florida State University.

At Florida State Gabby continued to play volleyball and to model. She spent six months of the year playing middle blocker in volleyball and spent the other six months in New York modeling for magazines like *Elle* and *Italian Vogue*. In 1990, she was named All-Southeastern Conference middle blocker and is still Florida State's all-time leader in blocks.

In 1992, Gabby began playing women's doubles beach volleyball (2 women per team), but struggled due to the differences in the style of play of this kind of volleyball versus the collegiate game (6 women on a team). Later in the same year, she was asked to join a new, professional circuit beach volleyball tour with four women on a team. In 1993, she led the league in kill shots and blocks, and she signed an endorsement contract with a major shoe manufacturer. The next year she was voted the league's best offensive and the most improved player.

Gabby has continued both her successful modeling and volleyball careers. She has been named to *Elle* magazine's "Five Most Beautiful Women in the World" list and is one of *People's* magazine's "50 Most Beautiful People." She has become a national celebrity promoting health and fitness.

Gabby has become a role model for many young men and women. She promotes participation in physical activities and sports as a way for adolescents to learn to control their bodies. Gabby feels that regular participation in physical activities and sports helps build confidence and self-discipline, and adds meaning to life.

Gabby works hard to maintain her own physical skills and good looks. In addition to playing competitive volleyball, she works out regularly at a gym. Her typical workout includes a 50-minute circuit of aerobics with strength and flexibility training. This has helped her develop a physique that has only 15 percent body fat. She also follows a sound nutrition plan to meet her daily energy needs and to control her weight.

Not everyone can be a super model and professional athlete like Gabrielle Reece, but Any Body Can learn to develop and maintain personal fitness for a lifetime of active living.

ABILITY LEVELS

Reteaching

Some students may need help mastering the concepts contained in this section. In your Teacher Resource Package, you will find the reproducible worksheet shown here. This worksheet should help students who have been absent and those needing additional help to improve their comprehension and retention of the content in this section.

evaluate reputable health and fitness information, including information on practicing sound nutrition or purchasing home exercise equipment. This section will also suggest some questions to ask when choosing a health and fitness club.

Finding Qualified Fitness Experts

At some point you will probably want to learn more about personal fitness or seek more in-depth, professional advice about nutrition, recreational activities, body building, or rehabilitation from injuries. It is important, as a wise consumer, that you seek out qualified and certified health and fitness professionals. Some examples of health and fitness professionals who are available to help you are physicians, physical therapists, athletic trainers, podiatrists, dietitians, exercise physiologists, health and physical educators, personal trainers, aerobic dance instructors, and fitness specialists.

Family physicians usually treat day-to-day health problems or injuries. These physicians train for many years in academic and clinical settings (settings where they are actually practicing medicine) and are licensed by the state. Other kinds of physicians have additional specialized training in specific medical areas, including surgery, cardiology (disorders of the heart), or orthopedics (bone and joint disorders).

Physical therapists are specially trained to work with people in rehabilitation (recovery from injury). They use a variety of treatments and techniques to help manage their patients' health problems.

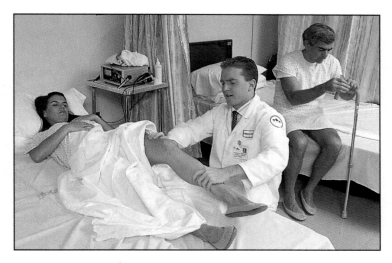

• *Physical therapists are specially trained to work with people who are rehabilitating from injuries.*

Teach & Apply

Discussion

Ask students if they have ever felt taken advantage of when purchasing health and fitness equipment or products. Did they get what they paid for? Ask them to share with you what types of claims they think might be misleading or false.

Activity

Have students look up articles in current newspapers and magazines that highlight various health and fitness products. Have them identify articles that appear to mislead consumers. This would make a good discussion topic in class.

Enrichment

This activity will allow you to provide a more challenging learning experience for some of your students.

Have the students find an advertisement that promotes health and fitness. The student is to apply critical thinking skills in assessing the truthfulness of the ad. Ask the student to show his or her advertisement, explain what product is being sold, whether he or she feels the advertisement is true or false, and on what evidence he or she has based his or her assessment. When the task is complete, the advertisements can be placed on poster board to create an advertising collage entitled "Fitness Fact or Fiction."

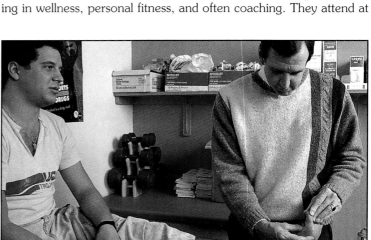

CNN® **Health and Fitness Updates**

You can update your coverage of health and fitness topics, as well as spark lively classroom discussion and deeper understanding, by using the **CNN Health and Fitness Updates.** These video updates are produced by Turner Educational Services, using the resources of CNN, the world's first 24-hour, all-news network.

With the introduction of the **CNN Health and Fitness Updates,** West Educational Publishing is proud to be the exclusive partner of CNN for textbook/video integration in high school fitness. By making use of the **CNN Health and Fitness Updates** you can bring the power of CNN, the network known for providing in-depth, live coverage and analysis of breaking news events, to your fitness class.

For assistance in using and incorporating the **CNN Health and Fitness Updates** into your classroom presentations, see the *Classroom Guide to the CNN Health and Fitness Updates.* The **CNN Health and Fitness Updates** are available with West Educational Publishing's *Foundations of Personal Fitness* by Don Rainey and Tinker Murray.

B ELIEVE IT? ... OR NOT?

The majority of people in the United States over the age of sixty-five are in nursing homes.

See page 389 for answer

Physical therapists undergo four to six years of academic and clinical training and must be licensed by the state. Clients are referred to physical therapists by physicians.

Athletic trainers usually work in the rehabilitation of athletes at the high school, college, or professional levels. Athletic trainers undergo at least four years of academic and clinical training before they can practice. They work under the supervision of physicians and are often licensed by the state.

Podiatrists are professionals trained specifically to treat disorders of the feet. They train at least five to six years in academic and clinical settings and are licensed by the state.

Dietitians specialize in providing nutrition advice and helping people control their weight. They undergo at least four years of academic and clinical training before they can practice. They are registered and licensed by the state.

Exercise physiologists are specially trained to understand the body's physical reactions to exercise. They complete at least four to six years of college and earn a degree with an emphasis in exercise physiology. They are not licensed by the state but usually earn **professional health and fitness certification** as fitness instructors or program directors by a national organization. To do so, individuals must pass written tests and demonstrate their skill as leaders of physical activity to be certified by national fitness and health organizations.

Health educators and **physical educators** have special training in wellness, personal fitness, and often coaching. They attend at

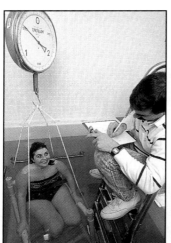

• *Personal trainers, exercise physiologists, and athletic trainers are just a few of the health and fitness specialists who can help you maintain or improve your personal fitness.*

CRITICAL THINKING

Select some of the best exercise equipment on the fitness market. Assign one piece of equipment to a group of four to five students. Be sure and include the Health Rider and Nordic Track. Have the groups gather information relating to cost, durability, positive aspects, negative aspects, and ease of operation. (Encourage the students to contact the manufacturer for information even though it will be biased.) Each student within the group should summarize the findings as to the equipment's usefulness and ability to provide an appropri-

least four to six years of college and earn degrees in health or physical education specialties. The instructor for the class you are now taking is most likely a health or physical educator. This professional is a very valuable first stop when you are seeking professional personal fitness advice. Health educators and physical educators are certified by the state to teach.

Personal trainers, aerobic dance instructors, and **fitness specialists** are individuals who specialize in working with people alone or in groups to help them achieve individual personal fitness goals. They may or may not have any formal academic or clinical training. Many organizations have programs that provide professional health and fitness certification for personal trainers, aerobic dance instructors, or fitness specialists who pass written and practical examinations. Unfortunately, some certification programs are very superficial. In fact, in some cases all an individual needs to do to receive a certification is mail in a fee. This type of certification is unethical, yet it occurs regularly.

Many excellent personal trainers and aerobic dance instructors are practicing their skills. You need to be aware, however, that others have little, if any, professional qualifications. If you choose a trainer or instructor who is not reputable, you probably will get inaccurate advice and may increase your risk for injury.

personal trainer

individual who specializes in working alone with people, instructing exercise sessions, and developing personal fitness programs for a fee.

aerobic dance instructor

individual who specializes in teaching aerobic dance activities to groups of people.

fitness specialist

individual (other than a personal trainer or aerobic dance instructor) who specializes in physical fitness and nutrition promotion.

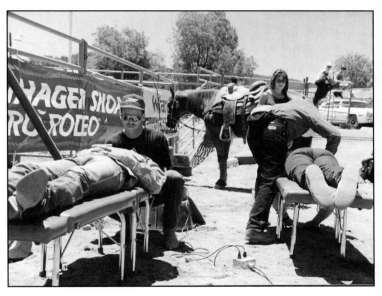

• *Health and fitness professionals are often seen at competitive events where they provide competitors with a variety of important services prior to and following the events.*

Discussion

Ask students if they are familiar with how the following health and fitness professionals can help them with obtaining personal fitness advice and services: physicians, physical therapists, athletic trainers, podiatrists, dietitians, exercise physiologists, health and physical educators, personal trainers, aerobic dance instructors, and fitness specialists.

Teacher Readings

Sizer, F. S., Whitney, E. N., and DeBruyne, L. K., *Making Life Choices: Health Skills and Concepts,* West Publishing Co., Minneapolis, MN: 1994.

ate fitness workout.

With the concept of using one piece of exercise equipment to provide a fitness workout, each student must create the "ultimate exercise machine." Once this is done, the student will develop a 60-second commercial (video or audio, depending upon available equipment) to sell this equipment to the consumer. Students must be creative and understand what the consumer would be looking for in any exercise device on the market.

Teacher Support Notes

You might want to remind students that there are a variety of different types of physicians that they might need to see for health problems or injuries. If they have more than minor problems, they will often be referred by their family physicians to a specialist. Some common specialists of whom they should be aware are: cardiologists (M.D.s that treat heart and blood vessel diseases), chiropractors (D.C.s treat spine and other joint problems), osteopaths (D.O.s manipulate bones and joints in addition to prescribing medicine and surgery), allergists and immunologists (M.D.s that treat allergies and asthma), internal medicine specialists (M.D.s that deal with diseases that do not require surgery), and orthopedic surgeons (M.D.s that perform bone and joint surgery and rehabilitation).

Consumer Corner

Have students read the Consumer Corner and discuss with them the concept of professional certification.

Evaluating Health and Fitness Information

Another important consumer issue has to do with health and fitness information claims that require you to be able to distinguish fact from fiction. As a consumer you are bombarded every day by advertisements in print, and on television and radio that promote health and fitness products (diets, fitness equipment, and so on). All these products claim they will make you fitter, look better, or feel better. You will also find many articles and books about health and fitness. Often the claims of these advertisements, books, and articles are false, misleading, unsafe, or ineffective.

You can become a better health and fitness information consumer by using the following guidelines:

- Look at the credentials (a list of a person's professional training and experiences) of the people making health and fitness claims, particularly if they are selling products.
- Be suspicious of claims of quick and simple results associated with health and fitness.

CONSUMER CORNER

Listening to the Experts

Many so-called health and fitness experts who look fit know very little about the whys and hows of developing and maintaining fitness. To find reputable professional personal fitness advice, follow these guidelines:

1. Ask your personal fitness course instructor to refer you to someone he or she respects professionally.
2. Ask your personal physician for advice.
3. Ask to see professional licenses or special training certifications.
4. Make sure a professional's certifications are from reputable organizations, such as the following:
   - American College of Sports Medicine, or ACSM (exercise physiologists and fitness specialists);
   - Young Men's Christian Association, or YMCA (fitness certifications);
   - American Council on Exercise, or ACE (aerobic dance instructors, fitness specialists);
   - Aerobics and Fitness Association of America, or AFAA (aerobic dance instructors, step aerobics instructors—individuals who teach aerobic dance with bench stepping routine, personal trainers);
   - National Strength and Conditioning Association, or NSCA (personal trainers and strength coaches—individuals who specialize in helping people build muscular strength and endurance).
5. Make sure the advice you get includes information that you can understand and use in your life.

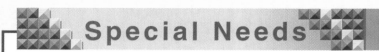

Special Needs

Osteoporosis is of particular concern in the disabled population, who tend to lead fairly sedentary lives. These students already exhibit signs of osteoporosis due to compromised movement and decreased muscle mass. As an individual ages, this can become even more of a problem for the disabled student.

For the disabled population, the following professionals can provide additional information regarding health-related fitness: therapeutic recreation specialists, adapted physical education specialists, and occupational therapists.

BELIEVE IT? ... OR NOT?

One goal of *Healthy People 2000* is to reduce the proportion of people aged sixty-five who have difficulty performing two or more personal care activities from 11 to 9 percent.

See page 389 for answer.

- Beware of miracle breakthroughs that you have not read or heard about elsewhere.
- Beware of individuals testifying that they got great results with a product, particularly if there is a label or disclaimer stating, "Results may vary."
- Check out home exercise equipment before you buy it. Make sure you know how to use it, that it is built to last, and that it is safe and effective. Seek professional advice before you buy if you have any questions.
- Beware of mail-order sales or infomercials that promote products or services that are not endorsed by qualified health and fitness professionals.
- Don't spend your money on a health and fitness product until you've had a chance to evaluate whether or not it is truly effective and practical for you.

Practice your skills at evaluating health and fitness claims by doing the exercise in the "Active Mind/Active Body" activity below.

Health and Fitness Facilities

At some point in your life, you may find it helpful to join a health and fitness club or center in order to restart or maintain your personal fitness program. If you do want to join a club or center, keep in mind that some are more reputable than others. A quality health and fitness facility should be a place where you can pursue your fitness conditioning safely and effectively, get sound professional advice, and achieve your personal goals.

Evaluating Health and Fitness Information

Identify and describe five different examples of misleading or false health and fitness information that you have seen in the last six weeks. If you need help, look for examples in your local newspaper, health and fitness magazines, television commercials, health and fitness club advertisements, and trade shows.

Teacher Support Notes

There are so many different types of professional certifications for the various areas of health, fitness, and rehabilitation that it is very difficult to keep track of which are reputable and which are not. If students or your colleagues ever have a question about the professional credentials of a health and fitness specialist, we recommend that you contact professional organizations like those mentioned in the Consumer Corner (ACSM, NSCA, AFAA, and so on) for more information.

Discuss

Ask students to discuss the latest health or fitness infomercial that they have seen on television. Ask them what it was about. How much did the product or service being promoted cost? What types of experts were shown?

The Americans with Disabilities Act (ADA) mandates accessibility to all facilities. The ADA also dictates that individuals with disabilities should be able to participate in the programs and activities of public facilities in the most integrated setting possible.

Facilities should allow access to all areas. When choosing a facility, the following should be kept in mind: Does the facility have a pool that can be accessed, ramps, elevators, bathrooms, and lockers that are wheelchair accessible?

Water activities are of utmost importance for the disabled student. Swimming is an excellent source of cardiovascular fitness and range of motion activity.

Activity

As homework, have students write a detailed description of an infomercial. The description should include the following: product or service marketed; whether the product or service is available elsewhere; cost of the product or service; promoted benefits of the product or service; credentials of the people promoting the product or service; whether there is a money-back guarantee on the product or service; and any other information you may think is worthwhile.

Teacher Support Note

You may want to tell students that the fifth part of NASPE's definition of a physically educated person is that the person "values physical activity and its contributions to a healthful lifestyle."

• *If you join a health and fitness center or club, find one that meets your specific needs.*

Kinds of Clubs. You can choose from many different types of health and fitness clubs or centers. These facilities often specialize in or cater to specific consumer needs or clients. For example, in your community you may find commercial gyms, commercial fitness centers, commercial dance studios, hospital-based wellness centers, corporate fitness centers, community recreational centers, college- or university-based fitness centers, or sports medicine clinic centers.

Commercial gyms are health and fitness facilities that are usually small in size and have relatively few members. These centers usually specialize in providing a few physical activities to the consumer. They cater to the serious weight trainer or high-performance athlete.

Commercial fitness centers are health and fitness facilities that offer a wide variety of resistance and aerobic training equipment and cater to all types of people. These centers are often found in neighborhood shopping centers. YMCAs and YWCAs are considered commercial fitness centers.

Commercial dance studios are health and fitness facilities that usually do not have much exercise equipment and cater to people interested in aerobic dance and jazz forms of exercise. These studios are often found in neighborhood shopping centers.

Hospital-based wellness centers are health and fitness facilities associated with neighborhood hospitals. These centers usually have

Wellness Connection

The human body has set limits on longevity. There are likely to be many causes of aging and, as a result, many factors involved with the aging process. Some of the biological theories on aging include the following:

Theory Of Aging By Program: Every species of animal has its own longevity that is programmed into its body cells.

Gene Mutation Theory Of Aging: Mutations (genetic changes) gradually build up in the body cells over a period of time until the cells can no longer function properly. While cells do have ways to

Answers to
B ELIEVE IT? ... OR NOT?

Pg. 369 False. If a claim sounds too good to be true or possible, it probably is. Don't fall for fitness claims that sound simplistic. Developing and maintaining personal fitness need not be painful or even uncomfortable, but it does take some discipline and time.

Pg. 372 True.

Pg. 375 False. You can find numerous examples of people in their forties, fifties, and beyond setting personal performance records in such diverse activities as weight lifting, golf, and target shooting.

Pg. 380 True.

Pg. 383 True.

Pg. 384 False. Only about 5 percent of people over sixty-five are in nursing homes. Most older Americans live independently and depend on their mental and physical abilities to function daily.

Pg. 387 True.

a wide variety of exercise and educational programs focusing on personal fitness. Hospital-based wellness centers cater primarily to clients who need medical screening before beginning a fitness program or medical supervision during their physical activity.

Corporate fitness centers are health and fitness facilities that are associated with businesses such as telephone companies or computer companies. These centers often offer a variety of recreational and fitness programs for employees and their families.

Community recreational centers are health and fitness facilities operated by a city park and recreation department. These centers offer a variety of recreational activities and programs to members of the community.

College- or university-based fitness centers are health and fitness facilities operated by state or private colleges or universities. These centers usually provide a variety of recreational and fitness programs for students, faculty, and staff from a particular school.

Sports medicine clinic centers are health and fitness facilities that focus on research promoting health and fitness, as well as on the development and operation of health, fitness, recreation, and educational programs. These centers are usually associated with large hospitals in large cities and cater to clients in the upper-middle socioeconomic class.

Figure 11.5 on the next page gives the advantages and disadvantages of the various types of health and fitness facilities that have been described. Study the figure carefully.

Choosing a Facility. How can you pick a health and fitness club from the many kinds available? To pick a quality health and fitness club or center for yourself, you need to determine your personal fitness needs and the type of facility that can best meet these needs. Visit several facilities to get an idea of what they offer. Always visit a health and fitness club or center before joining it.

As you visit a facility, ask yourself these questions:

- Is the facility conveniently located for you?
- What time does the facility open and close, and is it open on holidays?
- Is the facility clean and well maintained?
- Does the facility have a locker room? If so, are there towels and laundry service?
- Does the facility have enough showers, hot tubs, saunas, and steam rooms? Are they kept clean?
- What are the prices, and does the club have package deals or season specials?
- Is the facility very crowded when you want to use it?
- Can you fit in and socialize easily with the other members?

Discuss

Ask students whether they or other members of their families have ever belonged to a health club. If so, why did they join? What kind of club is it, and what kinds of services are available? Use information in the text to discuss with students the different kinds of clubs and services they provide.

Teacher Support Notes

The health and fitness clubs or centers listed in the text do not necessarily include every type of club or center available. The list is designed to give students an overview of what they can expect to see. The health and fitness club and center industry is constantly changing to meet consumer needs. It appears that as health and fitness consumers become more knowledgeable, they will request and require more service, flexibility, and convenience from their health and fitness clubs or centers.

repair damaged genes, over time these repair mechanisms become less efficient.

Cross-Linkage Theory Of Aging: Proteins are made up of smaller molecules called peptides. Chemical bonds (cross-links) between these peptides can cause permanent changes in proteins. With age, cross-links can build up until proteins can no longer function properly.

Free Radical Theory Of Aging: Substances released by polyunsaturated fats (free radicals) produce chemical reactions that alter and damage body cells.

Wear-and-tear Theory Of Aging: The body is simply a piece of machinery that wears out and ultimately breaks down.

Discussion

Use Figure 11.5 to ask students to compare the advantages and disadvantages of various health and fitness facilities.

Activity

Have students visit one or two health and fitness facilities. Have them use the list of questions at the bottom of page 389 and put together a report about each facility.

Assess

Use the Active Mind/Active Body activity on page 387 to assess student progress. Use the Section 3 Review questions to assess students' comprehension of the concepts presented in Section 3.

Health and Fitness Facility	Advantages	Disadvantages
Commercial gym	Is good for high performance	Has limited facilities; members may be too serious for your needs
Commercial fitness center	Has a large variety of activities	May be expensive or too crowded
Commercial dance studio	Usually has certified instructors	Has a limited number of fitness activities
Hospital-based wellness center	Has medical supervision and highly trained personnel	Has a relatively higher cost
Corporate fitness center	Has a variety of recreational and fitness activities	Is limited to employees and family members
Community recreational center	Has a variety of recreational activities and is economical	May have limited health and fitness activities
College- or university-based fitness center	Has a wide variety of programs and trained personnel	To join, you must be associated with the school (student, faculty, or staff); it may be very expensive for others to join
Sports medicine clinic center	Has comprehensive programs and medical supervision; is research based	Is expensive

• **Figure 11.5** *Comparison of Various Types of Health and Fitness Facilities.*

• Are the instructors or personal trainers certified and well skilled in correct resistance training?
• Are individual exercise programs available?
• Are educational programs available?
• Does the facility have a medical advisor for any special medical needs you have?
• Are the instructors certified in cardiopulmonary resuscitation (CPR) and first aid?
• Is the equipment well cared for and in top working condition?
• Is the exercise area uncluttered and well monitored for safety?
• Does the facility have a variety of both machines and free weights?

COOPERATIVE LEARNING

Following are resources for obtaining more information about how to incorporate cooperative learning into your classroom activities:
• *Cooperation in the Classroom* by D. Johnson, R. Johnson, and E. Holubec (Edina, MN: Interaction Book Co., 1988)

• *The Jigsaw Classroom* by E. Aronson (Beverly Hills, CA: Sage, 1978)
• *Designing Groupwork* by E. Cohen (New York: Teachers College Press, 1986)
• *Cooperative Learning: Resources for Teachers* by S. Kagan (Laguna Niguel, CA: Resources for Teachers, 1988)

- Does the facility have a variety of aerobic conditioning activities (swimming, cycles, treadmills, stair steppers, and so on)?
- Are aerobic exercise classes offered?
- Are racquetball, basketball, or tennis courts available?
- Are there indoor and outdoor hiking and jogging tracks or trails?
- Is there a system for evaluating your progress?
- Does the facility have computers to log or chart your progress?

All these steps should help you choose a health and fitness club or center wisely.

SECTION 3 REVIEW

Answer the following questions on a separate sheet of paper:

1. What is the difference between a physical therapist and a podiatrist?
2. List four ways to become a better health and fitness information consumer.
3. Discuss four factors you should consider before joining a health or fitness club.

SUMMARY

You can have some control over your aging process. You can maintain many of your mental and physical abilities, or even slow down their loss. A regular personal fitness program and sound nutrition can increase your chances for living a longer and more productive life. The maintenance of your functional health depends to a large extent on how active you are now and in the future. You should be prepared to make any necessary adjustments in your personal fitness plan to remain active as you age.

A wide variety or spectrum of physical activities, exercises, and sports can help you improve or maintain your functional health.

You should find the leisure and lifetime activities that work effectively for you in order to maintain your functional health and enjoy life more fully.

If you become a better health and fitness consumer, you will be able to spend your money more wisely on products and services that are available. By knowing how to seek professional health and fitness advice, you can save yourself time and money, as well as reduce your chances of getting poor service. Finally, if you desire to join a health and fitness club or center, choose it wisely. Visit several facilities, and choose one that meets your needs.

ANSWERS TO SECTION 3 REVIEW

1. A physical therapist is trained to work with people in rehabilitation. Clients are referred to physical therapists by physicians. Podiatrists are trained to treat disorders of the feet.
2. Answers may vary but might include: look at credentials; be suspicious of claims of quick and simple results; beware of mail-order sales; and make sure you evaluate a product or service before you buy.
3. Answers may vary but might include: Is the facility conveniently located for you? Is the facility clean and well maintained? Is the facility very crowded when you want to use it? Does the facility have a medical advisor for any special medical needs you have?

Close

Have students make posters to educate other students in their school about becoming wise health and personal fitness consumers. Display posters in early May during National Physical Fitness and Sport Month or in September for Family Health Month.

- *Team—Games—Tournament* by D. DeVries, et al (Englewood Cliff, NJ: Educational Technology, 1980)
- *A Guidebook for Cooperative Learning* by D. Dishon and P. O'Leary (Holmes Beach, FL: Learning Publications, 1984)
- *Joining Together: Group Theory and Group Skills* by D. W. Johnson and F. Johnson (Englewood Cliff, NJ: Prentice-Hall, Inc., 1987)
- *Cooperative Learning and Computers: An Activity Guide for Teachers* by M. Male, R. Johnson, D. Johnson, and M. Anderson (Santa Cruz, CA: Educational Apple-cations, 1988)
- *Cooperative Sports and Games Book* by T. Orlick (New York: Pantheon, 1982)

Chapter 11 Review

Answers

True/False

1. T
2. F
3. T
4. T
5. F
6. F
7. T
8. T
9. F
10. F

Multiple Choice

1. d.
2. a.
3. d.
4. a.
5. b.
6. c.

Discussion

1. Answers may vary but could include: A variety of mental and physical functions change with the aging process. Hair color can turn gray, bones become brittle, the conduction of nerve impulses slows, the resting metabolic rate decreases, reaction time slows, etc. By living a physically active lifestyle and eating a healthy diet, you can prevent or slow some of these processes.

2. Answers may vary but could include: Older persons who remain physically active can often do as much or more work than younger

True/False

On a separate sheet of paper, mark each question below either T for True or F for False.

1. You can have a positive impact on your risk for chronic diseases.
2. Leisure activities will not help you reduce your stress levels.
3. Aqua activities can reduce the pounding your body takes in weight-bearing activities.
4. Circuit weight training is an excellent way to develop a combination of health-related fitness components all at the same time.
5. If you live to be sixty-five, you can expect to live five more years at most.
6. Your resting metabolic rate does not decrease with age.
7. You reach your peak bone mass between the ages of twenty-seven and thirty-two.
8. Podiatrists are physicians who specialize in disorders of the feet.
9. Personal trainers are certified and licensed by states.
10. As you age, you will need to join a health and fitness club to continue your personal fitness program.

Multiple Choice

1. Which of the following can help you determine which lifetime activities are realistic for you?
   a. cost
   b. personality and attitude
   c. social needs
   d. all of the above
2. In-line skating will help you develop and maintain all but which one of the following?
   a. reaction time
   b. balance
   c. cardiovascular fitness
   d. body composition
3. By what percentage will your maximum breathing capacity decrease from ages thirty to ninety?
   a. 5 to 10 percent
   b. 15 to 25 percent
   c. 30 to 40 percent
   d. 50 to 60 percent
4. Which of the following changes associated with aging can you control by being physically active and eating a healthy diet?
   a. increased body fat
   b. graying of hair
   c. inherited diseases
   d. balding
5. Which of the following does not usually occur in people who remain sedentary as they age?
   a. They get depressed.
   b. They maintain functional health.
   c. They lose self-esteem.
   d. They lose bone mass.
6. With whom do physical therapists primarily work?
   a. athletes
   b. people with foot problems
   c. people in rehabilitation
   d. people who need to control their weight

CULTURAL DIVERSITY

Indonesia

Of the several Western sports played and watched in Indonesia, badminton is a particular favorite. Even people in remote villages play badminton, using rubber slippers as rackets and a clothes-line for the net if equipment is not available. Soccer, though, is the most popular sport. Like badminton, soccer can be played with makeshift equipment if the real thing is unavailable.

Several traditional games, originally played only by boys, are now played by

Discussion

1. Identify the mental and physical functions that change with the aging process. Describe how you can control to some degree the rate and amount that these functions will change.

2. Describe and explain why some older people can outwork or physically outperform much younger individuals.

3. Describe and explain how you can be a better health and fitness consumer.

Vocabulary Experience

Match the correct term in Column A to the definition in Column B by writing the appropriate number in each blank.

Column A

_____ aging process

_____ dietitian

_____ professional health and fitness certification

_____ leisure

_____ lifetime activities

_____ physical educator

Column B

1. Process where individuals must pass written tests and demonstrate their physical-activity-leading skills in order to be certified by national health and fitness organizations.

2. Free time.

3. How your body changes as you get older.

4. A professional with special training in wellness and personal fitness.

5. A professional who develops nutrition programs and works with people to control their weight.

6. Activities in which participation can last years to decades.

Critical Thinking

1. Develop a list of lifetime activities that you do now or would like to do now or in the future. Then explain why you enjoy them and how they can help you develop and maintain your personal fitness levels.

2. List and explain the changes in physical functioning that your parents and grandparents are facing as they age. How might staying physically active and eating a healthy diet help them cope with these changes?

3. React to this statement: *Education can make you a better health and fitness consumer and can prevent you from being the victim of rip-offs.*

individuals. This is due to the fact that good to better levels of functional health can be maintained in most people for several years if they are active.

3. Answers may vary but could include: You can be a better health and fitness consumer by knowing how to identify reputable fitness experts, being able to evaluate health and fitness information, and by knowing how to pick and choose a reputable fitness facility.

Critical Thinking

1. Answers will vary but should include activities from Figures 4.3 and 4.12 from Chapter 4.

2. Answers will vary but might include: A variety of changes occur with the aging process. By living a physically active lifestyle and eating a healthy diet, your parents and grandparents can prevent or slow some of these processes as compared to living a sedentary lifestyle.

3. Answers will vary.

Vocabulary Experience

_3_ aging process
_5_ dietitian
_1_ professional health and fitness certification
_2_ leisure
_6_ lifetime activities
_4_ physical educator

girls, too. One of them is *pencak silat,* a type of martial art with different styles, practiced all over Indonesia. There are over 800 *pencak silat* clubs in Indonesia, most of which are open to anyone who wants to join.

Sepak takraw is a team sport played in Sumatra and other places and is a little like volleyball. It is played on a court with a small, woven rattan ball, but players cannot use their hands to keep the ball in motion, only their heads, legs, and feet. In western Java the Sudanese people invented a game called *banjang*. In this form of wrestling, opponents hit each other on the legs with foot-long sticks until one of them is knocked down.

GLOSSARY

A

abdominal a muscle in the lower stomach area that is used in breathing.

acclimatization the process of allowing the body to adapt slowly to new conditions.

active warm-up a warm-up that attempts to raise the body temperature by actively involving the muscular, skeletal, and cardiovascular systems.

acute occurring over a short time.

adherence the ability to continue something, such as your chosen personal fitness program, over a period of time.

aerobic dance instructor individual who specializes in teaching aerobic dance activities to groups of people.

aerobic fitness level cardiovascular fitness level.

aerobic with oxygen.

agility the ability to change and control the direction and position of your body while maintaining a constant, rapid motion.

aging process how the body changes as a person gets older.

amino acid a class of compounds that are the basic building blocks for proteins.

anaerobic without oxygen.

anorexia nervosa an eating disorder in which people abnormally restrict their caloric intake.

antagonistic muscles opposing muscles.

antioxidant a vitamin or mineral that may help protect the body from various types of cell damage.

artery a blood vessel that carries blood away from the heart and branches out to supply oxygen and other nutrients to the muscles, tissues, and organs of the body.

asthma restriction of the breathing passages due to dust, allergies, pollution, or even vigorous exercise.

atherosclerosis a disease process that causes substances to build up inside arteries, reducing or blocking blood flow.

atrophy a loss of muscle size and strength because of lack of use.

B

balance the ability to control or stabilize your equilibrium while moving or staying still.

ballistic stretching exercises that involve quick up-and-down bobbing movements that are held very briefly.

biomechanics the study of the principles of physics applied to human motion.

blood pooling a condition, following exercise, in which blood collects in the large veins of the legs and lower body, especially when the exercise is stopped abruptly.

blood pressure the force by which blood is pushed against the walls of the arteries.

blood vessel in a muscle, the structure that provides oxygen, energy, and a waste removal system for each muscle fiber.

bulimia an eating disorder in which people overeat and then force themselves to vomit afterward or purposely overuse laxatives to eliminate food from their bodies.

C

caloric expenditure the number of calories expended or burned in daily physical activity.

caloric input the number of calories consumed in the diet.

capillary a small blood vessel that delivers oxygen and other nutrients to the individual muscle, tissue, and organ cells.

carbohydrate a nutrient that includes sugars and starches (like pasta).

cardiac muscle muscle in the heart and arteries.

cardiovascular cool-down a period after exercise in which you try to prevent blood pooling by moving about slowly and continuously for about three to five minutes.

cardiovascular disease heart and blood vessel disease.

cardiovascular fitness the ability to work continuously for extended periods of time.

cardiovascular warm-up a warm-up that gradually increases the heart rate and internal body temperature.

cartilage a soft, cushioned material that surrounds the ends of bones at a joint to prevent the bones from rubbing against each other.

center of gravity the area of your body that determines how your weight is distributed.

cholesterol a blood fat.

chronic occurring over an extended time.

circulatory system the heart and the system of blood vessels in the body, including the arteries, capillaries, and veins.

complex carbohydrate a carbohydrate that is starchy and broken down more slowly in the body than a simple carbohydrate.

compound set method a weight-training hypertrophy program that requires you to do two different exercises that use the same muscle group, without allowing for rest between the sets.

concentric contraction the contraction and shortening of a muscle, which results in the movement of bones and joints; also called *positive work*.

conditioning engaging in regular physical activity or exercise that results in an improved state of physical fitness.

connective tissue the "glue" for the body tissue that binds muscles and bones together while still allowing them to move more efficiently.

contract to shorten.

coordination the ability to use your eyes and ears to determine and direct the smooth movement of your body.

cross-train to vary activities and exercises from day to day to prevent detraining, especially after an injury.

D

dehydration excess fluid loss from the body; symptoms include weakness and fatigue.

detraining the loss of health and fitness benefits when a personal fitness program is stopped.

diabetes mellitus a chronic disease affecting the blood sugar.

diaphragm a muscle in the middle chest area that is used in breathing.

diastolic blood pressure the pressure on the arteries when the heart relaxes after contraction.

distress excess negative stress, such as fear, anger, or confusion.

diuretic a substance that promotes water loss through urination.

dose the amount and frequency of an activity or substance.

E

eating disorders behaviors that cause a person to overeat, undereat, or practice extreme unhealthy actions to control their weight.

eccentric contraction a muscle's slow release of a contraction as it becomes longer; also called *negative work*.

ectomorph a slender, lean somatotype.

elasticity the rubberband-like flexibility of the muscles, tendons, and other connective tissues.

electrolyte a mineral whose electrical charge helps control the body's fluid balance.

endomorph a heavier, rounder somatotype.

energy balance the balance between calories consumed in the diet and the amount of calories burned in daily physical activity.

energy cost the amount of energy required for you to perform different physical activities or exercises.

energy expenditure the number of calories you burn each minute.

essential fat the minimum amount of body fat necessary for good health.

eustress positive stress; an enjoyable type of stress.

excessive leanness a percentage of body fat that is too low for good health.

exercise physical activity that is planned, structured, repetitive, and results in the improvement or maintenance of personal fitness.

F

fast-twitch muscle fiber a muscle cell that is suited to anaerobic work.

fat a type of nutrient that is high in energy; found in animal tissues, nuts, seeds, and oils of some plants.

fat-soluble vitamin a vitamin that dissolves in the body's fat tissues and can be stored in the body; the vitamins A, D, E, and K.

fiber a type of carbohydrate that is not digestible by humans and provides no energy.

FIT the three components of the overload principle: Frequency, Intensity, and Time/Duration; a level of physical conditioning that is desirable and obtainable by everyone.

fitness specialist individual (other than a personal trainer or aerobic dance instructor) who specializes in physical fitness and nutrition promotion.

flexibility the range of motion that your joints have during movement.

Food Guide Pyramid a visual outline of what people should eat each day.

free weights objects of varied weights that can be moved without restriction and used for weight lifting; examples are barbells and dumbbells.

frequency in a personal fitness prescription, how often you work.

frostbite damage to the body tissues due to freezing.

functional health a person's physical ability to function independently in life, without assistance.

G

general active warm-up a warm-up tailored to individual physical activities. It is less structured than a specific active warm-up.

genetic potential inherited muscle characteristics that determine the percentage, type, and number of our muscle fibers.

glucose sugar; the basic form of carbohydrate and a valuable source of energy.

glycogen the stored form of glucose in the liver and skeletal muscle.

H

health a state of well-being that includes physical, mental, emotional, spiritual, and social aspects.

health-related fitness physical fitness primarily associated with disease prevention and functional health. Health-related fitness has five components: cardiovascular fitness, body composition, flexibility, muscular strength, and muscular endurance.

heart attack the blockage of vessels feeding the heart, causing the death of heart tissue.

heat cramps painful contractions of the muscles used during physical activity or exercise due, at least in part, to dehydration.

heat exhaustion an overheating condition that includes weakness; headache; rapid pulse, stomach discomfort; dizziness; heavy sweating; muscle cramps; and cool, clammy skin.

heat stress index a number that reflects a combination of high temperatures and high humidity.

heat stroke a life-threatening condition resulting from a buildup of body heat; can be fatal.

hemoglobin an iron-rich compound in the blood that helps carry oxygen from the lungs to the muscles, tissues, and organs.

heart rate the number of times your heart beats per minute.

high-density lipoprotein (HDL) "good cholesterol"; the type of cholesterol that is associated with a lower atherosclerosis risk.

hyperflexibility the condition of having too much flexibility.

hyperplasia a theory of muscle enlargement that says muscle growth is due to muscle fibers splitting and creating additional fibers.

hypertension high blood pressure.

hyperthermia overheating; body temperature above 98.6 degrees Fahrenheit.

hypertrophy muscle enlargement due to the thickening of each existing muscle fiber.

hypoglycemic having a condition in which the blood glucose level drops and the person feels dizzy, tired, and irritable.

hypokinetic physically inactive, or sedentary.

hypothermia a condition in which the body temperature drops below normal (98.6 degrees Fahrenheit).

I

ideal body weight the perfect weight for good health.

intensity in a personal fitness prescription, how hard you work.

intercostal a muscle around the ribs that is used in breathing.

interval training alternating higher-intensity physical activities or exercises with lower-intensity recovery bouts for several minutes at a time.

isometric contraction a muscle's pushing against an immovable object and having no movement occur as it attempts to contract. The muscle does not become shorter or longer but creates tension.

isotonic progressive resistance a combination of concentric and eccentric muscle contractions.

K

kilocalorie a unit used to measure energy; also called a *calorie.*

L

large muscle group muscles of large size or a large number of muscles being used at one time.

lean body weight the weight of the bones, muscles, and connective tissue.

leisure activity an activity, sport, or other experience that people participate in during their free (nonwork) time.

leisure free (nonwork) time.

life expectancy the number of years a person can expect to live.

lifetime activity a physical activity, exercise, or sport that a person can participate in for long periods of time (years to decades).

ligament a band of tissue that connects bone to bone and limits the movement of a joint.

longevity the actual length of a person's life.

low back injury injury to the muscles, ligaments, tendons, or joints of the lower back.

low-density lipoprotein (LDL) "bad cholesterol"; a type of cholesterol that is associated with higher atherosclerosis risk.

M

maximum heart rate the maximum number of times your heart can beat in a minute.

medical examination a more extensive evaluation than is done in a medical screening, assessing any or all of the following: exercise stress test, blood test, urinary analysis, or family health-risk history.

medical screening a basic evaluation of the eyes, ears, nose, throat, blood pressure, height, weight, and a check for possible hernia.

mesomorph a muscular somatotype.

metabolic rate the number of calories that is burned or expended as heat.

microtear a small tear in a part of a muscle fiber or connective tissue because of greater-than-usual resistance; causes muscle soreness.

mineral a chemical element that is important for the body's structure and function and for regulating metabolism.

mode in a personal fitness prescription, the type of activity or exercise you do.

multiple set method a weight-training strength program that uses the same amount of weight (a percentage of your maximum) for each set until you are fatigued.

muscle fibers (muscle cells) long, thin structures the size of human hairs that contract to create movement. They run the entire length of a muscle.

muscle imbalance an imbalance that occurs when one muscle group that controls a joint is too strong in relation to a complementary set of muscles (another set of muscles that helps control the same joint).

muscle intensity the amount of tension or stress placed on a muscle.

muscle pump the contraction of the muscles in the body (especially the legs) as the muscles squeeze the veins to help blood move back to the right side of the heart.

muscle/skeletal warm-up a warm-up that usually involves a series of static body stretches.

muscular endurance the ability to contract your muscles several times without excessive fatigue.

muscular strength the maximal force that you can exert when you contract your muscles.

myocardial infarction (MI) a heart attack; a blockage of a vessel that feeds the heart muscle.

N

negative workout method a weight-training strength program that uses very heavy weights at the end of a prescribed number of sets and repetitions.

nerve in a muscle, the part that delivers the messages from the brain to direct each individual muscle fiber to contract.

nutrient a substance in foods that the body needs for proper growth, development, and functioning.

obesity excessive body fat; excessive weight (20% or more above appropriate weight).

osteoporosis a condition in which the bones are porous and brittle.

overfat carrying too much body fat.

overload principle the principle that says to improve your level of physical fitness, you must increase the amount of activity or exercise that you normally do.

overtraining being too active or exercising too much. Overtraining leads to overuse injuries and addictive behaviors.

overuse injury an injury caused by doing too much,

too soon, too often in an exercise program.

P

passive stretching exercises in which a partner or device provides the force for a stretch.

passive warm-up a warm-up that raises the body temperature using outside heat sources such as blankets, and hot baths.

perceived exertion how hard a person feels he or she is working during physical activity or exercise.

percentage of body fat the percentage of your body weight that is fat.

percentage of maximum heart rate a method of calculating an exercise intensity; 60 to 90 percent of your maximum heart rate.

personal fitness prescription an exercise or physical activity plan that includes frequency, intensity, time/duration, mode, and other factors.

personal fitness the result of a way of life that includes living an active lifestyle, maintaining good or better levels of physical fitness, consuming a healthy diet, and practicing good health behaviors throughout life.

personal trainer individual who specializes in working alone with people, instructing exercise sessions, and developing personal fitness programs for a fee.

physical activity zealot; exercise zealot a person who is addicted to a physical activity or exercise program.

physical fitness a level of individual physical ability that allows a person to perform daily physical tasks effectively with enough energy reserves for recreational activities or unexpected physical challenges.

physically active lifestyle a way of living that regularly includes physical activity such as walking, climbing stairs, or participating in recreational movements.

plateau effect the leveling off of physical fitness improvement in a personal fitness program.

plyometric training exercises such as bounding and jumping movements that increase your ability to develop force more quickly in explosive movements; a kind of reflex-assisted stretching.

power the ability to move your body parts swiftly while at the same time applying the maximum force of your muscles.

predisposition susceptibility to increased health risk due to genetic makeup.

progression principle the rate at which you change the frequency, intensity, and time/duration (FIT) of your personal fitness prescription.

progressive resistance the continued, systematic increase of muscle stress through the use of weights or other forms of resistance.

pronation an inward rolling of the foot in walking or jogging.

protein a type of nutrient that is the basic building block of the body.

pyramid training a weight-training strength program for the large muscle groups that starts by using light weights during the first set and then increases the amount of weight and decreases the number of reps with each following set.

R

range of motion (ROM) varying degrees of motion allowed around a joint.

reaction time the ability to react or respond quickly to what you hear, see, or feel.

Recommended Daily Allowance (RDA) the amount of nutrients recommended daily for individuals by the U.S. Department of Agriculture.

recovery heart rate the gradual return of the heart rate to resting levels within 5 to 10 minutes of a session of normal cardiovascular physical activity or exercise.

recovery time time or rest between exercises.

reflex a response that the nerves and muscles provide to various movements.

reflex-assisted stretching exercises that challenge the reflexes to adapt so that they allow the joints to move at faster speeds and with more explosive power.

rehydration the process of replacing fluids that have been lost or excreted from the body.

relative muscular endurance how many times you can lift a given weight in relation to your body weight and gender.

relative muscular strength how much weight you can lift one time in relation to your body weight and gender.

repetition (rep) the completed execution of an exercise one time.

resting metabolic rate (RMR) the amount of calories you need and expend while sitting comfortably at rest.

risk factor a condition or trait that increases the likelihood that people will develop chronic diseases.

S

saturated fat a fat that is usually solid at room temperature, comes mainly from animal fat, and typically contains high levels of cholesterol.

sedentary lifestyle an inactive lifestyle.

set a group of consecutive reps for an exercise.

simple carbohydrate simple sugar; a carbohydrate that is absorbed quickly into the bloodstream and that provides a quick form of energy.

skeletal muscle muscle located around bones and joints that controls movement.

skill-related fitness the ability to perform successfully during games and sports; also called *performance fitness*. Skill-related fitness has six components: agility, balance, coordination, power, speed, and reaction time.

slow-twitch muscle fiber a muscle cell that is associated with a high ability to do aerobic work.

small muscle group muscles of small size or a small number of muscles being used at one time.

smooth muscle muscle located around internal organs that automatically controls many functions of the body.

somatotype the type of body you have in terms of your body composition related to heredity.

specific active warm-up a warm-up structured primarily for a specific skill or game activity.

specificity principle the principle that says improvements in your personal fitness will occur in the particular muscles that you overload during physical activity or exercise.

speed the ability to move your body or parts of your body swiftly.

split workout a weight-training workout schedule in which you do not work each muscle group at each workout session but, instead, exercise one-half of your body at each session.

spotters individuals who assist you with weight-room safety.

static body stretches stretches that are done slowly, smoothly, and in a sustained fashion.

static stretching exercises in which you assume a stretch position slowly and then hold it for several seconds (10 to 60 seconds), until you feel slight discomfort but no real pain.

stitch a sharp pain on the side or sides of the abdomen; a common form of muscle cramp most commonly caused by improperly conditioned breathing muscles.

strain a pull, tear, or rip in a muscle or tendon.

stress fracture a bone injury caused by overuse; also called *fatigue fracture.*

stress the physical and psychological responses of your body as you try to adapt to stressors.

stressor anything that requires you to adapt and cope with either positive or negative situations.

stretching cool-down a period after cardiovascular cool-down in which you perform stretching exercises for three to five minutes to minimize stiffness and muscle soreness.

stroke blockage of blood flow to the brain.

superset method a weight-training hypertrophy program that uses two different exercises that train opposing muscles, without allowing for rest between sets.

supination a movement of the foot when walking or jogging in which the foot strikes the ground on the outside of the heel.

systolic blood pressure the pressure on the arteries when the heart contracts.

T

talk test a test that uses a person's ease or difficulty in carrying on a conversation while engaged in physical activity or exercise to measure exercise intensity.

target heart rate zone the recommended intensity for aerobic conditioning; estimated to be between 60 and 90 percent of one's predicted maximum heart rate.

tendon a band of tissue that connects muscle to bone.

testosterone a male hormone that plays an important role in building muscles.

time/duration in a personal fitness prescription, the length of time you work.

trainability the rate at which a person improves personal fitness following physical activity or exercise conditioning. Trainability is determined, to a large extent, by genetic makeup.

training load the amount of weight a weight trainer lifts during his or her workout.

triglyceride a blood fat.

U

underfat carrying too little body fat.

unsaturated fat a fat that is usually liquid at room temperature, comes mainly from plant sources, and does not contain cholesterol.

V

vegetarian a person who eliminates meat, fish, and poultry (and sometimes eggs and milk products) from their diet.

vein a blood vessel that collects blood from the capillaries and carries it back to the heart.

very low density lipoprotein (VLDL) "bad cholesterol"; a type of cholesterol that is associated with higher atherosclerosis risk.

vitamin a nutrient that helps control growth and helps the body release energy to do work.

W

warm-up a variety of low-intensity activities that are designed to prepare your body for moderate to vigorous activities.

water-soluble vitamin a vitamin that is not stored in the body and needs to be replaced regularly; vitamin C and the B vitamins.

weight machines a system of cables and pulleys designed for the movement of weights as used in weight-training exercises.

weight training the use of such equipment as barbells, dumbbells, and machines to improve fitness, health, and appearance.

weight-training circuit a specific sequence of weight-training exercises.

weight-training cycle a change in your weight-training programs over a period of time.

wellness the attainment and maintenance of a moderate to high level of physical, mental, emotional, spiritual, and social health.

wraparound thumb grip (closed grip) a grip used in lifting in which the fingers and thumb go in opposite directions around the bar to help keep the bar from rolling out of the hand.

INDEX

Photo Credits

2a—David Madison 2b—David Madison 2c—David Lissy 3—David Madison 5a—David Madison 5b—David Lissy 10b—David Madison 13—Phyllis Dicardi, The Picture Cube 17—Pacific Rim, Mary Van de Ven 18—Shaffer/Smith, The Picture Cube 20—David Lissy 26—David Madison 27a—Bettmann 27b—Bettmann 30a—David Lissy 30b—David Lissy 36a—David Lissy 36b—David Lissy 36c—David Lissy 37—David Lissy 39—Gaye Hilsenrath, The Picture Cube 44—David Madison 47—David Lissy 50—Frank Siteman, The Picture Cube 54—John Coletti, The Picture Cube 62—David Lissy 73—David Madison 81—David Madison 82a—Spencer Grant, The Picture Cube 82b—David Lissy 95—David Madison 104a—David Lissy 104b—David Lissy 104c—David Lissy 105—David Lissy 107—The Kobal Collection 108a—Focus on Sports 108b—David Madison 108c—David Madison 109a—David Madison 109b—David Madison 110—David Lissy 115a—David Madison 115b—David Madison 116—David Madison 117—David Lissy 120a—David Madison 120b—David Madison 148a—Bettmann 148b—Bettmann 156a—David Madison 156b—David Madison 156c—David Madison 157—David Madison 167a—Focus on Sports 167b—Focus on Sports 169a—Reproduced by permission of ICI Pharmaceuticals Division, Cheshire, England 169b—Reproduced by permission of ICI Pharmaceuticals Division, Cheshire, England 170—W. B. Spunbarg, The Picture Cube 173b—David Madison 178—David Lissy 180—David Madison 182—David Madison 188a—David Madison 188b—David Madison 189—David Madison 192—David Madison 216a—Comstock 216b—David Lissy 216c—David Madison 217—Comstock 219—David Madison 221a—Hal Gage, The Picture Cube 221b—David Madison 221c—Tom McCarthy, The Picture Cube 232—Comstock 234—Comstock 239c—David Madison 273a—U.S. Weight Lifting 273b—U.S. Weight Lifting 300a—R. Michael Stucky, Comstock 300b—David Madison 300c—David Madison 301—R. Michael Stucky, Comstock 305c—Spencor Grant, The Picture Cube 305a—Wm. Thompson, The Picture Cube 305b—Tom Hannon, The Picture Cube 306—Cleo Freelance, The Picture Cube 307—David Lissy 308—Ed Malitsky, The Picture Cube 309—David Madison 316—Kindra Clineff 330a—Cleo Photography, The Picture Cube 330b—Renee Lynn 330c—Jeff Greenberg, The Picture Cube 331—Cleo Photography, The Picture Cube 333—Larry Lawter, The Picture Cube 334—Gaye Hilsenrath, The Picture Cube 335—David Madison 336a—Eric Roth, The Picture Cube 338a—Eric Roth, The Picture Cube 338b—Henry T. Kaiser, The Picture Cube 340a—Bettmann 340b—Bettmann 341—Eric Roth 343—David Madison 344—Nancy Sheean, The Picture Cube 345—Frank Siteman, The Picture Cube 347—Eric Roth 348—Renee Lynn 349a—Ray Stanyard, Photo Edit 349b—Ray Stanyard, Photo Edit 349c—Ray Stanyard, Photo Edit 349d—Ray Stanyard, Photo Edit 349e—Ray Stanyard, Photo Edit 349f—Ray Stanyard, Photo Edit 354—David Madison 364a—Renee Lynn 364b—Shelby Thorner 364c—Comstock 365—Renee Lynn 368a—Shelby Thorner 368b—Kindra Clineff 370—McDonald Photography, The Picture Cube 373a—David Madison 373b—David Lissy 374—Sunstar, The Picture Cube 375a—David Madison 375b—David Madison 376a—David Madison 376b—Fred Scribner, The Picture Cube 378a—David Madison 378b—David Madison 379a—Kindra Clineff 379b—David Madison 379c—David Lissy 382a—Steve Woltmann 382b—Steve Woltmann 383—Tom McCarthy, The Picture Cube 384a—Bob Kraemer, The Picture Cube 384b—Frank Siteman, The Picture Cube 384c—Bob Kraemer, The Picture Cube 385—Courtesy of Terry Weyman, D.C. 388—Tim Davis